volume II

History of the CANADIAN PEOPLES

1867 to the Present

Alvin Finkel
Athabasca University

Margaret Conrad
Acadia University

with

Veronica Strong-Boag
University of British Columbia

Copp Clark Pitman Ltd.
A Longman Company
Toronto

ISBN: 0-7730-5189-9

Editor: Barbara Tessman
Executive editor: Jeff Miller
Proofreader: Claudia Kutchukian
Photo research: Andy Carroll, Maral Bablanian
Design: Kyle Gell
Cover illustration: Rocco Baviera
Map illustrations: Allan Moon
Typesetting: Marnie Morrissey
Printing and binding: Best Gagné Book Manufacturers

Canadian Cataloguing in Publication Data

Main entry under title:

History of the Canadian peoples

Includes bibliographical references and index.
Contents: v. 1. Beginnings to 1876 / Margaret Conrad, Alvin Finkel, Cornelius Jaenen. – v. 2. 1867 to the present / Alvin Finkel, Margaret Conrad with Veronica Strong-Boag.
ISBN 0-7730-5346-8 (set)
ISBN 0-7730-4843-X (v.I) 0-7730-5189-9 (v. II)
I. Canada – History. I. Conrad, Margaret. II. Finkel, Alvin, 1947–   . III. Jaenen, Cornelius J., 1927–   . IV. Strong-Boag, Veronica Jane, 1947–   .

FC164.H58 1993   971   C93-093786-4   F1033.H58 1993

Copp Clark Pitman Ltd.
2775 Matheson Blvd. East
Mississauga, Ontario
L4W 4P7

Associated companies:
Longman Group Ltd., London
Longman Inc., New York
Longman Cheshire Pty., Melbourne
Longman Paul Pty., Auckland

Printed and bound in Canada

1   2   3   4   5   5189-9   97   96   95   94   93

For our students past and present.
We hope that this is the kind of text where
they can identify something of their personal past.

C O N T E N T S

LIST OF MAPS

LIST OF TABLES

P R E F A C E

Like Volume I, Volume II of the *History of the Canadian Peoples* devotes as much attention to the ordinary people of the past as to those who dominated the political and economic spheres of Canadian society. We have reprinted here the Introduction from Volume I, which explains our general approach to this project.

Volume II begins with a survey of British North America on the eve of Confederation as a review for those who have read Volume I and as an introduction for those who have not. The remaining twelve chapters are divided into four chronological sections, each section consisting of three chapters: one focussing on economic developments, another on society, and a third on political life. As in Volume I, we attempt to cover topics relating to class, culture, race, region, and gender in our analysis, and to make the connections between the economic, social, and political processes that characterize Canada's past.

The authors wish to thank Michael Behiels, Cornelius Jaenen, and Brian Henderson for their role in the initial conceptualization of this project. We owe a particular debt to Barbara Tessman, managing editor at Copp Clark Pitman, whose contribution to the organization, content, and writing of Volume II was above and beyond the call of duty. Douglas Baldwin, Michael Behiels, Jeff Miller, Maurice Tugwell, Brian VanBlarcom, and Brian Young suggested changes and saved us from many errors. As is usually the case in projects such as these, secretarial services were fundamental to the project, and we wish to thank Myrna Nolan and Claire Gemmell of Athabasca University and Brenda Naugler and Carolyn Bowlby of Acadia University for their help. Of course, the authors alone bear responsibility for any problems remaining in the text.

INTERPRETING

CANADA'S PAST

In 1829, Shawnadithit, the last surviving Beothuk, died of tuberculosis in Newfoundland. Several decades later, three British North American colonies united to form the Dominion of Canada. The second of these two events has always had a central place in Canadian history textbooks. The first, until recently, has been ignored. For students of history in the 1990s, it is important to understand why the focus of historical analysis changes and what factors influence historians in their approaches to the past.

• The New Social History

In its broadest sense history is the study of the past. In non-literate societies, people passed down oral traditions from one generation to the next, with each generation fashioning the story to meet the needs of the time. When written language was invented, history became fixed in texts. The story was often revised, but earlier texts could be used to show how interpretations of the past had changed over time. Although ordinary people continued to tell their stories, "official" history was embodied in orthodox texts. Some of those texts, such as the Bible and the Koran, were deemed to be divinely inspired.

In Europe and North America, history became an academic discipline in the nineteenth century. Scholars in universities began to compare texts, develop standards of accuracy, and train students to become professional historians. At first professional historians focussed on political and military events, but gradually they broadened their scope to include economic and social developments.

No matter how meticulously researched, most academic histories written before 1970 either ignored, or treated unsympathetically, women, people of colour, and issues relating to private life. For example, a lesbian Native woman reading published historical works would have found only disparaging or condescending remarks about Native people, virtually no information about women's culture, and complete silence on homosexuality. Working-class women and men and members of ethnic groups who were not English, Scottish, or French would have learned little about their forebears from reading Canadian history.

Part of the reason that history was so narrowly focussed lies in the sources of information available to historians. The literate few, and especially the powerful among them—kings, prime ministers, bishops, and the like—have left behind far more written records than the millions of people whose lives they dominated. Our knowledge of medieval Europe, for example, is largely based on the accounts of church officials. Their belief that religious convictions governed the lives of the masses can be neither confirmed nor denied by direct evidence from the serfs, who left no written sources. Although social historians have found indirect evidence suggesting that the clerical interpretation exaggerates the piety and subservience of the majority, the fact remains that serfs, slaves, labourers, and peasants have received far less attention from historians than have the elites who ruled them.

Another reason for the narrow focus is that history was written by a small elite of educated white men to be read by others like themselves. Their interests understandably turned to war and political developments in which they and their peers participated; and their interpretation was usually from the point of view of the people who dominated such events. When women, children of the working class, and minorities began entering universities in larger numbers in the 1960s, they demanded that "their" history also be taken into account. Their questions encouraged a different approach to the past. Instead of seeing history as a sequence of events orchestrated by a small and powerful elite, scholars began to interpret it as an arena in which classes, ethnic groups, and individual men and women struggled to control the values that shaped their collective lives.

When history is approached as a contested terrain, its events must be analysed from a variety of perspectives. For example, when we discuss the rebellions of 1837 in Upper and Lower Canada, we recognize the importance of understanding not only the actions and attitudes of British officials and the ruling cliques within the Canadas, but also those of the ambitious middle classes, the farmers, and the landless poor. The goals of the rebels in Lower Canada varied depending on whether the focus is on a habitante with no bread to feed her children or a wealthy seigneur like the rebel leader Louis-Joseph Papineau. Similarly, the conclusions reached about the significance of events such as the rebellions of 1837 depend upon which actor's—or group of actors'—point of view is being considered.

Because each historian brings individual values and concerns to the study of the past, it is important to know something about the people who write history texts. The region, ethnicity, social class, gender, and political perspective of the historian, as well as the time of writing, are often reflected, consciously or unconsciously, in decisions about what subjects to analyse, what documents to consult, and how to interpret their relative meaning and importance. As historians now realize, documents cannot "speak for themselves." They have to be analysed critically because the context in which they were produced is as complex as the historian's own background.

Over the past two decades, social historians have made a concerted effort to provide a broader view of Canada's past. They have drawn upon other disciplines, such as geography, demography, economics, political science, sociology, anthropology, archaeology, and psychology to fill the gaps in their written sources. By taking an interdisciplinary approach, it is often possible to learn something about the motives of the silent majority who are usually left out of textbooks. Material evidence from archaeological excavations, data from censuses and immigration lists, oral traditions passed down from one generation to the next: these sources have all helped historians to develop a more complex sense of the reality of people's lives in past times. When personal computers became widely available in the 1970s, historians were able to process larger amounts of historical information. The science of demography, which analyses population trends and draws upon vast quantities of data, has proved particularly useful in helping historians to trace changes in family size, life-cycle choices, and migration patterns.

At the same time that new methodologies extended the scope of history, scholars were being influenced by new theoretical perspectives. Historians who studied women, minorities, and the working class brought insights from Marxism, feminism, and postmodernism to bear on historical inquiry. In focussing on issues such as class, race, ethnicity, and gender, and by asking new questions about old texts, historians have revolutionized the way we look at the past.[1]

This two-volume text attempts to integrate the findings of "the new social history" with earlier work on the rich and powerful to produce a more comprehensive portrait of Canadian society. While social history is emphasized, political history is not ignored. Indeed, we make an effort to show the impact on ordinary Canadians of decisions made by elites both inside and outside Canadian geographic boundaries. For example, in our discussion of the complicated class structure within the fur-trading empire of the Hudson's Bay Company in the mid-nineteenth century, we note that decisions made in London as well as those made by Governor Sir George Simpson in Canada helped to put this structure in place. We also show that the men who created the structures could not always control them. The Hudson's Bay Company's ability to focus its profit-making attention on fur trading alone was weakened by Métis resistance to company rules, by changing fashions in European markets, and by changing relations between women and men on the fur-trade frontier. It is this interaction— leading at times to compromises and at times to conflict—that underscores our discussion of Canadian politics.

It would be misleading to suggest that the new social history has produced consensus on historical issues. It is more correct to say that it has widened the debate. At various points in this text we discuss *historiography*; that is, debates about historical interpretation. In a survey text we can only touch upon the range of historiographical discussion, but we want students to consider a few examples of common historical assumptions that recent writings have challenged.

WHAT'S IN A NAME?

Contemporary political movements have forced historians to think about the words they use to describe Canadians. Thirty years ago most textbooks used the term "negroes" to refer to people with black skin. In the 1960s "black" became the politically conscious way to refer to people of African descent. More recently "African Canadian" has become the more popular term. Similarly, the words used to describe aboriginal peoples have changed in recent years. "Savages" was quickly dropped from textbooks in the 1960s, and although the misnomer "Indian" is still widely used today— and has particular applications that as yet seem unavoidable—the preferred terms seem to be "Native peoples" and "First Nations." "Amerindian" is a scholarly term to encompass the wide range of Native peoples and cultures.

Women, too, have insisted on being described in more respectful terms. Feminists objected strongly to the use of the word "girl" when adult women were being discussed, and they dismissed "lady" as being too condescending or elitist. Because "man" was adequate for the male of the species, "woman" seemed the most appropriate term, although some radical feminists have used the spelling "wymyn." Only the most hidebound of scholars still insist that the word "man" can be used to describe the entire human species.

Many scholars complained loudly about being asked to abandon words long established in their vocabularies. A few even argued that "political correctness" restricted freedom of speech. We do not hold such views. Because English is a living language and changes over time, we see no reason why it should not continue to change to reflect the new consciousness of groups in Canadian society. Indeed the importance of language is obvious in the sometimes derisive phrase "politically correct." In our view, the words "politically conscious" more accurately describe the attempts by groups to name their own experience. Language, of course, is not only about naming things but about power. Attempts by oppressed groups to find their own language to fit their experiences should be seen in the context of their struggles for empowerment. In this text we attempt to keep up with the changing times while bearing in mind that people in the past used a different terminology. We are also aware that in the future we may have to revise the words we use as groups continue to reinvent their identities.

• Geography and History

Historians have long recognized that geography has played an important role in the understanding of Canada's past, if for no other reason than that we have so much of it. With Canada occupying over 7 percent of the global land mass, it is not surprising that regions figure prominently in the country's historical development, and that an individual's sense of place is defined locally and regionally more often than nationally.

The Canadian nation-state is a human, not a geographical creation. Nevertheless, geography and climate help to define our political boundaries. Ten thousand years ago, most of the area that makes up present-day Canada was covered by ice. The nation's rugged terrain reflects its ice-age origins and explains why the northern half of the North American continent was less attractive to the First Nations and European immigrants than the warmer and more fertile regions to the south.

Canada is a northern nation, dominated by the great Canadian Shield, which makes up two-thirds of its terrain. The east–west thrust of soils, forests, and climate reinforces much of Canada's southern boundary, as does the St Lawrence–Great Lakes heartland. At the same time, north–south divisions of mountain ranges and plains serve as a geographical countervailing force. Most Canadians live within a few hundred kilometres of the American border and have easier access to their southern neighbours by land, air, and water than they have to other parts of their own country.

While twentieth-century developments in transportation and communication have largely eliminated geographical barriers to the movement of people and ideas, the origins of Canada's provinces can be found in an earlier era. The nation's federal system reflects a politics of place that, as we shall see, existed even before the arrival of the Europeans. Despite modern distinctions based on ethnicity, gender, and class, people in the Maritimes, Quebec, and the North, for example, also possess an identity based on geographical location and a shared historical experience in their geographic home.

The reasons why humans react to their environment in certain ways are complex. It is not difficult to understand why the First Nations of Newfoundland in the pre-contact period failed to develop farming practices, while their counterparts in the Great Lakes basin depended on farming for 70 percent of their food supply. There is simply very little good farmland in Newfoundland, while there is excellent potential for agriculture in what is today Ontario and Quebec. But why did the First Nations on the northern Prairies, later the breadbasket of the world, rarely farm? Did they simply lack the imagination? Or did the abundance of game, especially buffalo, make it unnecessary to develop an alternative supply of food? Or were there technological hurdles that had to be overcome before the Prairies could be successfully turned into rich wheatlands? These kinds of questions need to be addressed if we are to fully understand the regional character of the country.

In the past, history texts tended to be written with a Central Canadian bias. Historians, most of them working in Central Canadian universities, focussed on people and events in Ontario and Quebec and saw historical developments from the perspective of this region. They structured their chapters around dates that reflected significant episodes in the St Lawrence–Great Lakes region, such as the conquest or the rebellions, rather than developments in the Atlantic colonies, the Prairies, or the North. In this text we openly acknowledge that the tensions between the St Lawrence–Great Lakes "heartland" and the "peripheral" regions to the east, west, and north play a part in Canadian historical development. We attempt not only to discuss topics relevant to the "peripheral" regions of the nation but also to introduce regional perspectives on national developments, along with time frames that reflect the larger Canadian experience.

Although there is a surprising amount of documentary evidence concerning Canada's changing ecological history, it was only with the growth of the environmental movement in the 1970s that historians began to explore the impact of humans on their natural environment. We can now see new significance in the statements made by New Brunswick historian Peter Fisher in the 1820s to the effect that moose were being indiscriminately slaughtered and lumber companies were stripping the land of trees. In attempting to trace the changes in the environment over the past five hundred years, we offer a historical perspective on the environmental crisis that Canadians face today.

• Onwards and Upwards

The questions raised about the relationship of human beings to the planet have also prompted Canadian historians to reevaluate their interpretations of human interaction. In the past, historians simply assumed that the European conquest of Canada represented a step in the upward progress of "Western civilization." They were conditioned to accept notions of European moral superiority over other groups, the value of technological progress, and the right of Europeans to establish dominion over "inferior" peoples. Such views no longer go unchallenged. Aboriginal leaders now reject the Eurocentric view of the contact between Europeans and the aboriginal people of the Americas. They suggest that the First Nations embodied more egalitarian and peaceful values than the technologically superior European societies of the time. They also argue that Native peoples had a more positive relationship with the environment.

There is much evidence to support the Native interpretation of the past. By the time of contact, the Europeans, or at least their elites, had embraced social values that stressed domination: domination of women by men, domination of certain strata of citizens by a relatively tiny ruling group, and domination of the natural world by humankind. By contrast, most Native societies—like many European societies in earlier stages of their development—emphasized harmony among their members and with nature. While European values promoted scientific developments, the Natives of North America avoided the environmental destruction that dogged European "progress."

Many scholars now accept the Native perspective of events relating to the contact period and no longer see the European path of development as having beneficial consequences for the planet. As we shall see in later chapters, there is evidence that Canada's Native peoples had rich cultures that were weakened by European influence. In some cases the contact turned egalitarian, self-sufficient tribes into poverty-stricken groups riddled by disease, drunkenness, and abuse of women and children. This insight developed in part because historians now have a greater appreciation of the devastation wrought by European diseases on the Native peoples of the Americas. Although pre-contact populations are difficult to estimate, it would appear that between 1500 and 1650 the Native populations of the Americas were reduced to a mere 10 percent of their original numbers. In the face of such human devastation it is not difficult to see why the Europeans were able to defeat their aboriginal "enemies." Europeans were not morally or even necessarily technologically superior to the aboriginal peoples; they were only more immune to the diseases they brought with them.

While a positive reevaluation of pre-contact Native life has emerged in recent years, many scholars warn of the danger of romanticizing Native culture. Some aboriginal nations are alleged to have been warlike, others clearly practised slavery, and the evidence regarding the treatment of women in various tribes is, at best, contradictory. The disappearance of various animal species in the pre-contact period and evidence of wasteful hunting practices suggest that small populations, rather than conscious environmentalism, account for the lesser destruction of the environment in the pre-contact period compared to the period of European trade and settlement. We explore aspects of this debate in chapter 1.

The history of Native peoples is only one of many topics that have been fundamentally reevaluated in recent years. The emergence of a large literature on women's history has done more than add women to the picture; it has challenged many of the conclusions reached by historians who examined only the rhetoric and behaviour of male elites. In Canadian history, we now see the winning of responsible government in the mid-nineteenth century as primarily the triumph of middle-class white men. Women had to wait another seventy years for the vote and even longer to exercise significant political power.

Historians of women are quick to point out, however, that women were not merely passive victims of the historical process. Throughout the nineteenth century, for instance, parsons and pundits proclaimed that woman's place was in the home. They also focussed upon motherhood as woman's primary function in society. Despite such admonitions, women entered the work force in increasing numbers and dramatically limited the number of children they produced. So concerned were male legislators about the decline in the birth rate that they passed a law in 1892 denying women access to birth control and making abortion illegal. Nevertheless, the birth rate continued to decline. As is often the case with the powerless in society, women in the nineteenth century left few records to indicate why or how they limited births, but statistical evidence clearly demonstrates that they did so.

The history of the working class has also provided a new perspective on the past. By looking at history "from the bottom up," historians have been able to explain more clearly how power is exercised in Canadian society. Class, of course, is a difficult concept that changes over time. In the eighteenth and early nineteenth centuries, old aristocratic notions of the class structure, emphasizing land and heredity, dominated colonial life. The Industrial Revolution in the mid-nineteenth century increased the power of the middle class and created a landless working class, which was itself highly stratified.

Despite—or more likely because of—the large number of studies conducted on the working class, there is disagreement on a number of important questions. Historians take different views on the extent to which the values of skilled workers differed from those of their employers, and they hotly debate the degree to which skilled workers embraced the cause of the labouring poor. As for the poor themselves, both men and women, their voices remain largely silent in the pages of our history books. Statistical evidence and the views of reformers outside their ranks have been more available to historians than have direct expressions by the poor about their own situation.

Another problem is that documents capture only a moment of reality. As historians, we know that circumstances do not stand still. Values change, people grow older, and new ways of doing things come into practice. It is important, therefore, when studying individuals, to think about where they are in their life cycles. The responses of children to famine migrations or head taxes might well be quite different than the responses of middle-aged adults—and still more different than the responses of people nearing the end of their lives. Only a few documents, such as personal diaries, remind us that individuals are moving through time and that where they are in their own lifetimes is a critical part of understanding their point of view.

The report of the Royal Commission on the Relations between Capital and Labour in 1889 assembled the testimony of child and adult workers from some of Canada's earliest factories. This testimony was influenced not only by the presence of mill owners and supervisors but also by the stage the workers were at in their own lives. Georgina Loiselle, who was beaten with a cigar mould by M. Fortier, her employer, reported the incident with little emotion and no sense of outrage. She may well have been relatively sanguine about the event, not only because Fortier was supposedly acting in place of her parents, but also because she saw her situation as transitory. Like many young women of her generation, she undoubtedly hoped to marry and leave the factory forever. Her testimony in the 1880s must be viewed as one part of an ongoing process, a part that makes only limited sense in isolation.

There is nothing inevitable about historical processes. At times in this text the limitations on an individual's behaviour set by age, class, gender, region, or race may appear to suggest that many, perhaps most, of our ancestors were hopeless victims of forces beyond their control. A closer reading should reveal that people sought in various ways to transcend the limits placed on their lives. Social struggles of every sort changed or at least sought to change the course of history. The American feminist historian Natalie Zemon Davis speaks for many social historians when she observes:

> I want to show how different the past was. I want to show that even when times were hard, people found ways to cope with what was happening and maybe resist it. I want people today to be able to connect with the past by looking at the tragedies and the sufferings of the past, the cruelties and the hatefulness, the hope of the past, the love the people had, and the beating that they had. They sought for power over each other, but they helped each other, too. They did things both out of love and fear—that's my message. Especially I want to show that it could be different, that it was different and that there are alternatives.[2]

As you read this book we hope that you will gain a greater appreciation of how earlier generations of people in what is now called Canada responded to their environment and shaped their own history.

Notes

[1] It should be pointed out, however, that in 1990 more than 85 percent of historians teaching in Canadian universities were white men.

[2] Interview with Natalie Zemon Davis in MARHU, *Visions of History* (New York: Pantheon, 1983), 114–5.

BRITISH NORTH AMERICA AT THE TIME OF CONFEDERATION

In April and May 1855, a strike wave hit the region of Montreal. It began with a violent shutdown of the Grand Trunk Railway operations in Pointe St Charles, during which eleven machines were destroyed. The workers demanded better wages and shorter hours, and these demands soon echoed throughout workshops in the Griffintown area, including Redpath's sugar refinery and a large number of foundries. The violence at Pointe St Charles proved to be only the first of fourteen serious worker–employer confrontations in British North America from 1855 to 1859, confrontations mainly involving unskilled, unorganized labour. There were other manifestations of worker unrest. In Quebec City in late 1857, a demonstration of over 3000 people called on municipal officials to create jobs for the growing army of unemployed. On 10 June 1867, just three weeks before the creation of the Dominion of Canada, over 10 000 Montreal workers, parading behind the patriote flag of the Lower Canadian rebels of 1837, took to the streets in a show of worker solidarity. The parade was co-ordinated by the Grande Association de Protection des Ouvriers, an organization representing twenty-six crafts. Although the association soon disbanded, its message lived on: workers would not be treated as mere commodities in the capitalist marketplace.

• Economy and Society

The increase in unrest among wage-dependent workers was a sign of the changes affecting the fast-growing British North American colonies in the mid-nineteenth century. There were about 3.5 million people in British

North America in 1867. While an overwhelming majority of British North Americans remained self-employed primary producers, all were affected to some degree by the Industrial Revolution. In the mid-nineteenth century, factories and steam-operated machines began to replace home workers and artisans in small workshops, who had used mainly manual skills. This revolution reduced the numbers of people who could claim to be part of self-sufficient households. At the same time it expanded production and enhanced the role of marketplace relations in providing for people's needs.

Industry required not only mineral resources to operate its factories and machines but also foodstuffs to feed a work force that had neither the land nor the time to supply its own food needs. By mid-century, though new areas were still opening up in several of the colonies, most agricultural areas had passed the pioneer subsistence stage. An ever-increasing percentage of the rural population produced surpluses for international markets and the growing colonial cities and towns. Expanded agricultural markets meant cash that enabled farm families to purchase consumer goods and, later, farm implements, which in turn stimulated the development of trade and manufacturing in the urban centres.

Interior of the Toronto Rolling Mills, 1864   (Metropolitan Toronto Reference Library/ J. Ross Robertson Collection/T10914)

Starting in the 1840s, railways helped to quicken the pace of economic exchange. They linked cities with their rural hinterlands, and soon offered the possibility of transportation networks on an intercolonial and even an international scale. In 1867, the Grand Trunk Railway, stretching from Sarnia to Lévis, was the longest railway in British North America, and there were plans afoot to extend it into the Maritimes. Portland, Maine, was the winter port for the Grand Trunk. Other railway lines, such as the Great Western, were also oriented toward the United States. Between 1854 and 1866, a Reciprocity Treaty was in effect, which permitted primary products from the colonies to enter the United States duty free. British North American producers of timber, wheat, fish, and coal found steady markets, especially during the American Civil War, which raged from 1860 to 1865. As the demand for colonial produce increased, railway promoters dreamed of more and longer railways.

The railway companies became the major example in the pre-Confederation period of firms organized along industrial lines: personnel departments, specialized division of labour, modern accounting practices, and quality control procedures all reflected the implementation of the capitalist practices associated with the Industrial Revolution. The machine-laden locomotive shop of the Great Western in Hamilton and the wide range of metal-producing shops in the Grand Trunk's sprawling Montreal operation symbolized the changes that were occurring in goods production in British North America.

Railways, like other industrial projects, were changing the British North American economies and societies. But one must not overestimate the degree of social change that most individuals experienced before 1867. At the time of Confederation, over 80 percent of the working adult population of British North America received its income not from industry or services but from farming, fishing, lumbering, and fur trapping, with farming the primary occupation of the majority. Farming families, who made up the overwhelming majority of Canadians in 1867, consumed much of what they produced. For them, and for most residents of British North America, the family rather than the factory was still the unit of economic organization.

The Industrial Revolution was a male-dominated affair: overwhelmingly, both capitalists and skilled workers were white Protestant men. Women, children, francophones, recent immigrants, and people of colour were usually labelled "unskilled" and given the poorest wages. While some women took jobs in the new factories, particularly in textile, shoe, and tobacco production, the majority remained at home, responsible for unpaid domestic labour, which left them dependent on wages earned by fathers, husbands, and sons. Within the household economy of the farms, the distinction between paid and unpaid work, which became increasingly important in urban households, was less evident. The plant and animal resources of the farm were used by rural women to provide many items that city housewives, living in cramped working-class quarters, had to buy rather than produce themselves. Even though sales of farm products allowed farmers to purchase more goods, it was a rare farm household in the 1860s that did not depend for its survival on a myriad of activities largely reserved for women, such as gardening, canning, dairying, poultry raising, bread making, spinning, weaving, and sewing. In fishing communities, women cleaned and dried the fish. Native women fished, trapped, prepared hides, sewed clothes, gathered nuts, berries, and herbs, and served as guides. Everywhere, women, aided by older children, had the major responsibility for raising children, for cooking, and for cleaning. More affluent households had servants, who were also mainly female and who were generally supervised by the mistress of the house.

The labour of women was crucial to family survival, but it could not always ensure the independence of family units in rural areas. Throughout the colonies, many families lived on land too poor to provide for all their needs, much less for outside markets. Many farmers and their older sons worked as fishers or loggers part of the year to supplement family income. Their search for cash sometimes took them away from the farm for long periods. The women then managed the farm and were responsible for all facets of its operation. Some farm families gave up trying to eke out a living on marginal land and moved to industrial towns to take work in expanding factories.

Availability of land was a key factor in attracting immigrants to British North America, and by the 1850s it was mainly Canada West (today's southern Ontario) that drew prospective farmers. While over 75 percent of the Atlantic colonies' population was native born, as was an even higher percentage of rural residents of Canada East (today's southern Quebec), over half of the population of Canada West were immigrants, most seeking to establish a farm. Many of these immigrants spent years as farm labourers before being able to afford to buy their own land. Others never shed their status as farm labourers or tenants.

The promise of financial independence attracted settlers to Canada West but, for many, the fulfilment of the promise proved elusive. A farm family in Canada West might hope to clear two acres per year; in ten years, if they worked hard and were lucky, they might be self-sufficient in food and clothing. In subsequent years, the sale of surpluses might allow the purchase of luxuries: some Canada West farmhouses in the 1850s and 1860s boasted pianos, fancy furniture, and English imports such as clocks, pottery, and glassware. All of the British North American colonies had a

Women spinning and weaving   (Provincial Archives of New Brunswick, P5/641)

Dog-powered butter churn, circa 1870   (New Brunswick Museum/63.51)

range of residents, from the wealthy to the destitute, but people in Canada West were probably the most prosperous.

In 1867, Canada West was the breadbasket of British North America, producing 84 percent of the nation's wheat, much of it destined for export. Canada East specialized in livestock, potatoes, and coarse grains, most of which was consumed locally. Surplus potatoes, apples, and other foodstuffs from Maritime farms found markets in Newfoundland and the Caribbean. Stimulated by mechanization, new seeds and breeds, and better methods of transportation, commercial agriculture grew dramatically in the mid-nineteenth century, its markets expanded by urbanization, reciprocity, and the American Civil War. Even the end of reciprocity did not slow the momentum of Canadian agricultural expansion.

Luck and the determination of individuals and families both played a role in deciding who would prosper. Individual misfortune could jeopardize the survival of a family in an era where the state gave little aid to victims of circumstance. The death of a farmer in his prime years could mean destitution for his family, particularly if his widow had only children too young to work and was unable to find a new husband. A farm accident that incapacitated either the farmer or his wife could prove equally disastrous. The early death of a farm wife might force the widower to board his younger children or to hire a domestic servant to replace some of his wife's labours. While average life expectancy was forty, this figure is somewhat misleading. One in five children died before their first birthday, primarily as a result of diseases spread by impure water. Those who survived childhood and adolescence could expect to live to sixty. Still, neither long life nor robust health could be assumed.

If it became impossible to survive on a farm, a family had to move to a town where waged work by one or more family members became the means of survival. Unless one had a needed skill, finding work could be difficult. While labouring jobs for men were plentiful in summer, particularly in construction and dock work, the winter presented a bleak employment picture. The wages earned during the months when work was available could not easily be stretched to sustain a family for the entire year. When winter came, families in Halifax, Saint John, Montreal, and other colonial cities were often hard pressed to pay for the food, shelter, and fuel needed to survive until spring. The poor—which comprised most urban residents outside the merchant, professional, and skilled-trades categories—helped one another as much as they could. Two families might double up in a single room, for example, or share childcare so that mothers could do piecework or take in laundry. Some families survived the winter months only by resorting to charities run by middle- and upper-class women and female religious orders.

Although some of the new factories hired female labour, few town women had job prospects outside domestic service, and few households would hire a woman with children for what was usually a live-in position. The financial security of most women was tied to their choice of husband. Widows and wives of invalids, alcoholics, batterers, and philanderers obviously faced a difficult life. For the men who built the canals and railways and hauled goods off ships for eleven or twelve hours a day, when there was work, life was equally unrewarding. Many men were tempted to seek refuge from a dreary life by visiting taverns or brothels. Their wives, in a period when divorce was universally denounced and almost impossible to obtain, had little recourse. Moreover, married women's property laws held that the husband controlled all family assets, including any wages earned by the wife. On rare occasions, women in intolerable marriages might take their children and flee to the urban workhouses that many local governments had established for the destitute, but these spartan shelters provided neither privacy nor a future. Widows with young children also turned to workhouses as last resorts. The discomforts of the workhouse were intentional: the administrators wanted the working poor to know that a worse fate awaited them if they refused to accept even badly paid jobs.

Newcastle, on the Miramichi River, New Brunswick   (Provincial Archives of New Brunswick/L-225)

Only the most skilled of male workers—a small minority of the labour force—had the protection of unions in the pre-Confederation period. Unions not only fought for better wages and working conditions, they also provided members and their families with insurance against the loss of income that accompanied illness, disability, and death. Still, for the working class generally, life was not as bleak in 1860 as it had been half a century earlier. The transition from a commercial to an industrial economy brought glimpses of a better life, even for the most menial labourers. Manufacturing operations, unlike construction projects and dock work, often offered year-round employment, sometimes for several family members. Working conditions were likely to be harsh and the wages modest, but, for an increasing number of working-class families, these jobs offered a degree of security once unknown.

The household of the 1850s and 1860s took different forms. According to the nineteenth-century ideal, a family consisted of a married man and woman with their natural children. In reality, one household in four had members outside the immediate nuclear family, including relatives or boarders sharing accommodation. Many were headed by widows or deserted wives. Although families averaged seven children in 1851, the birth rate was falling. Women born in British North America in 1825 bore on average 7.8 children, while those born in 1845 bore 6.3. Most men did not marry until they were over twenty-five; women, on average, had reached the age of twenty-three at the time of marriage. Age at marriage depended somewhat on ethnic background, with French-speaking Catholic men and women marrying younger than English-speaking Protestants of Scottish background.

Marriage was considered a prerequisite for having children in a society where "illegitimate" children and their mothers were stigmatized even if many blamed the situation on the father who refused to marry the mother of his child. Desperate women sought illegal abortions; some who took the pregnancy to term committed infanticide; most unmarried mothers gave their babies to church-run orphanages where overcrowding and poor nutrition resulted in horrific death rates: of the 600 babies abandoned at the doors of a Montreal foundling hospital in 1863, for example, fewer than sixty survived. Community proscriptions against premarital sex were part of a rigid sexual code that also included harsh legal penalties against homosexuals. Homosexuality was considered a crime punishable by imprisonment and even death, though in practice the latter penalty appears not to have been imposed in the colonies. Still, there were cases of men being imprisoned for a decade for engaging in homosexual relationships. Networks of homosexual men appear to have existed but, because the legal system forced them to keep their intimate lives secret, little of the history of gays and lesbians of this period has been recorded.

Families in mid-century British North America were more likely to make provision for formally educating their children than had their counterparts in 1800. Schooling, once seen as the responsibility of parents and left to the voluntary sector and private enterprise, was increasingly becoming a state responsibility, with government grants to help build and maintain schools and hire teachers. Under the new education acts in the United Canadas and Nova Scotia, taxes were assessed on all property holders to eliminate the fees that parents had to pay to enrol their children in school. The common schools, or "free" schools as they were sometimes called, were not equally accessible to all children, and were certainly not uniform in their curriculum and administration. In the United Canadas, Roman Catholics ran their own schools and shared government grants equally with the public schools. A similar accommodation was worked out in Halifax. The Newfoundland government provided assistance to a school system that was developed entirely along denominational lines. While school attendance under the new system increased dramatically, most children attended erratically and for only a few years. Parents in many families viewed children over the age of eight or so primarily as contributors to the family economy. Although no longer dismissed as irrelevant or unaffordable, schooling was not allowed to take children from their home duties such as farmwork and minding younger brothers and sisters. In the 1860s, compulsory school attendance was a goal of education reformers, but it was still too controversial a policy to force on reluctant citizens.

As this discussion of schools suggests, religion played a crucial role in defining individual identity in British North America. About 40 percent of British North Americans were Roman Catholics, although this faith accounted for the majority only in Canada East and Assiniboia (the vast Hudson's Bay Company administrative district east of the Rocky Mountains and west of its administrative headquarters in the Red River colony, near today's Winnipeg). Protestants accounted for most of the rest of the population, especially in Canada West where eight of every ten residents was a Protestant. The largest Protestant denominations were Methodists, Presbyterians, Anglicans, and Baptists, the latter's strength largely limited to Nova Scotia and New Brunswick. Outside Canada East, Catholics were largely shut out of the economic elite and even the skilled trades. In larger communities, religiously defined organizations exerted considerable power. The Orange Order, initially an organization of Irish Protestants, had broadened into a larger set of Protestant clubs, offering social services and camaraderie to those whose identity was often bound up in anti-Catholicism. Violent clashes between Orange and Green (Irish Catholic) groups frequently accompanied the parades marking important events in the history of Ireland. Employers belonging to the Orange Order often hired members of the order over other candidates, especially Catholics. Yet, compared to Ireland, the religious strife in British North America was relatively muted.

Brute strength often outweighed notions of Christian charity in motivating individual behaviour in the colonies, where political conflict, drunken public brawls, and family violence were common. It was assumed by parents and teachers that naughty children should be beaten, and patriarchal perspectives accepted that a husband might use physical force against a wife who refused to obey him. Cockfighting, bearbaiting, wrestling, and fisticuffs, popular pastimes in rural areas, carried violence into recreation. Along the waterfront in Lower Town in Quebec and Water Street in Halifax, for example, the incidence of violent crimes and brawls, along with prostitution and drunkenness, was an extreme manifestation of the generalized brutality that many British North Americans embraced and many more fell victim to.

British North Americans were also the victims of life-threatening diseases and equally life-threatening treatments. The germ theory of disease was a generation away from widespread acceptance. Governments took few steps to improve sanitation; water and sewer systems in towns were rudimentary, with most residents either hauling their water from public wells or depending upon carters. Epidemics of cholera killed thousands while diseases such as tuberculosis and diphtheria were common. Physicians espousing a "scientific" model of diagnosis and treatment of ailments vied with an array of homeopaths and home-care advocates for public approval. No consensus emerged, but the future seemed to be on the side of the physicians, whose organizations had convinced several universities to open medical faculties that taught modern techniques of health and healing to an elite of young men.

Members of the elite were not immune to disease, but they usually lived away from the congested city centres and had better diets than those below them on the social scale. They could also indulge in more refined activities than their less fortunate fellow citizens. Eschewing the fisticuffs of the rural masses, the colonial elite set up clubs for yachting, racing, rowing, curling, and cricket. They read the works of colonial authors such as Thomas Chandler Haliburton, Susanna Moodie, and François Xavier Garneau, as well as literature imported from the United States, Britain, and France.

Most members of the elite were white, English-speaking, Protestant men, although a considerable element of Canada East's elite was francophone and Catholic. Non-whites and women were excluded from the interlocking boards of banks and railways as well as from political parties. Perhaps 50 000 people of African descent lived in the British North American colonies in the 1850s. The first blacks in the colonies were

The Victoria Pioneer Rifle Corps, the first all-black militia in Canada (British Columbia Archives and Records Service/HP53094)

mainly slaves who gained freedom as the colonies abolished slavery early in the nineteenth century. A large community of free United Empire Loyalist blacks settled in Nova Scotia after the American Revolution (1776–83) and were supplemented by black refugees from the War of 1812. In the 1850s, the "underground railway," devised and operated mainly by African Americans who had escaped slavery, brought many blacks to the United Canadas. While they were not slaves in their adopted country, blacks faced discrimination in land grants, voting rights, and access to schooling and jobs. Disheartened, many would return to the United States after the slaveholders were defeated in the American Civil War of 1861–65.

The discrimination faced by blacks was also the fate of the Chinese in pre-Confederation British North America, most of whom had migrated from California to British Columbia after the first of a series of gold rushes began in that colony in 1858. At the height of the gold fever in the early 1860s, about 7000 Chinese lived either on Vancouver Island or in mainland British Columbia. Most of the Chinese were men who worked as merchants, prospectors, and servants, but there were a few women working as prostitutes or alongside their husbands as merchants. By the end of the decade, with the gold fields depleted, fewer than 2000 Chinese remained in the colony of British Columbia: the hostility of the whites and lack of work had encouraged a majority of Chinese to return either to California or to their homeland.

For at least 140 000 non-whites, there was no other homeland but the territories that Britain and its colonizers now claimed as their own. In the 1860s, there were approximately 100 000 Indians in British Columbia and the Northwest, along with perhaps 10 000 Métis, some 20 000 Indians in the settled Eastern colonies, and 10 000 Inuit in the North. The Native population had been decimated from pre-contact estimates of 500 000 by European diseases such as typhus, smallpox, measles, scarlet fever, and whooping cough, for which Natives lacked immunities. The Native peoples had enjoyed more independence in the period before they had come into contact with European traders and settlers than they would ever know again. Lured by the iron goods of the fur traders, most Indians agreed to trap furs and provide supplies in return for desired merchandise. While the trade began as a fairly equal partnership between European traders and Native trappers, the Europeans soon exerted their energies to transform and control aboriginal peoples.

Such efforts, aided by missionaries who hoped to convert Indians to Christianity and European cultural values, had varying degrees of success. Overhunting of fur-bearing animals and game, evident in the Atlantic provinces in the seventeenth century and throughout much of the rest of British North America in the nineteenth century, often left tribes without an adequate resource base either to return to traditional lifestyles or to live well off trade. Despite adversity, aboriginal nations clung to ancient beliefs and practices, to the dismay of government and church authorities. In the 1860s, the Métis—the progeny of European traders and Native women—along with the Blackfoot of the southwestern plains, apprehensively watched the advance of western settlement in the United States and the resultant destruction of the buffalo, the source of their livelihood. Coastal Indians in British Columbia, who thrived during the fur-trade period, lost much of their land as settlers poured in from the 1850s onward and demonstrated little concern about the rights of the first inhabitants.

• Political Developments to 1867

The expansionary goals of the United States provided a catalyst for British North American union. In the first half of the nineteenth century, the Americans had swept aside the Indians and Spanish to extend their borders to the Pacific. They argued that it was their God-given right, or "manifest destiny," to do so. If the belligerent statements of politicians and pundits following the Civil War could be believed, the boundaries of the United States would soon extend to the North Pole as well. Most British North Americans had little interest in becoming American citizens. In the 1860s they were proud members of the British Empire and intended to stay that way. It was true that the mother country was tired of pouring money into the defence of the struggling North American colonies, but by adopting a tighter political framework, they could arguably better repel American aggression and serve the interests of Great Britain as well as their own.

For most advocates of Confederation, the United States was less a military threat than a shining example of what British North Americans hoped to achieve: industrial progress. The wealth that American entrepreneurs on the Atlantic seaboard had gained from industrial development made them the envy of colonial capitalists. Montreal's business community in particular had long set their sights on developing the "empire of the St Lawrence," as historian Donald Creighton described their vision. Until the mid-1840s, they could rely on British protectionism and imperial preference. Under this system, Britain applied low tariffs or no tariffs at all to goods produced in the colonies while levying high tariffs on goods produced outside of the British Empire. The Montreal bourgeoisie hoped to become the wholesalers and shipping agents of products traded between Britain and the United States. As Britain moved towards a policy of free trade, the Montreal business vision collapsed, to be replaced by a concentration on the American market for Canadian lumber and wheat, which reciprocity had expanded dramatically. As it became clear that the United States, with a protectionist Republican government under President Abraham Lincoln, was unlikely to renew reciprocity, the Montreal tycoons searched for a new plan to guarantee their profits.

The American success story offered the outlines of that plan. Montreal could become New York, Philadelphia, and Boston all rolled into one—a huge metropolis that dominated the financial, industrial, and railway life of a nation that stretched from coast to coast. Perhaps then the Grand Trunk Railway, whose construction and operation had nearly bankrupted the United Province of Canada, could finally become financially viable. Instead of looking southwards, railway promoters in Canada looked east to the mainland Atlantic colonies and westwards to the Hudson's Bay Company territories.

Toronto capitalists also looked westwards and believed that, standing in closer proximity to the region, they stood a better chance of capturing these new markets. But before western markets could be exploited, the land had to be acquired from the Hudson's Bay Company, the Indians

removed or marginalized, and the region opened up to commercial farmers who would ship their produce on Toronto railroads and receive, in
return, Toronto-manufactured products. Farmers in Canada West, fearful
that their province could not provide a farming future for all their children, embraced the call for a confederation that would be committed to
agricultural development in the Hudson's Bay territories and to the link by
railway of those territories to the settlements of Canada West. George
Brown, leader of the Reform Party in Canada West, was the most vocal
advocate of this viewpoint.

In theory, the Province of Canada could have acquired the northwest
region controlled by the HBC and reached consensus with the Atlantic
provinces regarding railway connections and free trade without resorting
to formal political arrangements. But the fractious politics of the United
Province and the heavy debts of its government made business people and
financiers uneasy. British investors, led by the large Baring Brothers bank,
would only agree to finance large new ventures in British North America if
the colonies united. It would be easier to deal with one government in the
region than several, and projects would be more likely to succeed if intercolonial squabbling could be averted. If colonial politicians refused to
meet the terms of the international business community, they might never
be able to realize their dreams of economic development.

The most vocal proponents of this business perspective were
Montreal's Grand Trunk Railway officials. The Grand Trunk was built on
shaky financial foundations. Like many railway projects in North America
in this period, its founders made a fortune by selling stocks many times in
excess of their real values, arguing that economic expansion would soon
justify inflated stock prices. But such initial speculation, added to misman-
agement and lower-than-predicted volumes of rail traffic, made the company a big money loser. The government of the United Province had
guaranteed many of the Grand Trunk's loans and was responsible for many
of its bills. In 1863, some of the railway company's chief British investors,
speculating on the chances of Confederation, purchased control of the
Hudson's Bay Company. They expected that a united British North
America would receive the financing necessary to buy the company's lands
from them at a price that would ensure a tidy profit. They also hoped that
the new national government would allow the Grand Trunk to build railways linking the mainland Atlantic colonies with Canada and linking
Canada with the Northwest.

Because of the growing railway debt, many politicians in the United
Canadas saw Confederation as an economic necessity. For many it was also
the way out of a political impasse. The United Province had been created
in 1840 by Britain in the aftermath of the rebellions in Upper Canada and

Lower Canada. It was a shotgun wedding of two colonies with different linguistic and religious majorities: over 80 percent of Lower Canadians were French-speaking Catholics while Upper Canadians were predominantly English-speaking Protestants. The British hoped to encourage French-Canadian assimilation to the English language and to Anglo-Protestant values, but they failed to achieve their goals. Even before responsible government (the selection of a Cabinet with majority support from the elected legislature) was granted in the late 1840s, co-operation between the two linguistic groups, rather than domination of one by the other, was evident. The division of the Department of Education into two sections, one for Canada West and one for Canada East, agreed upon by both elected legislators and the British-appointed governor-general, suggested that the union would not become a vehicle for French-Canadian assimilation despite earlier British objectives.

Agreement between the two sections of the United Province on important issues proved elusive. In Quebec, a coalition of conservative elements—the *bleus*—emerged as the dominant political force by the early 1850s. A francophone bourgeoisie, whose political connections served as an entry onto the boards of otherwise anglophone enterprises, won popular support by championing clerical views on education and cultural matters. Meanwhile, small farmers in Quebec increasingly came under the sway of a reinvigorated church. The Catholic Church, itself a large institutional investor, found a natural affinity with opportunist business people and politicians willing to serve clerical interests, and it urged the faithful to support conservative politicians. Liberal factions continued to enjoy strength in Montreal and Quebec City with their denunciations of tariffs, subsidies to railway magnates, and church control of education. But the weighting of ridings towards the rural areas weakened the representation of liberal sentiment from Quebec.

Within Canada West, by contrast, reformist politicians usually won electoral majorities. The result was that governments throughout the Union period could rarely claim to represent a majority of the voters in both sections of the United Province. The Protestant majority in Canada West chafed at laws providing public support to Catholic schools in their half of the province, laws passed by an overwhelming number of legislators from Canada East but with only minority support in Canada West.

As the population of Canada West began to outstrip that of Canada East—in 1861, the balance was 1.4 million to 1.1 million, in Canada West's favour—demands for representation by population rather than the equal division of seats between the two Canadas became a mainstay of reform politicians in Canada West. Francophone legislators from Canada East flatly rejected anglophone Reformers' view that democracy demanded a reapportionment of seats. They had not wanted the union in the first place, they noted, and would do nothing to weaken the position of francophones within it if it must continue.

As sectionalism became entrenched, government in the United Canadas came to a standstill. Finally, early in 1864, upon the initiative of George Brown, a coalition government was established with the sole purpose of finding a solution to the constitutional impasse. John A. Macdonald, George-Étienne Cartier, and George Brown—leaders of the Canada West Conservatives, the Canada East *bleus*, and Canada West Reformers—were all included in the Great Coalition. By June they had formulated a proposal.

The political crisis in the United Canadas coincided with discussions in the legislatures of the Maritime provinces about the desirability of Maritime union. Primarily of interest to Nova Scotians and New Brunswickers who were riding high on their shipbuilding and shipping industries, Maritime union offered the prospects of creating a larger stage for local politicians and entrepreneurs who did not want to lose out on opportunities in the age of industry and railways. The ice-free ports of Halifax and Saint John would serve as the end point for any major railway project the union could mount, and the region's rich reserves of coal would fuel the engines that ran the trains and factories.

Despite its logic, the idea of Maritime union soon gave way to notions of a rather larger federation. By inviting themselves as observers to the Maritime union conference, the Canadians began a chain of events that led to three conferences: one in Charlottetown in September 1864, a second in Quebec City in October of the same year, and a final one in London in the fall and winter of 1866–67. In April 1867, the British North America Act, bringing Ontario, Quebec, New Brunswick, and Nova Scotia together as the Dominion of Canada, passed in the British parliament and came into effect on 1 July 1867.

The Confederation agreement was largely the handiwork of the politicans from the United Canadas. For them the most important goal was to preserve the principle of majority rule while at the same time satisfying the demands of the francophone minority. This was achieved through a federal system of government. In the new federation, representation roughly by population (though with rural ridings receiving better representation than urban) would be granted in federal elections. But there would also be a provincial level of government, and both Canada West and Canada East would have provincial status. Pro-confederates in Quebec argued that the control over cultural and educational policies granted the provinces effectively recreated the separate Quebec that the Act of Union had wiped out. Anti-confederates, mainly francophone liberals—the *rouges*, led by A.A. Dorion—claimed that the proposed Confederation was too centralist.

Dorion argued that the federal government, with control over trade, foreign affairs, interprovincial railways, justice, and defence as well as the right to take on extraordinary powers in times of emergency, would dictate to the provinces. Francophone Quebec would lose control over its destiny, and eventually its culture would be eroded and its people assimilated into an anglophone Protestant state. *Rouge* pressures for an election or a referendum on Confederation were rejected, and the *bleu* majority from Canada East joined the major political forces from Canada West to give the Confederation scheme a comfortable majority in the legislature of the Province of Canada.

The accusation that the proposed Confederation gave too much power to the central government was also widespread in the Atlantic colonies. There, opponents rightly noted that Confederation was a scheme of Canadian politicians and business interests who regarded the proposed new nation as an extension of the boundaries of the United Province. Central Canada, by virtue of the concentration of over three-quarters of the colonial population within its territory, would dominate the new federation. A majority of Atlantic residents probably opposed Confederation, at least on the terms offered under the British North America Act. Local tariffs would have to be abandoned if Confederation succeeded, and many saw no reason to subsidize a railway from the Atlantic to the Canadas when the important markets were in Britain and the United States, not in Canada East or Canada West. In addition, the proposed acquisition of the Northwest would benefit few Atlantic citizens. Ontario farmers might see the Northwest as an extension of their own region and a good place to establish younger sons so that family farms need not be subdivided. But Nova Scotians and New Brunswickers, like Québécois, looked southwards, not to the West, for new places to settle.

Despite these factors, there were many supporters of Confederation within Atlantic Canada. The emerging coal and iron interests and railway investors in Nova Scotia responded positively to a wider federation. Charles Tupper, Nova Scotia's premier, had substantial investments in coal mines and, like other Maritime capitalists, hoped that markets in the Canadas might provide a partial replacement for markets about to be lost in the United States when the reciprocity treaty ended. Tupper, like his Canadian counterparts, chose not to have an election on the issue of Confederation. Through careful manoeuvring, he managed to get the Assembly to authorize further negotiations on union, but neither the Nova Scotia voters nor their elected representatives gave their approval to the resolutions included in the BNA Act.

New Brunswickers were also initially unimpressed with the Confederation proposals. An election in the colony in 1865 gave anti-confederates a comfortable majority. But Lieutenant-Governor Arthur Gordon won support for political union from the Catholic bishops of the province as well as from the timber merchants. He forced a second Confederation election in 1866 after the end of reciprocity with the United States and raids on British North America by the American wing of the Fenian Brotherhood, an Irish nationalist organization, had unsettled many New Brunswickers. Leaving little doubt that Britain expected New Brunswick to join the new nation of Canada, Gordon was able to secure a reversal of the voters' judgment a year earlier.

• Conclusion

No one could be sure in 1867 if the federation, created in good part to guarantee that certain railways would be built, would ever become a nation in the sentiments of its residents. While John A. Macdonald and other supporters of Confederation spoke passionately of creating a "new nationality," most of the new Canadians of 1867 identified mainly with their own colonies, now provinces, or indeed with the local area in which they lived. Most were unsure what impact the new federation would have on their lives. Generally, the struggle for survival was paramount in people's minds. While many embraced the Confederation cause absolutely and many others rejected it out of hand, most simply went about their lives and hoped that the politicians had not simply created another fine mess.

• Selected Reading

This chapter summarizes materials in the later chapters of *History of the Canadian Peoples*, volume 1. These chapters include lists of readings that may be consulted for the various topics raised in this chapter. Following is an abbreviated list of books dealing with the political, social, and economic history of British North America from about 1850 to 1867.

On the societies of British North America during this period useful starting-points are: Jean Barman, *The West Beyond the West: A History of British Columbia* (Toronto: University of Toronto Press, 1991); Gerald Friesen, *The Canadian Prairies: A History* (Toronto: University of Toronto Press, 1987); J.M.S. Careless, *The Union of the Canadas: the Growth of Canadian Institutions, 1841–1857* (Toronto: McClelland and Stewart, 1967); Brian Young and John A. Dickinson, *A Short History of Quebec: A*

Socioeconomic Perspective (Toronto: Copp Clark Pitman, 1988); and W.S. MacNutt, *The Atlantic Provinces: The Emergence of Colonial Society, 1712–1857* (Toronto: McClelland and Stewart, 1965). On women's experience, see Alison Prentice, Paula Bourne, Gail Cuthbert Grant, Beth Light, Wendy Mitchinson, and Naomi Black, *Canadian Women: A History* (Toronto: Harcourt Brace Jovanovich, 1988); Clio Collective, *Quebec Women: A History* (Toronto: Women's Press, 1986); Marjorie Griffin Cohen, *Women's Work, Markets, and Economic Development in Nineteenth-Century Ontario* (Toronto: University of Toronto Press, 1988); Peter Ward, *Courtship, Love and Marriage in Nineteenth-Century English Canada* (Montreal: McGill-Queen's University Press, 1990); and Constance Backhouse, *Petticoats and Prejudice: Women and the Law in Nineteenth-Century Canada* (Toronto: Women's Press, 1991). On rural life, see John McCallum, *Unequal Beginnings: Agriculture and Economic Development in Quebec and Ontario to 1870* (Toronto: University of Toronto Press, 1980); J.I. Little, *Crofters and Habitants: Settler Society, Economy and Culture in a Quebec Township, 1848–1881* (Montreal: McGill-Queen's University Press, 1991); and David Gagan, *Hopeful Travellers: Families, Land and Social Change in Mid-Victorian Peel County, Canada West* (Toronto: University of Toronto Press, 1981). Urban studies include the opening chapters of books on Toronto, Ottawa, and Hamilton in the Lorimer "Cities" series; T.W. Acheson, *Saint John: The Making of a Colonial Urban Community* (Toronto: University of Toronto Press, 1985); Michael Katz, *The People of Hamilton, Canada West: Family and Class in a Mid-Nineteenth Century City* (Cambridge, MA: Harvard University Press, 1975); and Judith Fingard, *The Dark Side of Life in Victorian Halifax* (Halifax: Pottersfield Press, 1989). On the history of the working class, the major overviews are Bryan Palmer, *Working-Class Experience: The Rise and Reconstitution of Canadian Labour, 1800–1980* (Toronto: Butterworths, 1983); and Desmond Morton and Terry Copp, *Working People: An Illustrated History of Canadian Labour* (Ottawa: Deneau, 1980). On Native peoples the two survey texts are Olive Patricia Dickason, *Canada's First Nations: A History of Founding Peoples from Earliest Times* (Toronto: McClelland and Stewart, 1992); and J.R. Miller, *Skyscrapers Hide the Heavens: A History of Indian–White Relations in Canada* (Toronto: University of Toronto Press, 1989).

There is an extensive literature on Confederation. Some of the key titles are: Ged Martin, ed., *The Causes of Canadian Confederation* (Fredericton: Acadiensis, 1990); D.G. Creighton, *The Road to Confederation: The Emergence of Canada 1863–1867* (Toronto: Macmillan, 1964); P.B. Waite, *The Life and Times of Confederation 1864–1867: Politics, Newspapers and the Union of British North America* (Toronto: University of Toronto Press, 1964); Kenneth G. Pryke, *Nova Scotia and Confederation* (Toronto: University of Toronto Press, 1979); W.L. Morton, *The Critical Years: The Union of British North America 1857–1873* (Toronto: McClelland and Stewart, 1964); and Arthur I. Silver, *The French-Canadian Idea of Confederation, 1864–1900* (Toronto: University of Toronto Press, 1982).

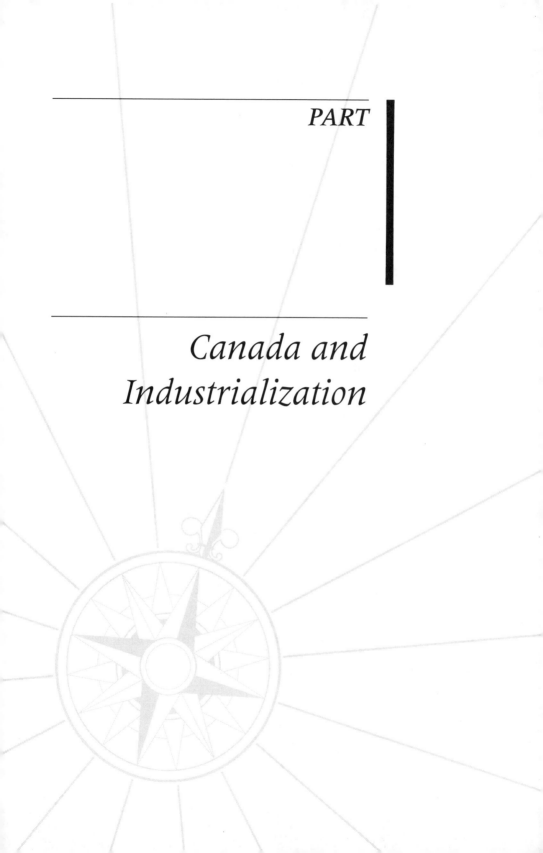

PART

Canada and Industrialization

Time Line

1859	–	Publication of Darwin's *On the Origin of Species*
1862	–	Establishment of Metlakatla
1867	–	Confederation; first federal and provincial elections; anti-confederates win in Nova Scotia
1867–73	–	John A. Macdonald serves as prime minister
1868	–	Canada First movement formed
1869	–	First Northwest Rebellion; Nova Scotia and federal government come to terms; Timothy Eaton opens his first store; beginning of Guibord affair in Montreal
1870	–	Province of Manitoba established; first branch of the YWCA opens in Saint John
1871	–	British Columbia joins Confederation; New Brunswick School Act; compulsory schooling for seven to fourteen year olds legislated in Ontario; Treaty of Washington
1871–77	–	Negotiation of treaties with Indians of Northwest
1872	–	Dominion Lands Act
1873	–	Prince Edward Island joins Confederation; Royal North West Mounted Police established; Pacific scandal
1873–78	–	Economic recession; Alexander Mackenzie serves as prime minister
1874	–	Creation of Woman's Christian Temperance Union in Canada
1875	–	Caraquet riot; union of Presbyterian churches
1876	–	Passage of Indian Act; creation of Toronto Women's Literary Club
1877	–	Saint John fire leaves 15 000 homeless
1878	–	Canada Temperance Act
1878–91	–	Macdonald's Conservatives return to power
1879	–	Increase in tariff marks implementation of National Policy; Provincial Miners' Association founded in Nova Scotia
1880	–	Canadian Pacific Railway contract granted
1881	–	Founding of the Société nationale des Acadiens

1883	–	Formation of Trades and Labour Congress of Canada; breakthrough of Knights of Labour; union of Methodist churches
1884	–	Creation of Imperial Federation League; Ontario passes the nation's first Factory Act
1885	–	Potlatch banned; pass system introduced for Native peoples in the Northwest; first head tax imposed on Chinese immigrants; major smallpox epidemic in Quebec; second Northwest Rebellion; Quebec Factory Act
1886	–	Parti national wins Quebec provincial election; "repealers" win Nova Scotia election; establishment of Royal Commission on Relations of Labour and Capital
1887	–	Provincial premiers' conference; British–American Joint High Commission on inshore fisheries set up
1888	–	Jesuit Estates Act passed in Quebec
1889	–	Federal government concedes that the area from Kenora to Thunder Bay forms part of Ontario
1890	–	Manitoba renounces official bilingualism and removes public support for separate schools
1891	–	Papal encyclical, *Rerum Novarum*, released; Goldwin Smith's *Canada and the Canadian Question* published
1891–92	–	John Abbott heads government
1892	–	North-West Territories legislative assembly restricts French-language education; St John's fire leaves 10 000 homeless
1892–94	–	John Thompson is prime minister
1893	–	Formation of National Council of Women of Canada
1894	–	Nova Scotia legislature defeats by one vote legislation to enfranchise women
1894–96	–	Mackenzie Bowell serves as prime minister
1895	–	Clara Brett Martin is Canada's first woman law graduate
1896	–	Charles Tupper serves briefly as prime minister until Conservatives defeated by Laurier Liberals

CHAPTER

NATIONAL GROWTH, NATIONAL DIVISIONS:
Politics and Protest, 1867–96

In 1881 a debate was raging in the House of Commons over Prime Minister John A. Macdonald's decision to grant the Canadian Pacific Railway a twenty-year monopoly on its route through the Northwest. In his speech, Macdonald evoked nationalism and economic self-interest and more than a hint of anti-Americanism. Edward Blake, the leader of the opposition, picked up on the latter when he replied:

> The views of hon. gentlemen opposite with reference to our North-West seem to me of the gloomiest character. They say, first of all, when you want to get an emigrant into that country, the only way you can do it is to practically blindfold him; because if you let him see or get within 100 miles of the American frontier he will be quite sure to go to the United States. They say, if you intend to keep him in our country, you have got to fetter his trade; if you build the railway close to the boundary both himself and his trade will go to Dakota and Minnesota and stay there too. If I thought that the future of the North-West depended on this drastic application, upon this compulsion, this forcing, upon this insisting upon particular measures, and lines and routes of railway, I should have very little hope in that future.[1]

There was little consensus on many of the crucial issues facing the new Dominion of Canada, as the debate between Blake and Macdonald makes clear. Regional, ethnic, class, and gender divisions ensured that the country's infancy would not be a peaceful one. In chapters 3 and 4 we will examine some of the conflicts that grew out of class and gender divisions. In this chapter we concentrate on Native peoples, who protested that their rights were ignored in the onrush of western and northern settlement; provincial

governments, which condemned federal actions as harmful to local interests; and the traditional hostilities between French-speaking Catholics and
English-speaking Protestants.

VOTING IN THE NEW DOMINION

The political system became the locus for many of the struggles within the
new political federation of Canada. Those with most to complain about
were least likely to have a vote. Voting at all levels of government was
largely restricted to male property holders. Women were denied the vote
at all levels until the 1880s when most provinces gave widows and single
women with property the vote in municipal elections. Status Indians,
regarded as wards of the state, had no vote. Property qualifications,
though gradually eased, kept most unskilled workers and farm labourers
off electoral lists. As a result of property, gender, and age restrictions,
only 15 percent of the Quebec population, for example, could vote in the
provincial or federal elections in 1871 and only about 20 percent had this
right by the end of the century. Today, by contrast, almost 70 percent of
the population has the right of suffrage, with most of the non-voters being
either children or immigrants who have not yet fulfilled the requirements
for citizenship. Municipal property qualifications were often stricter than
provincial requirements. In Winnipeg, for example, as late as 1906, only
7784 voters were registered in a city with a population of over 100 000.
Despite their disfranchisement, women, Indians, and the poor formed
organizations of their own which, as we shall see, did have an impact on
the political system.

•Parties and Patronage

By the mid-1870s, the two major parties in each province were the Liberal-
Conservatives (*bleus* in Quebec) and Liberals (or Reformers or Grits, as
they were often called). Party policy was set and candidates were chosen by
a small elite within each party. Constituency organizations, party memberships, and other characteristics of modern political organizations lay in the
future. The nineteenth-century party was an undisguised political machine
of key figures drawn from the business and professional communities. The
machine was well oiled by corporate contributions collected by party bag-
men who promised favours to donors should the party win election.

Government contracts, ranging from construction to printing, and government jobs, including plum appointments to harbour commissions and such lowly positions as rural postmaster, were reserved for the party faithful. Before World War I, only the barest attempts were made at any level of government to place competence above political loyalty in awarding contracts and posts.

Once in office, national parties were careful to use patronage to accommodate regional elites. In Quebec, the views of the clergy could not be ignored on political appointments; in Nova Scotia the coal owners and shippers had to be placated. Prime Minister John A. Macdonald allowed Joseph Howe, the repentant anti-confederate, as much influence in determining hirings and contracts in Nova Scotia as Charles Tupper, the loyal confederate, in order to broaden his government's support in the alienated province. In short, party loyalties were often bought rather than won through force of argument.

The majority of voters were not part of the partisan gravy trains and could choose their representatives on the basis of either support for the policies of a particular party or support for the integrity of a politician regardless of party. The latter way of choosing was in some ways futile. Members of a party caucus were expected to support their leaders. While the occasional dispute caused a breakdown in caucus voting, it was increasingly understood by ambitious MPs that to vote against the party leadership was to relinquish all hope of receiving a Cabinet post or other perks of office.

The issues dividing the two parties shifted over time, but on the whole the Conservative Party championed the powers of the federal government against the claims of the provinces. Macdonald's government, partly because it wished to maintain maximum patronage in its own hands but also because it believed on principle in a strong national government, clashed repeatedly with provincial administrations, particularly Liberal ones, over control of railway policy, river navigation policy, and many other issues. The tariff and railway policies of the Conservative administrations suggested that the party was not reluctant to intervene in the economy, albeit on the side of the most economically powerful.

Liberal parties in Ontario and the Maritimes included staunch free traders, mostly associated with the fisheries, agriculture, and the resource sector, who regarded interventionist governments as easily corruptible and distorters of the marketplace. The Liberals also included provincial rights defenders such as Oliver Mowat, premier of Ontario from 1872 to 1896, who was as eager as any Conservative to spend government money to promote industry in his province. Provincial rights became the rallying cry that held together the Liberals in a party whose members were divided regionally on the major Macdonald economic policies. Opponents of the original Confederation agreement who had balked at the apparent centralization of powers called for in the British North America Act generally favoured the Liberal Party over the Conservative Party.

• The Early Confederation Years

On 1 July 1867, by an act of the British Parliament, the Dominion of Canada was born. The Dominion's population, judging from the census conducted in 1861, was just under 3.1 million people: 1 396 091 residents in Ontario, 1 111 566 Quebeckers, 330 857 Nova Scotians, and 252 047 New Brunswickers. To Lord Monck, the governor-general, fell the task of choosing the nation's first prime minister. He selected John A. Macdonald, an opponent of Confederation before 1864, but thereafter its most energetic promoter.

Elections were held in different constituencies from July to September. By September 1867 it was clear that the Macdonald–Cartier party would form both the federal government and the provincial administrations of Quebec and Ontario. Led by Samuel Leonard Tilley, pro-confederates in New Brunswick had also carried a majority of that province's federal seats and were easily absorbed into the Conservative Party and government, both led by John A. Macdonald.

The opposition forces in Quebec and Ontario carried a relatively small number of seats in 1867. In Ontario, George Brown, who had left the Great Coalition in late 1865 over objections to the government's handling of negotiations of a new reciprocity treaty with the Americans, led a party of pro-confederate Reformers in opposition to Macdonald's Conservatives. But Macdonald was able to convince the remaining two Reform members of his coalition Cabinet to continue to support his government. The presence of Reformers in his entourage as well as the esteem he had won for leading the battle for a Confederation popular with most Ontario voters gave Macdonald a comfortable majority in Ontario.

The Quebec Liberals led by A.A. Dorion were in disarray, unwilling to accept Confederation but unable to undo it. The Roman Catholic Church's continued support of the *bleus* almost assured the defeat of Liberal candidates. But the extent of *bleu* support is often overstated by concentrating on the number of seats won rather than on popular vote. In the provincial election of 1867, the Liberals won 45 percent of the votes to 55 percent for the Conservatives. The vagaries of the electoral system trans-

Sir John A. Macdonald   (National Archives of Canada/PA12848)

lated this relatively close vote into fifty Conservative and fourteen Liberal seats, with one Independent. The federal result was forty-five Conservatives and nineteen Liberals.

Nova Scotia's Secessionist Movement

The Macdonald Conservatives' ability to win seats did not extend into Nova Scotia. Many farmers, fishers, and business people who had agitated for better terms for Nova Scotia's entry into Confederation continued to oppose the scheme. When the voters of that province went to the polls in September 1867 to elect both their federal parliamentary contingent and a new provincial house, they gave a decisive victory, particularly in seats, to the anti-confederates led by Joseph Howe. Charles Tupper narrowly carried his own federal seat, but the remaining eighteen Nova Scotia seats went to anti-confederates. With thirty-six of thirty-eight provincial seats held by anti-confederates, Nova Scotia's first post-Confederation provincial administration, headed by William Annand, was pledged to repeal the province's adherence to Confederation.

The secession threat posed a serious challenge to the new Dominion government as Tupper failed in his attempts to brand the Anti-union League, headed by Howe, as traitors to Britain and sympathizers of the Fenians. Many Nova Scotians believed that their interests would be sacrificed to those of Central Canada after Confederation and had reason to harbour such fears. In 1866 the British Colonial Office had, at the urging of the government in the Province of Canada, agreed to impose a licence system on Americans fishing inshore in the Maritimes. The Colonial Secretary was unwilling to keep the Americans completely out of the inshore fishery as the Maritimers were demanding because this would harm British–American relations, which the British government was attempting to repair. The black border around the front page of the Halifax *Morning Chronicle* and mock demonstrations against Confederation on 1 July 1867 expressed majority opinion in Nova Scotia that their colony's emerging autonomy had been snuffed out to be replaced by Central Canadian domination.

The first session of the Canadian Parliament opened on 8 November 1867 and endorsed several policies that reinforced Nova Scotian alienation from the new nation. When the 15 percent tariff rate of the Province of Canada became the rate for the post-Confederation Dominion of Canada there was a loud outcry from those who feared the impact of high tariffs on trade. Nova Scotia's rate had been 10 percent, and the West Indies import merchants of Halifax protested that they were being squeezed so that the sugar refineries of Montreal could be protected.

Nova Scotian alienation did not impress the Colonial Office, whose officials moved quickly to defeat the efforts of anti-confederates to repeal the union agreement. While Howe lobbied British politicians in London in June 1868, Colonial Secretary Lord Carnarvon made it plain to Canada's first governor-general, Lord Monck, that he would dismiss Nova Scotia's appeal. Although the formal request of the Nova Scotia legislature for repeal of its adherence to Confederation was officially rejected on 25 January 1869, its rejection had been assured months earlier.

Before the official boom fell on Nova Scotian aspirations for secession, Howe had begun to negotiate with the Canadians for better terms for Nova Scotia within Confederation. Such negotiations divided the anti-confederates, some of whom were prepared to resort to rebellion against Britain to undo the hated union. In contrast, Howe was neither a populist nor a republican: he was repulsed by talk of popular revolt or annexation to the United States as an alternative to the adhesion to Canada that Britain now demanded of Nova Scotia.

The major items in the "better terms" negotiated in 1868–69 by Howe with Finance Minister John Rose were the assumption by the federal government of an additional $1 million of pre-Confederation Nova Scotia debt and a grant of $82 698 per year for ten years from 1 June 1867 to help Nova Scotia meet its post-Confederation debts. The latter was a stopgap measure meant to deal with Nova Scotia's revenue shortfall since it would no longer collect its own tariffs and excise duties. Even so, at the end of the first year of Confederation, Ontario enjoyed a surplus on current account of $1 million while Nova Scotia faced a deficit of $100 000.

Resentment against the federal government remained strong. In 1871 Canada was represented as part of the British delegation in Washington that met with the Americans to resolve issues dividing the two countries. These included American access to Canada's inshore fisheries as well as American claims for compensation for damages inflicted during the American Civil War by Southern forces sailing British-built raiders such as

"Confederation! The much-fathered youngster." Cartoon by J.W. Bengough, 1886 (National Archives of Canada/C78676)

the *Alabama*. Macdonald hoped to trade the former for a new reciprocity treaty between Canada and the United States. That proved impossible with a protectionist Republican Congress south of the border. Canada had to content itself with the Washington Treaty's promise of $5.5 million in return for opening the fisheries. There would be no new reciprocity treaty.

The Nova Scotia government, charging a sell-out of Nova Scotia interests, called a general election for May 1871. It was re-elected but with a much-reduced majority. Gradually the government party came to identify with the Liberal opposition in the other provincial legislatures and in Parliament as this party shared its emphasis on provincial rights. Macdonald began awarding contracts for the construction of Nova Scotia sections of the Intercolonial Railway, and the resulting economic activity, not to mention patronage, assuaged anti-confederate sentiments. Talk of secession died down for about fifteen years, and the first threat to Confederation was averted. But Macdonald's troubles were not over yet.

Annexing the Northwest: The Red River Rebellion

The first parliamentary session of the Dominion of Canada moved swiftly to negotiate the transfer of the Northwest, also known as Rupert's Land, to the new country. By 1869 an agreement had been reached with the Hudson's Bay Company, which held legal title over the region, to sell its claim to the land for £300 000 (about $1.5 million) and one-twentieth of the lands of the fertile belt. This represented a major financial coup for the financiers who had bought control of the company in 1863 for £1.5 million since they recouped part of their initial investment in cash, retained their fur-trading operations, and stood to gain immensely from the sale of lands once the area was settled. Eventually, the land sales netted the company $120 million, or a profit of over fifteen times the 1863 investment.

The aboriginal peoples were treated less generously than the European "owners" of the land. Anxious to open the Northwest to Euro-Canadian settlement, the federal government moved quickly to establish its claim to Canada's new frontier. Public Works Minister William McDougall sent land surveyors to the Red River colony in August 1869 to prepare the first colony of the Government of Canada for an onrush of settlers, which was expected when the official transfer of title occurred in December. The Métis, aware that the Canada Act would soon place them under Canadian rather than Hudson's Bay Company control, feared the fate of the lands they farmed and, like the Ontario imperialists, wanted to ensure that land would be available to their descendants. Consulted by neither the company nor the Canadians, they feared the worst when they saw that the surveyors were using Ontario's square-lot system rather than the Quebec river-lot system used by the Métis to mark off land.

Since custom, not courts, determined Métis land title, they were afraid of losing possession of their land. Fears that they would be dispossessed by the Canadians were also buttressed by the behaviour of the Canadian arrivals of the 1860s. Largely land speculators who had come west to make their fortunes when Canada inevitably acquired the Northwest, these men were openly racist towards the non-white majority surrounding them. Unlike the fur traders, who were often paternalistic but rarely contemptuous towards the peoples who made the trade possible in the Northwest, the "Canadian Party," as they came to be called, regarded Native peoples, both Indian and Métis, as uncivilized people whose ungoverned presence in the region was a roadblock to European settlement. The newspaper the *Nor'wester* became a proponent of imposing Canadian law on "primitive" people who governed themselves without such civilized institutions as police, prisons, and poorhouses. The Canadian Party consisted of only a few hundred people in a population that the 1871 census recorded as just under 12 000: 5757 French-speaking Métis, 4083

Louis Riel (second row, centre) and the provisional government   (National Archives of Canada/C6692)

English-speaking Métis, 1500 whites, and 558 Indians. But only the "Canadians" had the ear of Ottawa.

On 11 October 1869, a group of unarmed Métis stopped a road-building party from its work, angry that the contract had been given to the Métis-baiting and land-speculating Canadian John Snow. Five days later a Métis National Committee was set up. The committee's goal was to block the Canadian takeover of Red River until firm guarantees for Métis land rights had been won. As secretary of this committee, the Métis chose Louis Riel, then only twenty-five years old. Riel had spent ten of the previous eleven years in Catholic educational institutions in Quebec and was seen as someone who could negotiate with the Canadians on their own terms but who, as a Métis, could be counted on not to sell out his people.

The federal government's initial reaction was not to negotiate with the Métis but to speed up its assertion of authority in Rupert's Land. Its intention was to create a single administration for a vast region that included all of today's Prairie provinces as well as the North. This region was called the North-West Territories. Over time the area of land referred to by this name was reduced as new provinces were created, sections of the Territories were annexed to new and existing provinces, and the Yukon was established as a separate administrative region. William McDougall, who was to be the first lieutenant-governor of the Northwest Territories, attempted to enter Canada's new fiefdom on 2 November but was repulsed by armed Métis defenders as he attempted to cross from Pembina, North Dakota, to Hudson's Bay territory.

In December, the Métis established a provisional government under John Bruce and Louis Riel to co-ordinate resistance to Canadian imperialism. Macdonald refused to negotiate with a governing body that he considered to be illegitimate. Instead he attempted to undermine the provisional government by using the influence of the Catholic Church over the French-speaking Métis and encouraging a rift between them and their English-speaking counterparts. He begged Britain to send a military expedition to suppress the uprising, but the British balked at doing so before Canada had negotiated with Riel's forces. An attempt by the Canadian party to oust the Riel government in December led the Métis to imprison sixty-five Canadians for three months. Yet another attempt to defeat Riel was nipped in the bud in February 1870 when the Métis arrested several conspirators. One of them, Thomas Scott, an itinerant Orangeman who had been employed as a road builder before the rebellion started, showed contempt for his Catholic, non-white guards and called on his fellow prisoners to break out of the makeshift prison. Riel, faced with vengeful guards and a threat to his government's legitimacy, agreed to have Scott executed in March 1870.

By that time, Macdonald, afraid that the Americans, who had agents at Red River, would take advantage of the political crisis to seize control of the region, reluctantly agreed to negotiate with representatives of the provisional government. They were led by Abbé N.J. Ritchot who had the confidence not only of Riel but of Rupert's Land Bishop A.A. Taché who opposed the rebellion but supported the Métis land claims. The demands of the French-speaking Métis for guarantees for their language and religion also had the Church's blessing.

Negotiations between the Canadian and provisional Red River governments concluded in May 1870 with an agreement that, on the surface, met Métis demands. The Red River colony and its environs would become the province of Manitoba. Like the other provinces, it would have an elected legislative assembly and an appointed upper chamber. It would have two official languages—English and French—for its legislative assembly proceedings and records as well as for its courts. Denominational schools, Protestant and Catholic, would be permitted. Unlike other provinces, Manitoba would, until such time as the federal government decided otherwise, have its lands controlled by the central government. For the Métis the major victory was the guarantee in the Manitoba Act that they would receive title for lands they currently farmed as well as 1.4 million acres of farmland for the use of their children.

This victory soon proved hollow. With a settlement in hand, Macdonald was able to convince Britain that a military expedition should be sent to Red River to assert Canadian control. That expedition was led by Colonel Garnet Wolseley and the Ontario Orangemen who loomed large in its ranks imposed a virtual reign of terror on the Métis. Riel fled to the United States, and other members of the provisional government went into hiding.

Over the next several years, as white settlers ringed their settlements and received title for land, the Métis waited in vain to receive their land grants. With the buffalo in Manitoba disappearing and no land settlement in sight, many Métis moved west to today's Saskatchewan where they could still hunt buffalo and where they could establish communities under their own control without being surrounded by hostile white settlers. The first Macdonald period of government ended in November 1873 without a fulfilment of land promises to the Métis.

The Indian Treaties

Anxious not to have a repeat of the Métis situation with the Indians, the Macdonald government decided to negotiate treaties with aboriginal people living in the newly conquered territory. Between 1871 and 1877, seven treaties were concluded with Indians east of the Rockies, whose estimated population was 34 000. Adams Archibald, the first lieutenant-governor of Manitoba and negotiator of Treaty One, which covered the Indians of Lower Fort Garry, made clear the intentions of the federal government, representing the British Monarch, to change the character of Indian society. He told the Indians: "Your Great Mother [Queen Victoria] wishes the good of all races under her sway. She wishes her red children to be happy and contented. She wishes them to live in comfort. She would like them to adopt the habits of the whites, to till land and raise food, and store it up against a time of want."[2]

Treaty One, like the six subsequent treaties, established reserves where the Indians would have their farms and homes, and promised implements, seed, and training to launch the Natives on agricultural careers. It also promised that their traditional hunting and fishing rights would be recognized. The Indians were soon frustrated by the failure of the Canadian government to provide promised farm aid. Weymss Simpson, the Indian commissioner, interpreted the Lower Fort Garry treaty to imply that implements and seed would be provided only when Indians had settled on reserves and built homes to demonstrate their readiness for an agricultural life. The distraught Lower Fort Garry Indians replied eloquently but with little impact: "We cannot tear down trees and build huts with our teeth, we cannot break the prairie with our hands, nor reap the harvest when we have grown it with our knives."[3] As historian Sarah Carter has suggested in her book *Lost Harvests*, officials in charge of Indian policy believed that the Indians were incapable of becoming commercial farmers. This became a self-fulfiling prophecy as the government established policies that made it difficult for Indian farmers to succeed.

The government's priority in the Northwest remained the provision of a framework for European, not aboriginal, settlement. In 1872, the Dominion Lands Act granted free homesteads of 160 acres to farmers who cleared ten acres and built a home within three years of registering their intention to settle. In 1873, the North-West Mounted Police, a semi-military organization, was established to act as peacekeeper in the Northwest. Though planning for the force was already in the works, its speedy approval by Parliament was assured after the massacre of twenty-two Assiniboine Indians in the Cypress Hills near today's Alberta–Montana border. American wolf hunters anxious to avenge the alleged theft of some horses were the perpetrators of this slaughter, and their action emphasized Canada's failure to assert authority over all of its western territories. The desire to prevent Americans from grabbing territories coveted by Canada also played a large role in Macdonald's anxious negotiations to ensure the speedy entry of British Columbia and Prince Edward Island into Confederation.

Railroading British Columbia
and Prince Edward Island

Although the gold rush on the Pacific Coast was over by the mid-1860s, coal mines were operating in Nanaimo, sawmills had been established on the timber lands of Alberni Canal and Burrard Inlet, and small agricultural settlements were scattered through mainland British Columbia and Vancouver Island. Britain had established Esquimalt, near Victoria, as its North Pacific naval base. Victoria continued its role as the centre of banking, commerce, and shipbuilding for both the mainland colony and the island. In all sectors, British capital prevailed, although the settlers included many Americans as well as British immigrants and migrants from other British North American colonies.

While the economic activity of the Europeans on the Pacific had been diversified, the decline of the gold fields resulted in a large outflow of prospectors and miners and the small business people that their earnings had supported. Before the slump, both Vancouver Island and the colony of British Columbia had spent liberally to build courts, roads, and other public works. After the gold rush, the two colonies were nearly bankrupt. With Britain's encouragement, they formed a legislative union in 1866, but with combined debts of $1.3 million, the united colonies were not in an improved position to initiate public projects. Mainlanders and islanders eyed each other suspiciously, New Westminster and Victoria fighting for two years over which would be the capital before the latter prevailed.

Some business people began to call for admission of the colony into the United States. Such a proposal was denounced by British authorities and British capitalists with an interest in the colony. Amor de Cosmos, a colourful Victoria newspaper editor whose outlandish adopted name (he was born William Smith) reflected his flamboyance, countered annexationist proposals with a resolution in the legislative council in March 1867 that British Columbia be included as a province of Canada.

Britain rejected de Cosmos's proposal at the time on the grounds that it was premature to incorporate the Pacific Coast into the new federation before the Northwest had been acquired by Canada. Once the deal for the Northwest had been made, Colonial Secretary Earl Granville was quick to let the colonists know that Britain favoured British Columbia's speedy entry into Confederation. Lieutenant-Governor Andrew Musgrave, following the pattern set by Britain's chief representatives in other colonies, actively promoted a Canadian future for the colony. After an inconclusive debate in the legislative council on the merits of union with Canada, it was agreed that a council delegation would meet with representatives of the Dominion government to determine whether the Canadians would accept the council's terms for British Columbia's entry into Confederation. These included the immediate building of a wagon road connecting New Westminster to Fort Garry, with a railroad along that route to follow in due course; the assumption by Canada of British Columbia's existing debt; and a grant to the province of $100 000 per annum to enable it to undertake necessary works.

The Canadians, led by Cartier during one of Macdonald's frequent illnesses, proved more than willing to meet these terms, offering to start building the railway within two years and complete it within ten years of British Columbia joining Confederation. This would obviate the need for a wagon road. The $100 000 per annum grant request raised some eyebrows in Ottawa. The grants to other provinces were only eighty cents per person per year, with Indians—Ottawa's responsibility under the British North America Act—excluded from the count. British Columbia would have needed a non-Indian population of 120 000 to justify its grant request; instead it had only about 10 500 (8576 whites, 1548 Chinese, and 462

Street scene in Barkerville, British Columbia   (Metropolitan Toronto Reference Library/TEC725)

blacks). The Macdonald government, anxious not to risk eventual annexation of the colony to the United States, agreed to pay $100 000 per year in perpetuity to British Columbia in return for a grant of a twenty-mile belt on each side of the proposed railway line.

The delegates from British Columbia met with the Canadian negotiators in June 1870. Elections in November 1870 gave every seat in the British Columbia legislature to supporters of Confederation on the terms worked out in the June negotiations. On 18 January 1871 the British Columbia legislative council unanimously decided to bring the colony into Confederation. Thus in June 1871, a sixth province became part of Canada.

Notwithstanding the election in 1870, Confederation in British Columbia did not involve consultation with the majority of that province's people. All women were excluded from the vote as were all Indians and Asians. Native people comprised almost 80 percent of the population. In short, only about 7 percent of the adult population—those not restricted by gender, race, or class—voted on Confederation. While few of them felt any real attachment to Canada, the economic stimulus of the proposed railway and Canadian government grants made Confederation appear to be a pragmatic economic arrangement.

Similar economic reasons led Prince Edward Island into Confederation in 1873. In the 1860s the promise of railway connections to the potential markets in Central Canada stirred interest in New Brunswick and Nova Scotia, but the railroad seemed irrelevant to residents of an island colony. The pro-confederates of the island, recognizing a losing issue, had dropped Confederation from their public agenda shortly after the Quebec conference of 1864. Elections in 1867 and 1870 were fought on the persistent land issue and on sectarian questions, such as education, not over union with Canada. In 1867, the Liberals, who had the allegiance of the majority of the colony's Catholics, defeated the Conservatives. Many rural Protestants voted Liberal to show their dismay at Conservative repression of the Tenant League—organized to intimidate landlords—and the government's inaction regarding the absentee-landlord issue. Since its establishment a century earlier, most of the colony's land had been granted to British landowners, few of whom took up residence on the island. These landlords extracted high rents and provided few services in return. Although over time some tenants were able to purchase land, most were too poor to do so, and collective opposition, often violent, developed against agents of the landlords who attempted to collect rents.

In office, the Liberals proved as unwilling as their Conservative predecessors to create publicly supported denominational schools. It was a dangerous position to take when 45 percent of the population was Roman

Catholic, and it resulted in significant Catholic defections from the Liberals in 1870. The Conservatives under James Pope, an ardent confederationist in 1864 and leading island businessman, formed the new government in alliance with the Catholic independents who had broken away from the Liberals. The provincial economy, when they took office, was strong. Fishing, farming, and shipbuilding created an export demand and local economy sufficiently strong to support several thousand manufacturing jobs in a population that had reached 94 021 by the time of the 1871 census. There were three banks administered by the local elite in Charlottetown, and a variety of newspapers.

For apostles of progress like Pope, something was missing: railroads. His government set out to fill the gap and soon found, as the Canadians, New Brunswickers, and Nova Scotians had learned earlier, that railway building and its attendant corruption were hard on the public purse. Faced with huge public debt, Pope argued to Prince Edward Islanders that only by joining Canada and letting that country assume the island's debt could they avoid the paralysis that repayment would entail. Canada, aware of American blandishments to Prince Edward Island (General Ben Butler of Massachusetts had come to the island in 1869 to offer a special trade deal, which appeared to be a first step towards luring it into the American union), was in a mood to negotiate. Macdonald agreed not only to assume railway debt but also to use federal monies to buy out the remaining absentee landlords so that tenants could become freeholders. So, in 1873, Prince Edward Island agreed to become the seventh province of Canada. There was little prospect that Newfoundland, the remaining Atlantic colony, would rush to be the eighth.

Newfoundland's Perspective

The Confederation proposal was presented by its Newfoundland supporters as a means of linking the colony's stagnant economy with the more vibrant economy of an emerging nation. This would provide new markets for Newfoundland products as well as grants that would allow the colony to build roads and other public works. As in Prince Edward Island, there was initial scepticism because a railroad could obviously not be built between an island and the rest of British North America.

The major merchants of St John's and Conception Bay opposed Confederation, which they feared would result in Canadian competition on their home turf. Looking to the sea and to trade with Britain, they saw little use for closer ties with the rest of British North America, which bought only 5 percent of their exports and sent them 16 percent of their imports. For Irish Catholics, and particularly the Church leaders in the colony,

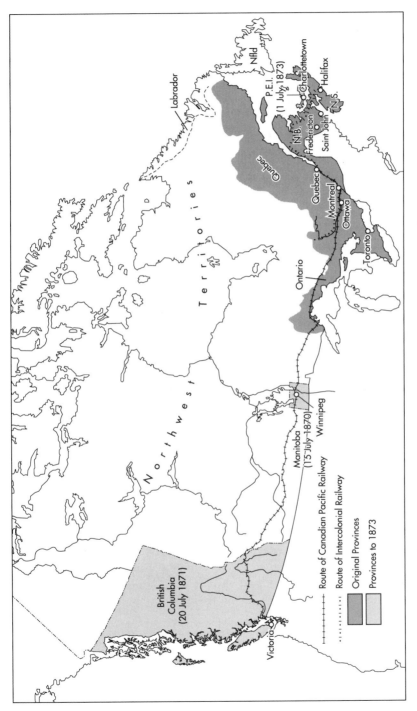

MAP 2.1 *Canada, 1867–73* (D.G.G. Kerr, *Historical Atlas of Canada* (Scarborough: Nelson, 1975), 55)

many of whom were recent Irish immigrants, the Act of Union that bound Ireland to Britain and the Act of Union that would bind Newfoundland to Canada were of similar vintage. Was not Ontario the home to thousands of Orangemen, including Prime Minister John A. Macdonald?

Unlike the three Maritime provinces, Newfoundland faced neither an overwhelming debt nor intense British pressure to join Confederation. In the colony's 1869 legislative election, twenty-one anti-confederates and nine confederates were elected. Several more generations would pass before Newfoundlanders debated the issue of Confederation again. In the 1880s, a railway development program inevitably arrived in Newfoundland with the usual accompanying public debt load. But by then, though Canada was once again putting out feelers, local politicians, smarting from their earlier defeat, did not wish to touch the Confederation issue.

• Pacific Scandal and the Defeat of Macdonald

In May 1871, the Macdonald government introduced legislation to allow for the construction of a railway from the Pacific to Lake Nipissing. The government would charter a company to build the line and grant it $30 million in cash and 20 million hectares of land as an incentive. The opposition members, led by the Ontario Reformers whose legislative leader was Alexander Mackenzie and whose eminence grise remained *Globe* editor George Brown, balked at such extravagance and confidently predicted that the awarding of a railway contract would be marked by political corruption. They were right.

Two consortia sought the lucrative railway-building contract. One was headed by Ontario Senator David MacPherson and included the leading lights of the Toronto business community. The other, headed by Hugh Allan, president of the Allan Steamship Lines, represented Montreal business interests and included representatives of the Northern Pacific Railway in the United States. Attempts by the Macdonald administration to effect a merger of these two groups and thus prevent political hard feelings between Montreal and Toronto stalled the awarding of a contract but bore no fruit.

Hugh Allan was determined that any merger would be on his terms. George-Étienne Cartier initially regarded Allan's demands as extreme and insisted that he make compromises. But Cartier was politically vulnerable, and Allan made clear his determination either to force Cartier's capitulation or to engineer his political defeat. As new federal elections loomed, a beleaguered Cartier, suffering from the Bright's disease that would cause his death the following year, gave his support to the railway charter request of "Quebec's first monopoly capitalist."[4] Allan gave at least $162 000 and perhaps as much as $360 000 to the Conservative re-election effort in recognition of Cartier's support.

The election of 1872 was a difficult one for Macdonald's government. Although it could present itself as the builder of the nation, it was vulnerable on many scores. It had failed to convince Washington to sign a new reciprocity agreement; it had, publicly, at least, been unable to resolve the question of who was to build the railway; and it had set aside a huge subsidy for private capitalists who would build the railway and reap its profits without a direct return to the public purse.

In Ontario, Alexander Mackenzie's Reformers—or Liberals as they were increasingly called—revived traditional Clear Grit criticisms of the Tories as corrupt spendthrifts. They also reminded Protestants that the federal government had not brought the Métis murderers of Thomas Scott before the courts.

In Quebec, the reformers had renamed themselves the Parti national in 1871, emphasizing their Quebec rather than Canadian orientation. While Ontario Liberals condemned the Métis, the Parti national denounced Cartier for having done nothing to settle Métis land claims or to win amnesty for Louis Riel. Quebec Liberals, somewhat opportunistically given their former emphasis on separation of Church and state, joined sections of the Quebec Roman Catholic hierarchy in castigating the federal Conservatives for standing idly by while New Brunswick in 1871 refused support to separate Roman Catholic schools.

In Nova Scotia and New Brunswick, criticisms were made of the Washington Treaty, of Canadian tariff rates, and of the slow progress of the Intercolonial Railway. The Nova Scotia members elected as anti-confederates in 1869 were, for the most part, running as Independents opposed to Macdonald but unwilling to throw in their lot with the loosely linked Reform or Liberal parties of the other provinces. Despite the support of both Tupper and Howe, the national government did not have a party machine in Nova Scotia capable of delivering confirmed Macdonald supporters.

The 1872 election, Canada's second last federal election with open balloting, lasted from July to October. Gathering in designated voting halls to publicly record their choice, electors' intentions were secret neither from neighbours nor political party workers. It was an election marked by fraud, intimidation, and violence. The Conservatives won a reduced majority, although its size was not clear due to the large number of members who were not clearly aligned either with the government or the opposition. In Ontario, where party lines were clearest, the arithmetic suggested fifty Liberals to thirty-eight Conservatives, while for Quebec thirty-eight presumed Conservatives sat with twenty-seven presumed members of the Parti national. The pre-Confederation political split between Upper and Lower Canada had been re-established. Cartier, despite the $85 000 that Hugh Allan had bestowed on his personal campaign, was badly beaten by a moderate liberal in Montreal East and was forced to re-enter parliament via a French-Canadian seat in Manitoba. New Brunswick, Manitoba, Prince Edward Island, and British Columbia returned mainly pro-government members, but Nova Scotia returned mainly incumbents, who would support the government only in return for favours to their province.

In February 1873 the new government announced the composition of the board of directors of the Canadian Pacific Railway Company. Sir Hugh Allan was the president, with the rest of the board representing a variety of regional interests. Two months later Lucius Huntington, a Liberal MP, charged that Allan had bought his presidency with $360 000 in donations to the Conservative machine. Macdonald reluctantly appointed a select committee to examine the charges. It soon became apparent that the Liberals had a mole in the Conservative organization: incriminating letters proved Cartier's corruption and left little doubt of Macdonald's as well. While most voters were aware that Canadian politics was corrupt, the extent of the Allan buy-out of the Conservative Party struck many people as scandalous. Even more damaging was the fact that Allan was being financed by American investors who were poised to assume control of Canada's major railway company. Sensing that the government was doomed, many independents, including a large block of Nova Scotians who had shown no previous interest in the Pacific railway issue, joined the Liberal opposition.

On 5 November 1873 Macdonald informed Governor-General Lord Dufferin that he no longer enjoyed a parliamentary majority and therefore, following the principle of responsible government, was resigning as prime minister. Dufferin invited Alexander Mackenzie to form a government. Mackenzie led a rather loose-knit Liberal Party consisting of old Ontario Reformers, Quebec *rouges* and moderate liberals, and Maritime Liberals and independents disillusioned by Macdonald's government.

An election was called in December 1873 by the new Liberal government, anxious to use the black mark against the Conservatives to win a big majority. Macdonald, who remained Conservative leader despite the scandal that wrecked his government, campaigned on a nationalist platform that emphasized the need for the Pacific railway to hold the Northwest and fulfil pledges to British Columbia. Mackenzie, heading a political organization whose supporters outside Ontario had been lukewarm or hostile to

Confederation, promised a new Pacific railway contract that did not involve large public expenditures for the benefit of private entrepreneurs. Emphasizing provincial rights and the need for economy, he presented a vision of the new Dominion markedly at odds with the "new nationality" that the Conservatives preached. Mackenzie's Canada would be decentralized and take into account that Confederation was an economic convenience for most former colonies rather than an attempt to create a centralized federation.

Mackenzie won the 1874 election handily, and the power and the patronage passed for five years from the Conservatives to the Liberals before returning to the Tories for seventeen years after elections in late 1878. The Liberals had their own national agenda, which included plans for a Supreme Court and electoral reform, but they were the victims of a worldwide recession that gripped Canada in 1873 and only gradually gave way to a rise in prosperity in the 1880s. Edward Blake, who served as Minister of Justice under Mackenzie, achieved some success in reducing the role of Britain in Canadian political life. Although he failed to make the new Canadian Supreme Court the final court of appeal—cases could still be sent to the British Judicial Committee of the Privy Council until 1949—he managed to enlarge Canada's area of jurisdiction, including the right to establish admiralty courts, exercise authority over shipping on the Great Lakes, and pardon criminals.

With his return to office, Macdonald began to enact what are often collectively referred to as the "national policies." Firstly, there was a policy of implementing tariffs high enough to protect infant industries in Canada. Secondly, Macdonald promised to rapidly complete the Pacific railway. The Liberals had proceeded slowly with this project, complaining that government revenues were insufficient during the recession to allow speedy construction of a 6000-kilometre line. Finally, the Conservative government pledged to significantly boost the country's population by attracting immigrants. These policies would form the framework of national development until the First World War.

The Northwest

Harsh government policy provoked strong feelings among the Indians and Métis of the Northwest, especially in what is now Saskatchewan. Plains Indians, aware that the buffalo and other game were becoming scarce and that the fur trade was increasingly concentrated northwards, begrudgingly accepted treaties that they believed guaranteed them government help to become farmers and assurances of a food supply in the transitional period before they became self-sufficient. As it turned out, not only was agricultural aid slow in coming, but food rations to the Indians were reduced after 1880 as a cost-cutting measure just as the buffalo were disappearing from the Canadian prairies. Such policies led to death by starvation of about 3000 of the Indians in the Northwest from 1880 to 1885.

In desperation, some Indians stole settlers' cattle once the buffalo were gone (the last Canadian hunt occurred in 1879 and the last Montana hunt in 1882). They were thwarted by the North-West Mounted Police, whose earlier good relations with the Natives had soured somewhat once it became clear that the Mounties had to act as the agents of the colonizers.

In addition to individual acts such as stealing, there were organized Indian responses to the desperate economic circumstances that the federal

Big Bear, Cree chief   (National Archives of Canada/C1873)

government had failed to alleviate. Cree chiefs such as Big Bear and Poundmaker played key roles in Native resistance. Big Bear had regarded the treaty provisions as insulting and had refused to sign Treaty Six until starvation among his band forced his hand in 1882. Big Bear continued to dream of a confederation of the Plains tribes to force the Canadian government to renegotiate the treaties and provide the Natives with ironclad assurances of their aboriginal rights. His attempts to win Blackfoot leaders over to his idea foundered on Blackfoot distrust of the Cree, dating back to their enmity during the fur-trading period. Even Blackfoot leaders like Crowfoot who were willing to pursue an all-Native alliance could not resist Indian Affairs pressure against such a union. The once-prosperous Blackfoot people, deprived of the buffalo, were completely dependent on government rations, which the government threatened to withdraw should the Blackfoot make common cause with dissident Cree.

In 1884, about 2000 Cree from several reserves gathered outside Battleford, the capital of the North-West Territories, to demand promised rations. Several Indian councils held that year demonstrated a growing cohesion of the Cree in resisting government mistreatment of the Indians. Increasingly, the influence of early leaders such as Poundmaker and Big Bear, who hoped to use collective peaceful pressure to force negotiations, gave way to leadership by younger militants who called for armed struggle.

The Métis living along the South Saskatchewan River also faced frustrations that peaceful protest failed to alleviate. South Saskatchewan settlements grouped both long-term residents and recent arrivals from Manitoba who hoped to continue a traditional lifestyle no longer possible as settlers took over the habitat of the Manitoba buffalo. It was clear by the mid-1870s that a transition from a buffalo-hunting existence supplemented by farming would have to give way to a largely agricultural existence. The Métis, encouraged by the clergy, began to petition Ottawa for a land base, agricultural aid, schools, and a locally run police force. In general, the Métis in the Saskatchewan territories wanted to make a transition to a European lifestyle but to maintain community control over new institutions and thereby preserve their distinct national existence.

Ottawa largely ignored Métis petitions. In 1884, the Métis decided to invite Louis Riel, still in exile in the U.S., to return to Canada to lead his people once again. Riel, by this time, was suffering from mental problems and had spent periods in various insane asylums. Initially he attempted to pursue the peaceful route of pressuring the Macdonald government for concessions. Predictably this achieved few results, and Riel, who believed he had a providential mission to lead the Métis to a New Jerusalem, proclaimed a provisional government on 18 March 1885. While he still hoped to force Ottawa to grant the moderate demands outlined in a "Bill of Rights" (see box) without resorting to violence, many Métis were convinced that government indifference would yield only to armed struggle. Gabriel Dumont, who became the military leader of the rebellion, advocated seizing government buildings and Mounted Police detachments and blowing up the railway tracks used by the federal government to send troops westwards.

THE "BILL OF RIGHTS," 1885

The rebel platform, published in the Toronto *Mail* on 13 April 1885, suggests that Riel's program was neither separatist nor racist, as Canadian opponents of Riel charged at the time. While the concerns of the Métis were uppermost in his mind, the "Bill of Rights" included calls for better treatment of all groups in the North-West Territories. Following is a condensed version of the rebels' demands:

1. That the half-breeds of the Northwest Territories be given grants similar to those accorded to the half-breeds of Manitoba by the Act of 1870.

2. That patents be issued to all half-breeds and white settlers who have fairly earned the right of possession to their farms; that the timber regulations be made more liberal; and that the settler be treated as having rights in the country.

3. That the provinces of Alberta and Saskatchewan be forthwith organized with legislatures of their own, so that the people may be no longer subject to the despotism of Lieutenant-Governor Dewdney; and, in the proposed new provincial legislatures, that the Métis shall have a fair and reasonable share of representation.

4. That the offices of trust throughout these provinces be given to residents of the country, as far as practicable, and that we denounce the appointment of disreputable outsiders and repudiate their authority.

5. That this region be administered for the benefit of the actual settler, and not for the advantage of the alien speculator; and that all lawful customs and usages which obtain among the Métis be respected.

6. That better provision be made for the Indians, the parliamentary grant to be increased, and lands set apart as an endowment for the establishment of hospitals and

schools for the use of whites, half-breeds, and Indians, at such places as the provincial legislatures may determine.

7. That the Land Department of the Dominion Government be administered as far as practicable from Winnipeg, so that settlers may not be compelled, as heretofore to go to Ottawa for the settlement of questions in dispute between them and land commissioners.

Source: Bill of Rights, 13 April 1885, Provincial Archives of Alberta.

Riel was only willing to countenance traditional battlefield strategy, and Dumont surrendered his guerrilla strategy to the tactics of a man increasingly devoured by hallucinations and incapable of pursuing a consistent strategy of either violence or non-violence. Once troops arrived in force from Central Canada under Major-General Frederick Middleton, Riel pulled all his supporters into Batoche for a last stand that lasted six weeks until Riel surrendered.

Riel was found guilty of treason and, despite a concerted campaign for clemency by French Canada, he was hanged in November 1885. His defence of his actions at his trial before an all-white jury in Regina was a mixture of a madman's ravings and clear-sighted analysis of the plight of Native peoples. Since his death, Riel has become a symbol of his people, and assessments of his behaviour have often varied greatly. It is more generally conceded now than a century ago that, whatever the merits of this complicated man, the cause for which he fought in 1885 was a noble one.

When word of the Métis rebellion reached Cree ears, moderate leaders such as Big Bear proved unable to restrain radicals who called for armed revolt. In March 1885, a hated Indian agent and eight others were killed as Cree warriors seized control of Frog Lake, north of Battleford. In another incident, two farming instructors regarded as hostile to the Indians were murdered in the Battleford district. The Indians paid dearly for their acts of frustration. Of eighty-one arrested, forty-four were convicted. Of these, eight were hanged, three given life imprisonment, and many others incarcerated for long periods. Even Big Bear and Poundmaker, who had tried to prevent violence, received three years imprisonment for felony-treason. The harsh prison regime in Western Canada meant early deaths for most of the convicted.

While the hanging of Louis Riel divided French and English Canadians for years to come, the hanging of the eight radical Indian leaders and the long jail sentences for many of their followers created little interest. But the Indians themselves did not forget. Though repression had

The Battle of Fish Creek, 1885, which preceded Batoche   (National Archives of Canada/ C2524)

broken organized resistance to white colonialism, individual acts of defiance still occurred and won sympathy from the Indians. In 1895, for example, Almighty Voice, who lived on a reserve east of Batoche, escaped custody after being charged with killing a settler's cow. After killing a Mountie attempting to arrest him, he escaped detection for two years, hidden by fellow Indians on various reserves. He died along with two companions in a shootout with the NWMP in which two Mounties also died. The grandson of Chief One Arrow, the first Indian to join Riel in rebellion in 1885, Almighty Voice was a link between Indian and Métis resistance to repressive national policies.

• French–English Conflict

Although the Confederation pact provided few guarantees for linguistic duality, there have always been politicians and historians who insist that Confederation involved a linguistic "compact" between two founding ethnic groups. Historian Ramsay Cook summarizes this thesis succinctly: "Confederation was an agreement, pact or entente, whichever of the words best describes the political rather than the legal character of the events of 1864–7. And the terms of that entente were that a new nation-state was to be founded on the basis of an acceptance of cultural duality and on a division of powers."[5] In practice, before 1900, legislatures outside Quebec proved resistant to the notion that French Canadians deserved protection of their language. These governments were hostile to francophone Catholic as well as anglophone Catholic calls for state support for separate school systems.

The Maritimes

The first school confrontation occurred in New Brunswick. The New Brunswick School Act of 1871 provided for public funding of only the public school system and gave municipalities the right to tax all ratepayers to support that system. Premier George King won a resounding victory in 1872 defending the schools legislation, campaigning on the slogan "Vote for the Queen against the Pope." In response to what they perceived as an unfair law, Catholics often refused to pay the school taxes, only to have constables seize property to be sold for unpaid taxes. Resistance to the taxes was especially fierce among the Acadians, who had accounted for the only concerted opposition to King in the 1872 election. Only one Acadian child in six at this time received any schooling, and few attended school for more than a few years. So most Acadians were unwilling to pay taxes to support any school, much less a school from which Catholic education was excluded. Most New Brunswick Acadians remained desperately poor in the late nineteenth century and could little afford to fund schools for others. Eking out a living from farming on infertile lands and lumbering and fishing, many were deeply in debt to the Robin family interests, long-time exploiters of the Gaspésiens and Acadiens from whom they bought fish and to whom they made loans at extortionate interest rates.

Matters came to a head in the town of Caraquet in 1875 when a small group of Protestants (there were only seventy-nine Protestants in a population of 3111 in Caraquet in 1871) tried to elect new parish officers after having the results of parish elections set aside on the grounds that most voters had been ineligible to cast ballots because they had not paid their school taxes. Acadians attempting to prevent the miniscule group of Protestants from taking over the county broke up their meeting on 15 January 1875. When constables and volunteers tried to arrest the "rioters," the Acadians resisted arrest. In the ensuing melee, one volunteer and one Acadian were shot. The resulting trial of a group of Acadians for murdering the volunteer became a cause célèbre for the Acadians. Their eventual discharge and the government's agreement to allow Catholics to congregate in a single school in an area and be taught by members of religious orders were victories for the long-ignored French Canadians of New Brunswick.

Some hard-fought concessions notwithstanding, French-language instruction in the Maritimes was inferior to English-language instruction. Nova Scotia in 1864 and Prince Edward Island in 1877 established a common curriculum for all schools. All instruction was to occur in English. In practice, teachers in areas with mainly Acadian populations taught in French, but the provincial Departments of Education provided them with no textbooks and conducted no normal school training in French. New Brunswick prepared a few elementary readers in French, but most textbooks made available to Acadian students were in English.

The confrontations over schools reflected a growing sense of political awareness among the Acadians. In the second half of the nineteenth century, Acadians experienced what in retrospect has been called a cultural renaissance. Curiously, it owed its beginnings in part to the publication in 1847 of the poem "Evangeline," written by Henry Wadsworth Longfellow, an American who had never visited the Maritimes. Taking inspiration from his romantic rendering of the expulsion story, Acadians rallied to create and preserve an identity entirely their own. This enterprise was encouraged by professors at Collège St Joseph in Memramcook, New Brunswick, founded in 1863, and by nationalist organizations in Quebec, including the Société Saint-Jean-Baptiste, which in 1880 invited all French-speaking communities in North America to a congress in Quebec. Impressed by the occasion, the Acadians held their own congress at Collège St Joseph in July 1881 with over 5000 in attendance. In this and a subsequent congress in 1884 at Miscouche, Prince Edward Island, the Acadians chose a national holiday (the Feast of the Assumption), a national flag (the French tricolour with the gold star), and a national hymn ("Ave Stella Maris"). Acadians were proud of their French heritage, but they were determined to develop cultural symbols distinct from those already established in Quebec.

Meanwhile, the Acadians were beginning to develop the numbers to sustain their cultural aspirations. Between 1871 and 1901 their representation in the population of New Brunswick increased from 16 to 24 percent, in Nova Scotia from 8.5 to 9.8, and in Prince Edward Island from 9.8 to 13 percent. So significant was the Acadian vote in a number of Maritime ridings that Sir Wilfrid Laurier made a point of attending the Acadian congress at Arichat in 1900.

Ontario

As in the Maritimes, the French-Canadian population of Ontario was grow-ing relative to anglophones in the late nineteenth century. Part of the growth occurred in Eastern Ontario, where French-Canadians had been con-centrated before Confederation, and part in the resource towns that grew up in Northern Ontario. The number of French speakers in the province jumped from 102 743 in 1881 to 158 671 in 1901 and 202 442 in 1911, repre-senting about 10 percent of the provincial population at the latter date.

With their rights to a Catholic education for their children protected by the British North America Act, Ontario francophones did not fear a threat to their religion as New Brunswick Catholics did. But their linguistic rights were at the whim of the Ontario legislature. Before 1885, provincial officials tolerated education in both French and German, but the second Northwest Rebellion created anxiety among imperial-minded citizens. The desire for uniformity within the province's schools and no doubt an ele-ment of anti-French feeling in the wake of Quebec campaigns against Riel's execution, led to provincial regulations limiting the numbers of hours of instruction in languages other than English and requiring teachers to be tested to ensure proficiency in English. But the local school boards were left to enforce this regulation and most chose to ignore it. The French lan-guage thrived in Ontario, causing English-only advocates to be on the watch for issues that might discredit non-anglophones.

Francophobes and anti-Catholics believed they had such an issue in the Jesuit Estates Act of 1888. The Quebec government had invited Pope Leo XIII to help to determine a monetary settlement for Jesuit properties confiscated by Britain at the time of the conquest. Although the settlement included funds for Protestant universities, Protestant extremists, ignoring the fact that the Pope's mission had been simply to arbitrate between vari-ous Catholic claimants, decried Vatican interference in Canadian affairs. A group misleadingly called the Equal Rights Association led by firebrand Dalton McCarthy campaigned against separate schools and for the assimila-tion of French Canadians. Responding to this campaign, the provincial Liberal government of Oliver Mowat in 1889 removed all French textbooks from the authorized list of books, but the province resisted calls for English-only instruction in Ontario schools.

French-language instruction could still be blocked at the local level. In Prescott County, francophone and anglophone Catholics acted as blocs in the election of local school boards. In Caledonia Township, for example, where francophones made up one-third of the population, the anglophone Catholics refused to establish any French-language schools to supplement the nine English-language schools established by 1871. In Alfred Township, no French-language schools were opened until the francophones became a majority and dominated the school board. Ironically, while anglophone and francophone Catholics fought for control within Ontario separate schools, their counterparts in Manitoba were forced to co-operate to defend the right to have publicly supported separate schools at all.

The West

The Manitoba Act of 1870 and the North-West Territories Act of 1875 provided for official bilingualism on the Prairies. But demography worked against the French Canadians. Although there were as many French speakers as English speakers in Manitoba in 1870, by 1891 francophones represented only 11 000 of the 152 000 residents in that province. Across the West, including British Columbia, only 4.6 percent of the population reported French as their mother tongue in 1901. Another statistic, from 1921, tells much of the story. While 292 000 Canadian-born westerners listed Ontario as their birthplace, only 53 000 named Quebec.

The Québécois avoided the West partly because their image of the region was based on negative reports from missionaries who had once hoped to prevent massive European settlement amongst their Native charges. When Ontario migrants began to move into the region in large numbers, the missionaries changed their tune and called for French-speaking Catholics to come to the area to offset the anglophone Protestant hordes. But the Catholic bishops in Quebec, anxious to preserve the ethnic balance in their province, encouraged colonization of infertile northern territories rather than emigration westwards. Most expatriates preferred in any case to go to New England or to francophone regions of Ontario rather than to risk a new life in the seemingly distant Prairies. The anti-French, anti-Catholic rhetoric that sounded from some corners in Protestant Ontario after the two Northwest Rebellions, and the ingrained image of the western lands as bleak and infertile, discouraged extensive Québécois migration to the Northwest.

Protestant Ontario transplants to the Northwest brought with them their antipathy to Ontario's separate school system and to public recognition for the French language. In the wake of the Jesuit Estates Act agitation, moves were made to humble Catholics and francophones in Manitoba. In 1890 the Manitoba legislature, ignoring the Manitoba Act, renounced official bilingualism. No longer would French be recognized as an official language in the province's courts or in the proceedings and official records of the legislature. French speakers were victims of an English-

French-Canadian settlers in Falher, Alberta   (Provincial Archives of Alberta/Ob.692)

Canadian nationalism that could not accept biculturalism or bilingualism and that equated proficiency in the English language with patriotism.

In the same session, the legislature passed the Manitoba Schools Act, which removed public financial support for separate schools. The Manitoba Act protected the rights that denominational schools had enjoyed in 1870 but such rights did not include a share of public grants simply because no such grants existed in the period of Hudson's Bay Company governance. The Catholic Church, more concerned about religious education than about language, made the Schools Act a point of contention in national politics, leaving the Manitoba francophones to fight a lonely battle on the language issue.

The right of the Manitoba government to legislate away public funding to denominational schools was challenged both by Anglicans and Catholics in the courts. French-Canadian Catholics, concentrated in areas where they could control the public school board and ensure both French-language and Catholic education, were in any case less affected than anglophone Catholics in Winnipeg. But, for both British-Canadian and Quebec nationalists, it became a Catholic–Protestant and Quebec–Ontario issue. It also became a divisive issue in national politics particularly after the

Judicial Committee of the Privy Council in Britain ruled that, while Manitoba had acted legally, the federal government enjoyed the constitutional right to pass remedial legislation that would restore public funding for denominational schools. The federal Conservative caucus, somewhat adrift when John A. Macdonald died shortly after his re-election in 1891, grappled with the Manitoba issue between 1891 and 1896, but failed to find a solution. When Wilfrid Laurier's Liberals came to power, they side-stepped the issue by coming to terms with the Liberal government of Manitoba and thereby avoiding a draconian intervention in an area of provincial responsibility.

While Catholic schools were not under attack in the North-West Territories, the French language was. In 1892 the North-West Territories legislative assembly, yielding to pressure from the Orange Order, legislated an end to education in French after the third grade. The same session followed Manitoba's lead to remove French as an official language in legislative proceedings.

Quebec

Because of their mutual suspicions, Quebec francophone Catholics and Ontario Orangemen had a tendency to view issues from the vantage point of conflict between the two cultures. Nowhere was this more obvious than in reactions to the Northwest Rebellion of 1885 and the hanging of Louis Riel. Because the Métis involved in the rebellion were primarily French-speaking Catholics, neither Orangemen nor Quebec nationalists were willing to see the 1885 rebellion as a battle for aboriginal rights. For Ontario imperialists, Riel, despite his heretical beliefs that alienated him from the Catholic hierarchy, was a French-Canadian Catholic who wished to deprive the British empire of the Northwest. For Quebec nationalists, he was a French-Canadian hero whose undoing proved that French-Canadian rights would not be respected outside of Quebec.

The latter belief encouraged *Quebec* nationalism as opposed to *French-Canadian* nationalism. After Riel's execution, an outpouring of grief and rage, including a 50 000-strong demonstration in Montreal where effigies of leading national Conservative politicians were burned, demonstrated the extent of Québécois alienation. In 1886, building on this alienation, Honoré Mercier led the Parti national, which included Quebec's Liberals along with Conservative dissidents, to a provincial election victory. The significance of Mercier's success has at times been overstated by historians. While the Riel agitation perhaps ensured a Liberal victory, the battle for power in Quebec had long been a close one.

It was less the hanging of Riel than the increasing stridency of anglo-phone imperialists within the party that weakened the Conservatives in Quebec. Macdonald had managed to keep both francophones and anglo-phones happy within one patronage-dispensing machine. His successors could hardly be faulted for failing to do so at a time when imperialist senti-ment was on the increase among English-Canadian opinion makers. Indeed Macdonald's decision to hang Riel was no doubt a calculated one designed to reassure anglophones that he was not a pawn of Catholic inter-ests. The clergy's hostility to Riel ensured that they would not retaliate against the Conservatives regardless of the opinions of their parishioners.

The victory of the Parti national suggested continued erosion of the political alliance that had taken power both nationally and in Quebec in the post-Confederation era. The word *national* in the party name was a reminder that the francophone majority in Quebec still regarded itself as a nation even if it was submerged within a larger nation-state. But the Parti national government was hardly alone in demanding greater provincial powers. The jealous defence of provincial interests against a federal regime which allegedly encroached on jurisdictions outside its authority was becoming general in Canadian politics by the 1880s.

• Provincial–Dominion Conflict
The West

The election of Alexander Mackenzie's Liberals in 1873, who were pledged to renegotiate the terms of British Columbia's entry into Confederation, created apprehension in the coastal province. Soon after taking office, Mackenzie informed the British Columbia provincial government that he would grant the initial demands made by the British Columbia delegation that had met with Cartier rather than the more generous terms that Cartier had agreed to. Instead of a railway link to the rest of Canada by 1881, British Columbia would receive a wagon road linking the province with Manitoba, a telegraph line, an intensive program of railway surveying, and a modest program of railway construction. If these terms were accepted, Mackenzie would use federal money to build a railway linking Esquimalt and Nanaimo.

George Anthony Walkem, premier of B.C. from 1874 to 1876 and 1878 to 1882, balked at any changes to promises already made to the province, but he was unable to budge Mackenzie. The prime minister was dependent on the Ontario Liberals who regarded British Columbia as the recipient of an unjustifiably large federal subsidy. Walkem's government supported a motion for secession of British Columbia from Canada, which passed that province's legislature in 1876. But the motion was largely a bargaining chip and was not followed up. When Macdonald returned to power in 1878, he was pressed by successive provincial administrations to make up for time lost during the Liberal years. The federal government caved in to British Columbia demands for a head tax on the Chinese in 1885 and completed the transcontinental railway to Vancouver in 1886. When Quebec Premier Honoré Mercier assembled the provinces to make demands on Ottawa in fall 1887, British Columbia was no longer interested in doing battle with the federal government.

Manitoba remained combative. Despite an increase in its debt allowance and in the subsidy it received as compensation for having its public lands under federal administration, federal–provincial tensions remained high. The federal government and the CPR continued to thwart Manitoba attempts to encourage the establishment of a railway linking Winnipeg with the Northern Pacific Railroad, which provided access to U.S. suppliers and markets. The administration of Tory Premier John Norquay, Canada's first premier of Métis descent, was sued by the CPR and harassed by the federal government, and Norquay was pushed out of office in 1887 over financial irregularities. Only in 1888 did the federal government finally buy out the monopoly clause in the CPR contract that had frustrated Manitoba's railway competition drive.

Western pressure on the federal government came not only from B.C. and Manitoba, but also from the North-West Territories. The North-West Territories Act of 1875 provided for gradual growth of elected representation within the advisory council of the territories as population grew. But the appointed governor alone was given the right to control the annual parliamentary grant to the territories. In 1889, the council, by then called the legislative assembly, resigned en masse, charging that the governor often ignored its advice. The federal government responded two years later by granting the assembly most powers held by provinces except the right to borrow money. By the mid-1890s, calls for the creation of one or two provinces within the territories became increasingly frequent.

The Maritimes

The national government faced demands from all three of the Maritime provinces. By the 1880s, New Brunswick complained that its federal subsidy was too paltry to allow the province to carry out its responsibilities. The Prince Edward Island legislature demanded that the Macdonald government improve steamship service to the Island as required in the terms of the union. Some provincial politicians pressed for a Northumberland Strait tunnel linking the Island to the mainland, but federal politicians dismissed such a scheme as too costly. The greatest hostility to Ottawa in the region still emanated from Nova Scotia. Once the ten years of additional subsidies that Joseph Howe had negotiated in 1869 had ended, the province found itself again short of revenue. In May 1886, Liberal Premier W.S. Fielding introduced a resolution in the Nova Scotia legislature calling for "repeal" of the British North America Act and establishment of a maritime union. He then called an election and increased his legislative majority. But Fielding found the other Atlantic premiers cool to his ideas of Maritime union, and when the Liberals won only seven of twenty-one Nova Scotia seats in the federal election of 1887, Fielding decided to simply push for greater recognition of the province's needs from the federal government. In an effort to mollify Nova Scotia, Macdonald raised tariffs on coal and steel and tried to secure American markets for the Maritime fishery.

Ontario

Because of Ontario's relative post-Confederation economic success, it may appear surprising that this province should have been a persistent critic of federal policy. More than partisanship divided Ontario (which was governed by Liberals from 1871 until early in the twentieth century) and the federal government (which was led by the Conservatives throughout most of this period). The two levels of government were locked in battle over who would dominate the new federation: the national government or the government of the province with half the nation's population.

While Macdonald's vision of Canada often ignored the hinterlands, his resistance to strong provincial authorities made him a natural enemy for the government of Ontario. In an attempt to prevent Ontario from looming too large in the federation, Macdonald tried to have the province's boundaries delimited by placing territories north and west of Lake Superior within the province of Manitoba. The federal government, under the Manitoba Act, had control over Manitoba's resources, and Macdonald argued that the decision making and the revenues pertaining to the rich storehouse of resources in the disputed territories should be under federal control. Ontario responded by proclaiming its right to occupy the western territories and imposing mining and timber licences and law enforcement in the disputed region. For individuals and companies in the area, the confusion created by the dispute was intolerable.

Arbitrators appointed by Mowat and Alexander Mackenzie agreed with Ontario's claim that the area from Port Arthur to Rat Portage (now called Kenora) had been under Canadian control before 1867 and therefore legally came under Ontario's control after Confederation. But Macdonald returned to power before federal legislation enacting the recommendation was passed. In 1881 he placed a bill before the Senate, which would have handed over the entire disputed area to Manitoba. Mowat defied Macdonald, and in Rat Portage in 1883 the dispute took on a comic opera character as constables appointed by the two levels of government arrested one another. Only after several decisions by the Judicial Committee of the Privy Council upheld Ontario's claim did Macdonald relent in 1889 to concede the boundary that Ontario demanded.

By then, Mowat was an implacable foe not only of Macdonald but of his centralizing vision of Confederation. Mowat insisted that Confederation was an agreement or compact of provinces in which the provinces retained the jurisdiction they once held except for specific responsibilities that they granted to the federal government. From this "provincial compact" point of view, there was no new "political nationality" formed in 1867. Thus the use in peacetime of the constitutional clause giving the federal government the power to legislate works for the "peace, order, and good government" of the nation should never intrude upon provincial jurisdiction. Provinces, claimed Mowat, had as supreme an authority in the areas granted them by the constitution as the federal government enjoyed in the areas specifically reserved for the central authority.

Mowat believed that the federal government's frequent disallowances of provincial legislation amounted to unconstitutional interference in Ontario's sovereign areas of authority. When Premier Mercier suggested a conference of the provinces, Mowat's major aim was to rally all the premiers to compel Ottawa to stay out of provincial affairs.

The Premiers' Conference

In October 1887, five of Canada's seven premiers—Conservative Prince Edward Island and a temporarily contented British Columbia administration stayed home—met in Quebec City to demand changes in federal–provincial relations. The twenty-two resolutions passed by the premiers included calls for a million dollar increase in subsidies to the provinces (which then stood at $3.2 million); the handing of the power of disallowance from the federal to the British government; provincial selection of half of all senators; provincial consent before local works could be placed under Dominion control; and recognition of Ontario's boundary. The power of disallowance was a particularly sore point. It allowed the federal government to set aside any provincial legislation that it believed to be outside provincial jurisdiction. Macdonald, making extensive use of his power to legislate for the "peace, order, and good government" of the nation, disallowed a great deal of provincial legislation. Often no greater issue was at hand than the respective rights of patronage of the federal and provincial governments. The provinces would appeal to the courts, which often decided in their favour, but the premiers were outraged over long delays before the various stages of appeal were exhausted and legislation could be implemented.

Macdonald ignored the premiers' proceedings, accusing the four Liberal premiers at the conference (the only Tory present was Manitoba's John Norquay) of partisan mischief. But the issue of what level of government should have the greatest say in running the Dominion of Canada would not disappear. Meanwhile, the federal government, as preoccupied as it was in attempting to assert its authority over the provinces, was also groping with the issue of how much authority it could exercise in the international arena.

• Canada and the World

Canada had no Department of External Affairs until 1909. The self-governing white dominions and colonies within the British Empire accepted British primacy in the international arena and had no desire to establish foreign policy at odds with British interests. Nonetheless, Canada's leaders made clear their expectation that Britain would consult Canada on diplomatic initiatives that affected Canadian interests. In the negotiations leading to the Treaty of Washington in 1871, and on several occasions thereafter, Britain included Canadian representatives on commissions dealing with issues important to Canada. Invariably, the issues at stake involved Canadian–American economic relations.

Fish, Seals, and Boundaries

Disputes about fish turned on interpretations of the Anglo-American convention of 1818 that excluded Americans from British North American inshore fisheries and from access to the harbours, bays, and creeks of British North America except for shelter, repairs, and supplies of wood and water. The Reciprocity Treaty (1854–66) and Washington Treaty (1871–83) periods provided the Americans with temporary free access to the inshore fisheries, but after 1883 the fisheries issue was again a point of contention. Canada seized American vessels allegedly fishing in Canadian waters during

1886 while an American congressional committee leisurely considered the issue of Canadian–American relations in the fishery.

A British–American Joint High Commission was established to deal with the problem. Canada, which wanted reciprocity in fisheries, was invited by Britain to name a representative to the British delegation when the commission opened in November 1887. But when the commission reported agreement three months later, it was clear that Sir Charles

The Fisheries: "The Goose and the Golden Egg," 1871   (Metropolitan Toronto Reference Library)

Tupper, the Canadian representative, had been unable to win a return to the reciprocity of 1854–66. The Americans, regarding Canadian inshore fisheries as less significant than they once had been, were unwilling to provide uninhibited Canadian access to the American fishery. Instead it was agreed that inshore waters in both countries would be set aside for fishers of that nation but that fishers of each country would have commercial privileges in the other.

Canada fared better with regard to its sealing industry in the North. The Americans, after buying Alaska from the Russians in 1867, believed that they inherited that country's claims in the Bering Sea. The U.S. government leased sealing rights off the Pribilof Islands to the North American Commercial Company, which was enraged when British Columbia interests also began sealing in the Bering Sea. The Americans charged that indiscriminate sealing was destroying the seal herd and seized Canadian vessels. But Britain, which had not recognized Russian claims in the area, countered that the North American Commercial Company was the major perpetrator of the slaughter. The two sides agreed to an arbitration panel, which met in Paris in 1893 and decided largely in Britain's favour. Canadian politicians had pressed Britain to be tough with the Americans on the sealing issue, but the fact that the British Columbia sealing interests were British firms undoubtedly played an equally significant role in determining the attitudes of the mother country. While Britain was key to resolving localized disputes between Canada and the United States in the area of trade, it played no direct role in resolving the biggest issue of all: free trade.

Reciprocity, Round One

The Macdonald government was reluctant to part with protection for Canadian manufacturing, the cornerstone of its National Policy of 1879, but it did not entirely abandon attempts to negotiate a trade treaty with the United States. With the Liberals still clinging tightly to their principle of free trade, a policy strongly supported by Canada's primary producers especially in the Maritimes and the West, the Conservatives were forced to make a public show of seeking easier access to American markets, especially for natural products. American politics, meanwhile, was dominated by a protectionist Republican Party unwilling to reduce tariffs on either primary or manufactured goods. When the Americans introduced the McKinley Tariff in 1890, the latest in a series of tariff hikes, Macdonald's hopes for a limited reciprocity were completely dashed.

In his last election in May 1891, Macdonald offered no new remedies for his divided country. The Conservative slogan in the campaign—"The

Old Man, The Old Flag and the Old Policy"—said it all. With Macdonald at the helm, the British flag as their inspiration, and the tariff as their crowning achievement, the Conservatives squeaked through. The Liberals, led by Wilfrid Laurier since their disastrous defeat under Edward Blake in 1887, boldly declared their support for "unrestricted reciprocity." Such a position, which retreated from the idea of commercial union, appealed to the radical wing of the party, but made many Liberals—and many Canadians—extremely nervous.

Opposition to unrestricted reciprocity usually rested on economic arguments, but often had a British imperialist flavour. There was a continuing fear among many Canadians of British descent that overly close commercial ties with the United States would weaken economic and cultural relations with Great Britain. Some people, of course, thought that the loosening of such ties was not a bad idea, but imperial sentiment was generally on the rise in the late nineteenth century. Even those who were not of British origin pointed to the British connection and the institutions it represented as one of the main pillars of the Canadian identity.

Such conflicting views over the future of the new nation were part of the subtext when Canadians went to the polls in 1891. Should Canadians seek closer ties with the United States or, failing that, with Great Britain? Perhaps they should dissolve their unwieldy federation and go it alone as separate dominions within the British Empire, as Newfoundland had done. Or was there something to be said for staying the course? Although a few visionaries saw Canada's future as that of an independent nation such as those emerging in Europe and Latin America, they were a definite minority in the late nineteenth century.

As Macdonald lay on his deathbed in June 1891, he must have wondered what manner of political entity he had helped to shape. Canadians were still at odds with each other and there were few signposts offering a clear direction for the future. Even the party he had worked so hard to build was in disarray and would break into squabbling factions following his death. From 1891 to 1896, Conservatives chose four leaders—John Abbott, John Thompson, Mackenzie Bowell, and Charles Tupper—but none of them seemed to have the leadership abilities of Macdonald. Canadians voted for the Liberals in 1896 for a variety of reasons. Laurier's success in improving the party's organization was one of them. Another was the party's retreat in 1893 from its rigid free-trade philosophy, which had alienated so many voters in Ontario where the tariff was credited with much of the province's economic growth.

• The Métis Rebellions:
A Historiographical Debate

Like contemporaries, historians have debated the justifiability of the two Métis rebellions, particularly the rebellion of 1885. Was Ottawa really planning to settle Métis land claims in Saskatchewan? Had the federal and Manitoba governments lived up to their promises in the Manitoba Act regarding the Métis in Manitoba?

Before the 1970s, most historians of the rebellions regarded the conflict between the government of Canada and the Métis as a conflict between nomadism and agriculture, even barbarism and civilization. The most exhaustive work on the Métis, Marcel Giraud's *Le Métis canadien*, published in Paris in 1945, was dismissive regarding the Métis' willingness or ability to make a transition to agricultural life.

There were a few dissenters to a historiography dominated by works that exalted European over Native values and displayed racist stereotyping of Native peoples. Writing in 1937, G.F.G. Stanley, while he employed conventional Eurocentric language, provided a sympathetic account of Métis society and suggested the Métis had rational, if not justifiable, reasons for rebellion in 1869 and 1885. Stanley blamed government incompetence and indifference as much as Riel for the two rebellions. But he clung to the view of the Métis as "primitive" peoples who were doomed in a contest with "civilization."

In his early work, W.L. Morton, one of the most influential historians of western Canada, dissented from the view of the Métis as "primitive." While he continued to view Indians this way, he observed that there were many European features to Métis life and he accepted the Métis view of themselves as a "nation." In his later work, however, Morton, who reviewed Giraud's work positively, proved largely hostile to the Métis cause. Both he and Donald Creighton, Canada's best-known academic historian from the 1950s to the 1970s, vindicated the Canadian government's treatment of the Métis.

The Métis, spurred by the dismissive and sometimes racist writings of academic historians, sponsored their own research into the events leading to the rebellions. The resulting work was attacked by academic historians as a series of conspiracy theories unsupported by evidence. The academics were relatively milder in their rejection of the work of popular historian George Woodcock. His biography of Gabriel Dumont stressed, among other things, a series of requests made by the Métis of Saskatchewan for government aid for a transition to a settled, agricultural life coupled with some recognition of Métis corporate identity. According to Woodcock, the government ignored these requests.

In the 1980s, several academic historians, particularly Douglas Sprague, weighed in on the side of the Métis. Sprague rejected racist stereotypes of the Métis and, using newly available archival evidence of government thinking in the 1870s and 1880s, went farther than Stanley in blaming governments for dispossessing the Métis. "The conclusion is that the North West Rebellion in 1885 was not the result of some tragic misunderstanding, but of the government's manipulation of the Manitoba Métis since 1869,"[6] wrote Sprague. He outlined a variety of stratagems that he claims governments used deliberately to deprive the Métis of lands promised them in 1870. Stalling was the major tactic. From 1870 to 1873, the Macdonald Conservatives ignored their promise to grant lands to the Métis, while the subsequent Mackenzie Liberal administration placed innumerable judicial roadblocks in the way of Métis who attempted to get title to land. Meanwhile, Ontario settlers who moved into Manitoba received land grants with little difficulty in areas the Métis believed had been reserved for their use. Their mistreatment of the Métis, to which both the federal and Manitoba governments turned a blind eye, caused many Métis to give up in frustration and move further west, abandoning or selling land claims in Manitoba. As settlement and the railway again began to stretch into their new territories, at the same time that the buffalo disappeared, the Métis demanded guarantees of land from the Canadian government. The government made a pretence of dealing with Métis demands but its previous duplicity in Manitoba and continuing inaction in Saskatchewan provoked a violent Métis reaction.

The "dispossession" thesis has been rejected by several scholars of the Métis, particularly political scientist Thomas Flanagan. While disowning the racist language of an earlier generation of Euro-Canadian historians of the Métis, Flanagan suggests that the Métis were, as a whole, more interested in hunting than farming. They sold titles and claims to land in Manitoba not because government delays, official hostility, and Euro-Canadian settlers pushed them out but because they did not want to farm. He argues that they received reasonable value for the lands they sold. The rebellion in Saskatchewan, from his point of view, may have been precipitated by Métis fears that their land claims in that territory would be ignored, but he blames government and Métis failure to communicate and Riel's agitation for the hostilities that produced the second rebellion. In Flanagan's view, delays both in the Manitoba and Saskatchewan land settlements resulted from disagreements and misunderstandings between the Métis and the federal government and not from deliberate stalling by the latter. From Flanagan's perspective, the view of the Métis as frustrated, dispossessed farmers has no basis in fact. The federal Department of Justice has made use of his expertise to rebuff Métis claims for compensation for wrongful removal of lands promised to them, while Sprague has been retained by the Métis to help make their case.

The Flanagan thesis makes little allowance for racism on the part of the governments dealing with the Métis. He concludes that the empirical evidence suggests that governments were willing to deal honestly with the Métis and did not regard these people as uncivilized primitives upon whom good land would be wasted. If he is correct and Sprague wrong, then the Canadian government's dealings with the Métis would stand out as a unique exception in the dealings between conquering Europeans and aboriginal peoples in the nineteenth century.

•Notes

[1] Canada, House of Commons, *Debates*, 17 Jan. 1881.

[2] Alexander Morris, *The Treaties of Canada with the Indians of Manitoba and the North-West Territories* (Toronto: Belfords Clarke, 1880; reprinted Coles, 1971), 28.

[3] Quoted in Manitoba Indian Brotherhood, *Treaty Days: Centennial Commemorations Historical Pageant* (Winnipeg: Manitoba Indian Brotherhood, 1971), 24.

[4] Brian Young and John A. Dickinson, *A Short History of Quebec: A Socio-Economic Perspective* (Toronto: Copp Clark Pitman, 1988), 126. Allan's financial interests centred on Merchants Bank, Quebec's second largest financial institution, and steamship lines. They also included Maritime and Ontario coal mines, the Montreal Telegraph Company, a Vermont marble company, and six fire, marine, and life insurance companies.

[5] Ramsay Cook, *Canada and the French-Canadian Question* (Toronto: Macmillan, 1966; reprinted Copp Clark Pitman, 1986), 178.

[6] D.N. Sprague, *Canada and the Metis, 1869–1885* (Waterloo: Wilfrid Laurier University Press, 1988), 184.

• Selected Readings

The standard surveys on the period are: W.L. Morton, *The Critical Years: The Union of British North America, 1857–1873* (Toronto: McClelland and Stewart, 1964); and P.B. Waite, *Canada 1874–1896: Arduous Destiny* (Toronto: McClelland and Stewart, 1971). Regional overviews are found in Gerald Friesen, *The Canadian Prairies: A History* (Toronto: University of Toronto Press, 1984); Margaret Ormsby, *British Columbia: A History* (Toronto: Macmillan, 1971); Jean Barman, *The West Beyond the West: A History of British Columbia* (Toronto: University of Toronto Press, 1991); Paul-André Linteau et al., *Quebec: A History, 1867–1929* (Toronto: Lorimer, 1983); Susan Mann Trofimenkoff, *The Dream of Nation: A Social and Intellectual History of Quebec* (Toronto: Gage, 1983); Brian Young and John A. Dickinson, *A Short History of Quebec: A Socio-Economic Perspective* (Toronto: Copp Clark Pitman, 1988); Joseph Schull, *Ontario Since 1867* (Toronto: McClelland and Stewart, 1978); David Alexander, *Atlantic Canada and Confederation: Essays in Canadian Political Economy* (Toronto: University of Toronto Press, 1983); and Morris Zaslow, *The Opening of the Canadian North, 1870–1914* (Toronto: McClelland and Stewart, 1971).

On the formation of political parties in Canada, see also R. Kenneth Carty and W. Peter Ward, eds., *National Politics and Community in Canada* (Vancouver: University of British Columbia Press, 1986). Ideological debates are traced in Denis Monière, *Ideologies in Quebec: The Historical Development* (Toronto: University of Toronto Press, 1981); Douglas V. Verney, *Three Civilizations, Two Cultures, One State: Canada's Political Traditions* (Durham, NC: Duke University Press, 1986); and Carl Berger, *The Sense of Power: Studies in the Ideas of Canadian Imperialism* (Toronto: University of Toronto Press, 1970). Biographies of key national political figures include Donald Creighton, *Sir John A. Macdonald: The Old Chieftain* (Toronto:

Macmillan, 1956); Dale C. Thompson, Alexander Mackenzie: Clear Grit (Toronto: Macmillan, 1960); and Brian Young, *George-Étienne Cartier: Montreal Bourgeois* (Montreal: McGill-Queen's University Press, 1981). On Canada's external relations see R.C. Brown, *Canada's National Policy, 1883–1900: A Study of American–Canadian Relations* (Princeton: Princeton University Press, 1964); and Edelgard E. Mahant and Graeme S. Mount, *An Introduction to Canadian–American Relations* (Agincourt, ON: Methuen, 1984).

Nova Scotia and Confederation 1864–1874 by Kenneth Pryke (Toronto: University of Toronto Press, 1979) provides detail on Nova Scotia politics in the 1860s and 1870s. The leading politician of the early post-Confederation period is portrayed in J. Murray Beck, *Joseph Howe*, vol. 2, *The Briton Becomes Canadian, 1848–1873* (Montreal: McGill-Queen's University Press, 1982). New Brunswick politics in the Confederation era are discussed in William M. Baker, *Timothy Warren Anglin: Irish Catholic Canadian* (Toronto: University of Toronto Press, 1977); and Alfred G. Bailey, "The Basis and Persistence of Opposition to Confederation in New Brunswick," *Canadian Historical Review* 23, 4 (Dec. 1942): 374–97. Prince Edward Island politics are discussed in Ian Ross Robertson, "Prince Edward Island Politics in the 1860s," *Acadiensis* 15, 1 (Autumn 1985): 35–58 and David Weale and Harry Baglole, *The Island and Confederation: The End of an Era* (Charlottetown: Ragweed, 1973). On Newfoundland's rejection of Confederation, see James Hiller, "Confederation Defeated: The Newfoundland Election of 1869," *Newfoundland in the Nineteenth and Twentieth Centuries: Essays in Interpretation*, ed. James Hiller and Peter Neary (Toronto: University of Toronto Press, 1980), 67–94. Newfoundland politics in the late nineteenth century are treated in S.J.R. Noel, *Politics of Newfoundland* (Toronto: University of Toronto Press, 1971).

There is a vast literature on the two Northwest rebellions. Among the better works relating to the 1869 rebellion are D.N. Sprague, *Canada and the Metis, 1869–1885* (Waterloo: Wilfrid Laurier University Press, 1988); Joseph Kinsey Howard, *Strange Empire: A Narrative of the Northwest* (New York: William Morrow, 1952); George Stanley, *The Birth of Western Canada: A History of the Riel Rebellions* (Toronto: University of Toronto Press, 1970); and George Stanley, *Louis Riel* (Toronto: McGraw-Hill Ryerson, 1963). The causes and events of the 1885 rebellion are detailed in the two Stanley works as well as Bob Beal and Rod Macleod, *Prairie Fire: The Northwest Rebellion of 1885* (Edmonton: Hurtig, 1984). A qualified defence of Canadian government actions is found in Thomas Flanagan, *Riel and the Rebellion: 1885 Reconsidered* (Saskatoon: Western Producer Prairie Books, 1983). The military aspects of the rebellion are outlined in Desmond Morton, *The Last War Drum* (Toronto: Hakkert, 1972). Biographies of the major Métis protagonists of the 1885 rebellion include Stanley's *Louis Riel* and George Woodcock, *Gabriel Dumont: The Métis Chief and His Lost World* (Edmonton: Hurtig, 1975). Life for Native peoples in the West following the defeat of the rebellions is the subject of several essays in F.L. Barron and James B. Waldrom, eds., *1885 and After: Native Society in Transition* (Regina: Canadian Plains Research Centre, 1986). An important community study focussing on the Métis is Diane Payment, *Batoche 1870–1910* (St-Boniface: Les Editions du Blé, 1983).

General background on French–English and Protestant–Catholic conflict is provided in Ramsay Cook, *Provincial Autonomy, Minority Rights and the Compact Theory, 1867–1921* (Ottawa: Queen's Printer, 1969) and Ramsay Cook, R. Craig Brown, and Carl Berger, eds., *Minorities, Schools and Politics* (Toronto: University of Toronto Press, 1969). The situation of French Canadians in the Maritimes is explored in Richard Wilbur, *The Rise of French New Brunswick* (Halifax: Formac, 1989) and Jean Daigle, ed., *The Acadians of the Maritimes: Thematic Studies* (Moncton: Centre d'études acadiennes, 1982).

A.I. Silver, "French Canada and the Prairie Frontier, 1870–1890," *Canadian Historical Review* 49, 1 (March 1969): 11–36 and Robert Painchaud, "French-Canadian Historiography and Franco-Catholic Settlement in Western Canada, 1870–1915," *Canadian Historical Review* 59, 4 (Dec. 1978): 447–66 seek to explain why relatively few French Canadians ventured to the Northwest. The conflicts embroiling those who did are examined in W.L. Morton, *Manitoba: A History* (Toronto: University of Toronto Press, 1957); Paul Crunican, *Priests and Politicians: Manitoba Schools and the Election of 1896* (Toronto: University of Toronto Press, 1974); and Kenneth Munro, "Official Bilingualism in Alberta," *Prairie Forum* 12, 1 (Spring 1987): 37–48. Ontario's linguistic conflicts are surveyed in Chad Gaffield, *Language, Schooling and Cultural Conflict: The Origins of the French-Language Controversy in Ontario* (Montreal: McGill-Queen's University Press, 1987).

On British Columbia's relations with the federal government, see Margaret Ormsby, *British Columbia* and Jean Barman, *The West Beyond the West.* On the Prairie provinces, see Lewis G. Thomas, ed., *The Prairie West to 1905: A Canadian Sourcebook* (Toronto: Oxford University Press, 1975), Lewis H. Thomas, *The Struggle for Responsible Government in the North-West Territories, 1870–97* (Toronto: University of Toronto Press, 1978), and W.L. Morton, *Manitoba: A History.*

On the Maritimes, see J. Murray Beck, *Politics of Nova Scotia*, vol. 1, (Tantallon, NS: Four East Publications, 1985); John G. Reid, "The 1880s: Decade of Industry" in *Six Crucial Decades: Times of Change in the History of the Maritimes* (Halifax: Nimbus, 1987), 125–57. Ontario's stormy relations with the federal government are the subject of Christopher Armstrong, *The Politics of Federalism: Ontario's Relations with the Federal Government 1867–1942* (Toronto: University of Toronto Press, 1981). Quebec City–Ottawa relations are discussed in Ramsay Cook, *Provincial Autonomy.*

CHAPTER

AN ECONOMY IN TRANSITION, 1867–96

}

Edwige Allard, a Montreal carpenter's wife, kept a one-acre garden that provided much of the food for her household of nine: Edwige, her husband, their six children, and Edwige's father-in-law. In 1871 she reported a crop of ten bushels of beans, ten bushels of potatoes, and four bushels of other root crops. By the end of the century, urban expansion had made families such as the Allards a rarity. Space was parcelled out unequally, and families with the lowest income from paid work were at the greatest disadvantage. Generally only the wealthy could afford an urban home with enough land for a garden and a house substantial enough to take in boarders without overcrowding. The wealthy rarely chose to take in boarders, but for the poor doubling up was often a necessity. As historian Bettina Bradbury notes:

> As new laws and restructured urban spaces curtailed access to subsistence, the ways in which married working-class women could contribute to the family's survival were narrowed down and altered. Where once she could make or save money raising animals, making butter, selling eggs or vegetables, now her contribution lay in sharing her living and cooking space with other individuals and families, taking in boarders, or going out to work occasionally for wages herself.[1]

During the last three decades of the nineteenth century, Canada experienced considerable industrial development, but slow population growth, stagnation in most resource sectors, and modest improvements in the standard of living disappointed those who had expected Confederation to usher in an era of economic expansion. Especially when they compared

Canadian progress with that of the United States, there seemed little basis for optimism. Economic recessions in 1873–78 and the early 1890s raised the level of unemployment and encouraged many people to move south of the border to find work. While European immigrants flocked to the United States, Canada's settlement frontiers remained empty. Was the new nation destined for failure after all?

Beneath the surface of Canada's discouraging economic performance, dramatic changes were taking place that would lay the basis for future growth. The 1901 census indicated that almost 35 percent of Canadians lived in communities with over one thousand residents, almost twice the percentage reported in 1871. By 1901 a vast network of rail lines stretched across the continent, linking cities, towns, and villages, many of which had not even existed thirty years earlier. The railway quickened the pace of economic life wherever it ran and laid the foundations for a national economy dominated by the business elites of Montreal and Toronto. Canada may have been beaten by the United States in the nineteenth-century race for economic growth, but it was still in the running.

Under the terms of the British North America Act of 1867, the federal government was the chosen instrument for promoting economic development. Ottawa collected the tariffs that were the main source of government revenue and a tool for protecting Canadian producers. Ottawa also regulated currency, chartered banks, and insurance companies, and controlled trade and commerce. Navigation, shipping, interprovincial ferries, fisheries, and marine services came under federal jurisdiction, while agriculture and immigration were shared between Ottawa and the provinces. Although natural resources remained under provincial control, the territorial resources of the old Hudson's Bay Company, representing over half the area of the new Dominion, were administered by Ottawa. Prairie lands were used to achieve a variety of national goals, including attracting immigrants, paying for railways, and even bankrolling the military. The cost to the Canadian taxpayer was surprisingly low. Extinguishing Native claims and Hudson's Bay Company charter rights had been largely achieved with the stroke of a pen.

Conservative governments in power in Ottawa from 1867 to 1873 and 1879 to 1896 encouraged integration of the provincial economies. Three policies—a protective tariff, transcontinental railways, and sponsorship of immigration—have generally been identified as the cornerstones of Conservative national development policy. By linking the provinces, the railways enabled tariff-protected goods to find national markets. Immigration provided both the railways and the manufacturers with markets. Although they characterized government efforts, these "national policies" only gradually became an integrated economic plan. They did not prevent Macdonald from continuing to pursue a reciprocity treaty for natural resources with the Americans whenever the opportunity arose.

•Industrial Growth

Macdonald himself used the term "National Policy" to describe the protective tariff promised in 1878. In 1879, the Conservative government raised the general tariff from 17.5 to 25 percent and boosted other tariffs over the 30 percent mark. Counting the Canadian Manufacturers' Association leaders among his principal supporters, Macdonald increased tariffs throughout the 1880s, reportedly relying on casual billiard room discussions with the manufacturers to determine appropriate levels of protection. Many manufacturers supported protectionism for at least a generation before 1879, but it was only in the 1870s that a federal political party organization chose to back their demand. Several factors contributed to the decision of the Conservatives to embrace protection. Firstly, an economic slump beginning in 1873 made promises to stimulate employment an attractive plank in any political platform. Secondly, manufacturers were increasingly well organized and able to make their demands felt. Finally, the greater weight of manufacturing in the economy made a policy geared to protecting manufacturers appear acceptable to a political party attempting to win office. By the late 1870s, the Tories embraced the tariff, while the Liberals remained free traders, giving Canadians a choice between two policy options rather than simply the choice between two rival patronage machines.

The importance of the National Policy in promoting industrial growth and economic expansion has long been debated. Detractors of the policy then and now charge that the tariff benefited inefficient producers at consumers' expense, and encouraged inexperienced, under-capitalized investors to establish firms destined for failure. Further, they argue, it allowed manufacturers to concentrate on the domestic market and deterred aggressive entrepreneurship aimed at international markets. From the point of view of their regional critics, Ottawa followed policies that favoured Central Canadian economic expansion to the detriment of the Atlantic provinces and the developing western region. Essentially, opponents of the policy have decried state intervention in the marketplace: business-oriented critics claim that such intervention distorts the allocation of resources while populist critics argue that it favours vested interests.

Supporters of the National Policy have argued that protection is necessary to allow infant industries to succeed against competition from larger established competitors in other countries. The importance of tariffs in American industrial development, for example, is generally conceded. In the Canadian case, the National Policy encouraged a 114 percent increase in capital investment in manufacturing in the 1880s over the 1870s. During the 1880s, total wages paid by manufacturers rose 68 percent. Individual wages rose a little, but most of the increase was explained by a rise in available jobs as the number of manufacturing establishments jumped 52 percent.

Most of these new establishments were in sectors such as boots and shoes, cotton, and furniture, where Canadians were already competing for the domestic market with foreign manufacturers. The leading Canadian manufacturers lauded such an import-substitution policy, rejecting the criticisms that tariffs discouraged specialization and aggressive international marketing. The *Canadian Manufacturer*, the publication of a leading group of Ontario industrialists, stressed in 1892: "We should not desire to import anything which we could manufacture to advantage at home, and we should not export anything which we ourselves could consume. This is the correct theory, and if it were elaborated and carried out to its fullest possible extent, our foreign trade might not be so large, but we would become richer and more independent."[2]

Production for a small protected home market may have discouraged technological innovation, particularly in the 1880s when competition was fierce in many industries. With a relatively small market, Canada had twenty-three cotton mills, five sugar refineries, and seven ropeworks. The dispersed character of industry in the country is also evident in the presence of over 200 sawmills in 1881. Every rural and urban district in Central Canada in 1881 had boot and shoe manufacturers and blacksmiths, while 167 districts had tailors and clothiers. Ownership of industry tended to be local until a wave of consolidations in the 1890s presaged a change in the ownership and location of Canadian manufacturing. Control over the textile industry, for example, passed into the hands of a small number of Montreal companies backed by the large financial institutions of that city.

Under the protective cloak of the National Policy tariff, Canadian entrepreneurs moved to fill needs hitherto met by American imports. Such products as Ganong chocolates, McClary ranges, and Wanzer sewing machines rose to national prominence in the last two decades of the nineteenth century. Toronto, in particular, became the centre of specialized industries that served a national market. One of the most impressive new Canadian products was the piano. In 1876, some 90 percent of the pianos that graced fashionable Victorian parlours in Canada were imported; by 1891 nearly all pianos were produced at home, many by Heintzman, R.S. Williams, or Mason and Risch of Toronto.

The agricultural implements industry also expanded under the tariff. Already well established in Ontario at the time of Confederation, the industry grew significantly after Confederation as farmers invested in machines for mowing, raking, reaping, and binding their harvest. Using American patents as well as developing their own lines, the Ontario firms of Massey Manufacturing and A. Harris and Son quickly emerged as leaders in the industry. The implementation of a 35 percent tariff on imported agricultural machinery in 1883 gave them a tremendous boost in the Canadian market. To press their advantage, they used aggressive sales techniques, including displays at county fairs, field contests, "delivery day" parades, catalogues, newspaper advertising, and easy credit terms. When in 1891 the two companies merged as Massey-Harris, capitalized at $5 million, they formed Canada's largest corporation, controlling over half the Canadian sales of agricultural machinery.

Such Canadian success stories notwithstanding, many of the larger firms that were established in Canada before 1900 were American branch-plant operations. Singer Sewing Machine, Gillette, Swift's, Coca-Cola, and American Tobacco were U.S. companies that set up Canadian manufacturing facilities in order to participate in a market that the Macdonald tariff made difficult to serve from across the border. The Conservatives welcomed foreign investors who sought to scale the tariff wall, regarding all firms in Canada as Canadian regardless of the nationality of their owners and the address to which profits were delivered. Towns anxious to share in the Industrial Revolution competed with bonuses and tax concessions to attract well-established international firms.

Like the agricultural implements trade, the steel industry created behind National Policy tariff walls was also Canadian-owned. In New Glasgow, Nova Scotia, for example, two blacksmiths, Graham Fraser and George Forest McKay, established the Nova Scotia Forge Company and in the 1880s began to manufacture open-hearth steel. In the 1890s, their firm, renamed the Nova Scotia Steel and Forge Company, built a large modern blast furnace and state-of-the-art coke ovens. In addition, the company bought iron ore deposits in Pictou County and built its own rail line to connect with the Intercolonial. Such vertical integration within an industry— that is, control by one firm of the manufacturing, marketing, and use of a product as well as of the natural resources necessary to produce it—was typical of the most successful new age industries.

Fraser and McKay might have had a greater market for steel products except that the railway companies had ensured there was no tariff on steel rails. In 1896, all steel rails were imported. The subversion of the National Policy by the railway builders demonstrates that the notion of a set of integrated "national policies" that linked railways and tariffs is easily over-stated. Even more than the manufacturing sector, railways became the model for monopoly, massive government subsidies, and corruption in Canadian political life.

In 1873 the Pacific railway scandal brought down the Macdonald government and exposed the unacceptably close relationship between politicians and the private interests that were proposing to build the railway. Macdonald's successor, Liberal Prime Minister Alexander Mackenzie, decided to make the Pacific railway, like the Intercolonial railway to the Maritimes, a state enterprise. When economic recession forced the government to move at a snail's pace, British Columbia, which had been promised a railway by 1883 as part of its Confederation agreement, threatened secession. Only 1000 of the 6000 kilometres of track needed to reach the Pacific Coast had been built by the time Mackenzie was voted out of office, and the challenging portion—the line through the Rockies—seemed indefinitely on hold.

Back in power, Macdonald used British Columbia's threat of secession to justify another generous offer to private business interests who were prepared to tackle the Pacific railway project. Headed by George Stephen, president of the Bank of Montreal, and Donald Smith, a major stakeholder in the Hudson's Bay Company, the Canadian Pacific Railway syndicate was made an offer by Ottawa that few self-respecting entrepreneurs could refuse. The CPR contract included: a cash grant of $25 million in aid of construction; a land grant of 25 000 000 acres (half of the land within thirty-two kilometres of the CPR's main line would be set aside until the company decided which parcels of land it wished to claim); an additional land grant for railway stations and road beds; the 1100 kilometres of completed track built in the Mackenzie years (value: $37 785 000); a guarantee of a twenty-year monopoly on western rail traffic; exemption of the company from the tariff on all materials required in railway construction; and a twenty-year exemption for all CPR properties from federal and provincial taxation and from taxation by municipalities not yet incorporated.

The building of the CPR has been the subject of a good deal of myth making in Canada. It did, after all, link the West with Central Canada through challenging terrain, and so its original owners and engineers have been presented as bold visionaries. Talented they may have been, but the public purse paid most of their bills. In addition to the original grants in 1880, monies were given to the CPR in 1885 at the time of the second Northwest Rebellion, and a government guarantee of a $15 million bond issue was provided in 1888 to win CPR agreement to void the monopoly clause in the original contract.

"The Syndicate's Christmas Tree; or, the Time for Giving Things Away," 1886 (J.W. Bengough/National Archives of Canada/C330740)

By 1891 Canada had over 20 000 kilometres of railway track, much of it subsidized by government grants and concessions. Telegraph lines were erected along the railway routes, making instantaneous transcontinental communication a reality by the 1880s. This conquest of time and space through developments in transportation and communication made traditional ways of telling time awkward. In 1867, clocks were set by astronomical calculations in each major locality. This meant that 12:00 noon was fifteen minutes earlier in Halifax than in Moncton. Few people in Halifax cared very much when it was noon in Toronto or Vancouver. The railway and telegraph demanded a more standardized approach, especially in a country as big as Canada. Appropriately, it was a Canadian, Sandford Fleming, who advocated a global system of telling time based on hourly variations from a standard mean. Fleming was instrumental in convincing those attending the International Prime Meridian Conference in 1884 in Washington to adopt such a system, which is still in use today.

Ontario and Quebec

Home to the nation's major transportation and banking interests, Montreal emerged as the nerve centre of the Canadian economy in the final decades of the nineteenth century. At the same time, Ontario surged ahead of Quebec in agriculture and manufacturing. Quebec farmers, who had increased food production in the 1850s, made slow progress thereafter. The nineteenth-century Ontario farm was about 2.5 times more productive than its Quebec counterpart. Though by 1900 its dairy production almost matched that of Ontario, Quebec continued to decline as a producer of grain and potatoes. Continued colonization in the Saguenay–Lac St Jean region, the St Maurice Valley, and the back country south of the St Lawrence

Quebec farmer, circa 1900   (National Archives of Canada/PA43304)

increased the land base by almost 40 percent, but much of that land was marginal and could only support a family through the sale of its wood products. Even with this agricultural expansion, in 1900 Quebec had only two-thirds as much land under cultivation as did Ontario.

Ontario's farmers, though modest producers by commercial standards, were in a far better position to sell a portion of their produce and to consume the wares of manufacturers. In 1871, for example, Ontario's farmers owned 37 874 reapers and mowers while Quebec's farmers owned only 5149, though the latter province had almost as many farmers as the former. Non-metropolitan Ontario could boast $1.5 million of value added in agricultural implements while non-metropolitan Quebec could claim only $300 000 of value added in that sector. With more capital to invest in animals, Ontario's farmers increased meat production more rapidly than their Quebec counterparts and were in a better position to exploit the heightened British demand for foreign bacon.

Manufacturers in Ontario sold not only to the farmers of that province but also to residents of the Prairies, where there was little local industry and where tariffs discouraged consumers from looking southwards for consumer

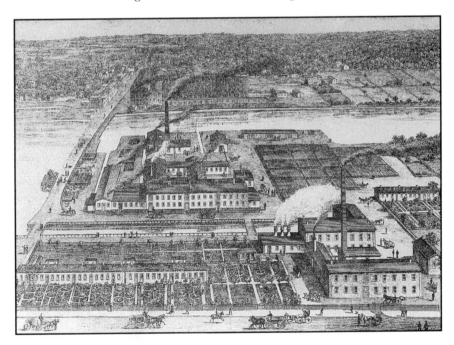

Paper mills at Valleyfield, Quebec, 1870s (E. Haberer/National Archives of Canada/ C16638)

goods and farm machinery. With markets at its doorstep, Ontario outdistanced Quebec and the Maritimes in manufacturing capacity. The increase in Quebec's manufacturing output was nonetheless impressive, doubling between 1871 and 1901 to $153 574 000. In Quebec, the tariff helped to create a strong textile industry and encouraged the expansion of sugar refining, meat curing, tobacco processing, and clothing manufacturing. The railways had become the basis for an $8-million-a-year transportation equipment industry and a $13-million-dollar iron and steel industry, both concentrated in Montreal.

Overall, Quebec's manufacturing output hovered around 60 percent of Ontario's from 1860 to 1900, and it could therefore be argued that, given the initial lag, Quebec held its own. The average annual growth rate of value added in the two provinces was virtually the same for the first three decades of Confederation. By 1881, Montreal workers, earning an average $268.60 per year, were paid almost as much as the workers of Ontario's five largest cities, who averaged $296.89. But outside Montreal, which was the home of the more technologically advanced industries, Quebec's workers were poorly paid and had much in common with Maritime workers whose region was increasingly dominated, like their own, by Montreal financiers.

The Atlantic Provinces

The Maritime provinces benefited less from the "national policies" than the rest of the country. While the Intercolonial railway, completed in 1876, brought welcome investment, it also made it easier for industries based in the St Lawrence area to compete with local output. Nevertheless, Maritime entrepreneurs invested heavily in manufacturing, especially in the years immediately following the 1879 tariff. During the 1880s, there was a 66 percent increase in industrial output in Nova Scotia. In the same decade, Saint John, the region's major shipbuilding and timber exporting centre, doubled its industrial capacity and emerged as the nation's main supplier of nails and brass products. By 1885 the Maritimes, with less than 20 percent of the nation's population, housed eight of Canada's twenty-three cotton mills, three of its five sugar refineries, two of its seven ropeworks, one of its three glassworks, and both of the Canadian steel mills.

Prosperity was concentrated in urban areas such as Halifax, Moncton, Amherst, Truro, and New Glasgow along the route of the Intercolonial. Cumberland County and Cape Breton benefited from a sevenfold increase in coal production between 1880 and 1913, fuelled by American demand. Nova Scotia's steel industry, aided by tariffs and federal subsidies, continued to be the province's hope for a high-technology future. Such prosperity, which came partially unstuck as the recession of the 1890s led to factory closures and industrial consolidations by Montreal financiers, largely passed over the outports, the former mainstays of the regional economy. In Prince Edward Island, nearly a quarter of all manufacturing jobs had disappeared in the first twenty-five years after the province entered Confederation.

Wooden shipbuilding had continued to be a lucrative venture in the 1870s if only because workers put in more hours for less pay. In the 1880s, the shipbuilders had to decide whether to invest in iron steamers or put their profits in other sectors. In all three Maritime provinces, the decision was to move away from shipbuilding. The bias of the national policies towards land industries and transcontinental trade proved decisive and left a legacy of bitterness in the region. Historians Eric W. Sager and Lewis R. Fischer note:

> It is not self-evident that [Maritime] economic and political interests were best served by the collective failure to sustain a shipping industry to serve Canada's export trades. There were politicians, both local and national, who wanted the National Policy to include a shipping industry and Atlantic seaports as part of a truly national economic structure. But the vision of Canada as a maritime power soon faded, even in the Maritimes. It is impossible to know how far a shipping industry might have contributed to prosperity in the Maritimes in the twentieth century. We are spared the knowledge by the decisions of the late nineteenth century, when Canadians pursued a landward development strategy and left the people of the Maritimes to dream of past glories and foregone opportunities.[3]

The landward strategy worked in a few sectors and then only briefly. Extensive competition from Central Canadian firms, whose economies of scale gave them a cost advantage, made it difficult for most Maritime firms to survive the boom and bust cycles of the late nineteenth century. First the cotton industry and then sugar, rope, and glass became victims of the consolidation movement. By 1895, the control of all secondary industries except for confectioneries and iron and steel had fallen into the hands of outside interests, most of them based in Montreal. Some industries continued to operate under distant management; others were closed down in efforts to "rationalize" production. By the first decade of the twentieth century, the trends were clear for all to see. Between 1880 and 1910, manufacturing in the Maritime region had grown at an annual rate of 1.8 percent compared to 3.1 for the nation as a whole. Overall, in the same period, the Maritime economy grew by only 2.2 percent, no greater than that of the holdout colony Newfoundland, and substantially less than the national growth rate of 3.8 percent.

The West and the National Policies

In the first three decades following Confederation, many of the resources of the new nation were invested in western development. Central Canadian boosters of western expansion believed that western settlers, most of whom came from Ontario before 1900, should be grateful to the federal government for buying up the Hudson's Bay Company lands, establishing the North West Mounted Police, putting the Indians on reserves, and spending the money needed to build a railway across the Prairies to the Pacific.

Instead, westerners complained that the tariff and CPR freight rates made life too expensive. CPR control of huge grants of land left large areas unsettled and produced a dispersed population pattern much as had occurred in Upper Canada in the era of the Family Compact. As in early Upper Canada, this resulted in a need for more roads and more schools than compact settlement would have necessitated. The fuss from Manitobans over the CPR monopoly was great enough that the provincial government decided to charter several rival railway lines to the United States in violation of federal opposition to such projects. Only the Macdonald government's buy out of the CPR's monopoly clause in 1888 prevented this threat to federal authority from becoming a showdown between the federal and provincial levels of government.

British Columbians, though they had demanded the Pacific railway, were no more enamoured of the tariff than were Prairie folk. With their economy largely dependent on exports of coal, lumber, and canned salmon, the National Policy was of little use to them. Their markets in the rest of Canada were negligible. It was to the western United States and to Britain that British Columbia business people looked for avenues for economic expansion. Challenging earlier views that the CPR link integrated British Columbia's economy with the rest of Canada, historian Robert McDonald comments:

> The province experienced no discernible influx of Canadian investment funds apart from capital from the CPR and its directors. The resource industries exporting to external markets from the coastal region continued to develop according to established patterns: the salmon canning industry, which grew rapidly during the nineties, remained clearly part of the old Pacific trade system; the traditional California market still purchased two-thirds of the coal produced on Vancouver Island; and increased lumber production, which doubled in the 1890s over the previous ten years, was sold primarily to traditional Pacific Ocean markets or was consumed locally by construction booms in Vancouver and the Kootenays. The developing prairie market, first for shingles and then for lumber, emerged only very slowly through the decade.[4]

RETAILING

Marketing the products of field and factory was the central function of industrial capitalism. As transportation improved and nation-wide markets emerged, retail operations grew and changed. These changes can be seen in the meteoric rise of the T. Eaton Company. In 1869 Timothy Eaton opened a dry-goods and clothing store on Yonge Street in Toronto. What distinguished Eaton from his many competitors was his method of selling, which included fixed prices, cash only, and money-back guarantees. The approach was so popular that Eaton moved to larger premises, equipped with an elevator, in 1883. Weekly "Bargain Days" and the latest technological innovations, such as elevators, electric lights, and escalators (the latter installed in 1907), drew curious crowds and increased sales. In 1884 Eaton reached across the country to grab business from local retailers when he issued his first mail-order catalogue. Telephone sales were instituted in 1885. By 1903 the Eaton mail-order business was so large that it moved to separate premises. The expansion in sales allowed Eaton to by-pass wholesalers and manufacturers. In 1890 Eaton's began manufacturing their own merchandise, and in 1893 they established their first overseas operation in London. Soon Eaton's wholesale operations circled the globe, with offices in such places as New York, Paris, and Yokohama and Kobe, Japan. Eaton's also opened a branch in Winnipeg in 1905, the first in a chain-store business that would expand dramatically in the 1920s. Robert Simpson, also of Toronto, paralleled the Eaton experience. No corner of Canada reached by the postal service was left unchanged by the rise of the great department stores and their catalogues.

Although it did cause some concern, the appearance of department stores and nation-wide chains on the scale of Eaton's or Simpson's did not destroy the local retail trade. The Wholesale Grocers' Guild, established in 1883, tried unsuccessfully to prevent direct sales from manufacturers, and retailers launched campaigns to urge customers to buy locally. In areas like the Maritimes and the Prairies, retailers painted lurid pictures of grasping Central Canadian mail-order stores sucking the lifeblood from the regional economy, but consumers bought the best product at the lowest price. Local retailers survived by providing specialties or services, such as long-term credit, unavailable from the big chains. Charles Woodward on the West Coast was the most conspicuous example of someone who defied the power of the Central Canadian retailers by establishing his own chain of department stores. In the final analysis, retailing expanded despite the activities of men like Timothy Eaton as more people and products were drawn into the market economy.

The salmon canning industry, for example, increased production from 55 000 to 200 000 cans between 1877 and 1882 and to almost 600 000 cans a year in the 1890s without a significant Canadian market.

Staples, Exports, and Growth

Between 1867 and 1901, Canada's Gross National Product (GNP) increased by over $300 million. Most of that growth came from railway construction and manufacturing. In the primary, or staple, sector of the economy, change was also taking place, but at a slower pace. The two great staples of the colonial economy—wood and wheat—faced sluggish export markets. In the 1890s, the demand for wheat began to increase, but it was not until the first decade of the twentieth century that wheat from the Prairies became a major factor in Canada's economic growth. In the meantime, farmers in the Eastern provinces began to produce cattle, cheese, corn, and apples for growing urban markets, and fishers turned from salted and dried fish to canned salmon and lobster.

Improved steamship services and cold storage facilities even made it possible for producers to supply the British market. One of the most successful entrepreneurs in the overseas trade was William Davies. An immigrant from Britain in 1854, Davies established a plant for curing and

---

MEASURING THE INDUSTRIAL ECONOMY

Economists divide the economy into three sectors: primary or staple industries such as hunting, fishing, forestry, farming, and mining; secondary or manufacturing industries, which add value through the processing of primary resources; and tertiary, or service industries, which facilitate the use and development of primary and secondary resources. The tertiary sector includes financial services, trade, transportation, utilities, and public administration as well as services ranging from street cleaning to teaching. Rents, investment income, indirect taxes, and income paid to nonresidents are often grouped separately. Together, the output of goods and services is called the Gross National Product. Since the goods and services produced outside of the market economy, such as housework and voluntary labour, are not included in calculations of GNP, the national output is considerably greater than the official figures indicate. In 1986 Statistics Canada switched to Gross Domestic Product (GDP) to measure the nation's economic performance. The GDP is calculated in a similar way to the GNP except that it excludes payments on foreign investment.

smoking meat in Toronto in 1861. The popularity of his bacon in Britain led to the opening of a larger plant in 1874. For a short time in the 1880s, until Ontario hog production could keep up with the demand, Davies was forced to buy hogs in the Chicago market.

Fur prices declined in the 1860s and 1870s, and the trade concentrated on northerly regions as southern supplies dwindled. Beginning in 1885, a worldwide decline in supply coupled with increasing demand caused prices to begin a rise that continued, with few interruptions, until World War II. Though competitors gradually moved into the Hudson's Bay Company's northern domains, the company's dominance in the fur trade continued. Native peoples provided most of the labour force and received better returns as fur prices went up. Despite the money paid by the fur trade companies, the increased activity in the North had a significant negative impact on the traditional Native economy. By the end of the century, caribou population in James Bay had diminished and subsistence survival as a way of life was threatened. Throughout the North, new railway lines brought surveyors, geologists, and prospectors, leading to outbreaks of measles, tuberculosis, and influenza among the northern Native population.

International competition kept demand and prices for Eastern Canadian fish from sharing in fur's economic revival. The major new developments were the lobster industry and the Bay of Fundy herring and sardine industry, both stimulated by improved canning technology. The Gaspé region suffered a major blow when Charles Robin and Company, the largest fishery firm in the Gulf of St Lawrence, closed down in 1886. Riots greeted the announcement of the closure, despite the company's history of gouging fishers through the "truck" system. Under this system, the company allowed fishers to run up debts in exchange for exclusive rights to buy their fish and serve as their suppliers. It inflated the price of supplies while paying bottom dollar for fish, but it guaranteed fishers a market for their catch. In Newfoundland, where truck was common, fishers frequently took advantage of opportunities to bypass the local company. In 1880, after an extremely hard winter, fishers and sealers in the Bay de Verde district ignored a local monopoly and sold seal pelts to eager buyers in exchange for pork, flour, molasses, butter, and biscuits.

Mining was still in its infancy. Only coal, mined primarily in Nova Scotia and British Columbia, emerged as a major area for investment in the years immediately following Confederation. In Ontario from 1870 to 1900, about $1 million a year worth of gold, silver, copper, and nickel was extracted from the Canadian Shield. Such minerals were mined without the province receiving a penny of revenue. The Ontario government spent over $8 million on subsidies and supported railway bond issues to build almost 4500 kilometres of track to connect Southern Ontario with the northern resource hinterland that would eventually provide a bonanza of mineral wealth. British Columbia also poured money into railways that would link the mineral-rich Kootenays with Vancouver. Gold mining began in the Yukon in the mid-1880s. Native peoples traded meat and fish to the miners in exchange for alcohol, guns, knives, and iron goods, and were employed by the mining firms as labourers. The Yukon gold rush began with the discovery of large gold deposits on Bonanza Creek in August 1896. Within a year thousands of men and women were making their way to Canada's North in hopes of striking it rich.

For lumbermen, the future appeared bleak. Poor management practices resulted in a rapid deforestation of areas that had previously supported the lumbering industry. The lumber barons of the Ottawa Valley, led by Ontario Cabinet Minister E.H. Bronson and federal MP W.C. Edwards, began to lobby for long-term leases over large areas as a means of providing stability for the industry. They argued that governments would be able to impose and enforce forestry conservation measures if timber cutting was restricted to a few companies.

Farmers in regions close to lumber operations often earned more from cutting timber on their properties than from farming. Their pressure to be allowed to remain in business as small timber operators defeated the timber barons' attempts to establish corporate control over the industry. The result was that the latter, whose real interest was profit rather than conservation, were unwilling to invest heavily in the expansion and rationalization of the pine lumber industry. Conservation generally appeared to be of minor interest to policy makers in this period. Economic expansion was their goal, and tree stumps rather than seeds for new trees represented money in the bank in the short term.

•The Lure of the City

In the vicinity of Manning Avenue and Bloor street, and within a radius of a quarter of a mile, there are situated 15 slaughter houses. These have all been visited at one time or another during the past summer and have always been found to be in a scrupulously clean condition. Notwithstanding this the residents in the locality complain most bitterly of the odors arising from them, especially in the summer months. The smell is so bad that even on warm evenings the residents are compelled to keep their doors and windows closed and to remain indoors. . . .

In certain sections privies are so numerous and so close to houses as to be a menace, if not positively dangerous to health. The denser the population the fewer the water closets, seems to be the rule, the more closely built portions having nearly all [privy] pits. In many cases there are houses built in the rear. These almost invariably have pits and in nearly every instance the privy is placed just where the kitchen door is located, or beside it. In warm weather, especially, the air is contaminated, and the smell is distinctly perceptible.[5]

Stench—from privies, from factories close to or within residential neighbourhoods, from rotting garbage placed in back lanes, and from barns housing substantial numbers of horses and even cows—was part of life especially in working-class districts of cities in the late nineteenth century. Noise, overcrowding, poor sewage systems, and inadequate roads also combined to make life unpleasant for many city dwellers. Conditions varied among neighbourhoods. In every city, by the end of the century, segregated residential patterns divided "the classes" (that is, the business and professional groups) from "the masses," people who increasingly experienced the worst features of urban life.

Unpleasant as the cities may have been for those who could not afford to live among the classes, they could be a refuge for those whom the farm economy could no longer support and for large numbers of immigrants without the capital or skills to farm. Cities also offered more entertainment than the villages: more bars and gambling dens and brothels; more commercial spectator sports; and for those with some spare cash, more opportunities to shop.

Character of Urbanization

Between 1871 and 1901, Montreal doubled its population, Toronto tripled its number of residents, and Winnipeg and Vancouver evolved from villages to major urban centres. By the turn of the century, 34.9 percent of Canadians lived in urban areas, compared to 18.3 percent in 1871, but urbanization was an uneven process. While 46.4 percent of British Columbians in 1901 lived in centres of 1000 or more, this was true of only 24.5 percent of Maritimers. The percentage of urbanization in the Maritimes in 1900 was relatively low, but it nonetheless was double the figure in 1871. Moncton, a railway centre, and towns in industrial Cape Breton and Cumberland County witnessed large population increases. Ontario, with just over 40 percent of its population classified as urban, and

Quebec, at 36 percent, were relatively urbanized provinces. The Prairie region, dominated by new farms, was the least urban region with only 19.3 percent of its residents living in cities and towns (see table 3.1).

Linked by the railways, cities increasingly dominated the economies of small towns and farming areas well outside their immediate vicinity. There was a hierarchy among the cities themselves. Increasingly, financial capital was concentrated in Montreal and Toronto, and the financial elites of these two cities became the source of much of the investment required for industrial and commercial undertakings throughout the country. In turn, Canada's major banking institutions acted as intermediaries for British financial investors. British investors made loans to Canadians that left projects under Canadian ownership when the loans were repaid. Americans, by contrast, tended to set up permanent branch plants. Nonetheless, before 1900, British investment in Canada was five times greater than American, though its impact on our urban and industrial development has been little explored.

The financial centres, with their chartered banks and insurance, mortgage, and loan companies, had the pools of capital necessary to carry out the industrial mergers that began in earnest in the 1890s. Family-owned Maritime firms, for example, were swallowed up in new corporations whose stocks traded on the Montreal Stock Exchange. The cotton and sugar companies of the region had already suffered this fate by the 1890s. Montreal capitalists also purchased coal mines and were involved with New England and Nova Scotia interests that joined in 1893 to create a virtual monopoly of the Cape Breton collieries. The flow of profits out of the Maritimes to Montreal further strengthened the economic power of that city.

Maritime financial companies, such as the Bank of Nova Scotia, that had once played an important role in the region, increasingly invested outside the area. Some historians claim that the failure of the Maritimes to generate a major metropolitan centre in the era of the National Policy contributed to the region's drift towards outside control and industrial stagnation. According to historian T.W. Acheson:

> Central to the experience was the failure of a viable regional metropolis to arise to provide the financial leadership and market alternative. With its powerful mercantile interests and its impressive banking institutions Halifax could most easily have adapted to this role, but its merchants preferred, like their Boston counterparts, to invest their large fortunes in banks and American railroad stocks than to venture them on building a new order. Only later, with the advent of regional resource industries, did that city play the role of financial metropolis.[6]

Table 3.1: POPULATION OF SELECTED CANADIAN CITIES AND RANK BY SIZE

City	1871 Population	Rank	1881 Population	Rank	1891 Population	Rank	1901 Population	Rank
Montreal	115 000	1	155 238	1	219 616	1	328 172	1
Toronto	59 000	3	96 916	2	181 215	2	209 892	2
Winnipeg	241	62	7 985	17	25 639	9	42 340	6
Vancouver	–			–	13 709	11	27 010	9
Hamilton	26 880	6	36 661	4	48 959	4	52 634	5
Ottawa	24 141	7	31 307	7	44 154	5	59 928	4
Quebec	59 699	2	62 446	3	63 090	3	68 840	3
London	18 000	8	26 266	8	31 977	8	37 976	9
Halifax	29 582	4	36 100	5	38 437	7	40 832	7
Saint John	28 805	5	26 127	9	39 179	6	40 711	8

Source: Alan Artibise, *Winnipeg: A Social History of Urban Growth* (Montreal: McGill-Queen's University Press, 1975), 132; George A. Nader, *Cities of Canada*, vol.2, *Profiles of Fifteen Metropolitan Centres* (Toronto: Macmillan, 1976).

Montreal, in addition to expanding its role as a centre of finance and transportation, became an important manufacturing city. While its industry was dominated by consumer goods firms, many of them small, it also boasted large companies that manufactured railway equipment. Though Montreal had an anglophone majority in 1867, migration from the countryside, extension of the city's boundaries, and the fecundity of the French-Canadian population restored the city's francophones to majority status by the 1890s. The city's wealth remained predominantly in anglophone hands, and most immigrants to the city were either anglophones or chose to learn English rather than French as their second language. There was a francophone professional and small business class including retail merchants, small entrepreneurs, notaries, doctors, curés, journalists, and teachers who lived well, if not as well as the anglophone corporate elite. Workers' lives were less pleasant. Sporadic employment at inadequate wages was a fact of life in Sainte-Marie and other east-end neighbourhoods.

Unskilled workers fared little better in Toronto, Montreal's only real economic rival in the late nineteenth century. A rail centre, Toronto benefited from the expansion of the rural sector in Ontario and the opening of the West and of the northern resource frontier. From 530 manufacturing enterprises with a work force of 9400 in 1871, Toronto's manufacturing base expanded to 2401 enterprises with 26 242 workers in 1891. Like other cities hoping to develop their manufacturing sector, Toronto lured new firms with promises of bonuses, free land, and tax holidays. Toronto's financial sector expanded with the city. The Bank of Commerce and the Bank of Toronto, active before Confederation, were joined by the Dominion Bank in 1871 and the Imperial Bank in 1873. With assets of $22.8 million in 1890, the Commerce, the city's biggest bank, was small relative to the Bank of Montreal with assets of $47.7 million.

The expanding scale of enterprises in Toronto, as in Montreal, led to gradual changes in the way business was conducted. In pre-industrial firms, the masters had worked alongside their apprentices; modern enterprises hired managers, line supervisors, and personnel officers to watch over employees and disseminate propaganda designed to make employees work harder for rarely seen owners. Still, even the largest firms were not yet mammoth operations. Massey Agricultural Implements, the largest Toronto manufacturer in the 1880s, employed about 700 people and remained family run, but it reflected the new corporate ideas of management, which would become widespread with the replacement of many family firms by corporate ownership in the next phase of the Industrial Revolution.

In the closing decades of the nineteenth century, Ottawa's fate was still tied to the fortunes of the lumber industry. Seasonal work made life difficult for the one-quarter of the city's population that could be classified as working poor. Among the city's more fortunate residents were members of the civil service, who represented 5 percent of Ottawa's population in 1871. With steady work and an average annual income of $1000, they faced a far more secure life than did lumber industry employees whose average annual income was $275.

Winnipeg's future rested on the fortunes of Prairie agriculture. A sleepy village of 241 people in 1871, with a variety of stores serving the local Red and Assiniboine River settlements, Winnipeg would have remained a backwater except for the determination of local merchants to have the Pacific railway put its main line through town and construct its western yards and shops there as well. The CPR Syndicate had planned to build through Selkirk, northeast of Winnipeg, but the railway directors could always be persuaded with gifts. Winnipeg had built a bridge across the Red River and secured two rail loops that could link a Pacific railway with the United States. It offered the CPR free passage on the bridge, a $200 000 bonus, free land for its station, and a permanent exemption from municipal taxes on railway property.

With the railway in place and Prairie agriculture under way, Winnipeg grew quickly to over 40 000 people by the end of the century. Though other Prairie cities, including Edmonton, Calgary, and Regina had begun to expand by the end of the century, the railyards and Winnipeg's position as the main distribution point for the region gave it an advantage in attracting new industry. It also became the home of the grain exchange whose speculators bid on farmers' crops. Despite its great impact on the Prairie region, Winnipeg was itself a vassel to the larger metropoles of Central Canada. The CPR made decisions affecting Winnipeg from its Montreal headquarters, and the manufactured goods that piled up in Winnipeg warehouses for distribution to Prairie points were usually the products of Central Canadian, rather than Winnipeg, factories. Nonetheless, by the turn of the century, there was a substantial manufacturing sector in the city, including clothing, furniture, and food processing firms as well as metal shops dependent on the railway.

Food processing also dominated Calgary's emerging manufacturing sector in the 1890s: a flour mill, Burns meatpacking, and Calgary Brewing were all in operation by 1893. Durable goods manufacture largely failed to get off the ground in the Prairie cities. In addition to shortages of capital, labour, and ready markets relative to Central Canadian cities, high freight rates on manufactured goods leaving the Prairies frustrated attempts to ship such goods from the region. Western manufacturers complained that the relatively low freight costs on shipments of manufactured goods into the West compared to the high costs on goods other than grain leaving the region amounted to discrimination. The CPR countered that it was simply good economics: cars entering the region with manufactured goods arrived full while those leaving with such goods were half-empty. Only by charging more per unit could the company make a profit from selling Prairie merchandise.

Vancouver, faced with the same CPR argument, had to be content with serving a market restricted to its own province and the Pacific northwest of the United States. Nonetheless, by 1891, 1084 of Vancouver's 13 709 residents worked in the city's manufacturing firms. Like Winnipeg, Vancouver owed its growth to the CPR. To become the terminus of that company's transcontinental line, Vancouver had also provided subsidies and tax holidays to the company. Competing with Victoria, whose commission merchants continued for another twenty years to control trade with Britain and California, Vancouver's merchants sought to dominate the British Columbia economy. Controlling city council—which was voted in, as in most Canadian cities, by an electorate restricted to male property

Shoe repair company in Edmonton   (Provincial Archives of Alberta/E. Brown Collection/B1417)

holders—the merchants provided a $300 000 subsidy to local promoters of a railway to the Upper Fraser Valley, spent $150 000 on a bridge across False Creek to connect the city with roads to the Fraser Valley, and gave subsidies to the initiators of a sugar refinery and a graving dock.

Cities in the West, as elsewhere, were dominated by an elite who were eager to foster economic growth. Winnipeg's leaders sought to attract new businesses, claiming that their city was the future "Chicago of the North." Speculating heavily in local real estate, boosters hoped to make big profits as the cities expanded and land values rose. Some were genuine in their expressed desires to provide a firm economic base for their municipalities, and they risked capital on consumer-goods factories that would only prosper if their city really grew.

Subsidies and free services for businesses absorbed most of the cities' property taxes. With no other source of revenue, municipalities had to skimp on social services. Early Winnipeg and Vancouver, as a result, lacked sewers and drains or any hint of neighbourhood planning to prevent overcrowding and leave some green areas for recreation. Only a few showcase areas such as Vancouver's Stanley Park, created in 1888, gave evidence of a concern for values other than growth and profits. Commercial, industrial, and residential pollution made most cities hazardous and unhealthy places to live.

Before 1900, municipal services were underdeveloped in all regions of the country. The Maritime provinces were particularly slow to give municipalities the authority to govern themselves. Although Charlottetown had received a special charter of incorporation as early as 1855 from the Prince Edward Island government, New Brunswick waited until 1877 to establish a Municipalities Act and until 1896 to implement a Town Incorporation Act. In Nova Scotia, a Municipalities Act was proclaimed in 1879 and the Towns Incorporation Act passed in 1888, the same year that the Newfoundland legislature declared St John's to be a town with the authority to govern itself on purely local matters.

Throughout the country, the laws governing creation of municipalities were, by the end of the century, patterned on Ontario's pre-Confederation model. Cities, towns, and villages were declared urban units, and cities that incorporated were given special rights to raise and spend money. Rural areas were divided into units called townships, rural districts, or parishes, depending on the province, and these became the basis of local elected government. In several provinces, counties were organized as a means of co-ordinating the interests of a group of townships in an area, but in Ontario and Quebec, county-level positions were filled by appointees of the provincial government rather than by elected officials. As the twentieth century dawned, many Canadians became interested in municipal reform. The services provided by municipalities touched the lives of ordinary people, who were bearing the brunt of the transformation taking place in the economic life of the country.

•Work and the Family

The shift from a pre-industrial to an industrial economy had an enormous impact on the Canadian family. While self-sufficiency was rare even in pre-industrial British North America, a majority of family units produced a substantial proportion of the goods they consumed. They relied only peripherally on the sale of their products and their labour in the marketplace. The extent of such marketplace participation rose throughout the nineteenth century and, by the time of Confederation, played a role in the lives of most families. Urban dwellers in particular lacked the resources to produce most of their own food, clothing, or shelter, but even in the countryside, the true subsistence farm family had become rare and was, in most cases, dirt poor.

Families responded to the new market economy in a gendered way. In Ontario, for example, women began in the mid-nineteenth century to increase their production for off-farm sales, becoming major producers in dairying, poultry raising, market gardening, and fruit growing. As these areas of farming expanded and wheat farming declined, men took over what had previously been considered women's work. Dairying in particular was entirely transformed in the second half of the nineteenth century. Canada's first cheese factory opened in Ontario in 1864. By 1871 there were 350 cheese factories in the nation, and by the end of the century 39 percent of Canadian cheese was produced in factories. Political economist Marjorie Cohen concludes that: "With the rise of cheese factories, the character of dairying on the farm, and in particular the division of labour in dairy work, changed considerably. The specialization of farms in production of milk to supply cheese factories meant males increasingly became involved in the production process. As large dairy herds developed, dairying ceased to be a part-time occupation for farm women and more and more became the major work of males on the farm."[7] Increasingly the pasturing, feeding, calving, and milking, once regarded as women's work, were appropriated by the legal head of the farm family household.

Farm families regarded children as an integral part of the family economy. From the 1860s to the 1920s, rural families without children or with few children were mainly, though not exclusively, responsible for sponsoring the immigration of over 80 000 destitute children from Britain to English Canada. Cruelly separated from their kin, these children often faced harsh treatment in their new homes. They, like the farm couple's natural children, were more likely to be viewed as labour to be exploited than as children requiring love and care. As historian Joy Parr has commented, "to be young, a servant, and a stranger was to be unusually vulnerable, powerless, and alone."[8]

Maggie Hall, a child immigrant, described a typical work day in a letter to a friend in 1890:

> I have to get my morning's work done by 12 o'clock every day to take the children for a walk then I have to get the table laid for lunch when I come in then after dinner I help to wash up then I have to give the little boy his lessons then for the rest of the afternoon I sew till it is time to get afternoon tea and shut up and light the gas then by that time it is time for our tea after which I clear away get the table ready for Miss Smith's dinner then put the little boy to bed & after Miss Smith's dinner I help wash up which does not take very long then I do what I like for the rest of the evening till halfpast nine when we have Prayers then I take Miss Smith's hot water & hot bottle, the basket of silver & glass of milk to her bedroom shut up & go to bed which by the time I have done all it is just ten.[9]

A romantic view of childhood innocence was maintained by middle-class families who could afford to keep servants to take on household chores and who did not depend on the wages of their older children. These people rarely extended such sentimental views to working-class children, nor could the working classes generally afford to view their own children this way. In farm and factory households, even if children brought in no wages, their work was necessary from an early age to ensure that the essential work of the household got done. Keeping the inhabitants and the inside and outside of the house clean required many hands in an age of wood stoves, coal furnaces, and dirt roads and before mechanized household appliances somewhat eased the strain of washing, cleaning, and cooking. Fetching water from wells, maintaining a family garden, babysitting, and caring for sick parents consumed many hours and often resulted in missed school days.

Children of the poor often entered the paid labour force at age eleven or twelve—and even younger—and lived with their parents for perhaps another fifteen years before marrying. In 1871, the census reported that 25 percent of boys between the ages of eleven and fifteen and 10 percent of girls that age had occupations outside the home. The Factory Acts passed in Ontario and Quebec in 1884 and 1885 repectively, and later

Farm children, circa 1900   (Glenbow Archives/NA2157-1)

replicated in other provinces, prohibited employment of boys under twelve and girls under fourteen in factories, but these laws were poorly enforced.

Given the importance of children to the family economy, it is not surprising that the economic security of a working-class family varied depending on its stage in the life cycle. Most working-class families headed by unskilled males were poor at some stage in their evolution. Generally, at the time of marriage, savings and two incomes allowed a couple to enjoy an acceptable, if modest, standard of living. Families with older children also enjoyed the possibility of second and third incomes that might make the difference between poverty and modest comfort. Poverty was especially pronounced for large families consisting of children too young to work or to be left unsupervised while the mother went off to work. In such instances the woman might still take in piecework, laundry, or boarders. Before it was outlawed by many municipalities, working-class wives also might raise pigs and chickens in their yards to reduce family food bills. These marginal earnings and savings often meant the difference between a family's subsistence and hunger. Some younger families lived with in-laws or other relatives until such time as their older children could help out the family.

Others simply lived badly. Overcrowded urban districts were filled with under-fed, badly sheltered, ragged young families.

Families headed by women—those who had never married, were widowed, or whose husbands had deserted them—as well as families where the husband was too ill to work or was an alcoholic were in a particularly precarious position. The state and even private charity made only minor contributions to a social safety net in a society where the individual and the family unit were largely left to sink or swim. In this respect, early industrial society was reminiscent of pre-industrial society where luck and good health played a greater role than planning in determining income levels.

In the urban family, it gradually became the ideal that married men earned incomes in the marketplace while their wives stayed home to do the housework and rear the children (or supervised servants who did this work) but earned no income. Professionals and unionized craftsmen could often earn a sufficient wage for a family, but the vast majority of the work force fell into neither of these categories. For them the notion that a male

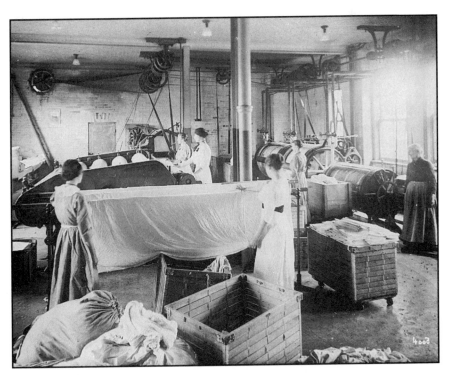

Women working in laundry   (National Archives of Canada/PA11262)

earner could feed, clothe, and shelter a family was a misconception, but it was a pervasive one that was used to justify underpaying women workers. The future prime minister, William Lyon Mackenzie King, writing in 1897 on the sweat shops of the clothing-manufacturing sector in Toronto, quoted an owner who noted: "I don't treat the men bad, but I even up by taking advantage of the women. I have a girl who can do as much work, and as good work as a man; she gets $5 a week. The man who is standing next to her gets $11. The girls, however, average $3.50 a week, and some are as low as two dollars."[10]

Male workers and perhaps their wives (the views of women of the popular classes are not well enough recorded for their attitudes to be described with any certainty) preferred to fight for so-called "family wages" for married men rather than to demand equal employment opportunities for women. Rather than trying to organize women in the work force, unions tried to convince employers to dismiss them. They argued that improving women's wages might encourage them to remain at work, taking jobs that could otherwise be done by men, and causing employers to depress the wages of married men. A married man, after all, could not ask for a wage large enough to support his whole family if more than one family member was in the paid labour force. As historian Craig Heron observes, late nineteenth-century craft unions "incorporated the new 'cult of domesticity' that urged women to stay in the household while the menfolk ventured forth in the world of paid work to earn the family's wages. Craftsmen tended to want their women at home, and deeply resented the ways that employers were using them as unskilled help in efforts to degrade crafts such as printing, shoemaking and tailoring."[11]

It is important to note that the notion of *skill*, while it arguably has an objective component, is also socially constructed. Certain jobs are treated as requiring special competencies or training while others are not. In the 1890s this meant that printing, though it required little talent or training, was a well-paid "skilled" occupation that excluded women, while dressmaking, which required considerable skill, was a poorly paid "unskilled" line of work that employed many women. Although women were the food manufacturers at home, in a candy-making factory such as Ganong Brothers in St Stephen, New Brunswick, only men were confectioners. Women were hired at low wages only to decorate the prepared centres of the candies and to put the candies in boxes.

On the railroads and in the more mechanized manufacturing sectors, employers in the late nineteenth century capitulated to male worker demands that women and children not be brought in as cheaper pairs of hands. In the labour-intensive sectors, such demands were often ignored:

Stonecutters collectively established work norms that contractors were forced to respect.
(Provincial Archives of Alberta/E. Brown Collection/B1380)

competition to provide goods at the lowest costs occurred mainly on the backs of workers. A workshop of men earning a family wage might have been the societal ideal, but it conflicted with the quest for profits.

The cigarmakers of London, Ontario, learned in the 1880s how easily a well-paid skilled job could be turned into a poorly paid "unskilled" occupation. While unionized workers marked their products with a blue label meant to signify quality and tried to restrict new entrants to the trade, their employers, anxious to reduce labour costs, tried to impose wage reductions. When that failed, they replaced so many of the union workers that by the mid-1880s, only thirteen of the 150 cigarmakers in town were adult males.

Young cigarmakers, like other child workers, were subjected to intense factory discipline. Often unable to keep up with unrealistic demands or unwilling to defer to the whims of management, they had their wages docked or their bodies beaten. One Montreal manufacturer, J.M. Fortier, not only beat recalcitrant child workers but locked them in a dark cellar closet for punishment. Defending his practices before the Royal Commission on the Relations of Labour and Capital in 1889, Fortier claimed that parents expected him to discipline their children and make them responsible, docile workers.

Given their value to the family economy, many children no doubt preferred workplaces to schools. In Cumberland County, Nova Scotia, where children made up 16 percent of the work force in the 1880s and 10 percent a decade later, young boys were proud to join the man's world of the mine. The coal mines were, in some ways, less oppressive places to work than most factories. Coal miners, working with primitive technology, produced an indispensable product, and their ability to shut down a mine gave coal miners power within the workplace and the community. Yet a coal mine, with its regular pay and high degree of workers' control, was a dangerous place to work. In 1891, the first of many Springhill, Nova Scotia, mining disasters resulted in the deaths of 125 men and boys.

Labour Struggles

The opposition of wage labourers to features of the industrial order led to the formation of unions of working people for the purpose of making collective demands on employers and providing mutual aid in times of hardship. Gradually, lobbying governments for legislative changes also became part of unions' agenda. The early unions were craft unions, alliances of men (and very rarely women) attempting to maintain control over working conditions and wages in the face of employer attempts to introduce new administrative methods and new technologies that would transform their craft. Labourers doing repetitive tasks were more easily replaced than craftspeople and proved largely unable to create lasting unions in the nineteenth century. Even the crafts had difficulty maintaining their organizations during recessions in which the oversupply of willing hands gave employers the advantage. Many early trade union organizations evaporated during the recession that began in late 1873.

Moulders in Toronto, working in stove, machinery, and agricultural implements industries, were able to dictate apprenticeship regulations, wage rates, and the pace of work in their factories. By contrast, Toronto coopers witnessed the destruction of their craft in the 1870s, and the city's shoemakers, despite a long struggle, lost the battle with their employers by 1890. Mechanization, employer hostility, and recession made it difficult for coopers and shoemakers to restrict entry into their profession as moulders continued to do.

The impact of technological and administrative innovation varied widely: the initial transition from a pre-industrial to a capitalist industrial economy was not always as dramatic as it was for the coopers and cigarmakers. Ironmakers in New Glasgow, Nova Scotia, and Hamilton, Ontario, were part of an industry that between the 1850s and 1890s began to replace simple tools and small shops with steam power, large factories, and mechanization of the labour process. Such changes created new groups of skilled workers: iron puddlers who manned the furnaces that refined pig iron into wrought iron, and "rollers" or lead hands whose decisions determined the pace of work and the quality of the product at rolling mills. Alongside these skilled workers, larger numbers of labourers continued to work at unskilled jobs as yet unchanged by technology.

In the building trades, carpenters generally no longer worked for master carpenters in small workshops or on building sites as they had in the early nineteenth century. Builders who integrated a variety of crafts in one operation emerged, and sashes, doors, and mouldings were increasingly factory produced. Steam power transformed the carpenters' craft and broke it down into its component parts. For all this, historian Ian McKay, in a study of Halifax carpenters, concludes:

> Partial mechanization, general contracting and a widening gap between employer and employed had all changed the carpenters' craft in the nineteenth century. In many other respects, however, the world of the craftsman had been modified but not transformed. The local craftsman still dealt with local employers, many of whom were still master carpenters, and he still saw the challenge facing the union as one of excluding the unskilled and the unmanly. He had limited dealings with the other building trades. There was as yet no visible "labour politics" and trade disputes were confined to very specific issues. There were important structural changes in the industry, but none had been of such scope as to destroy the traditional craft practices which the journeymen had evolved since the mid-nineteenth century.[12]

While many crafts workers held their own, the position of common labourers remained precarious. The poorly trained Chinese workers who performed some of the most dangerous jobs in building the CPR lines through the Rocky Mountains were paid one dollar per day. Many died while dynamiting rocks and others died from scurvy. Generally, navvies— the men who worked in construction gangs that built the railways and other public works—were victims of the sub-contracting system: the sub-contractor received a contract by bidding low and made that contract profitable by paying low wages and feeding and housing the workers in the cheapest way imaginable. Living in grim bunkhouses and eating stale bread, a navvy had experiences of the work world far removed from those of the proud craftsman.

Workers in bunkhouse   (National Archives of Canada/PA115432)

In the 1880s, the number of labour organizations in Canada rose from 165 to 760. Most of these were branches of American unions, and the most successful were those that represented skilled labourers. The craft unions were often quite powerful in maintaining on-the-job worker control. For example, the unionized moulders of Toronto had a large say not only about their wages but also about the number of pieces a foundry craftsman would produce per day. They fought to maintain control in factories against attempts to dictate production through management decrees or through new machinery that partially deskilled moulders' work. In 1890, moulders at the Gurney stove works began a successful sixteen-month strike against a pay reduction while workers in the Massey farm implements plant began a ten-month strike. Because mechanization in the moulding industry proved an expensive failure before 1900, craft solidarity usually resulted in victories for the moulders. Since their skills were demanded in a wide range of industries, these workers could find other positions elsewhere until their regular employer capitulated to their demands.

In the nineteenth century, unionized labour was still too weak to exert much political pressure. It was not until the Trade Union Act of 1872, passed by the Macdonald government, that common-law prohibitions against unions as combinations in restraint of trade were removed. The act legalized only unions that agreed to be liable for the individual acts of their members—including, for example, damages inflicted on company property during strikes—so few unions chose to register under its provisions. No laws forced employers to bargain collectively with their employees or indeed prevented employers from dismissing their employees without cause. Many employers simply refused to hire union labour and fired any employee who was suspected of advocating unions.

Nonetheless, workers organized in the early 1870s to force employers to implement a nine-hour day. In 1871, Toronto printers struck all of the city's newspapers in an attempt to force the nine-hour day on the publishing industry. The publishers, led by Reform Party notable George Brown, successfully prosecuted the strikers for seditious conspiracy, while 10 000 strike supporters paraded in favour of the accused and their strike demands. Throughout 1872, the movement for the nine-hour day reverberated throughout industrial Canada, only to be quelled by the crushing recession of 1873. But the movement produced a degree of solidarity among craftsmen and labourers that re-emerged once the recession lifted.

The 1880s and 1890s saw the strike firmly established as labour's chief method of attempting to win improvements for workers. While there had been only 56 strikes in British North America from 1815 to 1849 and 204 in the 1870s, there were 425 recorded strikes in the 1880s and 600 in the 1890s. A key player in the strike wave was the Noble and Holy Order of the Knights of Labour. Ironically, the Knights regarded strikes as a last resort in dealings with management, but they found that employer recalcitrance often forced them to such drastic action. The Knights originated in 1869 among Philadelphia garment cutters concerned about the loss of worker control in their industry. The group's emphasis on secret rituals, reminiscent of pre-industrial culture, appealed to workers, and the organization spread across the United States and into Canada in the 1880s. Unlike craft unions, the Knights were open to all workers regardless of skill. They attempted, like the nine-hour movement, to encourage workers to support each other's struggles.

In the preamble to their constitution, the Knights argued that workers must fight the "alarming developments and aggressiveness of great capitalists and corporations" to secure "full enjoyment of the wealth [workers] create, sufficient leisure in which to develop their intellectual, moral, and social faculties, all the benefits of recreation and pleasure of association, in a word, to enable them to share in the gains and honours of advancing civilization."[13] But they were unclear how best to work to this end. Their American leaders focussed on creating co-operatives as alternative workplaces, but capital for such ventures was always difficult to find.

The Knights' major breakthrough in Canada occurred in 1883 when they organized workers for a strike "against the monopolistic telegraph companies, symbol for much that was despised in the new industrial capitalist society."[14] Over the next several years they organized workers across Canada in a variety of industrial sectors and broke union taboos against including women and blacks—though not Orientals, whom prejudices branded as needing less to live on than other workers—in their ranks. In the late 1880s, about 16 000 Canadian workers were members of the Knights, with Toronto, Hamilton, and Montreal enjoying particularly large memberships. Locals in Toronto ranged from shoemakers, barbers, and plumbers to carpenters, journalists, and a group of women tailors.

While the Knights' efforts to organize workers according to industry rather than along craft lines appealed to many workers, it created enmity with the leaders of the craft unions who regarded the Knights as a dangerous rival. The class consciousness of the Knights contrasted with the group consciousness of the craft unions whose leaders claimed that the exclusive right of craftspeople to practise certain trades would be whittled away if all-inclusive workers' unions succeeded. Aided by repression in the United States, which weakened the Knights in the late 1880s, the craft unions began to force workers to choose between the Knights and separate craft unions. Throughout the 1890s, the Knights retained many locals, especially in Quebec, but their isolation was complete shortly after the turn of the century when the Trades and Labour Congress expelled Knights' locals from its ranks.

The TLC, created in 1883, was labour's political voice. The national organization and its municipal counterparts, such as the Montreal Trades and Labour Council, lobbied governments for such reforms as a nine-hour day, safer workplaces, and an end to child labour. Their efforts led to greater government regulation of the workplace, though workers constantly complained that governments were lax in enforcing such regulations. In the 1890s, for example, Ontario employed only two factory inspectors for the entire province.

Like the Knights, the Provincial Workmen's Association in Nova Scotia reflected workers' attempts to win collective guarantees within a system founded on capitalist values. The PWA began in 1879 as the Provincial Miners' Association but changed its name and broadened its focus in 1880. It shared with the Knights a decentralized organization and a solidarity amongst members based on participation in various rituals. Unlike the Knights, the PWA included only workers in recognized crafts. The association was dominated by Nova Scotia's large mining population, and its lobbying efforts led to mine safety legislation and other laws of benefit to miners. Although the organization became increasingly conservative after the turn of the century as radicals joined the United Mine Workers of America, the nineteenth-century PWA was quite militant. It shut down all the province's mines on two occasions, and its fiercely independent locals waged seventy other strikes before 1900. Although PWA leaders extolled settlement of disputes by collaboration rather than confrontation, the intransigence of many employers caused the locals to reject the rhetoric of their leaders.

Miner militancy on the East Coast was matched on the West Coast. Miners had spontaneously struck several times in British Columbia before a Mutual Protective Society was established in 1877 by the miners at Dunsmuir, Diggle and Company. The Society protested wage cuts and short-weighing of coal on company scales (the workers were paid by the

ONE HUNDRED AND TWO MUFFLED VOICES[15]

The Royal Commissioners studying the relations between labour and capital heard the testimony of nearly 1800 witnesses. Only 102 of those who testified were women. Although women made up over one-fifth of the paid labour force in 1891, nobody on the commission was very interested in hearing from them. As historian Susan Mann Trofimenkoff has revealed, it took a great deal of courage for working people generally and women in particular to speak before a formal body such as a royal commission. Saying something that offended employers might threaten a worker's job. Nearly half of the women testified anonymously; only 30 of the close to 1700 male witnesses did so.

The most dramatic testimony relating to women's work came from a woman identified as Georgina Loiselle. Beaten by her employer for her "impertinent" refusal to make 100 extra cigars, she was still employed at the factory five years later when she gave her testimony. Her employer justified his behaviour to the commissioners on the grounds that "her mother had prayed me . . . to correct her in the best way I could." With three of Georgina's brothers also employed by the company, the factory's owner had assumed the role of disciplinarian to the fatherless Loiselle children. Georgina was eighteen at the time of the beating and no one, including Georgina herself, seemed particularly surprised by her employer's brutality.

When the commissioners submitted their report, they indicated much greater concern over the moral consequences of women working in unchaperoned settings and using common washrooms with men than they did about the poor salaries and working conditions that were uniformly the lot of women in waged labour in Victorian Canada.

ton) and closed down the Wellington mine on Vancouver Island. Robert Dunsmuir, the province's leading capitalist, was able to convince the government to use the militia to force the miners back to work, but a long history of miner organization and militancy in British Columbia had begun. The miners had little support from the provincial government, while Dunsmuir received generous subsidies from the politicians on many occasions. In 1884, for example, the province granted Dunsmuir and his son James, along with four Americans, a charter for a 114-kilometre railway to link Wellington with Victoria. With the charter, they received federal subsidies of over 750 000 hectares of land and $750 000 in cash. The blatant bias of government towards employers only fanned the flame of class consciousness and made workers determined to take action against politicians as well as their exploitative employers.

Class conflict, and particularly the spread of both the Knights of Labour and of strikes, led the Macdonald Conservatives to create the Royal Commission on the Relations of Labour and Capital in 1886. The commissioners heard testimony from across the nation, but apart from the establishment of Labour Day as a national holiday in 1894, the commission led to few improvements in workers' lives.

• Conclusion

The Canadian economy of 1896 looked considerably different from the economy of British North America in 1867. Over this thirty-year period, characterized by boom and bust cycles, farmers, fishers, and trappers were increasingly being absorbed into an industrial economy. Farming still remained the most widespread occupation among Canadians, but the structure of farm life had been altered considerably, and outside the Prairie region its relative importance had declined significantly. On the Prairies, the Canadian Pacific Railway made commercial agriculture possible and spelled the end of the fur trade as a way of life. Railways and the tariff stimulated manufacturing and urban development in Central Canada and the Maritimes, but manufacturing was concentrated in few centres and by the 1890s was becoming even more highly focussed in the St Lawrence heartland. In less than thirty years, the Maritimes had lost a world-class shipbuilding industry and had witnessed the rapid rise and equally rapid decline of consumer industries. The region's population voted with their feet, with as many as one in three choosing emigration as their solution to economic underdevelopment.

National economic policies not only conferred unequal benefits on regions. They also discriminated on the basis of social class. Tariff-protected industries and subsidy-sustained railway companies were not required to pass on their benefits either to their workers or to consumers. With strikes, urban poverty, and outmigration becoming a feature of life in Canada, many Canadians began to weigh the advantages of moving to the United States.

•National Policies and Regional Development:
A Historiographical Debate

It is a commonplace in Western and Atlantic Canada that the national policies of the late nineteenth century were biased in favour of Central Canada. Some historians of these regions confirm popular perceptions and suggest that Central Canadian industrialization occurred at the expense of the outlying regions as a result of deliberate public policy.

There are also scholars, past and present, who argue that the national policies had negligible impact on the economic fate of these two regions. Historian S.A. Saunders argued in the 1930s that the economic problems of the Maritimes stemmed from decline in demand or price for the key staple exports. When British demand for timber and ships fell off in the 1880s, the region's economy began a decline from which it could not recover. The region's carrying trade meanwhile suffered a fatal blow from the competition of steam and steel ships.

This explanation, of course, does not address the issue of why the region's entrepreneurs did not adjust to changing economic times. According to historian T.W. Acheson, the dispersed character of Maritime capitalism served as a drag on regional economic development. The failure of any centre to become a regional metropolis, marshalling regional capital to take on the challenge of an industrial era, condemned the region to stagnation.

The authors of a recent economic history of Canada, economist Ken Norrie and historian Doug Owram, are sceptical about attempts to explain slow Maritime economic growth that presume that extensive industrialization of the region was possible in the late nineteenth century. They are even more sceptical of attempts to pin the blame on the national policies: "To find the argument credible, one would need to believe that fairly small changes in transportation rates or in Dominion subsidies could have had enormous effects on industrial prospects. Simply putting the issue in that manner suggests the probable answer."[16]

Norrie and Owram are equally sceptical of claims that the national policies discriminated against Western Canada, claims emphatically supported by most Western Canadian historians. T.D. Regehr, for example, states, "there has been deliberate and admitted freight-rate discrimination against the West."[17] Only constant battles by westerners resulted, over time, in partial amelioration of these rates, argues Regehr. But Norrie and Owram claim flatly, "rail freight rates in the development phase of the wheat economy were at least as low as they would have been under the next most likely alternative to the national policy."[18]

Norrie rejects the view that federal tariff and freight rate policies hindered western industrialization:

> In some instances, Prairie industrialization being perhaps the best example, the problem lies in being small and isolated rather than with discriminatory treatment. The present economic structure of the region is adequately explained by standard location theory concepts. It is incorrect to suggest that the federal government or other institutions have industrialized the East at the expense of the West. It must be recognized rather that any significant decentralization of industry in Canada can only be achieved by committing real resources to that end and that this means a subsidy for persons residing in the recipient regions at the expense of other Canadians.[19]

Norrie's argument perhaps makes too little allowance for the role the state has played all along in the marketplace, demonstrating, in its procurement policies, for example, a strong Central Canadian bias. But he does correctly point out a fallacy in the claims of many who focus on alleged discrimination against the regions: the assumption that the free market, left to its own workings, would have produced a more equitable distribution of industry in Canada. The tendency of capital left on its own to concentrate in a few areas with transportation and population advantages is a universal phenomenon of the capitalist system. Concentration has been obviated in several countries by state regimentation of industries that left little discretion in the hands of capitalists regarding location of industries. But there is little evidence that in late nineteenth-century Canada there were significant sections of popular opinion in any region who favoured more draconian intervention in the marketplace than that envisioned by John A. Macdonald and his business community supporters.

• Notes

[1] Bettina Bradbury, "Pigs, Cows, and Boarders: Non-Wage Forms of Survival Among Montreal Families, 1861–91," *Labour/Le Travail* 14 (Fall 1984): 46.

[2] Glen Williams, *Not for Export: Toward a Political Economy of Canada's Arrested Industrialization* (Toronto: McClelland and Stewart, 1983), 20.

[3] Eric W. Sager and Lewis R. Fischer, "Atlantic Canada and the Age of Sail Revisited," *Canadian Historical Review* 63, 2 (June 1982): 150.

[4] Robert A.J. McDonald, "Victoria, Vancouver and the Economic Development of British Columbia, 1886–1914" in *Town and City: Aspects of Western Canadian Urban Development*, ed. Alan F.J. Artibise (Regina: Canadian Plains Research Centre, 1981), 37.

[5] "Tenth Annual Report of the Provincial Board of Health," Ontario, *Sessional Papers*, 24 (1892), 5, 26, quoted in *The Workingman in the Nineteenth Century*, ed. Michael S. Cross (Toronto: University of Toronto Press, 1974), 148, 150.

[6] T.W. Acheson, "The National Policy and the Industrialization of the Maritimes, 1880–1910," *Acadiensis* 1, 2 (Spring 1972): 27–28.

[7] Marjorie Griffin Cohen, *Women's Work, Markets, and Economic Development in Nineteenth-Century Ontario* (Toronto: University of Toronto Press, 1988), 106.

[8] Joy Parr, *Labouring Children: British Immigrant Apprentices to Canada, 1869–1924* (Montreal: McGill-Queen's University Press, 1980), 82.

[9] John Bullen, "Hidden Workers: Child Labour and the Family Economy in Late Nineteenth-Century Urban Ontario," *Labour/Le Travail* 18 (Fall 1986): 181.

[10] Quoted in Ruth Frager, "Class and Ethnic Barriers to Feminist Perspectives in Toronto's Jewish Labour Movement, 1919–1939," *Studies in Political Economy* 30 (Autumn 1989): 148.

[11] Craig Heron, *The Canadian Labour Movement: A Short History* (Toronto: Lorimer, 1989), 10–11.

[12] Ian McKay, *The Craft Transformed: An Essay on the Carpenters of Halifax, 1885–1985* (Halifax: Holdfast Press, 1985), 26.

[13] "Preamble to the Knights of Labour Constitution" cited in Martin Robin, *Radical Politics and Canadian Labour* (Kingston: Industrial Relations Centre, Queen's University, 1971), 19–20.

[14] Gregory S. Kealey, *Toronto Workers Respond to Industrial Capitalism, 1867–1902* (Toronto: University of Toronto Press, 1980), 177.

[15] See Susan Mann Trofimenkoff, "One Hundred and Two Muffled Voices: Canada's Industrial Women in the 1880s," *Atlantis* 3, 1 (Fall 1977): 67–82.

[16] Kenneth Norrie and Douglas Owram, *A History of the Canadian Economy* (Toronto: Harcourt Brace Jovanovich, 1991), 402.

[17] T.D. Regehr, "Western Canada and the Burden of National Transportation Policies" in *Canada and the Burden of Unity*, ed. D.J. Bercuson (Toronto: Macmillan, 1977), 115.

[18] Norrie and Owram, *A History of the Canadian Economy*, 327.

[19] Kenneth H. Norrie, "Some Comments on Prairie Economic Alienation," *Canadian Public Policy* 2, 2 (Spring 1976): 222.

• Selected Reading

The major economic history surveys are: Kenneth Norrie and Douglas Owram, *A History of the Canadian Economy* (Toronto: Harcourt Brace Jovanovich, 1991); and W.T. Easterbrook and Hugh G.J. Aitken, *Canadian Economic History* (Toronto: University of Toronto Press, 1988). On the evolution of the National Policy tariffs, see Ben Forster, *A Conjunction of Interests: Business, Politics, and Tariffs, 1825–1879* (Toronto: University of Toronto Press, 1986). The economic impact of the tariff is discussed in J.H. Dales, *The Protective Tariff in Canada's Development* (Toronto: University of Toronto Press, 1966). On the CPR, see W. Kaye Lamb, *History of the Canadian Pacific Railway* (New York: Macmillan, 1977). Vernon Fowke's *National*

Policy and the Wheat Economy (Toronto: University of Toronto Press, 1957) makes the Prairie case against the national policies most strongly. An opposing view is presented in Kenneth H. Norrie, *The National Policy and the Prairie Region* (New Haven, CT: Yale University Press, 1971). Maritime assessments of national economic policies include: David G. Alexander, *Atlantic Canada and Confederation* (Toronto: University of Toronto Press, 1983); the much-reprinted essay by T.W. Acheson, "The National Policy and the Industrialization of the Maritimes, 1880–1910," *Acadiensis* 1 (Spring 1972): 3–28; and Eric W. Sager and Lewis R. Fischer, "Atlantic Canada and the Age of Sail Revisited," *Canadian Historical Review* 63, 2 (June 1982): 125–50. On Ontario economic development see Ian M. Drummond, *Progress Without Planning: The Economic History of Ontario from Confederation to the Second World War* (Toronto: University of Toronto Press, 1987); on British Columbia, Jean Barman, *The West Beyond the West: A History of British Columbia* (Toronto: University of Toronto Press, 1991). Quebec economic development in the late nineteenth century is the concern of Jean Hamelin et Yves Roby, *Histoire Économique du Québec, 1851–1896* (Montreal: Fides, 1971); J.I. Little, *Crofters and Habitants: Settler Society, Economy and Culture in a Quebec Township, 1848–1881* (Montreal: McGill-Queen's University Press, 1991); and Normand Séguin, *La Conquête du Sol au 19e Siècle* (Montreal: Boréal Express, 1977). The relative success of Ontario over other regions is explored in John Isbister, "Agriculture, Balanced Growth and Social Change in Central Canada since 1850: An Interpretation" in *Perspectives on Canadian Economic History*, ed. Douglas McCalla (Toronto: Copp Clark Pitman, 1987): 58–80; and N.R.M. Seifried, *The Regional Structure of the Canadian Economy* (Toronto: Nelson, 1984).

Business developments and ideology, with an emphasis on Ontario, are discussed in Michael Bliss, *Northern Enterprise: Five Centuries of Canadian Business* (Toronto: McClelland and Stewart, 1987); and his *A Living Profit: Studies in the Social History of Canadian Business, 1883–1911* (Toronto: McClelland and Stewart, 1974). A more critical assessment is Tom Naylor, *The History of Canadian Business, 1867–1914*, 2 vols. (Toronto: Lorimer, 1975). State-business relations in Ontario are illuminated in H.V. Nelles, *The Politics of Development: Forests, Mines and Hydro-Electric Power in Ontario, 1849–1941* (Toronto: Macmillan, 1974). Morris Zaslow, *The Opening of the Canadian North 1870–1914* (Toronto: McClelland and Stewart, 1971) outlines economic developments in northern regions. On the post-Confederation fur trade, see Arthur J. Ray, *The Canadian Fur Trade in the Industrial Age* (Toronto: University of Toronto Press, 1990). On changes in a major fishery, see Rosemary E. Ommer, *From Outpost to Outport: A Structural Analysis of the Jersey-Gaspe Fishery* (Montreal: McGill-Queen's University Press, 1991). The continuing importance of "truck" is examined in Rosemary E. Ommer, ed., *Merchant Credit and Labour Struggles in Historical Perspective* (Fredericton: Acadiensis Press, 1990).

Alan Artibise, *Winnipeg: A Social History of Urban Growth* (Montreal: McGill-Queen's University Press, 1975) provides a spirited history of the development of a new city. A series of illustrated urban histories published by James Lorimer is useful for studying the growth of the late nineteenth-century city. Included are *Winnipeg* by Alan Artibise (1977); *Ottawa* by John H. Taylor (1986); *Vancouver* by Patricia Roy (1980); *Calgary* by Max Foran (1978); and *Toronto to 1918* by J.M.S. Careless (1984). Also see Doug Baldwin and Thomas Spira, ed., *Gaslights, Epidemics and Vagabond Cows: Charlottetown in the Victorian Era* (Charlottetown: Ragweed, 1988); John English and Kenneth McLaughlin, *Kitchener: An Illustrated History* (Waterloo: Wilfrid Laurier University Press, 1983); and Judith Fingard, *The Dark Side of Life in Victorian Halifax* (Halifax: Pottersfield Press, 1989).

Among useful works on the late nineteenth-century family as an economic unit are Marjorie Griffin Cohen, *Women's Work, Markets and Economic Development in Nineteenth Century Ontario* (Toronto: University of Toronto Press, 1988); Joy Parr, *Labouring Children: British Immigrant Apprentices to Canada, 1869–1924* (Montreal: McGill-Queen's University Press, 1980); Bettina Bradbury, "The Family Economy and Work in an Industrializing City: Montreal in the 1870s," Canadian Historical Association *Papers* (Ottawa 1979): 71–96; Bettina Bradbury, "Pigs, Cows and Boarders: Non-Wage Forms of Survival Among Montreal Families, 1861–1881," *Labour/Le Travail* (Fall 1989): 9–48; and John Bullen, "Hidden Workers: Child Labour and the Family Economy in Late Nineteenth Century Urban Ontario," *Labour/Le Travail* (Fall 1986): 163–88.

The major overview of workers' struggles is Bryan D. Palmer, *Working-Class Experience* (Toronto: McClelland and Stewart, 1992). An overview focussing on unions is Desmond Morton, *Working People: An Illustrated History of the Canadian Labour Movement* (Toronto: Summerhill, 1990). First-hand accounts of working conditions are found in Greg Kealey, ed., *Canada Investigates Industrialism: The Royal Commission on the Relations of Labor and Capital, 1889* (Toronto: University of Toronto Press, 1973); and Michael Cross, ed., *The Workingman in the Nineteenth Century* (Toronto: Oxford University Press, 1974). Workers' lives in Quebec are examined in Jean Hamelin, ed., *Les Travailleurs Québécois, 1851–1896* (Montreal: Presses de l'Université du Québec, 1973).

Skilled workers' attitudes and activities are studied in Bryan D. Palmer, *A Culture in Conflict: Skilled Workers and Industrial Capitalism in Hamilton, Ontario, 1860–1914* (Montreal: McGill-Queen's University Press, 1979); Gregory S. Kealey, *Toronto Workers Respond to Industrial Capitalism, 1867–1892* (Toronto: University of Toronto Press, 1980); Craig Heron, *Working in Steel: The Early Years in Canada, 1883–1935* (Toronto: McClelland and Stewart, 1980); Ian McKay, *The Craft Transformed: An Essay on the Carpenters of Halifax, 1885–1985* (Halifax: Holdfast Press, 1985); Jacques Rouillard, *Histoire du Syndicalisme au Québec* (Montreal: Boréal Express, 1989); Eric

Sager, *Seafaring Labour: The Merchant Marine of Atlantic Canada, 1820–1914* (Montreal: McGill-Queen's University Press, 1989); Robert A.J. McDonald, "Working-Class Vancouver, 1886–1914: Urbanism and Class in British Columbia," *B.C. Studies* (Spring/Summer 1986): 33–69; Ian McKay, "Class Struggle and Merchant Capital: Craftsmen and Labourers on the Halifax Waterfront, 1850–1900" in *The Character of Class Struggle*, ed. Bryan D. Palmer (Toronto: McClelland and Stewart, 1986): 17–36; and Ian McKay, "The Realm of Uncertainty: The Experience of Work in the Cumberland Coal Mines, 1873–1927," *Acadiensis* 16, 1 (Autumn 1986): 3–57. On the Knights of Labour, see Gregory S. Kealey and Bryan D. Palmer, *"Dreaming of What Might Be": The Knights of Labor in Ontario* (New York: Cambridge University Press, 1982). On the Provincial Workmen's Association, see Ian McKay, "'By Wisdom, Wile or War': The Provincial Workmen's Association and the Struggle for Working-Class Independence in Nova Scotia," *Labour/Le Travail* 18 (Fall 1986): 13–62.

LATE VICTORIAN SOCIETY AND CULTURE, 1867–96

4

Felix Albert, born on a Quebec farm in the long-settled seigneurial belt along the St Lawrence River, moved to the colonization area of the Rimouski region with his family when he was a boy. In the 1860s and 1870s, he operated a farm there with his wife and family. Frequent crop failures resulting from bad weather often forced him to work in the lumberyards to supplement the family's income. Forestry companies throughout the colonization regions—the marginal agricultural areas whose settlement the Catholic Church supported as an alternative to migration from the province—paid their workers notoriously low wages, regarding such pay as simply a supplement to the subsistence workers gained from their farms. One winter, Albert went to work in Maine where his wife had relatives. He returned for the growing season but, after wheat rust destroyed their crop, the family permanently abandoned the farm and Canada in 1881, resettling in the textile town of Lowell, Massachusetts.

About the time the Alberts were leaving the country, two Polish immigrants, John Etmanski and Mary Kiedrowski, married and began to establish themselves on a farm. Etmanski had emigrated as a child with his parents who had settled in Sherwood Township on the Quebec–Ontario border. Kiedrowski had arrived in Canada as a teenager and had worked as a domestic before her marriage, which was held in 1876 in a log chapel of Canada's first Polish parish. The couple had twelve children, two of whom died during a diphtheria epidemic in 1893, and for the first nineteen years of their marriage lived in a two-room, scoop-roofed shanty. In 1895, agricultural prosperity and lumber revenues from trees felled on their property allowed the family to hire a Polish carpenter to build them a large, two-storey house.

The differing fortunes of these two families demonstrate the folly of debating whether Canada in the late nineteenth century was a land of opportunity or one of harshness and despair for the common folk. It was both. Some people prospered; others did not. The new Dominion of Canada was a nation of often-conflicting values: rejection of state help for individuals in distress co-existed with the national policies of state aid to railways and state protection of industries; a championing of individualism co-existed with racism and sexism that denied opportunities to many individuals; widespread gambling, drinking, and prostitution co-existed with religious rejection of these vices.

• Population Dynamics

Canada's population increased from 3 625 000 in 1870 to 5 074 000 in 1896, with natural increase and two new provinces accounting for much of the gains. While many immigrants came to Canada, some stayed only briefly before heading to the United States. By 1900, they were joined in that country by 1 179 922 Canadian-born persons, a figure equal to 22 percent of the Canadian population. The former Hudson's Bay Company territories on the Prairies proved a particular disappointment to Confederation boosters, as British settlers passed them by for the milder climes and allegedly better soil of the American West.

Canadians at the end of the nineteenth century lived longer and had fewer children than their counterparts at mid-century. Better nutrition and vaccines against smallpox meant that Canadians who survived their first year lived longer. A crude death rate of 21.6 per 1000 in British North America during the 1850s had declined to 16.2 per 1000 in the 1890s. Infant mortality rates remained high. In the major cities and towns of Ontario, 20 of every 100 babies born alive in 1880 died within a year. In the province of Quebec, 15 of every 100 babies born in 1871 died before their first birthday as did over 14 of every 100 born in 1900. In Montreal, the impure water supplies, slum housing, and inadequate diets of the working class contributed to a death rate of infants that was double the provincial average both in 1871 and 1900. Quebeckers, like Canadians generally, were trying to improve the lives of their families by limiting births: there was a decline from 48.9 to 36.7 births per 1000 in the province from the 1860s to the 1890s. The decline for the entire country was from 39.6 to 30.3 per 1000.

Population growth was uneven across the country. The Atlantic provinces, while experiencing a 13.5 percent increase in population in the

1871–81 period, had a growth of only 2.6 percent in the next two decades, thanks to outmigration. Prince Edward Island's population dropped from 109 000 in 1881 to 103 000 in 1901. By contrast, Ontario experienced a population increase of 18.9 percent from 1871 to 1881 and 12.9 percent in the next two decades. The Western provinces and territories, starting with small populations, gained the most people during the late nineteenth century in percentage terms. British Columbia's population, for example, jumped from 36 247 in 1870 to 98 173 in 1891 and 178 657 in 1901, while Manitoba's population rose from just over 25 000 in 1871 to 255 211 in 1901.

Although the drain of Quebec's population southwards was frequently commented upon, that province's population experienced about the same rate of growth as Ontario's from 1870 to 1900. There was a large migration of Ontarians westwards to Manitoba, the Northwest Territories, and British Columbia, regions that attracted a comparatively modest group of Quebec francophones. A larger group of Québécois moved into the eastern counties of Ontario to engage in farming and lumbering and later into Northern Ontario as its lumber and minerals began to be exploited. But most Quebec emigrants preferred work in New England's textile mills when they contemplated resettlement. A large percentage of the Quebec emigrants were either landless rural families or smallholders dependent on wage labour to survive. Family units were more prevalent than unattached individuals in this migration: a key consideration for families contemplating a move to textile towns was whether there were enough children in the family old enough to be hired in the mills to provide the family with an acceptable income. Between 1830 and 1900, it is estimated, about 700 000 Quebeckers had resettled in the United States.

•Immigrants and the Dominant Culture

Economic need rather than a desire for cultural diversity explains Canada's recruitment of people from outside the British Isles during the late nineteenth century. Even before Confederation, immigration agents were posted in Prussia as part of a campaign to boost agriculture and lumbering in the area between the lower Ottawa River and Georgian Bay. But until the late 1890s Canada's recruitment campaigns for immigrants focussed on the British Isles and the United States. In 1901, the census reported that 88 percent of Canadians were of British or French descent, just 4 percent fewer than in 1871. Still, diversity was in evidence.

The federal government's difficulties in attracting and holding large numbers of British farmers for the western territories created an interest in sponsoring block settlements for people from other areas of Europe. In the 1870s, about 7500 Russian Mennonites settled in Manitoba. Establishing themselves east of the Red River settlements, the Mennonites proved excellent farmers. They introduced crop rotation in the region and planted trees as wind breaks. The Mennonites struck many of their neighbours as peculiar because they divided farmland in their communities on an equal basis among families and grazed their stock on commonly owned pastures. In the 1870s, 250 Icelanders settled in Gimli, Manitoba. By the mid-1880s, that province also had several Hungarian settlements. Also during the 1880s, many Jews, fleeing persecution in the Russian Empire, established farming settlements in what is now Saskatchewan. It was a new experience for a people who had been barred by law and by feudal customs from farming in their homeland. Many other non-British, non-French people who settled on the Prairies and in Central Canada came by way of the United States. Among Canada's 5 000 000 people at the turn of the century there were 311 000 Germans, 34 000 Dutch, 31 000 Scandinavians, 20 000 Russians, 16 000 Jews, and 11 000 people from the Austrian Empire.

The new arrivals on the Prairies faced the back-breaking work, poor living conditions, and homesickness that pioneers in other regions had experienced. One of the sons of Maria Aho, a founding settler of a Finnish community established in southwest Saskatchewan in 1888, recalled:

> My mother was so homesick, she never allowed us to dismantle her trunk insisting that she would not stay in this bush with no roads, nothing, just a small two-room hut with branches as a roof. The roof leaked. But every second year she had a new baby until there were twelve of us. She worked all the time, I never saw her sleep and still she kept insisting we act civilized. I was not allowed out to the nearest town till I could read and write. She taught us all that and she told us about Finland, her hometown Lapua. We dug a well by hand, but it kept drying up. Still we had a sauna every week and we were all scrubbed. Then we read the Bible and sang from the hymn book. . . . Mother never saw Finland again, she died at seventy-six, and I have never seen that country, but still if people ask me I tell them that I am a Finn.[1]

Immigrants who settled in cities and towns generally found that there was little public provision for their welfare. If work was unavailable or only offered at below-subsistence wages, they had to depend on churches, ethnic organizations, and organized charities for survival. In Winnipeg, for example, a group of twenty Jewish immigrant families faced death from cold and lack of food in the makeshift government sheds where they were housed in 1883. Newspaper reports of their plight spurred the creation of a relief committee in the city as well as donations from well-established Jews in Central Canada.

Although Winnipeg Christians proved generous to this destitute group, Jews and other non-Christian groups were not welcomed by most Canadians. Many employers and landlords shunned them, and even the most successful Jewish business people were barred from the exclusive clubs of Toronto and Montreal. The most virulent discrimination was reserved for the non-white population. The Chinese, who performed the most dangerous jobs in the construction of the CPR, were almost universally despised. John A. Macdonald, while defending his policy of importing Chinese workers, revealed the contempt directed against these people, when he told a Toronto political meeting: "Well they do come and so do rats. I am pledged to build the great Pacific Railroad in five years, and if I cannot obtain white labour, I must employ other."[2]

Once the railway was built, Chinese labourers who did not return to China headed to different parts of British Columbia and, to a lesser extent,

Chinese houses, Victoria Harbour, British Columbia (National Archives of Canada/ C23415)

to points further east. Rejected by the broader society, the Chinese lived in segregated Chinatowns where support was available for the homeless, ill, and aged. Everywhere, angry white workers and small business people labelled them unfair competition, and the British Columbia government, which denied them the vote, began to lobby for their deportation. In 1885 the federal government, responding to that province's pressure, imposed a $50 head tax on Chinese immigrants. That was raised to $100 in 1901 and an astounding $500 in 1904, equivalent to a year's wages for steady work. Most of the Chinese in Canada were young men who had been unable to bring their families with them when they came to Canada; the tax forced them to decide whether to return to China or remain in Canada without realistic prospects of bringing family members to the country. Many stayed because their families depended on the monies sent back home. The result was a great gender imbalance in the Chinese-Canadian population. For years most of the small number of Chinese women in the country were wives of merchants who could afford to pay the tax or Chinese prostitutes already in the country, many of whom were the virtual slaves of merchants who offered the women to single Chinese workmen and white men who considered Chinese women exotic. Like most other first generation immigrants, the Chinese clung to their traditions, celebrating such important days in the Chinese calendar as Chinese New Year, the Dragon Boat Festival (commemorating the death of a famous poet); the Spring Festival (a feast in honour of one's ancestors); and the Moon Festival, when the night was lit up by lanterns.

Canada's poor treatment of non-whites extended to the black population, but prejudice was not uniform. W.P. Hubbard was a black baker in Toronto who marketed an oven that he had invented. Once the chauffeur for George Brown, Hubbard became a successful businessman and in 1894 was elected alderman. He was re-elected thirteen times and often served as acting mayor. With fewer than 1000 blacks in their city of almost 300 000, Torontonians proved able to judge Hubbard as an individual. In Victoria, by contrast, during the gold rush of the 1860s, a black community of about 700 in a town of 6000 was large enough to breed prejudice among the white majority. Churches, saloons, and theatres were segregated, and a riot occurred on one occasion when a black man sat in the "white" section of a Victoria theatre. Though some of Victoria's blacks were successful local investors, they found no acceptance, and most returned to the United States after slavery was abolished in that country. The largest concentration of blacks in Canada was in Nova Scotia where many African Americans, both slave and free, had fled during the American Revolution and the War of 1812. They were granted barren lands at Preston and Hammonds Plains but since the land provided little future, many moved to towns, especially Halifax, in search of work. From the 1840s, an area that came to be known as Africville provided a separate community for blacks trying to escape the discrimination in white neighbourhoods. Separated from the rest of the city by bush and rock, Africville had its own church and school and by the twentieth century was home to several hundred African Canadians.

Even small numbers did not guarantee racial harmony. In Calgary, where the Chinese formed less than 1 percent of the population before World War I, a smallpox outbreak in 1892 was blamed on the Chinese community because four of their members were included among those quarantined. When the four were released, a mob of three hundred tried to find them, destroying several Chinese-owned laundries in the process.

• Native Peoples and the Dominant Culture

Native peoples were also the victims of prejudice on the part of white settlers who coveted their lands. Once essential partners in the fur trade, first nations' peoples of southern Canada were now viewed as a nuisance in the path of "progress." Their numbers had been vastly reduced by the diseases the Europeans had brought with them. Although their natural immunities to these diseases had improved by the late nineteenth century, epidemics still took a heavy toll. The Cree of the Northwest suffered major losses as a variety of epidemics plagued them in the 1870s; northern Native peoples, whose contact with Europeans was still relatively recent, also suffered repeated fatal epidemics. The major goal of federal Indian policy became the removal of the Indians from their lands without provoking a violent reaction similar to the Northwest Rebellion. Under the Indian Act of 1876, Indians essentially became wards of the state. Officials of Indian Affairs had final say on all matters pertaining to reserve life, from public health to authority to cut timber or sell land. Chiefs and band councils framed legislation in certain areas, but ultimate authority rested with the federal government's appointed Indian agents.

Policies aimed at assimilating Native people into the dominant culture were largely doomed by first nations' unwillingness to abandon centuries-old beliefs and cultural practices. The racism of the whites dealing with Indians also hampered this objective. Southern Ontario Ojibwa attempting to create business opportunities faced bureaucratic resistance. In the 1890s, the request of the Ojibwa of Cape Croker to establish a lumber mill was rejected by the Indian agent, and a contract was given to non-Indians to harvest trees on the reserve. The Nawash band request for a dock for their fishing boats was rejected after white commercial fishers at Hope Bay petitioned against it.

Native industrial school students, with their father, Saskatchewan circa 1900
(National Archives of Canada/37113)

Education policies were characterized by similar contradictions. The government handed responsibility for Native education to the major churches, all of which had sent missionaries to reserves to convert the Indians to their brand of Christianity. While the churches professed support for assimilation of Natives into white society, their school curricula suggested that Indians were only wanted on the lower levels of that society. A limited amount of schooltime was devoted to academic subjects; instead, much of the day was divided between religious instruction and training in manual labour for boys and household work for girls. About two-thirds of the Native children enrolled in schools at the end of the century attended a day school on their reserve, but government policy favoured schools well away from reserves. Such residential schools were largely restricted to British Columbia and the Northwest and accounted for about a third of Native enrolments nationally in 1900. A Cabinet minister expressed the government's philosophy in 1883: "If these schools are to succeed, we must not have them too near the bands; in order to educate the children properly we must separate them from their families. Some people may say that this is hard, but if we want to civilize them, we must do that."[3] Indian parents complained that boarding schools and industrial schools not only separated children from their families but forbade children the use of their birth languages. In the industrial schools, where children worked in the fields and in shops learning trades, parents alleged that youngsters were overworked, subject to corporal punishment, which Native societies did not inflict on children, and poorly fed. There was a high mortality rate among the pupils of these harsh, church-run institutions, and parents often defied the Indian agents who pressured them to send their children to these schools.

There was widespread defiance of a variety of measures taken to restrict Indian freedom and suppress traditional ceremonies central to Native culture. A pass system was introduced on Northwest reserves after the rebellion of 1885, under which residents required written permission from an Indian agent before leaving a reserve even for short periods. This proved largely unenforceable. Attempts to ban the sun dances of the Prairie Indians in the 1890s simply drove them underground: the dances were an essential component of communion with the spirit world and, like all dances among Native peoples, were an expression of group solidarity.

British Columbia

British Columbia's coastal Indians similarly defied the ban on the potlatch, implemented by an amendment to the Indian Act in 1885. The potlatch involved the exchange of gifts during an elaborate ceremony and was a means both of redistributing wealth within a tribe and conferring honours and titles within the group. Traditionally, honours were mainly hereditary, and the gift-giving ceremony gave a ritualistic legitimacy to the social hierarchy. The large number of deaths due to diseases in the early period of European settlement opened a period of competition for vacant honours and titles, increasing the number of potlatches. The government regarded the time spent potlatching as a diversion from work and condemned the redistributive feature of the ceremony as inimicable to the cultivation of free-enterprise social values. It also claimed that it wished to end the practice of wife exchange, which it believed oppressed women. Among the Kwakiutl of Vancouver Island, however, a woman who had been married to several men reaped more honours than one with only one husband and was entitled to perform certain sacred dances at ceremonies. Kwakiutl women tended to ignore government attempts to restore them to their first husbands.

Not all Indians in British Columbia coped with the onrush of European settlement by asserting their traditional values. A minority joined Christian communities sponsored by the missionaries. The classic community was Metlakatla, established in 1862 near the mouth of the Skeena River by William Duncan of the Anglican Church Missionary Society. Duncan, like most of the missionaries, aimed to remould Indian society in the image of Victorian Britain. Appalled by the drunkenness, disease, and prostitution that the presence of white miners in the Skeena area let loose on the Tsimshians, he established a community in which liquor and prostitution were illegal. But Indian rituals were also forbidden in this authoritarian community where Duncan personally set the school curriculum and designed homes for the residents, who numbered 900 in 1876. The community collapsed when 600 of its residents moved to Alaska after disputes between Duncan and church authorities.

Most British Columbia Indians, of course, did not join church communities. Deprived of some of their former lands and their resource base, many were forced to become wage workers. In 1880 about 400 Native women worked in the Fraser River canneries, and by 1895 Native women composed most of the work force for northern British Columbia canneries as well. Proud workers who resisted arbitrary orders from managers, they worked ten-hour days for $1–$1.50 per day. Other women were agricultural labourers, fruit packers, knitters, and producers of art. Still others, along with their older children, accompanied fisher-husbands as boat pullers, can fillers, and net menders.

Native men were employed in most of the resource industries of the province and to a lesser extent in manufacturing as well. Like many non-Indians, they worked seasonally as fishers and loggers while others found more regular employment as miners. Those lucky enough to hold on to

THE MAJOR NATIVE DEMAND: LAND

Natives often expressed disbelief at the heavy-handedness with which both Euro-Canadian settlers and their governments dispossessed them of control over lands and resources. This letter to the *Victoria Daily Colonist* expressed views common among Native leaders. While the Natives were anxious "to live like white men by working in the fields," they were outraged that governments that had promised to make this possible did little to aid them to become farmers or even to prevent settlers from taking Indian lands away by means of force.

I am an Indian chief and a Christian. "Do unto others as you wish others should do unto you" is Christian doctrine. Is the white man a Christian? This is a part of his creed—"take all you want if it belongs to an Indian"? He has taken all our land and all the salmon and we have—nothing. He believes an Indian has a right to live if he can on nothing at all. . . .

The Indians are now reduced to this condition—THEY MUST ROB OR STARVE. Which will they do? I need not answer. An Indian is a man; and he has eyes. If you stab him he will bleed; if you poison him he will die. If you wrong him shall he not seek revenge? If an Indian wrongs a white man what is his humility? Revenge. If want compels us to execute the villainy they teach they may discover when it is TOO LATE that an Indian can imitate the lightning and strike in a thousand places at the same time. We are not beggars. In the middle of the magnificent country that was once our own we only ask for land enough to enable us to live like white men by working in the fields. If the Indians get no land this spring you MAY BE SURE the white man will have a very bad harvest this year, and the Indians will eat beef next winter. Fine talk won't feed an Indian. "Her Majesty's Indian subjects," whose rights are limited to living on nothing at all if they can, are prepared to face the worst—anything but death by starvation. In a court of justice we could prove that we are the only persons who have any right or title to this land. If the Queen has no power to aid us; if all the power belongs to the parliament, then I say again may the Lord have mercy on the Indians—AND ON THE WHITE-MEN.

WILLIAM,
Chief of the Williams Lake Indians[4]

good lands in the face of predatory settlers often prospered. In the 1880s, the Cowichan and Fraser River Valley Indians, for example, raised livestock, cereals, market produce, and fodder. On the reserves, carpenters, blacksmiths, cobblers, printers, and craftspeople made a reasonable living by 1900, while wealthy Indians owned trading schooners, hotels, inns, cafes, and small logging and sawmilling operations. But reserve life was always precarious in a province where settler and provincial government resistance had made impossible the negotiation of treaties to prevent the province from simply expropriating Native land at will.

Manitoba and the Northwest

The decline of the fur trade and the disappearance of the buffalo forced significant adaptation on the part of Native peoples in the Northwest. Reserves on the Prairies generally made a successful transition to agriculture despite the failure of the federal government to deliver fully on its promises of aid in this transition. Reserves in modern-day Saskatchewan practised mixed farming, with the Assiniboine Reserve reporting in 1893, for example, the harvesting of good crops of wheat, barley, oats, potatoes, turnips, carrots, and onions. This reserve also raised cattle and sheep. While the Natives were prepared and able to produce surpluses for commercial markets, the Department of Indian Affairs emphasized subsistence agriculture.

The woodlands Indians lacked viable agricultural lands and had suffered too much resource depletion in the heyday of the fur trade to revert fully to a pre-contact traditional economy. Some moved north with the fur trade while others engaged in commercial fishing to make up for lost income. By the 1890s in Manitoba, white-owned commercial fishing companies began to operate in the same lakes and rivers and began to deplete fish stocks.

Central and Eastern Canada

In 1885 Indians living east of Lake Superior were offered the right to full citizenship, including the vote, if they surrendered their Indian status. Few did. They opposed government attempts to replace communal land holdings with private plots and to replace traditional Indian forms of governance with European-style elected chiefs and band councils (who, in any case, the Department of Indian Affairs reserved the right to depose).

While all Native groups attempted to retain some of their cultural traditions, their economic activities depended on local resources and potential local employments. The Ojibwa of Southern Ontario trapped, fished, hunted, gathered wild rice, and tapped maple sugar, selling their surpluses in towns and cities of the region. Cree women in Northern Ontario worked as domestics and laundry workers while the men worked as guides, sawmill workers, and as packers for the railway and fur companies. In Quebec, the Cree and Montagnais of the North Shore remained a society of hunters while the Mi'kmaq of the Gaspé farmed and fished like their white neighbours. The Iroquois of Caughnawaga, near Montreal, took construction jobs in that city as well as in Ontario and the United States.

Mi'kmaq families in the Maritime provinces engaged in a variety of market activities in their attempts to make a living. Mi'kmaq women made and sold moccasins, baskets, chair seats, and fans, among other items. Women and children sold berries, fruits, and wild fowl door to door in Halifax and other places, and some Native women worked as domestics in the urban centres. The men made washtubs, buckets, ax handles, barrels, mast hoops, canoes, hockey sticks, snowshoes, and oars, and knocked on doors offering to do repairs of various kinds. Some also worked as commercial fishers, porpoise hunters, and as guides for European travellers and adventurers. A few found jobs in the coal mines and on the railroads, and some were employed in Pictou County discharging ore for ironworks.

Mi'kmaq settlement in Nova Scotia   (New Brunswick Museum)

While many Mi'kmaq farmed, the land that they had been granted consisted of small, infertile plots.

The Mi'kmaq of Newfoundland were also gradually forced to participate in a variety of market-based activities as the fur trade, their former commercial activity, declined. The predicament of the Native peoples of Newfoundland was described by Abraham Joe, an elderly Mi'kmaq, to the Earl of Dunraven in 1879, who reported his words as follows:

> Yes sir, things is very different from what they used to be. Lord! I mind the times when a man might travel from one end of the island to the other and never see nobody nowheres. Beavers were plenty then, and there was a good price for fur too; now there ain't no price, and beavers and otters ain't plenty like they used to be. Those d––d lumbermen be come up the rivers and scare the game. Why, there ain't a bay scarcely anywhere without one, mebbe even two liviers ["live here," a year-round settler] in it.[5]

The North

Canada's concept of the North was gradually changing in the years following Confederation. Although the provinces of Manitoba, Saskatchewan, and Alberta would not achieve their present configuration until early in the twentieth century, the general view that the "true North" was above the 60 degree parallel was beginning to emerge. In the late nineteenth century, the North still belonged to the aboriginal peoples. Before the Yukon gold rush, over half of the white population living in northern climates could be found in Labrador.

Although Canada's claim to much of the North was established by the purchase of the Hudson's Bay Company territory in 1869, there was some dispute about the extent of Canada's jurisdiction. In July 1880, the British government transferred to Canada its claims to northern territories including "all Islands adjacent to any such territories whether discovered or not." The doubts raised by such nebulous assertions were not relieved by the Colonial Boundaries Act of 1895 and remained to plague the Canadian government well into the twentieth century.

As the fur stocks in the south dwindled, aboriginal peoples living in the North were increasingly drawn into the fur trade. In the western Arctic, a variety of paid employments became as important as traditional subsistence occupations for the Indians. In the eastern Arctic, the Inuit continued to hunt caribou, walrus, and migratory birds in summer and seals in winter. The seals provided food and their blubber for fuel while caribou skins were used for winter garments. The Inuit continued to live in tents of caribou or sealskin in summer and in the winter either in igloos or stone and bone homes insulated with turf outside the walls and over the roof. Yet here, as in the western Arctic, the lure of luxury goods at the trading posts was causing more and more Native peoples to engage in the fur trade. In the central and western Arctic, an uncontrolled European slaughter of whales and walrus from the 1860s to the 1880s left starvation in its wake among a people already weakened by European diseases. The original Inuvialuit people disappeared from the region and were replaced by Alaskan Inuit. Since the Inuit were not included under the provisions of the Indian Act until 1939, they remained largely undisturbed by government bureaucracies.

• Urban Life

Most Canadians' struggle for survival may have been less precarious than it was for the Native peoples, but life was difficult nonetheless, especially for urbanites without capital or a marketable skill. By the 1890s cities were slowly becoming less dangerous places to live than they had been earlier in the century. Waterworks, sewer systems, and public health measures were slowly implemented by municipalities, and there was a gradual decline in the number of epidemics and uncontrolled fires. Still, progress was uneven: for many, the city remained a filthy, disease-ridden, and hazardous home. It was particularly dangerous for the newborns of the poor whose mortality rate was almost double that of their rural counterparts.

The best contemporary survey of living conditions in a Canadian city was carried out in 1896 by Herbert Brown Ames, a businessman and social reformer, in Montreal. Ames focussed on two areas of the city, areas he labelled "the city below the hill" and "the city above the hill." The former consisted of the part of west-end Montreal bounded by Westmount, the city limits, and the St Lawrence River, the latter the high terraces and plateaus along the base of Mount Royal. Ames was mainly interested in the poorer city below the hill, home to about 38 000 people divided almost equally among French, English, and Irish Canadians, but he studied the wealthier area as a point of comparison. Above the hill were "tall and handsome houses, stately churches and well-built schools" while below the hill "the tenement house replaces the single residence, and the factory with its smoking chimney is in evidence on every side."[6] Beautiful parks and abundant greenery added to the charms of the homes in the upper city while below, "one paltry plot of ground, scarce an acre in extent, dignified by the title of Richmond square, is the only spot where green grass can be seen free of charge."[7] Above the hill, all the homes had modern plumbing and looked out on wide, well paved, clean streets. Below the hill, half of all homes lacked modern plumbing and made use of pit-in-the-ground privies.

There were gradations of poverty within the city below the hill. Although its population density was more than double the city average, Ames concluded that most of the area was not overcrowded. In a sub-area called the "Swamp," however, space per family was low. According to Ames, the poorest of the poor were the residents whose homes faced a rear court and were not visible from the street. These homes were poorly built, and their residents suffered disproportionately from disease, crime, drunkenness, poverty, and early death. Summing up the conditions below the hill, Ames noted that for every ten families in the area, "One family might secure an entire house to itself, but nine families must needs share theirs with another. Nine families might dwell facing the street, but one would have to live in the rear. Five families might have proper sanitary accommodation, but as many more would have to put up with the pit privy. Three families might have six rooms, four families might have five rooms, while the homes of the remaining three would contain four rooms."[8]

Later studies of Montreal in the late nineteenth century have corroborated Ames' view that there were two cities in Montreal, with the rich and poor living completely different lives. The infant mortality rate in Montreal was among the highest in North America, and the infant death rates in the city's poorer wards were far above the city average. The ferocity of a smallpox outbreak in 1885 that killed 3000 Montrealers as well as 2600 other Québécois can be partly attributed to popular suspicions of vaccination, but poor water and sanitation in homes and workplaces contributed to even more deaths. Like infant mortality, overall death rates reflected class differences. In working-class, French-Canadian Sainte-Marie, the death rate per thousand in 1877–96 averaged 36.7; in upper-class anglophone Saint-Antoine, the rate was slightly below half that. Not all anglophones were part of the elite, of course, and the city below the hill had an English-speaking majority. So did the working-class neighbourhoods of Lachine and Pointe Saint-Charles, both English enclaves, and Griffintown, the Irish area. Workers in these and other areas of Montreal had an unhealthy diet in which fats and starches were prevalent. Common fare included peas, buns baked in molasses with bits of pork, potatoes, and bread. Milk, when available, was often full of contaminants that contributed to the high infant mortality rates.

Recreation varied with social class. For those people who lived in the city's wealthy enclaves such as Westmount and Mount Royal, there were

Milk wagon in St Roch, Quebec   (National Archives of Canada/PA1677)

opportunities for fine dining, theatre, operas, yachting, cricket, and camaraderie in exclusive clubs and philanthropic organizations. Working people
in Montreal had more entertainments available to them than were possible
in rural areas where small populations and church disapproval limited the
scope of leisure activities. Amusement parks, carnivals, dime theatres, lot-
teries, bazaars, dance halls, taverns, and brothels provided diversions of
which the church disapproved, particularly if such establishments operated
on Sundays.

Toronto was as divided as Montreal, but its standard of living for
working people was marginally higher. While few workers owned homes in
Montreal, by the end of the century in Toronto falling land prices brought
home ownership within the purview of an increasing number of working
families. Nonetheless, slum conditions prevailed in the backlane cottages
of St John's Ward and in areas close to railyards, factories, and packing-
houses. Working-class homes tended to be small, but many boasted
Victorian Gothic gables or Second Empire roofs. Middle-class areas generally had brick residences with verandahs while the upper-class areas featured mansions with broad arches on heavy pillars and embellished stone
or brickwork. The prosperity of the city's employers was evident not only in
their homes but in their enterprises and the institutional buildings they

sponsored. In the 1870s, Victorian versions of medieval or Renaissance buildings, often modelled on buildings in Napoleon III's France, became the fashion. The ornamental mansard roof on the Opera House was styled on a French model. Presbyterian Knox College and St Andrew's Church copied medieval models. In the 1880s the style turned to French Beaux Arts classicism, evident in the new Bank of Montreal at Front and Yonge, and "Richardson Romanesque," a Chicago import featuring huge round arches on thick pillars and great walls with sculpted detail. The latter style was evident in the provincial Parliament building and the city hall built that year. The city's wealth allowed the Toronto Philharmonic Society to prosper and Massey Hall to open for concerts in 1894. Of more interest to working people were the Woodbine race track, American baseball leagues, minstrel shows, and musical farces. As in Montreal, membership in exclusive gentlemen's clubs was a sign of success.

The gap between rich and poor was evident in the segregated neighbourhoods of all major Canadian cities and in the stark differences between the spectacular homes and office buildings of the wealthy, on the one hand, and the modest, sometimes substandard housing of workers on the other. The requirement that voters own property to acquire the municipal franchise ensured that municipal government attended mainly to the needs of the better off. Urban reformers argued that measures to reduce disease and the spread of fires benefited everyone, since neither germs nor flames spared the rich. Over time, their arguments carried the day, but ratepayer reluctance to foot more property taxes slowed the process. In Charlottetown, where waterworks, sewerage, and improved sanitation appeared in the late 1880s and the 1890s, the *Patriot*, a local newspaper, complained in 1874:

> The rich citizen can have his residence in the suburbs where the air and water are both pure, or if he chooses to live in the city he can afford to buy spring water, and he has always a doctor at hand to attend to any of his family who shows any symptoms of being unwell. [The poor man] must bring up his family in the neighborhood of reeking cesspools and filthy pig-sties. He can not well afford to buy pure water at a very expensive rate; and he has to think twice before he calls in a doctor.[9]

The extent to which clean water was restricted to better-off areas varied by the end of the century, despite the general recognition by the 1870s of the role of polluted water in carrying disease. Vancouver in the 1880s was an ugly, smelly city without sewers or drains or any hint of planned development. By the late 1890s, however, the city had acquired the water

works and extended water mains to most areas. With the mountains supplying pure water, Vancouver's water-related disease problems were minor
compared to most cities. Both Vancouver and Hamilton advertised their
comparatively safe water supplies in attempts to attract immigrants and
investors. In Winnipeg, by contrast, just 10 percent of the population had
sewers and waterworks in 1890: only in central Winnipeg, where the commercial elite lived and did business, was the water supply adequate. In the
working-class North End, no water mains were built until after 1900. River
water was delivered to homes, but the sewage system emptied into the river
with the result that deadly Red River fever (typhoid) was a continuing
problem for working families. The combination of wooden buildings and a
poor water supply translated into uncontrolled fires that destroyed many
homes. Winnipeg was not unique in this regard: in 1877 in Saint John, a
major fire left 15 000 homeless; in 1892, housing for 10 000 residents in
St John's was destroyed by fire.

Poor sanitation plagued nineteenth-century cities. In Ottawa, for
example, while a health officer was named in 1874 to demand that householders dispose of garbage, the city had no dump. Smallpox spread
through the tenements of Lower Town in 1875. It has been estimated that
one-quarter of the population of Ottawa were working poor, people able to
find work during part of the year, but unemployed and often destitute during the winter. There were also people who could not find work at all: men
maimed in mill, construction, and bush accidents; pregnant serving girls;
the handicapped and those ill with diseases such as tuberculosis. Both the
working poor and the unemployables required aid from private charities to
survive when relatives or friends were unable or unavailable to help.

Halifax was unique among Canadian cities for its military flavour.
While the British withdrew their troops from all other Canadian cities in
1871, they retained their garrison in Halifax, which served as Britain's
naval and military base for the North Atlantic. The Church of England
bishop declared in 1889 that "the military were a curse to this city and were
the cause of a great deal of demoralization among the poor."[10] Since cities
without military establishments also had demoralized poor in their midst, it
is doubtful that the good bishop was correct in laying the entire blame on
the military. It was nevertheless the case that grog shops, brothels, and disreputable boarding houses thrived on Barrack Street just below the Citadel
and helped to sustain the lifestyle of the repeat offenders committed to
Rockhead Prison, a substantial octagonal building located in the North
End of the city. After Barrack Street was closed to the military and its name
changed to South Brunswick in the early 1870s, "soldiertown" drifted to
adjacent Albermarle, Grafton, and City streets and continued to be a major
cause for concern among urban reformers.

•Community Responses to Industrialization and Poverty

The dislocation caused by industrialization and its attendant booms and busts demanded greater community responsibility for economic casualties. Many middle-class people blamed the poor themselves for their plight, observing that poor single men were often transient and poor married men were often heavy drinkers. Ignoring the economic causes that produced the transients (pejoratively labelled "tramps"), conservatives emphasized the need to make the tramping life unpalatable. Houses of Industry introduced work tests, usually involving breaking stones or sawing wood, to be performed by able-bodied men before meagre food and a place on the floor would be provided that evening. The medical profession, whose public legitimacy was rising in the late nineteenth century as the germ theory of disease gained credibility, encouraged such views by alleging that heredity rather than poverty created class conflict, crime, and mental illness. Flirting with *eugenics*—the notion of designating certain individuals and groups as genetically inferior and controlling their reproduction so as to ensure a genetically "superior" race—some physicians advocated strict social controls over the poor to decrease their supposedly hereditary tendencies towards unacceptable behaviour.

Demon drink was a favoured target of conservatives, although they were often joined in these attacks by trade unionists who thought that alcohol debased workers and by women's groups conscious of the economic strain and the increase in male violence towards women and children that alcoholism seemed to encourage. The Woman's Christian Temperance Union (WCTU), founded in the 1870s, was prominent in the prohibition movement and would later prove a driving force in the women's suffrage struggle. For many working men, the taverns were a source of entertainment and the only escape from grim workplaces and uncomfortable homes. Domestic servants, whose drinking was probably exaggerated by contemporaries, might imbibe to ease the pain of lives restricted by isolation and by subordination to an employer's whims for most of their waking hours.

The Canada Temperance Act, passed by the federal government in 1878 after pressure from temperance forces led by the Protestant churches, allowed municipalities to prohibit the sale of liquor within their boundaries after holding a plebiscite. A royal commission investigation in 1895 demonstrated that liquor flowed as freely in supposedly "dry" zones as in "wet" municipalities. In Moncton, for example, while the WCTU and the Sons of Temperance easily won a temperance referendum in 1879, bootleggers stepped into the breech left by the closing of the taverns. The local Methodists, Baptists, and Presbyterians might decry drinking as the sin of the Acadian Catholic minority in town, but many Protestant drinkers also helped to enrich the bootleggers. The municipality did not wish to pay the costs of enforcing prohibition, and the police soon tired of vain attempts to find witnesses who would satisfy a judge's call for proof that bootleggers had violated the law. Bootleggers moved easily from town to town, and the illegality of their trade was no deterrent to clients who resented the banning of taverns.

Prison reform was another prominent social movement, in the late nineteenth century, though, like prohibition, the cause predated Confederation. Prison reformers focussed on instilling the work ethic in prisoners as a means of rehabilitating them from lives of crime. Those who worked willingly in prison workshops had their sentences reduced. After Confederation, prisoners serving long sentences were sent to prisons under federal jurisdiction such as Kingston Penitentiary. Shorter sentences were served in provincial prisons. In Ontario, the first intermediate correctional facility, Central Prison, was established in 1874. Disgusted by the numbers of repeat offenders in the province, the government implemented a regimen of hard labour for the prisoners. Recalcitrance was punished with flogging or the withholding of food. A royal commission investigating charges of cruelty against prisoners supported the prison officers and suggested that they consider using even more force against prisoners. Reviewing the case of William O'Neill—kept in isolation for three months during which time he was provided with only bread and water, and after which he was declared insane—the commissioners suggested that even greater punishment might have been justified. Prison reformers' desire for social control was clearly greater than their sense of compassion.

The desire for social control was also evident in official attitudes towards homosexuality. Any sexual relations outside marriage were regarded as sinful by the churches, who still tended to view procreation as the only justification for sexual relations. Homosexuality was singled out as unnatural and treated as a serious crime, though the medical fashion by the end of the century was to label same-sex attraction as a form of insanity requiring confinement in a lunatic asylum rather than a prison. In Victoria two men convicted of sodomy in 1891 were each sentenced to fifteen years imprisonment, a sentence later commuted to seven years. Sentences of a year or two were more common. Sometimes the offenders were simply asked to leave town. In Regina, for example, Frank Hoskins, a leading merchant, was arrested in 1895 and charged with "gross indecency of an unnatural character" after being found engaging in sexual activity with two other men. As a result of a local petition that asked for leniency because of his sterling character prior to this incident, he was spared a prison sentence on the condition that he leave the Northwest Territories.

•Women's Struggles for Change

Women were becoming increasingly involved in the reform movements and charities of nineteenth-century Canada. As had been the case in the pre-industrial period, churches and middle-class women's groups made attempts to relieve distress within their communities. Many women regarded caring for the health and welfare of the destitute as an extension of their work as nurturers in the home. Some saw such work in terms of Christian sacrifice. Others argued that women's talents as care givers should be exploited more formally by encouraging women to become doctors and school prinicipals, by improving working conditions in the relatively new profession of nursing, and by establishing social work as a paid profession open to women.

The spread of volunteer organizations demonstrated women's desire for a greater role within the community. In the late nineteenth century, there was a conscious attempt on the part of women to organize separately from men to ensure that their efforts in charitable and political causes were not subordinated to those of men. Groups such as the Woman's

Women at a conference of Lutheran churches of Western Icelanders, Winnipeg, 1891 (Western Canada Pictorial Index/96-2978)

Christian Temperance Union, the women's auxiliaries of the Methodist and Baptist churches, the Women's Institutes, and Local Councils of Women formed part of this trend led by educated women who wished to expand established gender roles.

Women also sought to enter professional fields in which male monopolies were jealously defended. The legal and medical professions were particularly tenacious in resisting women's attempts to pursue professional training. Not until 1895 did Clara Brett Martin become Canada's first woman law graduate. She faced great resistance from the legal profession first in her desire to train and later in her attempts to practise. The legal system was unfair to women in more than simply resisting their bid to become lawyers. Property laws, divorce laws, and preconceived notions surrounding assault and rape clearly reflected a double standard that often left women with little recourse. Even on the Prairies, where women's crucial economic role within pioneer agriculture is often thought to have gained them greater equality than other women enjoyed, a woman's claim that she had been raped was generally discounted by the courts.

In medicine, Emily Howard Stowe and Jennie Trout were forced to train as physicians in the United States in the 1860s and 1870s because no Canadian medical school would admit women. Upon their return to Canada to practise in their chosen field, they successfully pressured Queen's University and the University of Toronto to open facilities to train women doctors, although these universities segregated the female medical trainees from the men. Unsurprisingly, in 1891, women represented only 1.6 percent of all doctors and 2 percent of dentists in Ontario. Women's exclusion from the medical profession prevented a challenge to the misogynist notions that permeated the medical textbooks and journals of the period. Women were presented as mere extensions of their wombs, biologically destined to have children, with childlessness a risk to their health. Advanced education, argued the medical ideologues, was wasted on a woman because her brain was inferior to a man's. Too much studying might reduce her fertility and lead to emotional and psychological problems.

Some who fought against the limitations placed on women wanting a career became active in the suffrage movement. Dr Emily Howard Stowe, for example, headed the Toronto Women's Literary Club, formed in 1876, which made votes for women a key goal. Pressure from women's organizations led to gradual municipal enfranchisement of unmarried and widowed women who met the property qualification. Ontario granted this right in 1884, New Brunswick in 1886, Nova Scotia in 1887, and Prince Edward Island in 1888. Votes provincially and federally would await the twentieth century. The lobbying of women's groups in Nova Scotia produced a narrow majority in favour of women's suffrage in the legislative assembly of that province in 1893, but clever manoeuvering by the anti-suffragist attorney-general forestalled passage of the relevant bill; when it was voted upon in the session of 1894, it lost by one vote.

The growth in women's activism in the late Victorian period was great enough to spark the creation of a Dominion federation of women's clubs in 1893. The National Council of Women of Canada (NCWC) linked together a large number of women's organizations concerned with a wide range of issues such as temperance, suffrage, child welfare, prostitution, and social purity, and improved working conditions and professional advancement for women. The NCWC was dominated by middle-class women who, while they espoused the conventional viewpoint that women's highest goals ought to be related to families, also endorsed careers for women. Stressing that women's role as nurturers in the home prepared them to undertake nurturing roles within the broader society, council spokespeople rejected the notion that a woman's place was solely in the home. The NCWC and other women's organizations, in calling for greater political and economic equality for women, often used "maternalist" arguments to justify their demands so as not to alienate the male legislators whose votes were needed. Even so, the Council met with considerable resistance. Some years after their encounter, Lady Drummond, a founding member of the NCWC, recalled meeting prominent journalist Goldwin Smith: "Someone introduced me to the late Mr Goldwin Smith, as the President of the Local Council, whereupon he appeared to take strong dislike to me and said, 'I distrust all such societies. They can only end in one way, to teach women to regard marriage as a sort of co-partnership to be dissolved at pleasure.' I fled from his cold and scrutinizing eye."[11]

Two of the largest women's organizations of the late nineteenth century were the Young Women's Christian Association (YWCA) and the WCTU. The first Canadian branch of the YWCA was established in Saint John in 1870 and, by the 1880s, the "Y" had become one of the major Protestant charitable organizations. It provided both philanthropy and job training for the poor, but its training for working-class girls was largely in domestic service. This reflected the perception by many in the YWCA that young women were at moral risk in the expanding factories and cities of late nineteenth-century Canada. They believed that girls could be better protected if they worked in private homes. Such paternalism ignored the number of female servants who were sexually exploited by their male employer or his sons.

Other evangelical groups included the Women's Missionary Aid Societies, which sponsored single women who went overseas to convert non-Christians in such places as India, Burma, and China. Missionary work abroad or among Native peoples in Canada and later also among non-British immigrants provided a source of employment as well as a cause that appealed to many single women. Wives of male missionaries also worked in the field. Missionary women, though they had careers, could be perceived as non-threatening because their work emphasized raising children, healing the sick, and giving moral guidance, the conventional role for women in families. The Salvation Army was a popular evangelical group that attracted large numbers of working-class women throughout the 1880s. Preaching a doctrine of spiritual equality, the Army "provided working-class women with an unprecedented public voice."[12] The Army evolved into a community service agency, "rescuing" prostitutes and providing food and shelter along with a generous dose of spiritual guidance to some of the destitute in Canadian society.

For French-Canadian Catholics in Quebec, the possibilities for community service for lay women were narrower. Religious orders took most of the responsibility for health, welfare, and education. Fifty-one new religious communities were established in Quebec from 1837 to 1899, thirty-four of them women's orders. Despite the patriarchal notions of church leaders, women generally ran their own communities. Marie-Elizabeth Casgrain, known as Sister Ste-Justine, for example, was chief trustee of the Congregation of Notre Dame in Montreal, which expanded from 440 women in 1870 to 1226 in 1901. Throughout the 1870s and 1880s, Casgrain established and administered the Congregation's budget, bought and sold property, and travelled to Europe to hire an architect for a new mother house.

Outside the church, such powerful and successful career women were almost non-existent in Quebec. One prominent exception was Maude Abbott, who completed a BA at McGill in 1890 but was refused admission into that university's medical school because of her sex. That same year, Bishops University opened its medical school to women, and Dr Abbott graduated from that institution in 1894. She went on to a distinguished career during which she was internationally recognized as one of the world's foremost authorities on "blue babies." Abbott's success story was uncommon. No women were trained as lawyers, notaries, engineers, or architects in nineteenth-century Quebec. Indeed, Quebec did not admit women to the bar until 1941. The expanding civil service likewise provided few opportunities for women. As late as 1911, fewer than 1 percent of the Quebec government's 17 787 employees were women.

By 1901, 6.1 percent of single women over twenty and 1.5 percent of all women over that age in Quebec were nuns. Historian Marta Danylewycz has accounted for the attraction of the nun's life of prayer and community service by reference to women's role in the family and to the limited options available to women outside the convent.

Maude Abbott   (National Archives of Canada/C9479)

The family economy, with its emphasis on the control of individualistic impulses and focus on collective need, schooled women in the principles of hard work and sacrifice necessary to life in a religious community. For middle- and upper-class women not so clearly subjected to the rigours of the family economy, secular society provided little room for social mobility and self-fulfilment. What could an ambitious woman do except seek social mobility through marriage or spiritual life?[13]

Nursing, which began to receive acceptance as a profession in the mid-nineteenth-century as a result of the efforts of Florence Nightingale in Britain, was also perceived as acceptable woman's work. Though formal training became increasingly necessary for nurses, the job remained poorly paid. The nurse was expected to be a selfless servant of patients, much like the idealized mother in the home. Religious conviction often brought women to the profession. Agnes Cowan, for example, a pioneering New-foundland nurse, daughter of Scottish immigrant farmers, was motivated by religious devotion to dedicate her life to nursing. She became matron first of St John's Hospital and later St John's Lunatic Asylum. In Quebec, most nurses were drawn from nursing orders and also combined professional pursuits with religious devotion.

The agitation for wider opportunities for women notwithstanding, the major responsibility for most Canadian women remained the home. But things were changing there as well. One of the key changes was the steady drop in the size of families. Women born in 1845 in British North America bore, on average, 6.3 offspring while those born in 1867 produced 4.8 children. In 1892 the Canadian government outlawed contraceptives and abortifacients, but women continued to share birth control information, and the trend towards smaller families continued unabated. Nonetheless, a married woman's child-bearing and child-raising years still consumed much of her life, and there was no diminution in women's responsibility for the household. Women's primary attachment to family and friends is revealed in the diaries of housewives and single working women: both wrote about personal friendships, anniversaries, shopping, visiting, and household chores, with workers saying little about their jobs.

In the countryside, women's economic contributions to the household economy remained crucial. Farm women worked extremely hard, engaged in what must have seemed like a never-ending round of sewing, weeding, milking, churning, cooking, baking, and scrubbing. Yet women were also key decision makers in the operation of the farm and household and producers of goods for farm consumption and off-farm markets. Though most successful farms required the labours of two adults and their older children, many women continued to operate farms after being widowed. Polly Scovill, who farmed with her husband in the Eastern Townships, was an example. Her husband died when she was forty-four and pregnant with her fourth child. Taking over the farm's management, she increased its productivity and sold large quantities of butter, cheese, and maple sugar, and opened a small clothing factory. When she was in her mid-sixties, Scovill entrusted the farm's management to her eldest daughter and her daughter's husband. She lived with the daughter until her death at the age of ninety-four. Her will divided the property equally among her four children and, unusually for the time, made explicit that her daughters' inheritance could not be included in a "community of property" arrangement—the practice by which a woman's property acquired before marriage became the property of the couple after marriage and therefore, in law, came under the husband's control.

In Western Canada, many farm wives were emigrés from Britain who had willingly chosen that life over the prospect of remaining at home where unfavourable sex ratios and discriminatory hiring practices limited their prospects of finding either husbands or jobs. Some of these "redundant women," as a contemporary British social critic labelled unmarried females, were middle-class women who required the grounding in domestic skills offered by emigration societies and training schools. In their diaries these women indicated the variety of their tasks in the farm family: they used skins to make hoods, mittens, and muffs and spun wool to make clothing, mattresses, and quilts; they made butter and raised chickens, both for sale; they made their own soap. Some women worked the fields. Harriet Neville, a Saskatchewan homesteader of the late nineteenth century, drove oxen while other women built sod barns or branded cattle. Women were unpaid nurses, doctors, and midwives. Daughters worked as both minders of young children and as field hands. Nellie McClung, as a young girl, had the responsibility of looking after the cattle, but she also attended school and, like many women of her generation, was employed as a schoolteacher for a period before her marriage.

• Schooling and Society

Increasing numbers of parents sought at least limited socio-economic mobility for their children by having them attend school. Even before a half-day of education for children between the ages of seven and fourteen became the law, school enrolments had increased dramatically from pre-1850 levels. But attendance remained irregular. Many children in rural areas continued to attend school only when the pressures of farmwork permitted, and the urban poor continued to pull their children from school when they reached the age where an employer would hire them. The middle-class atmosphere and values of the schools often alienated working-class children, and the strict discipline invited truancy. Nonetheless, by 1891, it was estimated that only 6 percent of Ontario residents and 13 percent of Maritime Canadians were totally illiterate. In Quebec, where compulsory schooling was enacted only in 1943, 26 percent of the population was deemed unable either to read or write; in Newfoundland, the figure was 32 percent.

Quebec's education system, unlike that of other provinces, was not directed by a Department of Education. Instead, as a result of religious pressures, two systems, one Catholic and one Protestant, were established, each eligible for provincial subsidies. A provincial Council of Public Instruction, which was initially merely an advisory body to a minister of public instruction, no longer reported to the minister after 1875: two denominational committees of the Council thereafter controlled education. The Catholic committee consisted of all Catholic bishops in the province plus an equal number of government-appointed lay Catholics. The presence of the bishops ensured that lay Catholics would not stray from the demands of the church for an education stressing Catholic values. The church's opposition to state involvement in education, and perhaps a belief that too much education was harmful to the spiritual good of the masses, doomed efforts to make education in Quebec either compulsory or free of tuition fees. As late as 1926, only 6 percent of Catholic pupils went beyond elementary school.

Elsewhere, education was also largely limited to the elementary grades where tuition fees were gradually eliminated. The curriculum concentrated on basic reading, writing, and arithmetic skills along with the inculcation of social values stressing deference to authority, different gender roles for boys and girls, and love of nation and empire. The introduction of high schools, beginning in Ontario in 1871, offered parents who could afford it a chance to further educate their children. Mechanical arts, bookkeeping, and agricultural science were available in addition to traditional subjects like literature, history, and mathematics, reflecting calls for more practical education for children.

Edmonton's first school, built in 1881   (National Archives of Canada/C3862)

The growth of professional schools in universities also indicated a growing demand for career-related education. Organizations of professionals, seeking to restrict entry into their fields and increase their legitimacy, pressured the state to grant them self-regulation; increasingly, a specific university degree became a condition for receiving a licence to practise a profession. Physicians, lawyers, and engineers succeeded in winning self-regulation in most jurisdictions by the end of the century and required university training as a condition of licensing. Critics of this trend warned against the creation of narrow professional monopolies that used education as a smokescreen to remove rivals. In the health field, for example, homeopaths, midwives, and other proponents of natural medicine complained that "professionalization" was a mask to bestow state favour on a single approach to medicine—the "scientific" approach stressing chemical-based medicines and surgical solutions espoused by the medical societies.

Despite an increased emphasis on professional training, the major focus of late Victorian universities was the creation of gentlemen scholars and of clergymen. Tuition fees restricted university education to a miniscule percentage of the population, many of them graduates of private schools. Among working people, attitudes to compulsory schooling varied. In Quebec, while the trade unions were on the side of free, compulsory schooling, many workers and farmers resisted the idea because they required the labour of their children either in the home or in the work force. In other provinces, where schooling was compulsory, labour spokespeople often complained about the rigid, conservative curricula prescribed by provincial departments of education and their emphasis on book learning over experience.

• The Victorian Frame of Mind
Imperialism and English Canada

After 1867, local and regional identities appear to have remained more important for most English Canadians than their identity as Canadians. Still, there were citizens who wished to give substance to the notion of a "new nationality" to which many supporters of Confederation had vaguely made reference. A year after Confederation, five affluent, public-spirited men held meetings in Ottawa to discuss ways to promote national feeling. The five were Ottawa civil servant and prolific author Henry J. Morgan, Nova Scotia Coal Owners' Association lobbyist Robert Grant Haliburton, poet Charles

Mair, Ontario militia officer and lawyer George Taylor Denison III, and barrister W.A. Foster. They became the nucleus of a movement called "Canada First," which claimed to promote Canadian pride and unity. Initially, this group was militantly pro-British and anti-American, but after the Washington Treaty was negotiated, resentment that Britain had sacrificed Canadian interests led them to focus on Canada's North American identity and its independence of both Britain and the United States. Canada was presented as a northern country peopled by robust Nordic races strengthened by their need to cope with a harsh environment. The *Canadian Monthly and National Review* and *The Nation*, journals spawned by the expanding circles of Canada Firsters in the 1870s, expounded this notion of a "new nationality" based on a combination of race and geography.

The place of French Canadians in the new nation confounded the Canada Firsters. While they at times stressed the common heritage of Canada's two dominant groups, they became the core of the movement to suppress the Northwest Rebellion in 1870. Their arguments against the rebels suggested hostility against both French Canadians and Native peoples. Mair, an Upper Canadian who had resettled in the Red River colony, proclaimed the superiority of English Canadians over French Canadians, the latter allegedly tainted by their intermarriages with the Native peoples.

In the 1880s, as European countries scrambled for control of the African continent, the "new nationality" took a British turn again. Canada's prosperity was being financed by the same interests benefiting from British territorial conquests and resource extraction from Africa. Bitterness at Britain's alleged abandonment of Canada gave way to a feeling of solidarity with this imperialist power whose citizens shared a common descent with English Canadians. The Imperial Federation League, established in London in 1884, called for a common foreign and defence policy for the white settler colonies of the British Empire. It soon had small but influential branches across English Canada as the desire to give substance to the notion of a "new nationality" merged with pride in Britain's achievements. Imperialists believed that the best future of the Dominion of Canada lay in attempting to convince Britain to include settler colonies in its imperial decision making rather than in Canada's dissociating itself from the empire and evolving a distinct foreign policy.

Support for imperialism among English Canadians was by no means unanimous. As the high degree of interest in closer economic links with the Americans suggests, many English Canadians were not uncomfortable with viewing Canada as essentially a North American nation. Goldwin Smith, a British-born intellectual who had lived briefly in the United States before moving to Canada in 1871, became a major proponent of not only commercial but political union. While Smith hoped for an eventual rapprochement between Britain and the United States to create a united Anglo-Saxondom, he deplored military conquest of territories, which, to him, was the essence of the imperialist movement. His provocative book, *Canada and the Canadian Question*, which appeared in 1891 during a hot political debate about reciprocity with the Americans, claimed that English Canadians were like Americans in every important respect. Joining the United States, he argued, would benefit Canadians economically and save them from following a road to war as defenders of British colonies.

Many propagandists for closer links between Canada and Britain ignored the exploitative character of British imperialism and claimed that it was, at least potentially, a means of spreading the message of a purified Christianity throughout the world. The leading imperialists were Methodists and Presbyterians, many of whom were born in the Maritime provinces. They were also social reformers, but their social critique tended to emphasize the lack of Christian values in institutions rather than the lack of state regulation to limit the damage that profit seekers might inflict on employees or consumers. The imperial goal, it was hoped, would rekindle spiritual values and bind Canadians together in a mission to unite with Britain to elevate the world.

Reverend G.M. Grant typified this imperialism. Born in Albion Mines, Nova Scotia, he became principal of Queen's University, a Presbyterian institution, in 1877 and remained in that post for two decades. Grant pressed for unity among Protestant churches to permit religion to permeate Canada's national existence. He played a key role in the union of four previously independent Presbyterian denominations into the Presbyterian Church in Canada in 1875 and foresaw possibilities for greater unity when the factious Methodists united in 1883. For Grant and others, religion, imperialism, and Canadian identity were inseparable threads in one cloth. Missionary societies subscribed to the imperialist outlook that justified conquest of African and Asian peoples in the name of Christianity and saw a potential national purpose in the struggle to convert "heathens."

Religion in Victorian Canada: A Changing Protestantism

The publication first of Charles Darwin's *The Origin of Species* in 1859 and then his *The Descent of Man* in 1871 provoked questioning of the literal truth of church teachings. If humans were simply evolutionary products rather than God's crowning achievement during a six-day creation, how could one accept the Old Testament account of creation? Some church leaders responded by rejecting Darwin's theory as speculative nonsense, unsupported by any evidence. They had support from some religious members of the scientific community, including geologist Sir William Dawson, principal of McGill University and the most influential scientist of his generation. Though Dawson attempted to reconcile the Bible's claims of a six-day creation with scientific knowledge of the variation in longevity of different animal and plant species (he suggested that the term "day" in Genesis ought to be understood as a longer period than a literal day), he rejected notions of humans developing from apes. Many other scientists, as well as theologians, tried to reconcile Darwin's views with Christian teaching, claiming that the Bible's stories were often figuratively rather than literally true. "Higher criticism," which treated the Bible as a historical document written by humans from a particular perspective, challenged the belief that the Bible was "God's word" and was therefore not open to interpretation or amendment. Divisions occurred within churches between the literalists and the higher critics.

The social problems accompanying industrialization sparked another major dispute within the churches on the causes and solutions of poverty. Many religious leaders continued to ascribe poverty to personal failings, and the churches generally supported both the punitive treatment of the poor and campaigns for temperance and prison reform that assumed that individuals rather than society required reforming. Newfoundland's Reverend G.S. Chamberlain, for example, reflected church traditions when, in 1880, he attributed the poverty of that colony's fishers to lack of thrift rather than the truck system. Nonetheless, consensus on the causes of poverty was cracking. In the 1880s the *Canadian Baptist,* under the editorship of Ebenezer William Dadson, called for such legislative measures as a guaranteed right to unionize, and legal protection for women, children, and Native people along with the usual demand for prohibition. Dadson called the law of supply and demand "unchristian." Methodist and Anglican leaders were also increasingly disposed to regard poverty as the fault, at least in part, of the socio-economic system. Of the emerging trend towards a social Christianity different from the individualist Christianity of the past, historian Ramsay Cook notes, "The religious crisis provoked by Darwinian science and historical criticism of the Bible led religious people to attempt to salvage Christianity by transforming it into an essentially social religion. The orthodox preoccupation with man's salvation was gradually replaced by a concern with social salvation; the traditional Christian emphasis on man's relationship with God shifted to a focus on man's relationship with man."[14]

While many Protestant leaders, like the Catholic bishops, denounced scepticism, intellectuals who remained strong in their religious attachments increasingly expressed humanist views. Reverend G.M. Grant, for example, in his book *Religions of the World* (1885), demonstrated great tolerance of non-Christian religions and called for Christian sectarianism to give way to a goal of global unity. Author Agnes Machar agreed that the churches must embrace reform so that working people were not driven towards atheistic communism. A keen critic of the oppression of women workers, Machar was in little doubt about the source of the problem. "The answer lies in the hard necessities of poverty which compels them to take the work on the terms offered, and makes them so much afraid of dismissal that they will seldom ever complain of oppression."[15]

The average church member was not directly involved in disputes over either the Bible or social philosophy. Although working-class attendance at church was worrisomely low to religious leaders, most rural folk and the middle and upper classes in towns and cities joined a church and attended Sunday services. The importance of religious beliefs in their daily lives is unclear. For example, though many became teetotallers and active prohibition advocates because of their church affiliation, there were clearly many churchgoers who drank liquor. In cities, in particular, activities frowned upon by the churches, such as gambling and prostitution, attracted a large percentage of the population, and only the force of law shut down theatres and shops that might compete with churches for Sunday attendance. On the other hand, the fact that legislators believed it necessary to accede to demands for Sunday closings does suggest church influence within society as a whole. The many women and men who joined temperance societies and foreign missionary societies clearly had more than "Sunday religion."

Yet there was less religious enthusiasm than there had been in the early nineteenth century. Revivalism, which emphasized intense personal experience, was downplayed by the established churches. Methodist camp meetings that had featured several days of open-air preaching and testimonies of devotion by people sleeping in tents gave way to "camps" featuring summer cottages, boat services, and other such amenities for middle-class Methodists who did not wish their religious observance to interfere with their creature comforts. The *Christian Guardian*, the official organ of the church, advertised its Thousand Island Park camp meetings in the 1870s in a way that would have been incomprehensible to people one hundred years earlier. "There is no more healthy and pleasant summer resort than Thousand Island Park, on the St. Lawrence. The scenery is picturesque and beautiful. The water is cool and clear. The air is pure and bracing. Good order and interesting services are maintained. Fishing, boating and bathing are available to any extent. The first of the series of services of the season was begun last Friday, under the direction of the Rev. Dr. Hibbard, and is now in full blast."[16]

The middle-class respectability that the established churches sought alienated some members and created a space for old-time revivalists. Phoebe Palmer, an American revivalist, had a strong following in Canada as did several Canadian evangelists such as John Hunter and Ralph C. Horner. Montreal-born Horner, expelled from the Methodist ministry, gained a following in Eastern Ontario and created a splinter church. The Salvation Army, an import from Britain, and Mormonism, an American sect, were among groups that attracted adherents in late nineteenth-century Canada. A variety of millenarian groups came and went during this period, attracting believers disillusioned with the apparent secularization of the established churches. These groups, in turn, often disillusioned their followers when the predicted Second Coming failed to occur.

Scepticism about church teachings was also evident in the spread of spiritualism and theosophy in the late nineteenth century. Spiritualists believed that the human soul remained alive after the death of the physical body and could be communicated with by the living. Some also believed in reincarnation. Theosophists embraced a theory that integrated religious and social reform. They proposed that there was a universal soul to which all individual souls were ultimately identical. Opposed to all forms of discrimination, including gender and race discrimination, theosophists proclaimed that individuals must find their identity in the universal soul. Among adherents of this movement were the suffragists Dr Emily Stowe, her daughter Dr Augusta Stowe-Gullen, as well as newspaper editor Albert Smythe and labour reformer and journalist T. Phillips Thompson. Unitarianism, which proclaimed the essential unity of all religious beliefs and, like theosophy, embraced social reform and an end to race and gender prejudices, also won some adherents. Most shocking to the churches was the creation by intellectuals in Montreal and Toronto of free-thought societies, whose meetings and newspapers equated Christianity with superstition.

A Combative Catholicism

The Roman Catholic Church was not without its sceptics and social reformers but, particularly in Quebec, the hierarchy attempted to check dissidence. An extreme faction of the hierarchy, the ultramontanes, went so far as to insist that Church teachings should form the basis of all social rules, including the laws promulgated by politicians. The church forbade Catholics from reading books that it considered irreligious, and it forbade the faithful from joining trade union organizations that it considered preoccupied with members' material life rather than their afterlife. Such rules did not prevent middle-class Catholics from finding banned literature in bookshops and libraries outside church control or from joining organizations such as the Knights of Labour. Indeed Pope Leo XIII lifted an ineffectual ban on Catholic participation in the Knights in 1887.

A celebrated case of the Church's confrontation with its critics was its refusal in 1869 to allow the burial of an activist of the liberal Institut Canadien in a Catholic cemetery. Even here, the church's authority was not unchallenged. The courts sided with the widow of Joseph Guibord and ordered that his remains be buried in the cemetery. The existence of the Institut demonstrated that scepticism was alive in intellectual circles in Quebec. Founded in Montreal in 1844 to foster French-Canadian culture, this organization sponsored public forums that championed secularization of education and freedom of conscience, and it established a library that ignored the church's index of forbidden readings. Although the Institut declined and eventually closed its doors in 1885, its ideas remained influential among middle-class and skilled working-class francophone Catholics.

The church's political influence in Quebec, while important, was never all-embracing. The Conservatives, who dominated Quebec politics in the years after 1867, were split between those who accepted the ultramontane ideology and those who believed that politicians must govern without a Church veto. The election of the Parti national as the provincial government in 1885, in defiance of continued Church support for the Conservative administration, demonstrated that many Catholics did not recognize the bishops' right to dictate their political decisions. In practice, despite its antecedents in the liberal *rouges*, which had been closely associated with the Institut Canadien in its formative years, the Parti national was not anti-clerical. It did not challenge church control over education or social services.

Yet Catholic teachings, most visible in the ubiquitous sisterhoods who taught in schools, nursed in hospitals, and looked after children in orphanages and homes for unwed mothers, were still evident in everyday life, even in the emerging cities where the church feared that its control over its flock was weaker than in the rural parishes. In turn-of-the-century Montreal working-class neighbourhoods, for example, there were "few common-law marriages, few illegitimate births, few voluntary separations of couples, and a high rate of participation of young girls in the congregation of Enfants de Marie."[17] Still, Edouard-Charles Fabre, archbishop of Montreal from 1876 to 1896, had little impact on the faithful as he denounced picnics, amusement parks, Sunday concerts and bazaars, gambling, and the presence of girls at public gatherings.

The church that presided over French-Canadian society was increasingly at odds with liberalizing trends in Rome. Leo XIII's encyclical of

1891, *Rerum Novarum,* regarded the unfettered marketplace as destructive of communities and of individual lives. While he supported private ownership of industry, the pope urged "a capitalism guided by government, that is to say a competitive market system hemmed in by laws, tariffs and taxes."[18] By contrast, the Roman Catholic hierarchy in Quebec distrusted the state as a competitor and made its influence felt in politics less to promote positive state action than to discourage state rivalry in education, health, and social services. The hierarchy's suspicion of state action made them unwitting allies of the Anglo-Canadian business people who were happy to accept state subsidies but unwilling to pay the costs of state social programs.

The Arts

Cultural production in British North America had been modest. By contrast, in late Victorian Canada there was an outpouring of novels, poetry, and works of fiction. Sparked by improved literacy, there was also a large increase in the number of newspapers and magazines. European works too found a larger audience than they had in the pre-Confederation period. From the point of view of some commentators, however, Canada's colonial past still inhibited the quality of its literary production. Sara Jeannette Duncan, novelist and essayist, commented towards the end of the century:

> In our character as colonists we find the root of all our sins of omission in letters. . . . Our enforced political humility is the distinguishing characteristic of every phase of our national life. We are ignored, and we ignore ourselves. A nation's development is like a plant's, unattractive under ground. So long as Canada remains in political obscurity, content to thrive only at the roots, so long will the leaves and blossoms of art and literature be scanty and stunted products of our national energy. . . . A national literature cannot be looked for as an outcome of anything less than a complete national existence.[19]

In Quebec, despite the church's thunderbolts against godless, republican France, there was a large audience for that nation's great authors such as Balzac and Stendhal as well as its popular writers of mysteries and melodramas. Most of the home-grown authors, anxious to please local patronage-dispensing politicians and clergy, stuck to clerical–conservative positions in their work. Quebec was presented in this literature as a devout Catholic nation with a mission to spread the Catholic word throughout the world. Glorification of the Papal Zouaves who fought to defend the Vatican against attempts to annex the Holy See to the new Italian state was especially popular, particularly as a contingent of Quebec volunteers had joined the Zouaves.

Newspapers ran serialized novels that were less circumscribed by religious values, but most featured larger-than-life Canadien heroes and beautiful, pure heroines. Set either in rural areas or in high society within the cities, none of these novels raised questions about urban poverty or life of the popular classes. One exception to a litany of novels and poems that recounted French-Canadian myths of the purity of rural life was Honoré Beaugrand's *Jeanne la Fileuse*, a romanticized presentation of the life of Quebec expatriates in New England.

Little enduring literature was produced during this period. An exception is Laure Conan's *Angeline de Montbrun*, which probes the mind of a woman in torment after her father's death and traces the development of a resolve to reject worldly life in favour of spirituality. In addition, in the 1890s, the young Emile Nelligan wrote much of his sad, nostalgic poetry that is still highly regarded in Quebec today.

Sculpture and painting of the period, while often captivating, also reflected the conservatism of Quebec society. The church and large businesses were the main markets for artists. Key sculptures erected during this period include Louis-Philippe Hebert's monument to Jacques Cartier and his monument to Maisonneuve in Montreal's Place d'Armes. Quebec painters of the late Victorian period focussed on landscapes and on romanticized portraits of peoples' lives. Cornelius Krieghoff, the Dutch-born painter whose vivid portrayals of the people and the countryside of rural Quebec remain popular today, had established his reputation by the 1850s and continued to paint until his sudden death in 1872. Aaron Allan Edson, a Quebec artist whose landscapes reflected the influence of British, American, and French styles of the period, was the best known of a variety of talented landscape painters who studied abroad and whose work attempted to synthesize various styles. A Society of Canadian Artists, formed in 1868, promoted Canadian work in a variety of exhibits. Before the end of the century, a number of art schools had been established.

English-Canadian cultural production was, on the whole, as conservative and prone to romanticizing the past as its French-Canadian counterpart. The Loyalist myth, common in works from the 1820s onward, remained popular. Both the initial Loyalist flight from the mad republic to the south and the defence of the Canadas in 1812 were mythologized in Egerton Ryerson's *The Loyalists of America and Their Times* (1880). The centennial celebrations of Loyalist settlements encouraged many such works. Even earlier, Charles Mair, the Manitoba stalwart against Métis rights, had won praise for his Loyalist poems. Ironically, Mair presented the Native leader, Tecumseh, who supported the British in 1812, as a hero in an 1886 drama. By the 1890s, Mair, who had seen the West as a garden for the taking, was nostalgic for the simple life of the Native people in "a golden age whose destruction he was himself helping to bring about."[20] Other poets made extensive use of Native subjects in their work. Pauline Johnson was the daughter of the chief of the Six Nations and an English woman. Her poems, which celebrated both Canada and her Native heritage, were enormously popular in her day. Another popular poet, Isabella Valancy Crawford, also drew extensively on Indian imagery and references in her imaginative poetry.

The yearning for simpler days and greater harmony with nature was a frequent theme in the works of the best-known English-Canadian poets of the late nineteenth century. Fredericton, a long-established college town, produced many of the leading lights of the period, notably Charles G.D. Roberts and Bliss Carman. Roberts, though a strong nationalist, was most celebrated for works that evoked the sea, hills, and orchards of his New Brunswick boyhood. Duncan Campbell Scott and Archibald Lampman, two Ottawa civil servants, shared with the Maritime poets a tendency to Christian moralizing and a focus on natural landscapes unblighted by human greed. Scott, in his second book of verse, *Labor and the Angel* (1898), sharply defended society's underdogs, and Lampman, who dabbled in socialist politics and rebelled against the inequalities that surrounded him, wrote several poems that contrasted the unspoiled beauty of nature with man-made hells. His "The City of the End of Things" was a futuristic creation of an urban nightmare where inhumanity was supreme.

Agnes Machar was a prolific writer of fiction and nonfiction works that fused reformist, feminist, religious, and patriotic concerns. Her novel, *Roland Graeme Knight*, an idealistic portrayal of a Knight of Labour and the woman who loved him, was a model of its kind. She was one of a small group of women who made a living either as writers of fiction or as journalists during this period. Another was Margaret Marshall Saunders, the daughter of a Baptist minister, who in 1894 published *Beautiful Joe*, the story of an abused dog. The book, which won first prize in an American Humane Society competition, became a bestseller, reputedly the first work by a Canadian author to sell a million copies. In 1886, Sara Jeannette Duncan became the first woman with a full-time appointment as a journalist to the Toronto *Globe*. Other women were occasional writers and a very few of these promoted feminist perspectives. Sarah Curzon, a Toronto suffrage and temperance advocate, produced a play in 1876 called *Laura Secord, the Heroine of 1812*, which used popular Loyalist mythologies to promote a positive view of women's abilities.

THE WRITING OF HISTORY

The mythologies of artistic creators were also evident in serious attempts to write about Canada's past. The notion of English Canada as a collection of peaceful Crown-loving former colonies and moderate advocates of responsible government figured prominently in the literature. In such accounts both oligarchies and radical reformers were given short shrift. John Charles Dent's *The Last Forty Years: Canada Since the Union of 1841* (1881) and *The Story of the Rebellion* (1885) were particularly influential.

A Whig view—the notion of the past as a straight line of progress—with large doses of support for British imperialism pervaded both the texts on Canada as a whole and on its constituent provinces and regions. A civil engineer, William Kingsford, produced the popular ten-volume *The History of Canada* from 1887 to 1898. Kingsford was touted as English Canada's counterpart to the famous French-Canadian nationalist historian François-Xavier Garneau. But while Garneau extolled *ancien régime* society and reviled the conquest, Kingsford and most English-Canadian historical writers regarded the conquest as a blessing in disguise for the French Canadians and a necessary step in the march towards civilization.

Such an uncritical evolutionary viewpoint also framed the major nineteenth-century accounts of the history of the Northwest and of British Columbia. Oddly enough, both books were written by historians named Alexander Begg, though the two men were unrelated. While the British Columbia Begg was somewhat restrained in his Whiggishness, the author of the three-volume *History of the North-West* (1894–95) extolled the replacement of the Native peoples and the fur trade with agriculturists as inevitable and highly significant for imperial development.

Only in the 1890s did the history of Canada become a subject for teaching and research by university professors. The naming of George Wrong to the chair of history at the University of Toronto and the introduction at Queen's of Adam Shortt's lectures on the economic and social history of Canada, both in 1894, marked the beginning of competition from the academy for the amateur historians who first raised interest in the nation's past.

In French Canada, the dominant position of the clergy had an important impact on the writing of history. The anticlerical, liberal history of Garneau in the 1840s with its openness to industrial development and ideological pluralism gave way to histories that emphasized the role of the clergy in developing French-Canadian society. Abbé Jean-Baptiste-Antoine Ferland's histories in the 1860s, for example, created a portrait of New France as a missionary colony whose history was guided by providence and its earthly representatives in the form of the self-sacrificing bishops, nuns, and priests. Even the few histories that challenged the view that the church's role had always been beneficial were rarely as liberal as Garneau's early work. Indeed Garneau himself modified his views in light of the clerical assault. Benjamin Sulte, an anticlerical historian in the 1880s, while championing secular forces, glorified rural life and paid little attention to the history of commerce in French Canada.

Journalism

The reading public with the education, time, and money to indulge in history books, novels, and books of poetry, while growing in the late nineteenth century, remained relatively small. But an increasing proportion of the population was sufficiently literate by the 1890s to read newspapers, and most could afford the time and money required to obtain and read an eight-page penny paper. Most papers were unabashedly partisan and reported the news in a way that made no pretence to political objectivity. While the nation claimed only forty-seven newspapers in 1873, that number had doubled to ninety-four by 1892.

Some papers were sombre enterprises such as the information-crammed *Globe* in Toronto, its rival, the *Mail*, and the ultramontane *Nouveau Monde* in Montreal. Increasingly, publishers saw the potential of newspapers for popular entertainment in a society where greater schooling meant more potential readers. The *Montreal Star*, founded in 1869, pioneered the sensationalist newspaper in Canada, focussing on gossip and events close to home rather than on serious politics and events in Europe. The *Telegram*, founded in 1876, brought the same formula to Toronto. *La Presse* of Montreal, which closed the century as Quebec's leading newspaper, also copied this formula, though it included more extensive and internationally oriented news coverage than its English-Canadian counterparts. Rapid printing, cheaper paper, the linotype, railways and telegraphs, and photocopying all made possible the provision of relatively recent news on a daily basis. Advertising by retailers, particularly the new large department store owners such as Timothy Eaton, made publishing lucrative and allowed publishers to keep newspaper prices cheap.

The views expressed by the newspapers were not greatly different from those found in the majority of serious works of fiction and nonfiction of the period. Though a small labour press struggled to survive with little advertising revenue, most papers by the end of the century were purveyors of the same ideology that their advertisers embodied: the ideology of capitalist economic expansion. Despite some partisan differences, most English-Canadian papers were jingoistic defenders of the privileges of established elites. Predictably there was a split between English-Canadian and French-Canadian newspapers on the subject of British imperialism.

Popular Entertainments

The readers of the mass press at the time were generally far more intrigued by the exploits of their sports heroes than by politics. Ned Hanlan, for the average Canadian in the 1880s, was a more fascinating figure than John A. Macdonald. From 1877 to 1884, Hanlan, son of a Toronto hotelier, defended fifteen rowing championships including the world championship in 1880.

Urbanization and the new capitalist ethic produced a greater commercialization of sport and drew in large numbers of people as paying spectators for professional teams. Baseball was the most popular spectator sport and attracted a huge working-class audience throughout English and French Canada. Toronto and Hamilton had professional baseball teams by the 1880s. Baseball was not only a spectator sport; large numbers of ordinary men played it as well. In Saint John, conductors' teams played the motormen, spinners played dyers, and longshoremen of the North Wharf played longshoremen of the South Wharf.

In winter, workers and their families took up skating, on ponds in rural areas and on commercial rinks in the cities. In the latter, competing owners hired bands, held carnivals, and sponsored skating shows to attract customers. Foot races and other activities that required no purchases of equipment were also popular among working people, but most sports that would later enjoy wide popularity were restricted to the middle and upper classes. Even ice hockey, whose popularity was on the rise by the end of the century, had not penetrated below the middle classes.

Popular games among the middle classes varied regionally and along ethnic lines. Cricket, soccer, and English rugby, associated with Britain, were popular in Victoria and Vancouver but of limited, though increasing, interest elsewhere. Curling was popular on the Prairies, and lacrosse, ice hockey, and Canadian football were the rage in Toronto and Montreal. While the amateur movement was well established, and included such groups as the Abegweit Athletic Association of Charlottetown and the James Bay Athletic Association of Victoria, it mirrored professional sports in its emphasis on winning as opposed to simply having fun. The amateur movement expanded the numbers of organized teams and leagues and earned income by leasing its sports facilities for commercial baseball, football, and lacrosse games.

Sporting activities were also beginning to open up for women. In the 1880s, bicycling joined tennis, curling, and skating to amuse middle-class women and to worry those who identified an increase in women's physical freedom with moral laxness and, worse still, feminist sympathies. Medical misinformation suggesting that physically active women would not give birth to healthy babies gave ammunition to those who warned that a sportswoman was in danger of losing her femininity. So while sports events became part of the male culture, most women sought relief from household drudgery through visits with families and friends, church events, and community carnivals.

Leisure activities were different for various social strata. Upper-class, middle-class, skilled workers', and unskilled workers' families had differing amounts of time and money to pursue recreational interests. Civic events such as parades temporarily united the social classes. Writes Michael Katz:

> The procession was the most important civic ritual in nineteenth century Hamilton. On every pretext work stopped and dignitaries, civic officials, representatives of societies, fire companies, even, on one memorable occasion, the mechanics of the Great Western Railroad, all carrying their banners, marched through the thronged city streets to a public place where eminent men made speeches to rousing cheers. Often after the procession came a mass dinner and carousing at one of

Curling in Ottawa   (National Archives of Canada/PA8498)

the local hotels, followed sometimes by a ball. . . . Processions signified urban civic festivals, the only real sources of release, refreshment and integration in the stratified, transient, and anxious world of the nineteenth-century city.[21]

By the 1880s labour in Hamilton sponsored its own processions and advanced its own slogans. It was one sign that, whatever the powers of the political, economic, and religious elites of late Victorian Canada, resistance to their authority could not be wholly suppressed. The early twentieth century, a period of economic expansion and general improvement in living standards, was, as we will see in Part II, also to be a period of increasing challenges against accepted authorities and their orthodoxies.

• Late Victorian Protestantism:
A Historiographical Debate

Should increasing concerns among Protestant churches about respectability and social problems in late Victorian Canada be viewed as signs of capitulation to an increasingly secular society? Certainly many historians view these developments in this manner. But others disagree.

The concern about respectability among the Methodists, for example, may be seen as having several causes. One approach emphasizes the reaction to external realities: a new urban environment provoked the fear that Methodism, with its roots in rural revivals, might become irrelevant. The church had to adapt to secular realities for the sake of its own survival.[22] But historian William Westfall suggests that internal church considerations were even more important. The revivals occurred in the period before a large church organization with many members had been established and was concerned with converting sinners to Christ. Once the church became a large institution with a mass membership of committed Christians to serve, revivalism of necessity became less important than ministering to the faithful. The membership itself remained closely attached to the traditions that had attracted them to Methodism and limited the extent to which the church leadership could change the direction of the church. The leadership, in its new emphasis on reasoned acceptance of church doctrines rather than emotional camp meetings, could claim authority from the church's founders, and were concerned about "moderation, gradualism, and the central place of the institutions of a well-established church in the religious life of the individual."[23]

For Westfall, growing church concerns about social problems reflected not a capitulation to secularism but a challenge to it. Setting aside differences that once kept various denominations at odds with one another, religious people and their church leaders worked together to assert a Protestant moral agenda, in the process creating a "Protestant culture":

> *Now arose the prospect that materialism would undermine the religious character of society as a whole and that large numbers of people might not enjoy the benefits of any religion. In the light of that possibility the former religious conflicts became much less important; secularism became the common and omnipresent enemy.*
>
> *In this way the new culture provided Christians with a new way of interpreting the world. Inspired by a powerful religious feeling, they caught a glimpse of a glorious future: they then sacrificed their own wealth and ambitions to take up the cause of Christ, and turn their talents to the moral reform of society.*[24]

Historian Ramsay Cook views the shift in emphasis from saving souls to reforming social institutions rather differently. He argues that "the most remarkable consequence . . . of the intellectual transformation that took place in English Canada between Confederation and the Great War" was that Protestantism became "'a mere sociological instead of a religious doctrine.'" As many nineteenth-century intellectuals suspected, "the path blazed by nineteenth-century religious liberals led not to the kingdom of God on earth but to the secular city."[25]

•Notes

[1] Varpu Lindstrom-Best, *Defiant Sisters: A Social History of Finnish Immigrant Women in Canada* (Toronto: Multicultural History Society of Ontario), 27.

[2] *Daily Globe* (Toronto), 7 June 1882.

[3] J.R. Miller, *Skyscrapers Hide the Heavens: A History of Indian–White Relations in Canada* (Toronto: University of Toronto Press, 1989), 298.

[4] *Victoria Daily Colonist*, 15 May 1880; quoted in Penny Petrone, ed., *First People, First Voices* (Toronto: University of Toronto Press, 1983), 68–69.

[5] Ruth Holmes Whitehead, *The Old Man Told Us: Excerpts from Micmac History 1500–1950* (Halifax: Nimbus, 1991), 278–79.

[6] Herbert Brown Ames, *The City Below the Hill* (Toronto: University of Toronto Press, 1972), 103.

[7] Ibid., 105.

[8] Ibid., 48.

[9] Quoted in Douglas Baldwin, "But Not a Drop to Drink": The Struggle for Pure Water" in *Gaslights, Epidemics and Vagabond Cows: Charlottetown in the Victorian Era*, ed. Doug Baldwin and Thomas Spira (Charlottetown: Ragweed Press, 1988), 110.

[10] Cited in Judith Fingard, *The Dark Side of Life in Victorian Halifax* (Porters Lake, NS: Potterfield Press, 1989), 16.

[11] National Archives of Canada, Montreal Council of Women papers, vol. 6, Alice L. Hooper, "The Montreal Council of Women: An Evaluation," 75th Annual Meeting, 1968.

[12] Lynne Marks, "Working Class Femininity and the Salvation Army: 'Hallelujah Lasses' in English Canada, 1882–1892" in *Rethinking Canada: The Promise of Women's History*, 2nd ed., ed. Veronica Strong-Boag and Anita Clair Fellman (Toronto: Copp Clark Pitman, 1991), 198.

[13] Marta Danylewycz, *Taking the Veil: An Alternative to Marriage, Motherhood and Spinsterhood in Quebec, 1840–1920* (Toronto: McClelland and Stewart, 1987), 70.

[14] Ramsay Cook, *The Regenerators: Social Criticism in Late Victorian English Canada* (Toronto: University of Toronto Press, 1985), 4.

[15] Ibid., 189.

[16] Neil Semple, "The Quest for the Kingdom: Aspects of Protestant Revivalism in Nineteenth-Century Ontario" in *Old Ontario: Essays in Honour of J.M.S. Careless*, ed. David Keane and Colin Read (Toronto: Dundurn Press, 1990), 112.

[17] Lucia Ferretti, "Mariage et Cadre de Vie Familiale dans une Paroisse Ouvrière Montréalaise: Saint-Brigide, 1900–1914," *Révue d'Histoire de l'Amérique Française* 39, 2 (Autumn 1985): 250.

[18] Gregory Baum, "The Relevance of the Antigonish Movement Today," *Journal of Canadian Studies* 15, 1 (Spring 1980): 111.

[19] Quoted in *The Canadian Essay*, ed. Gerald Lynch and David Rampton (Toronto: Copp Clark Pitman, 1991), 12.

[20] Dennis Duffy, *Gardens, Covenants, Exiles: Loyalism in the Literature of Upper Canada/Ontario* (Toronto: University of Toronto Press, 1982), 68.

[21] Michael B. Katz, *The People of Hamilton, Canada West: Family and Class in a Mid-Nineteenth Century City* (Cambridge, MA: Harvard University Press, 1975), 3–4.

[22] Works by Neil Semple stress this interpretation. See, for example, his "The Quest for the Kingdom," cited earlier.

[23] William Westfall, *Two Worlds: The Protestant Culture of Nineteenth Century Ontario* (Montreal: McGill-Queen's University Press, 1989), 78.

[24] Ibid., 80.

[25] Cook, *The Regenerators*, 229.

• Selected Reading

For an overview on immigration, see Jean Burnet with Howard Palmer, *"Coming Canadians": An Introduction to the History of Canada's Peoples* (Toronto: McClelland and Stewart, 1988). Works dealing with specific groups of immigrants include: Irving Abella, *A Coat of Many Colours: Two Centuries of Jewish Life in Canada* (Toronto: Lester and Orpen Dennys, 1990); Hans Lehmann, *The German Canadians 1750–1937: Immigration, Settlement and Culture* (St John's: Bassler Gerhard, 1986); and Frank H. Epp, *Mennonites in Canada, 1786–1920: The History of a Separate People* (Toronto: Macmillan, 1974). On forces drawing some groups into the country and others out, see Bruno Ramirez, *On the Move: French-Canadian and Italian Migrants in the North Atlantic Economy, 1860–1914* (Toronto: McClelland and Stewart, 1990). The experience of Chinese immigrants is discussed in Patricia E. Roy, *A White Man's Province: British Columbia Politicians and Chinese and Japanese Immigrants 1858–1914* (Vancouver: University of British Columbia Press, 1989); W. Peter Ward, *White Canada Forever: Popular Attitudes and Public Policy Toward Orientals in British Columbia*, 2nd ed. (Montreal: McGill-Queen's University Press, 1990); Tamara Adilman, "A Preliminary Sketch of Chinese Women and Work in British Columbia, 1858–1950," *British Columbia Reconsidered: Essays on Women*, ed. Gillian Creese and Veronica Strong-Boag (Vancouver: University of British Columbia Press, 1992), 309–39; and J. Brian Dawson with Patricia Dawson, *Moon Cakes in Gold Mountain: From China to the Canadian Plains* (Calgary: Detselig, 1991). The experience of blacks is traced in

James W. St. G. Walker, *Racial Discrimination in Canada: The Black Experience* (Toronto: Gage, 1985); and Robin Winks, *The Blacks in Canada: A History* (Montreal: McGill-Queen's University Press, 1971).

On Native peoples, the major overviews are Olive Patricia Dickason, *Canada's First Nations* (Toronto: McClelland and Stewart, 1992); and J.R. Miller, *Skyscrapers Hide the Heavens* (Toronto: University of Toronto Press, 1989). British Columbia studies include: Douglas Cole and Ira Chaikin, *An Iron Hand upon the People: The Law Against the Potlatch on the Northwest Coast* (Vancouver: Douglas and McIntyre, 1990); Helen Coderre, *Fighting with Property: A Study of Kwakiutl Potlatching and Warfare, 1792–1930* (New York: American Ethnological Society, 1950); Robin Fisher, *Contact and Conflict: Indian-European Relations in British Columbia 1774–1890* (Vancouver: University of British Columbia Press, 1979); Rolf Knight, *Indians at Work: An Informal History of Native Indian Labour in British Columbia 1858–1930* (Vancouver: New Star Books, 1978); Paul Tennant, *Aboriginal Peoples and Politics: The Indian Land Question in British Columbia, 1849–1989* (Vancouver: University of British Columbia Press, 1990); and Marjorie Mitchell and Anna Franklin, "When You Don't Know the Language, Listen to the Silence: A Historical Overview of Native Indian Women in British Columbia" in *Not Just Pin Money*, ed. Barbara K. Latham and Roberta J. Pazdro (Victoria: Camosun College, 1984), 17–34. On the Northwest, a good starting point is the treaties, detailed in Alexander Morris, *The Treaties of Canada with the Indians of Manitoba and the North-West Territories* (Toronto: Fifth House, 1991). Works on the Prairie provinces include Sarah A. Carter, *Lost Harvests: Prairie Indian Reserve Farmers and Government Policy* (Montreal: McGill-Queen's University Press, 1990); several essays in *As Long as the Sun Shines and Water Flows*, ed. Ian Getty and Antoine Lussier (Vancouver: University of British Columbia Press, 1983); David C. Mandelbaum, *The Plains Cree: An Ethnographic, Historical and Comparative Study* (Regina: Canadian Plains Research Centre, 1978); Richard Price, ed., *The Spirit of Alberta Indian Treaties* (Edmonton: University of Alberta Press, 1987); and F. Laurie Barron, "The Indian Pass System in the Canadian West, 1882–1935," *Prairie Forum*, 13, 1 (1988): 25–42. On Central Canada, see Peter Schmalz, *The Ojibwa of Southern Ontario* (Toronto: University of Toronto Press, 1990). On the Maritime provinces and Newfoundland, see Ellice B. Gonzalez, *Changing Economic Roles for Micmac Men and Women: An Ethnohistorical Analysis* (Ottawa: National Museum, 1981); and Ruth Holmes Whitehead, *The Old Man Told Us: Excerpts from Micmac History 1500–1950* (Halifax: Nimbus, 1991). On the North, key works include Keith J. Crowe, *A History of the Original Peoples of Northern Canada* (Montreal: McGill-Queen's University Press, 1991); and Ken S. Coates, *Best Left as Indians: Native–White Relations in the Yukon Territory, 1840–1973* (Montreal: McGill-Queen's University Press, 1991). Missionary work among Native peoples is discussed in John Webster Grant, *Moon of Wintertime: Missionaries and the Indians of Canada in Encounter since 1534* (Toronto: University of Toronto Press, 1984).

On city life, see the references cited in the selected reading for chapter 3. On urban reform, see also Paul Rutherford, ed., *Saving the Canadian City: The First Phase, 1880–1920* (Toronto: University of Toronto Press, 1974). On the standard of living in cities, an important study is David Gagan and Rosemary Gagan, "Working-Class Standards of Living in Late-Victorian Urban Ontario: A Review of the Miscellaneous Evidence on the Quality of Material Life," *Journal of the Canadian Historical Association*, new series, 1 (1990): 171–93. An intriguing essay on male working-class culture is Peter De Lottinville, "Joe Beef of Montreal: Working Class Culture and the Tavern, 1869–89," *Labour/Le Travailleur*, 8–9 (1981–82): 9–40. On epidemics, see Michael Bliss, *Plague: A Story of Smallpox in Montreal* (Toronto: Harper Collins, 1991). On the treatment of the unemployed see Stephen A. Speisman, "Munificent Parsons and Municipal Parsimony: Voluntary v. Public Poor Relief in Nineteenth Century Toronto," *Ontario History* 65 (1973): 55–70; and James M. Pitsula, "The Treatment of Tramps in Late Nineteenth-Century Toronto," Canadian Historical Association *Historical Papers* (1980): 116–32. On prison reform, see Peter Oliver, "'A Terror to Evil-Doers': The Central Prison and the 'Criminal Class' in Late Nineteenth-Century Ontario," *Patterns of the Past: Interpreting Ontario's History*, ed. Roger Hall, William Westfall, and Laurel Sefton MacDowell (Toronto: Dundurn, 1988), 206–37. On women and social reform movements, see T.R. Morrison, "'Their Proper Sphere': Feminism, the Family, and Child-Centred Social Reform in Ontario, 1875–1900," Parts 1 and 2, *Ontario History* 67 (1976): 45–64 and 68 (1976): 65–74.

The major overviews for women's history are: Alison Prentice et al., *Canadian Women: A History* (Toronto: Harcourt Brace Jovanovich, 1988); and Clio Collective, *Quebec Women: A History* (Toronto: Women's Press, 1987). On women and the family economy, see the selected reading for chapter 3. On women and paid work, see Joy Parr, *The Gender of Breadwinners: Women, Men and Change in Two Industrial Towns, 1880–1950* (Toronto: University of Toronto Press, 1990); Janice Acton, Penny Goldsmith, and Bonnie Shepard, eds., *Women at Work: Ontario 1850–1930* (Toronto: Women's Press, 1974); Claudette Lacelle, *Urban Domestic Servants in Nineteenth Century Canada* (Ottawa: Canadian Communications Group, 1987); and Wayne Roberts, *Honest Womanhood: Feminism, Femininity and Class Consciousness Among Toronto Working Women 1893–1914* (Toronto: New Hogtown Press, 1976). On women and reform movements generally, see Linda Kealey, ed., *A Not Unreasonable Claim: Women and Reform in Canada* (Toronto: Women's Press, 1979). On women and religion, important works include Marta Danylewycz, *Taking the Veil: An Alternative to Marriage, Motherhood and Spinsterhood in Quebec, 1840–1920* (Toronto: McClelland and Stewart, 1987); Ruth Compton Brouwer, *New Women for God: Canadian Presbyterian Women and India Missions, 1876–1914* (Toronto: University of Toronto Press, 1990); and Rosemary R. Gagan, *A Sensitive Independence: Canadian Methodist Women Missionaries in Canada and the Orient* (Montreal: McGill-Queen's

University Press, 1992). Victorian medical notions about women are dissected in Wendy M. Mitchinson, *The Nature of Their Bodies: Women and Their Doctors in Victorian Canada* (Toronto: University of Toronto Press, 1991). Women's dealings with the law are the subject of Constance Backhouse, *Petticoats and Prejudice: Women and Law in Nineteenth-Century Canada* (Toronto: Women's Press, 1991). The early suffrage movement is examined in Carol Lee Bacchi, *Liberation Deferred? The Ideas of the English-Canadian Suffragists, 1877–1918* (Toronto: University of Toronto Press, 1983). Bacchi's conclusions are disputed by Ernest Forbes, "The Ideas of Carol Bacchi and the Suffragists of Halifax," *Atlantis* 10, 2 (Spring 1985): 119–26. On women's home lives, see Margaret Conrad, Toni Laidlaw, and Donna Smyth, *No Place Like Home: Diaries and Letters of Nova Scotia Women 1771–1938* (Halifax: Formac, 1988); and Kathryn Harvey, "Amazons and Victims: Resisting Wife Abuse in Working Class Montreal, 1869–1879," *Journal of the Canadian Historical Association*, new series 2 (1991): 131–48. On farm women in Western Canada, works include Carol Fairbanks and Sara Brooks Sundberg, *Farm Women on the Prairie Frontier: A Sourcebook for Canada and the United States* (Metuchen, NJ: Scarecrow Press, 1983); Linda Rasmussen et al., *A Harvest Yet to Reap: A History of Prairie Women* (Toronto: Women's Press, 1976); and Nellie McClung, *Clearing in the West* (New York: 1936).

On sexual relations, see Gary Kinsmen, *The Regulation of Desire: Sexuality in Canada* (Montreal: Black Rose Books, 1987); Sharon Dale Stone, *Lesbians in Canada* (Toronto: Between the Lines, 1990); Angus McLaren and Arlene Tigar McLaren, *The Bedroom and the State: The Changing Practices and Politics of Contraception and Abortion in Canada, 1880–1980* (Toronto: McClelland and Stewart, 1986). On marriage, see Peter Ward, *Courtship, Love and Marriage in Nineteenth-Century English Canada* (Montreal: McGill-Queen's University Press, 1990).

On schooling, see Susan Houston and Alison Prentice, *Schooling and Scholars in Nineteenth Century Ontario* (Toronto: University of Toronto Press, 1988); Donald Wilson, ed., *An Imperfect Past: Education and Society in Canadian History* (Vancouver: University of British Columbia Press, 1984); Nancy Sheehan, David C. Jones, and Robert M. Stamp, eds., *Shaping the Schools of the Canadian West* (Calgary: Detselig, 1979); and Roger Magnuson, *A Brief History of Quebec Education* (Montreal: Harvest House, 1980).

On the intellectual history of late Victorian Canada, see Carl Berger, *The Sense of Power: Studies in the Ideas of Canadian Imperialism 1867–1914* (Toronto: University of Toronto Press, 1970); A.B. McKillop, *A Disciplined Intelligence: Critical Inquiry and Canadian Thought in the Victorian Era* (Montreal: McGill-Queen's University Press, 1979); Ramsay Cook, *The Regenerators: Social Criticism in Late Victorian English Canada* (Toronto: University of Toronto Press, 1985); Denis Monière, *Ideologies in Quebec: The Historical Development* (Toronto: University of Toronto Press, 1981); Mariana Valverde, *The Age of Light, Soap and Water: Moral Reform in English Canada,*

1885–1925 (Toronto: McClelland and Stewart, 1991); and Carl Berger, *Science, God, and Nature in Victorian Canada* (Toronto: University of Toronto Press, 1983).

On late nineteenth century religion, see Ramsay Cook, *The Regenerators*; William Westfall, *Two Worlds: The Protestant Culture of Nineteenth Century Ontario* (Montreal: McGill-Queen's University Press, 1989); John Webster Grant, *A Profusion of Spires: Religion in Nineteenth Century Ontario* (Toronto: University of Toronto Press, 1988); John S. Moir, *Enduring Witness: A History of the Presbyterian Church in Canada* (Toronto: Presbyterian Church of Canada, 1987); Harry A. Renfree, *Heritage and Horizon: The Baptist Story in Canada* (Mississauga: Canadian Baptist Federation, 1988); and Michael Gauvreau, *The Evangelical Century: College and Creed in English Canada from the Great Revival to the Great Depression* (Montreal: McGill-Queen's University Press, 1991).

Literary history is discussed in Carl F. Klinck, ed., *Literary History of Canada* (Toronto: University of Toronto Press, 1976); and Dennis Duffy, *Gardens, Covenants, Exiles: Loyalism in the Literature of Upper Canada/Ontario* (Toronto: University of Toronto Press, 1982). Paul Rutherford assesses the explosion in newspaper publication and newspaper readership in *A Victorian Authority: The Daily Press in Late Nineteenth-Century Canada* (Toronto: University of Toronto Press, 1982). On artistic developments, see J. Russell Harper, *Painting in Canada: A History* (Toronto: University of Toronto Press, 1977); and Dennis Reid, *"Our Own Country Canada": Being the Account of the National Aspirations of the Principal Landscape Artists in Montreal and Toronto, 1860–1890* (Ottawa: National Gallery, 1980). On the writing of history in the late nineteenth century, see M. Brook Taylor, *Promoters, Patriots and Partisans: Historiography in Nineteenth Century English Canada* (Toronto: University of Toronto Press, 1990); and Serge Gagnon, *Quebec and Its Historians, 1840–1920* (Montreal: Harvest House, 1982). A lively study of a key aspect of nineteenth-century entertainments is Alan Metcalfe, *Canada Learns to Play: The Emergence of Organized Sport, 1807–1914* (Toronto: McClelland and Stewart, 1987).

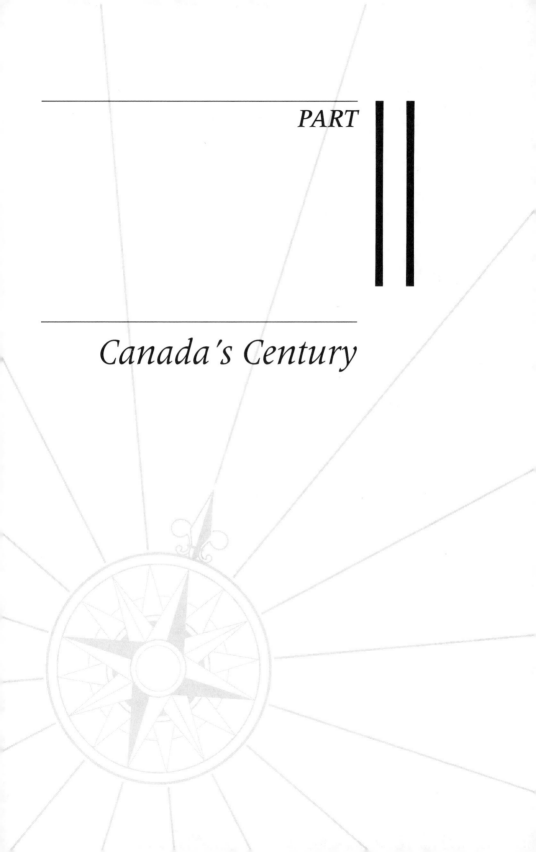

PART

II

Canada's Century

Time Line

1896	–	Canada's economy begins an extensive expansion; Klondike gold rush begins
1896–1911	–	Laurier Liberals form government
1897	–	Wheat boom begins
1898	–	National referendum on prohibition
1899–1902	–	South African War
1901	–	First transatlantic wireless signal received by Marconi in Newfoundland
1902	–	Formation of INCO
1903	–	Board of Railway Commissioners established; Laurier government provides loan guarantees and subsidies for two new transcontinental railroads; Quebec legislates compulsory vaccination for smallpox
1905	–	Saskatchewan and Alberta achieve provincehood
1906	–	Indian Act amended to make land surrenders easier; Ontario Hydro established; Cominco established
1907	–	Industrial Disputes Investigation Act passed; recession grips the Canadian economy; Anti-Asian riots in Vancouver; Doukhobors in Saskatchewan have half their land confiscated
1908	–	Founding of Moral and Social Reform Council of Canada; *Anne of Green Gables* published
1909–10	–	Miners' strike in Cape Breton
1910	–	*Le Devoir* begins publication; National Hockey Association formed; creation of Steel Company of Canada by mergers; Laurier government's Naval Service Bill
1911	–	Reciprocity treaty with United States rejected in federal election; École Sociale Populaire founded in Quebec

1911–20	–	Robert Borden is prime minister
1912	–	Ontario's Regulation 17 restricts education in languages other than English; Radical Doukhobors relocate from Saskatchewan to British Columbia
1913	–	Group of Seven begin their work together
1913–14	–	Major recession
1914	–	First workers' compensation act for Canada passed in Ontario
1914–18	–	First World War
1915	–	Saskatchewan leads the English-speaking provinces in banning alcohol
1916	–	Manitoba, Alberta, and Saskatchewan grant female suffrage; Manitoba government eliminates bilingual schools; National Research Council created
1917	–	Ontario and British Columbia women win the vote; conscription (Military Service Act) divides the nation
1917–23	–	Nationalization of interprovincial railways other than the CPR and incorporation, along with publicly owned railways, to form Canadian National Railways
1918	–	Saskatchewan makes English the only language of instruction beyond the first grade; League of Indians of Canada established; Nova Scotia concedes women's suffrage; women win right to vote federally
1919	–	Farmer–Labour government comes to power in Ontario; New Brunswick women win the vote; Winnipeg General Strike and other general strikes mark a year of labour radicalism

A MATURING INDUSTRIAL ECONOMY, 1896–1919

On 11 October 1910 crowds lined the streets of the Ontario town of Berlin (now Kitchener) to watch the motorcade carrying Adam Beck and Premier J.P. Whitney pass by on its way to the arena. As part of the ceremony marking the historic occasion, Hulda Rumpel, dressed in red, white, and blue, carried a button, which would summon electricity from Niagara, on top of a plush red cushion. Premier Whitney took the hand of Beck, his minister of power, and guided it towards the button, announcing: "Gentlemen, with this hand, tried and true, this hand which has made this project complete, I now turn on this power." Suddenly the arena blazed with light, Hulda Rumpel's crown of tiny light bulbs glowed, and the crowd cheered. The mayor of Berlin thanked Beck in German, and Beck responded with praise for Berlin's hydro pioneers, his own technical staff, the united municipalities, and the Whitney government. "You say our work is done. I say that it has only begun. We must deliver power to such an extent that the poorest workingman will have an electric light in his home," Adam Beck told the crowd. "No more oil and gas, soon, I hope, no more coal."[1]

Canada's "second industrial revolution" was built on electricity. Like the steam engine in an earlier period, electrical power stirred the imaginations of Canadian developers and attracted much public attention. Nowhere was there greater enthusiasm for electrical power than in Ontario and Quebec, which had abundant sources of potential electrical power locked inside rivers and waterfalls. The tremendous potential of Niagara Falls was initially harnessed by private corporations, but public distrust of developers resulted in the Ontario government creating a public corporation to distribute electricity in 1906. By the time of the ceremony in Berlin, the Hydro-Electric Power Commission of Ontario stood as a monument to the progressive business philosophy of Adam Beck and those who supported his dream for "the people's power."

Canada's obvious potential as an industrial nation inspired Prime Minister Wilfrid Laurier to claim: "As the nineteenth century was that of the United States, so I think the twentieth century shall be filled by Canada." Laurier was fond of such high-flowing rhetoric but, in 1904, when he made this statement to the Canadian Club's Ottawa branch, he had good reason to be optimistic. Spurred by a general quickening of the global economic pace, increased investment, technological innovation, and massive immigration, the Canadian economy entered the twentieth century on the crest of a boom that continued until 1912–13. The First World War also served as a catalyst for economic growth. When Canadians emerged from "the war to end all wars," they did so as citizens of an urban industrial nation.

• Economic Structures

In the half century following Confederation, Canada's Gross National Product multiplied five times. This was an impressive achievement for a young nation. Sustained economic growth is what distinguishes industrial from pre-industrial societies, and Canada's overall performance in this period suggests that an economic takeoff was occurring. While GNP is an important measure of economic growth, the GNP per capita is a more revealing indicator of economic performance. Table 5.1 shows that the overall GNP grew much faster than the per capita GNP. The increase in the population, which grew from 3.5 to nearly 9 million between 1867 and 1921, accounts, in part, both for the soaring GNP and for the less spectacular per capita growth. Nevertheless, the increase in per capita GNP *and* population offered undisputed evidence of improved productivity. Of course, in economies such as Canada's, where wealth is unequally distributed, the per capita GNP may bear little relationship to the actual income received by some, or even a majority of, people.

The emergence of mechanized factories in the mid-nineteenth century symbolized the advent of industrialism, but secondary industry was not the only sector of the Canadian economy transformed by the Industrial Revolution. Primary and service industries also felt the effects of new production processes. For example, the application of machines to agriculture increased farm output without requiring more labourers in the field. Similarly, the introduction of the typewriter in the late nineteenth century transformed the Canadian office. Moreover, changes in one sector often had important consequences for developments in another sector. Again

Table 5.1: GNP, REAL GNP, AND REAL GNP PER CAPITA, 1880–1920

Year	GNP*	Real GNP*	Real GNP Per Capita
1880	581	981	$231.00
1890	803	1366	286.00
1900	1057	1877	354.00
1910	2138	3085	441.00
1920	5543	3844	449.00

*Millions of dollars.

Source: William L. Marr and Donald Paterson, *Canada: An Economic History* (Toronto: Gage, 1980), 6.

agriculture offers a good example. As Canadian farms specialized and commercialized, the farm population bought more of the commodities produced in the secondary sector. At the same time, commercial farms became an important source of raw materials, savings, and labour for an expanding industrial economy.

During the course of the Industrial Revolution in Canada, the relative importance of the three economic sectors changed dramatically (see table 5.2). All sectors experienced growth, but secondary and tertiary industries expanded faster than primary industries. The timing of economic innovation and growth also differed widely from industry to industry. Footwear, for instance, industrialized quickly; jewellery making remained a craft industry well into the twentieth century. In some industries, such as baking, production at the domestic, artisan, and factory levels co-existed quite successfully. Other domestic and craft industries, such as textiles, were quickly overwhelmed by factory output. Not all industries thrived under the impact of new technologies and organizational processes. Wooden shipbuilding and sail making, for example, entered a precipitous decline in the age of iron and steam; carriage making was doomed to gradual extinction by the advent of the motor car.

Table 5.2: PERCENTAGE SECTORAL DISTRIBUTION OF THE GROSS NATIONAL PRODUCT

Year	Primary	Secondary	Tertiary	Other
1880	43.5	22.7	22.4	11.4
1890	36.6	28.1	26.7	8.6
1900	36.5	25.0	29.4	9.1
1910	30.2	27.8	33.6	8.4
1920	26.6	29.7	35.3	8.4

Source: William L. Marr and Donald Paterson, *Canada: An Economic History* (Toronto: Gage, 1980), 22.

Surprise soap cart   (Provincial Archives of New Brunswick/Taylor Collection/P5-423)

The first phase of Canada's Industrial Revolution, which occurred roughly between 1850 and 1900, was characterized by a rapid expansion of consumer goods industries, such as textiles, clothing, footwear, and cigars. The second phase, beginning around 1900, was fuelled by a surge in capital goods industries, such as machinery and equipment, and new technologies that spurred development in mining, pulp and paper, electrical and chemical industries. A strong tertiary sector, an indication that primary and secondary industries had reached a high level of efficiency, made its appearance in Canada as households looked increasingly to commercial outlets to provide goods and services once produced in the home.

Though Canada's manufacturing sector was large by 1914, its capital goods sector was weak relative to that of other major manufacturing nations. About three-fifths of capital investment in plants was imported, mainly from the United States. Charles M. Pepper, a special agent of the United States consular service, exaggerated only a little the significance of American equipment in Canadian factories.

> One striking fact is apparent, and this helps to explain why the imports from the United States have increased in spite of the steady development of Canadian industries and their partial success in supplying the

home demand. Not a factory of any kind is built in the Dominion that the installation is not made very largely from the United States. This was the case with the steel works at Sydney and Sault Ste. Marie. The electrical works at Hamilton are a speaking catalogue of manufacturers of hoists, cranes and machine tools on this side of the border. It is the case with the flour mills. . . . It is also true of the lumber mills. In mining machinery the United States may almost be said to have a monopoly, and the great smelters are its contribution to Canadian progress. So long as Canada continues to build new mills and establish new industries, the installation of the plants will be done largely by the splendidly equipped engineering works of the United States.[2]

A dependence on foreign technology led to a mediocre research record within Canadian corporations and an inability in most cases to compete in international markets against American and European products. With the tariff protecting the home market, most Canadian manufacturers seemed unconcerned about their relatively small share of global sales.

While Canadian economic growth was continuous from 1867 to 1921, economists have identified economic cycles that determined the rate of growth. Long-swing cycles in economic performance, relating to the opening of new economic frontiers and Great Britain's dominant role in the international capital market, were particularly important prior to 1914. The long-swing cycle rose after 1896 and had begun to slope downward in 1913 when the First World War sent it soaring. Shorter business cycles, reflecting rates of investment, also characterized this period. Between 1893 and 1896 and again in 1903 and 1907 the economy experienced a temporary slowdown. Shorter annual cycles were also important in the Canadian context where primary industries, construction, and transportation were influenced by seasonal considerations. In port cities such as Montreal the seasonal cycle of work and wages was particularly obvious as the winter freeze-up heralded higher unemployment rates and lower incomes for the city's working families.

During its rise to industrial maturity, Canada remained an open economy, one in which international trade was a significant component of national income. Moreover, the Canadian economy was small relative to that of its chief trading partners, Britain and the United States. With a small, open economy, Canadians in the industrial age remained as economically vulnerable as they had been under the mercantile system that preceded industrialization. Rising tariffs in the United States, fluctuating capital markets in Great Britain, and recessions in either country were immediately felt in Canada, and there was little Canadians could do economically or politically to alter that reality. Even in good economic times, the proximity of the United States could take the edge off the performance of the Canadian economy. When the Canadian economy was experiencing healthy growth, the American economy was often performing even better, encouraging people to move across the border to find work. More people emigrated from than immigrated to Canada between 1867 and 1900, and the massive immigration of the 1901–21 period was partially offset by continued movement of Canadians to the United States. In global terms Canada's economic performance in the fifty years following Confederation was spectacular but, compared to the United States where economic activity occurred on such a grand scale, the results seemed less impressive.

Private Initiative and Public Policy

In Canada as in the United States and Britain, private initiative was the preferred vehicle for undertaking risky economic ventures. Governments at all levels encouraged and assisted private enterprise—and accumulated huge public debts through grants and guarantees to private corporations—but only became directly involved as a last resort. Largely unfettered by government regulation before the First World War, private capitalists also reaped most of the profit of their risk-taking activities. Successful entrepreneurs paid no income tax whatsoever prior to 1917 and were subject to few estate or corporation taxes. A general view prevailed that the captains of industry were the authors of their own success and deserved to enjoy the wealth that their ability and hard work had earned them. By 1921 Canada had a charmed circle of multi-millionaire businessmen who capped their careers with palatial homes, knighthoods, and unprecedented power. The people who laboured in the mines, factories, and offices of industrial Canada received far less compensation for their long hours of work.

In the first decade of the twentieth century, entrepreneurs came under increasing attack and governments were encouraged to take action to protect the public against private greed. Regulatory commissions became a popular vehicle for establishing some control over the activities of private corporations. In 1903, a Board of Railway Commissioners was set up to serve as a buffer between the disgruntled public and the railways. Federally chartered telephone companies came under the commission's jurisdiction in 1906. In exceptional circumstances Ottawa was prepared to become directly involved in economic development. Under the War Measures Act, invoked in 1914, the federal government, aided by some of Canada's most successful entrepreneurs, took responsibility for co-ordinating the whole Canadian economy.

Public money also provided much of the infrastructure, or basic services, upon which private fortunes were built. Apart from involvement in railways, Ottawa sponsored the Geological Survey, established a system of experimental farms, and subsidized cold storage facilities to enhance economic development. In 1916, at the height of the First World War, the federal government created the Honorary Advisory Council for Science and Industrial Research (later renamed the National Research Council) to take initiative in scientific research, increasingly the key to economic development.

Provincial governments also enjoyed important economic powers, especially if Ottawa did not control their natural resources. Most provinces passed legislation to encourage settlement and disposed of timber and mineral rights by sale or lease. In 1897–1900, Ontario imposed an excise tax on export of unprocessed logs to encourage manufacturing in the province. As a result of this legislation, sawmills and pulp and paper plants were established in Ontario, leading other timber-producing provinces such as Quebec and New Brunswick to adopt similar legislative measures. As we have already seen, the Ontario government took the dramatic step in 1906 of establishing a provincially controlled Hydro-Electric Power Commission to regulate private power companies, to distribute power, and ultimately to generate its own power. Although promoted as a policy to bring "power to the people," Ontario Hydro was supported by entrepreneurs throughout southwestern sections of the province who wanted access to a cheap and reliable source of power for industrial purposes.

Like Ontario, the Prairie provinces experimented with government-owned utilities, but most provincial administrations preferred to avoid the political pitfalls of direct government ownership. Municipal governments could not afford the luxury of remaining so aloof. As cities grew and services became more complex, direct involvement seemed increasingly necessary. Private companies providing water, sewerage, street lighting, communication, and transportation services in urban settings were often granted monopoly powers under their charters and, in the opinion of consumers, abused their privileged position. Christopher Armstrong and H.V. Nelles point out that "monopoly's moment" in public utilities came in the 1890s but thereafter many municipal governments either assumed direct control over utilities or created regulatory commissions to keep an eye on private corporations.[4] The result of the spate of utility development in a burgeoning industrial economy was a typically Canadian system of mixed public and private services, reflecting the circumstances in individual localities.

Transportation and Communication

Canada's Industrial Revolution needed, above all else, a transportation network to weld the country into an integrated economic unit. During the economic boom of 1896–1913, two new transcontinental railway systems,

Intercolonial Railway workers   (Moncton Museum Collection)

the Canadian Northern and the Grand Trunk Pacific, spanned the continent. By 1915 Canadians boasted over 55 000 kilometres of track capable of
shuffling goods and people from the Atlantic to the Pacific and even into
the Yukon.

Most Canadian railways were built by private corporations—the Intercolonial Railway was an important exception—and were generously supported by federal, provincial, and municipal governments. Like the
Canadian Pacific Railway Company, the Canadian Northern and Grand
Trunk Pacific received fat concessions from the Canadian public. Although
the Canadian Pacific was completed a decade before traffic matched its
capacity, it managed to make a profit. The same was not true for its newer
rivals, which were faced with bankruptcy from the beginning. Products of
the unbounded optimism about Canadian, and particularly Western
Canadian, economic prospects, these companies came crashing down
when growth rates failed to match expectations. Their owners became rich,
selling stocks and bonds to speculators at home and in Britain, while
the government of Canada risked and then lost taxpayers' money to guarantee the loans that kept these companies afloat. Between 1917 and 1923,
the Canadian Pacific's rivals were amalgamated with other government-
sponsored railways to become the Canadian National Railway system.

Governments were prepared to subsidize railway development and bail railway companies out of their financial difficulties because an integrated transportation network was crucial to the growth of a national economy. By reducing transportation costs, railways expanded the geographic range in which products could be marketed. There was little likelihood of a bushel of wheat selling at a profit in the London market before the completion of the Canadian Pacific Railway. The cost of transporting grain by cumbersome boat and overland trails made it uncompetitive in international markets. With the introduction of lower freight rates on east-bound grain under the Crow's Nest Pass Agreement of 1897, and cutthroat competition resulting from the railway-building orgy of the early twentieth century, Prairie wheat farmers emerged as highly competitive players on international grain exchanges. Similarly, manufacturers in Montreal and Toronto would have had great difficulty capturing markets in the Maritimes and the West without the network of railways that fanned sales teams and products across the northern half of the continent. Economists might debate the cost advantages of investment in railways as opposed to some other opportunity, but Canadians knew that their community was doomed if it did not have a railway. The spectacular growth of Vancouver, Winnipeg, Moncton, and many lesser centres along railway lines was graphic proof of the economic stimulus provided by the "engine of industry."

Railways not only expanded their mileage; they also improved in efficiency and service. Standard gauge steel rails, new bridges, more powerful locomotives, and specialized cars—box, pullman, and refrigerator—brought railways into the golden age of freight and passenger service. By 1900 a train trip between Halifax and Vancouver took only six days, a far cry from the months required to travel the distance by ship around South America or overland by river and road. The increased efficiency of rail communication was reflected in the postal service. Daily mail service was inaugurated across the nation in 1886 and rural postal delivery was introduced in 1908.

Ocean travel was also improving in safety and capacity. Under the auspices of the federal government, which had responsibility for navigational aids, Canada's coasts and inland waterways sprouted lighthouses, channel markers, and wharves. When the ill-fated *Titanic* was sunk by an iceberg in 1912, it shocked Canadians who had become less accustomed to marine disasters than their grandparents had been. Reliable steamship and rail service carried Prairie wheat, Ontario bacon, and Nova Scotia apples to British markets on time and usually in good condition. A market for Maritime fish in Central Canada could only be secured with efficient and well equipped transportation facilities. Increased capacity and lower rates also encouraged the traffic in immigrants, as we will see in chapter 6. Not surprisingly, major railway companies such as Canadian Pacific soon acquired an integrated transportation and communication network that included grain elevators, steamship lines, telegraph systems, hotels, and port facilities. Such integration guaranteed a more efficient—and a more profitable—operation.

While the steam engine provided the original power for an industrializing Canada, electricity and gasoline made their debut prior to the First World War. Electrically powered transportation was too expensive to compete with the steam-powered train on a national level, but the proliferation of electric streetcars in Canadian cities in the 1890s transformed the urban landscape. With more efficient transportation, burgeoning industrial cities sprawled into suburbs where people fled to escape the congestion of the urban core.

The major threat to the supremacy of steam-powered transportation was the internal combustion engine. In 1904, the pioneer automobile manufacturer Henry Ford established his first branch plant in Canada at the behest of Walkerville carriage maker Gordon M. McGregor. By 1920 the Canadian automobile industry was producing 94 144 cars and trucks and employing over 8000 people. Most automobiles were still used for pleasure, but the commercial potential of motor vehicle transport was established, and provincial Departments of Highways were improving the roads to facil-

St Catharines Street Railway (CN)

itate the latest revolution in transportation. Notwithstanding the early aeronautical experiments by J.A.D. McCurdy and F.W. Baldwin near Alexander Graham Bell's estate in Cape Breton, Canadians remained on the periphery of the aircraft industry. An American subsidiary, Curtiss Aeroplanes of Toronto, produced aircraft for military purposes during the war, but it was not until after the Second World War that aircraft transport came into its own.

The new Dominion of Canada was united not only by rails of steel. In 1902 an underground cable linked Canada with Australia. Even before rails and telegraphs spanned the continent, Alexander Graham Bell had become a household name with his highly publicized telephone call between Brantford and Paris, Ontario, in 1876. Initially perceived as a novelty, the telephone quickly became a popular necessity for business and personal communication. Yet another communication first occurred in 1901 when a wireless signal was sent across the Atlantic. Guglielmo Marconi picked up the first signal by hoisting antennae on kites flown on Signal Hill in St John's. In 1902, Marconi's Wireless Telegraph Company of Canada began to operate a transatlantic radio link from Glace Bay, Nova Scotia. At about the same time, Canadian-born Reginald Fessenden was experimenting with wireless telegraph and voice transmissions, conducting ground-breaking work that would lead to the development of radio. Fessenden's first broadcast of the human voice by radio took place from his laboratory in Massachusetts on Christmas Eve 1906.

Mass Production and Modern Management

Developments in transportation and communication encouraged the growth of a national market for goods and services. In turn, market expansion led to reorganization of the structure of industry, encouraging small-scale, owner-operated businesses to evolve into bureaucratic, multinational, multipurpose corporations. Even the census categories were changed in 1901 to reflect new concepts of business activity. In calculating manufacturing establishments only those operations employing more than five people were enumerated. Three decades earlier the average number of people employed in an establishment had been under five.

In 1891, agricultural implements manufacturer Massey-Harris was the largest corporation in Canada, gobbling up the Canadian competition and increasing sales in the United States and Europe. Between 1890 and 1911 Massey-Harris accounted for 15 percent of the manufactures exported from Canada. Production was concentrated in Toronto, Brantford, and Woodstock and management "rationalized" into departments specializing in such areas as sales, advertising, and accounting. In its mechanized factories Massey-Harris produced a high volume of standardized products with interchangeable parts. Parts and service became an important selling point for the company, as it would later become for automobile manufacturers. Before the end of the century, Massey-Harris had established a major facility for research and development, explored the use of moving pictures for advertising, and diversified into bicycle production. Meanwhile, the Massey name graced the great concert hall in Toronto and the family fortune sustained such public charities as Toronto's Fred Victor Mission. Although International Harvester located in Canada in 1903, Massey-Harris survived the competition from the American branch plant and established its own branch plant in New York state in 1910.

The Massey-Harris story was repeated, usually with less success, in a variety of Canadian industries. As family firms and partnerships grew in size and complexity they usually turned into corporate enterprises. The limited liability corporation separated individual wealth from corporate wealth and made corporations independent legal entities. No longer tied to the fate of one or a few individuals, the corporation took on a life of its own. At the same time, ownership was divorced from management functions, which were increasingly carried out by salaried employees. No individual, no matter how energetic or gifted, could keep on top of the details of such rapidly expanding businesses. Nor was such control desirable. Chief executive officers needed their time to mobilize capital and plot long-range corporate strategy.

Control over day-to-day operations of large corporations was achieved through structural reorganization. At the turn of the century, management techniques became the focus of attention for business people trying to maximize the profits of their enterprises. *Scientific management,* a term coined by American Frederick W. Taylor, advocated that managers take responsibility for co-ordinating the work processes and that employees be deprived of any initiative or authority in deciding how to do their work. On the shop floor this meant that the labour process was broken down into simple repetitive tasks and that employee output was closely monitored by supervisors. At the management level, rigid hierarchies with clear lines of authority were developed and new accounting procedures implemented to control production and labour costs. When Henry Ford perfected the assembly line for his Model T in 1914, artisans who once performed the most skilled of manufacturing operations—the assembly of complex machinery—had been forced to submit to the dictates of management and the machine.

The bureaucratic structures in place, corporations could survive their founders. Indeed, control often passed out of the hands of founding families altogether if there were no talented sons or nephews to inherit the business (daughters and nieces being systematically excluded from corporate boardrooms). The only limit to the continued success of corporate enterprise was failure to compete in the marketplace. Driven by the Darwinian logic that held that only the fittest survived, successful corporate managers were forced to keep ahead of the competition. Yet historian Michael Bliss has revealed that Canadian entrepreneurs were decidedly unenthusiastic about unrestrained competition.[4] While giving lip-service to the god of free enterprise, they secretly agreed to fix prices and agitated publicly for policies that would guarantee them a "living profit." Nationwide associations, such as the Dominion Wholesale Grocers Guild, Retail Merchants Association, Canadian Manufacturers Association, and Canadian Bankers Association, tried to regulate the activities of their members. Restrictions on "unfair" trading practices often failed to bring order to the marketplace because it took only one entrepreneur to break an agreement. For most businesses, growing bigger meant becoming more efficient, reaping the benefits of economies of scale, and gaining an edge over competitors. The consequences of "bigger is better" thinking soon became obvious. If a company could become big enough, it might be possible to sweep all competition aside and establish a monopoly over the marketplace.

Monopoly was a bad word in industrializing Canada. It had unsavoury connotations reaching back to the mercantile era when monopolies had been granted to the King's favourites; it also flew in the face of the liberal doctrine of free enterprise. When American business people began using trusts and holding companies to dominate the market, their government passed anti-combines laws designed to prevent such monopolistic practices. Canada did likewise as early as 1889, though the combines tradition that emerged in Canada followed British precedents, which held that combination in itself was not illegal unless it was demonstrably against public interest. A spate of mergers in the 1880s was followed by an even bigger merger movement in the early twentieth century. Between 1909 and 1912, some 275 Canadian firms were consolidated into fifty-two enterprises, capitalized at nearly half a billion dollars.

The merger movement brought to the fore some of Canada's major corporate giants, including the Steel Company of Canada, the Canadian Cement Company, and Sherwin-Williams Paints. These vertically integrated companies were capable of handling all the functions of the industry, including supplying their own raw materials and shipping their products in company-owned boxcars. Their vast assets enabled them to mobilize capital on a scale hitherto unimaginable. Although such companies were technically not monopolies, their size gave them tremendous power in the reorganized marketplace. They could outbid and outlast their smaller competitors and make it difficult for new competitors to break into the industry. The fact that many of the companies established at the turn of the twentieth century are still household names in Canada—Imperial Oil, Bell Canada, General Electric—is visible testimony to their triumph over the "invisible forces" of the marketplace.

The longevity and stability of corporations has been a key feature of industrial capitalism. So, too, has been the emergence of an array of financial intermediaries whose chief purpose is to mobilize capital for investment. As the Canadian economy soared to new heights, conventional sources of capital—banks, governments, and wealthy individuals—proved inadequate to the task of financing large-scale ventures. New institutions and mechanisms, many of which developed around the financing of railways, emerged to fill the vacuum. By 1920, the Canadian financial community included two stock exchanges and a complex web of insurance, mortgage, and trust companies, bond brokers and securities dealers, all designed to move money to where it could reap the greatest return.

Much of the financial frenzy of the first decade of the twentieth century was fuelled by legislation that permitted companies to issue both preferred and common stock. Bonds and preferred stock had first claims on company dividends. Common shares were virtually worthless when issued but had the potential to return dividends if the profits of the company materialized. Stock issues were often much abused, with huge paper values piled high on shaky assets. Referred to as "watered" stock when based on speculation rather than assets, common shares were a gamble both for the buyer and the promoter. But the latter usually had inside information about the corporate issue and made money from commissions even if the stocks themselves proved worthless. Despite the potential for abuse, common stocks were a surprisingly effective vehicle for mobilizing domestic and foreign capital for investment. Stock exchanges, although they had existed in Montreal and Toronto from the middle of the nineteenth century, suddenly came to life, while securities companies joined bankers and insurance agents as important players in the financial field. When mergers were in the offing, such firms as Royal Securities, Dominion Securities, or Wood Gundy were often pulling the strings and arranging for the transfer—on paper of course—of the vast sums of money required to finance the transaction.

Canada's most flamboyant financier was Max Aitken. The son of a Presbyterian minister, Aitken grew up in northern New Brunswick and turned to selling bonds and insurance when he failed the entrance examination to Dalhousie Law School. As the protégé of Halifax businessman John Stairs, Aitken became president of Stairs's new holding company,

Royal Securities, in 1903. After speculating in utilities in the Caribbean and Latin America, Aitken moved to Montreal, used Montreal Trust to take over Royal Securities, and was a key figure in the merger movement of 1909–12. His crowning achievement was putting together the Steel Company of Canada in 1910, a conglomerate that included the Montreal Rolling Mills, Hamilton Steel and Iron, Canada Screw, and Canada Bolt and Nut. Having made his fortune, Aitken moved to London where he had marketed much of his speculative stock, became a member of Parliament, bought himself a title—Lord Beaverbrook—and continued to keep an eye on his Canadian interests. Among Beaverbrook's merger-making associates was a future Canadian prime minister, R.B. Bennett, whose millions were earned in part by collaborating with Aitken to merge grain elevators and hydro-electric stations on the Prairies.

Banks and institutions dealing in mortgages, trusts, and insurance also purchased industrial securities but were usually reluctant to speculate on the grand scale typical of securities houses. Nevertheless they felt the impact of the changing business climate. After expanding its interests throughout the last three decades of the nineteenth century, the Bank of Nova Scotia in 1900 moved its head office to Toronto to be at the centre of the Canadian business community. Six years later its chief Maritime-based competitor, the Royal Bank, moved its head office to Montreal. In banking, as in other businesses, consolidation was the order of the day. Between 1880 and 1920 the number of banks operating under Dominion charter declined from forty-four to eighteen, while the number of branches rose from under 300 to 4676. Although some twenty banks had failed in this period, many more had been absorbed by the giants in the field. Successful private bankers, such as Alloway and Champion in Winnipeg, sold out to the chartered banks, in this case the Bank of Commerce in 1919, when the partners became too old to continue the operation.

No longer simply vehicles for facilitating exchange, banks, by the early decades of the twentieth century, encouraged savings accounts by paying interest on deposited money, transferred funds from their many branches to profitable investment frontiers, and developed modern management structures. The major banks often figured prominently in mergers and takeovers and formed close relationships with trust and securities companies. By 1920 the Canadian banking community had developed a reputation for stability much like the solid buildings that dominated the main streets of most Canadian towns. And, like large corporations, they were built to last. By 1920, four of the five major banks of the second half of the twentieth century—Nova Scotia, Commerce, Montreal, and Royal—had established their position in the financial firmament.

Much of the capital required to finance Canada's industrial economy was raised domestically, channelled from personal and business savings either directly or through financial intermediaries to potential profit-making ventures. When it came to large projects such as railways or corporate mergers, Canadians tapped foreign capital markets, usually British or American, but in some cases French and German. The pattern was set in the mercantile era when British capitalists developed the fur, fish, and timber frontiers; it continued with the use of British capital to build canals and railways. At the turn of the century, foreign investment, more than half as large as domestic savings, was a significant factor in fueling the spectacular growth in Canada's age of industry.

Foreign investment in the Canadian economy rose to nearly $5 billion by 1920. For many Canadians, this was a source of pride rather than concern, visible proof that the National Policy had worked. Moreover, domestic investment far outstripped foreign investment in this period. Even as late as 1926, less than 20 percent of Canadian industry was controlled by foreigners.

•Economic Sectors

We don't need the marts of Europe, nor the trade of the Eastern
    Isles,
We don't need the Yankee's corn and wine, nor the Asiatic's smiles.
For what so good as our home-made cloth and under the wide blue
    dome,
Will you tell me where you have tasted bread like the bread that
    is baked at home?

Poet Pauline Johnson's domestic metaphor summed up the smug feelings of the members of the Canadian Manufacturers Association who commissioned her poem, entitled "Made in Canada," in 1903. By that time Canadians were producing a wide array of goods and services and had even entered the age of heavy industry with new steel plants in Nova Scotia and Ontario. Johnson also reflected the CMA's general view about foreign markets. The inward-looking philosophy of the manufacturers, however, limited the extent to which manufactured goods, outside of agricultural machinery and newsprint, were keyed to export markets. Nevertheless, Canadian producers, especially those in the primary sector, exported a significant portion of their output, and by 1903 were beginning to make their mark in global markets.

Staples: Old and New

In 1867 primary occupations absorbed the energies of over half of the Canadian population. Farming contributed one-third to the Gross National Product while hunting, fishing, lumbering, and mining added another 11.6 percent. Nearly three-quarters of Canada's exports came from the primary sector. Secondary industry in Canada was dominated by what are called primary manufactures—products such as flour and lumber that are closely tied to primary resources. Although other sectors of the economy grew rapidly during Canada's rise to industrial maturity, primary output increased at an especially impressive rate. Expansion to the west and north opened new frontiers to human and capital resources, while all primary industries became more productive under the influence of new technological and bureaucratic processes. By 1921 Canada was one of the world's great resource frontiers from which furs, fish, timber, wheat, and minerals poured forth to markets around the world.

Commercialization of farming first occurred in Ontario, where agriculture flourished, stimulated by the almost insatiable British demand for staple foods. With rail and steamship service offering more reliable transportation and lower freight rates, huge quantities of Ontario's bacon, cheese, butter, and eggs found their way to British larders by the end of the nineteenth century. Ontario farmers also branched into industrial crops such as sugar beets, grapes, and tobacco and provided most of the fruit and vegetables that were canned in Canada prior to 1920.

Cattle raising in Quebec's Eastern Townships proved a highly profitable venture, and butter and cheese were exported from that province to Britain. In the Annapolis Valley of Nova Scotia, apples became a remarkably successful crop. Apples had been a sideline of mixed farming activities in Nova Scotia since the early days of the French regime. Although apples sometimes supplemented cargoes of potatoes, fish, and lumber shipped to the United States and the West Indies, attempts to send them further afield meant that their quality upon arrival was, in the words of one commentator, "better imagined than described." With the inauguration of regular steamship service across the Atlantic and cheaper freight rates, the tyranny of distance was conquered. Valley apple production increased nearly tenfold between 1881 and 1911, and doubled again by 1921 as orchards planted during the prewar euphoria came to maturity. With an average annual output of over 5 million bushels, Nova Scotia grew nearly half of Canada's apple crop and sold most of it on the British market.

The Prairie wheat boom is perhaps the most spectacular success story of this period. Between 1901 and 1913 Prairie wheat production expanded from 56 million to 224 million bushels, grain exports increased by 600 percent,

WHEAT AND ECONOMIC GROWTH

The dramatic expansion of the Prairie wheat economy was once believed to have been the engine of Canada's economic growth from 1896 to 1913. While a debate among economic historians on the relative importance of this staple's impact on economic growth still rages, estimates of wheat's significance are now generally more modest than they once were. Some economists estimate that the wheat boom accounted for only about a tenth of the 23.6 percent growth in real per capita incomes in Canada in the first decade of the twentieth century. Others suggest a higher figure, but technological change in manufacturing as well as improved markets for hydro-electricity and pulp and paper together were far more important than the expanding wheat economy. Exaggerated expectations of profit from wheat's expansion led to an over-expansion of railway facilities in Western Canada and to an orgy of land speculation throughout the Prairies before World War I. Once more realistic estimates of the potential of wheat had been accepted, many individuals had gone bankrupt and municipal finances were shaky throughout the wheat belt.

and wheat soared from 14 to 42 percent of total Canadian exports. A variety of factors came together to make the wheat boom possible: faster maturing strains of wheat, the chill steel plough (which could handle the prairie sod), gas-driven tractors, rising world prices, lower transportation costs, a steady supply of immigrant labour, and encouragement from public and private agencies. Together, these factors transformed the Prairies from a fur trade frontier to the breadbasket of the world, its wheat production second in volume only to that of the United States.

Though significant, wheat was by no means the only product of Western agriculture. Dairy farming was important in Manitoba as was mixed farming in the Park Belt of the Prairies and in British Columbia. Between 1885 and 1905 cattle ranching flourished in the Alberta foothills. Canada's "wild west" was developed by "gentlemen farmers" such as Senator Matthew Cochrane, a pioneer cattle breeder and successful shoe manufacturer from the Eastern Townships. With an embargo on American imports, generous terms for leasing land, and the completion of the CPR—all provided by the obliging Macdonald government in the 1880s—ranching fever gripped Alberta. The first cattlemen's association was founded in 1882 and Calgary, the capital of ranching country, was incorporated in 1883. With stockyards, slaughterhouses, tanneries, and packing plants all catering to the domestic and overseas beef trade, Calgary was controlled by

Jasper Avenue, Edmonton, in 1890 and 1910   (Provincial Archives of Alberta/E. Brown Collection/B4755 and National Archives of Canada/C7911)

the elite cattlemen who communed together at the exclusive Ranchmen's Club. Cattle ranching also flourished in the Okanagan Valley in the wake of the gold rush. Despite their initial success, ranchers in both Alberta and British Columbia were soon fighting a rearguard action against farmers who, armed with dry land farming techniques, insisted on breaking up the cattle range. Battles between rancher and farmer were bitterly fought. One crusty rancher, in 1919, directed the executors of his will to use the money from the sale of his estate for "the extermination of that class of Vermin, commonly known as farmers."[5] By that time the days when the rancher reigned supreme had already gone, but livestock remained an important industry in the Western provinces.

Scientific and technological innovation had an enormous impact on agricultural production. It has been estimated that the development of the fast-maturing Marquis wheat by Dominion Cerealist Charles E. Saunders added over $100 million to farm income between 1911 and 1918. While horse and human power continued to be the chief sources of energy on Canadian farms, engine power was introduced as early as 1877 when the first steam threshing machine was used in Woodbridge, Ontario. Steam threshers could process more in a day than the average farmer produced in a year and soon transformed the harvesting process. Gasoline engines and tractors became practical in the second decade of the twentieth century, but few farmers actually owned one until the 1920s.

As farming evolved from a way of life to an industry, a number of patterns emerged. Commercial farms were on the average larger, more highly mechanized, and consequently more valuable than subsistence farms, which increasingly were abandoned. In marginal areas where farming had only been one of a variety of occupations including fishing and lumbering, commercial farming proved impossible. Not all commercial farms were successful even in prime agricultural areas. Usually small and undercapitalized, most commercial farms operated close to the margin, resulting in many failures both in the long-settled East and the booming West. Bad weather, bad markets, and just plain bad luck could make it impossible to carry on, especially if the farm were highly mortgaged to pay for new improvements. One of the major problems facing farmers was that large volumes and low prices prevailed as the productivity of the agricultural sector multiplied under the influence of new farming techniques. The decline in the relative importance of farming in this period reflects the fact that fewer farms were required to meet the Canadian and international demand for food.

The Canadian fishing industry, like agriculture, reeled under the impact of new economic structures. In the second half of the nineteenth century, salting, drying, and pickling as ways of preserving fish were supplemented by canning and cold storage. Nevertheless the production of salt cod, the mainstay of Latin American and southern European diets, absorbed most of the energies of the east coast fishery. Nova Scotians began exploiting the bank fishery early in the nineteenth century and, together with the Gaspé fishers, found markets for their low-grade but cheap saltfish in the Caribbean and Brazil. Although European markets for saltfish remained strong, Canadian, and even Newfoundland, fishers were unable to meet the competition from Norway, France, and other European countries. Part of the difficulty was that the ocean fisheries were a "free" resource, one that Canadians could not own, at least beyond a three-mile limit. With state-of-the-art vessels, government bounties, efficient marketing operations, and a superior product, the Europeans easily dominated the East Coast fisheries.

Undercapitalized, internally fragmented, and geographically dispersed, the east coast fishery failed to develop the abundant resource found at its very doorstep. Family-run operations made quality control difficult, while continued production of an inferior product in the saltfish industry put Canadian fish at a disadvantage in the European markets. The same problems developed when lobster canning factories began operating in the region in the second half of the nineteenth century. Because virtually every fishing port had a canning shed, the product varied widely in quality. Communication and cold storage facilities served to centralize the fresh fish operations in a few communities such as Yarmouth, Halifax, and Mulgrave, but the salt and canned fishery remained widely dispersed and unco-ordinated.

The fresh fish industry, which by the twentieth century was steadily gaining on the canned and saltfish trade, was hampered by an oversupplied local market, a small national market, and high American tariffs against imported fresh fish. Resistance on the part of the region's many inshore fishers to expensive technological innovations and new business methods also frustrated attempts to reorganize the industry. When steam trawlers were introduced in the first decade of the twentieth century, they were correctly considered a threat to the inshore fishery and subjected to restrictive taxes and regulations. The inshore fishery undoubtedly benefited from such policy decisions, but the Canadian fishery generally fell behind its more aggressive foreign competitors.

On the West Coast, the salmon fishery developed quickly in the final decades of the nineteenth century, and by 1900 salmon had surpassed cod in value. Steveston, where a large number of canneries were built, became known as the sockeye capital of the world, exporting its canned salmon largely to a British market. A complex division of labour based on race and gender characterized the British Columbia fishing industry. White managers, millwrights, and engineers supervised Chinese men and Japanese and Native women in the canneries while Native, white, and, later, Japanese men caught the fish. In 1902 much of the industry was centralized under the British Columbia Packers Association, a company backed by eastern Canadian and American capital and incorporated in New Jersey, a state whose liberal incorporation laws made it a popular base for companies avoiding anti-trust legislation. The new company consolidated and mechanized the packing process, increasing its profits by reducing the costs of both labour and fish supply. The Smith butchering machine, whose popular name, the "Iron Chink," reflected the racist attitudes towards Asian cannery workers, processed sixty to seventy-five fish a minute and encouraged the mechanizing of filleting, salting, and weighing. When the sanitary can and the double seamer were introduced in 1912, the automated assembly line became a reality.

British Columbia was also Canada's new timber frontier. By the 1880s, most of the white pine forests of Eastern Canada had been laid to waste. The demand for lumber for construction in rapidly growing North American cities was met by the majestic Douglas fir and cedar of the west coast. Between 1871 and 1880, some 350 million board feet of timber were cut in British Columbia; in the second decade of the twentieth century the figure had risen to a staggering 13.5 billion, and lumbering had emerged as one of British Columbia's most lucrative industries.

The forests of Eastern Canada continued to produce lumber, fine woods for furniture, pit props for mines, railway ties, shakes, shingles, and laths. They also came into their own in the production of pulp and paper. Although the first groundwood paper mill was established in Valleyfield, Quebec, in 1869, it was not until the end of the nineteenth century that the pulp and paper industry took off. The skyrocketing demand for newsprint in the United States and the expiration of important patents on newsprint production attracted capital investment, while legislation restricting the export of unprocessed logs encouraged a Canadian base for the industry. With the cost of newsprint soaring in the United States, the American government removed its tariff on pulp and newsprint from Canada in 1913. By 1920, Canada was rapidly emerging as the world's leader in newsprint production, over 80 percent of which was destined for the United States.

Canada's mining industry came virtually from nowhere in the nineteenth century to international prominence by 1921. As late as 1890, nearly 40 percent of Canada's mineral output consisted of non-metallic substances such as gypsum, grindstones, clay, and cement, but the twin impact of technological innovations and rising demand generated by new manufacturing processes brought rapid changes as the twentieth century dawned.

The new era of mining activity got off to a dramatic start when gold was discovered in the Klondike in 1896. Within two years the lure of instant wealth brought 40 000 people to the Yukon and transformed Dawson from a fur-trading post to western Canada's second largest city. Within another two years, a railway connected the Yukon with Skagway on the Pacific coast,

---

MARTHA MUNGER BLACK

The Yukon gold rush drew many people into the Canadian North, but few became permanent residents. One person who fell in love with the Yukon was Martha Munger. In 1898, she left polite society in Chicago—including her husband, who decided at the last minute not to accompany her—to make the difficult journey to Dawson. Only when she reached her destination did she realize that she was pregnant. In 1901, she set up a milling business. Three years later, she married lawyer George Black, who served as commissioner of the Yukon (1912–18) and a Conservative member of Parliament (1921–35; 1940–44). During the First World War, George was a captain in the Yukon Infantry, and Martha followed him to England. There she received the Order of the British Empire for her volunteer work with Yukon servicemen and was made a fellow of the Royal Geographical Society for her research on Yukon flora. When ill health prevented her husband from seeking re-election in 1935, Martha ran in his place and, at the age of seventy, became the second woman to hold a seat in the Canadian House of Commons.

---

and prospectors were being replaced by international corporations that continued to work the rich Yukon gold fields for another sixty years.

Since the Industrial Revolution was built on resources of coal, iron, and other base metals, the discovery and exploitation of these resources became the focus of much attention. Coal mining in the Maritimes, Alberta, and British Columbia expanded in the late nineteenth century to supply Canadian trains, factories, and homes. By the beginning of the twentieth century, huge quantities of coal and iron were processed in Canada's steel plants. Even so, the demand outstripped domestic supply. Meanwhile, surveys conducted for the CPR and the Canadian Geological Survey revealed the potential wealth locked in the Canadian Shield and the western mountain ranges. When the chemical and mechanical processes for separating complex ores were developed at the turn of the century the nickel–copper deposits around Sudbury and zinc–lead–silver deposits in British Columbia became profitable fields for exploitation. Capital poured into Canada from all over the world to bring the vast storehouse of mineral wealth into production.

The discovery of copper–gold deposits at the base of Red Mountain in 1887 created an instant boom town at Rossland, British Columbia, which a decade later boasted 8000 people. By that time an American promoter, F.A. Heinze, had built a smelter at Trail, which was connected to Rossland by a narrow gauge railway. The CPR's decision to build a line through the Crow's Nest Pass resulted in the CPR buying up Heinze's interests and the incorporation of the Consolidated Mining and Smelting Company of Canada (Cominco) in 1906. As a CPR subsidiary, Cominco had access to the extensive capital resources, which were used to develop hydro-electrical power in the region and to solve the metallurgical problem of separating the lead–zinc ores from the Sullivan Mine in the East Kootenay region. By 1910, British Columbia's mineral output was second in value only to Ontario's, much of it extracted from the fabulous Kootenay region.

Rich mineral resources were concentrated in "New Ontario," the area between Sudbury and Hudson Bay, which was granted in huge sections to Ontario by the federal government or the courts between 1874 and 1912. Following the discovery of copper sulphides in the Sudbury Basin in 1883, there was a rush to stake claims in the area. As in the Yukon and British Columbia, prospectors and speculators were soon replaced by large corporations. In 1886 American promoter Samuel J. Ritchie established the Canadian Copper Company to develop Sudbury's deposits for refining by the Orford Copper Company in New Jersey. Two years later a smelter was constructed at Copper Cliff to concentrate the nickel–copper matte prior

Union mine, Cumberland, British Columbia, 1889 (Provincial Archives of British Columbia/A-4531)

Table 5.3: MINERAL PRODUCTION BY PROVINCE AND TERRITORY, 1900–30

Province	1900	1910	1920	1930
Nova Scotia	$ 9 298 479	$14 195 730	$34 130 017	$ 27 019 367
New Brunswick	439 060	581 942	2 491 787	2 383 571
Quebec	3 292 383	8 270 136	28 886 214	41 215 220
Ontario	11 258 099	43 538 078	81 715 808	113 530 976
Manitoba		1 500 359	4 223 461	5 453 182
Saskatchewan		498 122	1 837 468	2 368 612
Alberta		8 996 210	33 586 456	30 427 742
Yukon	23 452 230	4 764 474	1 567 726	2 521 588
British Columbia	16 680 526	24 478 572	39 411 728	54 953 320

Source: *The Canada Year Book*, 1933, 345.

to shipping. Initially considered a nuisance, nickel was soon found to have valuable steel-hardening qualities. In 1902, Canadian Copper and Orford merged to form International Nickel Company, or Inco, of New Jersey. The increasing demand for nickel–steel armour plate in a rapidly militarizing Europe led Mond Nickel of Wales to establish a base in Sudbury, which soon became the world's major supplier of nickel. By that time, discoveries of gold, silver, and cobalt along the route of the Timiskaming and Northern Ontario Railway put the names of Cobalt, Timmins, Kirkland Lake, and Porcupine on the map. The value of minerals produced in Ontario increased four-fold between 1900 and 1910 and nearly doubled again in the next decade, making Ontario Canada's leading province in the mining industry.

Quebec's rich mining frontier was slow to develop, but the extraordinary range of mineral resources inspired a variety of initiatives. At the end of the nineteenth century, foreign companies began working the asbestos deposits in the Eastern Townships. Although Quebec quickly became the world's leading producer of this rare mineral, most of the processing was done outside of Canada, and the fierce competition between mining companies resulted in overproduction, gluts, and slowdowns that made the industry highly unstable. The copper and gold deposits of the Abitibi region of Quebec were known prior to the First World War but not seriously exploited until the 1920s.

One of the major attractions of Ontario and Quebec as mining and processing centres was the availability of cheap electrical power. Ontario's initiative in developing Niagara Falls gave the province a massive source of hydro-electric power. In Quebec, American capital developed the mighty Shawinigan Falls on the Saint-Maurice River, which was second only to

Niagara Falls in its generating capacity. Shawinigan soon attracted an aluminum smelter, pulp mill, and chemical factories. By 1903, hydro lines carried Shawinigan power to Montreal. Unlike Ontario, Quebec left the hydro industry to private enterprise, giving entrepreneurs free reign to charge lower rates to commercial customers if they chose to do so. Whether publicly or privately owned, the abundant supply of hydro-electric power served as a magnet to industry. With nearly 80 percent of Canada's generating capacity in 1918, Ontario and Quebec were in the vanguard of the second industrial revolution based on mining, chemicals, and pulp and paper, which relied on abundant energy resources.

Canadian furs continued to fetch premium prices on European markets after 1867, and Canadians, in particular Canada's aboriginal people, continued to hunt and trap furs. As in other primary industries, new technology and modern business practices had a transforming effect on the way the fur industry was conducted. The Hudson's Bay Company, faced with competition, introduced bureaucratic management structures, used railways and steamships where possible, and pushed into new fur trade frontiers. Under the direction of C.C. Chipman, who was appointed director in

Fur trader from Fort Chipweyan, Alberta   (National Archives of Canada/C1229)

1891, the trade was retrenched and reorganized, much to the disgust of the old commissioned officers who, according to historian Morris Zaslow, increasingly found their bureaucratic jobs bewildering and distasteful.[6] During the First World War the international market for Canadian furs shifted from London to New York. In 1920 Montreal held its first fur trade auction. Winnipeg and Edmonton were also centres of the rapidly developing fur trading industry. The value of Canadian pelts in 1920 was over $20 million, a figure that would not be surpassed for many years.

Canadians also briefly participated in the Bering Sea seal fishery, which attracted hunters from all over the world and soon threatened the herd with extinction. At American insistence, Canada signed a treaty in 1911 agreeing to abandon the hunt. By this time, fur farming had begun to emerge as an alternative to hunting and trapping. Based primarily in Prince Edward Island, the raising of fox, mink, and other fur-bearing animals in captivity was made more practical by the introduction of woven wire enclosures in the late 1890s. Thereafter the industry developed quickly, stimulated by improved breeding methods, the growing demand of the fashion industry, and the declining population of the world's wild fur-bearing animals. By 1910 Prince Edward Island breeders fetched as much as $15 000 a pair for their silver fox on the London market, and people were mortgaging their farms to invest in the industry.

Manufacturing and Construction

The dramatic development in Canadian staple industries was a direct result of the burgeoning manufacturing sector, both in Canada and elsewhere, which absorbed resources at a rate hitherto unimagined. As industrial processes were applied to more and more industries in Canada, small operations were consolidated into larger ones, and the industrial base of the country became geographically centred in the St Lawrence–Great Lakes heartland. By 1921, nearly 30 percent of Canada's GNP was derived from manufacturing and construction, a proportion that has remained virtually constant to the end of the twentieth century.

Economists divide secondary industry into three categories: consumer goods, such as processed food and clothing; capital goods, such as furniture and machinery; and intermediate goods, such as nails and chemicals, which are required to make a final product for the consumer. By 1921 Canadians produced a wide range of goods in all three categories, though the capital-goods sector was weak relative to that of most mature industrial economies.

Canadian companies, operating under the protective tariff, continued to supply most of the footwear and textiles sold in the nation. When

Garment factory interior in Quebec City (Archives nationales du Québec à Québec/ P535/N-79-12-43)

Dominion Cotton merged with three other companies to form Dominion Textiles in 1905, the Montreal businessmen who masterminded the consolidation had a virtual monopoly over the textile industry in Canada and healthy dividends to deposit in their bank accounts.

The growth of urban markets, both domestic and foreign, encouraged specialization in the food industry. Canadian factories refined sugar, packed spices, milled flour, distilled liquor, brewed beer, and made bread, biscuits, and candy. While production was geared to a domestic market, a few products did well in the export trade. One such product was Ontario pork, which could be shipped long distances once it had been cured in salt. Ontario farmers increased their production to supply the needs of the industry, and in 1899 William Davies' meat-packing company in Toronto slaughtered nearly 450 000 Canadian-grown hogs. With 300 workers and export sales of over $3.5 million, William Davies Company boasted that it was the largest pork-packing plant in the British Empire. In the first decade of the twentieth century Canadian bacon took second place to the Danish product, but by that time the domestic market had developed to take up the slack.

The cheese industry experienced an even more dramatic expansion. Once the Dairymen's Association solved their problems with quality control, Canadian cheese, like Canadian bacon, found a British market, and export sales skyrocketed from 8.3 million pounds in 1871 to 189.8 million in 1899. Canadian cheese production remained a decentralized activity and by the turn of the century had spread from Ontario to Quebec and the Maritimes. Although Canadian producers made their reputation with their cheddar, they also invented processed cheese, upon which A.F. McLaren of Ingersoll built a thriving business. Following the First World War he was bought out by another Canadian-born cheese maker, J.L. Kraft, who, in 1905, had moved to Chicago where he became the world's most successful cheese maker.

Even before the West really began to boom, the geographical structure of Canadian industrialization had taken shape. Montreal financial interests, as we have seen, had managed to exert their dominance over Maritime initiatives. Meanwhile, Ontario had gone from strength to strength, largely in response to its own expanding market. By 1900 Ontario accounted for fully 50 percent of the gross value of Canadian manufacturing, Quebec for 30 percent, the remaining 20 percent sprinkled throughout the Dominion. Once set, this pattern remained remarkably constant, although for a brief period between 1915 and 1925 Quebec's manufacturing sector dropped well below 30 percent as Ontario surged ahead under the twin impact of the war and western development. Neither the Maritimes nor the Western provinces managed to emulate the manufacturing success of the Central Canadians whose head start in the Industrial Revolution was evident even before Confederation.

One exception was the steel industry, which, at the turn of the century, was centred in Nova Scotia. In 1900 the Nova Scotia Steel Company of New Glasgow, which had been producing steel since 1882, acquired Sydney Coal Mines, built a new steel plant in Sydney, and reorganized as Nova Scotia Coal and Steel, capitalized at $7 million. Hard on the heels of this triumph came the Dominion Iron and Steel Company, the brainchild of Boston industrialist H.M. Whitney and a syndicate of Boston, New York, and Montreal businessmen. The capital of $15 million was raised largely in Montreal, and American interests soon withdrew in favour of Canadian shareholders. By 1902 the company employed 4000 men at its blast and steel furnace works in Sydney, which had temporarily become the centre of Canada's Industrial Revolution.

Ontario spawned two steel complexes of its own. After several false starts, the Hamilton Steel and Iron Company began pouring open-hearth steel in 1900 and established its dominance in the field following its reorganization as Stelco in 1910. Meanwhile, American visionary Francis Hector Clergue capped his industrial empire at Sault Ste Marie with a massive steel and iron works. In 1902, Clergue's Algoma Steel Company produced the first steel rails in the Dominion, but the following year Clergue ran out of money, and Algoma Steel became the sickly cousin of the big four steel companies of Canada. Algoma was only a minor setback in the otherwise rapid growth of Canada's iron and steel industry. Between 1877 and 1900 Canadian iron production increased over six-fold and multiplied ten-fold again by 1913, at which time Canadian plants poured over one million tons of iron, much of it converted to the steel required to run the wheels of modern industry.

Canada's capacity to produce capital goods expanded impressively during the first two decades of the twentieth century. In addition to the rails and rolling stock required for the railways, Canadian factories turned out binders and seed drills, bicycles and carriages, furniture and appliances to satisfy the Canadian market. Canadians also enthusiastically embraced the automobile age. No less than thirty-nine Canadian and eight American companies were established to build cars in Ontario alone prior to 1921. By that time, Ford, General Motors, and Chrysler, the "big three" American companies that would eventually dominate the North American automobile industry, were already well established, finding Canada a useful base from which to supply a British Empire market.

As manufacturing became more complex, intermediate goods required in the production process became a larger segment of secondary industry. Acids, alkalis, and heavy chemicals were essential ingredients in pulp and paper, iron and steel, oil refining, the electrical industry, and even in agriculture. Because chemical production often required vast quantities of electricity, plants were located near power sources. The Canada Carbide Company, for instance, became a subsidiary of Shawinigan Water and Power which controlled the vast Shawinigan dam in Quebec. Used in making everything from fertilizer to bleaching powder, calcium carbide was also a component in the manufacture of ammunition, an item in high demand during the First World War. Among the most successful intermediate goods industries were those producing the bolts, nails, nuts, screws, and similar products that quite literally held the products of industry together.

Given the economic growth in this period, it is hardly surprising that construction materials such as lumber, bricks, glass, stone, and cement figured prominently in the secondary sector. The demand for factories, public buildings, homes, and tenements sustained a construction industry that accounted for over 5 percent of the GNP by 1921. Although the construction industry itself was highly decentralized in this period, the same patterns of consolidation and centralization were at work in the manufacture of construction materials. A good case in point is Portland cement. Rock cement had a long history of use in construction, but Portland cement, or concrete, was only invented in the early decades of the nineteenth century.

Canadians began producing concrete on a commercial basis early in the 1890s, at which time output began to increase at a rapid rate. In an effort to control the industry, nine firms—five in Ontario, three in Quebec, and one in Alberta—were consolidated into the Canadian Cement Company in 1909 by the ubiquitous Max Aitken.

Serving the Industrial Economy

While the primary and secondary sectors provided much of the drama surrounding Canada's rise to industrial maturity, the service sector emerged as the major contributor to Canada's GNP by the end of the First World War. The Industrial Revolution in Canada and elsewhere was carried forward by a growing army of clerks, cleaners, cab drivers, cooks, and secretaries as well as managers, bankers, lawyers, engineers, and civil servants. In 1921 as many people worked in service industries as in the primary sector; they performed jobs, such as electrical repair, automobile sales, and switchboard operation, that could scarcely have been imagined in 1867. Since it is impossible to discuss the evolution of the many emerging service industries, we will focus on office workers as a case study.

The *Monetary Times* of 1 October 1920 offered the following observation: "The construction of the modern office grows constantly more like the construction of the factory. Work has been standardized, long rows of desks of uniform design and equipment now occupy the offices of our large commercial and financial institutions. With the increased division of labour each operation becomes more simple. The field in which each member of the staff operates is narrower." The modern office, like the mechanized factory and the limited liability corporation, was a hallmark of the industrial age. As industries became larger, efficient administration determined entrepreneurial success or failure. Managers and clerks staffed the new offices of corporate capitalism, taking orders, checking inventories, corresponding with suppliers, and generally ensuring that the company operated smoothly and at a profit. New notions of management efficiency were applied in the office much as they were in the factory. By 1921 the general bookkeeper and office worker had been replaced by accountants, stenographers, secretaries, filing clerks, and telephone operators, while typewriters, telephones, and Hollerith punch card machines were an integral part of the bureaucratic process. Those who worked in offices might wear white collars, but the structure of their work increasingly resembled that of blue-collar factory workers.

Clerical work was one of the fastest growing occupations in an industrializing Canada. While the general labour force grew by 10.4 percent between 1891 and 1901, the clerical sector rose 73.3 percent. The growth continued in the first decade of the twentieth century and reached an astounding 109.3 percent between 1911 and 1921. By the latter date clerical workers represented nearly 7 percent of the labour force. Another change had also taken place in this thirty-year period. In 1891 women comprised only 14.3 percent of those working in clerical positions; by 1921 41.8 percent of clerical workers were women, and the trend to feminization of clerical work continued throughout the twentieth century. Women were reputed to be better at the painstaking detail required by the modern office, but they were hired because they were paid less than their male counterparts. Since most women remained in the labour force only until they married, it was also unnecessary for employers to consider their long-term job prospects. Women office workers thus helped to increase the profitability of the modern corporate enterprise and soon became indispensable to its operations.

The Wartime Economy

Canada's productive capacity received a tremendous boost during the First World War. Although the war did not change the direction of the Canadian economy in any major way, it sped Canadians a little faster down the road to industrial maturity. Markets for a variety of Canadian products increased, at least temporarily, and the value of Canadian exports doubled in the first three years of the war and doubled again by 1919. In 1913 only 7 percent of Canadian manufactures were sold overseas, a figure that rose to 40 percent during the final two years of the war. Essential foodstuffs such as wheat were also in strong demand. When the war ended, overseas markets for manufactured goods contracted, restoring the prewar pattern of reliance on supplying consumer demands at home.

Canada's wartime economy, like that of peacetime, depended on private initiative, but the government found it necessary to intervene in the economy in a variety of ways. After a series of scandals and bottlenecks relating to munitions production, the government established an Imperial Munitions Board under the direction of Joseph Flavelle, Toronto financier and general manager of the William Davies Packing Company. Flavelle spurred private firms to new levels of productivity, enticed American companies to locate in Canada, and when all else failed, created government-run factories to produce everything from acetone to aeroplanes. As in peacetime, there were complaints about how federal policy was implemented. The board's patterns of granting contracts, for example, sparked accusations from Western Canada that Flavelle and his associates favoured Central Canadian firms over firms from the less industrialized regions of the nation.

Other commodities essential for the war effort were brought under similar government control. A Board of Grain Supervisors became the sole agent for Canadian wheat sales; a Fuel Controller decided the price and use of coal, wood, and gas; and a Food Board determined policy relating to the cost and distribution of food. The activities of the supervisory boards were many and various. In an effort to increase agricultural efficiency, the Food Board purchased 100 tractors from the Henry Ford Motor Company and distributed them at cost to farmers. The same board urged Canadians to eat more fish so that more beef and bacon could be released for overseas armies. Even children were encouraged to grow "victory gardens" as their contribution to the war effort.

By 1916 the Canadian economy was geared for war in a way that it never was for peace. Hostilities rejuvenated the Canadian shipbuilding industry, but in Montreal rather than Quebec City and Maritime ports. Moreover, the new shipbuilding industry gave employment to foundries and engineering companies not carpenters and woodworkers. During the war the British-owned Vickers Company employed over 15 000 people in their shipyards at Maisonneuve, a suburb of Montreal, while Davie Shipbuilding of Lauzon, Quebec, built submarines, submarine chasers, and steel barges. Between 1914 and 1918 Canada's steel mills doubled their capacity to meet British demands for shells and supplied as much as a third of British artillery needs. In addition to the stimulus provided to capital and intermediate goods industries, the war also increased the demands for food, clothing, and footwear. Farms and factories operated overtime to meet the demand, supplemented by the domestic labours of women and children who knit socks, preserved jam, and rolled bandages for the men at the front.

The twin demand for workers and soldiers resulted in a labour shortage by 1916 that required a temporary abandonment of the sexual division of labour. Women were recruited into jobs such as transportation and metal trades previously held only by men. In an effort to overcome the prejudices of employers against women, the Imperial Munitions Board published a photographic report praising the skills of women workers and offering assurances that there were "many operations in the Machine Shop which can safely be assigned to women." Over 30 000 women were hired in munitions factories during the war and many more in positions temporarily opened to women as a result of the exceptional conditions created by the war. When the war ended, women returned to their job ghettos, and the work force resumed its segregated character.

"We are justified in placing upon posterity the greater portion of the financial burden of this war, waged as it is in the interests of human freedom, and their benefit in equal if not in greater degree than our own,"

Canadian Finance Minister Thomas White opined in 1916. It was with this justification that the federal government under the sweeping provisions of the War Measures Act took a variety of economic initiatives that would have been unthinkable and, in some cases, unconstitutional, prior to the outbreak of hostilities. It suspended the Gold Standard, expanded the money supply, and engaged in deficit financing. For the first time the federal government floated loans in the New York bond market (not without some misgivings, both for economic and patriotic reasons); raised money domestically through the sale of "Victory Loans"; implemented business profit, corporation, and income taxes; established government-run industries; and nationalized half the country's railway capacity.

Strong wartime demand and expansionary monetary policies resulted in run-away inflation, which wrought havoc on those with low and fixed incomes. At the same time, inflation brought unprecedented profits to industry and made it easier for the government to finance the war effort. The long-standing tradition of borrowing from Britain was reversed during the war when British financial markets closed and the Canadian government extended credit to the mother country for the purchase of the necessities of war. Surprisingly even for Thomas White, the Canadian economy proved capable of generating nearly $2 billion in loans, and at no time during the war did government expenditures exceed 10 percent of the GNP.

The farm and labour movements let the Borden government know the extent of popular discontent at paying ever-increasing customs and excise duties while corporations fattened themselves on government wartime contracts. Borden responded with a war profits tax in 1916 pegged at 25 percent on all profits greater than 7 percent of capital for corporations and 10 percent of capital for other businesses with a capitalization of $50 000 or more. One year later, Canadians were hit with the first federal personal income taxes. The tax was a mere 2 percent on annual incomes up to $6000, a fabulous income at the time; single persons earning under $1500 and married men with family incomes under $3000 were exempted. Tax rates rose progressively to reach a maximum of 25 percent on income over $100 000.

The new taxes played a negligible role in paying for the war effort. Eighty-four percent of wartime revenues were raised via customs and excise duties while less than 1 percent came from the personal income taxes collected in 1917 and 1918. Throughout the 1920s, levels of federal corporate and personal income taxation were reduced, but in the 1930s, as all forms of revenue fell, the federal government began to rely more on the direct taxation methods introduced during the war. Nevertheless, as late as 1939, all forms of direct taxation, including sales taxes, yielded less than a third of government revenues.

When hostilities ended, the Canadian economy slumped alarmingly, and many industries failed to re-establish their prewar levels until well into the 1920s. Some industries, such as shell manufacturing, never recovered. At the same time, Canada was well on the way to becoming one of the world's great industrial nations, with all of the promise and problems associated with such a position.

• The Balance Sheet

For Canadians who had lived through the half century following Confederation, the revolution in the economy was patently obvious. Nearly half of Canadians lived in cities; manufacturing and service jobs employed three times the number of people still left in primary industries; and the material wealth of the nation had multiplied many times over. As one of the world's industrial nations, Canada had a higher status in world affairs than at the time of Confederation. Yet, the Canada of 1919 was more like the Canada of 1867 than superficial evidence might suggest. Although industrial maturity had brought the Canadian economy to a high level of efficiency, many characteristics of the pre-industrial economy had survived virtually intact, disguised by new rhetoric, perhaps, but nevertheless plainly Canadian in content.

In 1919, economic disparity between rich and poor continued to be a fact of Canadian life. The benefits of industrialism were no more equally distributed than land and wealth had been in the pre-industrial age. In every Canadian town and city hideous slums stood in sharp contrast to the elegant homes of the wealthy. William Mackenzie and Donald Mann, the swashbuckling financiers of the Canadian Northern, escaped from the collapse of their railway with a profit of $10 million while the public was left to pick up the tab. The American socialist and investigative journalist Gustavus Myers claimed in 1914 that fewer than fifty men controlled $4 billion, or one third of Canada's wealth. Certainly no one could have made such a claim in 1867. The total estate of Nova Scotia's Enos Collins, reputed to have been one of the wealthiest men in British North America when he died in 1871, was little more than $6 million. Although many Canadians were materially better off in 1919 than they were a generation before, others were not. Though the evidence is hotly debated, studies of both Montreal and Toronto, Canada's two largest cities throughout the period, suggest that the standard of living for working people did not improve during the turn-of-the-century economic boom. Indeed, the average working-class family remained poor, condemned to overcrowded housing, often inadequate diet, and resources too limited to cope with health emergencies and other crises.

The contours of poverty in industrial Canada also bore a shocking resemblance to earlier times. People of colour, especially aboriginal peoples and blacks, occupied the bottom rung of the economic ladder, as they had fifty years earlier, and every attempt was being made to ensure that Orientals did not set their sights too high. By 1919 a few men from most white ethnic groups managed to achieve economic success, but the business elite was dominated by the Canadian-born descendants of British immigrants, many of whom sent their children to the same schools and vacationed in the same fashionable waterholes—Murray Bay in Quebec, St Andrews in New Brunswick, and increasingly the Muskokas in Ontario. Although French Canadians constituted nearly one-third of the Canadian population, they made up less than 3 percent of the business elite.

Women were also systematically excluded from high-earning occupations, their primary economic functions curiously frozen in the unpaid world of the family. In 1920 less than 5 percent of married women worked

Building birch bark canoes, circa 1905   (Provincial Archives of New Brunswick/Taylor Collection/P5-381)

in the paid labour force, although an increasing number of single women held wage-paying jobs. No matter what their occupation or education, women in the labour force were paid less than men, and capitalists exploited the desperation of working-class women in the home. Clothing manufacturer H. Storey Company in Montreal had only 130 of its 1530 employees working on the premises in 1892. The remainder, all women, were scattered throughout the city and surrounding countryside doing piecework for a pittance in their "spare time" at home.

Stephen Leacock, who taught political economy at McGill University, poked fun at the new class of plutocrats who grew fat on the backs of the poor. In his *Arcadian Adventures of the Idle Rich*, published in 1914, pluto-crats were portrayed as crassly oblivious to the ironies in their discourse as they lingered over lunch at the Mausoleum Club:

> You may hear the older men explaining that the country is going to absolute ruin, and the younger ones explaining that the country is forg-ing ahead as it never did before; but chiefly they love to talk of great national questions, such as the protective tariff and the need of raising it, the sad decline of the morality of the working man, the spread of syndicalism and the lack of Christianity in the labour class, and the awful growth of selfishness among the mass of the people.

As with social class, the geography of Canadian development also reflected relative positions at the starting line in the middle of the nine-teenth century. Ontario, like its earlier manifestation Canada West, was the most populous and prosperous of the Canadian provinces, its ascendancy even more pronounced in 1919. Quebec, lagging economically behind its Central Canadian neighbour, was still tragically divided between its English and French inhabitants, though Montreal was now overwhelmingly French, because of the magnetic attraction to rural Quebeckers of jobs found in the city's booming industrial sector. The Maritime provinces, reluctantly drawn into such an unbalanced Confederation, continued to lag behind the rest of the country in standard of living and still harboured grievances against "Upper Canada." The West, now divided into provinces, showed signs of its frontier mentality—brash, optimistic, and open for develop-ment—despite the postwar slump that betrayed the vulnerability of its largely primary economy.

The tensions between town and country had survived the unequal race for development that saw wealth and population increasingly concen-trated in cities. The depopulation of rural areas and the material poverty of rural life in an age of opulence created a dramatic tension in Canada that was clearly stronger in 1919 than it had been earlier. The "rural problem"

THE CO-OPERATIVE MOVEMENT

One of the most significant challenges to the capitalist approach to industrial development came from the co-operative movement, which was particularly strong in rural Canada. Originating in Britain in the 1840s, co-operatives were organized on the principle of co-operation rather than competition and were owned by their members rather than by anonymous investors. Between 1860 and 1900, farmers in the Maritimes, Quebec, and Ontario developed over 1200 co-operative creameries and cheese factories. They also organized insurance companies to provide protection against crop failure and fires. Alphonse Desjardins in Quebec used co-operative principles to establish a chain of credit unions, or *caisses populaires*. In the West, grain farmers, led by E.A. Partridge, organized the Grain Growers' Grain Company in 1906 to market directly to buyers in Europe. The creation in 1909 of the Co-operative Union of Canada brought like-minded people together for education and lobbying activities. Although its early goal of eliminating capitalist competition was never achieved, the co-operative movement was a major political force in Canada by the second decade of the twentieth century.

was the subject of concern among politicians, parsons, and publicists who advocated a variety of remedies. Despite co-operative ventures, government programs, and efforts to provide rural uplift, Canada's population continued to drift to the cities, the pulsing heart of industrial society.

The Industrial Revolution had done little to make Canadians more respectful of their environment. Resources were exploited until they were exhausted with little thought to conservation or the impact on human health. Sawdust from lumber mills clogged rivers and destroyed fish stocks; the effluent from factories poisoned sources of drinking water; and factory smokestacks made breathing difficult, even hazardous. Only the example of the United States inspired the federal government to set aside Banff Hot Springs Reserve and Rocky Mountain Park for public use as the CPR reached completion. Following the North American Conservation Conference called by President Theodore Roosevelt in 1909, the Canadian government established a Canadian Commission of Conservation. Under the energetic direction of Clifford Sifton, the CCC investigated everything from fur farming and urban planning to power development and migratory birds. Most business people, however, saw little need for the planned management of resources and had no sympathy whatsoever with reformers who wanted to preserve rather than exploit the nation's wealth. Frustration with the Borden administration and jurisdictional disputes caused Sifton to resign in 1918. The Commission was abolished three years later, and Canadians entered the next phase of industrial development with as little concern for conservation as they had during their rise to industrial maturity.

A few Canadians in 1919 felt that lessons could be learned from the wartime experience in which centralized boards imposed some order on the unregulated marketplace, but many more saw the war as the triumph of economic democracy over the archaic forces of absolutism. As soon as it was safe to do so the Canadian government abandoned most of the wartime boards and regulations and left the marketplace to the free enter-prisers whose motto after the wartime experience could be summed up as "big is good but bigger is better."

• American Investment:
A Historiographical Debate

How important was American investment to Canada's industrial development before the First World War? What impact did it have on the character of that development? Could foreign control have been avoided?

For some economic historians, the answer is that American investment was unimportant before 1945. It was a fraction of British investment throughout the booms and recessions from 1896 to 1913, when most firms were Canadian owned. Others suggest that the pattern for future American domination of the Canadian economy was evident before 1919. While British capital in Canada was largely in the form of portfolio (or loan) capital, American investment was mainly direct investment aimed at starting up or buying out companies in Canada and exporting profits back home. Though American individuals and companies controlled only about 10 percent of all Canadian manufacturing in 1919, American predominance was greatest in new and expanding industries such as chemicals, electrical goods, petroleum refining, and automobiles, while Canadian control continued in older industries such as food processing and clothing and textile manufacture.

Political scientist Glenn Williams observes that direct investment, later the key to American control of Canadian industries, was not initially the way that American control was exercised.[8] Instead, licensing agreements that gave Canadian-based firms the right to manufacture an American firm's product for the Canadian market were more common. Such agreements usually restricted the licencee's right to export and encouraged Canadian manufacturers to produce for a national rather than an international market. Similarly, foreign-owned firms in Canada were restricted by their parents from exporting and had little incentive to do research to make their products internationally competitive.

As historian Michael Bliss has suggested, Macdonald intended that the National Policy tariff would induce American firms to set up branch plants in Canada. In the thinking of the time, it mattered little if a firm was Canadian or foreign owned. If it was located in Canada, it was a Canadian firm.[9] From the viewpoint of conservative economic historians such as Kenneth Norrie and Douglas Owram, one would be guilty of projecting the perspective of a later period backwards to criticize the view of foreign ownership espoused by Macdonald and those who agreed with his policies.[10] Canada was, after all, a late industrializer, and foreign investment speeded up its industrial maturation.

Williams and sociologist Gordon Laxer[11] take issue with this position. They note that notions of state–business collaboration to prevent foreign ownership and to maximize possibilities of capturing export markets were by no means unknown at the turn of the century. Both Sweden and Japan, late developers like Canada, followed economic development policies whose aim was to achieve autonomous ownership and viable exports. Both did so despite a host of foreign suitors anxious to establish or take control of local industries. Williams suggests that local elites in these countries were largely responsible for this economic model; Canadian elites, content with an import substitution model, lacked vision. Laxer suggests that agrarian nationalism was an important political force in those countries that eschewed foreign control. The patriotism (some would say xenophobia) of farmers in many countries was reflected in support both for a strong military and an economy with minimal foreign control. In Canada, however, agrarian political influence was dissipated by ethnic and regional antagonisms and openness to outside control established during the colonial era.

•Notes

[1] H.V. Nelles, *The Politics of Development: Forests, Mines and Hydro-Electric Power in Ontario, 1849–1941* (Toronto: Macmillan, 1974), 302.

[2] Glenn Williams, *Not for Export: Toward a Political Economy of Canada's Arrested Industrialization* (Toronto: McClelland and Stewart, 1983), 25–26.

[3] Christopher Armstrong and H.V. Nelles, *Monopoly's Moment: The Organization and Regulation of Canadian Utilities, 1830–1930* (Toronto: University of Toronto Press, 1986).

[4] Michael Bliss, *A Living Profit: Studies in the Social History of Canadian Business, 1883–1911* (Toronto: McClelland and Stewart, 1974).

[5] David H. Breen, "On the Range," *Horizon Canada* (Quebec: Centre for the Study of Teaching Canada, 1987), 1234.

[6] Morris Zaslow, *The Opening of the Canadian North, 1870–1914* (Toronto: McClelland and Stewart, 1971), 62.

[7] Williams, *Not for Export.*

[8] Michael Bliss, "Canadianizing American Business: The Roots of the Branch Plant" in Ian Lumsden, ed., *Close the 49th Parallel, Etc.: The Americanization of Canada* (Toronto: University of Toronto Press, 1970).

[9] Kenneth Norrie and Douglas Owram, *A History of the Canadian Economy* (Toronto: Harcourt Brace Jovanovich, 1991).

[10] H. Gordon Lazer, *Open for Business: The Roots of Foreign Ownership in Canada* (Toronto: Oxford University Press, 1989).

• Selected Reading

Canadian economic history for this period is outlined in the following general texts: Mary Quayle Innis, *An Economic History of Canada* (Toronto: Ryerson Press, 1945); W.T. Easterbrook and H.G.J. Aitken, *Canadian Economic History* (Toronto: Macmillan, 1956); William L. Marr and Donald G. Paterson, *Canada: An Economic History* (Toronto: Gage, 1980); Richard Pomfret, *The Economic Development of Canada* (Toronto: Nelson, 1981); Daniel Drache and Wallace Clement, eds., *The New Practical Guide to Canadian Political Economy* (Toronto: Lorimer, 1985); Michael Bliss, *Northern Enterprise: Five Centuries of Canadian Business* (Toronto: McClelland and Stewart, 1987); and Kenneth Norrie and Douglas Owram, *A History of the Canadian Economy* (Toronto: Harcourt Brace Jovanovich, 1991).

Studies that focus more specifically on the post-Confederation period include Royal Commission on Dominion–Provincial Relations, *Report*, Book I, *Canada, 1867–1917* (Ottawa: King's Printer, 1940); Michael Bliss, *A Living Profit: Studies in the Social History of Canadian Businessmen, 1883–1914* (Toronto: McClelland and Stewart, 1974); R.C. Brown and Ramsay Cook, *Canada, 1896–1921: A Nation Transformed* (Toronto: McClelland and Stewart, 1974); R.T. Naylor, *The History of Canadian Business, 1867–1914* (Toronto: Lorimer, 1975); O.J. Firestone, *Canada's Economic Development, 1867–1953* (London: Bowes & Bowes, 1958); Alan G. Green,

Immigration and the Postwar Canadian Economy (Toronto: Macmillan, 1976); Kevin Burley, ed., *The Development of Canada's Staples, 1867–1939* (Toronto: McClelland and Stewart, 1970); E.P. Neufeld, *The Financial System of Canada: Its Growth and Development* (Toronto: Macmillan, 1972); K.A.H. Buckley, *Capital Formation in Canada, 1896–1930* (Toronto: University of Toronto Press, 1955); G.P. de T. Glazebrook, *A History of Transportation in Canada* (Toronto: McClelland and Stewart, 1967); G.R. Stevens, *History of the Canadian National Railways* (New York: Macmillan, 1973); T.D. Regehr, *The Canadian Northern Railway: Pioneer Road of the Northern Prairies, 1895–1918* (Toronto: Macmillan, 1976); H.V. Nelles and Christopher Armstrong, *Monopoly's Moment: The Organization and Regulation of Canadian Utilities, 1830–1930* (Toronto: University of Toronto Press, 1988). On taxation a useful source is John Harvey Perry, *Taxes, Tariffs and Subsidies: A History of Canadian Fiscal Development* (Toronto: University of Toronto Press, 1955). On the foreign ownership/control debate, see Glenn Williams, *Not for Export: Toward a Political Economy of Canada's Arrested Industrialization* (Toronto: McClelland and Stewart, 1983); and Gordon Laxer, *Open for Business: The Roots of Foreign Ownership in Canada* (Toronto: Oxford University Press, 1989).

Geographically focussed studies include Chester Martin, *Dominion Lands Policy* (Toronto: Carleton Library, 1973); Morris Zaslow, *The Opening of the Canadian North, 1870–1914* (Toronto: McClelland and Stewart, 1971); V.C. Fowke, *The National Policy and the Wheat Economy* (Toronto: University of Toronto Press, 1957); John Herd Thompson, *The Harvests of War: The Prairie West, 1914–1918* (Toronto: McClelland and Stewart, 1978); J.H. Dales, *Hydroelectricity and Economic Development: Quebec, 1898–1940* (Cambridge, MA: Harvard University Press, 1957); William F. Ryan, *The Clergy and Economic Growth in Quebec, 1896–1914* (Quebec: Les Presses de l'Université Laval, 1966); Jean Hamelin and Yves Roby, *Histoire économique du Québec, 1815–1896* (Montreal: Fides, 1971); Paul André Linteau, René Durocher, and Jean-Claude Robert, *Quebec: A History, 1867–1929* (Toronto: Lorimer, 1983); Robert Armstrong, *Structure and Change: An Economic History of Quebec* (Toronto: Gage, 1984); Ron Rudin, *Banking en français: The French Banks of Quebec, 1835–1935* (Toronto: University of Toronto Press, 1985); H.V. Nelles, *The Politics of Development: Forests, Mines and Hydro-electric Power in Ontario, 1849–1941* (Toronto: Macmillan, 1974); Ian M. Drummond, ed., *Progress Without Planning: Ontario's Economic Development, 1867–1941* (Toronto: University of Toronto Press, 1987); S.A. Saunders, *Economic History of the Maritime Provinces* (Ottawa: Royal Commission on Dominion–Provincial Relations, 1940); David G. Alexander, *Atlantic Canada and Confederation Essays in Canadian Political Economy* (Toronto: University of Toronto Press, 1983); Jeremy Mouat, "Creating a New Staple: Capital, Technology, and Monopoly in British Columbia's Resource Sector, 1901–1925," *Journal of the Canadian Historical Association* 1 (1991): 215–37.

Urban development is the topic of G. Stelter and A.F.J. Artibise, eds., *The Canadian City: Essays in Urban History* (Toronto: Copp Clark Pitman, 1984); A.F.J. Artibise, ed., *Town and City: Aspects of Western Canadian Urban Development* (Regina: University of Regina, 1981); J.M.S. Careless, *The Rise of Cities: Canada Before 1914* (Ottawa: Canadian Historical Association, 1978); Paul André Linteau, *Maisonneuve: Comment des promoteurs fabrique une ville* (Montreal: Boréal Express, 1981).

Working-class life, described more fully in following chapters, is analysed in T.J. Copp, *The Anatomy of Poverty: The Condition of the Working Class in Montreal* (Toronto: McClelland and Stewart, 1974); Michael Piva, *The Conditions of the Working Class in Toronto, 1900–1921* (Ottawa: University of Ottawa Press, 1979); Bryan Palmer, *Working Class Experience: Rethinking the History of Canadian Labour, 1800–1991* (Toronto: McClelland and Stewart, 1992); Craig Heron, *Working in Steel: The Early Years in Canada, 1883–1935* (Toronto: McClelland and Stewart, 1988); and Jacques Rouillard, *Histoire du Syndicalisme Québécois: Des Origines à nos Jours* (Montreal: Boréal Express, 1989).

The impact of industrial capitalism on women's work is explored in Janice Acton, Penny Goldsmith, and Bonnie Shepard, eds., *Women at Work: Ontario, 1850–1930* (Toronto: Women's Press, 1974); Paula Bourne, ed., *Women's Paid and Unpaid Work: Historical and Contemporary Perspectives* (Toronto: New Hogtown, 1986); Beth Light and Joy Parr, eds., *Canadian Women on the Move, 1867–1920* (Toronto: New Hogtown, 1986); Marta Danylewycz, *Taking the Veil: An Alternative to Marriage, Motherhood and Spinsterhood in Quebec, 1840–1920* (Toronto: McClelland and Stewart, 1987); Graham Lowe, *Women in the Administrative Revolution: The Feminization of Clerical Work* (Toronto: University of Toronto Press, 1987); Marjorie G. Cohen, *Women's Work, Markets and Economic Development in Nineteenth-Century Ontario* (Toronto: University of Toronto Press, 1988); Joy Parr, *The Gender of Breadwinners: Women, Men and Change in Two Industrial Towns, 1880–1950* (Toronto: University of Toronto Press, 1990); Elaine Bernard, *The Long Distance Feeling: A History of the Telecommunications Union* (Vancouver: New Star, 1982).

Michael Bliss, *A Canadian Millionaire: The Life and Business Times of Sir Joseph Flavelle, Bart., 1858–1939* (Toronto: Macmillan, 1978) and A.J.P. Taylor, *Beaverbrook* (London: Hamish Hamilton, 1972) are readable biographies of early Canadian business tycoons.

On the aboriginal economy, in a maturing industrial economy, see Sarah Carter, *Lost Harvests: Prairie Indian Reserve Farmers and Government Policy* (Montreal: McGill-Queen's University Press, 1990).

RESHAPING CANADIAN SOCIETY, 1896–1919

Louis Kon was an educated Russian immigrant who arrived in Canada in 1908. In the following year, he recounted his early impressions of his adopted land.

> I inhabited in the Capitol of the golden North-West [Winnipeg].
>
> Broad streets and sidewalks, electric street-cars and light, fancy carriages and autos, very nice and big sensible hight buildings, up to date cafes, restaurants and hotels, most fashionable goods in lovely trimmed store-windows, a few theatres and every comfort charm and luxury of an modern city. . . .
>
> Some place in Alberta I met on the trail of a farmer driving a very nice teams. . . . [W]orking few years as in a factory he saved money enough to start the farming in proper way. Now beside a valuable property he has got few thousand dollars in bank.
>
> "Yes, my boy," said the farmer, "in my own country I would never be secure of my life. My children and grandchildren would be always poor laborers, uneducated people, living from day to the day without a prospect for better days and quiet hours."
>
> Lucky enough I found work on the C.P. as mason helper, carrying stones, cement, mixed concrete, learning again more English words and experiencing new kind of life in "box-car."
>
> Would somebody tell to me a couple of years ago, that I'll live in box-car, which suppose to serve for transporting cattle and freight, I would call him for duel. But now I blessed the hour I could get it.[1]

It is revealing that, in a land of prosperity, Kon felt grateful for a boxcar to call his temporary home. Why was there still such poverty in Canada during the years that have been characterized as the "Laurier boom"? This chapter explores the diversity of Canadian society during the early part of the twentieth century and attempts to explain why social tensions and poverty persisted in an age of overall economic growth.

Few Canadians in these years doubted that big was better: big meant that Canada could maintain its independence in North America, perhaps eventually challenging Britain and the United States for world leadership. A larger population was crucial to the hopes of both French- and English-speaking citizens. More births and more immigrants—preferably agriculturists from Great Britain, Northern Europe, and the United States—would help to guarantee future Canadian dominance, whether in trade and industry or culture and morality.

The meaning of the increase in population from 5.1 million in 1896 to 8.3 million in 1919 was nevertheless sorely debated. Was it a source of strength or did it bring with it more drawbacks than benefits? How were the traditional inhabitants of the Dominion to deal with newcomers who had very different origins and customs? What did being Canadian mean? Whatever their fears or hopes, Canadians, old and new, struggled to come to terms with a country whose farms and cities, families and homes, schools and churches, workplaces and culture were changing, often dramatically.

• Population

Unchanged was the fact that Canadians remained transient, moving in and out of regions and the country itself in response to the rise and decline of individual and family fortunes. Thousands of newcomers from Britain, the United States, Europe, and Asia—from a low of 16 835 arrivals in 1896 to a high of 400 870 in 1913—added to the picture of a nation and a continent in movement. In many ways, Canada in these years can be visualized as a gigantic railway station in which crowds mingled, often only for brief periods, then journeyed on to seek their fortunes in a wide variety of destinations. Despite relatively high levels of fertility and immigration, population growth nevertheless remained less than might have been expected since many Canadians, both native-born and immigrants, continued to try their luck in the United States. Still, in comparison to the thirty years after Confederation when Canada experienced a net migration loss, this period was one of growth and optimism.

In the late 1890s the upsurge in the world economy, gold discoveries in the Yukon, the disappearance of the American frontier of free land, and a major immigration campaign on the part of the Canadian government translated into unprecedented numbers flocking to the Dominion. While the number of Canadians had risen only 24 percent in 1881–1901, it increased 64 percent in the first two decades of the twentieth century. For the first time, Canada's attractions seemed to match, even to surpass, those of its southern rival. Ironically, this was also a time of increased American influence in Canada. With important resources of financial and human capital and dry lands expertise, Americans were well qualified to till the cheap and fertile lands of the "last best west." Also, as we saw in the previous chapter, American corporations entered the Canadian market in larger numbers, setting the standard in everything from food and automobiles to film production and publishing. Canada was faced simultaneously with questions of how to integrate large numbers of newcomers into the community and how to balance British and American influences in a society where the national identity was far from set.

The early twentieth century saw distinct shifts in the concentration of the population. While over half the Dominion's population continued to live in Quebec and Ontario, the proportion of Canadians calling these two provinces home dropped from 74.6 percent in 1891 to 60.3 percent in 1921. For the Maritimes, growth was disappointing: in 1891 the region had made

Galicians at immigration sheds in Quebec City   (National Archives of Canada/C4745)

up 18.2 percent of Canada's population; three decades later this figure had fallen to 11.4 percent. Indeed Prince Edward Island's 1921 population was smaller than it had been in any decade since the 1860s. The great beneficiary of national and international migrations was the West. Between 1901 and 1921, the percentage of the Canadian population living on the Prairies increased from 7.8 to 22.3 percent while the percentage in British Columbia rose from 3.3 to 6.0 percent. Increasing European populations in the Northwest Territories forced the federal government to accede to popular demands to create the provinces of Alberta and Saskatchewan in 1905.

Even more apparent than the dramatic shift in population was the emergence of distinctive regional demographic patterns. In the Maritimes, outmigration remained the dominant trend in all but a few industrial centres. Maritimers continued to be attracted to the New England states where jobs were plentiful and wages higher than at home. Because immigrants to Canada by-passed the Maritimes to concentrate on opportunities further west, the region's population remained largely native born. The only challenge to anglophone dominance in the Maritimes was the dramatic growth of New Brunswick's Acadian community, which between 1901 and 1921 increased from one-quarter to nearly one-third of the province's population.

In Quebec, the anglophone communities in Quebec City and the Eastern Townships were shrinking. Even in the rapidly growing industrial city of Montreal, the proportion of anglophones was dwindling under the impact of European immigration and the migration of French Canadians from the countryside. Emigration from rural Quebec to New England, so pronounced from 1870 to 1900, slowed to a trickle, ensuring the continued domination of French Canadians in the province. Ontario attracted more immigrants than its eastern rivals, but a substantial majority of its citizens continued to be of British stock. Thus, to a large extent, the Maritimes and Central Canada remained home to those of British and French origin, maintaining the dualism that was central to the Confederation agreements.

Only on the Prairies was this tradition significantly challenged. That region's original distinctiveness was confirmed by a deepening cultural diversity that would remain unknown to much of the rest of Canada until well after the Second World War. By 1921 the three Prairie provinces, with about one-quarter of the country's population, contained 54 percent of foreign-born Canadians. People of British stock lived side by side with Eastern and Western Europeans, each of whom contributed about 20 percent to the population of Manitoba, Saskatchewan, and Alberta. The result was not an idealized mosaic of different peoples or even the melting pot favoured in the United States. Rather, new arrivals were to be moulded to the values and institutions of the British majority, in what Howard Palmer has termed "Anglo-conformity."[2]

Native Canadians, for whom the pervasive controls of the Indian Act continued to apply, were similarly subject to pressures to conform to the culture of the majority. The residential schools continued to separate many children from their parents and to teach them to scorn traditional Native religious and cultural traditions and values. Diseases such as tuberculosis, resulting from overcrowding and malnutrition on many reserves, caused a continuing decline in Native populations in the Prairie region, which stopped only in the 1930s. With epidemics killing off Indians and Métis, and immigration increasing European settlers' numbers, the Native population of Alberta fell to a mere 3 percent in 1911. Fifty years earlier, Natives had made up an overwhelming majority of the population of the territory.

On the West Coast, the cultural mix varied again. In 1911, for example, Vancouver's population was 6.1 percent Asian and 73.7 percent British, with all other Europeans counting for only 11.5 percent. Chinese immigrants came first to the Fraser River gold rush in 1858, and their numbers climbed in response to employers' determination to take advantage of their cheaper labour in mines and railways. By 1921 the numbers of Chinese reached nearly 40 000. The first Japanese had arrived in 1877, but the peak of immigration from the mid-1890s to World War I brought almost 30 000 to the Dominion. Although most sent wages to their home villages and some returned to China or Japan, many Asian immigrants made their homes in British Columbia. The racist thinking and economic fears of those who wished to keep British Columbia "white forever" surfaced quickly. In 1907, whites marched through Japanese and Chinese sections of Vancouver, breaking windows and shouting racist slogans. While an isolated example, the incident indicated the depth of the antagonism faced by Asian immigrants. Antagonism was not limited to the West Coast, but that province was distinguished both by its relatively large group of Asian residents and the depth of its hostility to their presence. Racism also dogged the lives of the province's Native people, who often had their lands expropriated by the provincial government to make way for European settlers. As on the Prairies, West Coast Native populations had been decimated and their traditional subsistence economies shattered since Confederation.

The heterogeneous nature of immigration in the early years of the twentieth century did more than enhance differences among Canada's regions. Another consequence was a marked fragmentation of the Canadian labour force. The cultural cohesion that had spurred the efforts of the Knights of Labour in the 1880s shattered as the nation's workers too often found themselves without the shared traditions and language that had earlier encouraged a common front against North American capitalism. Yet the very diversity of Canada's working class, drawing as it did on every ethnic and racial group, distinguished it from the classes above it.

The more privileged the class, the more likely it was to resist entry by new-comers. Increasingly elaborate social, political, and economic networks interacted with powerful codes of behaviour to reserve power and status for a few citizens of British origin and a fewer still of French.

Under the direction of Clifford Sifton, Laurier's first minister of the interior, the federal government, hand in hand with steamship and railway companies, advertised heavily in Europe and the United States for agricultural immigrants to settle the Prairies. The government thereby hoped to provide consumers for the products of protected Canadian industry and encourage crucial agricultural exports to fuel the national economy. Immigrants, particularly women intending to take up domestic service, were equally in demand. Not only were they expected to relieve middle-class householders of the worst of domestic chores, but they affirmed the fundamental gender division of labour that most Canadians accepted as absolute.

Unlike many of his successors, Sifton was prepared to welcome Eastern Europeans, women and men in homespun and sheepskin coats, assessing them as good prospects to survive the rigours of pioneering on the Canadian Prairies. Industrialists and business people were similarly enthusiastic about such recruits, championing them as ideal candidates for the hard, low-wage labour needed in resource industries and in their own homes. Such immigrants were seen as a good deal more tractable than British or Americans who could draw on traditions of organized labour to counter corporate power. Sifton's ministerial successor after 1905, Frank Oliver, pursued much more restrictive policies. The mounting reservations about the character of newcomers could not stem the tide of those wishing to enter Canada before the First World War. In the course of roughly two decades, the Dominion changed from a society that was largely British and French to one with a much richer European and, to a lesser extent, Asian makeup.

Travel in steerage to the coast of North America and in colonist cars to the West introduced many immigrants to the hardships awaiting them in the new land. In the peak years of immigration, government officials and medical inspectors processed anxious thousands in Halifax or Quebec immigration sheds, sending most on to strange locations across Canada. A few unfortunates were rejected, chiefly for medical reasons, and families were broken up as individuals were forced to return to lands they had hoped were safely behind them. Once at their destination, settlers were left to fend for themselves, without public assistance. Ethnic solidarities proved invaluable to those attempting to make a start and to those stricken with poverty as a result of illness, family tragedy, indebtedness, a poor crop, or other misfortune. Mutual aid societies, co-operatives, and just plain neigh-bourliness rescued many families and individuals from destitution. Survival proved a good deal harder than the optimistic posters, films, and lectures supplied by the CPR and immigration recruiters had led settlers to expect. Successful farm settlement normally took years of back-breaking labour and self-sacrifice. Not surprisingly, just as in the past, many women and men decided that a better future awaited them and their children in the cities or in the United States.

Wherever newcomers ended up, their reception varied directly with their similarity to the numerically dominant ethnic group. When jobs were scarce or immigrants were believed to be morally or physically tainted, even a common heritage did not deter prejudice and discrimination. Signs in shop windows stating "No British need apply" testified to the nativism of people whose cultural roots were also British. Even children were not spared the chilly reception that awaited other immigrants. Between 1860 and 1930, some 80 000 poor British children, some as young as five years of age, were sent to homes in Canada. As historian Joy Parr has movingly documented, these "home children" encountered little sympathy and much exploitation as they were passed from hand to hand as agricultural labourers and domestic drudges.[3] Mistreatment and discrimination were not restricted to so-called paupers. An ethnic pecking order, based on the popular science of the day, placed British and American immigrants at the top of a racial hierarchy, followed closely by Western Europeans and Scandinavians. Considerably below such culturally similar communities were Central, Eastern, and Southern Europeans, Asians, and the Jewish, Mennonite, Hutterite, and Doukhobor religious groups. Last of all came American blacks, who were regarded as inferior and unassimilatable.

Despite the force of such prejudices, groups like Jews, escaping the anti-Semitic pogroms of tsarist Russia, and Chinese retreating from a homeland mired in rural overpopulation, joined other victims of religious persecution and economic disaster in coming to Canada. Men from underdeveloped southern Italy came as navvies in the 1880s and 1890s, working in mining and railway camps to send money back home. After 1900, they often settled in Toronto and Montreal and brought their families to Canada. As farmers, merchants, and labourers, the new "ethnic" immigrants quickly proved to be industrious members of their new communities. They nevertheless remained suspect in many eyes, bringing with them beliefs and practices that other Canadians did not understand.

Penalties for non-conformity could be severe. The refusal of the Doukhobors who arrived in Saskatchewan in 1899 to give up their objection to military service or their preference for communal living or to swear allegiance to the Crown—together with the nude protest marches conducted by the radical Freedomite sect—resulted in the confiscation of over half of their lands in 1907. Such treatment led the more radical members of this dissenting sect under Peter Veregin to move in 1912 to the Kootenays in

Doukhobor women winnowing grain   (National Archives of Canada/C8891)

British Columbia. The rapid settlement of that region by English-speaking immigrants meant that hostility soon followed the Doukhobors there as well.

Different practices in age of marriage and fertility were especially suspect. The fact that the first generation from Eastern and Southern Europe tended to marry earlier and to have larger families than those from Western and Northern Europe contributed to xenophobia among native-born Canadians who subscribed to doctrines of racial superiority and feared being overwhelmed by the "inferior races." The same concern about fertility lay behind the imposition of a head tax on all Chinese who entered Canada after 1886 and the general resistance to the entry of all people of colour. This tax prevented most Chinese men from bringing their families to Canada. Idolization of the family as an institution was a fundamental value for most Canadians, but it did not apply to persons of colour.

For many English-speaking Canadians, fear of being submerged beneath a tide of immigrants and their children was accentuated by anxiety about their relations with Quebec. French Canadians on average married earlier and produced more children than Canadians of British origin. As a result, Quebec's birth rate, although it fell, did so more slowly than Ontario's. While the long-term decline worried French Canadians who feared disappearance in North America's English-speaking sea, it was the immediate comparison that bothered those determined to keep Canada

British. Not surprisingly, the implications of comparative birth rates fuelled many of the debates over immigration, education, and urban development that disturbed Canadian public life.

Yet, for all the hard times and uncertain reception that characterized immigration to a new country, newcomers found crucial encouragement and support. Minority communities such as Vancouver's "Little Tokyo" and Saskatchewan's Jewish agricultural colonies near Wapella, Hirsch, Cupar, Lipton, and Sonnenfeld gave inhabitants opportunities to retain cherished customs and to work out collective ways of dealing, at least in part, with economic vulnerability and civil disability. In the Ukrainian settlements of east-central Alberta, over ninety community halls had been built by 1913 to host meetings, lectures, plays, concerts, dances, and choir practices. For navvies or sojourners—single males who commonly planned to return to home villages with their pockets full after working in Canada's mines, railways, and forests—the fellowship found in the boarding houses, stores, and restaurants run by their compatriots helped compensate for Canada's frequent inhospitality. Similarly, many of the 90 000 British women who emigrated as domestic servants in the decade before the Great War found friends and relatives to ease long hours and hard labour. In 1914 Ann Fisher, the daughter of a Scottish coal miner, set out alone to take up domestic service for a bank manager's family. She was far from defenceless, maintaining contacts with five other girls who came on the same boat and staying her first night in Montreal with a friend from Aberdeen. Such human resources helped to make the immigrant experience less daunting even when material advantages were slight or non-existent.

Wartime passions inflamed existing nativist sentiments. With the outbreak of war in 1914, previously favoured Germans found themselves, like former citizens of the Austro-Hungarian and Turkish empires, targets of suspicion and persecution. Enemy aliens were forced to register with local magistrates and to hand in all firearms, and over 8000 people were confined in internment camps across the country. Unemployment and police surveillance were common even when no disloyalty was evident. Feelings ran so high that Berlin, Ontario, voted to change its name to Kitchener after the British War Secretary, and in 1917 Robert Borden's Conservative Unionist government disfranchised residents who had been born in an enemy country, whose mother tongue was the language of an enemy country, and who had not been naturalized before 1902. The law had its intended effect because naturalization required five years residence in Canada and few "enemy aliens" arrived before 1897. Anti-immigrant sentiments thrived after the war as well, fuelling attacks on labour radicals everywhere, but especially in mine, lumber, and railway camps where recent immigrants were numerous. In 1919 the Winnipeg General Strike was also used as an occasion to link foreign agitators with labour protest, though the strike leaders were overwhelmingly of British origin.

• Farm Life

Although the Canadian homestead policy of 160 acres for a $10 fee and minor settlement duties seemed a bonanza to many, families settling on the land needed more than hope and industry to succeed. The minimum investment required in ploughs, oxen, milk cattle, poultry, wagons, and basic household utensils, as well as seed and sufficient supplies to tide families over until the first harvest, was reckoned to cost even thrifty families close to $1000. Few came with such a sum: it had to be earned in Canada. The solution for many immigrants was to work as labourers and domestics on more prosperous farms or to take jobs as railway navvies or miners or as servants in urban households. While husbands and older sons and daughters looked elsewhere for the cash stake to guarantee the family's future, married women regularly maintained homesteads, living for long, lonely winter months in what were often little more than shacks or in the somewhat less uncomfortable "soddies" constructed out of the prairie land itself, caring for young children and tending livestock.

While agricultural areas in the West and the North continued to attract settlers, homestead abandonment remained commonplace as settlers frequently found little in soils, climates, and markets to sustain their hopes. In parts of Central and Eastern Canada, poorer families regularly deserted the land, and small holdings were consolidated into larger, more capital-intensive operations. Rural depopulation was a cause taken up by the reform community at the turn of the century. It drew the attention of people as diverse as E.C. Drury, head of the Canadian Grange, an organization which lobbied on behalf of farmers, Henri Bourassa, a Quebec politician and journalist, and John MacDougall, a Presbyterian minister and the author of *Rural Life in Canada* (1913). For these people, rural living was as crucial to the nation's moral and spiritual well-being as it was to physical survival and food production. Farm women, discouraged by discriminatory homestead laws, unequal inheritance patterns, and the unending domestic toil that confronted their sex, contributed significantly to the female majority among the fifteen to twenty-nine age group found in many cities. The failure in these years of the homesteads-for-women movement conducted in the pages of the *Grain Growers' Guide* and the *Manitoba Free Press* helped to discourage women from taking up farming. The choice made by Louis Hémon's fictional heroine, Maria Chapdelaine, to stay to struggle with the harsh realities of settling the Canadian Shield was more rejected than imitated. By 1921 the stress of farm life had helped create a nation where the rural and urban populations were almost evenly matched.

Additional farm income tended to be ploughed back into agricultural machinery and additional acreage. The result began to transform the nature of male labour, at least on the more prosperous holdings. Men became the managers of large farm operations that increasingly developed the complexity of an urban factory. In contrast, female operations in and around the home frequently retained the character of the earliest days of settlement. Family resources often seemed to run out by the time it came to the domestic renovations, such as plumbing or wiring, that would have eased female labour. Women's efforts as mothers, housewives, and entrepreneurs nevertheless often maintained home and children on a day-to-day basis and generated essential cash through the sale of everything from butter and eggs on many holdings to the more exotic seneca root in southern Manitoba. Such earnings commonly went for store-bought essentials found in local towns and in Eaton's catalogues and helped send children to better schools and through more grades than they might otherwise have achieved.

The recession of 1912–13 threatened prosperity everywhere, but by 1916 the demands of a war economy contributed to an agricultural boom. When the promised military deferment of farmers' sons was cancelled soon after the election of the Union Government in 1917, farm women joined urban "farmerettes" to assume more responsibility for crucial wartime food production. Wartime farmers also bought more machinery in order to reduce their labour needs and expand production. In time, their purchases would sharply reduce essential income opportunities for marginal members of the farm community who laboured as wage earners on more prosperous holdings. By the end of the Great War many farmers found themselves with acreage, machinery, and production that could only be sustained by strong markets, low interest rates, and good weather, conditions that only too regularly failed to materialize.

• The Growth of the City

While rural areas and small towns often faced depopulation and stagnation, large cities grew dramatically. In the boom years from 1901 to 1911, the populations of Montreal and Toronto increased by 49 and 58 percent, respectively. Even this growth paled in comparison with that of Winnipeg, Calgary, Edmonton, and Vancouver where boosters enthusiastically pointed to respective increases of 224, 570, 216, and 324 percent in the same period. Cities offered unparalleled opportunities for money making and social and cultural development. While the new urban millionaires were invariably men, women were able to take advantage of new job opportunities in domestic service, teaching, nursing, and in the clerical, white-collar field. "New women" like Cora Hind of Winnipeg built up thriving careers, in her case first as a freelance stenographer, then as a wheat reporter for the *Manitoba Free Press*. The increasing numbers of young women who sought waged employment in these years might have shared Hind's ambitions or even her considerable talents, but they soon discovered that their careers in everything from banks to department stores were considerably shorter and lower paid than those of the men with whom they worked.

The city did not always live up to the hopes of inhabitants, but urban landscapes catalogued the exuberant optimism of these years. Banks and stores, universities and hospitals, museums and libraries, palatial private residences and apartment buildings provided architectural monuments to prosperity and ambition. To newcomer and long-time resident alike, many buildings must have seemed almost the equivalent of medieval cathedrals, highly visible symbols of the authority, power, and inspiration of modern industrial capitalism. Like the clothing and personal extravagances of Canadian business and government leaders and their families, lovingly displayed in the society pages of *Saturday Night* magazine and every local newspaper, architecture was part of the wave of conspicuous consumption on display in most Canadian cities. Railway hotels like Quebec City's Château Frontenac and Victoria's Empress, and private residences like Toronto's Casa Loma, reflected a romantic French influence, that spoke volumes for the social aspirations of the Canadian business class.

The attraction of French Second Empire style in Canadian architecture was succeeded by a monumental and equally arrogant Beaux Arts style with Roman columns, cornices, and vaults, of which Toronto's Union Station (1915–20), the Saskatchewan Legislature (1908–12), and Montreal's Sun Life Building (begun 1914) are some of the best examples. Construction advances, notably fire-proofed steel framing and reinforced concrete, changed the type of buildings that could be designed. Under the influence of the Chicago School of architects, early skyscrapers such as the Calgary Grain Exchange (1909) and Edmonton's Tegler Building (1911) began to alter the urban landscape in ways that made Canadian cities increasingly indistinguishable from their British and American counterparts. Such similarities were hardly unexpected since most important buildings were designed by American and British firms. Not until 1896 did McGill University establish the first Canadian department of architecture. Only in 1907 did the professional associations formed to control the practice of architecture in the provinces create a national organization. Two years later this became the Royal Architectural Institute of Canada. Notwithstanding such initiatives, Canadian architecture remained firmly wedded to international influences.

While the lucky few found aesthetically pleasing and comfortable surroundings in Vancouver's Shaughnessy or Montreal's "Golden Mile," many more were forced to cope with the "shame of the city" in the dirt and disease of Winnipeg's North End or Halifax's Africville. In Africville, the proximity of a tar factory, a leather tanning operation, slaughterhouses, stone-crushing industries, a fertilizer manufacturer, railway tracks, a coal port, a prison, and an infectious diseases hospital increasingly stigmatized its African-Canadian residents, just as similar developments encroached on poor areas elsewhere. The lack of water and sewerage hookups and fire protection, like the

One-room dwelling in Winnipeg, circa 1915   (Provincial Archives of Manitoba/Foote Collection/N2438)

absence of recreational facilities, which were readily available for the more well-to-do, also typified how class divided cities in visible ways. The rampant inflation of these years made it difficult, if not impossible, for many individuals to escape slums and shanties. Labour of the hardest and meanest sort brought little beyond housing that was likely to be a damp, dark, and crowded contrast to the homes of the middle and upper classes. Even such substandard housing could be lost if rents exceeded what were often inadequate or seasonal wages.

Rising urban populations quickly overran what amenities, natural and otherwise, the nineteenth-century city had to offer and proceeded to press hard on reserves of water, fuel, and space. Pollution and shortages were the order of the day for many families. The high infant mortality rate in poor districts of Montreal can be traced in large part to impure milk and water, hardly surprising since it was reckoned that 90 percent of milk shipped to Montreal in freight cars was unfit for human consumption. Richer families could afford to purchase milk that was certified pure. They were likely to live in areas served by adequate water, sewerage mains, and municipal parks. They could also escape to hideaways outside the city like those in Ontario's Kawartha District or Quebec's North Shore when weather or disease rendered urban life especially uncomfortable. In contrast, the mass of urban dwellers had to struggle to find ways of coping with the costs of city living.

Substantial differences in infant birth weight and mortality bore further witness to unequal prospects. In 1921, the infant mortality rate for Montreal's well-to-do suburbs of Outremont and Westmount was less than 6 percent. In contrast, that of west-end working-class districts was over 20 percent. Tuberculosis claimed hundreds of lives in Montreal that year. The city's working-class districts predictably saw the highest death rates. Improvements were often a long time coming. For example, Quebec did not require the pasteurization of milk until 1926. The threat posed by disease to wealthy residents did help to provoke some early public health efforts such as compulsory vaccination for smallpox in Quebec after 1903 and the opening of Montreal's water filtration plant in 1914.

The creation of the federal Commission of Conservation in 1909 and the appointment of Thomas Adams, one of the most prominent British planners of the day, as the commission's town planning adviser in 1914, signalled growing awareness that, unless Canadians were careful, their cities would repeat the problems of those elsewhere. As the commission noted,

> [industrial smoke] disfigures buildings, impairs the health of the population, renders the whole city filthy, destroys any beauty with which it may naturally be endowed and tends, therefore, to make it a squalid and undesirable place of residence, and this, at a time when economic

influences are forcing into our cities an ever increasing proportion of our population. These conditions press especially on the poor who must reside in the cities and cannot escape from these evils by taking houses in the suburbs.

•Family and Home

The primary group for most Canadians continued to be the family: kin united by birth or marriage. Those without relatives found themselves at a substantial disadvantage when the state and the private sector did little to protect the well-being of citizens. Recent immigrants often understood this reality, crowding together with distant kin in ways that offended even knowledgeable observers like J.S. Woodsworth, the Methodist superintendent of Winnipeg's All Peoples' Mission who summed up the dismay of many urban reformers in his social surveys, *My Neighbor* and *Strangers Within Our Gates* (1909). From the viewpoint of respectable society, the lack of privacy in overcrowded homes contributed to immorality. Yet sharing, as both earlier and later generations of immigrants discovered, was a sensible solution to economic uncertainty and social discrimination. Active membership in an ethnic community or labour union that in some ways functioned as an extended family also alleviated the plight of those facing ill health or unemployment. Organizations such as the Western Federation of Miners, the Sons of Scotland, and Toronto's Polish Ladies' Circle provided services that kept many compatriots afloat in bad times.

For all the significance of extended kin, the nuclear family of mother, father, and children supplied both the critical point of reference and the main form of material and emotional support for most individual Canadians. Migration, high death rates, and economic uncertainty regularly broke even intimate ties among larger groups. The benefits of family were not shared equally among all members. The husband exercised important customary and legal authority that gave him superior resources and power. British common law, despite amendments, placed wives' property and person under husbands' ultimate control. While wives had a right to dower—a lifetime interest in one-third of husbands' property upon widowhood—this was everywhere lost upon separation. After the West abolished dower rights in 1886, women's right to secure inheritance was not acknowledged until the years between 1910 and 1919 when all of the Prairie provinces legally guaranteed wives' inheritance rights and restricted husbands' ability to sell or mortgage property without spousal consent. Child custody for mothers was equally problematic. Only in the 1890s did

Canadian custody legislation grant women some redress from provisions favouring fathers, and even this concession was restricted. According to a 1907 law in British Columbia, mothers could not obtain custody of a child over the age of seven. Not until ten years later were mothers in the province given legal equality in custody matters.

The rarity of prosecution for crimes in which women were the overwhelming proportion of victims—rape, incest, battering—confirmed male authority in the bluntest possible way. Children were subject to the same authority until they reached the age of majority, married, or ran away from home. The prospect of beatings, which few police officers or neighbours dared to interrupt, ultimately kept many children and their mothers in accord with adult male desires.

Divorces were expensive and rarely granted unless adultery was proven. Between Confederation and the 1960s, divorce reform advocates in Canada were few, and the results of their efforts meagre. Notes historian James Snell:

> The absence of significant divorce reform is suggestive of the centrality of the ideal of the conjugal family and of the supportive role of the law. Family solidarity was so central to the belief system of the leaders of Canadian society that significant change in the divorce law could not easily be tolerated. The idea of the child-producing family and of the lifelong, sexually exclusive marriage was fundamental to social reproduction, economic organization, gender relations and sexual morality.[4]

People who did divorce, much like women who conceived a child out of wedlock, faced social opprobrium.

Unequal as the legal partnership was, most Canadians expected to marry, hoping to find economic, social, and emotional rewards. The domestic ideal envisioned a relationship where wives and husbands had different but complementary responsibilities. Male authority was vested in economic power, increasingly their ability to support a family through salary or wages. Women's ideal duties, at least among the middle class, were conceived as more moral, cultural, and social. While men in their roles as businessmen, lawyers, shopkeepers, and professionals might be contaminated by their contact with the world of profit, women were to protect humane values, especially in their role as mothers. Such idealized role differentiation was neither widespread nor perfect in its application. Few couples were either temperamentally or economically equipped to make such sharp distinctions. Farm women regularly worked in fields beside their husbands; wives of storekeepers were likely to be found behind the counter. Family survival often depended on women's practical economic contributions. They had little time to be the angel of the house.

Some men, such as John Moodie, father of suffragist Nellie McClung, provided essential emotional and psychological support for their wives and female children who sought less constricted lives. But most men defended the established gender roles. In Ukrainian farm households, as Helen Potrebenko observed, men would rather have sold their grain and bought back ground meal than have taken on the women's work of grinding and thus cast their manhood in doubt.[5]

Moral reformers, who were generally middle-class Protestants, generally supported clearly delineated gender roles, but they began to be concerned that men spent too little time at home. In attempts to get men out of the bars, brothels, and gambling dens, they recommended gardening and exercise as appropriate male leisure activities. The American sex educator, Sylvanus Stall, whose works were sold by the Methodist Church in Canada, advised, "In women, the love of home is usually more dominant than in men. By cultivating this in yourself you [men] will produce a harmony of thought and purpose which will contribute greatly to the comfort and well-being of both. Adorn your home with your own hands. Beautify the lawn, the shrubbery; and all external surroundings."[6]

Social ostracism and the Criminal Code penalized those who ventured outside the narrow bounds of acceptable sexual behaviour. Books and pamphlets warned against the evils of sexual intimacy outside of marriage, called for sexual moderation between husband and wife, and condemned masturbation as a "secret vice." Inevitably such literature expressed the values of the middle class and failed to have much impact on those who lived in less privileged circumstances. Couples often lived "common law," many babies arrived "early," prostitution was a fact of life on city streets, and masturbation continued to raise the hackles of doctors, parents, and preachers. Despite provisions in the Criminal Code used to prosecute them, homosexual men and lesbians were beginning to become self-conscious social groups with their own support systems.

The efforts to control sexuality sprang from a number of motives. Women anxious to eliminate the double standard of sexual behaviour advocated extending to men the strict codes that governed female sexuality. For most reformers, a life-long monogamous marriage—what the Woman's Christian Temperance Union described as "the pure white life for two"—was the bedrock of the nation. With correct family formation, the reformers argued, all manner of social evils would be eliminated, including wife battery, child abuse, divorce, and prostitution. The dominance of the middle-class family ideal was secured in industrial Canada only with difficulty. Laws made birth control illegal and divorce a remote possibility. Prostitutes, but not their male clients, faced arrest, fines, imprisonment, and social ostracism.

The hypocrisy surrounding sexual practices was exposed during the First World War. As opportunity for sexual experimentation of every kind increased, the incidence of venereal disease rose, and people began to talk more openly about sex and birth control. In the process, love became a little less romantic, a little more adventuresome, and, for some, a little safer. Nevertheless, it would take another generation and a prolonged economic depression to bring an open challenge to the Victorian laws relating to sexuality and still longer before they were eliminated.

While Canadians were coming to terms with the meaning and implications of sexuality in the industrial age, they were also systematically reducing their birth rate. Books like *What a Young Wife Ought to Know* (1908), *Searchlights on Health: Light on Dark Corners* (1894), *Karezza: Ethics of Marriage* (1896), and *Sane Sex Life and Sane Sex Living* (1919) circulated widely as Canadians tried to get information denied them by the Criminal Code. Abstinence, coitus interruptus, self-induced abortion, and the margin of safety provided by breast-feeding helped Canadian women and men space births. Canadians wanted reliable birth control not so much to indulge in the sexual excess that moralists feared but to improve family life, to preserve women's health, to give them some greater degree of freedom, and to provide better opportunities for children.

Smaller families were becoming fashionable because ideas about children were changing. Canadians were increasingly preoccupied with the manner in which children were reared and families organized. A rising standard of living and falling birth rate allowed parents, especially mothers, to devote more resources to children. While youngsters had long been, and many remained, important economic assets to their families, they became more than ever the focus of emotional and psychological expenditure by women whose domestic responsibilities were believed to centre on a perfected modern motherhood. For some children shifting views about mothering and childhood meant better health, more sympathy, and greater opportunity for individual self-expression.

Yet many youngsters, especially among the poor, failed to benefit from the modern ideas of childhood that centred on dependence, segregation, protection, and delayed responsibilities. Lucy Maud Montgomery's heroine in *Anne of Green Gables* (1908) was uncommonly fortunate as an orphan. Her early experience of economic exploitation and psychological repression continued to be the lot of many children. The young runaways, prostitutes, and labourers who haunt court records, royal commissions, and daily newspapers testify to the fact that children were not effectively protected. Remedies for the problems of poor and neglected children, although often well-intentioned, frequently tended to penalize this vulnerable group. The Juvenile Delinquents Act of 1908 is a case in point. Under the act, separate juvenile courts were created in an effort to combine crime control with child welfare. When children's courts were created—and they were far from universal depending as they did on federal–provincial co-operation—children were no longer tried alongside adults. They also lost many of their rights of due process, and they faced levels of indeterminate sentencing that adults largely escaped. They were also much more likely to be placed on probation or sentenced to separate institutions such as the Truro Girls' Home, Toronto's Mercer Reformatory, or Vancouver's Boys' Industrial School. The minimal training in agricultural, technical, and domestic skills that young inmates received rarely offered them a future of dignified independence, let alone economic comfort. Given the class bias that shaped such institutions, it is not surprising that they often became lit-tle more than high schools for the working class.

Class and racial biases were reflected in the pseudo-scientific theories of eugenics, which gained wide currency in this period. Drawing on scien-tific findings relating to reproduction in the plant and animal world, eugenicists argued that society could be reformed through improving the human species. If people with undesirable mental and physical traits could be prevented from reproducing, some eugenicists argued, then society as a whole would reach higher levels of progress. Those who embraced eugen-ics believed that individuals and ethnic groups had inherent traits that pre-disposed them to poverty and crime. Such a view did not allow for the possibility that social conditions and learned values created the problems of the industrial age.

Many homes were in no position to insulate their junior members from adult reality. Responsibilities usually came early on farms and in working-class homes. Parents hard-pressed for time or money regularly called upon children for assistance with those younger than themselves, and with house-hold chores, outside labour, and paid work. Tasks were often gender spe-cific. Daughters joined mothers engaged in home-based piecework for Canadian clothing manufacturers or cared for younger siblings. Sons ven-tured out as shoeshine boys, paper sellers, and petty pedlars or assisted their fathers in the fields or in the store. Laws setting the age at which school could be left and paid labour begun were regularly broken by families des-perate for additional assistance and children anxious for independence.

Whatever their situation, few children entirely escaped responsibility for domestic chores. With the exception of those who lived in bunk, boarding, or rooming houses, most Canadians followed a rigorous routine of household maintenance. Relatively few urban homes and only the rare farm were equipped with electricity and indoor plumbing. Coal and wood fires had to be supplied, kept up, and cleaned up. Water had to be carried, heated, and disposed of. Wash days with heavily soiled woolen or cotton clothing and bedding, hard cake soaps, heavy demands for water and heat, back-breaking scrubbing, and uncertain drying, were the bane of domestic existence.

Food preparation was equally labour intensive. In larger centres, food retailers like the Hamilton grocer William Carroll, who is credited with introducing the cash-and-carry marketing of groceries, provided customers with the advantages of meat slicers, prepackaging, refrigeration, and door-to-door delivery. By 1910 Theodore P. Loblaw was inaugurating his grocery chain in Toronto. Nine years later, Dominion Stores opened. Most Canadians, however, continued to rely on small local businesses, bulk foods, and a great deal of time-consuming home processing. Preserving large amounts of food not only required labour and skill, it involved substantial storage problems that many families, especially in the city, could not readily solve. Iceboxes, when available, held relatively little, and space was generally at a premium for both renters and owners. Inevitably, shopping and food preparation were daily tasks.

Ice delivery in Fredericton. Ice in blocks was harvested from the St John River in the cold weather and stored in sheds in sawdust insulation. (Provincial Archives of New Brunswick/Taylor Collection/448)

Housecleaning presented some of the same dilemmas. Dirt and grime were a part of making a living for most people. Yet hot water, cleansers, and domestic tools were in short supply, and only a minority of homes could afford regular domestic help. Elbow grease substituted when it could, but standards of cleanliness, like those of cooking, were necessarily much inferior to those that would be adopted after the introduction of vacuum cleaners, washing machines, synthetic fabrics, and water heaters. As they wrestled with the unrelenting demands of family feeding and cleaning, most married women and many children, especially girls, found themselves with little spare time.

•Schooling for Modern Life

Anxieties about family life contributed to the growth of schools and changes in curriculum. Faith in the malleability of youth, fear of social breakdown and political unrest, and some agreement that a modern labour market required new types of training, turned attention to the schools. Educational reformers were active in every province. By 1905, with the exception of Quebec, all provinces had legislated free schooling and compulsory attendance for youngsters aged seven to twelve. Between 1891 and 1922, elementary and secondary enrolments better than doubled from 942 500 to 1 939 700. The number of teachers grew still faster from 21 149 in 1890 to 54 691 in 1920. As a group, teachers' qualifications improved steadily, and women increased their numerical predominance in the profession. Demand for facilities was such that the T. Eaton Company advertised basic school building kits in its Winnipeg catalogue of 1917–18.

Under pressure from parents, teachers, and administrators, schools were slowly transformed to make them, on the one hand, more "humane, more child-centred, and more responsive to the way in which children grew" and on the other to make them "more practical and relevant to the later lives of their inmates."[7] Kindergartens, with their goal to improve the family life of the poor and to nurture originality and independence in the very young, expanded slowly from their Ontario urban base. In all grades more stress was placed on understanding the growing child and less on the value of corporal punishment. Schools were examined for minimum standards of health and safety, and school boards were encouraged to remedy their shortcomings. Montreal set the pace in 1906 with the Dominion's first regular and systematic medical inspection of pupils. By 1910 it was joined by Sydney, Vancouver, Halifax, Lachine, Toronto, Brantford, Winnipeg, Edmonton, and Nelson. Formal instruction in physical education entered schools at much the same time as an integral part of the wider reform effort to produce healthier children. For boys this often meant cadet training, an option that regularly pitted peace advocates against more militaristically inclined nationalists.

Other reformers advocated making the curriculum more applicable to the world of work. Under the leadership of Canada's first Dairy Commissioner, James W. Robertson, philanthropist Sir William Macdonald, and social activist Adelaide Hoodless, Canadian schools were encouraged to take up manual training and household science, the first directed at boys and the second at girls. Boys were encouraged to think in terms of practical pursuits, in particular a future in agriculture. Girls' training in up-to-date menus and housekeeping was to compensate for the shortcomings of family education, to reaffirm female responsibility for home and family, and to win recognition for the importance of traditional domestic labour. In Quebec, the *écoles ménagères* gave girls a non-academic education designed to make them good housekeepers and bearers of traditional Catholic values within families.

Of greatest interest to educators were new Canadians, whom the schools deliberately set out to assimilate, especially during the heightened nationalism of the First World War. The struggle for the loyalties of new arrivals was most visible on the Prairies. As anglophone Protestants became increasingly determined to control the shape of the new society, the French and Catholic school question apparently settled in 1897 came unstuck. The resolution of the Manitoba schools question had permitted a limited number of Catholic teachers, Catholic instruction at the end of the day, and bilingual teaching in English and any other language spoken by at least ten pupils in the school. What was not anticipated was the flood of new Canadians who would take advantage of the right to bilingual schooling.

Immigrant parents proved intensely interested in both preserving their native culture and securing the best schooling possible for their children. In urban areas they frequently established their own evening schools and sent their children during the day to learn English and Canadian ways in the public system. Of the newcomers, Ukrainian Canadians were among the most determined to establish a bilingual school system. Such efforts were resisted especially during World War I when British fears of European immigrants were at their height. In 1916, despite strong opposition from the French-Canadian, Polish, Mennonite, and Ukrainian communities, the Manitoba government eliminated all bilingual schools. In 1918 Saskatchewan eliminated instruction in languages other than English beyond the first grade. In Alberta, the Roman Catholic clergy had made separate schools, not language, its cause in 1905. The result was that, officially anyway, there were no bilingual schools to outlaw during the war. Nor were there any in British Columbia.

While the assimilation of immigrants motivated English-speaking nationalists in the West, in Ontario their concerns centred on the efforts of the growing francophone minority—about 10 percent by 1910—to secure education in its own language. In 1912 the ultra-Protestant Orange Lodges and English-speaking Catholics joined together to push Ontario's Department of Education to enact Regulation 17. Under this law, public funds were received only by schools with English-speaking teachers, where English instruction was begun upon admission, and where French was not used beyond the second year. Hostilities escalated to the point where thousands of francophone teachers and students paraded through Ottawa singing, in French:

> Little children, guard our language
> Never obey the oppressor!
> It is a sacred heritage from our ancestors
> Our young hearts must remain French
> O God of Jeanne d'Arc, protector of France,
> Save Canada, conserve forever
> In all our children's hearts the faith and courage
> In spite of everything to remain French-Canadian.[8]

Despite appeals, the courts supported the Ontario government. By the end of World War I bitterness was such that Quebec *nationalistes* compared Ontario to wartime Germany in its treatment of minorities. Heightened sensitivity to the survival of language and culture disrupted federal politics as both Borden and Laurier found their parties divided along language lines on the schools question. Ultimately, French Canada could not prevail when English-Canadian nationalism was fully aroused. When Canadian identity was being defined, bilingualism and biculturalism had frequently to give way to Anglo-conformity, as French-Canadian and immigrant parents discovered to their chagrin.

In Quebec, francophones from working-class and farm backgrounds continued to receive far less education than their anglophone counterparts inside and outside the province. As late as 1926, only one Catholic child in twenty in Montreal stayed in school beyond the primary grades. The Catholic Church opposed compulsory education, tuition-free schooling, and free textbooks. While the trade union movement battled for free, compulsory schooling, the church had the support of the textile, tobacco, and shoe industries, which employed many older children. Working-class and farm families also tended, on the whole, to regard the labour and wages of their children as necessary for family survival. Indeed, it has been suggested that rural Quebec migration to New England's textile factories largely stopped after 1900 because enforcement of laws against child labour in New England made survival impossible for poor families.

Although a national consensus emerged among English-Canadian educational reformers as to what changes were needed, the reality of schooling often varied dramatically. Funding, staffing, equipment, and accommodation differed markedly between town and city, private and public boards, between girls and boys, and among different grades, but a number of common features can be noted. Classes, especially those for younger children, normally held over forty pupils, and rural schools regularly grouped together children of several grades. Attendance, although a good deal better than it had been, continued to be a problem as youngsters came more or less regularly depending on their age, sex, and family circumstances. The scattered settlement characteristic of northern areas, with their isolated farmers, small mill operators, railway workers, and Native trappers, hunters, and fishers, for example, was never addressed adequately by the public school system. Equally problematic was the situation encountered by disabled youngsters. By 1914, school medical inspection meant that children with mental or physical handicaps were more likely to be identified. For those with minor dental, eye, and ear problems, remedies were possible. Children with serious disabilities found relatively few options. They were likely to be kept at home or to enter the labour force earlier than their contemporaries.

• Churches and the Struggle for Relevance

In the early twentieth century, Canada's churches were engaged in many of the same debates about social relevance that unsettled the educational system. Influential Protestant theologians emphasized the ethical rather than the dogmatic aspects of religion, in the process rejecting the infallibility of scripture and emphasizing the humanity of Christ. Books such as T.R. Glover's *The Jesus of History* (1919), which interpreted the life and teaching of Jesus and applied them to personal and social experience, became bestsellers as Canadians tried to grapple with the meaning of religion in a modern age.

Most Christian churches were drawn into the problems facing their membership. Influenced by developments in Britain and the United States, Protestant denominations in Canada—especially Methodists, Presbyterians, and Anglicans—spearheaded the social gospel movement, an attempt to apply the principles of Christianity to the problems of industrial society. Social gospellers argued that human misery and corruption were neither inevitable nor divinely ordained but direct products of human selfishness and greed. Social reform, they maintained, would bring the benefits of industrial society to all people, not just a fortunate few. By focussing on the physical and material condition of people on earth, social gospellers moved away from the evangelical preoccupation with individual spiritual development and life after death. Their programs for improving society soon brought them into contact with other reform groups organizing for change.

Early in the new century, church and labour groups formed an alliance to lobby for a Lord's Day Act to ensure a weekly day of rest for workers. Following the passage of the act in 1907, the alliance evolved into the Moral and Social Reform Council of Canada, an organization designed to bring together those who believed that religious energy should be brought to the task of social reform. Socialists, labour leaders, feminists, prohibitionists, and people from every Protestant denomination swelled the ranks of the social gospel crusade. Through their settlement houses, schools, congregations, and missions they carried the social gospel to inner cities, remote Indian reserves, and foreign lands. In their desire to spread spiritual and material improvement, social gospellers also served as agents of assimilation in Native and immigrant communities. The federal government, for instance, relied heavily upon missionaries such as the Anglican nuns at All Hallows School in British Columbia to inculcate Native children in the values of the dominant society. Supremely confident in the relevance of Christianity for all communities, social gospellers through their churches and associations such as the YMCA and YWCA contributed to overseas missions in China, India, and Japan. Medical missionaries, among them feminists like Margaret O'Hara and Agnes Turnbull, both graduates of Queen's Medical College, simultaneously spread the gospel and worked in hospitals and clinics.

Social gospellers were especially visible in Canada's inner cities. Methodists in Halifax's Jost Mission, for example, helped working-class women by combining religious instruction with practical assistance through sewing classes, an employment bureau, relief visits, and a day nursery. J.S. Woodsworth was perhaps the most energetic apostle of urban reform. Ordained as a Methodist minister in 1896, Woodsworth served as the pastor of All People's Mission in Winnipeg for a decade. His books on the immigrant community—*Strangers Within Our Gates* (1908) and *My Neighbour* (1910)—addressed the problems of immigrants in Winnipeg and betrayed Woodsworth's own biases against the customs and values of people who differed from his own white, Anglo-Saxon, middle-class background. At the same time, his religious sensibilities made him sympathetic to trade union-ism, pacifism, and socialism. Salem Bland, a professor at Wesley College in Winnipeg, shared Woodsworth's radicalism, as did a growing number of academics in Canada's church-sponsored colleges and universities.

In 1913, the Moral and Social Reform Council changed its name to the Social Service Council of Canada and hosted a congress in Ottawa the following year. The program testified to the broad range of interests that motivated the social gospellers: weekly day of rest, the Canadian Indian, the church and industrial life, the labour problem, child welfare, the prob-lem of the city, the problem of the country, social service as life work, com-mercialized vice and the white slave traffic, immigration, political purity, temperance, prison reform, and humanising religion. Wartime tensions would drive a wedge between the reformers and the radicals in the social gospel movement, but in 1914 great plans were afoot for a mass movement to establish "God's kingdom on earth."

The Roman Catholic Church also struggled to come to terms with the changing face of Canada. The 1891 papal encyclical *Rerum Novarum*, in which Pope Leo XIII argued that "some opportune remedy must be found

THE GRENFELL MISSION

In Newfoundland, the social gospel movement was represented in a dra-matic way by the mission of Wilfred Grenfell. Born in England in 1865, Grenfell was a student at London Medical School when he was converted to active Christianity by American evangelist Dwight L. Moody. He subse-quently joined the Royal National Mission to Deep Sea Fishermen. In 1892 he visited the coasts of Newfoundland and Labrador where he saw a great opportunity to combine medical and missionary work among people who rarely saw a doctor or a minister. The following year, he opened a hospi-tal in Battle Creek and, by the end of the century, had established his mis-sion headquarters at St Anthony's on the northern tip of Newfoundland. Backed by supporters in the United States, Canada, and Great Britain, Grenfell expanded his activities to include nursing stations, schools, co-operatives, and an orphanage. His well-publicized efforts to bring services to isolated areas—including a close brush with death on an ice floe in 1908—made him a popular hero and enabled him to earn more money for his mission through the lecture circuit. Following his marriage to a Chicago heiress in 1909, Grenfell spent less time in missionary work, which was carried on by dedicated men and women inspired by Grenfell's pioneering efforts.

quickly for the misery and wretchedness pressing so unjustly on the majority of the working class," had spurred a Catholic social action movement. In Quebec, where Catholics made up 85 percent of the population, this was centred in the Montreal-based École Sociale Populaire, established in 1911, which trained Catholic activists to work in the community. The growth of Catholic activism was also reflected in the expansion of the Catholic press as the clergy directly intervened to found or purchase newspapers, including *Le Droit* in Ottawa, *L'Action Catholique* in Quebec City, and *Le Bien Public* in Trois-Rivières. Quebec's social doctrine was heavily influenced by a mixture of Catholic values and French-Canadian nationalist ideology. In its rejection of a class-based society, the church also supported a Catholic trade union movement determined to shield workers from secularism and socialism. The result handicapped the union movement by, for example, dividing it from potential class allies in English-speaking unions.

For Catholic middle-class women in Quebec, *Rerum Novarum* inspired activities at odds with conservative Catholic views of women's roles. While women in religious orders had long held administrative and professional responsibilites, lay Catholic women increasingly also carved out important public roles for themselves. One family, the Lacoste-Gérin-Lajoies, illustrates the range of women's public activities at the turn of the century in Quebec.

> Marie Lacoste-Gérin-Lajoie used the Fédération nationale Saint-Jean-Baptiste, the organization she helped found, as a vehicle to push for access to higher education for women and for improvements in their legal status, and to provide organizational support to women workers. Her sister, Justine Lacoste-de Gaspé-Beaubien, was the founder of the Hôpital Sainte-Justine for children, and remained its president from 1907 until 1964. Marie's sister-in-law, Antoinette Gérin-Lajoie, was one of the co-founders of the École ménagère provincial, the first Quebec domestic science school formed by lay women. Marie's daughter, Marie Gérin-Lajoie, supplemented her religious commitment to Catholic social action by taking courses in social work at Columbia University and observing the British settlement house movement. She ushered in a new age of social service work for both lay women and nuns in her province, and eventually founded a religious order dedicated to training and supporting lay women in their social work.[9]

Although its influence remained the greatest in Quebec, the Roman Catholic Church expanded throughout Canada, building churches, hospitals, orphanages, and schools to serve its increasingly diverse flock. In the case of Polish immigrants, traditional Catholicism was closely allied to Polish nationalism, a connection that in 1901 turned the congregation of the Winnipeg Holy Ghost parish against the German-speaking Oblate Fathers. The Catholic Church played an essential role in language mainte-nance through networks of parochial schools. By 1916 there were as many as eleven Polish or Ukrainian schools in Manitoba. In contrast, Catholic work with Native peoples in schools and hospitals undermined aboriginal cultural traditions. In St Paul, Alberta, the Oblate Fathers and Grey Nuns operated Blue Quills Residential School, which tried to assimilate Indian pupils to European Catholic culture. Some Native parents accepted such schools as necessary evils. But while they may have acknowledged the value of Christianity and "white man's" skills, parents and students were dis-tressed by the enforced separations, loss of Native identity, and harsh regime of many residential schools.

Canada's established Jewish community, which was overwhelmingly British by national origin, also discovered its own version of culture shock. This small, relatively homogeneous and integrated group had suddenly to deal with newcomers who hailed largely from Eastern Europe, spoke

View of a carpenter's shop at Indian Residential School in Saskatchewan (Western Canada Pictorial Index/195-6190)

Yiddish as a common language, and espoused somewhat different religious practices. Between 1881 and 1921 the number of Jews in Canada jumped from 3000 to 125 000, most settling in existing enclaves in Montreal, Toronto, and Winnipeg. While these newcomers varied in their occupational backgrounds, ideologies, and religious practices, many shared the experience of poverty, finding employment in low-wage industries like garments and textiles. They were also much more likely than members of the older, more conservative Jewish community to be active critics of their society as Marxists, anarchists, and labour Zionists, the latter supporters of a Jewish homeland in Palestine established on the basis of co-operative principles. The result was a rich but divided culture. Anglicized Jews nevertheless provided critical assistance to their co-religionists through mutual aid societies, schools, and synagogues. The newcomers also quickly set up their own arrangements for charity and mutual aid in the segregated districts of Montreal's St Lawrence–Main district, the Ward in Toronto, and Winnipeg's North End.

• Life in the Workplace

Most Canadians spent a great portion of their day in the workplace, whether it be in the home, field, workshop, factory, store, or office. In many occupations, ten- to twelve-hour days were normal. People often worked in kin or ethnic groups, and hiring practices, particularly in many small businesses, often remained informal. Larger operations in factories, mills, or department stores could be more impersonal. Yet in Penman's textile mills in Paris, Ontario, which recruited large numbers of British weavers, workers were often able to develop a strong sense of community that found expression both in union activity and in a rich workplace culture. Immigrants who lacked English and any other common language laboured in the mines, railway construction projects, and mass-production industries where they might well be little more than a number on a pay envelope. In Alberta's coalfields in 1911, there were as many as fifteen to twenty separate ethnic groups. Many such bunkhouse men died anonymously, graves along rail tracks or near mines bearing only a fleeting testimonial to their existence.

Modern management techniques reduced the autonomy of many workers; so did the company town phenomenon. Mining and textile-mill towns of Nova Scotia, Northern Ontario, and Quebec were frequently owned lock, stock, and barrel by companies. Homes, stores, schools, doctors, and even churches were firmly under corporate control. Cape Breton coal, Quebec asbestos, Ontario gold, silver, and nickel, and Alberta and British Columbia coal were mined by workers who lived in company towns. While paternalism was sometimes espoused by factory owners, authoritarianism and exploitation were ever-present. In a 1909–10 strike, members of Cape Breton's United Mine Workers were summarily evicted from their homes and locked out of company stores. Company officials even ordered sympathetic ministers to stop sheltering the homeless in their churches.

Disease and injury often followed workers home. Although the 1889 Royal Commission on the Relations of Labour and Capital had reported dangerous working conditions and recommended remedy, little action was taken. Workers stricken by injury or disease were in the difficult position of having to prove employer negligence in order to sue for compensation. Ontario's Workmen's Compensation Act of 1914, followed by Nova Scotia in 1915, British Columbia in 1916, and Alberta and New Brunswick in 1918, conceded a limited right to industrial compensation. Nevertheless, many employees found no protection from the high levels of zinc, mercury, asbestos, dry-cleaning fluids, dyes, and other chemicals that went unregulated. Coal miners and textile workers regularly "retired" exhausted and prematurely aged, their lungs so damaged by coal dust and fabric fibres that they coughed themselves to death.

•Elite and Popular Culture

Canadians have often been self-conscious about their culture, and the early twentieth century proved no exception. The Dominion's youth, colonial inheritance, and proximity to the United States were advanced as reasons why Canadian writers, painters, and inventors rarely achieved international recognition. Intellectuals led regular laments about the disastrous state of culture and the difficulties of sustaining a national identity in the northern half of a continent dominated by the United States. The arrival of immigrants and the development of imperialist sentiments rooted in feelings of racial superiority accentuated this anxiety.

In French Canada, a Catholic conservatism opposed to liberalism, secularism, and radicalism in all forms was at odds with much of what was happening in the modern world, particularly in North America. Catholic clerical and lay leaders became outspoken champions and interpreters of French-Canadian culture. In 1903 priests teaching in Quebec's male classical colleges established the Association Catholique de la Jeunesse Canadienne-française (ACJC) to articulate and defend their vision of a French Catholic nation in North America. Not surprisingly, ACJC's motto was "notre maître le passé" (our master the past). A prominent member of this group was Lionel Groulx, a priest teaching at the Valleyfield Seminary. In his numerous publications beginning with *Croisade d'adolescents*, Groulx proclaimed a providential mission for French Canada in North America so long as it remained true to the Catholic faith. In 1910 the secular leader of the Catholic nationalists, Henri Bourassa, founded *Le Devoir*, the newspaper that quickly became the most prominent expression of the close ties between French-Canadian culture and religion. Although Bourassa himself was initially sympathetic to the idea of a bilingual and bicultural Canada, he increasingly saw English domination as a threat that required a retreat to the Catholic stronghold of Quebec.

Clerical nationalism flourished in every aspect of Quebec's cultural life, although it also had its challengers. Conservative novelists such as Laure Conan in *L'Oublié* (1900) celebrated the religious past. The peasant novel with its idealization of country life also achieved wide popularity, its best example being Louis Hémon's *Maria Chapdelaine* (1913). The realist challenge to this tradition found in Albert Laberge's *La Scouine* (1918) remained muted; indeed the novel's first edition was privately printed with only sixty copies. Only a few writers resisted clerical influence, notably bohemian Montreal poets like Émile Nelligan and members of the École Littéraire de Montréal who espoused a highly individualistic literature preoccupied with the meaning of life, death, and love, and who were highly influenced by French modernists like Baudelaire and Rimbaud. As a major sponsor of painting, sculpture, and architecture, the Church's support could make or break artists. A combination of church and private commissions supported fine contributions in the Art Nouveau tradition by such painters as Ozias Leduc and sculptors like Alfred Laliberté. Before the First World War, Quebeckers in search of more liberated artistic expression regularly turned to Paris.

Unfortunately, too little is known of what the French-speaking woman or man in the street made of this clerical nationalism. While they could hardly entirely avoid what the Roman Catholic Church endorsed, their songs and folklore owed something to old traditions that were critical of religious authority. Other elites were also subject to abuse as the criticism of merchants in a folk song suggests:

> "Marchand, marchand, combien ton blé?"
> "Trois francs l'avoin', six francs le blé."
> "C'est bien trop cher d'un' bonn' moitié."[10]

The urban proletariat also participated in a modern commercial culture emanating from the United States which, in its fascination with vaudeville, modern dance, and the movies, challenged many of the principles of clerical nationalism.

In English-speaking Canada, elite cultural life was similarly preoccupied with national survival. Since the centres of English-language publishing were located in London, and, increasingly, New York, "there was no market for 'Canadian' nationalism." Yet there was demand for stories "about the past or present in French Canada, maritime Nova Scotia, New Brunswick, domestic Prince Edward Island, rural Ontario, or the various localities of the great West."[11] Whatever the cause, the imaginative heart of much Canadian literature clearly lay in the regions. Exceptions to this rule tended to emphasize a northern, natural, aboriginal landscape and a past that for most Canadians savoured more of romance than reality. Dramatic readings by Pauline Johnson, Canada's "Mohawk Princess," on stages across the country drew on her Native heritage to conjure up a distinctive northern nationality that was far removed from the experience of most of her listeners. Similarly the animal stories of Ernest Thompson Seton—*Wild Animals I Have Known* (1898) and *Lives of the Hunted* (1901)—and Sir Charles G.D. Roberts—*The Kindred of the Wild* (1902) and *Red Fox* (1905)—sensitized adults and children to the claims of the natural world. Such writers generally neglected, except perhaps by implication, to go beyond the problem of individual conscience to scrutinize the institutional forces that threatened the environment for animal and human alike.

In general, popular writing in English revealed no common response to the changes that were transforming Canada. Writers could "pretend that the new age did not exist, and go on writing lyrics of nature and love; . . . withdraw to the areas of the country which were still untouched . . . and write regional idylls; . . . accept the vulgar prosperity of the age, flatter its tastes and echo its enthusiasms; or . . . could challenge it, satirize it and attempt to reduce its chaos to form."[12] Older writers like Roberts, Bliss Carman, and Duncan Campbell Scott virtually ignored the new age. Regional idylls focussing on the virtues of rural living provided the most popular form of escapism. Ralph Connor chronicled life in Glengarry, Ontario, to demonstrate the relevance of its Scottish Presbyterian morality to the new lands of the West. Lucy Maud Montgomery's *Anne of Green Gables* poked fun at traditional rural values but stopped short of serious criticism. Norman Duncan looked for inspiration to Newfoundland's fishing villages and W.H. Drummond to old Quebec. The new West appeared in fiction such as Nellie McClung's bestseller, *Sowing Seeds in Danny* (1908) and M. Ellis's *Tales of the Klondike* (1898). Such writers combined a pervasive sense of regional identity with an equally strong dose of Protestant secular moralism. With few exceptions, such as H.B. Blanchard's *After the Cataclysm*

(1899) and Mabel Burkholder's *The Course of Impatience Carningham* (1911), writers refused to grapple with the harsher realities of urban industrial life. Other writers like Robert Service, in rollicking verses such as "The Shooting of Dan McGrew" and "The Cremation of Sam McGee," celebrated the energy and enthusiasm of the northern frontier.

Yet a new realistic tradition was also emerging, most obviously in work by Sara Jeannette Duncan, a disciple of the American novelist Henry James. Her novel *The Imperialist* (1904) dissected the reality of small-town Ontario life and explored the need to balance British sentiment with the reality of North American living. Only one major popular writer, Stephen Leacock, in heavily ironic volumes like *Sunshine Sketches of a Little Town* (1912), questioned the values and virtues of North American liberal capitalism. In his *Literary Lapses* (1910) he used a humorous interview to condemn North American business ethics:

> So one evening I asked one of the millionaires how old Bloggs had made all his money.
>
> "How he made it?" he answered with a sneer. "Why, he made it by taking it out of widows and orphans."
>
> Widows and orphans! I thought, what an excellent idea. But who would have suspected that they had it?
>
> "And how," I asked pretty cautiously, "did he go at it to get it out of them?"
>
> "Why," the man answered, "he just ground them under his heels, and that was how."

Ultimately, however, for all Leacock's willingness to target the conventions of the age, his solutions too turned backwards, to a Tory conservatism that was highly authoritarian and often violently anti-Semitic, nativist, and misogynist.

Leading periodicals of the day were somewhat more inclined to express liberal sentiments but the nationalism of *Saturday Night* (established 1887), *Busy Man's Magazine* (1896–1911), which became *Maclean's Magazine*, and especially *Canadian Magazine* (1893–1939) spoke largely to WASP Ontario, failing to include Quebec, the Maritimes, or the West, except as reflections of Ontario interests. World War I tended to accentuate such narrow sentiments, frequently giving full rein in works like Ralph Connor's *The Major* (1917) and Robert Stead's *The Cow Puncher* (1918) to an evangelical Protestant and tribalistic British nationalism. Only an unusual writer like Francis Beynon in *Aleta Dey* (1919) dared to question the chauvinism and militarism of the Great War, and her reward was exile to the United States.

While many homes boasted volumes by these authors and regularly subscribed to Canadian as well as British and American newspapers and magazines, an important oral tradition also flourished. Edith Fowke's collections of folk songs, notably *Folk Songs of Canada* (1954), *Ring Around the Moon* (1977), and *Sally Go Round the Sun* (1969), document how Canadian voices drew on a rich variety of traditions stemming from aboriginal cultures, Europe, and the United States. In some ways the whole course of Canadian history was replayed through the medium of folk songs and in this manner spread through lumber camps, fishing fleets, and city bars, school playgrounds, and domestic parlours. Then and now they provide a glimpse of worlds of work, poverty, and conflict, that were not so readily available in the conventional literature of the time. A song from southeastern Newfoundland sums up the costs of marriage for the poor:

> Oh mother dear, I wants a sack
> With beads and buttons down the back . . .
> Me boot is broke, me frock is tore,
> But Georgie Snooks I do adore . . .
> Oh, fish is low and flour is high,
> So Georgie Snooks he can't have I.

Other popular songs described the hardships of life for working people and championed the right of legitimate protest. In the historical ballad "Let Us Recall, Brethren, Our Struggle" Doukhobors told the story of their persecution and courageous resistance in tsarist Russia and steeled themselves to withstand assaults from Canadian critics.

Folk art included practical handicrafts like quilts and woven fabric, some of which reached a high order of design and complexity, elaborate images on barns and taverns, and carefully crafted collages of shells and paper. Such work was rarely recognized by the artistic elite of the day, which distinguished sharply between conventional forms of "high" art and those dismissed as handicrafts, which, not coincidentally, were often the special preserve of women.

Overwhelmingly, professional artists were men who, like William Brymner, Robert Harris, and George Reid, trained either in the academic style of the Paris Salon school or later, like Edmund Morris and Curtis Williamson, found inspiration in the atmospheric Hague School. An exception to the habit of European training was Homer Watson, who, like the French-Canadian Ozias Leduc, was self-taught and visited Europe only later in life. Painters regularly took up identifiably Canadian subjects, particularly landscapes of more settled areas of the country. In 1907 the creation of the Canadian Art Club encouraged showings by early Canadian impressionists like Maurice Cullen, Clarence Gagnon, and James Wilson Morrice. By its last exhibition in 1915 the CAC was being overtaken by men such as Lawren Harris and J.E.H. MacDonald who were searching for new ways of presenting Canadian subjects. In 1912 they found their inspiration in an exhibition of contemporary Scandinavian landscapes. A year later, along with Tom Thomson, Frank Carmichael, Frank Johnston, Arthur Lismer, Fred Varley, and A.Y. Jackson, they were applying these insights in sketching Algonquin Park. The war and the death of Thomson in 1917 postponed the public arrival of the painters who came to be known as the Group of Seven, but they were part of a significant prewar effort to find artistic expression for what was deemed uniquely Canadian. On the West Coast, Emily Carr was beginning to develop her own powerful, post-impressionist style to convey the majesty of Native life and the coastal landscape. Lacking the sympathetic community available to her eastern male contemporaries, she was forced to support herself by running an apartment house. Both Carr and the Algonquin Group, like the great majority of earlier Canadian painters, avoided the city and its problems. Their world, like that of many writers, most often symbolized an effort to come to terms with the natural rather than the human world of early twentieth-century Canada.

And yet in the booming atmosphere of turn-of-the-century cities, many Canadians discovered tremendous cultural vitality. Immigrants brought with them a taste for new foods and amusements that even the harsh judgments of long-term residents could not entirely quell. Atwater Market in Montreal, St Lawrence Market in Toronto, and the City Hall Farmers' Market in Winnipeg offered a range of sights, sounds, and smells that enriched urban life. Newspapers and magazines, many with small circulations in ethnic communities, added variety to intellectual life. The circulation of the English and French press grew by leaps and bounds as households regularly subscribed to several newspapers and magazines. By 1913 the number of daily newspapers reached an all-time peak of 138. After that date their numbers dwindled in the face of pressure to curb competition and concentrate ownership.

Overleaf—top left: ***Kwakiutl Mask***, *c. 1900* (wood, cedar bark, and paint; 29.0 x 20.3 x 86.0 cm; McMichael Canadian Art Collection, Purchase 1977; 1977.2.3); bottom left: *Clarence Gagnon, 1881–1942*, ***Twilight, Baie St Paul***, *c. 1920* (oil on canvas; 49.9 x 65.0 cm; McMichael Canadian Art Collection, Gift of Mr. Syd Hoare; 1975.61); top right: ***Ice Bridge over the St Charles River***, *1908, by James Wilson Morrice* (Montreal Museum of Fine Arts); bottom right: *J.E.H. MacDonald, 1873–1932*, ***Beaver Dam and Birches***, *1919* (oil on panel; 21.5 x 26.4 cm; McMichael Canadian Art Collection, Gift of the Founders, Robert and Signe McMichael; 1966.16.49)

Canadians were also enthusiastic spectators at a host of foreign and domestic touring theatre companies, which benefited from the proliferation of railways in the first decade of the twentieth century. In 1897, Corliss Powers Walker, an impresario with a string of small theatres in North Dakota, settled in Winnipeg from which he controlled bookings and theatre management throughout the West. His flagship theatre was the Walker, which seated 2000 people and hosted productions, some of them direct from Broadway, six nights a week, fifty-two weeks a year. The seven touring companies of the Marks Brothers entertained in small towns across the Dominion. Parisian companies toured Quebec and in the 1890s the first local, professional French-language companies were established. The British Canadian Theatrical Organization Society (1912) attempted to balance extensive American influence by organizing tours of British theatrical troupes. The Trans-Canada Theatre Society (1915) was Canadian owned but stayed in business by organizing tours by foreign companies. By the First World War, British and Americans had acquired controlling interests in Canadian theatres, effectively monopolizing this aspect of cultural life.

The difficulties faced by Canadian talent did not escape notice. In 1907 Governor-General Earl Grey created the Earl Grey Music and Dramatic Competition for the dramatic arts, but this collapsed in 1911 and had only a minimum influence. There was also significant progress in amateur little theatre, notably with the creation in 1905 of the Toronto Arts and Letters Players and in 1913 of the Ottawa Drama League. The opening of the Hart House Theatre at the University of Toronto in 1919 capped national development, providing the forum for many distinguished Canadian actors, directors, and playwrights. Canadian audiences were also introduced to the international world of dance. In 1896 Lois Fuller performed her famous fire dance at the Vancouver Opera House. From 1910 on Anna Pavlova could be seen on Canadian stages. In 1917 Nijinsky and the Diaghilev Ballet Russe made a Canadian appearance in Vancouver.

Many performances were aimed at more well-to-do audiences, but the crowds they drew included Canadians from many walks of life. Spectators also found much to entertain them in dance halls, burlesque theatres, and taverns. There hypnotists, magicians, circuses, and vaudeville drew audiences into a rich world of political satire, popular music, and broad comedy. These years also saw the appearance of a popular entertainment that would soon outdraw all others. In 1896, 1200 citizens of Ottawa paid ten cents each to watch Belsaz the magician and—the forerunner of a technology that would put many such performers out of business—a production of Thomas Edison's Vitascope. The Dominion's first public showing of movies included *The Kiss*, a short of less than a minute, "four coloured boys eating watermelons, the Black Diamond Express, a bathing scene at Atlantic City and a coloured film of Lo Lo Fuller's Serpentine Dance." The controversy, excitement, and moral outrage provoked in these few minutes quickly became characteristic of the medium, which just as rapidly found a hearty welcome in vaudeville theatres. Shows were seen from one end of the Dominion to the other, even in pioneer settlements. The theatre in turn-of-the-century Cochrane, Ontario, was thronged every day not only by locals but "by gangs of workmen passing to and from the great railway construction camps."

By World War I mobile screenings were beginning to give way to permanent theatres. Vancouver's Schulberg's Electric (1902) and Crystal (1904), Winnipeg's Unique and Dreamland (1903), St John's York (1906), and Montreal's Nationale and Palais Royal (1904) charged each enthusiastic customer a nickel. Hence the name nickelodeon. Most pictures were silent, but early innovations in accompanying sound came to Canada in 1914, just in time to see service in patriotic wartime newsreels. By then movies had become a major form of entertainment. With more comfortable and elaborate theatres, more developed narratives, and somewhat higher prices, films were also making significant inroads among the middle class, who had at first scorned the medium's supposed vulgarity. Ironically enough, it was in the confines of the early dream palaces, which were increasingly dominated by American celluloid, that Canadians who otherwise had little in common and much to disagree about came together. In its own way, the repetition of this shared experience united audiences, if only in a moment or two of vicarious pleasure, as little did in the high culture of the day.

The Growth of Sports

The evolution of modern mass culture was also increasingly visible in the variety of athletic activities pursued by Canadians. Games and pastimes began to develop strict regulations and regular seasons as the expansion of railway and road networks permitted more inter-community and inter-regional play than ever before. The emergence of specialized sports pages, common to most newspapers by the 1890s, popularized many events and, in the process, helped make some commercially viable. An increase in the number of electrically lit indoor facilities, such as curling and skating rinks, indoor tracks, and gymnasia, made athletic activities accessible year-round to many urban residents. As a result sport was frequently transformed from an outdoor to an indoor pastime, at least for many adult urbanites. In rural areas, sporting occasions remained more intermittent and less highly structured, but they too felt the impact of new technology and commercial sponsorship.

Sport assumed an important role in delineating social classes. The ideology of amateurism reflected the self-interest and the privileged position of the urban anglophone middle class. Their increasingly rigorous definition and defence of "amateur" status, with its prohibition of payment and its precise codes of behaviour and training, effectively eliminated most people from serious competition. Middle-class views of the nature and purpose of sports dominated not only the Olympic Games, which were inaugurated in 1896, but also the administration of athletic programs in schools and universities and the social clubs that sprang up in most Canadian cities.

Less well-to-do Canadians found leisure time and money in short supply. Until late in the nineteenth century, laws prohibited sporting events on the sabbath, often the only day a worker was likely to have free. Mounting regulation of the urban landscape, such as parks where no ball playing was allowed, added to the constraints upon leisure pursuits. As one critic pointed out in the 1890s, "To the young, the strong, and the rich, the choice is wide and varied; to the poor, the busy and the woman who is [no] longer young, the problem of athletics on ever so modest a scale is a difficult one."[13] Thus, sport reflected the social inequality that was so much a feature of Canadian life in general. Yet stratified as sports largely remained, opportunities to play and to watch expanded in these years. Somewhat shorter work weeks, at least for skilled male labourers, and the rising influence of school-based sports gave more adults and children the opportunity to experience the enthusiasm of athletic contest.

Games continued to be strongly associated with certain ethnic groups and particular regions. On the West Coast cricket, soccer, and English rugby were taken up by those with strong British ties. Canadian football, a curious amalgam of British and American rules, took firmest root in the English-speaking urban heartland of Ontario, Manitoba, and the city of Montreal. Lacrosse found its home, although by the end of this period it would be in decline, in Montreal, Ontario, and the lower mainland of British Columbia. With enthusiasts from coast to coast, ice hockey and curling came the closest to reflecting a national sport. Even then, hockey, like lacrosse and Canadian football, was relatively little played in the Maritimes. Baseball and basketball flourished across the country, suggesting the pervasiveness of American influence. Although basketball was developed by a Canadian—James Naismith from Almonte, Ontario—it was pioneered at the YMCA International Training School in Springfield, Massachusetts, where Naismith was a student and later a teacher. Softball emerged as a Canadian adaptation of indoor baseball and, with the help of churches, schools, and city playgrounds, spread quickly. It seems that French Canadians' rejection of English values included their games as well. Among organized sports only baseball and ice hockey provoked much enthusiasm among the francophone community.

The development of track and field owed much to the traditional games of various Scottish societies. Events included pole tossing, weight and hammer throwing, running, and jumping. Schools, universities, and organizations like the Young Men's Christian Association also sponsored early events and helped to keep track and field firmly within the amateur camp. With the creation in 1900 of Canada's first formal track and field association, the Ontario Amateur Athletic Association, this area of athletics was well on its way to assuming its present form. Canada's track and field athletes soon won medals: Tom Longboat—a rare exception to the exclusion of Native peoples from competitive athletics—came first in the 1907 Boston Marathon; George Goulding first in the 10 000 metre walk of the 1912 Olympics; Duncan Gillis second in the hammer throw in the 1912 Olympics. Track and field enthusiasm was merely slowed by the war; by 1919 all provinces were holding track and field championships.

Despite middle-class strictures regarding amateurism, professionalism in everything from ice hockey to boxing and wrestling found a strong Canadian market. By the mid-1890s a marked expansion in the number of ice rinks and teams effectively transformed ice hockey into a commercial success. In 1908 the Montreal Wanderers, after winning the last amateur Stanley Cup, immediately turned professional. With the creation two years later of the National Hockey Association and in 1912 of the Pacific Coast Hockey Association, professional hockey largely eclipsed its amateur rivals. Nevertheless its success ultimately drew on strong amateur play in clubs and universities and on a raft of industrial teams from towns like Halifax, New Glasgow, Glace Bay, Cobalt, and Haileybury.

By the 1890s social proscriptions against female involvement in sports were breaking down; indeed, women were allowed to compete in the 1900 Olympics. Tennis, golf, and bicycling were increasingly available to women with leisure time. The inauguration of school sports like basketball and field hockey created new female enthusiasts. The increased entry of female students into universities also prepared the way for young women who, like their brothers, found intercollegiate play a rewarding part of life. By the end of the war, women were participating in golf, curling, basketball, softball, tennis, and even hockey. Canada's outstanding sports story in the first third of the century was supplied by a female basketball team, the Edmonton Grads, students and alumnae of that city's Commercial High School. Beginning in 1915 and continuing for twenty-five years, the Grads put together an unrivalled record of wins over domestic and international opponents.

Edmonton Grads, Dominion champions, 1922   (Provincial Archives of Alberta/A11,428)

With the war, some sports teams folded and players went overseas, yet athletic activity of various kinds continued to flourish. Army camps, with their support for military boxing championships and military baseball leagues, provided an important recreational outlet for many young men. While the conflict cancelled golf championships, this sport continued its recreational success and others like lawn bowling and tennis moved westward and drew larger numbers of women. The abandonment of swimming facilities by male athletes offered girls and women unprecedented opportunities for competition. The war ushered in other changes as well. Baseball, like cricket, English rugby, and lacrosse, failed to thrive, a casualty it seemed to the appeal of other sports, the attractions of American professional players, and the absence of the high school feeder programs that benefited other sports. By 1920 the prevalence of school athletics and the multitude of programs run by groups such as the YWCA, YMCA, the Canadian Girls in Training, and the Boy Scouts, had given sports an unprecedented place in the lives of most Canadians. Similarly, the discovery by sports promoters that good money could be made presenting professional football and hockey on a regular basis meant that Canadian sport was well on its way to becoming a major North American industry. For all the predominance of the anglophone middle class in many areas of sporting life, a shared interest in sporting activity may well have helped to begin to knit together diverse classes and groups of Canadians.

• The Progressive Spirit

In the first two decades of the twentieth century, Canadian society became more culturally diverse and socially stratified. Tensions between native-born and newcomer, rich and poor, men and women, English and French, Catholic and Protestant thrived. Yet, prior to the First World War there was an air of optimism about the future. Most Canadians, consciously or not, imbibed the spirit of progressivism that swept the North American continent, encouraging people to believe that society could be improved through hard work, judicious laws, scientific management, and reformed political structures. Those in the vanguard of progressivism (not to be confused with the Progressive Party, which in 1919 took the name of the larger movement) were a mixed lot: unionists, co-operators, feminists, prohibitionists, social gospellers, and socialists. Many were urban professionals—doctors, journalists, lawyers, and parsons—eager to provide all citizens with the chance to live the good life as they experienced it.

The First World War deepened the divisions and dampened the optimism of the progressives. The fate of the social gospel movement, which had united disparate strands of Protestant thought, was a case in point. Class tensions challenged elitist notions of the social structure, and the Russian Revolution of 1917 offered a still untested alternative to incremental reform. The chasm between radicals and reformers widened. Those on the left of the political spectrum, like J.S. Woodsworth and Salem Bland, were pushed out of their churches because of their political views. Beatrice Brigden, a sex educator for the Methodist Church, became a socialist and a feminist, abandoning earlier attempts to reconcile her beliefs with the increasingly right-wing notions preached from the pulpit.

The seeds of social disharmony were planted well before the outbreak of the war, but the stresses that the war produced exposed the divisions and, as we shall see in the next chapter, changed the face of Canadian politics forever.

• The Suffragists:

A Historiographical Debate

As outlined in this and the following chapter, efforts to reform industrial society proliferated at the turn of the twentieth century. Middle-class reformers, imbued with the progressive spirit of the age, were convinced that political action and social reform could eliminate many of the "social evils" that they saw around them. For many historians, these reformers have become the heroes of Canadian history, and people such as social gospeller J.S. Woodsworth and feminist Nellie McClung have been praised for their clarity of vision. Other historians have taken a more critical approach to reformers who are viewed less as people of vision than as a privileged group who tried to impose their narrow middle-class values on all Canadians. The clash of opinion is clearly drawn around the women's movement, which culminated in the granting of suffrage to women during and immediately following the First World War.

In 1950 Catherine Cleverdon published her pioneering study of the women's suffrage movement. "Political equality is a prize not to be lightly held," she maintained. "Though it came to Canadian women without the harshness and bitterness of the struggle in Great Britain, it was won by the hard work and heartaches of small groups of women throughout the dominion who had the courage and vision to seek it."[14] Cleverdon's perspective was shaped by her strong commitment to the democratic process and her identification with the suffrage leaders, many of whom she interviewed while conducting her research.

When interest in women's history resurfaced in the 1970s and 1980s, scholars were less inclined to see Canada's suffragists as only people with "courage and vision." Carol Lee Bacchi, following the direction taken by feminist scholars internationally, concluded in her study of some 200 suffrage leaders that "Most Canadian suffragists were social reformers and members of a social elite. They asked that women be allowed to vote in order to impress certain values upon society, Protestant morality, sobriety and family order."[15] In many suffrage circles, it was revealed, racist and class-bound solutions—including eugenics, exclusive immigration laws, and restrictive voting practices—were openly advocated. Even more damning, especially from the point of view of left-wing scholars, was the fact many middle-class suffrage leaders had the time to devote to "good causes" because they exploited an underclass of household servants. Since a narrow "maternal feminist" vision—many suffrage leaders saw women's primary role and rationale for public action being rooted in their status as mothers—seemed to motivate most Canadian suffragists, they were ultimately seen as unworthy predecessors to the more purposeful feminists of the modern women's movement. To quote Bacchi, "the female suffragist did not *fail* to effect a social revolution for women; the majority never had a revolution in mind."[16]

The rejection of the early suffrage leaders as "foremothers" to modern feminism has elicited a vigorous response. In a critique of Bacchi's book, historian Ernest R. Forbes used the experience of women in Halifax, who were described by both Cleverdon and Bacchi as being invariably "conservative" in their approach to female suffrage, to expose the parochialism and present-mindedness of such a position. Halifax suffrage leaders took on a whole range of feminist reforms, Forbes argued, and used any available argument to promote their clearly radical goals. "Reading only the leader's statements in the newspapers one might conclude that the scheme was motivated chiefly by class interests and social control. Having read the minutes [of the Local Council of Women] I do not believe it. Neither, apparently, did the men who rejected their proposals."[17]

Contemporary political concern about what constitutes modern feminism clearly motivates such a debate and may obscure more important questions that should be asked about the suffrage movement. Australian scholar Judith Allen, for instance, has called upon scholars to adopt a comparative and international approach to suffrage. By looking at such issues as temperance and sexual consent laws, as well as suffrage, Allen shows that feminist causes were rooted in time and place. For example, developments following the granting of the vote to women in New Zealand and parts of Australia in the 1890s were different from those that followed the success of suffrage in Great Britain, Canada, and the United States where suffrage was granted a generation later. Allen concludes that momentous demographic changes—including the decline in family size, the narrowing in the age gap between spouses, the vast increase in the rate of divorce, the dramatic fall in mortality rates, and the change in women's labour force participation rate—signalled altered negotiations between men and women. By seeing suffrage and other reform activities in the context of the larger changes taking place within society and the values shaping responses to those changes, individual reform leaders can be better understood. The question then becomes not whether suffrage leaders were heroes or villains but why they responded to their world the way that they did.

•Notes

[1] Quoted in Irving Abella and David Millar, eds., *The Canadian Worker in the Twentieth Century* (Toronto: Oxford University Press, 1978), 32, 35, 36.

[2] Howard Palmer, "Reluctant Hosts: Anglo-Canadian Views of Multiculturalism in the Twentieth Century" in *Readings in Canadian History: Post-Confederation*, ed. R.D. Francis and D.B. Smith (Toronto: Holt, Rinehart and Winston, 1986).

[3] Joy Parr, *Labouring Children: British Immigrant Apprentices to Canada, 1869–1924* (Montreal: McGill-Queen's University Press, 1980).

[4] James G. Snell, *In the Shadow of the Law: Divorce in Canada, 1900–1939* (Toronto: University of Toronto Press, 1971), 262.

[5] Helen Potrebenko, *No Streets of Gold: A Social History of Ukrainians in Alberta* (Vancouver: New Star, 1977).

[6] Quoted in Mariana Valverde, *The Age of Light, Soap and Water: Moral Reform in English Canada, 1885–1925* (Toronto: McClelland and Stewart, 1991), 31.

[7] Neil Sutherland, *Children in English-Canadian Society* (Toronto: University of Toronto Press, 1976), 156.

[8] Robert Craig Brown and Ramsay Cook, *Canada, 1896–1921: A Nation Transformed* (Toronto: McClelland and Stewart, 1974), 258.

[9] Gail Cuthbert Brandt, "Postmodern Patchwork: Some Recent Trends in the Writing of Women's History in Canada," *Canadian Historical Review* 72, 4 (1991): 453–54.

[10] Edith Fowke and Richard Johnston, *Folk Songs of Canada* (Waterloo: Waterloo Music Company, 1978).

[11] Gordon Roper, "New Forces: New Fiction 1880–1920" in *Literary History of Canada*, vol. 1, 2nd ed., ed. Carl Klinck (Toronto: University of Toronto Press, 1976), 287.

[12] D. Pacey, *Creative Writing in Canada* (Toronto: Ryerson Press, 1961), 91.

[13] Elizabeth Mitchell, "The Rise of Athleticism Among Girls and Women," *National Council of Women Yearbook* (1896), 106.

[14] Catherine L. Cleverdon, *The Woman Suffrage Movement in Canada*, rev. ed. with an Introduction by Ramsay Cook (Toronto: University of Toronto Press, 1974), 267.

[15] Carol Lee Bacchi, *Liberation Deferred? The Ideas of the English Canadian Suffragists, 1877–1918* (Toronto: University of Toronto Press, 1983), 3.

[16] Ibid., 148.

[17] Ernest Forbes, "The Ideas of Carol Bacchi and the Suffragists of Halifax," *Atlantis* 10, 2 (Spring 1985): 122.

• Selected Reading

Many of the major economic, women's, labour, Native, and urban histories are cited in chapter 4.

On immigration and immigrants, the major survey is Jean Burnet with Howard Palmer, *"Coming Canadians": An Introduction to the History of Canada's Peoples* (Toronto: McClelland and Stewart, 1988). Among other key works are Donald Avery, *Dangerous Foreigners: European Immigrant Workers and Labour Radicalism in Canada* (Toronto: McClelland and Stewart, 1979); Howard Palmer, *Patterns of Prejudice* (Toronto: McClelland and Stewart, 1982); Barbara Roberts, *Whence They Came: Deportation from Canada 1900–1935* (Ottawa: University of Ottawa Press, 1988); Orest Martynowych, *The Ukrainian Bloc Settlement in East Central Alberta, 1890–1930: A History* (Edmonton: Alberta Culture, 1985); Patricia E. Roy, *A White Man's Province: British Columbia Politicians and Chinese and Japanese Immigrants 1858–1914* (Vancouver: University of British Columbia Press, 1989); W. Peter Ward,

White Canada Forever: Popular Attitudes and Public Policy Toward Orientals in British Columbia (Montreal: McGill-Queen's University Press, 1978); and George Woodcock and Ivan Avakumovic, *The Doukhobors* (Ottawa: Carleton Library, 1977).

On out-migration see Patricia A. Thornton, "The Problem of Out-Migration from Atlantic Canada, 1867–1921: A New Look" in *Acadiensis Reader*, vol. 2, ed. P.A. Buckner and David Frank (Fredericton: Acadiensis Press, 1988), 34–65. On out-migration of French-Canadians to the United States and in-migration of Italians to Canada, see Bruno Ramirez, *On the Move: French-Canadian and Italian Migrants in the North Atlantic Economy, 1860–1914* (Toronto: McClelland and Stewart, 1991). On child immigrants, see Joy Parr, *Labouring Children: British Immigrant Apprentices to Canada, 1896–1924* (Montreal: McGill-Queen's University Press, 1980).

On the homesteading experience, works include Eliane Silverman, *The Last Best West: Women on the Alberta Frontier, 1880–1930* (Montreal: Eden Press, 1984); David Jones and Ian Macpherson, eds., *Building Beyond the Homestead* (Calgary: University of Calgary Press, 1988); Georgina Binnie-Clark, *Wheat and Women* (Toronto: University of Toronto Press, 1979); Howard Palmer with Tamara Palmer, *Alberta: A New History* (Edmonton: Hurtig, 1990); and David Jones, *Empire of Dust: Settling and Abandoning the Prairie Dry Belt* (Edmonton: University of Alberta Press, 1987). Other useful works on the social history of the developing Prairie communities are Paul Voisey, *Vulcan: The Making of a Prairie Community* (Toronto: University of Toronto Press, 1988); Elizabeth B. Mitchell, *In Western Canada Before the War: Impressions of Early Twentieth Century Prairie Communities* (Saskatoon: Western Producer Prairie Books, 1981); David Breen, *The Canadian Prairie West and the Ranching Frontier* (Toronto: University of Toronto Press, 1983); and Susan Jackel, ed., *A Flannel Shirt and Liberty: British Gentlewomen in the Canadian West* (Vancouver: University of British Columbia Press, 1982). Pioneer experiences in British Columbia are discussed in Jean Barman, *The West Beyond the West: A History of British Columbia* (Toronto: University of Toronto Press, 1991).

Social histories dealing with changing notions of families and of sexuality include: Angus McLaren and Arlene Tigar McLaren, *The Bedroom and the State: The Changing Practices and Politics of Contraception and Abortion in Canada, 1880–1980* (Toronto: McClelland and Stewart, 1986); Neil Sutherland, *Children in English-Canadian Society: Framing the Twentieth Century Consensus* (Toronto: University of Toronto Press, 1976); Patricia Rooke and Rudy Schnell, *Discarding the Asylum: From Child Rescue to the Welfare State in English Canada, 1800–1950* (Lanham, MO: University Press of America, 1983); James G. Snell, *In the Shadow of the Law: Divorce in Canada 1900–39* (Toronto: University of Toronto Press, 1991); and Angus McLaren, *Our Own Master Race: Eugenics in Canada 1885–1945* (Toronto: McClelland and Stewart, 1990). Women's histories, in addition to those cited in chapter 4, include Denise Lemieux and Lucie Mercier, *Les femmes au tournant du siècle, 1880–1940: Ages de la vie, maternité et quotidien* (Quebec: Institut québécois de recherche sur la culture, 1989); Barbara K. Latham and Roberta J. Pazdro, eds., *Not Just Pin Money: Selected Essays in the History of Women's Work in British Columbia* (Victoria: Camosun College, 1984); Linda Rasmussen et al., *A Harvest Yet to Reap: A History of Prairie Women* (Toronto: Women's Press, 1974); Franca Iacovetta and Mariana Valverde, eds., *Gender Conflicts: New Essays in Women's History* (Toronto: University of Toronto Press, 1992).

On schooling, see Alison Prentice and Marjorie Theobald, eds., *Women Who Taught: Perspectives on the History of Women and Teaching* (Toronto: University of Toronto Press, 1991); Nancy Sheehan et al., ed., *Schools in the West: Essays in Canadian Educational History* (Calgary: Detselig, 1986). On the issues of separate schools and language of instruction see Manopoly Lupul, *The Roman Catholic Church and the North-West School Question: A Study in Church–State Relations in Western Canada* (Toronto: University of Toronto Press, 1974); John Herd Thompson, *The Harvests of War: The Prairie West, 1914–18* (Toronto: McClelland and Stewart, 1978); Ramsay Cook, Craig Brown, Carl Berger, eds., *Minorities, Schools and Politics* (Toronto: University of Toronto Press, 1969).

On religion and moral reform, major works include Richard Allen, *The Social Passion: Religion and Social Reform in Canada, 1914–1928* (Toronto: University of Toronto Press, 1990); Valverde, *The Age of Light, Soap and Water*; Ronald Rompkey, *Grenfell of Labrador: A Biography* (Toronto: University of Toronto Press, 1991); Ruth Compton Brouwer, *New Women for God: Canadian Presbyterian Women and Indian Missions, 1876–1914* (Toronto: University of Toronto Press, 1990); Rosemary R. Gagan, *A Sensitive Independence: Canadian Methodist Women Missionaries in Canada and the Orient, 1881–1925* (Montreal: McGill-Queen's University Press, 1992); and Allen Mills, *Fool for Christ: The Political Thought of J.S. Woodsworth* (Toronto: University of Toronto Press, 1991). On clerical nationalism, useful sources are Susan Mann Trofimenkoff, *L'Action Française: French-Canadian Nationalism in the Twenties* (Toronto: University of Toronto Press, 1975); Joseph Levitt, *Henri Bourassa and the Golden Calf: The Social Program of the Nationalists of Quebec, 1900–1914* (Ottawa: University of Ottawa Press, 1969); Denis Monière, *Ideologies in Quebec: The Historical Development* (Toronto: University of Toronto Press, 1981); and Jean Hamelin and Nicole Gagnon, *Histoire du Catholicisme québécois*, Part 3, *Le XXe siècle* (Montreal: Boréal Express, 1984).

On bunkhouse men and company towns, see Edmund Bradwin, *The Bunkhouse Men* (Toronto: University of Toronto Press, 1972); Ian Radforth, *Bushworkers and Bosses: Logging in Northern Ontario 1900–1980* (Toronto: University of Toronto Press, 1987); and Ian McKay, "The Realm of Uncertainty: The Experience of Work in the Cumberland Coal Mines, 1873–1927," *Acadiensis*, 16, 1 (1986). Other good social histories of labour in this period include Ian McKay, *The Craft Transformed: An Essay on the Carpenters of Halifax 1885–1985* (Halifax: Holdfast Press, 1985); and Working Lives Collective, *Working Lives: Vancouver 1886–1986* (Vancouver: New Star, 1987). See also Bryan D. Palmer, *Working-Class Experience* (Toronto: McClelland and Stewart, 1992).

On cultural developments see Maria Tippett, *Making Culture: English-Canadian Institutions and the Arts Before the Massey Commission* (Toronto: University of Toronto Press, 1990); J. Russell Harper, *Painting in Canada: A History*, 2nd ed. (Toronto: University of Toronto Press, 1977); Guy Robert, *La peinture au Québec depuis ses origines* (Ste-Adèle, PQ: Iconia, 1978); Laurent Mailhot and Pierre Nepveu, *La poésie québécoise des origines à nos jours* (Montreal: L'Hexagone, 1986); Carl Klinck, *Literary History of Canada* (Toronto: University of Toronto Press, 1976). Sport is discussed in Alan Metcalfe, *Canada Learns to Play: The Emergence of Organized Sport, 1807–1914* (Toronto: McClelland and Stewart, 1987).

CHAPTER 7

EXPANDING POLITICAL HORIZONS, 1896–1919

Senefta Kizima arrived in Canada on a cattle boat in 1912. The fourteen-year-old girl was accompanied by her parents, who were immigrants from the Ukraine. Her father had initially intended to homestead, but the family settled in Calgary instead. Senefta began work as a domestic labourer while she was still fourteen.

> In 1915 at the time of the First World War, I got a job washing dishes in a restaurant. One time some drunk soldiers broke into the restaurant and demanded that the owner fire "Austrians" because they were "enemies." The owner, afraid the drunk soldiers would break windows, had to fire us. Because of his "Austrianness," my father also lost his job.
>
> Someone began rounding up workers for a coal mine in the area near Canmore. Father had once worked in a mine. He hired on at Georgetown. . . . [H]e sustained a serious injury in the mine—his leg was crushed and he was an invalid for the rest of his life.
>
> At that time there was no compensation; once you were ignored you had no reason to live. . . .
>
> We returned to Calgary to our house which had stood empty for a year. I got a job in a restaurant as a waitress. I was paid $7 a week. One time two people came into the restaurant and asked me how many hours I worked and how much I earned. They were organizing restaurant workers into a union. This was 1916 or 1917. Having organized the workers, they called a strike in restaurants and hotels in Calgary.
>
> At the time of the strike I understood many things, experienced injustice, and saw great dishonesty among people. The results of this struggle were higher wages for restaurant workers.
>
> Therefore, to the Ukrainian progressive movement I came, because of the union, because of the strike battle.[1]

The union movement that attracted Kizima was only one of many organized groups that drew the allegiances of Canadians in the first decades of the twentieth century. In *Sunshine Sketches of a Little Town* (1912) Stephen Leacock poked fun at contemporaries who belonged "to the Knights of Pythias and the Masons and the Oddfellows . . . to the Snow Shoe Club and the Girls' Friendly Society." But elected politicians ignored the expanding plethora of community groups at their peril. While the elites who headed up the political system continued to distribute government appointments and contracts within a narrow circle, they increasingly recognized the need to placate grass-roots demands.

Pressure from below manifested itself in movements that assembled on Parliament Hill, conducted elaborate petitions, buttonholed mayors and their councils, marched in May Day parades, and sometimes fought the Mounties and militia on city streets. Reformers focussed on municipal and provincial solutions. Notions regarding the federal role, if any, in dealing with problems created by urbanization and industrialization divided reformers as much as they did the two major political parties. Limited identities of gender, race, ethnicity, class, province, and region shaped a Canadian politics that, while vibrant, mitigated against nation-wide programs. Yet reformist notions of various kinds penetrated municipal, provincial, and federal politics and transformed Canadian political institutions.

•The Demand for Woman's Suffrage

By the 1890s, increasing numbers of reformers favoured the idea of female suffrage. Supporters came to the movement from many different causes: from lengthy struggles to open universities, medical schools, and business on an equal basis to women; from groups condemning women's unfavourable legal position in matters of property inheritance and child custody; and from organizations like the Woman's Christian Temperance Union whose members recognized that women were uniquely subject to the violence that sometimes accompanied alcohol abuse.

Two feminist perspectives were evident in the suffragists' arguments: equal rights and social feminism. Equal rights advocates hoped to sweep away the unfair laws and attitudes that discriminated against women. Social feminists wanted special laws to support women in their roles as wives and mothers. Feminists such as Dr Emily Howard Stowe of Toronto and Dr Eliza Ritchie and Anna Leonowens of Halifax had begun to link up with an international woman's movement seeking full legal, social, and economic equality. In this they were influenced by natural rights theories stemming from the French and American revolutions, by progressive religious views, and by liberal thinkers such as Mary Wollstonecraft and Elizabeth Cady Stanton. Increasingly women beyond the initial intrepid band of equal rights feminists grew anxious to play a more direct role in social development. Expanding on the view that a woman's place was in the home, social feminists argued that the propagation of Christian values in the home required reinforcement of these values throughout society's institutions. They approached woman's suffrage from the perspective of the disturbing changes in private and public life that had been wrought by industrial capitalism. Like Nellie McClung and Emily Murphy on the Prairies, Elsie Gregory McGill in B.C., Dr Elizabeth Smith Shortt in Ontario, Marie Gérin-Lajoie and Josephine Dandurand in Quebec, and Edith Archibald and Ada Powers in Nova Scotia, these feminists used the widespread belief in women's distinctive nature to justify greater public and private power for their sex. They particularly pointed to a sense of altruism and nurturing believed to spring from women's biological capacity to mother.

British suffragist Emmeline Pankhurst (first row, fifth from left) stands between Nellie McClung and Emily Murphy during Pankhurst's North American war tour (Provincial Archives of British Columbia/39849)

Many middle-class suffragists believed that women's innate moral superiority was more evident in their own class, whose wives and mothers had the time and correct moral views to devote to good causes. Advocates of this point of view were likely to see female suffrage as one expedient method, like prohibition, of reshaping the behaviour not only of the male sex in general but of the unrespectable and undisciplined members of the urban working class, particulary immigrants. Whatever the precise justification offered by suffrage advocates, the demand for the vote remained fundamentally radical, offering as it did the unconventional prospect of women seeking a direct connection with the state rather than allowing male family members to act as mediators for them.

Not surprisingly, in view of the close association between champions of temperance and suffrage, similar tactics were employed by the two groups to force governments into action. Letter writing, personal appeals, petitions, and the use of satire characterized their efforts. Tireless canvassing by organizers and the determination of petitioners not to be silenced allowed women's groups across the nation to present petitions with thousands of signatures to provincial legislatures.

Western Canada produced the one individual most identified with the Canadian suffrage cause. Nellie L. McClung, born in Grey County, Ontario, inspired hearts and hopes across the Dominion in campaign speeches published in 1915 as *In Times Like These*. In 1914, Manitoba's Political Equality League financed its campaign by packing Winnipeg's Walker Theatre for a performance of "How the Vote Was Won." To thunderous applause, Nellie McClung, as premier of a Women's Parliament, punctured the pretensions of the Conservative regime of Sir Rodmond Roblin in her speech to an imaginary group of franchise-seeking males: "We wish to compliment this delegation on their splendid gentlemanly appearance. If, without exercising the vote, such splendid specimens of manhood can be produced, such a system of affairs should not be interfered with. . . . Another trouble is that if men start to vote they will vote too much. Politics unsettles men, and unsettled men mean unsettled bills— broken furniture, broken vows and divorce." Although suffrage in school board and municipal elections was often won earlier, forty years and more of such tactics preceded the passage of the first provincial female franchise act in Manitoba in 1916. Alberta, Saskatchewan, and British Columbia followed later that year, Ontario in 1917, Nova Scotia and the federal government in 1918, New Brunswick in 1919, and Prince Edward Island in 1922. Even then, some women remained disfranchised: women in Quebec could not vote in provincial elections until 1940; status Indians and Asian Canadians—both male and female—had to wait until after World War II for the right to cast ballots as full citizens. Canadians of South Asian and Chinese ancestry were enfranchised in 1947, Japanese Canadians in 1949, and status Indians only in 1960.

Women were far from unanimous on the use of their new political rights. A few chose independent feminist politics, but a much larger number favoured integration into existing political parties. As it turned out, co-operation in male politics generally meant that women conducted fund raising and organizing for male candidates rather than running for office themselves. A familiar pattern soon emerged of female representation being inversely proportional to the prestige and power held by an office: comparatively large numbers of school board trustees were women but next to no Cabinet ministers and of course no premiers or prime ministers.

The hardships of the suffrage campaigns wore out several generations of women and deterred the less brave from expressing opinions publicly. The strength of anti-feminism and misogyny has rarely been studied, but it tarred media and institutions of every sort. Efforts to bring about equality roused fierce opposition. Determination to keep women "in their place" was a widespread phenomenon. Henri Bourassa's tirades against feminism and suffrage as foreign imports of an Anglo-Saxon secular and materialistic culture that could destroy Catholic Quebec were more than matched by rantings from such respectable English-Canadian intellectuals as Andrew Macphail, Stephen Leacock, and Goldwin Smith. Within the labour movement and the workplace, male workers continued to insist that most jobs be gender-segregated, with the men's jobs receiving higher status and greater economic rewards. Women worked alongside men in printing, telegraphy, and hosiery, but a hierarchy of skills, supported by employers and male employees, was largely unchallenged. Equality for women called into question deep-seated beliefs about human nature, the privileged position of men, and the organization of the Canadian community. It is little wonder that only the valiant questioned sex roles and that champions were regularly outnumbered by the fearful and the angry.

• The Claim for Native Rights

The rapid development of Canada in these years also pressed hard on the Native peoples. In many areas of Canada, and particularly in the West, supposedly protected reserve lands were confiscated by governments eager to assuage population pressure and the demand of white settlers for the best land. The government's unwillingness to spend money to either train or equip Indian farmers meant that only subsistence farming, requiring little machinery and the use of a fraction of reserve land, was encouraged. When immigrant commercial farmers coveted reserve land, the low productivity of Indian farming was used as an excuse to deprive Indians of their birthright. In 1906 the Indian Act was amended to make sale of reserve lands easier. At times they were sold even when Indians, despite state policies, had become successful farmers. The Blood of southern Alberta, for example, were forced to sell off lands in 1916 and 1917 after the Department of Indian Affairs, to the consternation of the progressive local Indian agent, withheld funds needed for Blood farming operations until they consented to the sale. British Columbia Indians frequently had their lands seized. The McKenna–McBride Commission, created in 1912 to resolve federal–provincial differences regarding Indian land claims in the province, ignored Indian wishes and exchanged 14 400 hectares of reserve land for larger but significantly less valuable holdings.

Native people responded to encroachments on their resource base by seeking jobs within the industrial economy developing around them. In regions that experienced the economic boom of the Laurier years, Natives took advantage of greater demands for their skills. Reports from Indian agents before World War I indicate, for example, extensive and well-paid employment of Ojibwa and Swampy Cree near Lake Manitoba in fishing, lumbering, and gypsum mining. In Chapleau, Ontario, Cree women and girls did laundry and cleaning for wages while the men worked on railway construction. In Fort Francis, occupations included work in sawmills, on steamboats, and on farms. Women and men from Native communities in British Columbia continued to work in lumber mills, canneries, mines, and the commercial fishery, as they had before 1896. Yet, as Morris Zaslow notes regarding the Indians of the Pacific Coast: "even when Indians were successful workmen, they still were not masters of their own economic destiny; they worked mainly for wages or sold their produce to middlemen who reaped the profits."[2]

Remedies for injustice did not come easily. As litigants in a European-based judicial system, Indian people faced major social, cultural, and economic obstacles. Yet Native organizations arose to challenge official policy in these years. While often subservient to the Department of Indian Affairs, which held the purse strings for many bands, the Grand General Indian Council of Ontario met biennially to debate and to send resolutions to the federal government. Anger at developments such as a 1911 Ontario act permitting reserve lands adjacent to towns of 8000 or more to be expropriated spurred protests even from the conciliatory-minded council. Pan-Indian revival movements such as the Council of the Tribes were still more outspoken, stating bluntly that whites had demoralized and defrauded Native peoples who should now fight back. Regional protests included a sophisticated campaign by the Nishga of the Northwest Coast to obtain recognition of aboriginal land rights. In 1906 the chief of British Columbia's Capilano Band travelled to England to petition King Edward and, nine years later, the Allied Tribes of British Columbia was established to force the British Privy Council to settle Native land claims. The unrelenting hostility of the Department of Indian Affairs and the indifference or outright opposition of most other Canadians doomed such protests, but the First World War empowered a generation of Native champions who proved harder to ignore.

The patriotism of Indian servicemen, whose enlistment numbers exceeded their proportion in the general population, was rewarded by the grant of the federal franchise to ex-servicemen without loss of status, but their military service produced results unexpected by the white community. Pan-Indian consciousness was fed by the shared experience of military life. In 1918 a charismatic veteran and member of the Six Nations' reserve, F.O. Loft, was elected president of the new League of Indians of Canada. In the hope of bettering the condition of Native peoples, the League championed Indian autonomy. Loft observed that, "the day is past when one band or a few bands can successfully . . . free themselves from the domination of officialdom and from being ever the prey and victims of unscrupulous means of depriving us of our lands and homes and even deny[ing] us of the rights we are entitled to as free men under the British flag." Such statements prompted police surveillance, accusations of bolshevism, and harassment by Indian Affairs. The League itself did not long survive Loft's death in 1934, but it helped give birth to militant Native associations in both Alberta and Saskatchewan.

Organization of the Métis beyond the local level proved difficult to re-establish in the years following the defeat of the 1885 rebellion. Although the Métis continued to demand land as their aboriginal right, government indifference and the pressures of white settlers forced them to inhabit mainly fringe areas with little agricultural potential. They hunted, fished, and trapped in unsettled territories and moved on if white settlements forced them to do so. The result was that instead of the "Métis nation" that the rebels of 1885 had hoped to create, the Métis were dispersed across the Prairies in places like Green Lake, Saskatchewan, and Lac Ste Anne and Lac la Biche in Alberta. The Métis of Batoche finally won a land settlement in 1899–1900, receiving individual land grants as opposed to a reserve. Since farming required capital that the Métis lacked, many sold their lands. In 1896, the Catholic Church, spurred by the missionary Albert Lacombe, established a Métis reserve, St Paul des Métis, one hundred kilometres northeast of Edmonton. Promises of livestock and equipment failed to materialize as it became clear that neither the Church nor the federal government wished to invest much money in this project. By 1908 most of the Métis farmers had moved away, and the community was gradually transformed into a French-Canadian settlement. The Métis became a forgotten people, invisible even in the census until 1981 when, for the first time, "Métis" was recognized as an ethnic group.

• Organizing Working People

In the early twentieth century, workers confronted business people increasingly hostile to their claims. Meanwhile, the state, despite its pretence to impartiality, gave substantial advantages to capitalists. The Canadian working class had to face these challenges just as the Anglo-American cultural homogeneity that had strengthened the Knights of Labour in the 1880s was slipping away. New immigrants from Europe and Asia penetrated and fractured the working class without making similar inroads within the capitalist class. Labour's attempts to come to terms with this new diversity, and the uses it was put to by capital, sometimes deteriorated into racism. With honourable exceptions like the One Big Union (OBU), a besieged labour movement readily excluded Asians, blacks, and even Eastern and Southern Europeans. While the shared predicament facing all workers did not escape notice, deepened cultural divisions interacted with the distinctiveness of regional economies to pit wage earners against one another and to obscure the common features of modern industry. Meanwhile, as historian Bryan Palmer argues, "in the workplace, managerial innovations, technological change, and newly developing industrial sectors diluted many skills, created a new hierarchy of job classifications, and increased the need for unskilled workers."[3] Such developments made collective action difficult. Yet the rapidity of economic concentration and of the reorganization of work forced increasing numbers of men and women to defend their interests collectively, at times taking on both governments and business.

International craft unionism was the most obvious beneficiary of workers' awareness of the need to address their disadvantages in an economy that was increasingly subject to the power of big business. In 1900, about 60 percent of Canada's 20 000 union members were in international unions. The Trades and Labour Congress of Canada (TLC) displayed its determination to heed the pragmatic call of Samuel Gompers and the American Federation of Labor for higher wages rather than systemic change. "Gomperism," the notion that organization by trade was preferable to organization by industry, and that job action was preferable to political action, had won over Canada's major central organization of labour. Yet TLC/AFL hegemony was never total. Many different philosophies continued to vie for the favour of the Dominion's working men and women. The TLC exiles quickly established a rival nationalist labour centre, the National Trades and Labour Congress, which became the Canadian Federation of Labour in 1908. Although its small numbers never challenged TLC dominance, it offered a nationalist alternative. In Quebec, many French-Canadian workers looked for assistance to the Catholic Church and distrusted the American ties of the TLC. In British Columbia, radical American unions like the Western Federation of Miners and unionists familiar with the development of the British Labour Party continually challenged the prerogatives and the perspective of TLC affiliates. Even within the TLC, a radical contingent pressed for industrial unionism, which would organize all workers, regardless of their trade or alleged skill level, and for socialist politics. Unionists from Western Canada and the Cape Breton coal fields were most prominent in this radical minority.

The benefits of international unionism have been much debated by historians. There is little doubt that Gomperism discouraged impulses towards a complete restructuring of capitalism and offered relatively little opportunity to the unskilled or to women. Only 5.6 percent of Ontario's labour force and 8.4 percent of Quebec's was organized in 1911 despite widespread organization of skilled groups. Yet individual craft unionists were often at the centre of demands for socialist reform and industrial action. Nor could the exclusivism of craft unionism completely undermine the larger principle of labour solidarity. Recognition of the international nature of labour's struggle was spurred not only by unions spanning national frontiers but by awareness of the influence of American models of business management and the spread of American branch plants.

In the face of management's determination to monopolize the advantages of increased efficiency, workers resorted increasingly to strikes. Continuing the pattern established in the 1880s and 1890s, most conflicts flared up during periods of relative prosperity, such as 1904–5 or 1909–11, when labour benefited from being in especially short supply. Impersonal monopoly capitalism was leading to the breakdown of older paternalistic structures that, to a limited degree, had acknowledged a shared, if hierarchical, community of skill and interest between master and wage earner. In such a climate, working-class protest proliferated across the Dominion.

Between 1901 and 1914, Nova Scotia, New Brunswick, and Prince Edward Island were home to at least 411 strikes. Many such confrontations, unlike those in Central Canada, were staged by unskilled labourers rather than crafts workers, refuting the image of conservatism that has often plagued historical accounts of this region. Steady increases in prices of food, fuel, and other necessities often made wages the chief bone of contention in strike action. In other cases, like the twenty-two-month strike by coal miners in Springhill in 1909–11, where the United Mine Workers of America lost the battle, union recognition was a major objective. Closely related strike issues involved worker demands for greater control over apprenticeship, forms of payment, work systems, and the behaviour of supervisors. The more than 421 labour struggles that unsettled Southern Ontario in the same period repeated many of the same demands. There in the nation's industrial heartland, craftsmen, particularly those in the building and metal trades, were outspoken critics of low wages and high profits. They also contested the prerogatives of management, insisting on their own traditional right to control apprenticeship and to challenge arbitrary supervisors and new systems of payment. The 1907 strike of Toronto Bell Telephone operators rejected the company's right to unilaterally change and, in effect, to worsen the conditions of employment. Like carpenters, garment workers, painters, and moulders, the telephone operators recognized that innovation was being used as an excuse to deskill and to wrest authority and autonomy from the worker.

South Porcupine miners' strike, circa 1910–15   (Ontario Archives/S13722)

In Quebec, conflict centred on the labour-intensive light industries—textiles, boots and shoes, and clothing—where wage cuts, long hours, and underaged employees drove workers to test their strength against capital. In 1900 female spoolers in Valleyfield's cotton industry walked off the job when apprentices were hired to perform their work. Overall, Quebec lost more workdays per worker to strikes than did Ontario in the period from 1901 to 1921. The Catholic Church, concerned that materialistic, "atheistic" unions were attracting Catholic workers, began to sponsor confessional unions, in which priests advised the workers' representatives and ensured that workers' actions met with Church approval. Priests assigned to the unions were often sensitized to labour's plight when recalcitrant employers resisted even modest union demands. Gradually, the Catholic unions developed an outlook similar to that of the TLC unions.

In the West, coal miners and railway workers led protests against arbitary management from companies like Canadian Collieries on Vancouver Island and the Canadian Pacific Railway, which the United Brotherhood of Railway Employees battled from one end of the line to the other. Powerful corporations, like the CPR and coal companies in Cape Breton and Vancouver Island, subjected workers to long contests that drained union resources. Where employers were less powerful, as in the coal fields of southeastern British Columbia and Alberta, labour's representatives often did better, securing in 1905–6 an important foothold for radical unionists in District 18 of the United Mine Workers of America.

Wage labourers were not alone in their struggles. Spouses and children, indeed whole communities, especially in single-industry towns where divisions between companies and their employees were most sharply exposed, took every opportunity to demonstrate their political solidarity. In Cape Breton's coal fields women joined their menfolk in protest against Dominion Steel and Coal. On one occasion, when physically prevented from interfering with the strikebreakers, women called on their Scottish Presbyterian heritage and "knelt down on the road and appealed to God with genuine fervour to cause the rocks in the pit to fall upon the objects of their hatred," a divine intervention with which many local clergymen would have been in sympathy. During the 1906 strike of Hamilton's street railway workers, "We Walk" ribbons symbolized that many local citizens, from doctors who donated services to strikers to shoe dealers who offered free boots, sided with workers and their demands for improved wages and union recognition and against the unregulated authority of the civic monopoly.

The increased visibility of such conflicts and the political threat that they represented to the established order prompted governments to develop policies to forestall a complete breakdown in industrial relations.

Intervention was far from even-handed. Corporate power was reflected in the frequency with which politicians permitted businesses to employ troops, militia, and police to coerce labour. In 1899, militia cleared the streets of Londoners rioting in sympathy with the Amalgamated Association of Street Railway Employees against the Cleveland corporation that ran the streetcars. A year later, fishers on the Fraser River saw militia and provincial police help canning companies break their strike against low prices for their catch. In the same year, Valleyfield, Quebec, labourers building a cotton mill fought alongside mill operatives against militia summoned by the mayor at the request of the employers. Nova Scotia's coal towns, like those in the West, were particularly susceptible to such official intervention. In 1909–10, the Dominion Coal Company employed most of Canada's small permanent militia guarding mines and strikebreakers, in the process defeating the efforts of the United Mine Workers to challenge the Provincial Workmen's Association.

For all its short-term results in forcing labour to toe the company line, military or police intervention in capital–labour disputes tended to be expensive, to provoke sympathy for workers, and to exacerbate class conflict. The alternative, less obviously smacking of class warfare, was an industrial relations strategy worked out by William Lyon Mackenzie King. In 1900 after King's exposé of sweatshops manufacturing military uniforms, Ottawa agreed to insert a fair-wage clause in federal contracts. Much more influential was his engineering of the Industrial Disputes Investigation Act of 1907 (the Lemieux Act) prohibiting strikes and lockouts in public utilities and mines until the dispute had been investigated by a tripartite board of arbitration representing capital and labour, with government as "an impartial umpire." By establishing a compulsory cooling-off period, the act deprived organized labour of its strongest weapon, the surprise strike, without any compensatory protection against retaliation by the employer. The Trades and Labour Congress asked Robert Borden's newly elected Conservative government to repeal the act. But Borden appeared unperturbed by labour's evidence that employers used the cooling-off period to build up inventories and hire strikebreakers so that any strike would prove ineffectual.

The state's overt favouritism towards business, evidenced by the use of the military and by legislation like the Lemieux Act, made many labour leaders question traditional political loyalties. In the nation's largest cities, prewar May Day rallies drew thousands. Labour politics and parties had emerged in the 1870s and 1880s, and, during the Laurier years, many union locals in the TLC moved away from the American Federation of Labor notion that, while unions could endorse old-party candidates, they ought not to run labour candidates. The example of Britain's Independent

Labour Party provided an alternative model to AFL non-partisanship. In 1900, A.W. Puttee, a Winnipeg Labour Party founder, and Ralph Smith, TLC president, were elected to Parliament. In 1906, rejecting the more radical Socialist Party of Canada, the TLC endorsed the creation of provincial labour parties. While the Socialists preached the total abolition of capitalism, Labour focussed on amelioration of its impact upon working people. Although they supported public ownership of railways, utilities, and monopolies, labourites' main emphasis was on state enforcement of safe working conditions, implementation of social insurance programs, and so on. Nevertheless, labourites backed Socialist Jimmy Simpson's election to Toronto's Board of Control in 1914 and the election of Labour members to city councils in Winnipeg, Edmonton, and Calgary, among other cities, before 1919. After the war, such victories became even more frequent.

Some radicals within the labour movement rejected both parliamentary process and traditional unionism altogether. The Industrial Workers of the World (IWW), whose major base of strength lay in railway construction camps throughout Western Canada and Northern Ontario, called on workers to make the strike a political weapon. The "Wobblies," as they were called, believed that workers should collectively lay down their tools when a fellow worker was unjustly treated by an employer. Eventually, the IWW leadership hoped, when workers had become accustomed to acting in solidarity with one another, general strikes of all workers could be used to force employers to hand over their properties to their workers. The IWW message found support among the exploited bunkhouse workers whom conventional unions ignored and whose plight could safely be forgotten by politicians, since these transients rarely stayed long enough in one place to qualify to vote. IWW strength declined significantly once the railway-building period wound down after 1910. Persecution of the organization's leaders in Canada and the United States during and after the First World War left only a shell of an organization. But syndicalist notions—the view that workers could achieve more through job actions, particularly general strikes, than through parliamentary politics—would remain popular in the immediate postwar period.

Working-class dissatisfaction with governments continued to grow once the initial patriotic excitement of the "war to end all wars" subsided. Despite the models of both France and Britain which, upon the declaration of war, had quickly consulted union leaders and Socialist politicians, Canada's politicians largely ignored organized labour, turning instead to the business people who had long been familiar councillors. By the middle of the war, the stage was set for renewed confrontation between Canadian workers and governments.

•Organizing to Defend
Agrarian Interests

While women, Indians, and workers found their criticism of Canadian development regularly ignored, policy makers were more hesitant in dismissing the claims of the nation's farmers. In their struggles to influence policy, farmers wielded significant advantages: they represented important blocks of voters—indeed their electoral strength was increasingly out of proportion to their numbers—and defended a vision of Canada to which many contemporaries were emotionally attached. Their self-portrait as independent sons and daughters of the soil, rejecting the material and political corruption of their time and representing the moral and cultural wealth of their nation, appealed to observers already anxious about modern development and somewhat nostalgic about the simpler virtues associated with a more agrarian past.

This electoral strength and emotional appeal helps explain why organizations like the Women's Institutes, les Cercles Fermières, the Farmers' Institutes, and a host of other farm-initiated associations found a ready audience in, and frequently financial assistance from, governments, especially at the provincial level. Support for experimental farms, the assisted immigration of cheap farm labourers, the school garden and manual training movement signalled the relative strength of agrarian forces. Meanwhile, a new generation of farm leaders was being educated in institutions such as the Nova Scotia Agricultural College (1905), Macdonald College of McGill (1907), Manitoba Agricultural College (1906), and the faculties of agriculture of the University of Alberta (1915) and the University of British Columbia (1915).

Continuing problems with rural depopulation, especially in Central and Eastern Canada, combined with the burgeoning economy of the newly settled West to produce a farm movement demanding major changes in Canada's politics. Farmers turned quickly to collective action and, in 1902, the Ontario Farmers' Association appeared as a critic of high transportation costs, the protective tariff, and inequitable tax policies. By 1907, it had merged with the Grange, a farm organization which dated back to the 1870s, to form what became the more militant United Farmers of Ontario, led by E.C. Drury and J.J. Morrison. Two years later, Ontario's farmers met with western grain growers to establish the Canadian Council of Agriculture as a national lobbying body.

In the West, farm organizations were early critics of the national government, especially its policies on tariffs and railways. Laurier's Liberals were to prove uncertain defenders of agrarian interests, but farmers reaped immediate benefits from the Conservative defeat in 1896. The Crow's Nest Pass Agreement of 1897 subsidized the CPR to build a line from Lethbridge, Alberta, to Nelson, British Columbia, in return for reduced rates on grain and flour moving east and settlers' effects and agricultural machinery going west. In 1900, the Manitoba Grain Act's tougher regulation of grain loading, warehousing, and the allocation of railway cars attempted to dampen grain farmers' anger with the CPR and eastern interests in general.

Agrarian discontent led to the creation of the Territorial Grain Growers' Association in 1901; after 1905 the association became the basis for provincial grain growers' groups in Alberta and Saskatchewan. By the First World War, organizations such as the United Farmers of Alberta and Saskatchewan Grain Growers' Association were powers that the provincial governments had to reckon with. Growing disenchantment with the system was also demonstrated in agrarian enthusiasm for economic co-operation: by World War I, Saskatchewan and Alberta farmers had created grain elevator co-operatives. The case for producer and consumer co-operation was effectively presented in Winnipeg's *Grain Growers' Guide*, which began publication in 1908. Agrarian activists also agitated for better schools, roads, and medical care for country people and reforms to improve the plight of farm women. Recognition of women's contribution to farm life led to early agrarian support for female enfranchisement, a significant factor in the earlier suffrage victories in the West.

Tariff policy emerged as the outstanding common grievance of Canadian farmers. Protective tariffs were roundly condemned as a charge upon society's producers for the benefit of manufacturers who, according to many farmers, were materialistic, greedy, and corrupt. This sense of moral superiority was captured in a 1913 speech by the master of the Dominion Grange: "A class of idle rich has grown up in our cities, to whose love of ostentation commerce and industry are now pandering. These enervated and miserable specimens of humanity rush about the country in great cars, flaunt their wealth in our faces, tear up our roads and cast their dust upon our fields." No wonder every revision of the tariff and every general election occasioned the drawing of lines between the business and farm communities. Other issues capturing agrarian attention included rural depopulation, the spread of monopolies and combinations, the limited availability of storage elevators, and the need for a Hudson Bay Railway. When Laurier set out on his triumphal pre-election tour of the West in 1910, tariff policies were paramount. The message was forcefully reiterated in December of the same year when a thousand Ontario, Quebec, Prairie, and Maritime farmers protested on Parliament Hill.

• Managing the City

Cities were at the heart of many of the concerns voiced by Canadian reformers. While cities had always been difficult places in which to live, by the twentieth century they had become even more dangerous and less pleasing to the senses. To be sure, their problems were not yet on the scale of those found in New York, Manchester, and Glasgow, but Canadian cities nevertheless had appalling rates of crime, death, and overcrowding. Muckraking journalists in such newspapers as Montreal's *La Presse*, Toronto's *Telegram*, Ottawa's *Journal*, and Hamilton's *Herald* kept the stories of danger and social dislocation ever before the public eye and offered ample evidence to strengthen the campaigns of urban reformers.

Coalitions urging urban reform included many of the people involved in other reform efforts: middle-class professionals, women's rights activists, and social gospellers, most notably J.S. Woodsworth, Methodist superintendent of Winnipeg's All People's Mission, and Adelaide Plumptre, Toronto Local Council of Women activist and prominent civic reformer. They were led by a new generation of civic experts—individuals such as Herbert Ames, businessman and author of *The City Below the Hill*; S. Morley Wickett, a Toronto municipal politician and the author of an anthology on civic government; and W.D. Lighthall, Montreal lawyer and mayor of Westmount.

Toronto Department of Health well baby clinic instructed new mothers on how to care for their infants   (City of Toronto Archives/RG8-32-234)

Urban reformers enlisted in voluntary organizations ranging from the Salvation Army and the YWCA to Montreal's City Improvement League and the Union of Canadian Municipalities. These groups subjected urban life, with its racial and ethnic diversity, crowding, and largely unregulated commerce and industry, to hard scrutiny. Solutions varied, but critics were unanimous in concluding that, without immediate treatment, urban ills doomed the Dominion to recreate the worst of the old and the new worlds.

Remedies often focussed on improvements in municipal health, especially in water and milk supplies. Crises—like Montreal's 1914 typhoid scare, which led to a municipal system of water filtration—often were the immediate spur to change. Children were a particular focus of concern. Newly appointed public health doctors and nurses provided municipalities and school boards with graphic illustrations of the need for vaccination, medical inspection, and better nutrition. For middle-class women, the special appeal of local politics lay in its potential to help poor mothers and children. In Montreal Justine Lacoste-de Gaspé-Beaubien and others founded Sainte-Justine hospital for children in 1907. In Vancouver the Women's Auxiliary to the General Hospital helped the poor with services and goods, from arranging adoptions to supplying infant layettes. Methodist and Presbyterian deaconesses, clergy, and lay people enabled church-sponsored settlement houses such as Toronto's Fred Victor Mission and Halifax's Jost Mission to offer welfare programs that governments were not yet equipped to manage. Such efforts, often involving extensive negotiations with local politicians as well as church boards and other private agencies, reduced infant mortality from one end of the country to another, although poor districts like Montreal's St. Henri, Toronto's Ward, or Vancouver's Strathcona remained dangerous places in which to be born.

Growing awareness of the problem of the cities fuelled the "City Beautiful" movement, with its ideal of rational planning, handsome buildings, and public spaces. Experts like Thomas Adams, planning adviser to the Commission on Conservation, and Herbert Ames catalogued and condemned pollution, disease, crowding, corruption, immorality, and visual ugliness. Proposed parks, sewers, public baths, and water filtration plants promised more attractive environments as well as better health for all inhabitants. With such civic improvements, middle-class reformers hoped to produce not only a more healthy environment, but a more productive and law-abiding population. Middle-class planners' dreams of a sober new world of efficiency, rationality, and order left little room for such working-class institutions as the poolroom, the open-air meeting, or the saloon. Nor, for the most part, did they come to terms with the demand for cheap housing or with the differing needs of non-Anglo-Saxon, non-Protestant immigrants. The challenge for reformers was to find solutions that did not bring them into conflict with cost-conscious governments, powerful business interests, and increasingly diverse inhabitants of the growing cities.

Urban progressives were particularly suspicious, not only of the working class and immigrants, whom they ranked low in a complex racial and social hierarchy, but of private utilities in water, power, telephones, and transport. Consumer grievances with fares and service and with high-handed corporate management that ignored public dissatisfaction fuelled campaigns for municipal regulation and ownership. Results differed across the country. In 1906 a coalition of urban reformers in southern Ontario, angry about the costs and inefficiency of private electrical generation and transmission, helped create Ontario Hydro, the Dominion's first provincially owned utility. By 1909, municipal streetcars were operating in Calgary and, two years later, had begun service in Regina. By 1914, Edmonton provided its citizens with their own electricity, streetcars, and telephones. Toronto's Transit Commission took over a combination of private and public street railways, but Bell was left to manage telephone operations. In Montreal, private utilities weathered the tide of complaint. Widespread disenchantment with urban monopolies made Canadians more receptive to some form of corporate regulation and more cynical about business operations in general.

Feelings of confidence in the solutions posed by urban experts and dissatisfaction with urban utilities were accompanied by strong distrust of local democracy. Poorer citizens in particular were often portrayed by reformers as passive, potential tools of corrupt politicians. Ward politics were particularly suspect. To counter the power of local interests, Winnipeg (1906), Ottawa (1907), Montreal (1909), Hamilton (1910), and London (1914) adopted Boards of Control elected on a city-wide franchise. Because middle-class voters had a much higher turnout at the polls than working-class voters, city-wide systems often deprived workers of the representatives that the ward system gave them. An arguably more extreme attempt to wrest influence from poorer urban residents was the trend to "expert" city managers or commissioners as adopted in Edmonton in 1904, Saint John in 1908, and Regina, Saskatoon, and Prince Albert in 1911 and 1912. Handing over power to unelected officials who had no contact with the working poor was seen as a way of depoliticizing urban politics. The faith in expert urban management came naturally to an anxious middle class uncertain about its ability to guarantee peace and order on its own terms. Ironically enough, just when a widened franchise promised input from more citizens, urban reformers experimented with modern methods of imposing their will on the electorate, methods mainly imported from the United States.

Not surprisingly, the class bias of much of the reform agenda limited support from poorer districts. As the 1914 mayoralty victory of Médéric Martin—the candidate of French-speaking, working-class Montreal—illustrated, dissidents sometimes mobilized resistance to middle-class directives. While some benefits of the reform movement were undeniable, notably in public health, it was equally clear that the effort to change the Canadian city too often asserted the superiority of middle-class, Anglo-Saxon ways of life without considering the concerns and interests of the city's diverse population. It was easy for cynics like Stephen Leacock, in "The Great Fight for Clean Civic Government," to caricature reformers as creatures of a self-complacent business class and their politics as merely those of self-interest.

• Sobering Up Canada

Perhaps no struggle better summed up the contradictions of reform politics than that for temperance and prohibition. Huge numbers of predominantly Protestant, Anglo-Celtic, middle-class Canadians—at least 40 000 in Ontario alone in the 1890s—joined temperance lodges or groups like the Woman's Christian Temperance Union. The Odd Fellows, the Knights of Pythias, and the Knights of Columbus, like the Knights of Labour, closed their ranks to those involved in the liquor business. Some insurance companies offered non-drinkers preferential rates. The Methodist, Presbyterian, and Baptist churches threw their weight behind the crusade against the sale and consumption of alcohol. By the end of the nineteenth century, the Dominion Alliance for the Total Suppression of the Liquor Traffic was a formidable nation-wide organization that politicians could ignore only at their peril.

For some prohibitionists, alcohol was at the root of many of the ills of industrializing Canada: poverty, violence, crime, ill health, and family breakdown. Only by banning the sale and consumption of alcohol, the prohibitionists argued, could society be fully reconstructed. By focussing on alcohol as the problem, many prohibitionists failed to address the larger causes of social dislocation. Alcohol consumption among the working class, for example, offered a convenient explanation for both middle-class prosperity and the desperate situation of the poor, but it did little to change the class structure of industrial society. Similarly, women in the WCTU moved easily from a condemnation of alcohol to a critique of the men who did most of the drinking, but they were unable to mount a sustained attack on the patriarchal structures that dominated Canadian society.

In 1898, a national referendum on prohibition, preceded by much hard campaigning by advocates and opponents, produced a majority for the drys everywhere but in Quebec. The relatively small overall majority and a low voter turnout, both reflections of an appeal limited to certain groups, allowed Prime Minister Laurier to sidestep an issue that bitterly divided the country and to maintain the existing system of local option. His position helped to convince prohibitionist critics not only to turn their attention to the provinces, but to demand a wholesale cleansing of Canadian politics, corrupted as it was by the liquor traffic and the amoral voter. Victory for such views waited until the First World War when intoxication was perceived to threaten both domestic production and the war effort. In 1915, Saskatchewan went dry, followed by every province but Quebec. In 1918, the federal government prohibited the importation of liquor into Canada for the duration of the war. The triumph of temperance politics was short-lived. In the 1920s Canadians rejected the appeal to Victorian middle-class ideals of thrift and sobriety and, with government sale of liquor, in effect embraced a modern consumer society that glorified expenditure and indulgence. In the process, the WCTU's insight into the nature of violence against women and children largely disappeared from public view, to survive only as part of the private politics of many Canadian families.

• Provincial Rights and the Management of Progress

While Canadians identified strongly with particular social and economic groups, geography and history also made many strong provincialists and, sometimes, regionalists. Confederation was still a relatively recent phenomenon, even for its first recruits.

In the Maritimes, regional resentment flourished as all three provinces fell behind the rest of the nation in economic growth. The expansion of industries related to coal and steel in the first decade of the twentieth century masked some of the deep structural problems facing the region's economy, but no one could deny that the Maritimes generally was losing power within Confederation. In the 1890s the region held 18 percent of the seats in the House of Commons; by 1914 its representation had dropped to 13 percent. Declining representation made it difficult for the Maritime region to wrest concessions from Ottawa to meet its special needs or to exert influence in federal–provincial conferences. Faced with stagnant economies and continued outmigration, provincial governments in the region had difficulty mounting the programs increasingly demanded by the voters.

As was the case in the 1860s and 1880s, economic uncertainty and political frustration stirred Maritimers to action. In 1905, the region's business community established the Maritime Board of Trade, which resurrected the idea of Maritime union. Politicians soon followed their lead. In 1908, New Brunswick premier H.D. Hazen called for a "united Acadia" to resist decreases in Maritime parliamentary representation. The premiers of the three provinces co-ordinated their efforts to restore the absolute number of seats held at the time of Confederation, but little was achieved. The only concession to Maritime concerns was an amendment to the British North America Act in 1913, which guaranteed that representation in the House of Commons would not be less than the number of senators representing a province. For Prince Edward Island, this meant that its elected representation could not be reduced to fewer than four, scarcely the contingent required for dramatic parliamentary manoeuvres.

Limited economic prospects were reflected in the region's provincial politics. In Nova Scotia, the Liberal Party remained in office between 1882 and 1925. Farmer and Labour parties emerged to challenge mainstream politics in the provincial election of 1920 but were soon eclipsed. In New Brunswick, provincial politics were fractured by bitter sectional, religious, and cultural rivalries. The Acadian vote figured prominently in the Liberal victory of 1917, while Farmer, Labour, and Independent candidates all scored successes in 1920. In contrast, a property and municipal franchise system and a voice voting system prior to 1913 made it difficult for third parties to gain a foothold in Prince Edward Island. Other signs also pointed to the island's determination to chart its own way. In 1906, after intense debate, Prince Edward Island became the first province to embrace local option throughout its entire jurisdiction. Two years later, the assembly unanimously banned the use of automobiles in the province. Not until 1913 could cars operate, and then on a limited number of highways; it would be some years before local plebiscites sufficiently overcame rural hostility to permit automobile traffic throughout the island.

Newfoundlanders also maintained their distinctive political agenda. The building of an island railway and the settlement by 1911 of fishery disputes with France and the United States removed issues that previously had encouraged thought of a Canadian alliance. In 1908–09, the Fishermen's Protective Union, under the leadership of William Coaker, emerged as a strong political force. The FPU established cash stores to undermine the truck system that kept most fishing communities constantly in debt to the merchants. Despite the hostility of the Roman Catholic church, the FPU had 20 000 members by 1914, most of them in the Protestant areas of northeastern Newfoundland. It fielded successful candidates in the 1913 election and joined the National Government in 1917. In 1919 Coaker became minister of fisheries, but support for the FPU declined when Coaker proved unable to implement major reforms in fishery policy.

During Laurier's tenure as prime minister, many French-speaking Quebeckers nurtured hopes about their place in a federal state, but they also maintained strong, often overriding, loyalties to their own community. During their uninterrupted reign from 1897 to 1936, the provincial Liberals gave priority to economic development and private enterprise. In this they were supported by an elaborate system of public patronage, a highly partisan press, and an electoral system favouring rural constituencies. Nevertheless, the Quebec government was not entirely indifferent to problems created by industrialization and urbanization and by the growth of monopoly capitalism. With the substantial revenues accruing from natural resource development and new taxes, cautious Liberal administrations undertook a modest expansion in government services. Most notable were the provision of railroads and roads to resource sites, and the creation of educational innovations such as new technical programs, a surveying and a forestry school, and the École des Hautes Études Commerciales. Spending initiatives were very much designed to aid Quebec's economic development: before 1920, contributions to public health and welfare remained less than 10 percent of government expenditures.

Prosperity and faith in private enterprise fortified Liberal premiers like Lomer Gouin (1905–20), who concentrated on modernizing the state with new commissions and departments while regulating capitalism's worst abuses. In response to criticisms, the Liberal government agreed to lease rather than sell valuable hydraulic resources and to follow Ontario's lead in restricting the export of pulpwood in order to stimulate Quebec's paper industry. Only opposition from the Roman Catholic Church stood in the way of the Liberals' long-time hope of introducing compulsory education.

For a time it seemed as if a new nationalist party might challenge the Liberal stranglehold on the province. The leader of the nationalist movement was Henri Bourassa, the grandson of Louis Joseph Papineau and one time protégé of Laurier. In 1899 Bourassa resigned his seat in the House of Commons to protest the Liberal Party's decision to send troops to the South African War. He returned to the House of Commons in 1900 as an independent and soon emerged as the intellectual and moral leader of French-Canadian nationalism. Fortunately for Laurier, Bourassa's suspicion of party discipline meant that he concentrated on influencing public opinion and existing parties rather than forming a new organization to promote his policies. His attraction to a bilingual and bicultural Canada also put him at odds with nationalists who felt that Quebec should pursue a destiny independent from the rest of Canada.

Henri Bourassa and Wilfrid Laurier   (National Archives of Canada/C27360 and A119)

In 1907 Bourassa resigned his federal seat to enter provincial politics. There he maintained a loose alliance with the Conservative nationalists but after 1910 devoted much of his energy to his newspaper *Le Devoir*. In 1911 a strong contingent of French-Canadian nationalists was elected under the Conservative banner, but they split with the party over Canadian contributions to the British navy. As long as the provincial Conservatives suffered from guilt-by-association with their strongly pro-British federal counterpart, the Liberal government in Quebec had little to fear from them.

The only other challenge in Quebec to the Liberals was the Montreal-based Parti Ouvrier whose platform called for the nationalization of banks and utilities, government unemployment insurance, health insurance, and old age pensions, and free compulsory education. Opposed by the Roman Catholic Church, such a party had little hope of gaining a victory at the polls.

Even in Ontario, political leaders only slowly came to terms with urban–industrial development. The long Liberal reign that had begun in 1871 continued until 1905. Although reluctant to intervene in the economy, Liberals were protective of Ontario's industrial prospects, insisting that all pine timber cut on Ontario lands be sawn in Canadian mills and attempting to place a licence fee on all exported ore. In the face of the federal threat of disallowance and unrelenting hostility from mine and smelter interests, the latter initiative failed. More traditional government intervention in the form of provincial guarantees to the Timiskaming and Northern Ontario Railway opened up the northern clay belt with its promising timber and ore reserves and its potential value for colonization. In an effort to curb the worst abuses of economic individualism, successive Liberal governments increased funding to public welfare and education, bringing improvements to some factories and schools. By 1905, the Liberals were floundering. Their Victorian creed provided few answers to urban industrial distress or increasing class conflict. Scandals, mounting rural disenchantment, and a growing reputation for inefficiency finally undermined a tired Liberal administration.

Under Conservative Premiers James Whitney and William Hearst, the worst electoral abuses and political patronage were abolished. The province's educational system received a boost, notably in improved support for the University of Toronto, new normal schools, better teachers' salaries, additional funding for technical education, and the creation of the Royal Ontario Museum and the Ontario College of Art. Conservative governments also wooed rural voters with better roads, drainage programs, assistance to specialized agriculture, and support for Ontario Hydro. The Conservative vision remained more limited when it came to winning the loyalty of urban workers. Despite bitter strikes and the rising cost of living, Whitney opposed a minimum wage and saw little role for unions. In 1914, Hearst became premier. Although Hearst searched for new policies, breaking new ground in plans for mothers' allowances and setting aside the first funding for public housing, his attempts at innovation alienated traditional Tory voters without winning new support. Farmers remained unhappy with a government that seemed insensitive to their concerns and organized workers resented the failure of the government to act on the recommendations of the Ontario Unemployment Commission to appoint a minister of labour and to introduce some form of unemployment insurance. Women were offended by Hearst's slow conversion to suffrage. The stage was set for the 1919 victory of the United Farmers of Ontario and a new premier, Ernest Charles Drury.

On the Prairies, much of political life revolved around conflict with the federal government. Politicians often appealed to the electorate not so much on the basis of policies or party allegiance but as champions of the territory or the province against Ottawa. In Manitoba, debates revolved around the extension of boundaries (not finalized until 1912), the rights of separate schools (only temporarily settled with the Laurier–Greenway Agreement in 1897), and the natural resources question (unsettled until 1930). Prairie politics also testified to the rising power of organized farmers. Manitoba forced the Winnipeg Grain Exchange to rescind its expulsion of the Grain Growers' Grain Company co-operative, experimented briefly with the public ownership of grain elevators, and, to ensure rural service often unavailable from commercial firms, created North America's first publicly owned telephone company.

Ethnic divisions bedevilled Manitoba politics. Sir Rodmond Roblin's Conservative administration (1900–15) nurtured a patronage machine increasingly dependent on the votes of non-British immigrants. In the 1914 election, a government majority was maintained only by sweeping non-British ridings. The Liberals' triumph a year later owed much to a largely Anglo-Saxon reform movement frustrated by supposed immigrant influence over the administration. The new government, inspired both by the social gospel and the Great War's heightened nativism, embraced civil service reform, temperance, the eight-hour workday, improvements in labour legislation, compulsory primary education, and woman suffrage. Little sympathy was spared for the organized working class, whose protests were often traced to so-called foreign agitators and sometimes associated with events in revolutionary Russia. For all the middle-class nativist fears, the first provincial seat for Labour was in fact won in 1914 by an English immigrant, Fred Dixon, and the labour movement itself was, as elsewhere, far from immune to racist and anti-immigrant sentiments.

By the late 1890s sizeable population increases in the Northwest Territories produced calls for schools, roads, and other services that the territorial treasury, limited to federal subsidies, could not easily grant. A movement for provincehood, led by the territorial legislature and newspapers, gained wide support, and both national political parties felt obliged to accede to the demand. Laurier's decision to create two provinces rather than one, while officially explained with reference to the sheer size of the Northwest Territories, was in reality due to the popularity of the Conservative territorial government leader, F.W.G. Haultain. The Prime Minister feared that if only one province were created, this vast region might become a Tory fiefdom. Division into two provinces would mean that, in at least one province, the Liberals would not face Haultain in an election. Laurier invited Liberals to form the government in both new provinces, giving his party a substantial patronage advantage over the rival Conservatives. He also created a continuing source of federal–provincial friction in deciding, contrary to British constitutional practice, to hold public lands and natural resources for the benefit of Ottawa. Laurier's efforts to retain the independent Catholic and French school system of the 1880s were successfully resisted by Manitoba MP Clifford Sifton who, rejecting a bilingual/bicultural future for his region, resigned his cabinet position in protest.

Despite growing resentment of eastern domination, most readily visible in attacks on the CPR, regional sentiments were for a long time

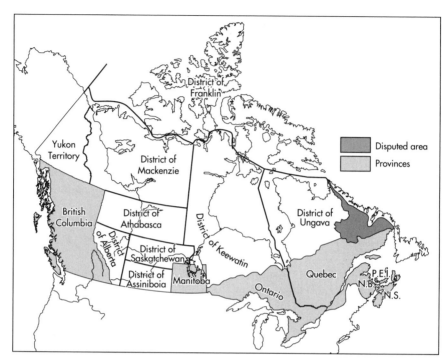

MAP 7.1　*Canada, 1898*　(D.G.G. Kerr, *Historical Atlas of Canada* (Scarborough: Nelson, 1975), 67)

contained within the two-party system and by an optimistic faith in the ultimate triumph of Prairie democracy. Agrarian leaders were respectfully consulted and frequently brought into provincial governments where they guaranteed legislation such as that providing for the Saskatchewan Co-operative Elevator Company owned and operated by farmers. Liberal administrations also listened to reform coalitions of women, farmers, and professionals, responding with such progressive measures as female suffrage and mothers' pensions. Workers were substantially less welcome, finding few legislative benefits coming their way. Middle-class optimism about shaping the new Prairie community was hard hit by the First World War. The anxious uncertainty of that conflict strengthened elite determination to suppress all challenges to British-Canadian rule from immigrants and the organized working class.

In British Columbia, federal–provincial politics centred on disagreement over federal subsidies and Ottawa's disallowance of legislation designed to restrict Asian immigration. For many years after the province

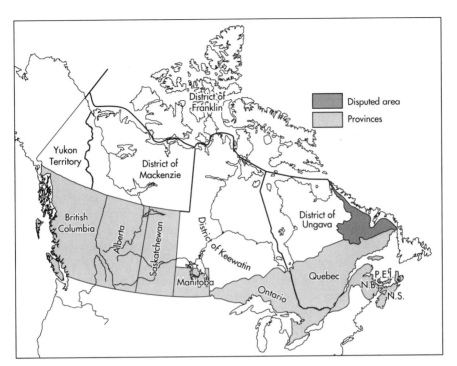

MAP 7.2   *Canada, 1905*   (D.G.G. Kerr, *Historical Atlas of Canada* (Scarborough: Nelson, 1975), 67)

joined Confederation, the British Columbia legislature, much like the legislature of the Northwest Territories, was characterized not by strict party lines but by loose personal and sectional coalitions. Transportation and business interests were especially noticeable, although a few pro-labour MLAs were also elected. In 1903 a series of unstable administrations gave way to party government on the federal model under Conservative Premier Richard McBride. By the election of 1909, his platform of railway promotion, Asiatic exclusion, and better terms for the province in Confederation routed all but two Liberals and two Socialists from the legislature. A prewar depression that stretched to 1915, and Liberal effectiveness in taking up the progressive causes—notably temperance, female suffrage, and clean government—brought victory for Harlan Brewster's Liberals in 1916. The early period of Liberal rule saw the heyday of reform hopes, with the introduction not only of an extended franchise but of mothers' pensions, a minimum wage, public health laboratories, schools for handicapped children, and longer compulsory school attendance.

• The Federal Government and Laurier Liberalism

Laurier's talent for political management as well as his awareness of the strength of provincial sentiments was evident in the formation of his first cabinet. His ministers, who included powerful local chieftains—W.S. Fielding of Nova Scotia, Oliver Mowat of Ontario, and A.G. Blair of New Brunswick—and rising newcomers like Clifford Sifton of Manitoba, reflected an updated liberalism stripped of its *rouge* and Clear Grit radicalism. Also deserted was the traditional Liberal adherence to free trade. In 1897 the new tariff promised to offer the best of old and new, protection but with a so-called "British preference" that applied lower tariffs to any country admitting Canadian products at a rate equal to the minimum Canadian tariff. Little changed from the old National Policy with the ongoing emphasis on railway expansion and western settlement. The eastern-based Grand Trunk and the western-based Canadian Northern were both encouraged to complete transcontinental lines, at considerable cost to the taxpayer. The vast sums involved meant that Liberal railway policy often brought in its wake the political corruption that had accompanied construction of the CPR.

• Imperialism, Nationalism, and Reciprocity

Compromise proved equally elusive in international relations. Queen Victoria's Diamond Jubilee of 1897 and the South African War (1899–1902) roused fierce feelings in both English and French Canada. As historian Carl Berger has argued,[4] the nationalism of men such as Stephen Leacock, George Grant, George Parkin, and George Denison could not readily be distinguished from a high-minded, if often jingoistic, British imperialism. For such nationalists, the lessons of race and history dictated closer association with Great Britain. As the natural heir to the "greatest empire the world has ever known," Canada would inevitably assume a major role on the world stage and support Britain's efforts to exert control over the Dutch settlers—known as Boers—in South Africa and nationalists in Ireland. In contrast, French Canadians like Henri Bourassa identified with the Boers and the Irish nationalists.

In the Imperial Conferences of 1897, 1902, 1907, and 1911, Laurier defended Dominion autonomy, but finding a middle ground was often difficult. Once official hostilities broke out in South Africa in 1899, French Canada found itself pitted against English-Canadian demands for participation, lobbying from the British-appointed General Office commanding the Canadian militia, and pressure from the British Colonial Office for an official Canadian presence. Laurier offered a compromise: Ottawa would equip and raise volunteers, but once in South Africa they would be paid by the British. More than 7000 Canadians eventually saw service. Laurier was also lukewarm to proposals from the British Colonial Secretary, Joseph Chamberlain, for an imperial council on defence. Neither Canadian imperialists nor French-Canadian nationalists were satisfied. The founding of the Imperial Order Daughters of the Empire and passionate celebrations of Empire Day in English Canada, and the strong stand against imperialist sentiment taken by Henri Bourassa in Quebec, promised an uncertain future for Laurier's effort to find a middle path. Yet, so long as his opponents remained in disarray, no rival could match Laurier's ability to manufacture a fragile political consensus.

Laurier was doubly careful about imperial defence because he needed British support in negotiating with the rising American empire. By the late 1890s, Klondike gold discoveries made the Yukon's disputed boundary with Alaska a key area of concern. Canada's dependence on Britain was reflected in the makeup of an international judicial tribunal to decide the issue in 1903. Two Canadians found an uncertain ally in the British appointee, Lord Alverstone, in negotiating with three American commissioners, loyal appointees of President Theodore Roosevelt, whose commitment to territorial expansion was common knowledge. The British decision to side with the United States over the boundary demonstrated that Anglo-American accord was more important to Britain, worried by the increasing military might of imperial Germany, than were good relations with its former colony. This hard lesson about their relative importance sparked anti-British outbursts and strengthened an autonomous nationalism among Canadians.

By 1907 the crisis created by an escalating Anglo-German naval rivalry tested Canada's relationship with Great Britain once again. Was the Dominion to make a direct financial contribution towards the cost of dreadnoughts to the Admiralty or to establish its own navy? In 1910, Laurier's Naval Service Bill proposed a Canadian navy that, in times of war, could be placed under imperial control, and rejected any regular contribution to the Admiralty. United in their disdain for Laurier's "tinpot navy," the Conservatives were nevertheless deeply divided between an English-Canadian majority demanding a direct contribution and a small band of French Canadians who opposed both a contribution to Britain and a separate Canadian navy. The debate over naval policy deepened the division carved by the South

African War and the Autonomy Bills—which created the new provinces of Alberta and Saskatchewan—between Laurier and Henri Bourassa.

Just as matters looked increasingly difficult for Laurier, the United States seemingly provided an issue to unite the country and defeat the prime minister's enemies. Under President Taft, the Americans proposed a comprehensive trade agreement that allowed the free entry of most natural products and set lower rates on a number of commodities, including agricultural implements. Federal Liberals were jubilant. Here, it seemed, was the solution to farm grievances and a means of satisfying those who had long treasured positive memories of the pre-Confederation period of reciprocity.

•The 1911 Election and the Conservative Agenda

At first glance, the phlegmatic Robert Laird Borden, federal Conservative leader since 1901, was not the man to challenge the charismatic Laurier. Yet this respectable Halifax lawyer had managed to rebuild a party shattered by the divisions of the 1890s. His progressive Halifax Platform of 1907 included endorsement of a degree of public ownership, rural free mail delivery, and civil service reform. By 1911, the Conservatives, unlike the Liberals, were also backed by effective local organizations. Conservative spirits were raised further still by the desertion of two key groups of Liberals. Enraged by the prospect of reciprocity, eighteen prominent Toronto businessmen and financiers, along with long-time Liberal allies like the Canadian Manufacturers Association, dropped the party they had formerly supported so generously. Together with dissident Liberal MPs like Clifford Sifton and Lloyd Harris, they denounced reciprocity as a threat to Canadian survival, a step towards absorption by the United States and, not so incidentally, a threat to the Dominion's manufacturing interests. Laurier's Quebec stronghold also crumbled as Bourassa's nationalists, damning the naval policy as a sell-out to English Canada, found common cause with Quebec francophone Conservatives.

Months of heated debate and pamphleteering preceded the federal election of 1911. Reciprocity and the naval policy, the two issues that more than any other posed the question of Canada's future, combined with the usual appeal of patronage, local issues, and local candidates to defeat the Liberals. Their 623 554 votes only slightly trailed the Conservatives with 666 074, but the distribution of seats was decisive. The Liberals won only eighty-seven, going down to humiliating defeat in Ontario; the Conservatives took 134 seats, including twenty-seven in Quebec where the alliance with nationalists boosted Conservative fortunes. Neither Laurier's individualist Liberalism nor his efforts to steer a middle course between differing visions of Canada proved sufficient to the problems of the day. Borden soon found that his course would not be an easy one. With the nation sorely divided over national policy, his efforts to implement election promises often faced stiff opposition not only in the House and Senate but within his own party.

Once in office, Borden moved quickly to reward Quebec, Ontario, and Manitoba with grants of federal lands, which nearly doubled the size of those provinces. He also attempted to take the politics out of tariff policy by establishing a Tariff Commission. Meanwhile, western farmers were wooed by construction of the first leg of the long-promised Hudson Bay Railway, which provided an alternative port at Churchill for grain shipments, and the Canada Grain Act, which regulated the inspection and marketing of grain and authorized the federal government to build or acquire and operate terminal elevators. In keeping with their progressive philosophy, the Conservatives introduced legislation that would provide federal funding for agricultural education, provincial highways, and extended rural mail delivery. Unfortunately for Borden, the policies he championed received rough treatment in the Liberal-dominated Senate. Many of the government's bills were severely amended, and both the Highways Bill and Tariff Commission Bill were rejected.

The dead weight of the Senate also hampered Borden's foreign policy. Taking on the External Affairs portfolio himself, Borden slowly introduced reforms into the department, which had been created by the Laurier administration in 1909. In exchange for a contribution to British defence, Borden demanded a greater voice in shaping imperial foreign policy. His French-Canadian followers remained unreconciled, even by the promise of a permanent independent navy. The Conservative Naval Aid Bill finally went down to defeat in the Liberal-dominated Senate, leaving Canadian defence policy in shambles.

The efforts to transform the civil service from an inefficient, uncoordinated institution staffed by friends of the government to an efficient corps of professionals also ran into roadblocks. Having grown over many years in response to a variety of demands, the Canadian civil service was anything but the efficient bureaucratic machine that its critics felt it should be. Its problems could only partly be blamed on Conservatives who wanted their turn at the trough after so many years out of office. Even when patronage was not an issue, it was difficult to find highly trained people for relatively poorly paid and seemingly unexciting jobs.

Partisan politics and bureaucratic inefficiency were not Borden's only worries. In 1913 the nation sank into a severe depression that continued into 1916. As early as 1912, it was clear that prices were rising faster than wages and that the average worker was being caught in the squeeze. By 1913 the London credit market had tightened, crippling farmers, business people, and wage earners alike. Unemployment rose alarmingly. Borden appointed a commission to look into the high cost of living and urged the railways to maintain full employment over the winter. Plans for Senate reform and policies to address the economic crisis were much on Borden's mind as he contemplated an election in 1914. Events in Europe caused him to set everything aside.

•The Great War
The War at Home

Canada was automatically at war when Great Britain responded to Germany's invasion of Belgium with a declaration of hostilities in August 1914. Yet neither the Canadian state nor its people were prepared for what lay ahead. Struggling to deal with unprecedented demands, Conservatives and Liberals united to pass the War Measures Act, which massively increased the powers of the federal government, giving it full authority to do everything deemed "necessary for the security, defence, peace, order and welfare of Canada." Such legislation could not compensate for the inexperience, corruption, and confusion that dogged the mobilization of the Canadian Expeditionary Force under Sam Hughes, Borden's minister of militia and defence. Hughes was finally dismissed from his portfolio in 1916, but by that time his administrative incompetence had brought an avalanche of criticism against the government's handling of the war effort.

While Canadians celebrated the courage of troops at battlefields from Ypres to Vimy Ridge, they also confronted renewed divisions at home. The fact that the majority of the First Division consisted of recent immigrants from Great Britain was conveniently forgotten as English Canadians focussed on Quebec's lacklustre recruitment. French Canadians were generally sympathetic to the Allied cause, but their alienation from the British Crown and remote connection with France left few interested in joining the armed forces. Anger at Ontario's 1912 legislation restricting French-language instruction, and at the military's reluctance to create French-speaking regiments, reinforced feelings of estrangement from a cause that became identified with Britain and English Canada. As the casualty lists published in Canadian papers lengthened, Borden resorted to conscription to make good his 1916 promise of 500 000 Canadian recruits. Opposition among western farmers was reduced by generous exemption provisions, especially for agricultural workers, in the Military Service Act of 1917. A year later, losses in Europe brought the cancellation of all exemptions.

In their refusal to support the war effort wholeheartedly, Quebeckers were not alone. At least as difficult was the situation facing almost 90 000 "enemy aliens," many of whom were long-time residents of Canada and were hostile to their country of origin, but who were forced to register with police. Over 8000 were interned, including over 3000 Canadian citizens. Radicals, like labour leader Ginger Goodwin, who was eventually murdered by police, condemned the war as the product of capitalist rivalries. Conscription radicalized the western labour movement as moderate labourites joined socialists in demanding that wealth be conscripted (that is, that all industrial profits be confiscated during wartime) before men. Pacifists like J.S. Woodsworth and Francis Marion Beynon took issue with the government because they believed war to be a totally inadequate means of ensuring international peace. Official measures did little to address such grievances, leaving them to fester and their memory to divide subsequent generations.

Canadians were also divided by the fact that the war economy touched groups very differently. Governments lacked professional civil servants capable of equitably managing an economy suddenly on a war footing. As a result, Ottawa was critically dependent on the expertise and good will of business people like Joseph Flavelle, general manager of the William Davies Packing Company, who became chair of the Imperial Munitions Board. Companies, especially those producing munitions, but also suppliers of food, clothing, and military goods of all types, recorded huge profits. Criticism of such heavy profits and charges of corruption in the awarding of military contracts made Canadians increasingly sceptical about businesses' patriotic claims, all the more so when they compared the prosperity of those like Flavelle to the deprivation suffered by the servicemen's families who relied on the charity of the Canadian Patriotic Fund.

By 1916, war production had ended unemployment, and factories and farms competed with the military for recruits. Prompted by patriotic desires to increase production and to free men for military service as well as by the need to support themselves and their families, women left paid and unpaid work in the nation's homes to labour in factories, fields, department stores, and banks. Like the male workers they joined and replaced, albeit at lower wages, women confronted wartime inflation and a soaring cost of living. Canada's War Labour Policy, which was proclaimed in 1918, prohibited strikes, lockouts, and discrimination against union members. It affirmed the right to organize and called for fair wages and equal pay for equal work, but ultimately it was largely ineffective. The failure of the government to address glaring inequities in the impact of the war contributed to union expansion, rising levels of strike activity, and, despite the outlawing of various radical organizations, radical protest.

Labour shortages from 1916 to the end of the war blunted employers' strongest weapon in the battle to prevent unionization and strikes: the threat of the sack. There was no desperate reserve army of labour willing to take the jobs of striking workers, and, in the period before another recession struck in 1920, workers recognized their potential power in bringing employers to heel. In Trenton, for example, Nova Scotia workers formed an industrial union that included labourers in the steel and car works and the Pictou County coal mines. The steelworkers, following the coal miners, demonstrated militancy in their demands for better wages and a cleaner, safer plant, but their union collapsed after the war when munitions contracts dried up. The company, taking advantage of farmers and fishers available for work for part of the year, held out against union demands. Ultimately, its decision to avoid improving labour productivity by maintaining a low-wage policy made the company increasingly uncompetitive.

In Newfoundland, as in Canada, wartime labour shortages led to a spread of industrial unionism followed by its collapse in the postwar recession. The Newfoundland Industrial Workers' Association organized railway shops, longshoremen, street railway workers, and factory workers. Its Ladies' Branch in St John's organized a series of militant strikes in manufacturing operations in 1918 and 1919. But postwar unemployment broke the union and allowed employers to roll back wage gains. Wartime hopes of transcending traditionally poor employment prospects that caused thousands of Newfoundlanders to resettle in New England and New York gave way to a new out-migration.

Increasing unhappiness with Ottawa's ability to deal with the war was reflected in a string of provincial victories for the Liberal Party between 1915 and 1917. The Conservatives, motivated by Borden's ill-considered pledge of half a million recruits and by mounting losses in Europe, pressed on with the Military Service Act drafting single men between the ages of twenty and thirty-five in August 1917. The result split both old parties: Quebec Conservatives deserted party ranks, and many English-Canadian Liberals voted against their leader and in favour of conscription. Borden's awareness of Conservative weakness and his heartfelt belief that conscription was essential if Canada was to meet its obligations led him to propose a wartime coalition to Laurier. The seventy-eight-year-old Liberal chief rejected the proposal, concluding "If I were now to take a different attitude, I would simply hand over the province [Quebec] to the Nationalists, and the consequences may be very serious." Inspired by the nationalist sentiments of their own community, enough English-Canadian Liberals accepted Borden's offer to enable him to form a so-called Union Government in late 1917. Success in the subsequent election was further assured by the exemption of farmers' sons from conscription, by the Military Voters Act, which enfranchised all members of the armed forces regardless of sex or length of residence in Canada, and by the Wartime Elections Act, which enfranchised all female relatives of servicemen and disfranchised all conscientious objectors and those immigrants who had arrived from enemy countries since 1902. As Dr Margaret Gordon, President of the Canadian Suffrage Association observed, "it would have been more direct and at the same time more honest if the bill simply stated that all who did not pledge themselves to vote Conservative would be disfranchised." In Quebec all but three ridings supported Laurier. Beyond that province, the Liberals carried only ten of twenty-eight seats in the Maritimes, eight of eighty-two in Ontario, and two of fifty-seven in the West.

The division of the country along cultural lines appeared to be complete as anti-conscription riots rocked Quebec in 1918 and the provincial legislature debated a secessionist resolution. Five civilians shot by soldiers in Quebec City in a protest against conscription provided martyrs to the francophone cause. But many anglophones also opposed conscription. The labour movement, particularly in Western Canada, demanded that all war profiteering end before any consideration could be given to conscription.

Canadian nurses at a hospital in France voting in 1917   (National Archives of Canada/PA2279)

Civilian voters in the Maritimes gave a slight majority of their votes to anti-conscription candidates. Even in Ontario, anti-conscriptionists, though winning only 10 percent of the seats, won almost 40 percent of the civilian vote.

Whether conscription served even its military purpose has been much debated not only at the time but by subsequent generations of historians. Of 400 000 men who registered under the legislation, defaults, desertions, and tribunals sympathetic to local boys meant that fewer than 125 000 were successfully drafted and less than 25 000 went to France. A year after the election, Canada's soldiers were lining up to come home and rioting over the slowness of demobilization. The political costs of conscription lasted into the next three decades. There was ultimately no satisfactory answer to the question posed by critics like Francis Beynon and J.S. Woodsworth as to why labour was conscripted before wealth.

The Battlefield

While patriotism motivated many young men who joined the armed forces, many others went overseas in search of adventure. As Larry Nelson, a Toronto enlistee in 1914, recalled, "most of us were young and saw it as a wonderful opportunity to throw off the shackles of working in an office or a factory or on a farm or what-have-you."[5] Still others, victims of the 1913–14 recession, enlisted to have a steady job. Most, raised on a diet of pro-British propaganda that suggested the Empire's military invincibility, were unprepared for a protracted war of unspeakable slaughter on both sides. A small group, of whom the best known was Lieutenant-Colonel W.A. "Billy" Bishop, would join the Royal Flying Corps, making use of the relatively new "aeroplane" to spy on enemy movements and to shoot down enemy planes. But most Canadian recruits went to the European front, and that meant the trenches in France and Belgium.

Life in the trenches was horrendous. Men remained in the pits for a week or more at a time in all kinds of weather before they were relieved briefly to go to makeshift rest camps. Covered with lice, many developed "trench fever" and frostbite. Rats nibbled the corpses of fallen comrades while the infantrymen dug new trenches and maintained existing ones, moved supplies, and tried not to think of their hunger and fear. Charles Yale Harrison, an American in the Canadian Expeditionary Force, recalled his reaction to a German shelling:

> I am terrified. I hug the earth, digging my fingers into every crevice, every hole.
>
> A blinding flash and an explosive howl a few feet in front of the trench. My bowels liquify. Acrid smoke bites the throat, parches the

mouth. I am beyond mere fright. I am frozen with an insane fear that keeps me cowering in the bottom of the trench. I lie flat on my belly waiting. . . .

Suddenly it stops.[6]

Fear was justified. Of just over 650 000 Canadians who enlisted or were conscripted, about 60 000 died, and at least as many were wounded, whether physically or mentally, severely enough to be unable to resume a normal life. The mentally wounded, or "shell shocked" as they came to be known, returned to a society that was ill-prepared for such casualties. While a soldier whose wounds put him in a wheelchair received a government pension and the sympathy of other Canadians, there was little comfort for the many returnees who seemed unfit to resume their family or work life, and who stared vacantly into space or sought comfort in the bottle.

Canadians generally applauded the heroism of their soldiers. Several battles were particularly important in galvanizing English-Canadian opinion

---

"MANPOWER" AND THE WAR

The shortage of soldiers for the war effort was compounded by the exclusionary policies practised by the Canadian military. Despite the eagerness of some Canadian women to serve overseas, they were unwelcome on the front lines. The only official role for women in the armed forces was as nurses in the Canadian Army Nursing Service, a branch of the Canadian Army Medical Corps. Some 3000 nursing sisters served in the First World War, and forty-seven lost their lives in active duty, victims of enemy attack and disease contracted from patients.

When Indian, Japanese, or African-Canadian men offered their services, they, too, were often turned away. The commander of the 104th Overseas Battalion, for instance, rejected fourteen black would-be recruits in Saint John because, he argued, accepting them would have been unfair to his white recruits. As the manpower shortage became critical, and blacks became more insistent, military leaders decided to create a segregated unit that would not offend the racist sensibilities of the men at the front. The No. 2 Construction Battalion was established in July 1916 with its headquarters in Nova Scotia. Commanded by white officers, its rank and file was recruited from black communities across Canada and included some 145 African Americans who crossed the border to participate in the war. The battalion was attached to the Canadian Forestry Corps, a labour unit whose job was to support the men fighting at the front.

Trench warfare (National Archives of Canada/PA1326)

and creating support for conscription. Ypres was the first. It was during this battle in 1915 that the Germans first used chlorine gas in an attempt to asphyxiate enemy forces. There were more than 7000 Canadian casualties at Ypres. Although most of the fatalities were from artillery shells rather than chemicals, the introduction of chemical weaponry added another danger for soldiers at the front. It was the battle of Ypres that inspired Lieutenant-Colonel John McCrae, a Canadian doctor, to write the poem "In Flanders Fields," a moving call to keep faith with the soldiers who had given up their lives.

Canadian forces were responsible for a major allied victory on 9 April 1917 at Vimy Ridge in France. The capture of this piece of high ground came at the cost of 3598 Canadian dead and 7004 wounded, but the strategic importance of the victory raised morale among the war's supporters. It also likely helped to garner public support for Borden when he announced his intention to introduce conscription a month later. The next major assault involving Canadians was less successful: 15 654 Canadian casualties were reported at the Battle of Passchendaele, although it brought the Allies no closer to victory.

For many Canadians, the heavy casualties underscored the futility of war generally and the "Great War" in particular. Even if most people were unswayed by socialists' claims that the war was simply a contest between two rapacious groups of capitalist imperialists, many Canadians had no real idea what the war was about. Some never doubted the justice of the British cause and believed that the sacrifices Canada had made demonstrated its right to a larger share in imperial decision making.

• Canada on the World Stage

Borden's willingness to smash the nationalist–Conservative coalition that had elected his party in Quebec in 1911 owed much to his faith that Canada would emerge from the First World War with new international status. Right from the beginning, he pressed hard to give the Dominion a voice in imperial war planning. British governments, reluctant to share imperial power, but eager for an economic and military commitment from Canada and its sister dominions and colonies, slowly gave way but only after they had proved irritatingly insensitive to Canada's emergence as a major combatant and contributor to the war effort. The Dominion's disillusionment deepened with early German victories and mounting proof of incompetence among the British military leadership. Borden argued passionately that Canadians would be unwilling to make greater sacrifices if they were not given a voice in policy making. In 1917 when British Prime Minister Lloyd George called an Imperial War Conference and created the Imperial War Cabinet, Canadians seemed on the way to winning a formal role in setting a common foreign policy.

In the same year, the United States entered the war as an ally of Britain and Canada. For some time, Canada had been instrumental in defending British policies to Americans suspicious of British imperialism and angered by the violation of the freedom of the seas represented by the British blockade of Germany. Following the American entry into the war, the co-ordinated defence of the North Atlantic began an unprecedented military relationship between the two North American nations. A German military resurgence early in 1918 and the British failure to make good on promises of adequate consultation with the dominions combined to make the North American alliance all the more critical.

When Germany surrendered, and Armistice was declared on 11 November 1918, efforts to institute meaningful military consultation between Britain and its empire collapsed. The struggle for appropriate recognition of Canadian sacrifice shifted to Borden's demand for Canadian representation at the peace conference. It was acknowledged by separate Dominion representation on the British Empire Delegation to the Paris peace conference, separate membership in the new League of Nations and the International Labour Organization, and separate ratification of the Versailles peace treaty.

At home, Canadians disagreed about the meaning of their new status. Divided on how to pursue the war they had joined so naively, they were equally divided on the meaning of their commitment to the international security system embodied in the League covenant. In distancing them from Great Britain, bringing them closer to the United States, and introducing them to the dilemmas of international security, World War I raised questions of status and independence that would disturb Canadians deeply over the next two decades.

•What Brave New World?

Many Canadians, particularly those who had long been committed to the reform of their society, believed that the war offered an unprecedented opportunity for national regeneration. Social gospellers like the Methodists Salem Bland and Nellie McClung interpreted the struggle against Germany as a classic conflict of good against evil. In the crucible of conflict, old apathy and materialism would disappear and a better nation would emerge. United in patriotism and committed to self-sacrifice, citizens would discover the will to remake society in the image desired by middle-class progressives. The wartime triumph of prohibition and woman suffrage for a time raised reform hopes. A flood of publications, like McClung's *In Times Like These* (1915), *The New Era in Canada* (1917), Bland's *The New Christianity* (1920), J.T.M. Anderson's *The Education of New Canadians* (1920), Stephen Leacock's *The Unsolved Riddle of Social Justice* (1920), and William Lyon Mackenzie King's *Industry and Humanity* (1918) asked contemporaries to take up the war's challenge of creating a more just world.

Not coincidentally, given their class and ethnic background, the society these writers had in mind was fundamentally British in character and "progressive" in ideology. Although French Canadians were generally far less optimistic about postwar prospects, reform-minded Catholics also developed a progressive social critique. Activists like Father Joseph Archambault, author of *La Question Sociale et Nos Devoirs de Catholiques* (1917) and the founder of the Catholic-action magazine *Semaine Sociale* in 1920, pointed to the poverty, the class conflict, and the secularism that needed solutions if French Canada was to survive and prosper.

For many, the war proved a lesson in disillusionment. Higher profits for a few were accompanied by low wages, bad working conditions, and a spiralling cost of living for many. Governments, desperate to mobilize resources for war and with few close ties to labour, did little to rectify abuses. Political tensions mounted quickly when crises at home as well as losses in Europe dampened morale and found governments ill-equipped to aid their citizens. Public confidence faltered badly with the Halifax explosion of December 1917. In that horrifying event, more than two square kilometres of the city's north end disappeared after a French ship carrying almost 2000 tonnes of explosives blew up in Halifax harbour, killing 1600 people and injuring another 9000 out of a population of 50 000. The great flu epidemic of the winter of 1918–19, which took its worst toll among Canadians aged twenty to forty, carried off at least 50 000, leaving citizens everywhere reeling with shock. Such disasters contributed to a rising tide of discontent that would sweep Borden's successor, Arthur Meighen, and his party from power in 1921.

Domestic conflicts may have developed in response to specific Canadian conditions, but they did not develop in isolation. The Bolshevik Revolution in Russia in 1917 and the rising tide of socialist and communist protest in Europe and the United States terrified Canadian politicians and business people just as they inspired the Canadian left. The dispatch of Canadians to Murmansk and Vladivostok as part of a combined allied endeavour to put an end to the Russian Revolution was fiercely protested by a labour movement that saw yet one more instance of state support for a status quo that gave immense advantages to the rich and powerful.

Unhappy as it might be with the Union Government, the labour movement was also deeply divided. Conservative eastern craft unionism took control of the Trades and Labour Congress at the 1918 convention, but the Western Labour Conference held shortly thereafter in Calgary broke with TLC policies of conciliation and restraint, resolving to create a single industrial union, the "One Big Union" (OBU), to challenge conservative unionists, hostile employers, and unsympathetic governments. Unlike the anti-electoral IWW, the leadership of the fledgling OBU included many socialists who saw strike action as one arm of class struggle and electioneering as its complement. But before the fledgling OBU could hold its founding convention, its strike philosophy had an unanticipated dry run. On 5 May 1919, the Winnipeg Trades and Labour Council called a general strike following the breakdown between management and labour in the metal and building trades in the city. At stake were the principle of collective bargaining and better wages and working conditions. Although only 12 000 of Winnipeg's workers belonged to a union of any kind, about 30 000 workers joined the strike within hours of the call for action. They included female telephone operators and department store retail clerks who had waged successful wartime strikes and hoped to consolidate their gains by working to strengthen the labour movement as a whole.

Winnipeg's strike sparked a series of general strikes of varying lengths across the country. Although these strikes were ostensibly held in support of the Winnipeg workers, local grievances came to the fore everywhere. Poverty and internal divisions caused most of these strikes to come to an end within a month. The Winnipeg strike was the longest, stretching from

Demonstrations during Winnipeg General Strike, June 1919   (Provincial Archives of Manitoba)

May 15 to June 26. Its leaders made every effort to keep it orderly, agreeing to have essential services such as milk delivery continue throughout the strike. But strike opponents, drawn mainly from the employer and professional groups in the city, organized a citizens' committee to crush the strike

---

BLOODY SATURDAY

The events of 21 June 1919 in Winnipeg were a reminder of the state's willingness to use violence against those it deemed too radical. Following is the official strikers' view of the events of that afternoon as reported in *Strike Bulletin*, the newspaper published by the Strike Committee.

One is dead and a number injured, probably thirty or more, as a result of the forcible prevention of the "silent parade" which had been planned by returned men to start at 2:30 o'clock last Saturday afternoon. Apparently the bloody business was carefully planned, for Mayor Gray issued a proclamation in the morning stating that "Any women taking part in a parade do so at their own risk." Nevertheless a vast crowd of men, women and children assembled to witness the "silent parade." . . .

On Saturday, about 2:30 p.m., just the time when the parade was scheduled to start, some 50 mounted men swinging baseball bats rode down Main Street. Half were red-coated R.N.W.M.P., the others wore khaki. They quickened pace as they passed the Union Bank. The crowd opened, let them through and closed in behind them. They turned and charged through the crowd again, greeted by hisses and boos, and some stones. There were two riderless horses with the squad when it emerged and galloped up Main Street. The men in khaki disappeared at this juncture, but the red-coats reined their horses and reformed opposite the old post office.

Then, with revolvers drawn, they galloped down Main Street, turned, and charged right into the crowd on William Avenue, firing as they charged. One man, standing on the sidewalk, thought the mounties were firing blank cartridges until a spectator standing beside him dropped with a bullet through the head. We have no exact information about the total number of casualties, but these were not less than thirty. The crowd dispersed as quickly as possible when the shooting began.

and discredit its leadership. Insisting that the strike was Bolshevik-inspired, the so-called Citizens' Committee of One Thousand refused to let the issue of employees' right to collective bargaining become the sole focus of the debate. When it became apparent that the city's police supported the strikers, the committee influenced the mayor in having the entire force replaced by people unsympathetic to the strike. With encouragement from the anti-strike forces, the federal government sent the Royal North West Mounted Police to Winnipeg, allegedly to maintain order. On 21 June—a day that became known as "Bloody Saturday"—the Mounties attempted to disperse war veterans holding an illegal demonstration in support of the strike. The demonstrators refused to leave and the police therefore fired a volley of shots into the crowd. By the end of the day, two men were dead and many other protesters were injured.

Strikers were also arrested by the score. Included among those jailed were two Winnipeg aldermen and a member of the Manitoba legislature. Recognizing the state's determination to crush the strike, those leaders who had not yet been imprisoned capitulated on 26 June. Winnipeg would remain a class-divided city for generations to come. Its working-class residents north of Portage Avenue were as divided politically as they were culturally from the wealthier citizens in the city's south end.

A heightened awareness of class division, like the differences that increasingly separated French and English Canada, was a long-term legacy of the First World War. One hero of the Winnipeg General Strike, J.S. Woodsworth, who was imprisoned as editor of the strike newspaper, went on to represent Winnipeg's working-class north end in Parliament as a member of the Labour Party. Eventually he would lead the Co-operative Commonwealth Federation to contest the right of the two old parties to monopolize the formal political choices available to Canadians. Other veterans of the strike would join the Communist Party of Canada after it was formed clandestinely in 1921. As historian Richard Allen has suggested, the experience of the Winnipeg Strike and the war itself helped quench the Protestant middle class's desire for social reform.[7] An idealistic liberalism no longer seemed a sure solution to the problems of racial and class conflict in an industrial world.

The Labour and Communist parties were not the only expression of political diversity that followed in the wake of the war. When Laurier died in 1919, he was replaced as party leader by William Lyon Mackenzie King, a former minister of labour who personified the progressive spirit of the age. Borden, exhausted by the war, also withdrew from politics, leaving his successor, Arthur Meighen, the impossible tasks of running the divided country and pulling the Conservative Party together to fight a postwar election.

Neither the Liberals nor the Conservatives proved sufficiently progressive to capture the support of the nation's alienated farmers. In 1916 the Canadian Council of Agriculture developed the "Farmers' Platform," which included a call for free trade; graduated income, inheritance, and corporation taxes; nationalization of railway, telegraph, and express companies; and reform of the political process to eliminate the problems created by patronage, corruption, and centralized party discipline. The success of Farmers' parties in the Ontario provincial election and in by-elections in Prairie constituencies in 1919 encouraged efforts to form a party to fight on the national level, and the National Progressive Party was born.

Anyone surveying the political scene on the New Year's Eve ushering in the 1920s must have wondered what kind of revolution was taking place. So much had changed since 1911, the last time that Canadians had voted in a peacetime election. With the enfranchisement of women, the potential electorate had doubled. So, too, had the number of political parties. Many voters in the next federal election would have the opportunity to choose Progressive, Labour, or various independent candidates instead of representatives of the old-line parties. And as we will see in the next section, almost a third of them would do so.

• Conscription:
A Historiographical Debate

Why was conscription introduced? Was it a military necessity? Did its introduction signal Canada's desire to assert itself in international affairs or did it reflect subservience to Britain? Did its proponents carry the 1917 election by deliberately employing anti-French-Canadian messages? Historians of conscription have offered varied answers to these questions and, perhaps unsurprisingly, much of the division has been between francophone and anglophone historians.

According to one perspective, political pressure from English Canada forced the government's hand. Borden was "responding to the will of the English-speaking majority," write the authors of the authoritative history of Quebec in this period.[8] English-Canadian historians agree that there was pressure on the government for conscription, but they note that the government was aware that English Canadians were divided on the issue and feared that conscription might be a vote loser for a government already in difficulties.[9] Borden and his key ministers, they argue, imposed conscription because of British pressure for a greater Canadian commitment to the war effort. Moreover, Borden's own conviction that Canada should do more left the government few options when voluntary recruitments failed to meet the government's targets for fighting men.[10]

From this viewpoint, conscription was a military necessity. Military historian A.M. Willms claims that, proportionate to its population, Canada before 1917 had contributed fewer military recruits than the other white-settler Dominions. More recruits were necessary because of the heavy casualties of war.[11] But French-Canadian historians have argued that this interpretation accepts the Allied view that a peace treaty was not negotiable. Robert Rumilly's biography of Henri Bourassa stresses the view that negotiations were possible if both sides gave up the idea that there had to be a clear victor.[12]

Rumilly and other French-Canadian historians have generally accepted Bourassa's view that no great principles were at stake in the war. But English-Canadian historians have rejected the view that Canada simply subordinated itself to British imperialism. Ramsay Cook, explaining the support for conscription by *Winnipeg Free Press* editor, John W. Dafoe, suggests that many English Canadians who fought for greater Canadian autonomy from Britain believed the war was being fought over "cherished values" of democracy and not from motives of "sycophantic colonialism or aggressive imperialism."[13] The government's embrace of the view that this was a battle for "Canadian liberty and autonomy" is noted in a recent history of World War I that emphasizes Borden's insistence on Canadian involvement both in war planning and in shaping the postwar world.[14]

How did the government win the election that allowed it to impose a measure it deemed necessary in this battle for "liberty?" Most historians agree that the Wartime Elections Act did not respect the liberty of all citizens, but there is less agreement about the extent to which the government resorted to ethnocentric appeals in its attempts to overcome anglophone divisions about the fairness of imposing conscription. Roger Graham, who wrote a biography on the influential Cabinet minister and later prime minister Arthur Meighen, claims that the government attempted to avoid having the election contribute to national disunity.[15] French-Canadian historians dismiss this claim, noting that the whole purpose of conscription was to assuage English-Canadian opinion that French Canadians were not doing their share.[16] Some anglophone historians also disagree with Graham's suggestion that the government took the high road in the election of 1917. Note J.L. Granatstein and J.M. Hitsman: "The Union Government campaign, founded on the Military Service Act and the War Time Elections Act, deliberately set out to create an English-Canadian nationalism, separate from and opposed to both French Canada and naturalized Canadians. No other conclusion can be drawn from this election campaign, one of the few in Canadian history deliberately conducted on racist grounds."[17]

•Notes

[1] Helen Potrebenko, *No Streets of Gold: A Social History of Ukrainians in Alberta* (Vancouver: New Star, 1977), 131–32.

[2] Morris Zaslow, *The Opening of the Canadian North, 1870–1914* (Toronto: McClelland and Stewart, 1971), 234.

[3] Bryan Palmer, *Working Class Experience* (Toronto: Butterworths, 1983), 137.

[4] Carl Berger, *The Sense of Power: Studies in the Ideas of Canadian Imperialism, 1867–1914* (Toronto: University of Toronto Press, 1970).

[5] Quoted in Daphne Read, ed., *The Great War and Canadian Society: An Oral History* (Toronto: New Hogtown, 1978), 100.

[6] Quoted in Desmond Morton and J.L. Granatstein, *Marching to Armageddon: Canadians and the Great War, 1914–1919* (Toronto: Lester and Orpen Dennys, 1989), 55–56.

[7] Richard Allen, *The Social Passion: Religion and Social Reform in Canada, 1914–28* (Toronto: University of Toronto Press, 1971).

[8] Paul-André Linteau, René Durocher, and Jean-Claude Robert, *Quebec: A History 1867–1929* (Toronto: Lorimer, 1983), 524.

[9] See, for example, J.L. Granatstein and J.M. Hitsman, *Broken Promises: A History of Conscription in Canada* (Toronto: Oxford University Press, 1977), 67.

[10] Ibid., 61.

[11] A.M. Willms, "Conscription 1917: A Brief for the Defence" in *Conscription 1917*, ed. Ramsay Cook, Craig Brown, and Carl Berger (Toronto: University of Toronto Press, 1969), 1–14.

[12] Robert Rumilly, *Henri Bourassa: La Vie Publique d'un Grand Canadien* (Montreal: Les Éditions Chantecler, 1953), 544.

[13] Ramsay Cook, "Dafoe, Laurier and the Formation of Union Government" in *Conscription 1917*, 15–38.

[14] Morton and Granatstein, *Marching to Armageddon*, 145.

[15] Roger Graham, *Arthur Meighen*, vol. 1, *The Door of Opportunity* (Toronto: Clark, Irwin, 1960), 194–95.

[16] Linteau, Durocher, and Robert, *Quebec*, 524.

[17] Granatstein and Hitsman, *Broken Promises*, 78.

• Selected Reading

Major works on the struggle for women's suffrage include Carol Lee Bacchi, *Liberation Deferred? The Ideas of the English Canadian Suffragists 1877–1918* (Toronto: University of Toronto Press, 1983) to which a critical response is Ernest Forbes, "The Ideas of Carol Bacchi and the Suffragists of Halifax," *Atlantis* 10, 2 (Spring 1985): 119–26. See also Catherine L. Cleverdon, *The Woman Suffrage Movement in Canada* (Toronto: University of Toronto Press, 1950) and Veronica Strong-Boag, *The Parliament of Women: The National Council of Women of Canada 1893–1929* (Ottawa: National Museum of Civilization, 1976). On Nellie McClung's views, see *In Times Like These* (Toronto: University of Toronto Press, 1972) with an introduction by Veronica Strong-Boag. Women's political involvements once the vote was won are examined critically in Sylvia Bashevkin, *Toeing the Lines: Women and Party Politics in English Canada* (Toronto: University of Toronto Press, 1985) and Linda Kealey and Joan Sangster, eds., *Beyond the Vote: Canadian Women and Politics* (Toronto: University of Toronto Press, 1989).

On Native politics versus the politics of the government officials dealing with Indians, see Olive P. Dickason, *Canada's First Nations* (Toronto: McClelland and Stewart, 1992); J.R. Miller, *Skyscrapers Hide the Heavens: A History of Indian–White Relations in Canada* (Toronto: University of Toronto Press, 1989); Brian Titley, *A Narrow Vision: Duncan Campbell Scott and the Administration of Indian Affairs in Canada* (Vancouver: University of British Columbia Press, 1986); F. Laurie Barron and James B. Waldram, eds., *1885 and After: Native Society in Transition* (Regina: University of Regina Press, 1986); Sarah Carter, *Lost Harvests: Prairie Indian Reserve Farmers and Government Policy* (Montreal: McGill-Queen's University Press, 1990); and R.E. Cail, *Land, Man and Law: The Disposal of Crown Lands in British Columbia 1871–1913* (Vancouver: University of British Columbia Press, 1974).

Major studies of unionization and working people's lives in the period 1896–1919 are mentioned in chapters 5 and 6. On worker radicalism, see A. Ross McCormack, *Reformers, Rebels and Revolutionaries* (Toronto: University of Toronto Press, 1977); David Bercuson, *Fools and Wise Men: The Rise and Fall of One Big Union* (Toronto: McGraw-Hill Ryerson, 1978); and James Naylor, *The New Democracy: Challenging the Social Order in Industrial Ontario, 1914–1925* (Toronto: University of Toronto Press, 1991). On the 1919 strikes, see David Bercuson, *Confrontation at Winnipeg: Labour, Industrial Relations, and the General Strike* (Montreal: McGill-Queen's University Press, 1990); Alan Artibise, *Winnipeg: A Social History of Urban Growth, 1874–1914* (Montreal: McGill-Queen's University Press, 1975); Paul Philips, *No Power Greater* (Vancouver: B.C. Federation of Labour, 1967); and Gregory S. Kealey, "1919: The Canadian Labour Revolt," *Labour/Le Travail* 13 (Spring 1984): 11–44.

On agrarian struggles, Vernon Fowke, *National Policy and the Wheat Economy* (Toronto: University of Toronto Press, 1957) provides the major theoretical framework for understanding western discontent while Ernest Forbes, *The Maritime Rights Movement, 1919–1927: A Study in Canadian Regionalism* (Montreal: McGill-Queen's University Press, 1979) explains why Maritimers regarded westerners as far more favoured by the federal government than themselves. On the creation of the new provinces of Alberta and Saskatchewan, see David J. Hall, *Clifford Sifton: The Lonely Eminence 1901–1929* (Vancouver: University of British Columbia Press, 1981); Douglas Owram, ed., *The Formation of Alberta: A Documentary History* (Calgary: Alberta Historical Society, 1979); John H. Archer, *Saskatchewan: A History* (Saskatoon: Western Producer Prairie Books, 1990); and Howard Palmer with Tamara Palmer, *A New History of Alberta* (Edmonton: Hurtig, 1990). On the thorny schools issue in the new provinces, see Manopoly Lupul, *The Roman Catholic Church and the North-West School Question: A Study in Church–State Relations in Western Canada, 1875–1905* (Toronto: University of Toronto Press, 1974). For political developments in British Columbia, see Jean Barman, *The West Beyond the West: A History of British Columbia* (Toronto: University of Toronto Press, 1991).

Politics in the Maritime provinces and Newfoundland at the turn of the century is discussed in P.A. Buckner and David Frank, eds., *Atlantic Canada After Confederation* (Fredericton: Acadiensis Press, 1988) and James Hiller and Peter Neary, eds., *Newfoundland in the Nineteenth and Twentieth Centuries* (Toronto: University of Toronto Press, 1980). On Quebec politics, see Paul-André Linteau et al., *Quebec: A History 1867–1929* (Toronto: Lorimer, 1983). On Ontario politics, see Christopher Armstrong, *The Politics of Federalism: Ontario's Relations with the Federal Government 1867–1942* (Toronto: University of Toronto Press, 1981) and H.V. Nelles, *The Politics of Development* (Toronto: Macmillan, 1974). Federal political developments are outlined in R.C. Brown and Ramsay Cook, *Canada 1896–1921: A Nation Transformed* (Toronto: McClelland and Stewart, 1974).

On Canada during wartime and the immediate aftermath, see Daphne Read, ed., *The Great War and Canadian Society: An Oral History* (Toronto: New Hogtown, 1978); Barbara M. Wilson, *Ontario and the First World War* (Toronto: University of Toronto Press, 1977); R. Craig Brown, *Robert Laird Borden*, vol. 2 (Ottawa: Carleton University Press, 1969); Frances Swyripa and John Thompson, eds., *Loyalties in Conflict: Ukrainians in Canada During the Great War* (Edmonton: University of Alberta Press, 1983); John Herd Thompson, *The Harvests of War: The Prairie West 1914–18* (Toronto: McClelland and Stewart, 1978); Desmond Morton and J.L. Granatstein, *Marching to Armageddon: Canadians and the Great War, 1914–1918* (Toronto: Lester and Orpen Dennys, 1989); Desmond Morton and Glenn Wright, *Winning the Second Battle: Canadian Veterans and the Return to Civilian Life, 1915–1930* (Toronto: University of Toronto Press, 1987); G.W.L. Nicholson, *Canada's Nursing Sisters* (Toronto: S. Stevens, 1975); and Calvin W. Ruck, *The Black Batallion, 1916–20* (Halifax: Nimbus, 1987). On pacifists, see Thomas Socknat, *Witness Against War: Pacifism in Canada, 1900–1945* (Toronto: University of Toronto Press, 1987).

Works dealing with conscription include J.L. Granatstein and J.M. Hitsman, *Broken Promises: A History of Conscription in Canada* (Toronto: Oxford University Press, 1977); Ramsay Cook, Craig Brown, and Carl Berger, eds., *Conscription 1917* (Toronto: University of Toronto Press, 1969); and Linteau et al., *Quebec: A History.* On the major battles, see G.W.L. Nicholson, *Canadian Expeditionary Force, 1914–1919* (Ottawa: Queen's Printer, 1964); Daniel G. Dancocks, *Legacy of Valour: The Canadians at Passchendaele* (Edmonton: Hurtig, 1986); and Daniel G. Dancocks, *Spearhead to Victory: Canada and the Great War* (Edmonton: Hurtig, 1987).

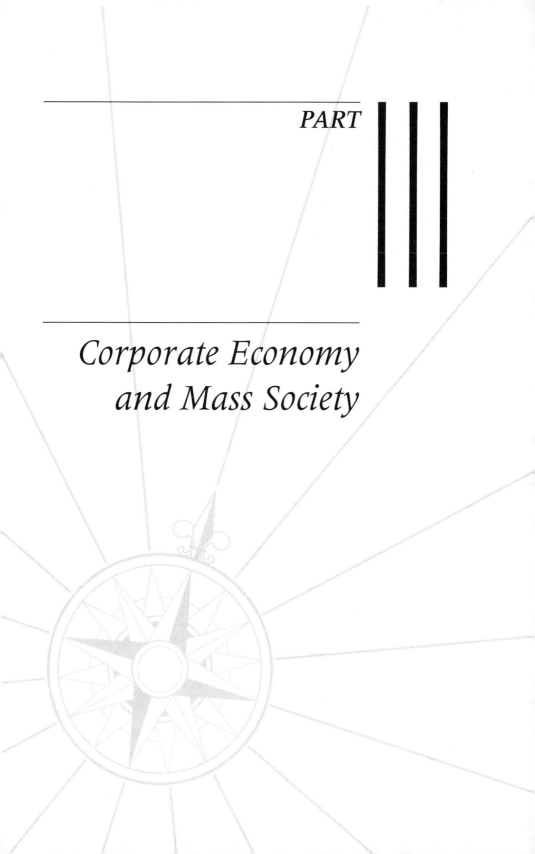

PART

III

*Corporate Economy
and Mass Society*

Time Line

1920–21	–	Arthur Meighen heads federal government
1920–24	–	Recession grips Canada
1921	–	Progressive Party wins second largest block of seats in House of Commons; United Farmers of Alberta form provincial government
1921–26	–	William Lyon Mackenzie King serves as prime minister
1922	–	United Farmers of Manitoba form provincial government
1925	–	Formation of United Church of Canada; coal miners' strike in Cape Breton; Maritime Rights election in Nova Scotia
1926	–	Appointment of Duncan Commission; Arthur Meighen returns briefly to power
1926–30	–	Mackenzie King's Liberals form government in Ottawa
1928	–	St Francis Xavier Extension Department begins co-operative programs
1929	–	Crash of New York stock market
1930–35	–	R.B. Bennett serves as prime minister
1930–39	–	Great Depression
1931	–	*Quadragesimo anno*; Statute of Westminster
1932	–	Imperial Economic Conference in Ottawa; establishment of federal relief camps; creation of CCF; Canadian Radio Broadcasting Corporation Act
1934	–	Bank of Canada Act
1935	–	Bennett New Deal; creation of the Canadian Wheat Board; On-to-Ottawa trek; election of Social Credit in Alberta; Canada–United States trade agreement
1935–48	–	Third King administration
1936	–	Election of Union Nationale government in Quebec
1939	–	Establishment of National Film Board
1939–45	–	World War II
1940	–	Quebec women get the vote; unemployment insurance established as national program; Permanent Joint Board on Defence established
1942	–	Kirkland Lake gold miners' strike

1943	–	Compulsory school attendance legislated in Quebec
1944	–	Establishment of facilities at Chalk River to create plutonium; PC 1003 recognizes right to collective bargaining
1945	–	Major Ford strike; end of war; Gouzenko revelations; United Nations established
1946	–	Special joint committee of House and Senate reviews Indian Act
1947	–	Marshall plan; GATT Agreement; oil strike at Leduc, Alberta, begins western oil boom
1948–57	–	Louis St Laurent's Liberals form government in Ottawa
1949	–	Creation of NATO; Asbestos strike; Newfoundland joins Canada
1950–53	–	Korean War
1951	–	Federal universal old-age pension approved by Parliament; Massey Commission reports; federal grants to universities begin
1952	–	Atomic Energy of Canada created; first Canadian television stations begin operation
1954	–	Canada joins International Control Commission for Indochina; NATO proclaims a nuclear-centred strategy; St Lawrence Seaway agreement
1956	–	Suez crisis
1957	–	Murdochville strike; hospitalization insurance and equalization grants approved by Parliament; Canada Council created
1957–63	–	John Diefenbaker serves as prime minister
1958	–	Canada signs NORAD agreement; Board of Broadcast Governors established
1959	–	Defence Production Sharing Agreement; Newfoundland loggers' strike; opening of St Lawrence Seaway; cancellation of AVRO Arrow development
1960	–	Agriculture Rehabilitation and Development Act

THE ECONOMY IN THE MODERN AGE, 1920–60

8

On 16 July 1945, scientists and other observers gathered in bunkers near Los Alamos, New Mexico, one of the locations where work on the top secret Manhattan Project had been carried out. At its peak the Manhattan Project employed 600 000 people based at thirty industrial sites. Dr J. Robert Oppenheimer headed the team of international scientists who had brought the world to this fateful day. When the first atomic bomb—nick-named "Fat Man" because of its shape—exploded with a force of over 15 000 tonnes of TNT, it produced a huge mushroom cloud and outshone the sun. It also dug a huge crater and fused the desert sand into glass. Oppenheimer, perhaps more than anyone, understood the significance of that day's event. Overwhelmed by the bomb's frightening power, he recalled the words from the sacred Hindu text, the *Bhagavad Gita*, "I am become death, Destroyer of Worlds."

The atomic bomb was the culmination of the powers unleashed by science, technology, and industrial enterprise that characterized the so-called modern age. It was not by chance that Canadians had a part to play in the Manhattan Project. Rich in uranium, a necessary ingredient of atomic energy, Canada was a key in the successful production of nuclear weapons. Early in the Second World War, a team of British, European, and Canadian scientists under the umbrella of the National Research Council had begun working on aspects of the atomic energy puzzle in laboratories based in Montreal. The Canadian government agreed to make uranium resources available for American research. On 19 August 1943, American President Franklin Roosevelt and British Prime Minister Winston Churchill met with Mackenzie King in Quebec City where an agreement was reached

Mackenzie King with Franklin Roosevelt and Winston Churchill at Quebec Conference, 1943   (National Archives of Canada/C31186)

to ensure "full and effective interchange of information and ideas" on scientific research relating to atomic energy. A Combined Policy Committee consisting of three Americans, two British, and one Canadian—C.D. Howe—was established to oversee the international effort. In the summer of 1944, Chalk River, Ontario, was chosen as the site of Canada's first nuclear reactor and by September of the following year the facility was up and running. But by that time, Oppenheimer's team had already made history. Two of their bombs had been dropped on Japan in August 1945, ushering in the atomic age.

Between 1920 and 1960 Canada arrived as a modern industrial nation. Corporate capitalism consolidated its position as the driving force of economic growth, and the state increasingly intervened to reduce the severity of economic cycles and to provide a safety net for the casualties of the private enterprise system. Politically, Canadians moved gradually towards independent nationhood and assumed a larger role in international affairs in alliance with the United States, which had replaced Britain as Canada's major trading partner. As nuclear weapons proliferated in the name of deterrence, nations like Canada sought desperately to align themselves with superpowers in the hopes that strong alliances would forestall aggression. Meanwhile, a communications revolution based on radio, movies, and television brought the consumer values of corporate capitalism into every corner of the nation. Mass culture, manufactured in metropolitan centres and sold like any other commodity, broke down local identities and isolation. By the 1950s all Canadians were drawn into an interlocking web of multinational corporations, complex bureaucracies, international alliances, and mass culture that directly influenced their every thought and deed.

• Riding the Economic Roller Coaster

As the second industrial revolution based on the internal combustion engine, resource development, electrical power, and new chemical processes worked its way through the economy, Canadians experienced both the best of times and the worst of times. Recovery in the second half of the 1920s from a prolonged postwar recession was followed by the Great Depression of the 1930s. In turn, the "dirty thirties" gave way to a period of spectacular growth sustained by the demands of World World II and the Korean and Cold Wars. Canada's economy survived the roller coaster ride remarkably well. Over the forty-year period between 1920 and 1960, the population doubled, the GNP increased five-fold, and by the 1950s all sectors of the economy recorded high levels of productivity (see tables 8.1 and 8.2). Only in the final years of the "fabulous fifties" were there indications that the postwar boom might not last forever.

Table 8.1: GNP, REAL GNP, AND REAL GNP PER CAPITA, 1920–60

Year	GNP*	Real GNP*	Real GNP Per Capita
1920	$ 5 543	$ 3 844	$ 449
1930	5 728	5 119	501
1940	6 743	6 743	592
1950	18 006	10 475	764
1960	36 287	19 199	1 074

*Millions of dollars.

Source: William L. Marr and Donald Paterson, *Canada: An Economic History* (Toronto: Gage, 1980), 6.

Table 8.2: PERCENTAGE SECTORAL DISTRIBUTION OF THE GROSS NATIONAL PRODUCT, 1920–60

Year	Primary	Secondary	Tertiary	Other
1920	26.6	29.7	35.3	8.4
1930	15.9	26.1	52.3	5.7
1940	17.6	26.9	45.7	9.8
1950	15.6	31.1	44.6	8.7
1960	9.6	28.0	51.0	11.4

Source: William L. Marr and Donald Paterson, *Canada: An Economic History* (Toronto: Gage, 1980), 22.

The Turbulent Twenties

Despite a persistent recession that gripped the country between 1920 and 1924, the Canadian economy in the 1920s recorded a higher rate of growth than in the previous decade. The roaring success of the American economy, which was increasingly relying on foreign markets and resources in this period, encouraged investment in Canada. As in the first decades of the twentieth century, much of the growth in the Canadian economy came from the staples of wheat, pulp and paper, minerals, and hydro-electric power. Automobiles and electrical appliances were the leading manufactured products, while the service sector continued its steady rise to undisputed dominance, accounting for over half of the GNP by 1930.

The transition from a wartime to a peacetime economy was a difficult one for Canadians. Export markets, which absorbed over one-third of the value of Canadian output between 1916 and 1918, contracted sharply. In 1920, near-drought conditions in the southern Prairies and a precipitous drop in wheat prices spelled disaster for the wheat economy. Protectionist sentiment in the United States led to increased tariffs, which were particularly hard-felt in Canada. In 1921, manufacturing, construction, and transportation industries stagnated, and the GNP dipped an ominous 20.1 percent.

As the effects of the slump reverberated throughout the economy, companies went bankrupt at an unprecedented rate, unemployment rose sharply, and migration to the United States increased dramatically. Even banks were brought to their knees, resulting in desperate mergers and the messy collapse in August 1923 of the Home Bank with its seventy branches. The Canadian government, anxious to return to "normalcy," did little to cushion the grim effects of market forces. Finance Minister William Fielding's budget in 1922 was aimed at reducing the deficit accumulated during the war, not at stimulating the economy through government spending. Besieged by angry petitioners, Ottawa agreed to pay $3 million in compensation to depositors of the Home Bank and in 1924 created the office of Inspector General of Banks as a step towards restoring confidence in the badly shaken banking system, but there were no dramatic departures from the charted course.

From its trough in 1922, the economic barometer began to rise, and by 1924 the clouds of recession had lifted. Massive investment in old and new staple industries in response to foreign demand, and often with foreign capital, helped to spur the recovery. As in the prewar era, the exploitation of Canada's farming, forest, and mining frontiers was made possible through technological advances. During the 1920s, tractors became more common on Canadian farms, airplanes served as a valuable aid to mineral exploration, and the selective flotation process proved an effective way of separating base and precious metals from compound ores. The automobile and radio, accessible to a wide range of Canadians, symbolized the seemingly endless possibilities of the industrial age.

As markets for wheat in Britain and Europe began to return to their earlier buoyancy, Prairie farmers expanded their acreage, and immigration to the West resumed. Between 1925 and 1929, the Prairie provinces brought nearly 24 million hectares under cultivation, produced an average of over 400 million bushels of wheat annually, and supplied 40 percent of the world's export market. After three decades of expansion, the wheat economy was a complex network of growing, harvesting, and marketing mechanisms. Farmer-owned co-operatives competed with private corporations to market the grain and secure the best prices on volatile world markets. Encouraged by orderly marketing procedures established during the war, western farmers in the 1920s experimented with a system of wheat pools. Producers agreed to sell their wheat to a common pool and share the returns, rather than gamble individually on the Winnipeg Grain Exchange. With high prices in the late 1920s, the system worked well, and just over half of the wheat crop was sold through co-ops in 1929. When markets glutted and prices fell during the Great Depression, neither pools nor private companies could save farms from ruin.

The most spectacular new staple industry of the 1920s was pulp and paper. Following the abolition of the American tariff on imported newsprint in 1913, Canadian output grew from 402 000 tons in 1913 to 2 985 000 in 1930, making Canada the world's largest producer of newsprint. The meteoric rise of the industry was capped during the 1920s when pulp and newsprint began to rival King Wheat as Canada's most valuable export. Much of the investment in pulp and paper came from the United States, which also absorbed the bulk of the output. At the end of a decade of hectic investment, Canada supplied over 60 percent of the newsprint consumed in the United States. Although pulp and paper operations were scattered from Nova Scotia to British Columbia, over half of the productive capacity was located in Quebec, where abundant and accessible forest resources, cheap labour, and attractive power rates attracted capital. The demand for pulp and paper breathed new life into the forestry industry of the Ottawa, St Maurice, Saguenay, and Miramichi Rivers, and animated declining villages such as Liverpool, Nova Scotia, and Kapuskasing, Ontario.

Unplanned growth in the newsprint industry resulted in cutthroat competition and unstable market conditions. The "Big Three"—the International Paper Company, Abitibi Power and Paper, and the Canadian Power and Paper Company—together with the "Little Three"—Backus-Brooks, St Lawrence Paper, and Price Brothers—controlled 86 percent of Canada's newsprint industry but were unable to bring order to the market. Between 1920 and 1926, the price of newsprint dropped from $136 to $65 a ton. In 1927–28, the Canadian Newsprint Company, and its successor the Canadian Newsprint Institute, tried to control output, allocate tonnage, and set prices, but the American-based International Paper Company defied such organizations, offering to supply the Hearst newspaper interests at $7 to $10 per ton below cartel prices. In December 1928, Quebec's premier, Louis-Alexandre Taschereau, travelled to New York to persuade the big interests not to undermine the industry that was so crucial to the economy of his province. By threatening to "change the timber duties overnight," rebating to the mills who lived up to the agreement, he managed to secure a $5 per ton increase, but the International Paper Company persisted in its breakaway pricing policies. During the Depression, newsprint dropped below $40 a ton, causing chaos in the industry.

As in pulp and paper development, Quebec also surged ahead in electrical generating capacity. By the early 1930s Quebec accounted for nearly 50 percent of Canada's electrical energy. Private capitalists in Quebec developed power primarily for industrial purposes: in 1933, 96.5 percent of the province's capacity was devoted to industry, compared to 82.6 percent in Ontario. Other provinces lagged far behind Quebec and Ontario, although British Columbia had huge hydro potential and, together with the Yukon, produced nearly 10 percent of Canada's electrical generating capacity. Because of the availability of abundant hydro-electric resources, Canada became the site of aluminum manufacture. Bauxite from the West Indies was imported to Quebec where intensive electrolysis isolated aluminum for industrial use. By the 1930s the Aluminum Company of Canada, originally established in 1902 as a subsidiary of an American corporation, had emerged as the world's second largest aluminum producer, its new reduction plant in Arvida, Quebec, one of the marvels of Canada's industrial age.

During the 1920s Canada's mining frontier continued to attract investment. The gold- and copper-rich ores in the Abitibi region of Quebec around Rouyn–Noranda were developed by a Toronto-based corporation, Noranda Mines. In 1927, Hudson Bay Mining and Smelting, a creation of the Whitney syndicate of New York, began to work the copper–zinc ores near Flin Flon, Manitoba. New uses for nickel in the appliance and automobile industry, as well as in the Canadian five-cent piece, kept Sudbury booming. In 1928, Inco and Mond merged as Inco (Canada), controlling 90 percent of the world nickel market. The demand for gasoline and oil products rose quickly with growing sales of automobiles. Canada's largest petroleum company, Imperial Oil, a subsidiary of the American corporate giant Standard Oil, expanded its operations in Turner Valley, Alberta. By 1925 Alberta oil fields accounted for over 90 percent of Canada's petroleum output, but only 5 percent of Canadian consumption was supplied by Canadian wells. The rest was imported from the United States, the Caribbean, Latin America, and even Borneo. Imperial's oil discovery in 1920 at Fort Norman on the Mackenzie River was considered too remote to be commercially viable.

In the manufacturing sector, what economists call "consumer durables"—automobiles, radios, household appliances, and furniture—were the big success story of the 1920s. Since Ontario had the largest number of consumers, it is perhaps not surprising that most of the companies producing consumer durables were located in that province. Canadian entrepreneurs were quick to fill the huge demand for automobiles. During the 1920s, most of Canada's independent automobile manufacturers were left in the dust by the "big three" American firms—Ford, General Motors, and Chrysler—which controlled two-thirds of the Canadian market. Ford's economical Model T was particularly popular until GM's Chevrolet managed to capture the lion's share of the automobile market in the late 1920s. High tariffs on imported cars encouraged the American giants to establish branch plants to supply the Canadian market as well as the British Empire market in which Canada had a tariff advantage. By the 1920s, Canada's automobile industry was the second largest in the world and exports accounted for over one-third of its output. The spectacular growth of Oshawa, Windsor, and Walkerville, where the assembly plants of the big automobile manufacturers were located, was proof enough of the significance of "the great god Car."

At its pre-Depression height in 1928, automobile manufacturing employed over 16 000 people directly and many more in parts and service.

The burgeoning industry gobbled up iron, rubber, plate glass, leather, aluminum, lead, nickel, tin, and, of course, gasoline. In 1926–27, the federal government reduced tariffs on automobiles in an effort to bring down prices and introduced Canadian content rules to encourage more parts manufacturing in Canada. Despite the uncertainty introduced by such policies, the big three and their parts suppliers continued to maintain a vigorous trade. Thus, transportation continued to be an important component of industrial growth, with automobiles rapidly gaining on trains as the leading sector in the transport industry.

Automobiles also stimulated growth in the service sector of the economy. Sales outlets and service stations sprang up across the country. No longer tied to train routes, restaurants and cabins appeared along busy highways to cater to the "motoring public." Tourism developed to new levels. Trucks and cars replaced the horse and wagon in making commercial deliveries. Although Canada's roads were still too primitive to make a cross-country tour anything more than a gruelling marathon, the public demand for better roads led provincial governments to construct hard-surfaced highways along much-travelled routes. Taxes levied on gasoline and cars helped to finance the ribbons of asphalt that cost even more to build and maintain than railway lines.

The electrical appliance industry was another area of postwar growth. Radios were particularly popular, but so, too, were washing machines, toasters, electric ranges, and vacuum cleaners. Like the automobile, household appliances were falling in price during the 1920s, coming increasingly within reach of the middle-class consumer. Canadian General Electric and Westinghouse were the giants of appliance manufacturing, and during the decade Hoover, Philco, and Phillips became household names. Only a few Canadian-owned companies, such as Moffatt and Rogers Majestic, managed to carve out a niche for themselves in the rapidly expanding appliance market. Whether wholly Canadian owned or American branch plants, Canadian companies drew most of their product designs and production technologies from the United States. A notable exception was the "battery-less" radio—capable of running on alternating current—developed by Toronto-born Edward Samuel Rogers in 1927.

In the new age of consumerism, the tertiary sector came into its own. Wholesaling, retailing, banking, and insurance expanded as never before, while the paper work associated with corporate enterprise kept offices growing. Spurred by the power of advertising and by low prices achieved through mass purchases, chain operations grabbed over 20 percent of the Canadian retail market by the end of the 1920s. In the variety store business, chains accounted for an astounding 90 percent of sales. Indeed, chains became the symbol of consumer society, promoting mass taste and uniformity in culture. Eaton's invested in chain operations, and outlets of such American companies as Woolworth, Kresge, and Metropolitan stores could be found on the main streets of most Canadian towns. In the grocery business, Dominion and Safeway became prominent names, while Famous Players, a subsidiary of the American film company, established a dominant position in the business of screening movies, edging out once-thriving Canadian-based film distributors. Direct sales by such companies as Imperial Oil, Kodak, and Singer also became a feature of the retailing scene in the 1920s.

The impressive growth in consumer durable, service, and staple industries masked problems in other areas of the Canadian economy. In the Eastern provinces, farming and fishing were crippled by falling prices. Market gardening remained a lucrative activity near large urban centres but farmers and fishers who depended on international markets faced stiff competition, soft markets, and the constant threat of exclusionary tariffs. Primary producers experimented with co-operative marketing organizations and attempted to improve their efficiency by investing in new machinery but they were always at the mercy of market forces over which they had little control. The frustration of Prince Edward Island farmers is revealed in the following tongue-in-cheek account, published in the Charlottetown *Patriot*, in March 1928:

> Potatoes are seeds that are planted and grown in Prince Edward Island to keep the producer broke and the buyer crazy. The tuber varies in colour and weight, and the man who can guess the nearest to the size of the crop while it is growing is called the "Potato Man" by the public, a "Fool" by the farmer, and a "Poor Businessman" by his creditors.
>
> The price of potatoes is determined by the man who has to eat them, and goes up when you have sold and down when you have bought. A dealer working for a group of shippers was sent to Boston to watch the potato market, and after a few days' deliberation, he wired his employers to this effect: "Some think they will go up and some think they will go down. I do too. Whatever you do will be wrong. Act at once."[1]

Having invested labour and capital in an attempt to improve their efficiency, farmers and fishers could no longer retreat into comfortable subsistence to ride out hard times. Nor would they want to. Like everyone else in the modern age, they wanted the comforts and advantages that the new consumer society offered. If they could not get them by farming and fishing, then they would become part of the stream of labour moving into the city. Nearly a million Canadians moved to the United States in the turbulent twenties, many of them from the rural areas of Eastern Canada.

RUM RUNNING

One of the occupations that supplemented the incomes of both rich and poor in the interwar years was "rum running." With the United States committed to a rigorous policy of prohibition between 1920 and 1933, Canadians, especially in provinces where prohibition laws had been lifted or where they were imperfectly enforced, could not resist the opportunity to make big money in the illicit alcohol trade that flourished south of the border. The Maritime provinces were well situated to supply the eastern seaboard with liquor produced in the West Indies and St Pierre and Miquelon. By 1925, half the Lunenburg fishing fleet was reputedly engaged in the rum trade. It was during this period that Canadian distillery owners such as Samuel Bronfman laid the basis for a thriving Canadian export industry and vast personal fortunes. In an effort to stop clandestine activities and to tap some of the wealth generated by the liquor trade, most provincial governments quickly abandoned prohibition and assumed direct control over the sale of alcohol.

A modern kitchen in 1921, with an electric washing machine and iron, although the sink still has a hand pump   (Ontario Hydro)

Eastern farmers and fishers were not the only ones who faced uncertainty in the 1920s. In many of the industries that defined the first phase of the Industrial Revolution, including railways, coal, and iron and steel, atrophy had set in. Canada's two national railways embarked on an orgy of spending on branch lines, steamships, and hotels, piling up debts when they should have been retrenching to meet the fast-developing competition from automobiles. When retrenchment finally came and the demand for rails and rolling stock decreased, the iron and steel industry languished. Only the Hamilton-based companies Stelco and Dofasco, fattened by the demands of the nearby automobile industry, survived the 1920s unscathed. Algoma and Besco, the new Montreal-based holding company for Maritime iron and steel industries, were dependent on railway orders and faced trying times. Their managers were unable or unwilling to make the investments necessary to retool their operations for the second industrial revolution. Besco was a particularly ill-fated corporation. Under the presidency of Roy "the Wolf" Wolvin, Besco initiated a series of layoffs, wage reductions, and production cutbacks that brought industrial Cape Breton to the brink of civil war. In the meantime, over half of the rolled steel used in the manufacture of consumer durables in the 1920s was imported. The crisis in iron and steel, in turn, reduced the demand for coal. Since the Ontario-based companies increasingly purchased their coal from the United States, the share of the market held by Canadian coal producers actually fell from 50 to 40 percent during the 1920s.

The Dirty Thirties

The problems experienced in some industries and in some regions in the 1920s became the concern of everyone from 1929 to 1933. Although Canadians had become accustomed to economic cycles, there was nothing in the past to compare to the Great Depression of the 1930s. Capitalism had finally met its Waterloo, or so it seemed, and no one was in a position to stop the suffering caused by collapsing export markets, falling prices, and widespread unemployment. As businesses failed, banks teetered on the brink of collapse, and even the federal government faced insolvency, everyone asked the same question. What had happened to precipitate such a calamity?

The crash of the New York stock market on 29 October 1929 signalled the beginning, but was not the cause, of the Great Depression. A symbol of the underlying problems in the global economy, the crash reflected the shaky foundations upon which the prosperity of the period from 1924 to 1929 had been based. That foundation was the unprecedented

productivity made possible by new technologies and continuing reorganization of corporate practices. Since investment in the production of more
commodities only made sense if there were consumers for these products,
the purchasing power of workers and farmers was of critical importance to
the success of the industrial sector. Studies now show that in most countries
the income of the working class lagged far behind the availability of new
goods. In the United States, for example, the Brookings Institute estimated
that productivity increased by 40 percent in the 1920s boom but workers'
wages rose only 8 percent while profits soared by 80 percent. Monies not
distributed as profits often went into new investments and, for a time,
before inventories piled up, speculators bid up the price of stocks in expectations of continued economic growth. With stock issues largely unregulated by the state, a variety of countries witnessed gigantic sales of watered
stocks. Such business practices, when they became publicly known in 1929,
scared many investors away from the stock market.

Trade with other countries offered the possibility of finding consumers abroad for items that home markets could not afford, but the 1920s
was a period of global overproduction. There were no international bodies
that could orchestrate a slowdown in production in the 1920s or ease the
fall in production in the 1930s. The United States, the one country with the
economic clout to assume a leadership role in the international economy
was, as yet, unwilling to do so. As panic set in, the United States followed
tight-money policies that squeezed not only its own borrowers but also
international borrowers dependent on American loans. Once the global
downward spiral started, it took on a life of its own. Prices dropped dramatically and then dropped again and again, as producers tried to convince
someone, anyone, to buy their products. Governments reacted by erecting
high tariff barriers against imports.

Canada was particularly hard hit by the Depression. Its small and
open economy was buoyed by exports of primary products, which the
world now decided it no longer needed. Because the American market had
played such an important role in the expansion of the 1920s, the collapse
of the American economy could only mean disaster for its major trading
partner. To make matters worse, in 1930 the American Congress passed
legislation providing for the highest tariff barriers in the country's history.
But that was only the beginning. Competition from Argentine and
Australian wheat, a problem throughout the 1920s, became increasingly
serious in the 1930s as wheat prices dropped to their lowest in over a century. As the price of basic foods eroded, the market for fresh and salt fish
collapsed. Automobile sales slipped to less than a quarter of their 1929
level, the contraction of the empire market compounding a shrinking

domestic demand. By 1933 the value of Canada's exports was less than half what it had been in 1929. Although export volumes resumed their earlier levels by the late 1930s, values remained below the inflated 1929 figure (see table 8.3).

Table 8.3: ECONOMIC INDICATORS, 1926–39

	1926	1929	1933	1937	1939
GNP*	5152	6134	3510	5257	5636
Exports*	1261	1152	529	997	925
Farm income*	609	392	66	280	362
Gross fixed capital formation*	808	1344	319	809	746
Automobile sales (thousands)	159	205	45	149	126
Common stock prices (1935–39=100)	200.6	203.4	97.3	122.4	86.1
Unemployment (thousands)	108	116	826	411	529
Unemployment (percent of labour force)	3.0	2.8	19.3	9.1	11.4
Cost of living index (1935–39=100)	121.7	121.6	94.3	101.2	101.5
Wage rates (1949=100)	46.1	48.5	41.6	47.3	48.9
Corporation profits (millions pre-tax)	325	396	73	280	362

*In millions, current dollars.

Source: Michael Bliss, *Northern Enterprise: Five Centuries of Canadian Business* (Toronto: McClelland and Stewart, 1987), 418–19.

With companies firing workers, unemployment reached unprecedented levels. The two national railways alone laid off 65 000 employees in the first four years of the Depression. Although unemployment figures are elusive for this period, nearly 20 percent of the labour force was officially classified as unemployed in 1933, the worst year of the Depression. Many more Canadians were underemployed, working part time and in menial jobs that did not utilize their skills and training. As had always been the case in Canada, seasonal unemployment added greatly to the misery of working people. Hidden unemployment was rife in the 1930s as women were forced into early retirement and, in the case of married women, actually fired from their jobs, ostensibly to provide more work for men supporting families. During the Depression, the average wage in the clerical "pink collar" sector, where women now predominated, dropped below the average wage in the male-dominated blue collar sector. Since rural poverty and underemployment were never measured by statistical analyses, it is impossible to measure the exact level of misery that prevailed outside the cities.

In the first four years of the Depression, per capita income, like everything else, dropped sharply (see table 8.4). Saskatchewan, staggering under the double assault of the collapse of the wheat economy and massive crop failures, experienced the greatest descent. Drought plagued the southern Prairies for most of the decade and raised fears that the region might swirl away with the dust storms that characterized the hot, dry summers. Grasshopper infestations added more hardship. The increasing number of gophers, who flourished in this climate, provided food for many poor families. Government bounties on gopher tails also provided many a child with pocket money. In every western province, the decline in staple exports had devastating consequences. The Maritime provinces could ill-afford to sink any lower, but they did. Even in "good years," average incomes on the East Coast had barely reached the level attained by the wealthier provinces during the depths of the Depression. While the region's destitute had been left to their own devices in the 1920s, the generalized crisis throughout the nation during the 1930s led to relief programs that benefited some Maritimers, but only after a decade of misery.

Table 8.4: PER CAPITA INCOME BY PROVINCE, 1928–29, 1933

Province	1928–29 Average Per Capita Income	1933 Average Per Capita Income	Decrease %
British Columbia	$594	$314	47
Ontario	549	310	44
Alberta	548	212	61
Saskatchewan	478	135	72
Manitoba	466	240	49
Quebec	391	220	44
Nova Scotia	322	207	36
New Brunswick	292	180	39
Prince Edward Island	278	154	45

Source: *Rowell–Sirois Report*, Book 1, *Canada: 1868–1939*, 150.

It did not take long for the economic crisis to assume national proportions. In September 1931, Canada's dollar began dropping in relation to American currency and the New York capital market refused to make any more Canadian loans. Since corporations and governments at all levels borrowed in New York, the situation was critical. In October, three big Montreal brokerage firms went into receivership when panicky American creditors called in their loans. Sun Life, Canada's largest insurance company, and most of Canada's investment and brokerage firms were on the verge of bankruptcy. Forced to declare their real profit and loss positions, many Canadian corporations would have had to admit insolvency. Most were not called upon to do so, agreeing among themselves, with government approval, to accept the paper value of their increasingly worthless assets. In order to pay its bills the federal government resorted to wartime precedents of borrowing money from the public. A "National Service Loan" of $150 million—over-subscribed by $72 million—helped to pull Canada through the crisis. Ottawa also came to the rescue of the provincial governments, most of which were deeply in debt. Newfoundland was not so fortunate. Its treasury bare, the proud Dominion was forced in 1933 to suspend responsible government and submit to a commission government administered by Britain.

Nothing disappeared as quickly during the 1930s as support for the liberal notion of laissez-faire. Suddenly unable to find work, people blamed profit-seeking capitalists for their plight and no longer found the ethos of "free" enterprise so captivating. Even business people abandoned their rugged individualism when faced with personal bankruptcy and the failure of their private cartels to hold the lines on prices. Everyone turned to governments to save them from their problems, proposing marketing boards, central banks, public works, easy money, anything to put order and sanity back into the faltering industrial economy. Canadian governments were slow to react to the public pressure for action, primarily because they did not know what to do. Under the Conservative administration of R.B. Bennett, which came to office in July 1930, more money was spent on relief for the unemployed, but relief was an inadequate response to the problem of unemployment in the industrial age. With only a small proportion of the population engaged in subsistence activities, most Canadians were dependent either on wages or on the sale of commercially produced products. When jobs and markets disappeared, they had no means of keeping body and soul together.

Bennett promised to create jobs by blasting his way into foreign markets and raising tariffs as a means of forcing Canada's trading partners to sue for mercy. This was an inadequate response to the immediate crisis, but one that had redeeming features. Britain was the first country to respond to Bennett's initiative. Having been forced by the Depression to abandon its free trade policy, Britain agreed to preferential treatment for

Canadian apples, lumber, wheat, and a variety of meat and dairy products at the Imperial Economic Conference held in Ottawa in 1932. The agreement did little to help Canada's floundering manufacturing sector or the devastated wheat economy, but it was welcome news to the apple growers of the Annapolis Valley, lumbermen in British Columbia, and Ontario's beef and dairy farmers. In 1935 the United States began its retreat from high tariffs when it signed a comprehensive trade treaty with Canada, the first since 1854.

There was also pressure on the government to manipulate the money supply as a means of stimulating the economy. Ottawa resisted most of the "soft money" proposals that circulated during the decade, but provided relief to hard-pressed farmers through the Farmers' Creditors Arrangement Act. As banking practices became increasingly restrictive, there was widespread agreement that Canada needed a central bank such as the Bank of

R.B. Bennett's trade policy, as seen by cartoonist Arch Dale   (Winnipeg *Free Press*, 14 April 1931)

England or the Federal Reserve Bank in the United States to convince the public that someone was in control. In 1934, the Bank of Canada Act made provision for a central bank. Its major function, in the words of the preamble to the act, was "to regulate credit and currency in the best interests of the economic life of the nation." The Bank's first governor, Graham Towers, was recruited from the Royal Bank at the astounding salary of $30 000 a year (about twenty times the average industrial wage).

Responding to pressing problems relating to wheat exports, municipal funding, and housing, Ottawa pumped money into the economy through programs established under the Prairie Farm Rehabilitation Act, the Municipal Improvement Assistance Act, and the Dominion Housing Act. The federal government also passed the Natural Products Marketing Act, providing a legal framework for marketing boards, and created the Canadian Wheat Board to manage the sale of Canada's most troubled staple. Given the magnitude of the crisis, it no longer seemed wrong to fix prices and regulate output in the farming sector. Nor was the notion of a government-sponsored social security system, already in place in many European countries, irrelevant in the Canadian context. In 1935, R.B. Bennett, facing widespread criticism and an imminent election, introduced legislation to regulate hours of work, minimum wages, and working conditions and to provide insurance against sickness, industrial accidents, and unemployment. Of course, many voters recognized that Bennett's innovative policies, which laid the foundations for a national social security system, provided more relief for the federal treasury than it did for Canada's destitute, who had no jobs to which such regulations might apply.

No matter what his motives, Bennett received few benefits from his conversion to social security. He lost the 1935 election, and the courts declared most of his program unconstitutional. Under the British North America Act, the provinces were responsible for social policy, and even marketing boards were deemed a matter for provincial rather than national legislation. Bennett's successor, William Lyon Mackenzie King, resisted appeals for dramatic action. In typical King fashion, he had the situation studied, appointing a National Employment Commission to investigate and recommend policy on unemployment and relief, and a Royal Commission on Dominion–Provincial Relations as a means of resolving the constitutional impasse.

The general drift of economic thinking during the 1930s was towards economic planning and government intervention as a means of solving the problem of boom and bust cycles. Although a variety of experts came forward with solutions to the economic crisis, the most influential was British economist John Maynard Keynes. His book, *The General Theory of Employment,*

Interest and Money (1936), became the bible of a new generation of academics, politicians, and bureaucrats attempting to understand the causes of, and to find solutions for, the Great Depression. Arguing that rigidities in the capitalist system prevented the laws of supply and demand from functioning in practice as they were outlined in classical theory, he advised that the state play a stabilizing role by increasing expenditures and lowering taxes during the downside of the business cycle. In this way, he maintained, depressions would be less severe and recovery more immediate. For those seeking a middle way between the increasingly polarizing positions on the economy, Keynes was a godsend. His analysis was less radical than the solutions of Marxian economists who advocated the complete abolition of the capitalist system, and more purposeful than the prescriptions of die-hard laissez-faire liberals who remained true believers in self-adjusting economic forces. In the Keynesian economy, governments could play a larger role in economic planning, but capitalism would continue to be the driving force of economic development. Surely, this was the best of all possible worlds.

During the Depression, Keynes was read by only a few Canadians and understood by even fewer. No government in Canada in the 1930s practised Keynesian economic policies. Most of the pump priming activities pursued in the public sector were influenced by Franklin D. Roosevelt, the flamboyant president of the United States, whose New Deal had captured the imaginations of people all over the world. Canadians were impressed by New Deal programs to encourage public works, cultural development, and a more humane workplace for Americans, and they simply wanted their government to spend its way out of the Depression too.

The path to economic recovery in Canada proved to be long and difficult. By 1934 the economic cycle had begun to edge upward, and most economic indicators showed a slow but steady rise until 1938 when a sharp recession brought them tumbling down again. Unemployment still hovered around 11 percent in 1939. Only with the demand created by the Second World War did the economic clouds finally lift. For a few Canadians they had never descended. The social pages of the newspapers reported the European cruises and the posh parties of the Southams and the Eatons. As the cost of living dropped, those on fixed incomes and those who managed to keep their jobs—and their wage levels—also found that their purchasing power increased. Reflecting the brutal irony of poverty in the midst of plenty, many people remember the 1930s as the time when they bought their first car or radio. Others knew only the humiliating experience of going on the dole, standing in soup lines, or riding the rails.

The "self-regulating" aspects of free enterprise manifested themselves in the speed with which various industries recovered from the Great

Soup kitchen in Edmonton, 1933   (Glenbow Archives/ND3-6523B)

Depression. While most entrepreneurs were slow to gamble on new investment, the automobile industry rebounded quickly. Radio stations, cinemas,
and oil and gas companies showed steady growth. When the price of gold
was artificially raised from $20 to $35 during the Depression, mining companies had little difficulty attracting investors. Ontario and British
Columbia were the main beneficiaries of the gold mining boom, but many
provinces—and the territories—experienced their own gold rushes in the
1930s. Discoveries of the mineral pitchblende near Great Bear Lake made
Eldorado Gold Mines one of the success stories of the Depression. The
source of radium used in the treatment of cancer, pitchblende also contains
uranium, initially considered a useless by-product of the mining process.

The Great Depression served as a serious shock to western capitalism.
It did not, however, dislodge that system; nor did it seriously impede its
momentum. In many respects, the liberal economists were right: the downward swing cut out the economic deadwood and let the strongest survive.
By the end of the 1930s a handful of huge corporations dominated most of
Canada's productive capacity. Nevertheless, as the Depression ran its
course, many Canadians came to the conclusion that survival of the fittest

was not the best policy by which to run a nation. A new social contract was necessary to create an economic order in which everyone was guaranteed at least the bare necessities for survival. In 1938 the National Employment Commission issued a report advocating unemployment insurance as a means of preventing the kind of insecurity experienced by wage earners during the Great Depression. This suggestion had the support of both organized labour and reform-minded business people such as Arthur B. Purvis, who chaired the commission. Similarly, the Royal Commission on Dominion–Provincial Relations (more often cited by the names of the men who chaired it, Newton Rowell and Joseph Sirois) recommended that Ottawa assume greater control over economic and social policy. By the time that the Rowell–Sirois report was submitted in 1940, the Second World War had become the focus of public attention, and the powers that the commission recommended were temporarily made possible under the War Measures Act.

The Business of War

"It drives one mad to think that any old Canadian boor, who probably can't even find Europe on the globe, flies to Europe from his super-rich country which his people don't know how to exploit, and here bombards a continent with a crowded population," Joseph Goebbels, Hitler's minister of propaganda, complained in his diary on 3 March 1943. Goebbels had some reason to be concerned. By 1943 Canada, with a population of only eleven million people, was turning out fighter planes, pilots, and bombs at a rate few could have imagined in 1939. In addition, Canadians were producing military vehicles, war ships, mine sweepers, grenades, depth charges, and anti-tank mines that would cause Germany and its allies considerable grief. The sad irony of war was recognized by people other than Joseph Goebbels. What Canadians seemed unable to do in peacetime they did with surprising ease during World War II: they produced their way out of the Great Depression.

On the surface, the Second World War had much the same impact as the First World War on the Canadian economy. It pulled the nation out of an economic slump, expanded production in all sectors of the economy, and dramatically increased export sales. On closer inspection, it was obvious that the country that declared war on Germany in 1939 was vastly different from the one that rode to war on Britain's coattails in 1914. First, the experience of World War I had taught some lessons about the need for tighter controls on a wartime economy. The system of planning, rationing, taxation, and wage and price controls imposed by the federal government

Letter carrier delivering ration books to Ontario family, 1942   (National Archives of Canada/C26110)

in the early stages of the Second World War prevented the devastating inflation that had seriously disrupted the economy during the First World War. Second, the federal government, following a decade of increasing intervention in economic matters, was better equipped to co-ordinate a major war effort. Under the guidance of a sophisticated cadre of civil servants, economic policy was centralized and orchestrated to achieve desired ends. The Department of Munitions and Supply, run like a commando unit by its energetic minister C.D. Howe, was given sweeping powers. With the help of members of Canada's business community who were seconded to Ottawa, Howe expanded existing industries, created new ones, and focussed the total resources of the country on the successful prosecution of the war.

The federal government's role in the war economy was pervasive. In its twenty-eight Crown corporations, the government produced everything from synthetic rubber to airplanes. Prairie farmers were delighted when Ottawa suspended the operations of the Winnipeg Grain Exchange in 1943 and made the Canadian Wheat Board the exclusive international sales agent for the nation's precious wheat crop. Under the auspices of the Wartime Prices and Trade Board, an army of controllers, regulators, and trouble shooters fanned out across the country allocating output, rationing consumer purchases, and cutting through bottlenecks and red tape. During the course of the war the number of federal civil servants more than doubled, from 46 000 in 1939 to 116 000 in 1945. Ottawa would never return to its prewar size and sleepy pace. In the First World War federal spending represented about 10 percent of the GNP. By 1944 Ottawa accounted for nearly 40 percent of the GNP, which translated into the staggering sum of $4.4 billion. All this was accomplished without resorting to the massive foreign borrowing that had characterized public policy during World War I. Extensive taxation of both corporate and personal incomes, the sale of Victory Bonds, and the careful regulation of the money supply through the Bank of Canada enabled Canadians to finance their own war.

Despite the impressive record, Canada's wartime economy encountered both short- and long-term problems. Before the war, Canada balanced its trade deficit with the United States by selling a surplus to Britain. Sterling was converted into dollars and the deficit easily covered. Once locked in a life-and-death struggle with Germany, Britain imposed exchange controls, which included restrictions on the convertibility of sterling into dollars. As Britain's wartime purchases in Canada escalated, Canadians were left with the daunting prospect of having a huge surplus of sterling and a crippling deficit in American dollars.

In an effort to deal with the crisis, Ottawa established stringent exchange controls, which were monitored by a Foreign Exchange Control Board. The dollar was pegged at 90.9 cents in relation to American currency and imports were permitted only under licence. By 1940 restrictions were placed on travel to the United States, and an embargo was imposed on the importation of a long list of commodities from countries outside the sterling bloc. Although Britain released gold and American dollars to the tune of $248 million for Canadian purchases in 1940, the Canadian trade deficit with the United States continued to mount alarmingly. There was little Canada could do to solve the dilemma. During the interwar years, Canadian and American industry had become so hopelessly integrated that virtually everything Canada produced included American components. Canadian automobile manufacturers imported parts from their parent companies; Stelco's furnaces were fuelled by coal from Pennsylvania; and mining companies required complex machinery manufactured in the United States. With over 30 percent of Canada's wartime output consisting of components imported from the United States, the nation's war effort would be compromised unless some solution was found to the exchange crisis.

The problem was eventually solved when the United States entered the war in December 1941. In the meantime, the Americans, concerned about their own military preparedness, began to behave more like allies than neutrals. An exchange crisis was averted in 1940–41 when the United States embarked on a series of measures by which war materials could be obtained through barter rather than purchased with elusive American dollars. In August 1940 the United States signed an agreement with Britain to exchange destroyers for bases in Newfoundland. Early in 1941 the American Congress empowered the president to have manufactured "any defense article for the government of any country whose defense the President deems vital to the defense of the United States." These articles he could "sell, transfer title to, exchange, lend, lease, or otherwise dispose of" to the governments involved. In March 1941, a Lend–Lease arrangement was concluded between the United States and Britain. It was extended for any goods or components Canada produced for Britain by the Hyde Park Agreement of April 1941. Under the terms of the agreement, the United States also promised to make extensive purchases in Canada for its wartime production, and both countries expressed a willingness to co-ordinate their defence production programs. By the time the United States formally entered the war, North America was already functioning as an integrated unit in defence production, and the problem for Canada became too much rather than too little American exchange.

World War II tended to reinforce rather than alter economic trends. Before the war, Canadian industrial capacity was concentrated in Central Canada. Wartime production was initially expanded in existing industries, and virtually all of the plants built and operated by the government were located in the industrial heartland of the country. There were some notable exceptions. Winnipeg became a centre for munitions and communications industries. Adjacent to Alberta's oil and natural gas reserves, Calgary was the obvious site for nitrogen and high octane fuel production. So important was oil to modern warfare that a Crown corporation, Wartime Oils, was created to develop Canada's oil potential. Vancouver sprouted a Boeing aircraft factory and a modern shipbuilding industry. New military bases quickened the economic pace in communities from Summerside to Esquimalt, while such projects as the Alaska Highway, the Canol pipeline from Norman Wells to Whitehorse, and the Air Ferry to Britain brought development to the Yukon and Northwest Territories. As the economy reached its full productive capacity, Ontario's industrial output actually declined slightly relative to the other Canadian provinces, but the war demonstrated that industry, whether fuelled by private or public enterprise, had a tendency to concentrate in the St Lawrence heartland.

To a considerable extent, the decision not to use wartime policy to solve the problem of regional disparity was made in the interests of efficiency. Nevertheless, it was clear to those on the losing end of the wartime investment boom that political rather than strategic interests often governed economic decisions. There was no obvious reason, for example, why the constituency of Digby–Annapolis–Kings in Nova Scotia became the location for two military bases other than that its member of parliament was Finance Minister J.L. Ilsley. Similarly, the languishing Algoma Steel Corporation in Sault Ste Marie, which had the support of C.D. Howe, fared better in the race for contracts than the equally languishing Dominion Steel and Coal Corporation based in Cape Breton. Because H.R. MacMillan, chair of Wartime Shipping Limited, took a special interest in British Columbia, shipbuilding facilities were developed on the West Coast. They proved useful when the Pacific war moved into high gear in 1942. For the most part, however, decisions relating to shipbuilding and repair were notoriously ill-conceived. Even British officials failed to understand why the ice-free ports of Halifax and Saint John were treated as secondary to Montreal, which was ice-bound during the winter and whose narrow access was infested with German U-boats. As historian Marc Milner has pointed out, the failure to develop repair facilities in the Maritime provinces not only consolidated regional disparity but also seriously impeded the effectiveness of the Canadian navy.[2]

Traditional attitudes towards labour were also called into question by the wartime experience. When war was declared, those involved in military recruitment and wartime production could draw upon a pool of over half a million unemployed Canadians. Many more gladly left their uninspiring jobs for better prospects in the armed forces or work relating to the war. By 1941 the labour pool had dried up, and a shortage of workers was looming. Even conscription for military service, a policy that the government wanted to avoid if at all possible, suddenly seemed a national necessity. In 1942 the government embarked upon a campaign to recruit women into the paid labour force. Before the war, only 20 percent of women between the ages of fifteen and sixty-five worked outside the home and, of these, only 4 percent were married. At first only unmarried women between the ages of twenty and twenty-four were targeted, but by 1943 all women, married or single, with or without children, were strongly encouraged to do their patriotic duty. In Quebec and Ontario a government-sponsored day-care system offered support for a handful of mothers. The number of women in the work force increased from 638 000 in 1939 to over one million by 1944, some 255 000 of whom were engaged in what were defined as war industries. As in peacetime, women were paid less than the men whose jobs they

The Toronto Transit Commission offered women drivers "full rates" during wartime labour shortages   (Toronto Transit Commission)

assumed. Similarly, most of the 43 000 women who served in the armed forces did "women's work" as clerks, cooks, and telephone operators. When the war ended, the day-care facilities were closed and women "retired" from their paid positions, except, of course, from the service jobs that they traditionally dominated.

Because of the labour shortage and huge increase in productivity stimulated by wartime production, workers had more bargaining power than had been the case during the Depression. They also found themselves subject to wage controls and stiff resistance by employers to unionization. As conflict between labour and capital escalated, strikes became more frequent, many of them related to the issue of union recognition. In 1943, Canadian workers engaged in over 400 strikes involving more than 200 000 workers and the loss of over one million worker-days. The government, anxious to keep its war industries functioning smoothly and its political popularity high, was forced to act. In February 1944 Order-in-Council P.C. 1003 ushered in a new era of labour policy in Canada. The order guaranteed workers the right to organize and to bargain collectively, established procedures for the certification and compulsory recognition of trade unions, defined unfair labour practices, and established an administrative apparatus to enforce the order. Designed initially as a war measure, P.C. 1003 became the Magna Carta of the union movement, and most of its provisions were extended in postwar legislation. With this legal and administrative apparatus in place, the way was paved for organized labour to join big business and big government in the three-cornered power structure of modern industrial society.

The crisis atmosphere that prevailed during the war also made it easier for the federal government to embark on a series of policies advocated by planners imbued with Keynesian principles. In 1940 Ottawa introduced a national unemployment insurance program after provincial consent was forthcoming for the requisite amendment to the BNA Act. An insurance plan rather than a welfare scheme, the program required earners and employers to make contributions to a fund from which employees could draw if they were laid off work. Since everyone expected that hard times would return when the war ended, such compulsory saving was considered wise planning. Moreover, contributions to the unemployment insurance fund helped to dampen wartime inflation by drawing money out of the pockets of consumers in a period of rapid growth, presumably to be spent when hard times returned.

There were many Canadians who felt that Ottawa's plans to stabilize the economy should go beyond insurance policies and labour legislation. Among the many proposals for postwar reconstruction was a system of social security to serve as a "safety net" for Canada's less fortunate citizens. In August 1944 the King administration introduced family allowance legislation, by which mothers of children under sixteen received a monthly stipend. The first cheques, amounting to $5 to $8 per child, were sent out in 1945. Universal old-age pensions and state-supported health care were considered by Cabinet but initially rejected by the Department of Finance as too costly. Nevertheless, the idea of the welfare state, nurtured by the suffering of the Depression and the seemingly spectacular success of wartime planning, had come to Canada to stay.

• Consolidating Continental Capitalism, 1946–56

The anticipated postwar depression failed to materialize. In the decade following the war, pent-up consumer demand, technological innovation, increased business investment, and high levels of government spending kept the Canadian economy booming. Export markets returned to their wartime levels by the mid-1950s and foreign investment—most of it American—continued to rise impressively. Productivity and per capita income sustained unprecedented increases. Although free enterprise remained the engine of growth, federal officials, armed with their Keynesian textbooks, were prepared to intervene in the economy to ensure a high level of employment and productivity. The role of the state was also enhanced by the outbreak of the Korean War in 1950. Military spending rose to 45 percent of the federal budget in 1953 and remained an important feature of government spending priorities throughout the decade as capitalist countries aligned themselves against the communist bloc in a protracted Cold War.

The Welfare and Warfare Economy

Some Canadians hoped that wartime controls would continue to govern the peacetime economy. Despite its many problems and the constant demand for exemptions, the Wartime Prices and Trade Board had kept a lid on inflation and profiteering while seeming to provide a fairer distribution of scarce resources than had been the case in the prewar period. Not surprisingly, there was little enthusiasm either from government or business for abandoning the free market system. The bureaucratic nightmares that bedevilled the WPTB's activities were still fresh in the minds of those who had stalked the corridors of power during the war. Unlike Europeans, whose economies had been shattered, Canadians had emerged from the war unscathed and confident in their productive capacity. They would not follow the British electorate in letting socialism win the peace.

The King administration did not give up its economic powers completely. Immediately after the war, production slowed, exports contracted, and inflation reared its ugly head. The federal government kept the economy moving through tax incentives to industry and programs targeted at veterans, housing, and municipalities. Soon, consumer demand, fuelled by a decade and a half of depression and denial—and a well-orchestrated advertising campaign honed on wartime propaganda techniques—picked up the slack. Industries geared for war hardly skipped a beat as plants were quickly converted from producing troop carriers, uniforms, bombs, and barracks, to making cars, clothes, appliances, and housing materials. Emerging from the war with shiny new plants and equipment, some of them purchased at fire sale prices from the federal government, the Canadian business community continued its orgy of investment in capital stock until 1957.

Canadian officials may have been leery of controls, but they were enthusiastic about the level of multilateral trade that had developed during the war. Since Canada's economic prosperity depended on a healthy export trade, "trade liberalization" became a cornerstone of Canadian postwar foreign policy. Canadians participated in the creation of the International Monetary Fund and the World Bank, institutions designed to stabilize the postwar global economy. In November 1947 Canada signed the General Agreement on Tariffs and Trade (GATT), which bound its twenty-three signatories to consultation aimed at reducing trade barriers. Ironically, the intent of the agreement was immediately compromised in Canada by a series of restrictive trade measures announced by Finance Minister Douglas Abbott late in 1947. Another exchange crisis precipitated by a binge of postwar spending on American products forced the government to re-impose import controls and secure a $300 million loan from the American Import–Export Bank. With a trade deficit amounting to over a billion dollars a year, and exports dwindling to their lowest levels since the beginning of the war, the situation looked bleak.

Canada was not the only country facing a shortage of American dollars. Britain suspended sterling convertibility six weeks after implementing it in 1947, adding measurably to Canada's own exchange crisis. European and Japanese economies were in total ruin. Most Latin American economies limped along on one cylinder. Only the United States, which in the immediate postwar period accounted for nearly half of the world's industrial output, could rescue its allies from a long, slow process of economic recovery. Fearing that poverty might increase support for communism, the American Congress early in 1948 adopted the Marshall Plan, named after its sponsor, Secretary of State George Marshall. By this plan, the democracies of Western Europe were provided with funds to rebuild their shattered economies. The Americans, anxious to restore their northern neighbour to economic health, included Canada under the plan, allowing Europeans to buy Canadian goods with American dollars. It has been argued that had the Marshall Plan not provided Canadians with the export markets that they so desperately needed in the immediate postwar period, they might well have been forced to seek a free trade agreement with the United States. Such an agreement would have been highly controversial in both countries at this time, but it was seriously discussed by officials as one of the only ways to solve Canada's recurring exchange crises.[3]

By 1949 controls were being lifted, foreign investment resumed, and exports began to rise. The cyclical upswing was reinforced by massive military spending associated with the Korean and Cold wars. Between 1950 and 1953 defence expenditures rose from 16 to 45 percent of the federal budget, and a new ministry was created to orchestrate the business of war. C.D. Howe became the minister of defence production, and in this guise he continued to play godfather to the business community. With well over a billion dollars spent annually on defence in the 1950s, every aspect of the

Canadian economy was shaped by military considerations. As late as 1960 when defence had slipped back to a quarter of the federal budgetary expenditures, military purchases accounted for 89 percent of the shipments in the aircraft industry, 41 percent in electronics, and 21 percent in shipbuilding. Research and development in both Canada and the United States was increasingly related to defence priorities. Strategic stockpiling by the American military led to large-scale purchases of Canadian primary products, particularly minerals. In the United States the term *military–industrial complex* was coined to describe this new era of defence-induced growth. It was equally applicable to Canada.

Contrary to the Keynesian theory they professed to be following, federal planners failed to tailor their policies to cyclical swings. Admittedly, Ottawa ran budget surpluses for most of the years between 1949 and 1956, but they were not sufficiently large to offset private investment or the profligate spending policies of provincial and municipal governments. In the heady atmosphere of postwar prosperity, politicians and the public came to believe that both welfare and warfare could be accommodated. Their treasuries fattened by higher personal and business taxes, governments at all levels spent money at an unprecedented rate, investing in infrastructure (roads and electrical power facilities) and building up social capital (schools and hospitals). Ottawa, in co-operation with provinces and private industry, became involved in several mega-projects, including the Trans-Canada Highway, the St Lawrence Seaway, the Trans-Canada Pipeline, and Beechwood Power. In the early 1950s the federal government felt confident enough of its spending powers to implement universal old-age pensions and to enter negotiations with the provinces to establish a hospital insurance plan. Little wonder that between 1946 and 1956 output increased by 5.3 percent a year and consumption by 5.1 percent.

Economic Growth in the Fabulous Fifties

While the new economy was constrained by considerations of welfare and warfare, the direction of economic development in the 1950s bore a marked resemblance to the trends of the 1920s. Spectacular growth occurred in the construction, consumer durable, staple, and service industries, while innovation and mass marketing sustained a high level of productivity. In 1957 economic indicators began to slump, and a public debate erupted as to the best means of getting the economy moving again. Many people were afraid that the boom would end in a bust as it had in the 1920s. Such fears proved unfounded. The recession was mercifully brief, and Canadians entered the 1960s with a sense of power buoyed by their magnificent economic achievements.

Much of the productivity in the postwar period was stimulated by technological innovation leading to new product lines. Although many innovations such as synthetic fibres, plastics, and pesticides had been stimulated by wartime needs, others, including televisions, the self-propelled combine harvester, and the snowmobile, had been developed prior to the war but became commercially viable only in the improved postwar economic climate. In the iron and steel industry, the "basic oxygen furnace," introduced in 1954, improved efficiency. Metropolitan Life installed elephantine computers in their offices in 1956, at the same time that the Department of National Revenue decided to enter the electronic age. Developments in the chemical industry revolutionized agriculture and sparked massive forest spraying programs. Homemakers were even using DDT to rid their houses of annoying insects. The pharmaceutical industry could hardly keep up with the demand for new products, including such miracle drugs as penicillin and polio vaccines. The stream of innovations, encouraged by the postwar boom and the explosion of scientific research, seemed endless.

The rapid pace of economic change took its toll in the primary sector. While production in farming, fishing, forestry, mining, and trapping remained high, the secondary and tertiary industries grew even faster. By 1960 the primary sector contributed less than 10 percent of Canada's GNP (see table 8.2). The numbers employed in primary activities declined

MEDICAL RESEARCH IN CANADA

Although Canadians were not usually in the forefront of research and development, there were exceptions. Canadians made headlines in the field of medicine when a team at the University of Toronto, headed by Frederick Banting, discovered insulin, a lifesaving therapy for diabetes mellitus. Banting and one of his co-researchers, J.J.R. McLeod, shared the 1923 Nobel Prize for their efforts. Banting gave half of his prize money to C.H. Best who was a key researcher on the investigative team. In 1934, Wilder Penfield established the Montreal Neurological Institute, which rapidly became internationally renowned for its research, teaching, and treatment related to diseases of the nervous system. Penfield established the "Montreal procedure" for the treatment of epilepsy and was a tireless student of the brain, which he argued was the most important unexplored field of scientific inquiry.

sharply in the 1950s as productivity rose under the impact of mechanization and innovation. Meanwhile, the last pockets of subsistence survival were invaded by the values and institutions of industrial capitalism. In Newfoundland, which joined Canadian Confederation in 1949, families in outport communities were given grants to move to anticipated "growth centres." Even Canada's Inuit were incorporated into the North American market economy through their painting and sculpture, which had become popular in the art market in southern climes. For children educated in consolidated schools equipped with gymnasiums, workshops, and televisions, subsistence survival made no sense at all. The transformation from subsistence to consumer society was perhaps best reflected in the experience of a vacationing antique dealer who in a short period in the late 1950s bought 1200 spinning wheels in rural areas of Cape Breton.

The relative decline in agriculture was accompanied by momentous changes in the structure of the industry. During the war, federal subsidies encouraged Prairie farmers to diversify their output. Oats, barley, and flax soon became as important as wheat to western producers. Although the volume of postwar wheat sales was maintained through special agreements with Britain, the price of wheat remained low on international markets throughout the 1950s, discouraging further expansion of the wheat economy. A similar transformation occurred in the Annapolis Valley where farmers were paid to uproot their apple orchards and concentrate on other fruits as well as vegetables, poultry, and dairy products for a domestic rather than a British market. In the St Lawrence heartland, producing food for urban markets was big business, but farm land was fast disappearing under the impact of urban sprawl. With the high wages paid in other occupations, only those farmers who could run a successful commercial operation bothered to stick with farming.

In the postwar period, marketing boards revolutionized farming in Canada by establishing quotas, setting prices, and defining market boundaries. A larger percentage of farm products was destined for canning and, increasingly, freezing. Such novelties as the potato chip and the "TV dinner" gobbled up the output of Canadian farms. For those who survived the "rationalization" process, farming became a full-fledged business enterprise, part of a delicately balanced continental network of production, processing, and marketing required to feed an increasingly urbanized North American society. Giant American corporations, such as Hostess Foods, Stokely Van Camp, Swift's, and Swanson's competed with domestically based processors such as McCains, Aylmer, E.D. Smith, and Schneider's for the produce of Canadian farms. Increasingly, too, corporations established vertically integrated operations by growing the crops required for their processing plants. With corporate production aggressively challenging the family farm, and fewer than 10 percent of Canadians making their living in agriculture, the industry no longer exerted the influence in political circles that it did at the beginning of the century when over one-third of Canadians were classified as farmers (see table 8.5).

The transformation of the East Coast fishing industry in the postwar decade parallelled that of agriculture. As European markets for saltfish disappeared, sales of fresh and frozen fish were increasingly geared to an oversupplied North American market. At the same time, technology revolutionized productivity in the fisheries. The stern trawler, introduced on the Grand Banks in the 1950s, could harvest 180 000 kilograms of fish in a two-week period. In 1953, Britain built the *Fairtry*, a factory freezer trawler with unsurpassed fishing power. Within a decade there were 1400 trawlers of various shapes and sizes engaged in the Bank fishery, taking an unprecedented 2 600 000 metric tons of fish. These developments sealed the fate of inshore fishers. Their catches dwindling because of excessive fishing on the Banks, they were forced to concentrate on more valuable species such as scallops and lobster, which in turn became depleted. The real choice for most inshore fishers was between becoming a labourer on a corporate trawler or changing occupations. Not surprisingly, the number of Canadian fishers in the Atlantic fishery declined by nearly 40 percent between 1951 and 1961.

Table 8.5: WORK FORCE BY INDUSTRY, 1911 AND 1961

Industry	1911	1961
Agriculture	34.19	9.90
Fishing and trapping	1.28	0.54
Forestry	1.57	1.68
Mining	2.14	1.85
Manufacturing	17.38	21.81
Electricity and gas	0.39	0.97
Construction	7.31	7.22
Transportation	6.65	7.02
Trade	9.54	15.34
Finance, insurance, real estate	1.35	3.54
Personal services	12.11	19.49
Public administration	2.87	8.21
Others	3.22	2.45
TOTAL	100.00	100.00
	(2 725 140)	(6 458 156)

Source: William L. Marr and Donald G. Paterson, *Canada: An Economic History* (Toronto: Gage, 1980), 198.

Canadians seemed helpless to stop the unco-ordinated exploitation of the Bank fishery, which was still defined as an international resource. In 1949 an International Commission for the Northwest Atlantic Fisheries (ICNAF) was created to co-ordinate the fisheries, but it had no authority to bind its membership to comply with conservation measures. Nor was the law of the sea, formulated over 300 years earlier by the Dutch jurist Hugo Grotius, of much value in regulating the new uses of the ocean in the industrial age. Interest in resources in and under the ocean finally led the United Nations to institute the Law of the Sea Conference. At conference meetings in 1958 and 1960, Canadian officials demanded a twelve-mile limit, which, in retrospect, seems to have been excessively modest. In 1964 Canadians made a unilateral declaration of a twelve-mile limit, which remained in effect until the 200-mile limit was established by the third Law of the Sea Conference in 1977.

As the fisheries developed into a modern industry, co-operative organizations founded by fishers prior to the war lost control of processing and marketing structures. During the 1950s and 1960s, large domestic and foreign corporations, including National Sea Products (Halifax), Booth Fisheries (Chicago), Atlantic Fish Processors (Toronto), and B.C. Packers (Toronto) emerged as integrated trawler–processing firms selling mainly through Boston, New York, and Chicago. The East Coast fishery, like its West Coast counterpart, became part of the great continental corporate universe. Most fishers earned a wage rather than being self-employed. In 1956 the remaining poverty-prone self-employed fishers became eligible for unemployment insurance.

While the 1950s forced hard decisions on the nation's farming and fishing communities, impressive growth occurred in mining and hydroelectrical power generation. Private companies developed copper deposits at Murdochville on the Gaspé Peninsula, lead–zinc–copper ores in the Dalhousie–Bathurst region of New Brunswick, and potash in Saskatchewan. In 1949 a consortium of six American steel companies and two Canadian resource groups formed the Iron Ore Company to bring the vast deposits on the Ungava–Labrador border into production. The company built a 570-kilometre railway from Sept-Îles to the new resource town of Schefferville and were enthusiastic about improvements to the St Lawrence–Great Lakes transportation system so that ores could be easily moved to mills in the industrial heartland of North America.

In 1954 the United States and Canada concluded an agreement to jointly fund the St Lawrence Seaway, a massive project designed to enlarge the canals and develop the power potential along the inland waterway. Nearly 3800 kilometres from Anticosti Island to the head of Lake Superior, the Seaway was an impressive engineering and construction feat when completed in 1959. Highways, railways, and even towns were moved to make way for Lake St Lawrence, which was created as part of a massive hydro development in eastern Ontario. Built and operated as a public corporation, the Seaway was an expensive venture, costing the Canadian government over a billion dollars. Sales of electricity covered the outlays for the system's power stations, but the tolls on transportation through the canals never brought in enough money to pay the Seaway's operating costs, let alone repay the capital debt incurred in its construction. For many of the 6500 people who lived in Morristown, Iroquois, and other villages destroyed to build the Seaway, no amount of money could compensate for the loss of their communities.

The development of the atomic bomb and the nuclear reactor stimulated the Canadian uranium market. Because of the strategic importance of the element, the Canadian government nationalized Canada's major uranium mining company, Eldorado Mining and Refining, in 1944. Following the war, Eldorado served as a compulsory marketing agent for all private Canadian uranium companies, selling most of the Canadian output at fabulous prices to the United States Atomic Energy Commission. In 1952 another Crown corporation, Atomic Energy of Canada Limited, was created to develop peaceful uses for atomic energy, in particular the Candu reactor. Ontario was the first province to enter an agreement with AECL to build nuclear power stations, and the first demonstration plant at Rolphston came into operation in 1962. With major finds at Beaverlodge and Blind River in Northern Ontario, Canada supplied a third of the world's military and civilian uranium requirements in the 1950s. Eldorado Nuclear, Rio Tinto-Rio Algom and Dennison Mines became both literally and figuratively some of Canada's hottest companies, while Uranium City, Saskatchewan, and Elliot Lake, Ontario, were added to the pantheon of boom towns on Canada's resource frontier.

Canada's energy resources seemed to know no bounds in the postwar decade. On 3 February 1947 Imperial Oil's Leduc No. 1 well, near Edmonton, struck oil, and ten days later 500 Albertan dignitaries were invited to the official production test. Like the railways and the hydro developments of earlier eras, oil in the mid-twentieth century sparked people's imaginations and demanded high ceremony. Once the geological base of Alberta's vast oil reserves was understood, oil discoveries became regular fare. Capital poured into Alberta from all over the world, and by 1956 over 1200 companies were exploring for oil in Canada's West.

In the early 1950s, four corporate giants, Imperial, Shell, Texaco, and British American, dominated the Canadian oil and gas industry. Gulf Oil entered the picture when it bought out British American in 1956. The last integrated Canadian-owned oil company, Canadian Oil, which operated the White Rose chain of service stations, was taken over by Shell in 1962. Canadians remained active on the production side of the industry, through such companies as Pacific Petroleums, Home Oil, Husky, and Hudson's Bay. With world oil and gas prices remaining low—less than $2 a barrel in the mid-1960s—the big problem for Canadian producers was to find a market for their abundant product.

By 1952, pipelines in which Imperial Oil was a major shareholder funnelled oil from Alberta either to Vancouver or through Wisconsin to Sarnia, Ontario. Canadian-owned Westcoast Transmission Company's

Oil well at Leduc, Alberta, 1947   (Imperial Oil Archives)

1000-kilometre gas pipeline was completed to Vancouver in 1951. In 1956 the Canadian government entered an agreement with an American company, Trans-Canada Pipelines, to build a gas pipeline to Montreal. In addition to a generous loan to the company, Ottawa agreed to create a Crown corporation to build the uneconomical section of the pipeline through northern Ontario. Predictably, it was C.D. Howe who, as minister of trade and commerce, backed the ambitious project against the wishes of many people, including members of the Liberal Cabinet. Alberta refused to have anything to do with Trans-Canada, building its own pipeline to the Saskatchewan border. While the ownership and control of the all-Canada pipeline gradually fell into Canadian hands, an American consortium including Trans-Canada eventually built a larger line south of the Great Lakes. The United States absorbed about half of the Canadian output of oil and gas, but cheap imports of crude oil from the Middle East and Venezuela kept the industry lean until the early 1970s.

There were campaigns by independent petroleum companies for an oil pipeline from Alberta to Montreal that would replace the north–south energy grid with an east–west one. But Imperial, controlled by Standard Oil of New Jersey, which also had large investments in Venezuela and the Middle East, prevailed with the government, thwarting such plans. Standard's international marketing strategy doubtlessly determined Imperial's position but, lacking an infrastructure that could provide reliable data on the industry, the federal and Alberta governments relied on Imperial for information and advice.

Ontario, with its state-owned hydro plants, seaway, and nuclear power stations, and Alberta, with its oil and natural gas operations, set a high standard for other provinces to follow. Yet follow they did. Newfoundland Premier Joey Smallwood convinced British and European capitalists to develop the mighty Churchill Falls in Labrador, while New Brunswick Premier Hugh John Flemming wrung $30 million out of the federal government to help him complete his Beechwood Power complex on the St John River. Nova Scotia put its energies into developing coal-generated thermal power plants. British Columbia's energy potential came into its own in the postwar period. In the early 1950s Alcan built a huge generating station at Kemano to supply its $450 million aluminum smelter at Kitimat. Social Credit premier W.A.C. Bennett was determined to make his province rich by developing the potential of the Rocky Mountain Trench and the Columbia River. Even Saskatchewan's socialist premier, Tommy Douglas, had plans to build a power-generating project on the South Saskatchewan River and demanded that the province get equal treatment from Ottawa when generous subsidies were being handed out.

Questioning Canadian Capitalism

By the mid-1950s "development" seemed to be the top priority of both business and government. In the private sector, entrepreneurs were weaving and darting from one opportunity to another, building up corporate empires at a dazzling rate, succeeding in one venture, failing in another, moving fast enough to avoid bankruptcy and public criticism. H.R. MacMillan graduated from his wartime duties to put together MacMillan-Bloedel in 1953, one of the largest forestry companies in the world, with integrated timber reserves, sawmills, and shipping operations. E.P. Taylor, another of Howe's wartime recruits, engineered his investment firm, Argus Corporation, into one of North America's major conglomerates, with controlling interest in everything from Canadian Breweries and Orange Crush to Massey-Ferguson and Domtar. The Bronfmans used their commanding position in the distilling industry to create their own investment companies. In New Brunswick, K.C. Irving was constructing an empire based on oil, timber, and communications that would make him one of the richest men in the world.

Most Canadians had little understanding of the wheeling and dealing that accompanied the world of corporate finance, but what they saw made them uneasy. They were even more distressed by the cozy relationship

MINISTER OF EVERYTHING

C.D. Howe, "the minister of everything," epitomized the development ethic that had seized Canadians in the heady atmosphere of postwar expansion. Prior to the war, he had held various transportation portfolios in the Cabinet and had launched Trans-Canada Airlines. During the war he was minister of munitions and supply, the nerve centre of wartime production. As the war came to an end he was appointed minister of reconstruction and presided over the privatization of the Canadian economy. Howe kept a watchful eye on his wartime companies, selling most of them, retaining a few, like Polymer in Sarnia which produced synthetic rubber, as Crown corporations. He also helped to keep Canada's aircraft industry aloft with generous subsidies and government orders. This paternalism continued in 1948 when he became minister of trade and industry. Following the outbreak of the Korean War, Howe added the Ministry of Defence Production to his many responsibilities and was a key figure in determining the recipients of Canada's massive defence expenditures.

Howe's insistence on pushing the unpopular Trans-Canada Pipeline Bill through Parliament in the spring of 1956 was a contributing factor in the downfall of the St Laurent government the following year. In turn, one of

Howe's pet projects, the AVRO Arrow, survived long enough to cause crippling embarrassment for St Laurent's successor, John Diefenbaker. A supersonic jet interceptor commissioned by the Department of Defence, the Arrow was contracted to A.V. Roe, Canada (AVRO), the ambitious subsidiary of British-based Hawker-Siddley, which Howe had convinced to take over the government's Victoria Aircraft Plant at Malton after the war. Using its defence contracts as a springboard, A.V. Roe soon became one of Canada's largest conglomerates. Meanwhile, the Arrow cost six times more to produce than its American counterpart by the time it made its first test flight in 1958. No one, not even the Canadian Air Force, wanted to buy it. When the federal government finally announced the cancellation of the Arrow contract in February 1959, it was an action long overdue but nevertheless controversial because it spelled disaster for Canada's aviation industry and made Canadians more dependent on the United States to supply their military needs.

C.D. Howe, 1943　(National Archives of Canada/68669)

between politicians and big business that had developed during and after the war.

By the 1950s, the growing American involvement in the Canadian economy and Canada's increasing dependence on American trade also became a topic of public debate. Close economic relations between the two nations were nothing new, but since the Second World War they had become more intense. In the 1950s, strategic considerations bound the United States even closer to Canada. The Paley Commission established by President Truman in 1951 noted in its report, *Resources for Freedom*, that the United States was fast running out of the raw materials required to fuel its military and civilian economy. Where better to invest than in the vast friendly hinterland to the north? During the 1950s American investment poured into Canada, and American branch plants reinvested much of their earnings in Canadian industries.

The shift in economic dependence from Britain to the United States had occurred with remarkable speed. In less than half a century, Canadians had replaced one economic metropolis with another. By 1960 the United States accounted for three-quarters of Canada's foreign investment and absorbed two-thirds of the nation's exports (see tables 8.6 and 8.7). Meanwhile, Britain's share of Canadian foreign investment had dropped to 15 percent, and exports to Britain declined in direct proportion to the growth of the American market. Since much of the American money came in the form of direct investment in branch-plant operations or stock purchases, control of Canadian industry in important resource and manufacturing sectors was moving south of the border. The remark made by political economist Harold Innis that Canada had "moved from colony to nation to colony" seemed particularly apt.

Table 8.6: FOREIGN CONTROL AS A PERCENTAGE OF SELECTED CANADIAN INDUSTRIES, 1926–63

Industry	1926	1930	1939	1948	1958
Manufacturing	35	36	38	43	57
Petroleum and natural gas*	—	—	—	—	73
Mining and smelting	38	47	42	40	60
Railways	3	3	3	3	2
Other utilities	20	29	26	26	5
TOTAL	17	20	21	25	32

*Petroleum and natural gas combined with mining and smelting to 1948.

Source: John Fayerweather, *Foreign Investment in Canada: Prospects for National Policy* (Toronto: Oxford University Press, 1974), 7.

Table 8.7: FOREIGN CONTROL FOR SELECTED CANADIAN MANUFACTURING INDUSTRIES, 1963

Manufacturing	Percent
Beverages	17
Rubber	97
Textiles	20
Pulp and paper	47
Agricultural machinery	50
Automobiles and parts	97
Other transportation equipment	78
Primary iron and steel	14
Electrical apparatus	77
Chemicals	78
Other	70
TOTAL	60

Source: John Fayerweather, *Foreign Investment in Canada: Prospects for National Policy* (Toronto: Oxford University Press, 1974), 7.

Canadians were not certain how to respond to this transformation in their economic relations. They had long courted American capital investment and had boasted about the success of the tariff in encouraging American companies to locate north of the forty-ninth parallel. Now the degree of American control of Canada's economic destiny began to take on sinister overtones. In 1955 the Canadian government appointed a Royal Commission on Canada's Economic Prospects to inquire into and report on the long-term prospects of the Canadian economy. Chaired by Walter Gordon, a partner in one of Toronto's major accounting firms, the commission called attention to the problems caused by the "Americanization" of the Canadian economy in its report, which was tabled in 1957. The commissioners urged the government to exercise closer control over the activities of foreign companies operating in Canada and suggested that foreign corporations be required to employ more Canadians in senior management positions, include Canadians on their boards, and sell an "appreciable interest" in their equity stocks to people in the country where they did their business. With Canadians becoming more confident in their abilities to control their economic destiny, the stage was set for a new wave of economic nationalism, which would crest in the 1960s.

Walter Gordon's was a voice from the heart of Canada's business establishment. After a decade of hectic growth, others also raised questions about the Canada that corporate capitalism had built. Economists only measured things like GNP and per capita income; they failed to weigh the qualitative value of the goods produced; nor did they count the cost of resource depletion and environmental damage. Should scarce resources be used to produce guns rather than butter? Was economic growth in the present so important that the well-being of future generations should be sacrificed for it? Walter Gordon ended his report, not by focussing on economic questions but by raising the spectre of nuclear war. "If we are to avoid annihilation and the destruction of civilization as we know it, the main effort of all civilized peoples must be devoted to the creation of some kind of international organization with power to control these forces of destruction," he concluded. Such troubling issues would not go away no matter how affluent Canadians became.

• Conclusion

In little more than a century, Canada had been transformed from a group of isolated pre-industrial British colonies to one of the world's most productive industrial nations. Four out of five Canadians in the labour force earned a wage or salary rather than being self-employed or employing the labour of others. No longer a rural people, most Canadians now lived in cities. The industrial workday had been reduced from twelve to eight hours and still Canadians could boast a standard of living second in the world only to the United States. Because Canadians had come so far so fast, there was a need to take stock, to ask questions about where they were going as a nation. Of course, some of the changes were more apparent than real. While it was true that over six million Canadians were counted in the labour force by 1960, as many survived by engaging in unpaid domestic work, voluntary labour, or subsistence production. Others were only involved in the market economy on a part-time basis. Still others remained on the bottom rung of the economic ladder, for no other reason than their gender, the colour of their skin, or their ethnic origin. Like Canadians generally, those on the margins of industrial society became more empowered in the prosperous decade of the 1950s and would make their voices heard as Canada entered the post-industrial age.

• Origins of the Welfare State:

A Historiographical Debate

Social scientists generally agree on the various factors contributing to the evolution of the welfare state in Canada, but the relative weight of these factors is in dispute. So is the extent to which Canada's version of the welfare state compares favourably with the regimes established in other industrial countries.

Historians and political scientists have identified a variety of pressures that merged to create new federal social insurance programs: pressures from the unemployed; from business groups; from municipalities and provinces; from the more liberal churches; from within the state bureaucracy. The impact of key politicians has also been noted. Books and articles stressing the primacy of each of these forces present conflicting views of the character of political life in Canada in the recent past and the degree of social justice in the country. Some of the evidence of these works is summed up in future chapters, but it is worth noting here that scholars, by focussing on different phenomena, have come up with quite opposed views of the reform process in Canada.

Unemployment insurance can serve as an example. Alvin Finkel has suggested that pressure from big business was largely responsible for producing an unemployment insurance program.[4] These business people, who wanted the payouts to be modest, were interested in preventing public finances from being besieged by unplanned expenditures when unemployment rose. They stressed that the scale of payments must be modest and the funds for the program must come, in large part, from working people.

James Struthers argues that this scenario is too one-sided, suggesting that popular pressures played a large role in securing unemployment insurance.[5] Indeed, some argue that the business community, though divided, was largely opposed to unemployment insurance. According to sociologist Carl Cuneo, unemployment insurance was an example of the state implementing reforms to save capitalism from itself rather than trying to reduce the power of the business community.[6]

The role of specific politicians and of state bureaucrats is stressed by other historians. R.B. Bennett's need to appear reform-minded before the election of 1935 is often mentioned.[7] Bennett had promised unemployment insurance as early as 1931, and it was an unsurprising item in his "New Deal" package of reforms in 1935. J.L. Granatstein attributes Mackenzie King's reintroduction of unemployment insurance in 1940 to his desire to plan for expected postwar unemployment.[8]

Some scholars believe that the emphasis on outside pressures upon politicians is overstated and that the state bureaucracy shaped the character of the unemployment insurance program. Political scientist Leslie Pal, while admitting that a variety of forces caused politicians to accept the need for some form of social insurance, suggests that a state-centred rather than society-centred perspective explains the character of the program itself.

> *In its formative years, UI became grounded in an actuarial ideology and administrative logic. Contributions, benefits, duration, coverage, and administrative autonomy all had roots in this bureaucratic perspective on the program. Whereas employee groups tended to view UI in terms of rights, and employers saw it in terms of costs and economic effect, officials were preoccupied with administrative feasibility, actuarial soundness, and strict insurance principles. It is true that in many respects this led to a similarity of views between employers and officials, particularly on the abuse question, but this similarity was coincidental in that officials' views were arrived at independently. They were not the result of "pressure."[9]*

Can society and the state be so neatly hived off from one another? Studies suggest that the state bureaucracy shares many similarities in background with the economic elites. Recent literature on unemployment insurance, examined from the perspective of gender, also suggests a happy coincidence between the views of state bureaucrats, involved in drawing up unemployment insurance legislation, and the views of corporate leaders, at the expense of women workers.[10] Indeed, as Ruth Pierson has pointed out, neither progressives nor conservatives organised to defend married women workers' rights to receive fair compensation when they lost jobs.

•Notes

[1] *Patriot*, 26 March 1928, cited in Ruth A. Freeman and Jennifer Callaghan, "A History of Potato Marketing in Prince Edward Island, 1920–1987," prepared for the Royal Commission on the Potato Industry, April 1987.

[2] Marc Milner, *North Atlantic Run: The Royal Canadian Navy and the Battle for the Convoys* (Toronto: University of Toronto Press, 1985), ch. 9.

[3] Robert Bothwell, Ian Drummond, and John English, *Canada Since 1945: Power, Politics and Provincialism* (Toronto: University of Toronto Press, 1981), 89.

[4] Alvin Finkel, *Business and Social Reform in the Thirties* (Toronto: Lorimer, 1979).

[5] James Struthers, *No Fault of Their Own: Unemployment and the Canadian Welfare State, 1914–1941* (Toronto: University of Toronto Press, 1981).

[6] Carl J. Cuneo, "State, Class, and Reserve Labour: The Case of the 1941 Canadian Unemployment Insurance Act," *Canadian Review of Sociology and Anthropology* 16 (May 1979): 147–70.

[7] See, for example, Larry A. Glassford, *Reaction and Reform: The Politics of the Conservative Party under R.B. Bennett, 1927–1938* (Toronto: University of Toronto Press, 1992).

[8] J.L. Granatstein, *Canada's War: The Politics of the Mackenzie King Government, 1939–1945* (Toronto: Oxford University Press, 1975).

[9] Leslie Pal, *State, Class and Bureaucracy: Canadian Unemployment Insurance and Public Policy* (Montreal: McGill-Queen's University Press, 1988), 109.

[10] Ruth Roach Pierson, "Gender and the Unemployment Insurance Debates in Canada, 1934–1940," *Labour/Le Travail* 25 (Spring 1990): 77–103.

•Selected Reading

In addition to the sources cited in chapter 5 that also cover the period from 1920 to 1960, the following titles should be consulted: John Thompson and Alan Seager, *Canada, 1922–1939: Decades of Discord* (Toronto: McClelland and Stewart, 1985); Ian Drummond, Robert Bothwell, and John English, *Canada, 1900–1945* (Toronto: University of Toronto Press, 1987); *Canada Since 1945* (Toronto: University of Toronto Press, 1982); Tom Traves, *The State and Enterprise: Canadian Manufacturers and the Federal Government, 1917–1931* (Toronto: University of Toronto Press, 1979); Douglas Owram, *The Government Generation: Canadian Intellectuals and the State, 1900–1945* (Toronto: University of Toronto Press, 1986); Ian MacPherson, *Each For All: A History of the Cooperative Movement in English Canada, 1900–1945* (Ottawa: Carleton University Press, 1979); Trevor J. Dick, "Canadian Newsprint, 1913–1930: National Policies and the North American Economy" in *Perspectives on Canadian Economic History*, ed. Douglas McCalla (Toronto: Copp Clark Pitman, 1987); J.L. Granatstein and Robert Cuff, *American Dollars and Canadian Prosperity* (Toronto: Samuel-Stevens, 1978); Melissa Clark Jones, *A Staple State: Canadian Industrial Resources in Cold War* (Toronto: University of Toronto Press, 1987).

On the economy during the Depression and the Second World War see Douglas Owram, "Economic Thought in the 1930s: The Prelude to Keynesianism," *Canadian Historical Review* 66, 3 (Sept. 1985): 344–77; A.E. Safarian, *The Canadian Economy in the Great Depression* (Ottawa: Carleton University Press, 1970); Ian M. Drummond, *British Economic Policy and the Empire, 1919–1939* (London: Allen and Unwin, 1972); Ian M. Drummond and Norman Hillmer, *Negotiating Freer Trade* (Waterloo, ON: Wilfrid Laurier University Press, 1989); Alvin Finkel, *Business and Social Reform in the Thirties* (Toronto: Lorimer, 1979); James Struthers, *No Fault of Their Own: Unemployment and the Canadian Welfare State, 1914–1941* (Toronto: University of Toronto Press, 1981); Larry A. Glassford, *Reaction and Reform: The Politics of the Conservative Party Under R.B. Bennett, 1927–1938* (Toronto: University of Toronto Press, 1992); Robert Bothwell and William Kilbourn, *C.D. Howe: A Biography* (Toronto: McClelland and Stewart, 1980); Robert Bothwell, *Nucleus: The History of Atomic Energy of Canada Limited* (Toronto: University of Toronto Press, 1988); J.L. Granatstein, *Canada's War: The Politics of the Mackenzie King Government, 1939–1945* (Toronto: University of Toronto Press, 1975); A.F.W. Plumptre, *Three Decades of Decision: Canada and the World Monetary System, 1944–1975* (Toronto: McClelland and Stewart, 1977); E.R. Forbes, "Cutting the Pie Into Smaller Pieces: Matching Grants and Relief in the Maritime Provinces during the 1930s" and "Consolidating Disparity: The Maritimes and the Industrialization of Canada during the Second World War" in *Challenging the Regional Stereotype: Essays on the Twentieth Century Maritimes* (Fredericton: Acadiensis Press, 1989).

On women in this period see Veronica Strong-Boag, *The New Day Recalled: Lives of Girls and Women in English Canada, 1919–1939* (Toronto: Copp Clark Pitman, 1988); Andrée Lévesque, *La norme et les déviantes: des femmes au Québec pendant l'entre-deux-guerres* (Montreal: Les éditions de remue-ménage, 1989); Jean Burnet, ed., *Looking into My Sister's Eyes: An Exploration in Women's History* (Toronto: Multicultural History Society of Ontario, 1986); Ruth Roach Pierson, *"They're Still Women After All": The Second World War and Canadian Womanhood* (Toronto: McClelland and Stewart, 1986).

THE GROWTH OF THE STATE, 1920–60

Ed Bates, a rural Saskatchewan butcher, responded to his vanishing clientele as the Depression gripped Saskatchewan by moving his family and shop to Vancouver. Again the Depression claimed the Bates family for victims and they were forced to seek relief. Denied welfare by the Vancouver authorities because of their recent arrival in that city, they attempted to get social assistance in Saskatoon, only to be told they must return to their small town to apply for help. Too proud to return home to live on welfare, they decided to rent a car and kill themselves by carbon monoxide poisoning. Mr and Mrs Bates survived the suicide attempt, but their son Jack did not, and they were charged with his murder. Local citizens blamed the politicians, rather than the parents, for Jack's death. A defence committee was formed, and a coroner's jury found the Bateses innocent in the tragic death of their son. The incident revealed that, while some people blamed themselves for their economic failures, a growing group blamed the political and economic system rather than the individual for widespread poverty. These people began to demand that the state intervene to ensure that others never reach the desperate straits of the Bates family.

The growth of the state at all levels—federal, provincial, and municipal—from 1920 to 1960 was a response to a variety of social pressures. This chapter focusses on popular calls for reform and state reaction to these pressures. As we shall see, the reforms demanded by protest movements and parties were taken seriously by the established political and economic elites. But the actual reforms implemented, while they partially met demands from below, were usually in a form conservative enough to ensure that little redistribution of wealth and power actually occurred.

As we study the interaction of reform groups and conservative political forces, it is important to bear in mind that the state in a democratic

Destitute family in Saskatchewan, 1934　(Glenbow Archives/ND3-6742)

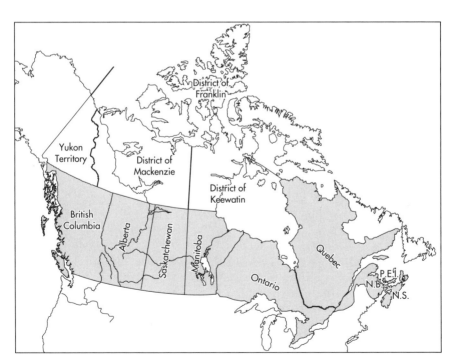

MAP 9.1　*Canada, 1931*　(D.G.G. Kerr, *Historical Atlas of Canada* (Scarborough: Nelson, 1975), 67)

capitalist society is a complex phenomenon. On the one hand, the political parties contending for state power require voters' support, and this tends to make them far more sensitive to ordinary people's desires than the parties of an earlier era when the franchise was more restricted. On the other hand, politicians who accept the ideology of marketplace supremacy in the economy must be careful not to offend the interests of the corporate leaders who dominate that marketplace. The vote is only one way to pressure governments. As this chapter makes clear, protest movements of various types abounded in Canada both before and after the Second World War. These groups agitated for everything from an end to Catholic immigration to Canada to the overthrow of the capitalist system.

• Regional and Class Protest in the 1920s

The federal election of 1921 produced a surprising result. The Conservatives under Arthur Meighen suffered a crushing defeat, and the Liberals under their new leader William Lyon Mackenzie King emerged with a minority government. A new political party called the Progressive Party, which embraced the farmers' platform of the Canadian Council of Agriculture, had come second to the Liberals in parliamentary seats. Indeed, the Progressives had won more seats in English Canada than the Liberals, who had swept Quebec. The Progressives' call for a speedy elimination of all tariffs and for public ownership of utilities, particularly railways, apparently struck a positive chord among rural residents in English Canada.

This result followed a trend that began in 1919 with the election of a minority United Farmers of Ontario government supported by the province's Independent Labour Party. Two years later, the United Farmers of Alberta produced a majority government even though they had run candidates only in rural seats and had won just 28 percent of the popular vote. In 1922, it was Manitoba's turn to elect a farmers' government. In all three farmer-run provinces, a healthy labour component in the legislature suggested that old-party dominance in urban and industrial areas was as unsteady as it was in the countryside. In the early postwar elections in the Maritimes, as well, particularly in Nova Scotia in 1920, the popularity of class-based parties appeared to be rising. Yet, by 1939, the Progressive Party was long dead and the only remaining farmers' government was in Manitoba, where the Progressive Party had merged with the Liberals in 1928 and no longer presented itself as the voice of only one segment of the community. Maritime complaints had been taken up by the provincial wings of the old-line parties and, outside industrial Cape Breton, the class-based parties in the region had largely been abandoned. New voices of class and regional protest emerged in Canada in the 1930s, but they proved in the short term to be weaker threats to the hegemony of the two main parties than the movements of the early 1920s.

The Progressive Party

With 65 of 245 seats in Parliament in 1921, the Progressives made clear the determination of farmers in Canada not to be left out of national decision making. As we saw in chapter 7, farmers became increasingly concerned that their status as the bedrock of the nation was being eroded as the country became more industrialized. Frustrated by business dominance of the Liberal and Conservative parties, and convinced that these parties were corrupt patronage machines, farmers had become disillusioned with the political choices before them. In Western Canada, farmers' economic grievances joined with traditional regional complaints, such as federal control over Prairie resources, to make the idea of a new party particularly attractive.

Wartime inflation had increased farmer indignation with high tariffs on imported industrial goods. The protectionism of the Union government in Ottawa convinced many that the Conservatives, who led that government, were irretrievably beholden to big business interests in Central Canada for whom the tariff was sacred. But many Anglo-Canadian farmers, for reasons of chauvinism and economic self-interest, were also resentful towards the federal Liberals. That party's majority had opposed conscription, to the chagrin of loyal imperialists of all classes, including the farmers. Worse, the conscription issue had temporarily detached much of the non-francophone leadership of the Liberals from the party, leaving a Quebec rump apparently dominated by protectionists.

T.A. Crerar, the Progressives' first national leader, had been a Unionist Cabinet minister and conscriptionist Liberal, which limited his appeal in rural Quebec, where resentment against conscription ensured vast support for the federal Liberals in the first postwar election. Quebec's Liberal Party, dominated by the francophone economic elite, was an uneasy alliance of low and high tariff interests, the latter unwilling to join the Conservative Party because of the party's perceived imperialism and hostility to francophone perspectives.

Disenchanted imperialist Liberals formed the conservative wing of the Progressive Party. This group dominated the party in both Manitoba and Ontario. It was mainly in Alberta that a radical wing proved influential within the farmers' political movement. Led by Henry Wise Wood, the United Farmers of Alberta rejected the party system altogether and claimed that elected representatives ought to be free to vote their constituents' interests rather than forced to support the party line. Wood, sharing a belief common in Western Canada and the Maritimes, felt that regional and local interests had been subordinated to Central Canadian business concerns. He called for a reorganization of Parliament so that constituencies would be based not on geography but on social class. In Wood's "group government," farmers, workers, entrepreneurs, and professionals would have representation commensurate with the weight of each occupational grouping within the population. The radical wing of the farmers' movement emphasized free co-operation among individuals as an alternative to domination by capitalist monopolies. While the radicals believed that the state could play a positive role in implementing social justice, before the 1930s they regarded the co-operative movement rather than the state as the key to creating a more egalitarian society.

The women's sections of the farm organizations were particularly strong proponents of co-operation as an alternative to competition. Irene Parlby, president of the United Farm Women of Alberta (UFWA) from 1917 to 1921 and later the first female member of the Alberta Cabinet, argued that rural communities could only be strong if their residents

POLITICAL WOMEN

During the interwar period, many Canadian women continued the political activism that, prior to the First World War, had led them into the suffrage and temperance movements. Women were involved both in party politics and in reform movements agitating for women's rights, child welfare, prison reform, and world peace. In 1929, five Alberta women were instrumental in convincing the Judicial Committee of the Privy Council in the United Kingdom (then the last court of appeal for the Canadian legal system) that women were "persons" under the law and were therefore entitled to sit in the Canadian Senate. The five were: Nellie McClung, the reformer, writer, and former Liberal MLA who had been prominent in the woman suffrage movement; writer and reformer Emily Murphy, who in 1916 had become the first woman magistrate in the British Empire; Alberta Cabinet Minister Irene Parlby; activist and former Alberta MLA Louise McKinney; and Henrietta Muir Edwards, who had helped to found the National Council of Women and the Victorian Order of Nurses. Despite considerable feeling that Judge Murphy should be rewarded with the post, the Liberal government of Mackenzie King appointed Cairine Wilson, a long-time Liberal Party organizer, as the first woman senator in Canada.

Along with McClung, Parlby, and McKinney, Agnes Macphail was a distinguished member of a relatively small group of women who served in the House of Commons or in provincial legislatures before 1960. A teacher from Grey County, Ontario, in 1921 she became the first woman elected to Parliament. As a member of the Progressive Party, she soon made her mark as an outspoken defender of farmers, workers, women, and prisoners. She advocated bringing more women into political life, and championed peaceful solutions to international conflicts. Her long career in federal politics came to an end when she was defeated in the election of 1940. By then an activist in the Co-operative Commonwealth Federation, she later served as a CCF member of the Ontario legislature from 1943 to 1945 and 1948 to 1951, during which time she was responsible for the enactment of the first equal pay legislation in Canada.

Agnes Macphail   (Yousuf Karsh/National Archives of Canada/C21562)

worked together and in concert with other rural communities to provide health, educational, and recreational facilities. Rural women throughout the West took upon themselves the task of establishing rural hospitals and clinics, improving local schools, and setting up local community centres and theatres. Having won their battle for the vote, women's organizations used their political influence to convince governments to spend money to improve community life rather than to focus purely on economic development. The UFWA was committed not only to co-operation among farm people but to co-operation among all nations to end war. Joining with women's peace groups in other regions, it called on the schools to shape curricula so that students were exposed to the values of tolerance and peaceful settlement of disputes as alternatives to bigotry and war.

The UFWA, like other farm women's organizations in the West, also took up the battle for better protection of women's property rights both within marriage and during divorce. They also attempted to persuade the provincial government to establish family planning clinics, but they made little headway on either of these issues with the largely male UFA government. The government's insensitivity to feminist demands was hardly surprising. Despite the radicalism within the UFA movement, the government itself followed conventional parliamentary procedures and implemented few radical pieces of legislation. The gulf between the movement and government bearing the UFA name grew ever wider. By the early 1930s, the UFA government was practising fiscal conservatism while the UFA organization called for a socialist restructuring of society.

Federal members of Parliament from Alberta remained, on the whole, radicals committed to more democratic, participatory politics. But they had little influence over other Progressives who simply wanted the Liberal Party to get rid of tariffs. First Crerar, and later Robert Forke, the party's second parliamentary leader, crossed over to the Liberal Party when the radicals frustrated their efforts to create a traditional party machine and Mackenzie King's Liberals proved willing to pass some reforms demanded by the moderate Progressives. King lowered tariffs on farm machinery and equipment, and acceded to Prairie demands to complete a rail link to the port of Churchill. The rail link was supposed to create an alternative to shipping via the Great Lakes–St Lawrence route, which farmers believed to be monopolized by a few price-gouging shippers, but it proved to be too costly an alternative. King also restored the Crow rate, which had been suspended in wartime, and negotiated the surrender of federal control over the Prairie provinces' natural resources.

The Progressives were divided on questions of economic restructuring. Opposition to tariffs was general in the party, but there were strong disagreements on the merits of public versus private operation of railways, utilities, and the marketing of grain. While Crerar was a strong free enter-priser, many Progressives had won elections promising their constituents to press for nationalization of the CPR. In the West, many of those who voted against the old-line parties were grain farmers who had approved of the orderly marketing of grain by the Canadian Wheat Board during the war.

Within the provinces they governed, the farmers' movements appeared to follow the same economic policies as the traditional parties. The United Farmers of Ontario, unfortunate enough to be in power through a recession (1919–23), proved mainly interested in cutting govern-ment expenditures. Their lacklustre performance resulted in a third-place finish when they faced the electorate in 1923. Their Independent Labour Party allies, hard-pressed to indicate what advances working people had won from the Farmer–Labour government, also suffered an ignominious defeat. The UFA and its allies in the Canadian Labour Party proved more durable, though their eventual defeat in the 1935 provincial election left both organizations without a seat in the legislature. While the UFA had a fairly positive record in the areas of health and education in the 1920s, by the 1930s many thought it more solicitous towards finance companies than to their financially strapped debtors, particularly farmers.

The Progressive movement, although powered by genuine feelings of economic exploitation and by farmers' determination to assert their politi-cal power, demonstrated the absence of a coherent ideology in the 1920s. At times, the movement appeared to be a national anglophone farmers' protest party; at other times it appeared mainly a Prairie protest movement (though it made little headway in Saskatchewan provincial politics, where a superb Liberal organization kept it at bay); at still others, it seemed a con-fusing alliance of bitterly opposed factions. Many Prairie farmers turned away from debates about the role of the state in protecting farmers' inter-ests and instead created huge pools to market farmers' grain.

The failure of both the Progressives and the farmers' marketing ven-tures caused Prairie farmers in the 1930s to seek new political avenues for reform. In Ontario, where they were less dependent on the fortunes of a single cash crop, farmers proved content to return to lobbying old-line par-ties for legislation supportive of farm interests. In the Maritimes, the Progressives had never made much headway, despite shared resentment towards Central Canadian interests.

The Maritime Rights Movement

As Maritimers watched their commercial and manufacturing establishments either close or move to Montreal or Toronto, their resentment grew not only against Central Canada, but against Western Canada, which they regarded as the spoiled child of Confederation. While the western provinces decried exploitation by Central Canada, the Maritimers denounced the Crow rates and the comparatively generous provincial subsidies to the West (the result of rapidly expanding populations and of compensation payments for federal control of local resources). The Maritime premiers had opposed the huge territorial grants given to Manitoba, Quebec, and Ontario in 1912, claiming that the wealth of these territories ought to belong to the Dominion as a whole.

As the population of the Maritimes declined relative to the rest of the nation, there was a drop in the proportion of seats the region held in the House of Commons. This created fears that Maritime complaints, already largely ignored, would be shunted aside completely. Eastern business leaders, in particular, decided that only a united regional effort could exert sufficient pressure on Ottawa to achieve results. In the past, local rivalries, including the battle for economic dominance between Saint John and Halifax, had precluded Maritime solidarity. But, led by the Maritime Board of Trade, significant regional solidarity emerged in the decade following the war. Labour leaders, middle-class reformers, and farmers, deciding that the regional economy's very existence was in jeopardy, joined forces with business leaders to fight for Maritime rights.

The Maritime Rights Movement centred around several demands. The key one, first voiced by the Maritime Board of Trade in 1919, was for the Canadian National Railways to be divided into two autonomous regional sections, with the eastern section headquartered in the Maritimes. The inclusion of the Intercolonial in the CNR in 1917 and the removal of its head office to Toronto confirmed the region's worst fears. Not only were jobs lost and freight rates increased, but service levels were cut and East Coast cities abandoned as major terminals of the import–export trade. Maritime rights also embraced such issues as more equitable subsidies for the Maritime provinces so that they might improve educational and health services, better parliamentary representation for the region, and greater protection for the Maritime manufacturing sector.

The Progressive Party and the labour parties in Ontario and Western Canada, conveniently forgetting the regional bases of many of their own demands, were largely uninterested in what they perceived as the parochial program of the Maritime Rights Movement. Their unwillingness to incorporate Maritime claims into their programs meant that their organizations, initially well received in the Maritimes, largely evaporated. Most Maritime workers and farmers joined the business community in campaigns to lobby the traditional parties. They did so not because they were innately conservative and unwilling to consider class-based parties, but because the established parties appeared more receptive and were more likely to have the power to heed calls for reform in the country's most stagnant region.

In 1926, Mackenzie King, having largely pacified western and Ontario farmers and reduced the Progressives to a rump in Parliament, turned his attention to the Maritimes. He set up a Royal Commission on Maritime Claims, naming as its head the British lawyer-industrialist, Sir Andrew Rae Duncan. Duncan recognized that Maritime governments were forced to tax their citizens more than other provincial governments just to maintain a minimal level of services and called for a series of grants to the region's governments. He also recommended a revision of railway rates to provide more regional equity and to allow industrial improvements to port facilities at Halifax and Saint John to encourage international trade through the region. While King appeared to embrace the Duncan Report, his government refused to fully implement its recommendations. As historian Ernest Forbes observes: "Unfortunately for the Maritimes, the King government turned it into a program for political pacification; only gradually would Maritimers realize how much of the substance of Sir Andrew Rae Duncan's program had been removed in its supposed implementation."[1] Like the Progressive movement, popular agitation for Maritime rights largely dissipated in the late 1920s and proved difficult to re-ignite even during the Depression.

• Protest by Other Means: Communists, Fascists, and the KKK

During the 1920s, the mainstream labour parties steered an uneasy course between socialism and reformism. While several provincial labour parties espoused gradual nationalization of major industries and greater worker control in their operation, the struggle for immediate reforms for workers—minimum wages for women, improved workers' compensation, federal unemployment insurance—absorbed most of the time of elected Labour representatives. Their alliance with conservative farmers' administrations in Ontario and Alberta even placed their commitment to reform in question. Within the labour movement, craft union leaders had reasserted their supremacy and forestalled the advance of industrial unions. The major industrial unions that survived, such as the United Mine Workers and Amalgamated Clothing Workers, were increasingly conservative and often collaborated closely with management. In the case of the UMW, this resulted in temporary breakaway movements both in the Cape Breton and the Alberta coal fields.

The Communists

Recession and postwar state repression, which reduced the size of the labour movement in Canada by about 40 percent in the first four years of the 1920s, were major factors in labour's increased conservatism. A marked contrast to this trend was the Communist Party of Canada (CPC). Organized furtively in a barn outside Guelph in 1921, the CPC, though it never enrolled more than 30 000 members at any time in its history, included many of the nation's most committed labour radicals. Communist leadership in the coal fields, in garment shops, in hard-rock mining, and among northern Ontario bushworkers brought a spirit of militancy to many groups either ignored or poorly represented by established unions. Immigrant unskilled labour, particularly Ukrainians and Finns, formed the backbone of Canada's Communist Party. The CPC also established Women's Labour Leagues to help educate and organize women workers.

Communist doctrines appealed to labour leaders like Scottish immigrant J.B. McLachlan, whose organizational work among the coal miners of Cape Breton during the 1909–10 strike had led management to blacklist him. When he urged coal miners to conduct a sympathy strike in support of Sydney steelworkers in 1923, he was removed from his position as president of District 26 of the United Mine Workers by John L. Lewis, the president of the UMW. Convicted in court of seditious libel, McLachlan spent a few months in prison before returning to Cape Breton in 1924 to edit the *Maritime Labour Herald*. During the 1930s, he served as president of the Workers Unity League, a communist-inspired union organization. Disgusted by Stalin's totalitarian regime in the Soviet Union and its tight surveillance of party members in Canada, McLachlan resigned from the party in 1936.

Communist ideas, meanwhile, helped to shape local opinion during the violent and protracted coal miners' strike that rocked industrial Cape Breton in 1925. As the living conditions of the struggling miners and their families became more widely known, there was a great outpouring of sympathy across the country. Even miners in the Soviet Union sent assistance. When Progressive member of Parliament Agnes McPhail visited the conflict-ridden area, she found a situation that she claimed would make her adopt views more radical than any she detected among the starving miners.

The Depression created more situations in which communism could take root. In 1932, Prime Minister Bennett decided to create relief camps to house single, unemployed, transient men, who were travelling from city to city in search of work. At the time, it seemed to Bennett and his advisors that these unfortunate people were a potentially explosive group who

Cartoonist Donald McRitchie depicted the 1925 coal miners' strike in Cape Breton as a conflict between agitators and the hard-line policy pursued by the British Empire Steel and Coal Corporation (BESCO), which owned the mine. (*Halifax Herald*)

should be segregated from society until the economy improved. The transients were to be denied welfare unless they agreed to go to remote camps, which Bennett placed under military control. Within the camps, spartan living conditions and an allowance of twenty cents per day awaited inmates. While they sometimes performed useful work such as highway construction, the inmates' isolation and lack of pay bred hopelessness. As Irene Baird's powerful novel *Waste Heritage* (1939) vividly illustrated, Communist organizers had little difficulty convincing these desperate young men to organize to demand "work and wages" and the closing of the camps.

Depression demonstration   (National Archives of Canada/C29397)

Communist agitators were evident in the city, too, where they were instrumental, though hardly alone, in helping to organize protest against injustice in welfare and housing. Many married men, who received pitiful vouchers to maintain their families, demonstrated for higher relief payments. Married women, angry with a system that generally offered only purchase-specific vouchers, demanded cash payments so that they could exercise some discretion in meeting their families' needs and were not stigmatized when they shopped. Women and men joined together to prevent the eviction of families so poor they could no longer pay even the meagre rent for substandard housing.

As the authorities watched thousands of unemployed men and women demonstrating for social justice, their first instinct was to suppress dissent. The use of state violence to protect the *status quo* was hardly new in

Canada, and in the 1930s many strikers and demonstrators were jailed or beaten. Their leaders, if they were not citizens, were often deported. The Communist Party was declared illegal in 1931 and seven of its members including its leader Tim Buck were imprisoned. It was re-legalized in 1936, only to be banned in Quebec under the infamous Padlock Law of 1937, a law disallowed by the Supreme Court twenty years later because it violated the federal government's exclusive right to make criminal laws. Banned yet again in 1940, the party reorganized as the Labour Progressive Party.

While there were several tragic instances in the 1930s of strikers being killed by the police, the clash between the authorities and the victims of the Depression that gained the most national attention occurred in Regina in 1935. An On-to-Ottawa Trek, organized primarily by Communist relief camp workers in British Columbia, moved by rail eastwards to Ottawa, gathering new demonstrators to pressure Bennett to implement a "work and wages" alternative to the camps. Bennett, concerned with the momentum that the trek had gained, decided to use the RCMP to stop the demonstrators in Regina. Predictably, the RCMP's attempts to disperse the strikers resulted in violence, with one constable dead and hundreds of strikers and constables injured. The next year, Mackenzie King abolished the camps, which by that time had provided temporary homes and education in the politics of despair to about 100 000 Canadians.

Communist effectiveness in organizing relief workers as well as many industrial workers translated into only limited electoral success. Even during the Depression, most Canadians remained uninterested in socialist alternatives, and few saw the repressive Soviet Union, the model state espoused by the CPC, as a society that Canada should emulate. Fewer still wished to emulate fascist Italy or Nazi Germany, where dictators Benito Mussolini and Adolf Hitler were producing another kind of revolution.

The Extreme Right

National pride led sizeable numbers of German and Italian Canadians to support the dictators who had seized power and seemingly restored national dignity in their native countries. While few supported the use of violence to bring fascism to Canada, coteries of fascists did organize in most major Canadian cities and in some small towns. Most of their leaders were of British or French descent, and their followers were drawn from all classes and cultures.

Attracted by Adolf Hitler's glorification of violence, white supremacy, and hatred of Jews, Communists, and homosexuals, Nazis battled with Communists and union groups and attempted to keep Jews off beaches and away from other public places. In Quebec, the Nazis claimed to represent the last stand of Catholicism against decadent forces, and the right-wing leadership of the province's churches turned a blind eye to fascist attempts to use the church to promote racism and anti-Semitism. In Western Canada, anti-communist Ukrainian nationalist organizations sympathized with the racial exclusiveness and militarism of the Nazis, conveniently ignoring Hitler's estimation of the Slavs as an inferior race fit only to be slaves to the "Aryan" races.

The racism of the extreme right reflected the dark side of a heritage of several centuries of European imperialism in which claims of racial superiority played an important role in justifying the conquest of non-Europeans. In North America, no organization has been more identified with racism than the Ku Klux Klan, the secretive, violent brotherhood of hooded white men who took up the cause of white supremacy in the American South after the Civil War. The Klan proved the most influential right-wing organization in Canada in the 1920s and early 1930s, though details of its operations remain sketchy. With few blacks to terrorize, the Canadian Klan became a Protestant extremist organization with Catholics as its target. The Klan called for an end to immigration of non-Protestants

The Ku Klux Klan in Saskatchewan   (National Archives of Canada/PA87848)

and for deportation of those Catholics born outside Canada. Strongest in Saskatchewan and Alberta, the Klan's influence proved that prewar nativist sentiments in the West had not disappeared. In Saskatchewan, Klan membership in the late 1920s has been estimated at 10 000 to 15 000.

The Klan exercised influence within the Saskatchewan Conservative Party, which led a coalition government from 1929 to 1934. Klan pressures led the government to end French-language instruction in the early grades of school and to dismiss nuns teaching in public schools. E.E. Perley, a Saskatchewan Conservative MP, informed R.B. Bennett that only Protestants should be appointed to the Senate from Saskatchewan. He wrote Bennett in 1931: "Possibly you are aware that the Ku Klux Klan is very strong in this province and no doubt was a great silent factor both in the provincial and in the last federal election, in favour of the Conservatives. They are very much worked up over the fact that one of the first major appointments is to go to the Roman Catholic Church, and it certainly will do us a great deal of harm."[2] Fortunately only a minority believed that the Depression could be ended, and further economic crises averted, by deporting or persecuting Catholics, Jews, or Communists. Yet an increasingly large section of the population was open to political action that the old-line parties, controlled by the financial elites, rejected.

• Third Parties

The Co-operative Commonwealth Federation, Social Credit, and the Union Nationale were all born in the Dirty Thirties, each with its own formula for preventing capitalist boom–bust economic cycles. With as much as one-third of the nation facing destitution, Canadians looked to new political parties to find a solution to their problems.

The CCF

The Co-operative Commonwealth Federation (CCF), formed in 1932, enjoyed modest success in the 1930s. Unlike the Union Nationale and Social Credit, it formed no governments during the Depression decade. Less than one voter in ten cast a ballot for the CCF in 1935; almost as many voted for the short-lived Reconstruction Party, led by renegade Conservative Cabinet Minister H.H. Stevens and dedicated to favourable legislation for small businesses. Yet the CCF, the forerunner of the New Democratic Party, ultimately proved more influential than the other new parties of the 1930s.

The CCF was a democratic socialist party formed as the result of a decision by progressive members of Parliament to capitalize on grass-roots pressure to unite the disparate left-wing labour and farm organizations in the country. It inherited the often contradictory traditions of labourism, socialism, and farm radicalism in Western Canada, and early election results demonstrated that, outside of industrial Cape Breton, the CCF had taken root mainly in the West. By 1939, it formed the opposition in British Columbia, Saskatchewan, and Manitoba.

Led by Winnipeg Labour MP, J.S. Woodsworth, the CCF rejected both capitalism and the revolutionary rhetoric of the Communists. The CCF's Regina Manifesto in 1933 proclaimed the possibility of a parliamentary road to socialism. The manifesto suggested that major industries ought to be under either government or co-operative control and that the state, rather than the marketplace, should determine levels of investment to bring an end to boom–bust cycles. The manifesto reflected compromise among the party's constituents. The farmers were promised that a democratic socialist government would not nationalize land and indeed would have as a goal the preservation of family farms. The socialists were assured that the CCF's ultimate goal was an egalitarian nation. The manifesto, after outlining a set of public-spending measures to get the unemployed back to work, ended on a radical note: "No C.C.F. Government will rest content until it has eradicated capitalism and put into operation the full programme of socialized planning which will lead to the establishment in Canada of the Co-operative Commonwealth."[3]

The CCF established a democratic internal structure that gave local constituency members the power to choose electoral candidates without central party direction and the annual convention the power to set party policy. Women activists from the farm and labour movements, such as Louise Lucas in Saskatchewan and Beatrice Brigden in Manitoba, struggled to make women's rights a concern of the new socialist party. These women, like those in other farm and labour organizations, found the workings of party politics persistently patriarchal. Women were generally expected to stay out of policy making and remain in subordinate, supporting roles. Nonetheless, several CCF women, such as Dorothy Steeves, Agnes Macphail, and Laura Jamieson, were elected to provincial legislatures. Thérèse Casgrain, who had been a leading activist in the struggle for women's suffrage in Quebec, became leader of the province's CCF in 1951, barely ten years after Quebec women secured the provincial franchise.

The CCF formed the government in Saskatchewan from 1944 to 1964. There Premiers T.C. (Tommy) Douglas and Woodrow Lloyd pioneered the first public hospital insurance and medicare programs in Canada. They also successfully expanded the public sector to include gas distribution, automobile insurance, an inter-city bus company, and marketing boards that regulated northern resources. During its first term in office, the Saskatchewan CCF operated several manufacturing plants that had gone bankrupt under private owners and made plans for public involvement in the resources sector. By its second term, the resistance of outside investors and buyers to dealing in products emanating from Crown corporations caused the CCF to shelve plans for greater state involvement in the economy. The focus of the party increasingly became the extension of welfare programs.

Social Credit

Not all western Canadians who rejected the mainstream political parties turned towards socialism for a solution to economic ills. When popular Alberta radio evangelist William "Bible Bill" Aberhart began in 1932 to inject "social credit" into his weekly radio broadcasts, he found a receptive audience. Aberhart, re-interpreting doctrines espoused by a British engineer, Major C.H. Douglas, and building on traditional suspicion towards Central Canadian financial institutions, claimed that the Depression had been caused by the banks' failure to print enough money so that consumer spending could match industrial production. To many free enterprisers, disillusioned by the severity of the Depression, Aberhart's nostrums proved appealing. If only the banks could be forced to supply consumers with money, they believed, prosperity could be restored.

Social credit meant that governments would replace financial institutions as the arbiters of how much money should be in circulation and in whose hands. It claimed to offer a scientific formula to determine the shortfall in purchasing power, advocating that the government simply credit all citizens equally with a share of this shortfall to keep the economy healthy. Opponents suggested that such money would have to be borrowed, thereby increasing government debt, or the currency would be devalued. Social Credit rejected charges that their policies promised either inflated prices for imported products (following currency devaluation) or large government deficits, but their arguments against such charges were, at best, vague. Aberhart attempted unsuccessfully to convince the UFA government in Alberta to embrace social credit ideas such as the social dividend and the just price. Under the former, the state would issue money to all adults so as to boost purchasing power, while state regulation of prices would ensure that social dividends were not eaten away by price-gouging business people.

In 1935, Aberhart turned the social credit study clubs spawned by his radio appeals into a political movement that won fifty-six of sixty-three seats in that year's provincial election. Once in power, he failed to deliver on his promises to issue social dividends or to control prices, and he only attempted to regulate banks and currency when a backbenchers' revolt in 1937 forced him to stop procrastinating. Legislation to this end in 1937 and 1938 was disallowed by the federal government and ultimately by the courts, which upheld federal jurisdiction over banking and currency. Thus, Aberhart was able to blame the federal government for his failure to implement his election promises.

Many Social Credit supporters in Alberta in 1935 regarded the party as quasi-socialist. An energetic Social Credit movement with a charismatic leader promised not only money for nothing but also a new deal for the unemployed and protection of citizens against money lenders. The government legislated moratoria on debts, earning it the eternal gratitude of many farmers. Beyond this, its record was spotty. Aberhart was a prickly authoritarian and ignored popular pressure for better treatment of welfare recipients and for improved workers' compensation. His attempts to legislate the press to print government propaganda alongside the regular content of newspapers was struck down by the courts, revealing anti-civil-libertarian tendencies of the Social Credit movement.

The Alberta Social Credit Party, initially a mass movement with a diverse membership and a diffuse but left-leaning program, had become, by Aberhart's death in 1943, a right-wing organization with a relatively restricted membership in which religious fundamentalists and monetary cranks loomed large. The party leaders, always receptive to conspiracy theories, began to believe that bankers, communists, socialists, and unionists were all part of an international conspiracy to suppress the human freedom that only Social Credit philosophy could create and protect. A section of the party was convinced that the Jews were the glue that stuck this strange Bolsheviks-and-bankers alliance together. Ernest Manning, the premier of Alberta from 1943 to 1968, would not allow the party to support such bigotry, and in 1947 he purged influential anti-Semites from the party and government. Buoyed up by revenues that grew apace after the discovery of huge oil reserves in 1947, Manning provided conservative, business-oriented government. The blandness of his programs provided a strong contrast with the party's populist origins.

Union Nationale

In Quebec the reform movement resulted less from workers' and farmers' pressures, though both existed, than from clerical responses to a 1931 Papal encyclical that, while reaffirming Church objections to "godless communism," supported state intervention to achieve social justice. The Jesuit-sponsored École Sociale Populaire, an organization that propagated church teachings, assembled representatives of lay Catholic organizations, including unions, *caisses populaires* (credit unions), and professional groups, to produce a document on desirable social reforms in line with the Pope's thinking. In 1933 they published *Le Programme de Restauration Sociale*, a program of non-socialist reforms including government regulation of monopolies, improved working conditions in industry, a system of farm credits, and a variety of social insurance measures. The program suggested that if regulation proved insufficient to lower prices, the state might have to set up companies in certain sectors in competition with private industry.

The big-business-oriented Liberal regime of Alexandre Taschereau proved uninterested in reform. In frustration, liberal-minded Liberals, led by Paul Gouin, formed a breakaway party, the Action Libérale Nationale. Maurice Duplessis, a Trois Rivières lawyer who led the province's moribund Conservative Party, sensed a political opportunity and formed an electoral alliance with the renegade Liberals. The so-called Union Nationale contested the 1935 provincial election with the *Programme de Restauration Sociale* as its platform and with the two component parties maintaining organizational autonomy.

Disillusionment with the long-governing Liberals produced a close result: forty-eight Liberal and forty-two Union Nationale seats. Shortly after the election, the Union Nationale was able to capitalize on evidence of government corruption and nepotism to force Taschereau's resignation. The hastily formed new government, forced to call an election in 1936, was badly mauled by the Union Nationale, which made corruption rather than reform the theme of its campaign. Duplessis out-manoeuvered Gouin to take full control of the Union Nationale, submerging its two founding parties into a new organization under his personal control. Gouin and other reformers, realizing that Duplessis was uninterested in change, denounced the new political *chef* of the province. But Duplessis was unstoppable as voters, disgusted with the corruption of the Liberal leaders, turned to the strongest available option.

In power, the Union Nationale delivered only on its promises to aid farmers with cheap loans and to colonize remote (and generally infertile) areas of the province with unemployed people willing to become farmers. Such relocation was reminiscent of the Bennett work camps, which isolated the unemployed in an attempt to ward off dissent. The coal, gasoline, and bread companies, whose prices the 1935 Union Nationale program promised to control, faced no regulation. The power companies, which the Union Nationale suggested might be socialized, remained in private hands and without additional regulation. Employers, not labour, received a sympathetic ear from the government, and the Padlock Law of 1937, giving the government the right to lock the doors of organizations allegedly engaged in communist subversion, demonstrated that dissent from below would not be tolerated.

Duplessis attempted to win popular support with a strong rhetorical assertion of Quebec nationalism and opposition to federal interference in the province. His government rejected the view that the federal government must expand its programs to cope with an increasingly industrial society. The "provincial compact" view of Confederation served his purposes well. His government told the Royal Commission on Dominion–Provincial Relations: "Under our federal system, each province, within its own jurisdictions, constitutes an autonomous state, enjoying all the prerogatives of a sovereign state without any subjection to the federal power."[4]

Such views echoed the perspective of Ontario's Liberal premier, Mitchell Hepburn. Though he and Duplessis ultimately parted ways on the question of how Canada should react to the outbreak of war in Europe, the

Premiers Maurice Duplessis (left) and Mitchell Hepburn   (National Archives of Canada/C19518)

two men collaborated closely on several issues. These included an unsuccessful attempt to convince Ottawa to allow hydro-electric exports and a successful bid to prevent Mackenzie King from introducing a national unemployment insurance bill after the Bennett legislation for such a program was overturned by the courts.

When the Second World War began in September 1939, Duplessis resisted the proclamation of the War Measures Act on the grounds that the provinces, not the central government, had jurisdiction over civil liberties. At the same time, he called an election, expecting that his stand against the federal government would guarantee him victory. His plans backfired when federal Liberal ministers from the province threatened to resign from Cabinet if Duplessis were re-elected. Francophone voters, afraid that this might make conscription more likely, and disillusioned with the failure of their new provincial masters to deliver on their promises, handed a massive majority to the Liberals.

The Union Nationale defeat was temporary. Adelard Godbout's Liberal government was reformist but too willing, from the point of view of many Québécois, to surrender provincial jurisdiction to the federal government. A reformist nationalist alternative, the Bloc Populaire Canadien, emerged during the war and attracted support from intellectuals and unionists. The split in reformist forces led to Duplessis' return to office in 1944. There he remained until his death fifteen years later, using patronage and a strident nationalism to win support for a government that ironically gave English-speaking capitalists carte blanche to exploit both the province's workers and resources. Duplessis may have preached provincial autonomy, but with the emergence of the welfare state, he was largely unsuccessful in resisting the expansion of federal powers.

•World War II

The road to Duplessis' return to power was paved by King's ambivalence on the issue of conscription. Before World War II erupted in September 1939, King had solemnly promised Quebec that his government would not impose conscription for overseas service. After Canada declared war, King repeated this pledge, and his government's re-election in early 1940 suggested general support for voluntary recruitment. But in June 1940, France surrendered, raising fears that Britain might also be defeated, with the victorious Germans then turning their military might to North America. King moved swiftly to enact the National Resources Mobilization Act (NRMA), which gave the government broad powers to ensure domestic security, including creating a conscript army for the defence of Canada's coasts.

As the war dragged on, pressures from within Cabinet, from opposition members, and from many English Canadians caused King to re-evaluate his position. In 1942, he called a national plebiscite to have himself released from his pledge. While 64 percent of Canadians agreed to let King do as he saw fit regarding conscription, at least 85 percent of Quebec francophones demanded that he honour his original promise. Although conscription was not proclaimed until November 1944, its threat was the catalyst for the formation of the Bloc Populaire Canadien and for the return of the Union Nationale to office in Quebec.

While King continued to resist pressures in favour of conscription, he was unwilling to reduce Canada's commitment to the Allied war effort. The government passed an order-in-council allowing the armed forces to conscript 16 000 NRMA men, about 37 percent of whom were French Canadians who had been posted in units mainly in British Columbia. Demonstrations, including a mutiny in Terrace, B.C., in which recruits seized anti-tank guns, followed King's announcement, although such actions were never reported in the media, whose war reporting was subject to censorship. Eventually 13 000 NRMA men were sent overseas, though their conscription appears not to have been a military necessity. As in World War I, conscription strengthened the credibility of Quebec nationalists and added to feelings of betrayal among French Canadians.

French-Canadian enlistment in World War II was significantly higher than in the First World War. About 19 percent of the overseas forces were French Canadians, compared to 12 percent in the earlier war. Like their English-Canadian counterparts, French Canadians who enlisted in the early stages of the war often did so to seek adventure. Others simply wanted employment. Eventually, the wartime economy led to a labour shortage, and recruitment became more difficult. Nonetheless, overall Canadian participation was impressive: about 920 000 men and women joined the forces, from a population of 11 000 000. Most served in the army, although about 100 000 joined the Royal Canadian Air Force and 93 000 served in the Royal Canadian Navy. Over 42 000 died in service, including more than 17 000 members of the RCAF.

Canadian forces were dispersed among several theatres. In December 1941, Canadian forces were involved in a futile effort to dislodge the Japanese from the British colony of Hong Kong. Almost 300 Canadians lost their lives and another 1700 were taken prisoner. Mistreatment in prison camps in Hong Kong and as forced labour in Japanese mines killed another 300 before the end of the war. In 1942, an ill-conceived landing at Dieppe in France left 907 Canadians dead and almost 2000 prisoners.

Canadians also participated in the liberation of Europe, including the invasions of Sicily in 1943 and Normandy in 1944.

Although only men participated in combat, 43 000 women in uniform worked behind the lines, some as nurses and many more as drivers, stretcher bearers, cooks, secretaries, and machine operators. The members of the Canadian Women's Army Corps, the Women's Royal Naval Service, and the Women's Division of the Royal Canadian Air Force faced a great deal of sexism, but their services were essential to the war effort. For the women who kept the field hospitals going, comforting the dying was a daily task. Not all the wounded were anonymous. A Red Cross Corps worker recalled, "I remember seeing a flash [a shoulder patch] on one jacket lying across the foot of the bed and I knew that flash because it was the regiment which came from my home town. . . . I had to look at the face and he was unconscious and it was Billy C— and I nearly dropped what I was carrying. I'd gone on skating parties with him, hayrides. I think I had a crush on him once. I don't think I ever knew what war and battle was until then."[5]

Women's Royal Naval Service member operating direction-finding equipment in New Brunswick, 1945   (National Archives of Canada/PA142540)

Most Canadians, whether or not they enlisted, supported the war effort, but people of German and Italian origin were often regarded with suspicion. Hundreds were imprisoned without trial under the provisions of the War Measures Act on the basis of flimsy evidence connecting them to the Nazis or fascists. Undoubtedly, the group that faced the greatest injustice during the war were Japanese Canadians. The Japanese of British Columbia had managed, despite the racism of their neighbours, to establish themselves as successful market gardeners, fishers, and canners. Shortly after Japan attacked Pearl Harbor in December 1941, the Canadian government evacuated approximately 23 000 Japanese, many of them born in Canada, from the coastal areas of the province. The state seized their assets and resold them to local white folk. Although the government had no evidence that more than a handful of Canadians of Japanese descent might be disloyal, it denied civil liberties to the entire Japanese-Canadian population. Postwar recompense to these victims was insignificant, but for many years few dared to complain for fear of provoking a revival of King's plan to deport all Japanese Canadians, which was announced at war's end but later abandoned.

Japanese-Canadian internees   (Tak Toyota/National Archives of Canada/C-47393)

• The Welfare State

As we saw in the previous chapter, the state in Canada, particularly at the federal level, began to expand the scope of its operations in the 1930s and, by the postwar period, had emerged as an important player in the economy. Expansion of state power occurred in all countries undergoing increased industrialization, but the particular configuration of state institutions and policies varied depending upon the strength of contending social forces. The emergence of reformist third parties and the explosion of militancy on the part of the unemployed made it impossible for the Conservatives and the Liberals to merely recycle used rhetoric. Reform was necessary if these parties and, indeed, the capitalist system were to be preserved. Prime Minister R.B. Bennett gave backhanded credit to the Canadian Communist Party's general secretary for influencing the Conservative government to initiate its ill-fated New Deal of 1935: "Tim Buck has today a very strong position in the province of Ontario and he openly demands the abolition of the capitalist system. A good deal of pruning is sometimes necessary to save a tree and it would be well for us in Canada to remember that there is considerable pruning to be done if we are to save the fabric of the capitalist system."[6]

An extraordinary rise in popular support for the CCF during the war, as measured by the polling organizations that made their first Canadian appearance at this time, became a particular catalyst for action. Mackenzie King, cautious by nature, watched the growth of the CCF and of trade unions and decided the time had come to implement reforms to which his party had nominally been committed since the national convention in 1919, which had chosen him as party leader. King and politicians generally had to contend as well with the social gospel tradition and the pressures from the social welfare agencies that had become increasingly professionalized and outspoken in the 1920s and 1930s.

Unemployment insurance provides an example of a program that was won by popular struggles but implemented in such a way as to prevent redistribution of wealth. Throughout the 1930s, campaigns by Communists, the CCF, and Social Credit for federal non-contributory unemployment insurance—that is for direct payments by the federal government to unemployed people—drew gasps from conservatives. Insurance, after all, meant that the receiver of a benefit had made payments towards that benefit. According to the conservative view, the problem with the traditional practice of relieving the unemployed through municipal welfare, funded from property tax collections, was precisely that those taxed and those receiving benefits were generally different people.

The struggles of the unemployed persuaded many municipal councils to increase relief payments, often leaving them unable to pay municipal debts. Bankers and industrialists called for relief to become a federal matter to make local pressures less onerous. The popular prescription of the capitalists who supported reform was contributory unemployment insurance. The scheme introduced by the federal government in 1940 adhered to insurance principles: employees and employers made equal contributions to the unemployment insurance fund to which the government made a smaller contribution from general revenues.

There was a host of groups exempt from this unemployment insurance scheme. Some of these exemptions were testimony to the influence of special interest groups. The exclusion of farm labourers, for example, could be traced to the strength of the farm lobby. Other rules and exemptions reflected patriarchal notions of women's place in the economy. Married women were excluded from coverage: few people regarded such job loss as of consequence to the woman or her family. Domestic work, still a frequent occupation for single women, was also excluded from coverage. By gearing the size of benefits to the wages earned and by tying eligibility to weeks of continuous work, the system also discriminated against women workers for whom paid labour generally meant job insecurity and poor wages.

Unemployment insurance was only one of the government's programs that were designed in such a way as to avoid left-wing demands for real redistribution of wealth. More than any one program, though, it was the change to the taxation system itself that ensured that the wealthy would not be taxed too heavily for programs to help workers, farmers, and the poor. In 1930, only households earning $3000 or more per annum were required to pay income tax. R.B. Bennett lowered that figure to $2000, and, despite inflation, it fell even further in the postwar period. Thus, by the 1950s, most working families were paying income tax, while in 1930 only 3–4 percent of households had been required to do so.

Newly instituted marketing boards provided benefits to primary producers, but they did not become the means, as some radical producers' groups had hoped, of eliminating third parties and forcing processors to accept smaller profits. Instead, as economist Lloyd Reynolds observed in 1940:

> There is a tendency under these plans to fix not only the price paid to farmers but the price charged to consumers. Processors and distributors argue that they can guarantee a fixed price to the farmer only if their own returns are guaranteed, and for this reason are usually able to secure farmer support for their proposals. There is thus a marked tendency towards complete cartelization of the food industries, with prices fixed at every stage from the grower to the final consumer.[7]

Even the Canadian Wheat Board, re-established in 1935 as a temporary agency and given permanent status in 1943, guaranteed prices not only to farmers but also to private elevator companies and export firms that continued to be the backbone of the grain trade. Arguably, such reform programs, much as they may have been a response to pressures from below, provided sophisticated forms of corporate welfare.

Corporate leaders did not believe so. Even those who supported increased state involvement in economic regulation and in social programs lamented the increased levels of government spending and decried increases in corporate taxation. In general, the growth of the state has been marked less by consensus than by constant rivalry among groups for legislation in their own interests. Ironically, the "national interest" is always invoked by each sector as it presses its own group or class interests on a particular matter of federal jurisdiction. Political parties act as mediators between the contending groups, attempting to piece together programs that satisfy critical numbers of voters as well as influential party financial contributors.

• The Party System and Political Leadership

As the war dragged on, Canadians began to fret about the nation's postwar agenda. Memories of the Great Depression and of the major recession that had followed World War I caused many to believe that the end of this war would usher in a new depression. Government planning of the economy during wartime, relatively successful price controls, and rationing had resulted in full employment and a higher standard of living for ordinary people. Why, they asked, could governments not continue in peacetime to act as the chief economic regulator and provide a measure of security to citizens that seemed available only in wartime?

The two major parties appeared at first to ignore such concerns. King argued that plans for reconstruction must await the defeat of the Axis powers. The Conservatives, meanwhile, having followed a reformist path from 1935 to 1940, selected as their leader in 1941 the more traditional Arthur Meighen, who had led the Conservative Party in the 1920s and served as prime minister in 1920–21 and from June to September 1926. While Meighen had supported some of the more cautious Bennett reforms, by 1941 he opposed all social insurance schemes. In early 1942, Meighen sought a parliamentary seat in a by-election in the supposedly safe Conservative riding of York South. King, who feared Meighen's pro-conscription campaign, did not run a

Liberal candidate, leaving the CCF to challenge Meighen. The CCF had carried only eight seats in 1940 and appeared to be no threat to the federal Liberals. Throughout the by-election, Meighen talked of the need to impose conscription; the previously unknown CCF candidate, Joseph Noseworthy, spoke of the need to plan employment and insurance programs for the postwar era. The majority of constituents liked his message. Meighen's defeat and subsequent resignation as Conservative leader had repercussions throughout the political system. By the end of 1943, the Gallup poll revealed that slightly more Canadians would vote CCF than Tory or Liberal.

Reformist Conservatives led by J.M. Macdonnell, president of National Trust, argued that the country could not be allowed to fall to the socialists. They drew up a reform platform that went beyond Bennett's New Deal to embrace universal pensions and medical insurance and guarantees of workers' rights to form unions and engage in collective bargaining. In 1942, they persuaded John Bracken, the reformist Liberal–Progressive premier of Manitoba, to become leader of their national party. At his insistence, they changed the name of the party to Progressive Conservative in the hope of shedding their reactionary image.

Despite attempts to steal their thunder, the CCF advance continued. In 1943, the party went from no seats to thirty-four seats in the Ontario legislature compared to thirty-eight for the Conservatives, two for the Communists, and fifteen for the Liberals, who had been discredited by their recently departed leader, Mitchell Hepburn. Provincial Conservative leader George Drew, later an opponent of social insurance programs, had blithely promised cradle-to-grave social security in an attempt to blunt the CCF advance. In the same year, in a Montreal by-election, communist Fred Rose won a federal seat, running under the banner of the Labour Progressive Party. Mackenzie King, who had established an advisory committee on reconstruction in 1941 to mollify concerns about the postwar period, decided it was time to act. Correctly reasoning that voters were wary of the socialists but willing to turn to them if the traditional parties remained wedded to the status quo, he decided that the Liberals could not yield to the Conservatives the image of reformers of capitalism.

CCF fortunes were bright enough in western Canada to allow it to win the Saskatchewan election of 1944. The party enrolled over 30 000 members in a province of 900 000 souls and capitalized on its own reformist policies as well as disenchantment with federal Liberal refusal to raise grain prices. But in the Ontario election of 1945, a massive anti-socialist campaign by business interests, and a commitment by Conservative Premier George Drew to a package of reforms, reduced the CCF to eight seats and third place in the provincial legislature. Six weeks later, the party won only twenty-eight of 245 seats in the federal election, with 15 percent of the popular vote. The Liberals were re-elected with a reduced parliamentary majority. The socialist hordes had been kept outside the gates of the government ministries.

• Labour and the State

One reason for the Liberal government's success in fending off the CCF threat was its official recognition that the state could no longer ignore the demands of trade unions. Its position had been otherwise when the war began. The Industrial Disputes Investigation Act, found to be unconstitutional in 1925 when applied to industries outside federal jurisdiction, was vastly extended under the War Measures Act to allow the government to use conciliation to avoid strikes. A 1940 order-in-council advocated that management recognize unions and engage in collective bargaining with them, but it gave no legislative teeth to this statement.

During the Depression a new militancy developed among Canadian workers, and they were no longer prepared to silently submit to the dictates of government. In the United States, workers began to join a brash new federation of industrial unions, the Congress of Industrial Organizations (CIO), which soon also had branches in Canada. A CIO strike called against General Motors in Oshawa in 1937 brought 4000 workers to the streets. In 1939, CIO affiliates were expelled from the craft-dominated Trades and Labour Congress and joined the All-Canadian Congress of Labour, a grouping of Canadian-controlled unions, to form the Canadian Congress of Labour.

Industrial and craft unions took full advantage of improved wartime employment conditions to organize workers no longer afraid of being fired for union activities. In highly mechanized industries, including steel production, automobile manufacturing, electrical parts production, meatpacking, and the pulp and paper industry, skilled male workers, generally of Anglo-Canadian background, led the drive for industry-wide unionism. While mechanization had, at times, enhanced the demand for skilled labour relative to late-nineteenth-century requirements, organizational changes in industry gave these workers less autonomy than they once had enjoyed. The result was that skilled workers, aware of the precarious character of the labour market, began to identify more closely with the semi-skilled production workers. This shift in the views of those recognized as skilled was key to the success of the industrial union movement.

Many employers continued to refuse to negotiate with unions even when the latter could demonstrate that they represented an overwhelming majority of a company's work force. In 1941 Dominion Steel and Coal refused to recognize a local of the Steelworkers' Organizing Committee, forerunner of United Steelworkers of America, even though 93 percent of the work force in their Montreal mill had signed union cards. Then in 1942, labour alienation reached new heights as the federal government aided gold mine operators in Kirkland Lake, Ontario, to keep unions out of their mines, first by using conciliation to delay a strike and then by refusing to intervene as the miners and their wives futilely walked picket lines.

In the 1943 provincial election, the Ontario wing of the Canadian Congress of Labour proclaimed the CCF the party that represented labour's interests and poured personnel and funds into that party's campaign. King, by now, could see the writing on the wall, and, as we saw in chapter 8, passed P.C. 1003, which recognized workers' rights to collective bargaining. In 1948, with the War Measures Act and government by order-in-council over, the Industrial Relations Disputes Act, which incorporated the key clauses of P.C. 1003, was passed to apply to workers in the federal sector. Provincial governments introduced their own labour legislation, much of which was modelled on the federal legislation. Labour historians regard this legislation as a watershed for trade unions because it recognized the right of workers to organize. But some analysts suggest that the legislation represented an attempt to pacify an increasingly militant working class by co-opting its leaders into the planning mechanisms of corporations. Under all the new labour laws, workers found their rights to negotiate limited to wages and narrowly defined working conditions. Unions were expected to enforce contracts and to keep their members in line. Decisions to reduce the size of the work force, to speed up production, or to use hazardous materials in the workplace were generally not covered by contracts, and union leaders were obliged to inform their members that strikes or slowdowns meant to force management to reconsider these issues would not be tolerated. Even when management appeared to violate a contract, workers were not allowed to strike. Instead they had to use often drawn-out grievance procedures to seek redress. Employers generally found that "management's right to manage" had been preserved.

While organized labour began to wonder about the advantages of its new bureaucratic processes, most Canadian workers had no such luxury. As late as 1960, less than a third of the work force was organized. There were many impediments to unionization. Some corporations attempted to distract workers from organizing by developing corporate welfare programs, including schemes for pensions, profit sharing, industrial councils, and health insurance. Women and immigrants, particularly those performing unskilled jobs, were notoriously difficult to unionize. Many feared for their jobs. Such fears were real: after World War I, thousands of workers were fired for supporting unions; even after the federal government recognized workers' right to organize, the labour boards that administered such legislation generally accepted employers' claims that an employee had been dismissed for reasons other than supporting a union. Some women, viewing paid work as only a brief interlude before marriage and child rearing, were not susceptible to union promises of better things to come. In any case, many unions were male-dominated organizations that showed little sensitivity towards the concerns of women workers, sometimes viewing them with contempt if not outright hostility. Workers in small factories and throughout the service sector understood that the "right to organize" was in reality protected by the state for only specific groups of workers from which they were excluded.

Even in sectors where workers felt confident enough to unionize, they soon learned that employers would not easily concede to demands for better wages and working conditions. Wartime wage freezes created pent-up demands for increases at war's end. Many working-class families had fared well in wartime because of overtime pay and two salaries. But the closure of government-funded day-care centres and a resurgence of patriarchal arguments that women return to their homes so that men could find jobs initially caused the number of married women in paid work to decline precipitously. Their husbands, if they worked in the mass-production industries, then demanded "family wages," which they believed employers could well afford to pay. In 1946 and 1947 about 240 000 workers struck for a total of almost 7 000 000 workdays. Automobile, steel, rubber, textile, packing, electrical manufacturing, forestry, and mining companies all felt the sting of such action. Average wages rose from 69.4 cents per hour in 1945 to 91.3 cents per hour in 1948, though inflation ate up some of the increase.

Women workers, largely without unions, did not share in the gains. In the late 1940s, a few attempts were made to enrol service workers, increasingly women, into a union movement that seemed to have lost momentum. In 1948, the Retail, Wholesale, and Department Store Union, aided by the Canadian Congress of Labour, initiated a three-year drive, headed by Eileen Talman, to organize Toronto's Eaton's store. The company pulled out all the stops to oppose the unionization, linking unions with communism, raising wages just before the vote on unionizing took place, and warning part-time workers that unionism would cost them their jobs. When only 40 percent of the workers supported affiliation with the RWDSU, the CCL leadership, almost exclusively male, concluded that women were too passive to unionize and ceased its attempts to organize sectors dominated by female labour. Such stereotypical views were at the same time being exploded in Quebec where women endured a bitter and ultimately successful strike at Dupuis Frères department store in 1952 to win better pay and working conditions. Members of the increasingly secular Confédération des Travailleurs Catholiques du Canada, these women were a harbinger of things to come in postwar Quebec.

Quebec workers who struck were well aware that their provincial government often came to the armed defence of strike-bound employers. In 1949, for example, workers in the town of Asbestos, unwilling to delay a strike until a government-appointed board of arbitration reported, struck so that the company would not have time to stockpile asbestos before the inevitable walkout. During the five-month strike, the workers faced a large contingent of provincial police who protected replacement workers hired by the company. Many workers were arrested or beaten in clashes with the police.

The brutal state response to the strike galvanized considerable resistance to the Union Nationale. Liberal and liberal-nationalist intellectuals,

Demonstration during Asbestos strike, 1949   (National Archives of Canada/PA130357)

including the future prime minister, Pierre Elliott Trudeau, were increasingly united on the need to defeat Duplessis and to protect workers' interests. Even within the church, there were dissenters against Duplessis. Rank-and-file clergy who supported the Asbestos strikers briefly had a champion in Archbishop Charbonneau of Montreal, but the church transferred Charbonneau out of the province. The Roman Catholic Church had a longstanding role in mediating labour conflict in Quebec, but its rigidity during the Asbestos strike destroyed that role forever.

It was not only in Quebec that striking workers were confronted by police. In November 1945, the Ontario government sent provincial police and reinforcements from the RCMP into the gates of the Ford plant at Windsor to end a five-week-old strike. The strikers responded by blockading the plant with cars. The federal government appointed Justice Ivan Rand in an attempt to bring the two sides together. The major issue was the "closed shop," or compulsory union membership for employees. Rand successfully proposed a formula for union membership: in a bargaining unit where a majority voted to join a union, all members of that unit must pay union dues whether or not they joined the union. A less happy ending greeted the loggers of Newfoundland who struck in 1959, only to have Premier Joey Smallwood use the RCMP to enforce his decision to decertify the International Woodworkers' Association as the bargaining agent of the loggers. Three people died during this violent strike.

Limitations on the right to organize and the right to strike varied throughout the country. Saskatchewan's CCF government led a province where urban and industrial workers were a minority of the population, yet it had the most liberal attitude towards unions. Alberta, whose Social Credit government in the postwar period regarded unions as part of a Communists-and-bankers conspiracy to snuff out individualism, passed fairly restrictive legislation. Quebec Premier Duplessis, who had allied his nationalist party with conservative business interests, passed the most restrictive legislation of all.

•Federal–Provincial Relations

As we have seen, the growth of the state led to greater tensions between some provinces and the federal government on the division of powers. During the war, the provinces had agreed to abandon their own collection of income taxes in return for federal grants. This method of collecting revenues won favour in the poorer provinces because it provided them with more funds than they might otherwise have been able to collect, but

Ontario argued that it was being forced to subsidize the rest of the country. Though Quebec was a net beneficiary, the Union Nationale argued that the provincial Liberals, who had agreed to this arrangement, had sold out the interests of a province that had to protect its jurisdictions in order to preserve Quebec's francophone, Catholic character.

After the war, the provinces gradually restored their old tax systems and regarded tax monies received from Ottawa as only one component of their revenues. The percentage of federal corporate and personal income taxes collected that was rebated to provinces rose gradually from a mere 5 percent just after the war to 24 percent by the early 1960s. The provinces claimed that with increasing demands upon them for schools, universities, hospitals, and highways, an expanded revenue base was crucial. The federal government, unwilling to abandon its power over revenues or its perceived responsibilities in areas of provincial jurisdiction such as health, education, and welfare, introduced programs of insurance and shared-cost grants in an attempt to equalize or at least reduce the disparity in services available in the provinces. A universal old-age pension was introduced in 1951; a hospital insurance program with costs shared by the provincial and federal governments passed in 1957. One year earlier, the federal government agreed to pay half the costs of welfare for the unemployable, a group once the responsibility of municipalities but increasingly the charges of the provinces. Federal–provincial shared-cost grants to universities and technical schools were also introduced in the 1950s in an effort to match other industrial countries in providing the educated work force necessary for managing and improving the performance of an economy where new technological developments were increasingly important.

While George Drew remained premier from 1943 to 1948, Ontario was as loath as Quebec to accept federal intervention in areas of provincial jurisdiction. Its stance softened somewhat when Drew left the premiership to become national Conservative leader and was replaced by Leslie Frost. Until the death of Maurice Duplessis in 1959, Quebec continued to resist most federal proposals. Indeed Duplessis, under pressure from nationalist intellectuals, spurned over $200 million in federal monies earmarked for Quebec universities on the grounds that the federal government had no responsibility for education. Nationalists feared that federal funding might lead to interference in university affairs within Quebec.

Quebec and Ontario apprehension regarding federal intervention arguably delayed the introduction of welfare state measures in Canada. Shortly after the 1945 federal election, Mackenzie King called a dominion–provincial conference on reconstruction. The federal government Green Book of proposals prepared for the conference called for national programs to take care of the old, the sick, and the unemployed. Declaring unemployment a problem that the federal government must handle, the conference proposals also embraced Keynesian notions on public works. To fund these costly endeavours, the federal government suggested it would require exclusive rights to personal and corporate income tax and to succession duties. But Ontario and Quebec balked. Premier George Drew argued that the provinces could not surrender all major taxes and still fulfil their responsibilities. It was they, not the federal government, who needed greater revenues. Opposed to state medical insurance and other measures of universal coverage, Duplessis was able to reject the federal proposals both on grounds that they represented centralization and embodied socialism.

After several attempts at compromise, the federal government contented itself with a piecemeal approach to welfare-state policy. It is not clear, in any case, that the federal government would have proceeded with the full Green Book agenda had there been no provincial obstructions. By 1945, corporate Canada was generally convinced that reforms had gone far enough, and Duplessis and Drew had received much encouragement from business in opposing the federal proposals. Mackenzie King's enthusiasm for comprehensive reform had peaked when the CCF was high in the polls; it fell as quickly when CCF support began to dwindle. With influential voices in Cabinet, particularly that of C.D. Howe, echoing the views of Drew and Duplessis, it is a moot point whether the latter two gentlemen were the cause or merely the pretext of federal government inaction on welfare and state planning issues.

Part of the Green Book philosophy had been the redirection of public works to poorer areas of the country. While the failure of the federal–provincial conferences of 1945 and 1946 need not have diminished this goal, in practice it was ignored in the years that followed. The premiers of the Maritime provinces, Saskatchewan, and Manitoba continued to pressure Ottawa to use its taxing and spending powers to provide greater aid to their provinces and thus supplement their attempts to provide decent social services and to attract industry. In 1956, the St Laurent government announced a system of fiscal equalization grants. This program, which provided grants to all provinces other than Ontario, British Columbia, and Alberta, was designed to allow poorer provinces to provide education and health services comparable to the wealthier provinces. But better services alone could not convince people to remain in provinces with declining industries and few jobs for young people.

John Diefenbaker's Conservative government, first elected in 1957, responded with Atlantic Provinces Adjustment Grants and measures intended to lure businesses into depressed areas. The 1960 budget allowed firms double the normal tax advantage for capital expenditures if they located in areas designated as slow-growth, high-unemployment zones. Within a year, the government had also passed the Agriculture Rehabilitation and Development Act (ARDA), which poured money into rural areas to improve efficiency in resource bases and to create alternative employment in depressed regions. This became the prototype for ambitious, though largely unsuccessful, efforts to correct the tendency for private industries to locate in developed metropolitan areas, which were closer to markets and had the advantage in infrastructure and availability of skilled labour.

There were limits to the federal government's willingness to equalize opportunities among provinces. Newfoundland had joined Canada in 1949 after a small majority of its residents chose Confederation over independence. In the postwar period, Newfoundland's strategic position caused British and American military planners to support the colony's integration with Canada, a stalwart of the emerging Cold War alliance. Canada offered the underdeveloped island the chance to participate in social programs that local finances could ill afford. Under the terms of Newfoundland's

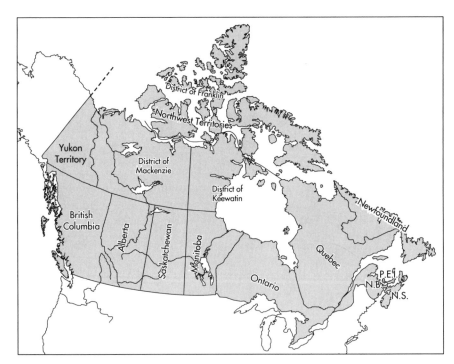

MAP 9.2 *Canada, 1949* (G.J. Matthews and R. Morrow Jr., *Canada and the World: An Atlas Resource* (Scarborough: Prentice-Hall, 1978), 5)

union with Canada, a Royal Commission was established to determine the level of subsidies required to provide services of similar quality to those in the Maritime provinces. When the commission reported in 1958, it claimed that $6.6 million a year was the magic figure. Newfoundland insisted that $15 million was needed, but Diefenbaker accepted the commission's viewpoint and, to the dismay of Premier Joey Smallwood, announced that the special payments would end in 1962.

•Foreign Affairs

Handling Canadian relations with the rest of the world was a growth sector in the expanding postwar state. While Canada had only eighteen foreign service officers in 1930, it had 132 in 1946 and 414 in 1960. The budget of the Department of External Affairs had been under $25 000 in 1912 but had risen to almost $5 million in the 1945–46 fiscal year and over $83 million in 1967–68. During and after the Second World War, many brilliant male minds joined the department which by 1949 was headed by one of its former officers and a future prime minister, Lester Pearson.

Canada's increased involvement in foreign affairs reflected the nation's new status. Following the First World War, the international focus was increasingly on the self-determination of nations, and Canada opted for greater autonomy. In a series of meetings during the 1920s, the foundations were laid for a new British Commonwealth of self-governing nations to replace the old British Empire of dependent colonies. By the Statute of Westminster, passed by the British Parliament in 1931, Canada and the other Dominions were given full legal freedom to exercise their independence in domestic and foreign affairs. Because Canadians could not agree on an amending formula, the alteration of the constitution was specifically exempted from the statute. Canadians also continued to carry British passports and allow legal appeals to the British Judicial Committee of the Privy Council until after the Second World War. Nevertheless, the Statute of Westminster paved the way to complete independence for Canada in foreign affairs.

In the interwar years Canada, unlike the United States, was a full member of the League of Nations, an international organization based in Geneva, Switzerland, designed to protect the world from another war like the Great War. The League fell short of these goals, and Britain was soon urging its Dominions for assistance in efforts to keep peace in Europe and the Middle East. Under Mackenzie King's government, such a policy was stoutly resisted. Indeed, when Walter Riddell, Canada's representative at the League, called for stronger measures against Italy, which had invaded Ethiopia in 1935, he was told by Ottawa to change his position. Canada must be kept out of European conflicts.

Despite the failure of the League, Canadians again pinned their hopes on an international organization to keep the peace following the Second World War. In the spring of 1945, Canadian politicians and diplomats participated in meetings that led to the founding of the United Nations, and they were eager to see it work. As a "middle power" below the "big five"—Great Britain, France, the United States, the Soviet Union, and China—Canadians could play a mediating role in international affairs.

The Cold War

The making of foreign policy could not be separated from domestic realities. With Britain weakened by the war, and the United States a growing influence in Canadian economic life, Canadian foreign policy began to mirror that of the Americans. In this respect, Canada was in step with the major European industrial powers, which depended on American aid to reconstruct their shattered economies and rarely questioned American foreign policy. That policy was dominated by a militant anti-communism.

The Soviet Union under Stalin appeared to be undermining the fragile democracies in Europe and using its position on the Security Council of the United Nations to frustrate efforts to keep the peace. Soviet agents seemed to be everywhere, including Ottawa. In 1946 Igor Gouzenko, a cypher clerk in the Soviet embassy, revealed that a Soviet spy ring had been in operation in Canada throughout the war. Given Canada's close involvement with research relating to the atomic bomb, this was perceived as a serious matter. Canadians were drawn into the so-called Cold War, which pitted communist states against capitalist democracies.

In dramatic contrast to its isolation in the interwar years, the United States became the champion of the so-called "free world." Its chief policy goal, trumpeted in classrooms, from the pulpit, and by the ubiquitous media, was the containment of communism at home and abroad. America's exclusive possession of nuclear weapons from 1945 to 1949, followed by a decade of clear nuclear superiority over the Soviet Union, encouraged American political leaders to enunciate a policy of so-called deterrence: the Soviets and their communist allies throughout the world would have to behave, or the Americans and their allies would drop nuclear bombs on their territory.

In Canada, most External Affairs officials, while appalled by Stalin and the police apparatus central to the Soviet state, regarded American claims regarding Soviet intentions in foreign policy as vastly exaggerated.

WHO STARTED THE COLD WAR?

In retrospect, Soviet ambitions in the postwar period appear to have been more conservative than the Americans claimed. Scholars have revised analyses of various Communist and left-wing revolutionary insurrections to suggest that nationalism, rather than Soviet-sponsored communism, was the determining factor in grass-roots struggles against western-supported regimes. But the Americans, despite having had their own revolution against foreign control, distrusted nationalist forces elsewhere.

Historians will long debate the degree of blame to be attached to the United States and the Soviet Union for launching and continuing the Cold War. Defenders of American behaviour stress Stalin's bloody-minded policies and the bellicosity of the Soviets. Defenders of the U.S.S.R point out that the Soviets had lost over twenty million people to the Nazi war machine and were understandably paranoid about the postwar intentions of a nuclear West that had refused to share the secrets of the atom bomb with its wartime ally. They claim that American ideological blinkers made impossible an appreciation of Soviet demands for security and destroyed the possibilities of peaceful relations with a nation that might have enjoyed greater liberalism at home if it were not forced to become a militaristic state. Some opponents go further and claim that America's Cold War posturing reflected "free-trade imperialism"—the need of its capitalist economy for untrammelled access to cheap resources and unprotected markets. Nationalism within former colonies threatened the success of American imperial objectives and therefore had to be snuffed out. It has also been noted that military pump priming of the economy was more ideologically acceptable to American business than welfare pump priming. As *Business Week* magazine explained, "military spending doesn't alter the structure of the economy" whereas welfare and public works spending "changes the whole economic pattern."[8]

Publicly, however, Canada supported American views: "Given the importance of Washington's politics to Canada's economic future, a public declaration of a cautious, balanced assessment of Russian policy . . . would not in fact have served the Canadian interest."[9]

In military terms, Canada and the United States were closely linked from 1940 when, in the wake of Nazi victories over France and Norway, President Roosevelt and Prime Minister King established the Permanent Joint Board on Defence to co-ordinate the defence policies of the two nations. The Board continued to operate after the war and, while the Canadian government balked at its military planners' suggestions in 1946 that the two nations mesh their defence forces, Canada was increasingly drawn into American defence strategy. In 1949, Canadians joined the North Atlantic Treaty Organization (NATO), a military pact that included the United States and Britain as well as Western European nations. Despite Canada's insistence on the formal acknowledgement of NATO's goals of economic as well as military integration, the organization soon became primarily an American instrument for co-ordinating the defence policies of its allies, rather than a club of equals that could restrain American initiatives.

In 1950, Canada agreed to contribute troops to the United Nations force sent to hold the line against communism in Korea. Following World War II, Korea had been divided into two zones, North Korea under the supervision of the Soviet Union, and South Korea under the control of the United States. The two zones were slated for amalgamation, but were frozen in their antagonistic divisions by the Cold War. When troops from North Korea invaded South Korea in June 1950, the United States manoeuvred the United Nations into sending a peacekeeping force into the region. Canadians worked furiously behind the scenes to restrain their aggressive allies, and the war ended in 1953 with Korea seemingly permanently divided. In total about 25 000 Canadians participated, and 300 lost their lives in Korea.

Meanwhile, Canada and the United States were pouring billions into an elaborate defence system to protect North America from a Soviet air attack. Between 1949 and 1957, three radar defence systems, including the Distant Early Warning (DEW), were built. The DEW line stretched from Alaska to Baffin Island and did much to open the North to southern influences. The co-operation between the two nations in this project helped to pave the way for the North Atlantic Air Defence Treaty (NORAD), which produced a unified air command for North America, with headquarters in Colorado Springs. Negotiated by the Liberals under St Laurent, the NORAD agreement was formally signed by the Progressive Conservative government in 1958, indicating the wide degree of consensus in Canada in support of close Canadian–American co-operation in defence matters. The agreement would create difficulties for John Diefenbaker because it placed pressure on Canada to adopt nuclear weapons, something the government had decided against in 1945. Canada did participate in the Atomic Energy Commission, which was created in 1946 to find ways of ensuring that the atom would be used only for peaceful purposes. Ultimately, it failed to find common ground between the Americans who wished to preserve their monopoly of nuclear knowledge and the Soviets who wished to match American nuclear abilities.

Nuclear superiority was, in the 1950s, the strategic key to American foreign policy. In 1954, John Foster Dulles, the hawkish Secretary of State in the administration of President Dwight D. Eisenhower, proclaimed that Americans would resort to "massive retaliation," including possible use of nuclear weapons, against aggression. That year NATO agreed to make nuclear deterrence the mainstay of defence strategy. Ignoring the likelihood that a nuclear war, once begun, would not be contained, NATO decided to build up stocks of "tactical" nuclear weaponry, intermediate-range weapons designed for battle in a particular region, as opposed to "strategic" weapons designed for a full-scale nuclear war. In December 1957, in line with this NATO policy, Canada agreed to play a role in surveillance of possible military strike plans by the Communists. In 1959 and 1960, Canada ordered a variety of aircraft and missiles meant to serve this role. In 1959, Canada agreed to permit storage of American nuclear weapons at Goose Bay and Harman Air Force bases, which, though on Canadian territory, were controlled by the Americans. That same year, Canada received a reward for its close co-operation with American defence policies: under the Defence Production Sharing Agreement, Canadian companies won the right to bid for American military contracts on an equal basis with American contractors. Canada offered the Americans the same privileges for this country's rather less impressive military procurements.

Despite its co-operation in American military policy, Canada attempted to cultivate an image as a peacemaker. When Britain, France, and Israel attacked Egypt to undo its efforts to seize control of the Suez Canal, Minister of External Affairs Lester Pearson's role in ending the conflict won him a Nobel Peace Prize. Canada was one of a number of nations that sent peacekeeping forces to the region and, in subsequent years, Canada proved more than willing to send peacekeeping troops to hot spots. In retrospect, it seems clear that Canada was able to play the peacekeeping role only when the Americans did not feel their vital interests were at stake. This was not the case in Vietnam, a French colony since the nineteenth century. In 1954, Communists under Ho Chi Minh forced the French out and established control over the northern half of the partitioned country. Negotiations in Geneva that year produced an accord calling for reunification of North and South Vietnam after elections to be held in 1956. An International Control Commission (ICC), with Canada, Poland, and India as its members, was established to monitor the implementation of the provisions of the Geneva accord. But the Americans decided to violate the accord in order to provide time for the new, pro-American rulers of South Vietnam to gain popular legitimacy. In practice, this regime oversaw a reign of terror, murdering suspected sympathizers of the Communists and uprooting peasant villages.

In monitoring the developing conflict in Vietnam, members of the ICC were guided more by their own political views than by attempts at neutrality. Poland seemed able to see only South Vietnamese violations, while Canada, after briefly trying to prevent breaches of the accord, came to notice only violations by the North Vietnamese side.

In Vietnam and elsewhere, makers of foreign policy argued that they had to publicly support the broad outlines of Washington's external policies if they hoped to moderate these policies via "quiet diplomacy." Ottawa would have no moderating influence on the White House if Canada were not seen as a reliable ally. Scholars are divided as to whether this perspective reflected a sober assessment of geo-political realities or was simply a self-serving rationalization for kowtowing to a nation whose ability for economic retaliation was painfully clear. The foreign policy community was, in any case, not monolithic: a minority within the Department of External Affairs prodded their colleagues to support nationalist objectives in the Third World and not to reduce all issues to Cold War polarities.

The Domestic Cold War

The Cold War was, in part, an ideological battle, and its participants, hoping to impose their values on other countries, would not countenance defeat on the home front. The Soviets and their allies crushed dissent ruthlessly. Western countries claimed that they allowed completely open discussion, but McCarthyism in the United States suggested otherwise. Though Senator Joseph McCarthy was hardly the first important American politician to equate dissent with treachery, his pursuit of communists and critics of his rabid brand of anti-communism was so relentless, that he gave his name to the witchhunts of the early 1950s.

McCarthyism in Canada was less virulent than in the United States, but it infected Canadian institutions nonetheless. Anti-communism became a key ingredient in immigration policy. While restrictions on former Nazis were lifted to the point where the RCMP complained that war criminals were being admitted to Canada, no such tolerance was extended to communists and ex-communists. Communists were not only deported and kept out as permanent immigrants, they were even prevented from making visits to Canada. The federal government meanwhile attempted to root radicals out of the civil service. After all, it was just such people who had handed information to Soviet Embassy officials about nuclear programs during World War II. The civil libertarian argument that individuals ought to be judged by their actions and not their beliefs or associations was rejected in such an environment.

Communists who had been democratically chosen to head unions were denounced so stridently by editorialists and their non-communist union opponents that the state confidently persecuted them and, in some cases, destroyed their unions. In 1946, Duplessis jailed Kent Rowley and Madeleine Parent, organizers for the Trades and Labour Congress local of textile workers in Valleyfield. In 1949, the RCMP helped to force striking seamen who belonged to the Canadian Seamen's Union into the Seafarers' International Union, headed by convicted American thug Hal Banks. A year later, the Canadian Labour Relations Board revoked the CSU's certification, claiming a Communist-led union could not be recognized under the Industrial Relations and Disputes Investigation Act.

Communists and ex-communists faced constant surveillance and harassment. Roscoe Fillmore, active from the early 1900s with the Socialists and Communists, and later a founding member of the Labour Progressive Party, was a prominent horticulturalist in Nova Scotia. Even though he gave up his LPP membership in 1950, years later the RCMP was still following him to horticultural conferences and filing reports, complete with licence plate numbers, on the cars stopping by the Fillmore Valley Nursery on summer weekends. RCMP agents even spied on the funerals of Fillmore's comrades, sitting in the back row, noting the names of those attending.

The suicide of a veteran Canadian diplomat, E.H. Norman, in Cairo in 1956, after repeated but unsubstantiated charges that he was a Soviet agent, demonstrates the tragic side of McCarthyism. Lives could be ruined if individuals were suspected of being communists or being soft on communism. Representatives of the peace movement, such as the Women's International League for Peace and Freedom, founded in 1915, also suffered severely from red-baiters who smeared anyone who opposed them. In such an atmosphere those leery of the Cold War philosophy or of particular actions that flowed from such a philosophy generally kept their mouths shut. Both in Canada and the United States, fundamental criticism of Canadian and American foreign policy or of red baiting was rare, both in scholarly and journalistic media. The notion that democracy versus communism was a simplistic assessment of a complicated world situation would take hold only in the late 1960s.

• Conclusion

In 1960 the state in Canada played a much larger role both in the economy and in international relations than it had in 1920. As the country industrialized, both its farmers who feared being left behind and its workers who feared exploitation by employers pressured for state legislation to make the conditions of life more secure. The corporate elite, while enjoying close links with the two main political parties, was suspicious of plans for state interventionism. It was nonetheless willing to embrace its own version of reform, partly to secure corporate stability but also to mollify demands from below that might become menacing if ignored.

Political leaders, even more than the corporate elite, recognized the need to pacify popular demands. Their goal was to do so without impinging greatly on the economic power or wealth of the entrepreneurial class. That they seemed to succeed in balancing goals of legitimation and accumulation in the postwar period was largely luck: great economic growth allowed the state to provide tidbits for the poor without actually giving them a greater slice of the economic pie. The quiescence of the 1950s relative to the militancy of the Depression and wartime era made it unnecessary for Canadian governments to go as far as countries such as Sweden, Austria, and West Germany in creating a welfare state. The Cold War, which kept the American economy strong, helped the inextricably linked Canadian economy immeasurably. While this resulted in a cautious, sometimes cowardly Canadian foreign policy, Canadians as a whole, generally enamoured with the "American way of life," were not disturbed. Indeed, after the poverty of the early 1920s and the Dirty Thirties and the privations of wartime, Canadians, as we suggest in the next chapter, were hardly in the mood for listening to prophets of doom. Though a quarter of Canadians remained desperately poor, many of the rest were enjoying lifestyles barely dreamed of by their ancestors. Concerns about environmental degradation, Third World distress, and poverty at home were not the sort of thing many Canadians wanted to think about.

• Right-wing Populism Versus Left-wing Populism:
A Historiographical Debate

The view presented in this chapter that the CCF and Social Credit were polar opposites is not shared by all scholars. Some point to the similarity in origin of these movements: both had urban origins but found a mass audience among Prairie farmers; both claimed a national platform but focussed on regional and indeed provincial strategies for political change; neither had an important base outside Western Canada in the 1930s. Both parties were populist; that is, they claimed to be people's movements against the interests of the entrenched political and economic elites.

The CCF's populism was directed against all big capitalists while Social Credit's populist attack targeted only financial institutions. The CCF may therefore be described as a "left-wing populist" movement because it identified farmers' interests with workers' interests against the interests of big business. Social Credit may be described as "right-wing populist" because it was suspicious of unions and suggested that workers and farmers had interests in common with capitalists other than bankers.

But were these two parties very different in practice? Some scholars say yes. While the CCF nationalized auto insurance and the distribution of natural gas and established a provincial intercity bus company, among other initiatives, the Alberta government denounced all state ventures in the economy. While the CCF pioneered universal free hospital and medical care insurance in Saskatchewan, the Social Credit regime in Alberta insisted that medical care schemes must be voluntary and must involve some direct payment for services by subscribers to prevent abuse of the program. While the CCF passed labour legislation that favoured union organization in Saskatchewan, Social Credit produced a labour code that made unionization difficult. Welfare recipients were subjected to mean-spirited treatment in Alberta, but some sympathy in Saskatchewan.[10]

Yet many scholars believe the gap in performance between the CCF in Saskatchewan and Social Credit in Alberta has been exaggerated. They claim that the farm programs of the two governments were similar and that, whatever philosophical differences existed between the two governments, both spent lavishly on health, education, and roads. The provincial takeovers in Saskatchewan are held to have had a negligible impact on overall private ownership and direction of the provincial economy.[11]

The claims of the two sides are difficult to adjudicate in part because the Alberta government, awash in oil revenues by the 1950s, had a vastly superior financial base to its Saskatchewan counterpart. It could afford to spend extravagantly, all the while deploring the tendencies of governments generally to spend more than they earned. Nonetheless, left-wing critics of Alberta Social Credit suggest that the poor in Alberta were largely passed over in the orgy of public spending.[12] Their point of comparison is usually Saskatchewan, which they allege had more humanitarian social policies. But left-wing critics of the Saskatchewan CCF suggest that, in office, that party attempted to appease powerful elite interests at the ultimate expense of the poor.

• Notes

[1] Ernest R. Forbes, *Maritime Rights: The Maritime Rights Movement, 1919–1927: A Study in Canadian Regionalism* (Montreal: McGill-Queen's University Press, 1979).

[2] E.E. Perley to R.B. Bennett, 6 Jan. 1931, R.B. Bennett papers, Public Archives of Canada.

[3] From "Programme of the Co-operative Commonwealth Federation adopted at First National Convention held at Regina, Sask., July 1933."

[4] Canada, Royal Commission on Dominion–Provincial Relations, *Hearings* (1938), 8129.

[5] Barry Broadfoot, *Six War Years, 1939–1945: Memories of Canadians at Home and Abroad* (Toronto: Doubleday, 1974), 144.

[6] Quoted in Alvin Finkel, *Business and Social Reform in the Thirties* (Toronto: Lorimer, 1979), 92.

[7] Lloyd G. Reynolds, *The Control of Competition in Canada* (Cambridge: Harvard University Press, 1940), 43.

[8] Quoted in Noam Chomsky, "The Drift Towards Global War," *Studies in Political Economy* 17 (Summer 1985): 12.

[9] R.D. Cuff and J.L. Granatstein, *American Dollars–Canadian Prosperity: Canadian–American Economic Relations 1945–1950* (Toronto: Samuel Stevens, 1978), 199–200.

[10] The view that there are sharp differences between Social Credit's performance in Alberta and the CCF's performance in Saskatchewan is defended in Alvin Finkel, *The Social Credit Phenomenon in Alberta* (Toronto: University of Toronto Press, 1989), 202–13 and Walter D. Young, *Democracy and Discontent: Progressivism, Socialism and Social Credit in the Canadian West* (Toronto: McGraw-Hill Ryerson, 1978). On the general distinction between left and right variants of populism, see John Richards, "Populism: A Qualified Defence," *Studies in Political Economy* 5 (Spring 1981): 5–27.

[11] The best case for a convergence in the behaviour of these two parties in office is made in John F. Conway, "To Seek a Goodly Heritage: The Prairie Populist Responses to the National Policy" (PhD thesis, Simon Fraser University, 1978). Peter R. Sinclair argues that the Saskatchewan CCF had lost its early radicalism before winning office: "The Saskatchewan CCF: Ascent to Power and the Decline of Socialism," *Canadian Historical Review* 54, 4 (Dec. 1973): 419–33. An opposite point of view is found in Lewis H. Thomas, "The CCF Victory in Saskatchewan, 1944," *Saskatchewan History* 28, 2 (Spring 1975): 52–64.

[12] See Finkel, *The Social Credit Phenomenon.*

•Selected Reading

On the major works on national political and economic developments from 1920 to 1960, see the Selected Reading section in chapter 8.

On the treatment of immigrants, incisive accounts include Barbara Roberts, *Whence They Came: Deportation from Canada 1900–1935* (Ottawa: University of Ottawa Press, 1988); Reginald Whitaker, *Double Standard: The Secret History of Canadian Immigration* (Toronto: Lester and Orpen Dennys, 1987); Irving Abella and Harold Troper, *None Is Too Many: Canada and the Jews of Europe, 1933–1948* (Toronto: Lester and Orpen Dennys, 1982); Donald Avery, *Dangerous Foreigners: European Immigrant Workers and*

Labour Radicalism in Canada, 1896–1932 (Toronto: McClelland and Stewart, 1979); James Morton, *In the Sea of Sterile Mountains: A History of the Chinese in British Columbia* (Vancouver: Douglas and McIntyre, 1974); and Howard Palmer, *Patterns of Prejudice: A History of Nativism in Alberta* (Toronto: McClelland and Stewart, 1982).

On Western protest, see David Laycock, *Populism and Democratic Thought in the Canadian Prairies, 1910–1945* (Toronto: University of Toronto Press, 1990); Alvin Finkel, *The Social Credit Phenomenon in Alberta* (Toronto: University of Toronto Press, 1989); W.L. Morton, *The Progressive Party in Canada* (Toronto: University of Toronto Press, 1950); Vernon C. Fowke, *The National Policy and the Wheat Economy* (Toronto: University of Toronto Press, 1957); J.R. Mallory, *Social Credit and the Federal Power in Canada* (Toronto: University of Toronto Press, 1954); John A. Irving, *The Social Credit Movement in Alberta* (Toronto: University of Toronto Press, 1959); C.B. Macpherson, *Democracy in Alberta: Social Credit and the Party System* (Toronto: University of Toronto Press, 1962); David R. Elliott and Iris Miller, *Bible Bill: A Biography of William Aberhart* (Edmonton: Reidmore, 1987); L.H. Thomas, ed., *The Making of a Socialist: The Recollections of T.C. Douglas* (Edmonton: University of Alberta Press, 1982); Seymour Martin Lipset, *Agrarian Socialism: The Co-operative Commonwealth Federation in Saskatchewan* (Berkeley: University of California Press, 1971); Kenneth McNaught, *A Prophet in Politics: A Biography of J.S. Woodsworth* (Toronto: University of Toronto Press, 1959); and Allen Mills, *Fool for Christ: The Political Thought of J.S. Woodsworth* (Toronto: University of Toronto Press, 1991); Robin Fisher, *Duff Pattullo of British Columbia* (Toronto: University of Toronto Press, 1991); Ronald Liversedge, *Recollections of the On-to-Ottawa Trek* (Ottawa: Carleton University Press, 1973).

On protest in the Atlantic region important works include Ernest R. Forbes, *Maritime Rights: The Maritime Rights Movement, 1919–1927* (Montreal: McGill-Queen's University Press, 1979); David Frank, ed., *Industrialization and Underdevelopment in the Maritimes 1880–1930* (Toronto: Garamond, 1985); Margaret Conrad, *George Nowlan: Maritime Conservative in National Politics* (Toronto: University of Toronto Press, 1986); Robert J. Brym and R. James Sacouman, eds., *Underdevelopment and Social Movements in Atlantic Canada* (Toronto: New Hogtown, 1979); Gary Burrill and Ian McKay, eds., *People, Resources and Power: Critical Perspectives on Underdevelopment and Primary Industries in the Atlantic Region* (Fredericton: Acadiensis Press, 1987); and Verner Smitheram et al., *The Garden Transformed: Prince Edward Island, 1945–1980* (Charlottetown: Ragweed, 1982).

On Canadian Communists see Ian Angus, *Canadian Bolsheviks* (Montreal: Vanguard, 1981); Ivan Avakumovic, *The Communist Party in Canada: A History* (Toronto: McClelland and Stewart, 1975); and William Beeching and Phyllis Clarke, eds., *Yours in the Struggle: The Reminiscences of Tim Buck* (Toronto: NC Press, 1977). On the national CCF, see Walter Young, *Anatomy of a Party: The National CCF,*

1932–61 (Toronto: University of Toronto Press, 1969); Norman Penner, *From Protest to Power: Social Democracy in Canada 1900–Present* (Toronto: Lorimer, 1992); and William Brennan, ed., *Building the Co-operative Commonwealth: Essays on the Social Democratic Tradition in Canada* (Regina: Canadian Plains, 1984). On women in the CCF and Communist Party, a critical account is Joan Sangster, *Dreams of Equality: Women on the Canadian Left, 1920–1950* (Toronto: McClelland and Stewart, 1989). A biography of a major woman founder of the CCF is Terry Crowley, *Agnes Macphail and the Politics of Equality* (Toronto: Lorimer, 1990). Provincial CCF histories include: Nelson Wiseman, *Social Democracy in Manitoba: A History of the CCF–NDP* (Winnipeg: University of Manitoba Press, 1983); Gerald L. Caplan, *The Dilemma of Canadian Socialism: The CCF in Ontario, 1932–1945* (Toronto: McClelland and Stewart, 1973); Seymour Martin Lipset, *Agrarian Socialism*; and Dorothy Steeves, *The Compassionate Rebel: Ernest E. Winch and His Times* (Vancouver: Douglas and McIntyre, 1960). On intellectuals and the Left: Michiel Horn, *The League for Social Reconstruction* (Toronto: University of Toronto Press, 1980). On the extreme right, see Lita-Rose Betcherman, *The Swastika and the Maple Leaf* (Toronto: Fitzhenry and Whiteside, 1975).

On Quebec political and social developments in this period, see Paul-André Linteau, René Durocher, Jean-Claude Robert, and François Ricard, *Quebec Since 1930* (Toronto: Lorimer, 1991); Evelyn Dumas, *The Bitter Thirties in Quebec* (Montreal: Black Rose, 1975); Yves Vaillancourt, *L'évolution des politiques sociales au Québec 1940–1960* (Montreal: Presses de l'Université de Montréal, 1988); Andrée Lévesque, *Virage à gauche interdit: les communistes, les socialistes, et leurs ennemis au Québec, 1929–1939* (Montreal: Boréal Express, 1984); Conrad Black, *Duplessis* (Toronto: McClelland and Stewart, 1979); Bernard L. Vigod, *Quebec Before Duplessis: The Political Career of Louis-Alexandre Taschereau* (Montreal: McGill-Queen's University Press, 1986); Herbert F. Quinn, *The Union Nationale* (Toronto: University of Toronto Press, 1979); Pierre Elliott Trudeau, *The Asbestos Strike* (Toronto: James Lewis and Samuel, 1974); Jacques Rouillard, *Histoire du syndicalisme québécois* (Montreal: Boréal Express, 1989); Gerard Boismenu, *Le duplessisme* (Montreal: Presses de l'Université de Montréal, 1981); Kenneth McRoberts, *Quebec: Social Change and Political Crisis* (Toronto: McClelland and Stewart, 1988); and Francine Berry, *Le Travail de la femme au Québec: L'évolution de 1940–1970* (Montreal: Presses de l'Université du Québec, 1977).

On labour, corporations, and the state, key works include Irving M. Abella, *Nationalism, Communism and Canadian Labour* (Toronto: University of Toronto Press, 1973); Bryan D. Palmer, *Working Class Experience: Rethinking the History of Canadian Labour, 1800–1991* (Toronto: McClelland and Stewart, 1992); Jeremy Webber, "The Malaise of Compulsory Conciliation: Strike Prevention in Canada During World War II," *Labour* 15 (1985): 57–88; Laurel Sefton MacDowell, *Remember Kirkland Lake*

(Toronto: University of Toronto Press, 1983); Ian Radforth, *Bushworkers and Bosses* (Toronto: University of Toronto Press, 1987); Craig Heron, *Working in Steel* (Toronto: McClelland and Stewart, 1988); and Michael Earle, ed., *Workers and the State in Twentieth-Century Nova Scotia* (Fredericton: Acadiensis Press, 1989).

On World War II, see J.L. Granatstein and Desmond Morton, *A Nation Forged in Fire: Canadians and the Second World War* (Toronto: Lester and Orpen Dennys, 1989); J.L. Granatstein and J.M. Hitsman, *Broken Promises: A History of Conscription in Canada* (Toronto: Oxford University Press, 1979); Ann Gomer Sunahara, *The Politics of Racism: The Uprooting of Japanese Canadians During the Second World War* (Toronto: Lorimer, 1981); and Barry Broadfoot, *Six War Years: Memories of Canadians at Home and Abroad* (Toronto: Doubleday, 1974). On Canada and the early Cold War, see Denis Smith, *Politics of Fear: Canada and the Cold War, 1941–1948* (Toronto: University of Toronto Press, 1988); James Eayrs, *In Defence of Canada*, vol. 4 (Toronto: University of Toronto Press, 1980) and vol. 5 (Toronto: University of Toronto Press, 1983); George Ignatieff, *The Making of a Peacemonger* (Toronto: Penguin, 1985); Denis Stairs, *The Diplomacy of Constraint: Canada, the Korean War and the United States* (Toronto: University of Toronto Press, 1974); Douglas Ross, *In the Interests of Peace: Canada and Vietnam 1945–1973* (Toronto: University of Toronto Press, 1985); Victor Levant, *Quiet Complicity: Canadian Involvement in the Vietnam War* (Toronto: Between the Lines, 1986); and Robert Bothwell, *Canada and the United States: The Politics of Partnership* (Toronto: University of Toronto Press, 1992). On the domestic Cold War, see Len Scher, *The Un-Canadians: True Stories of the Blacklist Era* (Toronto: Lester, 1992).

CHAPTER

SOCIETY AND CULTURE IN
THE MODERN AGE, 1920–60

Helen Burgess had separated from her husband and was working to support herself and her two children when she wrote a desperate letter to Prime Minister Mackenzie King in June 1947. The Toronto woman was a victim of the critical urban housing shortage that had resulted from a virtual halt in residential construction during the Depression and Second World War. While urban populations increased, the quantity and quality of available accommodation deteriorated. Wrote Burgess:

> I make clear a week $26.09. Out of this I have to live, pay rent for one little room, street car fare and personal expenses. I had to send my little children to an orphanage as I couldn't keep them with me in a room as nobody will give you a room if you have children. Now please would you help me, tell me what I should do in order that I could have my babies with me. My heart is breaking for them as I need them and want them with me. I miss them terribly and they miss me too.[1]

One year earlier, Irene Walker, arguing on behalf of an organization of parents fighting to maintain the government-subsidized day-care centres that had opened during the war, emphasized the problems posed by inadequate housing. She wrote Ontario Premier George Drew:

> In some cases, the family's home consists of one room, where they have to eat, sleep and live. The meals are prepared on a one or two burner gas plate. In some cases there are as many as 21 people in one home where they have to share one bathroom and sometimes the kitchen. There is no place for the children to play. We read every day of children being hurt or killed by traffic accidents. If the services of the Day Care Centres had been made available to those children, their lives would have been saved.[2]

Helen Burgess and Irene Walker would have found incomprehensible the scorn that intellectuals would pour on the new suburbs that sprang up after 1945. Five rooms plus a small yard where children could play seemed a fantasy to most working families in 1920 or even 1945, but such homes had materialized for many by 1960, a symbol of postwar prosperity that optimists proclaimed would soon be available for every citizen. Although more than one Canadian in four, even in 1960, lived in poverty, for the rest, including the millions only a step up from poverty, life had never been better.

The promise of technologically provided abundance, which enticed Canadians in 1920, appeared to be within the reach of a majority in 1960. While a recession, a depression, and a war had forced delays in purchasing the appliances and gadgets for which advertising effectively created markets, consumers in the 1950s earned the wages necessary to buy—usually on time payments—automobiles, televisions, refrigerators, and washing machines. Consumption became, arguably, the major pastime of society, and status increasingly was bestowed on individuals solely on the basis of the goods they owned.

Materialist values permeated society at every level. Not surprisingly, there was also a reaction to such values among those who believed that

This postwar float encouraged women to think of themselves as consumers and ornaments (Provincial Archives of Alberta/B1.20021/1)

unbridled individualism and acquisitiveness were destroying community and spiritual values. Such voices received little attention from a population tired of poverty and insecurity and anxious to create a modern world in which instant gratification was possible.

•Population

Canada's population more than doubled between the census years 1921 and 1961, rising from 8.8 million to 18.2 million (see table 10.1). Immigration, which occurred in higher volumes during prosperous periods, accounted for a significant portion of the increase. The late 1920s and the years after World War II were the major periods of new immigration. From 1946 to 1962, 1 761 505 new immigrants came to Canada, including 47 783 war brides and their 21 950 children. Postwar immigrants were primarily European; only 4 percent came from Asia and Africa, and many of these were white South Africans and Israelis. Although in theory the government no longer barred immigration of non-whites after the Second World War, in reality it was extremely difficult for people of colour to come to Canada. Overseas officers of the Department of Immigration were confined to Europe, as were visa offices, and the minister of citizenship and immigration enjoyed substantial discretionary power in granting entry. Such practices made specific legislated interdictions unnecessary. The proportion of Asian and black Canadians actually fell from 1921 to 1961; by the latter date, there were 121 573 Asians and 32 127 blacks in Canada.

Table 10.1: POPULATION GROWTH OF CANADA, 1921–61

Period	Natural Increase (percentage)	Immigration (percentage)	Population at Beginning of Interval
1921–31	15.5	+2.6	8 787 949
1931–41	11.8	−0.9	10 376 786
1941–51	20.2	+1.5	11 506 655
1951–61	22.5	+7.7	14 009 429
1961–71	14.3	+4.0	18 238 247

Source: Daniel Kubat and David Thornton, *Statistical Profile of Canadian Society* (Toronto: McGraw-Hill Ryerson, 1974), 14; William L. Marr and Donald Paterson, *Canada: An Economic History* (Toronto: Gage, 1980), 153.

Many Anglo-Canadians continued to encourage the government to give preferential treatment to immigrants from Britain. The federal government pandered to nativist sentiment during the recession of the early 1920s but later in the decade bowed to pressure from railway companies, manufacturers, and farmers, all facing labour shortages, and opened the door to wider European immigration. Still, not all Europeans were welcomed. Canada's doors were firmly closed against European Jews, desperate to escape Nazi oppression in the 1930s. The anti-Semitism of government officials proved stronger than the urgent appeals of the Canadian Jewish community on behalf of their persecuted co-religionists. After World War II, there was an initial reluctance to accept Germans and Italians as prospective citizens. From 1946 to 1950, only 9984 Germans and 20 052 Italians were permitted entry. But the explosion in labour needs led to acceptance of 189 705 Germans and 166 397 Italians from 1951 to 1957.

Canada's population increased twice as fast from 1941 to 1961 as it had from 1921 to 1941. While immigration was part of the story, much of the rest came from the baby boom of the postwar period. Women had limited the size of their families during the Depression and the war. The fertility rate, measured by births per 1000 women aged fifteen to forty-nine, fell from 120 in 1921 to 94 in 1931 and 87 in 1941. It rose to 109 in 1951 and 117 in 1956 to fall back to 112 in 1961. Birth control continued to be illegal in Canada during this period, but it was practised nonetheless. Industrialist A.R. Kaufman even established a birth control service—the Parents' Information Bureau—in Kitchener, Ontario, in the early 1930s. He hired nurses to provide birth control information and to arrange for the distribution of contraceptives to women in many parts of the country. Although his goal seems to have been specifically to limit the fertility of the "lower classes"—the PIB began as a service to workers laid off from Kaufman's own factory—he was a key figure in the birth control movement in Canada.

Children born in 1961 had a life expectancy a decade longer than children born in 1931, although Native people, on average, survived only half as long as other Canadians, testimony to the dire poverty in which they continued to live. The average boy born in 1961 could expect to live 68.35 years (against 60 in 1931) while the average girl had 74.17 years before her (as opposed to 62.1 in 1931). Better nutrition, preventive medicine, and the use of antibiotics all contributed to increased life expectancy. Infant mortality rates dropped dramatically. Based on calculations per 100 000 births, diarrhoea and enteritis killed an average of 1227 babies each year from 1931 to 1935, but only 19 in 1960. Similarly, communicable diseases annually carried off 743 babies per 100 000 in the early 1930s; by 1960, the death rate had dropped to 57. The same period saw the increased medicalization of childbirth: hospital births, supervised by a physician, became the norm, although rural, outport, and Northern women often continued to give birth at home, attended by a midwife.

While more open immigration and a higher birth rate led Canada's overall population to increase fairly dramatically, the main increase, as table 10.2 suggests, was in Central Canada and the two westernmost provinces. Indeed, even though Canada had over one million more immigrants than emigrants in the 1950s, six provinces experienced a net migration outwards to other parts of Canada as well as to the United States. Saskatchewan, with its precarious one-crop economy, did particularly poorly. Between 1941 and 1961, about 350 000 residents of the province packed up and left. Both new Canadians and those who had moved from one province to another were to be found disproportionately in the four fastest-growing provinces—Ontario, British Columbia, Alberta, and Quebec.

Table 10.2: POPULATION OF CANADA, ITS PROVINCES AND TERRITORIES, 1921, 1961

	1921	1961
Canada	8 787 949	18 238 247
Newfoundland	(not part of Canada)	457 853
Prince Edward Island	88 615	104 629
Nova Scotia	523 837	737 007
New Brunswick	387 876	597 936
Quebec	2 360 510	5 259 211
Ontario	2 933 662	6 236 092
Manitoba	610 118	921 686
Saskatchewan	757 510	925 181
Alberta	588 454	1 331 944
British Columbia	524 852	1 629 082
Yukon	4 157	8 143
Northwest Territories	14 628	22 998

Source: F.H. Leacy, ed., *Historical Statistics of Canada*, 2nd ed., Series A2-14.

The slow-growth provinces—the Maritimes, Newfoundland, Manitoba, and Saskatchewan—saw little change in their ethnic distribution during this period. Atlantic Canada continued to be dominated by people of British origin, although there was a significant Acadian minority. Saskatchewan and Manitoba continued to see significant immigration from Southern and Eastern Europe, as they had before World War I. Southern Ontario, by contrast, which had been largely a white Anglo-Saxon preserve before 1920, became home to tens of thousands of Southern and Eastern European immigrants. Most Ukrainians who came to Canada before 1945 settled in Western Canada, but 80 percent of those arriving in the postwar immigration wave settled in Ontario, mainly in Toronto. Metropolitan Toronto was also home to 90 000 Italian immigrants. Montreal, too, attracted a cosmopolitan population, and, to the chagrin of francophones, most of the new arrivals chose to learn English, the language of economic power in Quebec, rather than French, the language of the majority.

As in the past, family contacts played an important role both in attracting immigrants to Canada and in determining their settlement patterns. But there were also many single men, drawn by the promise of a better life, who took work in the bush, in mines, and in urban construction. Single Finnish women in the 1920s and northern Italians after 1945 took jobs as domestics and seamstresses. Single women had been recruited during the 1920s and earlier from the East Midlands in England to work at the Penmans knit-goods factory in Paris, Ontario.

Most ethnic groups formed organizations to preserve elements of their cultural tradition and to provide mutual support in attempts to adapt to a new country. Women's groups offered opportunities for both ethnic and gender solidarity. Ukrainian women's organizations sponsored charitable activities and raised funds to build and equip Ukrainian museums. Jewish women established the National Council of Jewish Women and a variety of other organizations, including an organization to educate themselves and to raise funds for the creation of a Jewish state in Palestine. Sometimes ethnic organizations were mainly oriented to life in Canada rather than to preservation of Old World customs and goals. Finnish domestics in Ontario, for example, established maids' meeting rooms and employment exchanges to increase their bargaining power with employers.

Some of those entering Canada were fleeing religious persecution at home. Between 1922 and 1930, over 20 000 Mennonites arrived from the Soviet Union, sponsored by the Canadian Mennonite Board of Colonization in co-operation with the CPR. Most settled on farms in Saskatchewan and Manitoba. Some of these families relived the harsh lives of earlier generations of settlers, clearing and cultivating the land and living in houses with sod roofs and dirt floors. Daughters often went into domestic service, either on neighbouring farms or villages or in cities like Winnipeg, where two Girls' Homes were established for Mennonite domestics in the 1920s.

By 1941 there were over 100 000 Mennonites in Canada, despite the fact that, in the 1920s, almost 8000 had left the country for Latin America to protest the imposition of unilingual education in the Prairie provinces. They feared that failure to educate their children in German would expose them to secular influences from the larger society. For the Mennonites, fears of secularism ran deep. Many Mennonites had abandoned their communities for city life and, while most of these émigrés still identified with their religion of origin, they also embraced secular urban values. In this they joined most Canadians, leaving the churches in a quandary as to how to assert the primacy of spiritual values over consumerism.

• The Secular Society: The Impact of War and Materialism on Religion and Values

The Protestant Church

After his discharge from the military at the end of World War II, writer Pierre Berton, once a devout Anglican, attended church with his mother. The contents of the sermon in the Anglican Church in Victoria convinced him not to return.

> We had just come through a long depression and a long war, and the world was topsyturvy. I had been to Europe and back and had seen some of the real problems that distress the human animal. My head was crowded with questions, ideas, vague longings, half-formed resolves, and some small troubles. Whatever it was I was seeking, I did not find it in that church. Instead, I was subjected to a string of religious clichés which, while doubtless comforting to those who seek solace in the repetition of old, familiar phrases, was maddening to me.[3]

The problem of the relevance of religion was not new to the years following the Second World War. During and after World War I, Labour Churches, led by activists such as William Ivens and J.S. Woodsworth, operated in Winnipeg and other Canadian cities. The Labour Church offered little separation between political and religious concerns and, ultimately, it lost its religious identification. Its focus on social class encouraged its members to question the assumptions built into Christian theology, including the notion that God, rather than human labour, provided people with the necessities of life. J.S. Woodsworth, in a table prayer meant to replace a traditional grace, expressed the credo of this unorthodox religious movement: "We are thankful for these and all the good things of life. We recognize that they are a part of our common heritage and come to us through the efforts of our brothers and sisters the world over. What we desire for ourselves we wish for all. To this end may we take our share in the world's work and the world's struggles."[4]

The churches were confronted with a dilemma: they could become active participants in society to satisfy secularists like Berton or they could call their parishioners to arms in a battle against spreading materialism. For the most part, they did neither. While the social gospel message suffused many reform movements, it did not appeal to wealthy parishioners or to worshippers who wanted their religious experience to be otherworldly. Antimaterialism, on the other hand, appealed to few of the devout, since most people, however regular their church attendance, did not want the church to interfere in their everyday lives. Religious leaders watched as trade unions and political organizations stole their thunder for reform, the welfare state rendered some of their charitable causes obsolete, and movies, radio, and television replaced entertainment activities offered by the churches. Embattled but never humbled, the churches, particularly the Protestant sects, responded by tacitly accepting a Sunday-only role in the lives of most of their members. For many, churches did not fulfil even this function: only about one in three nominal Protestants was active in the church by 1960.

The merger of the Methodist, Presbyterian, and Congregationalist churches into the United Church of Canada in 1925 was motivated by lofty notions of the churches' mission in Canada. Its sponsors dreamed of a re-unified Christianity that would have the power to win a confrontation with modernism for the hearts and minds of Canadians. But a large element of the lay Presbyterian population, particularly in Ontario and the Maritimes, was more concerned with preserving its ethnic (Scots and Scots-Irish) traditions than with pursuing the exalted goals of its ministers. For fourteen years, the United Church and the Presbyterian Church struggled, consulting the courts as to who had the right to which assets. A particularly galling point for the Presbyterians was the removal of their name by the Act of Parliament that incorporated the new United Church. Finally, in 1939, the United Church relented and agreed to ask Parliament to recognize the reality that the Presbyterian Church had not disappeared.

The founders of the United Church hoped that a united Protestant-dom could influence legislators in such areas as temperance, censorship, Sunday observance, and gambling, but the churches enjoyed only modest success. Prohibition pressures had caused many jurisdictions to ban taverns and to close liquor stores before World War I. In 1918, the federal government passed an order-in-council that outlawed the manufacture or sale of alcoholic beverages in Canada, but a year later it yielded to distiller pressure and left the provinces to decide the fate of demon rum within their own borders.

British Columbians voted in 1920 for a government monopoly on hard liquor sales, with beer to be sold in grocery stores. Within four years, Quebec and the three Prairie provinces had restored liquor sales, though the Prairies chose to keep out barrooms and to restrict liquor consumption to private homes. In Ontario, the puritanism of the Farmer government on the temperance issue, as well as on questions such as legalizing horse racing, proved an important factor in its humiliating election defeat in 1923. Nova Scotia maintained prohibition until 1929. Prince Edward Island was the last holdout, but it finally abandoned prohibition in 1948.

Apart from attempting to influence legislators, the Protestant churches tried to maintain their hold over their communicants by providing leisure activities such as picnics, plays, and exhibitions. As community organizations and service clubs increasingly built facilities, the need for church-sponsored events declined. Commercial entertainments, particularly television, which came to Canada in the early 1950s, also competed with church-sponsored recreation.

The churches continued to attract women to their active ranks. Although the ministerial and lay leadership of the churches was almost exclusively male, women's auxiliaries and missionary societies enjoyed a great deal of autonomy and gave women, still relatively powerless in Canadian society, an opportunity to demonstrate leadership skills in social and charitable activities as well as in missionary roles. The United Church, the largest Protestant church, reported 401 757 members in its Women's Auxiliary and Women's Missionary Society in 1955. Efforts to give women the status that their participation warranted were largely unsuccessful. In 1929 the Baptist Assembly, after noting the "unspeakably valuable" role of women to the church, rejected ordination of women as "a practice which is so entirely new to us as a people."[5] Although the United Church accepted its first female minister, Lydia Gruchy, in the 1930s, the Presbyterian church set up a committee on the role of women in the church in the 1950s and found little support for ordination of women or even election of women elders.

Conservatism was widespread among the Protestant churches and gave way only gradually. One area that saw considerable liberalization was birth control. By the 1930s, both the Anglican and United churches cautiously endorsed the use of mechanical contraceptives to limit family size. By contrast, in 1960 the churches remained completely opposed to abortion and begrudging in their acceptance of divorce. This did not prevent the divorce rate from rising sixfold between 1920 and 1960 though, at 39 per 100 000 population in 1960, divorce remained an uncommon fate for couples. Church attitudes regarding homosexuality and pre-marital sex also relaxed little in the first half of the twentieth century.

A growing minority of Canadians were unhappy with the decreased fervour of the established churches. Several fundamentalist sects grew rapidly between 1921 and 1961. Pentecostals, for example, who numbered barely 7000 in 1921, had won the allegiance of almost 144 000 Canadians by 1961. The millenialist Jehovah's Witnesses, who attracted attention by distributing church publications door-to-door and on street corners, jumped from 6689 adherents in the 1921 census to 68 018 in 1961. Two fundamentalist radio ministers, William Aberhart and Ernest Manning, occupied the premier's office in Alberta from 1943 to 1968. Charismatic ministers like Canadian-born Aimee Semple McPherson, who preached from her California temple, won the hearts of those who missed the energy and conviction of old-time religion. Millions of Canadians, including contented members of established churches, had been impressed in the 1950s by the intense television performances of American Protestants Billy Graham and Norman Vincent Peale and the Catholic bishop Fulton Sheen.

The Catholic Church

With 8 342 826 nominal adherents in 1961, the Roman Catholic Church was not far from outnumbering all Protestant denominations combined. Its position on a number of social issues was generally more conservative than that of the Protestant churches. Although during the Depression the Catholic Church had ceased its opposition to the rhythm method of birth control, in 1960 it remained unalterably opposed to all mechanical forms of contraception. It was also implacably against divorce. On political issues, there was evidence of growing liberalism. In 1931, Pope Pius XI issued an encyclical called *Quadragesimo anno*, which attacked monopoly capitalism and called for co-operatives, state intervention, and, in extreme cases, nationalization to break up huge, non-competitive concentrations of capital. The encyclical strengthened the hand of reformist Catholics who, following an earlier encyclical issued by Pope Leo XIII in 1891, claimed that the church had an obligation to protect the poor.

Co-operatives were particularly favoured by Catholic reformers. Under Father Moses Coady, the founding director of the Extension Department of St Francis Xavier University in Antigonish, Nova Scotia, attempts were made from 1928 onwards to spread co-operatives through communities dependent on farming, fishing, coal mining, and steel production. Concentrating on the Atlantic region, Coady's achievements included the United Maritime Fishermen's Co-operative, which comprised local co-operatives for processing fish and a central organization to provide supplies and to market the final products. The Acadians in the region proved particularly receptive to the call for co-operatives. In Quebec, Pêcheurs Unis du Québec, founded in 1939, followed the same principles as its Maritime counterpart. By the 1940s the UMFC counted about 4500 members and the PUQ about 3000.

In Quebec, reformists in the Catholic Church had been responsible for the creation of the École Sociale Populaire, whose reform program, as noted in chapter 9, was hijacked by Maurice Duplessis. But, on the whole, the Roman Catholic Church in Quebec could not be called liberal. It resisted all efforts to provide greater equality for women and opposed compulsory education for young people. Whatever the École Sociale Populaire believed, the church hierarchy continued to mistrust the state and to regard it as a competitor. Duplessis' unwillingness to establish new state programs in the social services, while raising the ire of liberals, ensured his support by the church establishment. Continued church control over educational, health, and charitable institutions was seen as a shield to protect the faithful from the temptations that secular society constantly placed before them.

The church enrolled a small army to achieve its mission. In the early 1950s, for example, with 2 600 000 Catholics in the province, the church had at its disposal about 7300 priests, 10 000 other male members of religious orders, and almost 60 000 nuns in 140 religious communities. The nuns, motivated by church doctrine, worked tirelessly to provide health services to the poor and to care for the aged and infirm, groups the church regarded as both needy and virtuous. The church was harsh in dealing with those it regarded as sinful, as evidenced in the operation of homes for unwed mothers in Montreal and Quebec City, run by the Sisters of Miséricorde. Pregnant women were hidden from society and required, after giving birth, to work in the home for several months as penance and as a way of paying for their care. Both the mother and her child were stigmatized.

Church attendance on the part of Quebec Catholics was near universal, and many believed that, in Quebec and throughout French Canada, the church could dictate popular values. But there were suggestions that many Quebec Catholics, like other Canadians, listened selectively to their clerical leaders. Quebec's legendary fertility rate, which in 1921 was more than 50 percent higher than Ontario's, by 1961 had fallen below the Canadian average, despite pro-natal church propaganda. Workers ignored church denunciations of godless non-Catholic unions, and the Catholic unions became increasingly secular, severing their link with the church in 1960.

• The Communications Revolution

In 1920 radio made its first appearance in Canada. In 1940, three Canadian households in four owned a radio. In 1960, eight years after the first Canadian television stations made their appearance, three households in four owned a TV, and their sets were switched on an average six hours per day. Homemade and community entertainments, while they did not disappear, became less important in most people's lives than radio and, later, the "tube."

Radio was introduced in North America by electrical companies who, having manufactured receiving sets, began to broadcast programs to sell these appliances. Ten years after radio's introduction, Canada had over sixty stations, many owned by electrical retailers or newspapers, which depended upon private advertisers for revenue. Most of the stations had weak signals; over 40 percent of Canadians had access only to American stations. In the 1930s, several key metropolitan stations in Canada, unwilling to pour dollars into developing Canadian material to compete with popular American shows, affiliated with the major American radio networks to win the privilege of broadcasting American shows to Canadians from within Canada. Thus, by the mid-1930s, private radio station broadcasts in Canada consisted "to a considerable extent of American re-broadcasts."[6]

Fears that unregulated radio would contribute to the Americanization of Canadian culture sparked the formation of the Canadian Radio League, an organization dedicated to the creation of a Canadian version of the publicly operated British Broadcasting Corporation. The League popularized

An early radio broadcast   (National Archives of Canada/C29468)

the slogan that in broadcasting, Canadians must choose "the state or the United States." Mackenzie King responded to pressures for government regulation of radio by creating a royal commission to advise the government on the future control, organization, and financing of broadcasting. Sir John Aird, president of the Bank of Commerce, chaired the commission. His 1929 report called for a public broadcasting company to own and operate all radio stations and to build seven 50 000-watt stations across the country.

In 1932, the Privy Council awarded exclusive control over radio to the federal government, and Prime Minister R.B. Bennett established the Canadian Radio Broadcasting Commission, which in 1936 was reorganized as the Canadian Broadcasting Corporation (CBC). While private stations were not to be banished, as Aird had recommended, the CBC would have broad powers of control over their operation. The CBC's own stations were given a mandate to unite Canadians, much as the building of railways had united earlier generations.

When television made its commercial appearance after World War II, the federal government decided to extend licensing power over the new medium to the CBC's Board of Governors. The CBC was to establish a television network and initially would be given a monopoly over Canadian TV so as to make the network cost effective. By 1960, nine CBC stations and thirty-eight affiliates were on air. While they gave over much of their prime time to American shows such as "I Love Lucy" and "The Ed Sullivan Show," CBC-TV also produced Canadian dramas and variety shows that provided an outlet for many Canadian actors, musicians, and entertainers. "Front Page Challenge," a sedate guess-the-name-in-the-news show, was introduced in 1956. "Country Hoedown" introduced a generation of country music entertainers, notably Tommy Hunter, while "Don Messer's Jubilee," which was first aired in 1959, earned a devoted following. While American sitcoms and teleplays proved more popular than their Canadian-produced equivalents, "The Plouffe Family," a teleplay focussing on the lives of a working-class Montreal family, was a huge success in both its French and English versions.

In 1958, the federal government responded to pressure from private broadcasters to end the CBC monopoly over television. They were supported by many Canadians who wanted more American offerings and resented the geographical unfairness that allowed Torontonians to tap into a variety of Buffalo stations while Winnipegers and Edmontonians had only the CBC. Under new legislation, private channels became eligible for licences, and a Board of Broadcast Governors (BBG) was set up to license radio and television stations. As the first private stations went on air, featuring almost non-stop American entertainment, nationalist pressures forced the BBG to establish a 55 percent Canadian content guideline in the 1960s.

Cheaply produced game shows, modelled on American programs, were the private stations' answer to the rule, and hopes that content regulations would stimulate a viable Canadian television production industry were largely unrealized.

While most television shows, whether produced in Canada or the United States, constituted light entertainment, they embodied a set of conservative social values and stereotypes. "Family shows," including "Father Knows Best" and "Leave It to Beaver," extolled middle-class patriarchal families in which father earned the money while mother cared for the household. A woman's purpose in life was presented in innumerable commercials that explained how, by purchasing the advertised products, a housewife could fulfil herself and be the envy of neighbours by staying young and attractive while keeping a spotless house with impeccably well-groomed and well-nourished inhabitants. Ironically, the impossibility for most families of both maintaining traditional gender roles and purchasing the products advocated in commercials forced Canadians to choose between one or the other.

American content and American models were evident in other areas of mass culture besides radio and television. Movies had become a favourite pastime for Canadians of all social classes after World War I. The average Canadian went to twelve movies per year in 1936 and eighteen in 1950 before television caused a drop in movie attendance. Most of these films were Hollywood productions: in 1953, 74.6 percent of the 1289 feature films that were distributed in Canada originated in the United States, 16.9 percent originated in France, and 5.8 percent in Britain. There was only one Canadian film in movie houses that year. Even newsreels and cartoons, which theatres screened before the main attraction, tended to be American imports.

Canadian marginalization in the film industry was apparent by the early 1920s as major American studios came to dominate the distribution as well as production of films. In 1923, Famous Players bought out the Allen company, the major chain of Canadian theatres that had started with a cinema in Brantford, Ontario, in 1906. By 1930, when a Combines Investigation Act report on the film industry was released, Famous Players distributed about 90 percent of all feature pictures shown in Canada. Nonetheless, the combines report concluded that Famous Players was not a "combine" under Canadian law: it did not collude with anyone to forestall competition in its industry because it controlled too much of that industry to combine with anyone!

The federal government resisted pressures from Canadian film producers and nationalists to place quotas on imported films and create a market for Canadian products by requiring that the distributors feature Canadian films. In 1939, on the eve of war, the government created the National Film Board as a vehicle for wartime propaganda. Under its first head, John Grierson, the NFB achieved acclaim as a producer of short films and documentaries, but in its early years its resources were too thin to make feature films. After the war, C.D. Howe and his officials decided to avoid quotas on Hollywood movies by entering an agreement with the major studios to include mentions of Canada in major American films.

Canadian entertainers sought success in the larger American market, and their reputations among the home folk were enhanced when they achieved it. Oscar-winning actors Mary Pickford, Marie Dressler, Norma Shearer, and Walter Huston were acclaimed in Canada for their Hollywood successes; former CBC newsman Lorne Greene was lionized for his role as the patriarch of the Ponderosa ranch in television's "Bonanza." "Cross-Canada Hit Parade" exulted in 1957 when two songs recorded by Canadians—"Diana" by Ottawa's Paul Anka and "Little Darlin'" by Halifax's Diamonds—topped the American charts. Johnny Wayne and Frank Shuster, about to lose their Canadian television series, were renewed after American audiences cheered their comic portrayal of Julius Caesar's murder on "The Ed Sullivan Show" in May 1958. Almost alone among Canadian entertainers who achieved American success, Wayne and Shuster remained Canadian residents.

The magazine industry was dominated by American publications. In 1925 it was estimated that American magazines outsold their Canadian counterparts by eight to one. In 1931, after R.B. Bennett responded to Canadian publishers' pressures for protection with a hefty tariff on American magazines, Canadian magazine sales rose 64 percent over four years, and American magazine sales in Canada fell 62 percent. General-interest magazines such as *Maclean's* and *Liberty* were major benefactors, along with magazines aimed at rural Canada. Under Mackenzie King, such protection fell victim to trade deals, and American magazines regained their former market shares, boasting 80 percent of the Canadian market in 1954. Because of economies of scale and greater advertising revenue, American magazines were cheaper and glossier and attracted Canadian consumers.

Newspapers, while increasingly bought up by chains such as Southam and Thomson, remained largely Canadian owned. Yet foreign news in all but a few dailies was produced by cables from American news services. The *Canadian Annual Review* complained in 1922 that not only were Canadians reading foreign news items with American biases, but stories about Canadian participation in European events displayed ignorance about the workings of Canada's political system.

The bombarding of Canadians with American messages disquieted some Canadian scholars, particularly the country's most celebrated political economist, Harold Adams Innis. In a number of essays, collected in *Empire and Communications* (1950) and *The Bias of Communications* (1951), Innis suggested that media empires centred in the United States were shaping the thinking of people the world over. Democracy, he suggested, required a balance between centralization and decentralization, but democratic discussion was being subverted by the limited number of individuals who controlled access to information. As historian Mary Vipond observes, Innis's "thesis has provided the theoretical groundwork for contemplation of one of the central paradoxes of Canadian history: how technology in general and communications technology in particular have acted as a double-edged sword that simultaneously facilitates the promotion of national unity and serves as the highway on which the culture of another nation rides into our homes."[7]

Concerns about the overwhelming American influence on Canadian culture, particularly in anglophone Canada, led to the creation in 1949 of a royal commission to study national development in the arts, letters, and sciences. Headed by Vincent Massey—scion of the farm-implements giant Massey-Harris, wealthy Liberal party backer, and former Canadian high commissioner to Britain—the royal commission recommended government programs to stimulate the arts. In the 1950s the federal government responded by establishing the Canada Council and other bodies to dispense modest funds to the nation's writers, painters, musicians, and scholars. The result was that, while profitable popular culture remained Americanized, there was a strengthening of the Canadian presence in literature, music, and art.

While governments failed to intervene to ensure greater Canadian content in the popular media, they had no scruples about censoring what they felt was unsuitable material. Critics like French feminist Simone de Beauvoir were barred from the CBC in the 1950s due to government apprehension about their corrupting influence and books such as *Peyton Place*, *Lady Chatterley's Lover*, and *The Tropic of Cancer* were seized by customs officials at the border. Film censorship boards existed across the country. During the Social Credit years, Alberta's board banned material that it considered either communistic or nihilistic. A British Information Office film extolling the United Nations and condemning racism ran afoul of the communist witchhunters, and popular American films *The Wild One* and *The Blackboard Jungle* were banned for not being uplifting. Quebec's censorship board snipped not only explicit sexual scenes but also depictions of burglaries, gambling, divorce, suicide, or unpatriotic behaviour.

Quebec's harsh censorship resulted from effective lobbying by the Catholic Church. In that province, the church hierarchy proved at least as damaging as foreign control in preventing the media from becoming a means of democratic communication. Language provided some protection against the overwhelming American message that confronted English Canada, but dubbed and subtitled American movies and television programs, along with France's exports, formed an important component of Quebec's culture in the age of mass communications. Information programs on Radio-Canada, the French-language CBC radio and television network, increasingly gave an audience to liberal elements in Quebec. Duplessis complained bitterly about the coverage that the television show "Conférence de presse" gave to his opponents. Radio-Canada produced a number of celebrities in French Canada, one of whom was René Lévesque, the future premier, who in the 1950s hosted a popular weekly information show on international events. A bitter Radio-Canada strike in 1959, in which Lévesque played a key role, took on nationalist overtones as the striking producers and technicians accused the Diefenbaker government, in which French-Canadian ministers exerted little influence, of being uninterested because the strikers were francophones.

Whatever their differences, French and English Canadians seemed equally fascinated by American society. American styles of dress and American products, advertised everywhere, were in demand, especially by younger Canadians. Older Canadians, too, in the 1950s, having lived through depression and war, regarded American society with its massive economic output and its vast array of consumer products as a model worth imitating.

• Wealth, Poverty, and Power in Canada

While the Depression of the 1930s, which forced vast numbers of Canadians onto relief, stands out as the worst period of privation in Canada before World War II, most Canadians only scraped by even during the "roaring twenties." Historian Michiel Horn suggests that during the interwar period "it is likely that more than half of the Canadian people were never anything but poor."[8] In 1929 the average annual wage of $1200 per year was $230 below what social workers estimated a family required to live above poverty level. Credit helped many to get by, though it often led to an unending debt trap. Department stores such as Simpson's and Eaton's encouraged credit shopping in the 1920s, and household finance companies sprang up everywhere. In 1931, 28.4 percent of all store sales were credit purchases. This credit boom contracted spectacularly when consumers were unable to meet payments, and their goods were repossessed.

Despite the Depression, there were wealthy people who profited while others suffered. Cattle and hog raisers barely recouped their costs of operation when they sold their animals to the packers, but heads of packing firms, like J.S. McLean of Canada Packers, still raked in considerable profits. The Eaton family, heirs to the merchandising fortune, graced the social pages as they travelled the globe and hosted swank receptions. But Annie Wells, a seamstress who did piecework for Eaton's in Toronto, told the Royal Commission on Price Spreads and Mass Buying that she earned $9\frac{1}{2}$ cents for sewing twelve dresses; each dress sold for $1.59. Gray Miller, chief executive officer of Imperial Tobacco, earned $25 000 a year while clerks in the company's United Cigar Stores earned as little as $1300 a year for a fifty-four-hour week. The spread between rich and poor would not change much by the 1960s, when John Porter's *The Vertical Mosaic* (1965) established that most wealth was concentrated in a handful of families in Canada.

Postwar prosperity meant that the pie was bigger, even if its division remained inequitable. By 1956, with average wages in Canada at $62.40 per week or about $3250 per year, the purchasing power of the average family had doubled since the Great Depression. Home ownership, affordable to only a third of Canadians in 1948, had risen to 60 percent in 1961. Government guarantees of mortgages for middle- and upper-income earners under the National Housing Act helped to spur an increase of 500 000 dwellings across Canada between 1945 and 1951 alone. The Canada Mortgage and Housing Corporation, which administered the act, played a role both in aiding acquisition of land for development and the mortgage guarantees that made a rapid increase in suburbanization possible. Passenger automobile registrations, which had numbered 333 621 in 1921 and 1 028 100 in 1931, reached 4 325 682 in 1961, or almost one automobile for every four Canadians. While only 24 892 washing machines had been warehoused in 1921, there were 294 622 such machines shipped in 1961. Household refrigerator shipments numbered only 1590 in 1927, but 239 436 in 1960.

These dazzling consumption figures could easily disguise the continued presence of poverty in Canada. According to the Economic Council of Canada, in 1961 more than one household in four lived in poverty, although rates varied according to region, ethnicity, and gender. Households in Atlantic Canada and the northerly regions of all provinces experi-

In 1922, hundreds of homes in Haileybury, Ontario, were destroyed by a fire. The Toronto Transit Commission donated old streetcars to shelter the town's residents until their homes could be rebuilt.   (Toronto Transit Commission)

enced greater poverty than the populous industrial corridor of Southern Ontario or the lower mainland of British Columbia. Native peoples, African Canadians, francophones, and some recent immigrants also had disproportionately high poverty rates, as did many women-headed households with children.

The wage gap between wealthy and poor provinces tells part of the story of regional disparity. While the average of weekly wages and salaries in Canada in 1961 was $78.11, in British Columbia the figure was $85.20, in Ontario $81.14, in Alberta $80.45. In Nova Scotia the average was only $63.98, in New Brunswick $63.55, and in Prince Edward Island $57.03. In Newfoundland the figure was $71.41, but the prevalence of allegedly independent operators in the fishery, whose low earnings were excluded from calculations of employee incomes, makes this figure misleading. The disparity in unemployment rates, indicated in table 10.3, also demonstrates regional imbalances in prosperity.

Women workers, regardless of region, earned substantially less than men. In 1960, men's average wages in the manufacturing sector were $80.34 per week for hourly workers while women averaged only $43.96 per

Table 10.3: UNEMPLOYMENT NATIONALLY AND BY REGION
(Percent of non-agriculture labour force unemployed in selected years)

Year	Canada	Atlantic Provinces	Quebec	Ontario	Prairies	British Columbia
1946	3.4	5.5	4.0	2.8	2.2	3.9
1950	3.6	7.8	4.4	2.4	2.3	4.4
1955	4.4	6.5	6.2	3.2	3.1	3.8
1960	7.0	10.7	9.1	5.4	4.2	8.5

Source: F.H. Leacy, ed., *Historical Statistics of Canada*, 2nd ed., Series D 491-497.

week. Women worked fewer hours generally, but they also were paid less per hour—$1.14 as opposed to $1.93 for men. Salaried males in the manufacturing sector were paid on average more than double what their female counterparts received.

As we saw at the beginning of this chapter, single mothers trying to support a family were perhaps most deeply affected by such discrimination. After 1944, they benefited somewhat from family allowances, although, with monthly payments of $5 to $8 per child, the allowances were pitifully inadequate. As one advocate of an increase in the allowance rate noted, "given the actual price of milk—19 cents for a pint—the monthly allowance of $5.00 given for children of less than six years does not even pay for the pint of milk that doctors recommend as the daily requirement for children and adolescents to ensure the normal development of their bodies. . . . The allowances are ineffective in helping workers' families in large cities."[9]

Small as these allowances were, for the neediest families, such as those in Northern Canada, they could make the difference between starvation and survival. Poverty could be extremely harsh in the North where, between the wars, "the most consistent features of northern society were limited growth, federal government neglect, dependence on a small number of mines, a vibrant fur trade and a bicultural society."[10] White trappers from the south in the 1920s and 1930s overtrapped, ignoring exclusive Native rights to hunt in certain territories. While Native hunters could still generally get by, the Inuit who were drawn into the whaling industry off Herschel Island in the western Arctic suffered first massive epidemics and then technological displacement. By the 1920s, three in four Inuit in the western Arctic were Alaskan migrants, the indigenous population having been decimated.

Health, education, and infrastructural improvements occurred in the late 1950s as part of the Diefenbaker government's largely illusory attempt to unlock a storehouse of northern resources. But Native self-sufficiency in

Issuing family allowance cheques to Natives at a Hudson's Bay Company store in the Northwest Territories, 1950 (S.J. Bailey/National Archives of Canada/PA164744)

the region was under attack in the postwar period from Indian Affairs officials who made assistance conditional on parents sending children to school. This encouraged families who previously had moved their homes from trapline to trapline to limit their hunting activities and remain sedentary in a settlement with a school.

In the south, Indian children continued to be deliberately separated from their parents by Indian Affairs and church officials determined to use residential schools to assimilate Native peoples to European ways. Overcrowding in the dormitories of these schools, and poor nutrition and housing on reserves, resulted in early deaths and a continued decline in the number of status Indians in Canada from 1880 to 1930. By the latter date, Native immunities had strengthened and the population began to rise. Indians began to organize to demand better treatment and, while their internal differences prevented the emergence of a truly national organization, the presence of church-educated Indians among Native-rights advocates first shocked and later caused a reassessment by churches of their assimilationist policies. The League of Indians of Canada, formed by Ontario Indians in 1919 but later dominated by Prairie Natives, at first called for better schools and greater agricultural assistance. In its dying days in the 1930s it advocated a return to traditional Native ways and condemned federal repression of Native traditions.

In 1930 the federal government transferred to the Prairie provinces jurisdiction over their natural resources, beginning an escalation of pressures on Native peoples. Thousands were arrested for violating provincial fish and game laws even though their treaties with the federal government had granted them such rights in their traditional territories. In 1946–48, a special joint committee of the Senate and House reviewed the Indian Act, but its report demonstrated continued Euro-Canadian disregard for the traditions of Canada's first peoples. The old assimilatory goals were to continue, but there would be reforms. In 1951, ineffectual bans on the potlatch and Sun Dance were lifted. Elected band councils could make decisions in areas that traditionally concerned municipal governments, but Indian Affairs could overrule these decisions. Neither Native poverty nor subordination to the whims of Indian Affairs officials were alleviated in the 1950s, but status Indians were finally enfranchised federally in 1960, and from the 1950s the provinces began to grant Natives this token of citizenship.

The right to work and to live healthily, as important as the vote, eluded the Métis peoples. In Alberta, a provincial commission established in 1934 to investigate conditions among the Métis heard shocking medical evidence suggesting that the group, still victims of intense discrimination, was facing extinction. As much as 90 percent of the Métis population was infected with tuberculosis; paralysis, blindness, and syphilis were rampant. The province responded in 1939 by establishing six Métis colonies where schools and health care were provided, but no attempt was made to give these colonies a real economic base. Saskatchewan Métis fared little better even after the election of the CCF in 1944. The new government did nothing to provide sewer and water services or housing to Métis communities. It did establish marketing boards for timber and furs, but these did not operate to Native benefit. In cities, Native people faced discrimination in housing and employment. Even without a formal policy of segregation, schools, reflecting common prejudices, streamed Native students into non-academic pursuits.

African Canadians faced similar discrimination. In Dresden, Ontario, where blacks made up 17 percent of the town's 2000 people in 1950, restaurants, poolrooms, and barber and beauty shops refused patronage from non-whites. Nova Scotia blacks fought for their rights through the Nova Scotia Association for the Advancement of Coloured People (NSAACP), founded in 1945. In 1946 the NSAACP raised money to help Viola Desmond fight segregation in movie theatres. Desmond, a Halifax beautician, was arrested in a New Glasgow theatre for sitting downstairs rather than in the balcony to which blacks were usually restricted. She was thrown in jail and fined for attempting to defraud the government of one cent in amusement tax—seats in the balcony were less expensive than those downstairs. Sentenced to thirty days in jail or a $20 fine, she paid the money but appealed the decision. Although the case was thrown out on a technicality, the incident resulted in so much negative publicity that such discriminatory laws were soon abandoned. Nevertheless, blacks in Nova Scotia faced dismal prospects. A report prepared for the National Council of Women of Canada in the 1950s on the position of women in Nova Scotia observed that African-Canadian women—and men—had few job opportunities in that province. Elsewhere, discrimination on the basis of race was upheld by the courts. In 1949, the Appeal Court of Ontario ruled that there was nothing legally wrong with a clause in property deeds that barred Jews and blacks from buying property in Beach O'Pines near Sarnia. Denied entrance at every door, non-whites loomed large among the poor.

Blood woman curing beef, 1928   (National Archives of Canada/A13148)

The relative poverty of francophones, while less dramatic than Native or African-Canadian destitution, occurred despite significant francophone representation in the federal government and domination in the Quebec legislature. In Montreal in 1961 male workers of Anglo-Canadian descent earned an average 50 percent more than francophones; francophone wages in the province compared unfavourably to those of most immigrant groups as well. Poorly educated relative to English Canadians, and often recent migrants from farms, French-Canadian workers confronted an indus-

---

THE URBAN POOR IN CANADIAN LITERATURE

In the 1940s, French-Canadian writers began to examine the lives of the urban poor. One of the most celebrated works of this kind was *The Tin Flute* by Gabrielle Roy (1945). In the novel, despite the heroic efforts of Rose-Anna Lacasse to encourage her many offspring to be hopeful, despair is more common in the 1930s in Saint-Henri, a railway factory slum district of Montreal. Florentine, the eldest, whose work at a five-and-dime store's restaurant accounts for most of the family's income, is cold and cynical, desperately searching for any means to escape the poverty that confronts her. Her chosen vehicle, Jean Lévesque, a machinist, is equally determined to escape poverty, and he shuns the pregnant Florentine because she is a stumbling block to his aspirations. Rose-Anna nobly struggles on, but her life is one of misery, as this excerpt suggests.

> They were all old enough to go to school except little Gisèle, but Rose-Anna had been keeping them at home for several weeks, Lucille because she had no overshoes and Albert because he had a bad cold. As for little Daniel, he had been wasting away for two months now, without any outward signs of serious illness. Philippe, who had reached the age of fifteen, obstinately refused to go back to school. . . .
>
> During all her married life two events were always associated with the spring: she was almost always pregnant, and in that condition she was obliged to look for a new place to live. Every spring they moved. . . . [T]hey reached the point where they never moved of their own volition, but because they were behind in their rent and must find something less expensive. From year to year, they looked for cheaper and cheaper lodgings, while rents went up and habitable dwellings became more and more scarce.[11]

trial structure in which anglophone employers predominated in the higher-capitalized, better-paying workplaces and favoured anglophones for supervisory functions. At the top ranks, an old-boys' network marginalized French speakers: a study of directorates of 83 of the largest corporations headquartered in Montreal in 1943 revealed that 768 directorships were held by English Canadians and only 93 by French Canadians. According to a study by John Porter, French Canadians, who composed about 30 percent of the country's population, accounted for only 6.7 percent of its economic elite. Francophone presence in Quebec's corporations varied by sector. In 1961, just over half of the province's construction workers worked for companies that had majority francophone control, but only 6.5 percent of miners were in such firms. In manufacturing 21.7 percent of workers were in companies controlled by French Canadians, 47 percent in firms controlled by English Canadians, and 31.3 percent worked for foreign employers.

Outside Quebec, the association between poverty and retention of the French language induced many to assimilate to the majority anglophone

Tenants being evicted in Montreal during the Depression   (National Archives of Canada/C30811)

group. The assimilation rate—the percentage of Canadians with French as their first language who later became primarily English speakers—was reported as 22.1 percent in Ontario in 1931 and 37.7 percent in 1961. In Nova Scotia and Prince Edward Island, the 1961 rate was over 55 percent, and on the Prairies assimilation rates ranged from 30 percent in Manitoba to almost 50 percent in Alberta. The small French communities in British Columbia and Newfoundland assimilated at rates of 65 and 85 percent respectively. The assimilation rate was a less threatening 12 percent in New Brunswick where a high Acadian birth rate and lower emigration rate relative to that of anglophones resulted in an increase in the proportion of French Canadians in the province. Nevertheless, franco-phone poverty in New Brunswick remained widespread. Francophone school counties, unable to collect property taxes on the scale possible in other areas, could afford only about two-thirds of the educational outlay of anglophone counties, despite aid from provincial education grants.

Relatively poor education appeared to dog francophones everywhere in Canada. Church control over Catholic education in Quebec remained intact throughout the period. The Church had long supported education beyond elementary schooling only for select males destined for the priesthood and the professions. By the 1950s it was forced to accommodate greater parental pressure for higher education by building and staffing a wider range of secondary schools. More vocational and business education programs were established, but the system was underfinanced because of its overreliance on property taxes. As late as 1958, only about one-third as many francophone Catholic pupils as Protestant students completed grade 11.

Outside Quebec and New Brunswick, francophones were hampered by lack of official support for instruction in languages other than English. In 1927 Ontario abandoned its effort to put an end to French instruction, but only for elementary schools. In any case, the province provided French-language schools with none of the planning or co-ordination that English-language schools received. The western and Atlantic provinces (except for New Brunswick) either forbade or made little provision for French-language education. By 1960 instruction in Canada's second language was generally tolerated, but funds for producing and acquiring textbooks and for training teachers were withheld. Many francophone community leaders believed that educational inferiority, as well as popular prejudice and government indifference, condemned them to ghettoization and poverty.

Immigrants who did not speak English often faced the same fate when they arrived in Canada, although many, particularly in the prosperous 1950s, learned English and made good in their new homeland. Immigrants were often recruited for particular jobs. Because of labour shortages following the Second World War, some were forced to sign labour contracts with farmers or resource companies that restricted their mobility for their first year in Canada. Church leaders complained that immigrant workers suffered a great deal of illness owing to overwork and poor housing, and that they were usually unable to pay for medical services and often unwilling to seek doctors' charity.

Health Care

Canadians had differing access to medical attention depending on their class and region. Late nineteenth-century infant mortality rates were higher in cities than in rural areas. This began to change once cities provided safe water supplies and better sanitation services to their residents. Relative availability of medical services meant that urban areas began to replace the countryside as the safer place for children to grow up. In 1943, in British Columbia, which had the lowest overall infant mortality rate in Canada, 30 urban infants per thousand died before their first birthday, compared to 63 rural infants. This trend was repeated across the country, although numbers were much higher in the poorer provinces. In Manitoba, the urban figure was 43, the rural figure 76; in New Brunswick, the rates were 55 and 79 respectively.

Interestingly, the province with the lowest infant mortality rate in rural areas was Saskatchewan with 52 deaths per thousand. The explanation appears to be that, in the interwar period, much of rural Saskatchewan had implemented a "municipal doctor" scheme, in which the municipality hired and paid doctors. With medical care prepaid through property taxes, the economic inhibitions that kept many people from seeing doctors were less prevalent. Doctors, who in other provinces often left rural areas when they realized how few of their patients could affort to pay medical bills, were attracted by the stability of income that the municipal doctor plan provided.

Even the presence of a public health unit within a county—providing counselling and, where necessary, nutritional aid for expectant and new mothers—could have a significant impact on rural health. In Quebec, in the first two months of 1937, rural counties with health units reported an infant mortality rate of 86.2 per thousand while counties without health units had a rate of 118.6. This trend was duplicated in the overall death rate, which was 10.5 and 12.9, respectively, in counties with and without public health units.

Rural Canadians were generally united in their support for a national medical care program. During a national radio farm forum in 1943, local groups of listeners wrote descriptions of their medical services and how they could be improved. All thought that a national medical care program was the answer. Wrote the Seaforth, Ontario, group: "The government

THE DIONNE QUINTUPLETS

The fate of the Dionne quintuplets provides an extreme example of the increasing intervention of the state and medical experts in the lives of families. Born on 28 May 1934, Annette, Émilie, Yvonne, Cécile, and Marie instantly became famous, and almost as quickly the state removed the infants from the care of their poor, rural, francophone parents. Two months after their birth, the Ontario government placed the girls under the control of a board of guardians and soon thereafter moved the babies to a specially equipped hospital so their upbringing could be overseen by Dr Allan Roy Dafoe, who had delivered them. He and other medical practitioners monitored the babies' every movement. Parental wishes were ignored, and only after a long battle, which enlisted the aid of the Roman Catholic Church and Franco-Ontarion nationalists, were the girls restored to their parents.

It was little wonder that everyone wanted custody of the quints. The girls were a major economic asset: they had endorsements of over $1 million, were the subjects of Hollywood films, and became a major tourist attraction—three million curiosity seekers flocked to view them from behind a one-way screen. The girls never fully recovered from their traumatic first years. Émilie died in a convent in 1954, and the four survivors recorded their unhappy stories in We Were Five, published in 1965.

sponsors the TB testing of cattle, pays for loss and has blood testing every year free of charge. What about humans? Let's take our hats off to Russia as far as health is concerned."[12]

The regional distribution of medical personnel paralleled regional patterns of wealth distribution. In 1959, although Canadians collectively had one doctor to serve every 938 people, much more favourable ratios were found in Ontario, British Columbia, and Alberta. In Newfoundland, there was only one doctor for every 2190 residents. The gap in dental services, which were generally deemed inadequate everywhere in the country, was more extreme—one dentist to every 2400 British Columbians but only one for every 11 000 in Newfoundland, and if St John's and Corner Brook were excluded, the figure for dental care in the province was one dentist for every 30 859 people.

The lack of local medical services caused the Newfoundland Federation of Labour to mock the slogans on the posters that Ontario public health organizations sent around to schools throughout the country.

"Brush your teeth three times a day and see your dentist twice a year" say posters in the school. The dentist is 150 miles away.

"Fight cancer with a checkup and a cheque." The checkup means a trip by coastal boat to a doctor with no training or equipment to diagnose cancer.

"Prize your eyes" says the CNIB. But on the coast of Labrador or at the head of Bay D'Espoir, there has never been an eye specialist, not even in transit.[13]

According to the National Committee for Mental Hygiene in 1939, a quarter of all Canadians depended on charity for their medical services, while a tenth had no difficulty spending whatever money was deemed necessary to maintain good health. The rest of the population could pay normal medical bills but were faced with an impossible situation if a family member required long-term care or a major operation. By 1960, almost half of Canadians had purchased prepaid medical care, though most plans covered only diagnostic and curative services, with no payment for dental care, prescription drugs, preventive services, or mental health care. Unsurprisingly, in Atlantic Canada, coverage was 50 percent less than for the country as a whole. In the rural areas of the Prairie provinces, coverage was much lower than in the cities. Only the introduction of the national hospital insurance scheme in 1957 marked an advance in which all Canadians could claim some share.

Women, Work, and the Family

Work did not always mean the same thing to both men and women. Aside from the obvious distinction industrial society makes between unpaid work in the home, done largely by women, and work in the paid labour force, there were differing attitudes towards waged work itself. These attitudes, notes historian Joy Parr, were reinforced by the different socialization that girls and boys received:

> Through waged work, boys learned manliness; they mastered discipline and discrimination, ways of appraising their work and one another, which they would practice through their adult lives; varied though these ways of being manly were, they shared one trait: they were lessons males alone might learn. Girls did not learn womanliness through paid employment. Their experience of waged work . . . was important in their growing into womanhood because it became them to remain under the protection of male kin while they waited for their life's work, in marriage and outside the market, to begin.[14]

For many young women, the time spent inside the market was indeed dismal. Before World War II, most were underpaid store clerks, office workers, and domestics. During the Depression, the lot of women workers, mostly single or heads of one-parent households, was particularly precarious. Some were forced into prostitution because of a lack of alternative work and the difficulties single women faced in convincing relief authorities to provide them with aid. Cafeteria workers in Edmonton were not alone in being paid far below the legislated but laxly enforced minimum wage for women. Aided by demonstrations of unemployed men on relief,

Day care was a problem even during the war. This Mi'kmaq woman brought her child with her to the Pictou shipyards in 1943. (National Film Board/National Archives of Canada/PA116254)

the Edmonton women were able to strike for the modest pay that was legally their minimum due.

Lack of day-care facilities made wage labour impractical for mothers unless they had kin to help out. Stella Beachey, a knit-goods worker in Paris, Ontario, bore three children after her marriage in 1942, but never stayed out of the labour force for longer than a year at a time. Her mother, with whom she, her husband, and her children shared a home until 1950 when they bought their own house across the street, cared for the children.

Immigrant women whose first language was not English fared even more poorly in the work force than their English-speaking counterparts. They were clustered in occupations such as sewing for extremely low piece rates and in minimum-wage jobs as cleaners and launderers. With the advent of such labour-saving devices as vacuum cleaners and washing machines, and the availability of higher wages in other occupations, fewer women were employed as domestics. Those who did such work, which was exempt from minimum-wage regulations, were usually immigrant women. Married immigrant women with large families usually remained home and added to family income in cash or kind as best they could. Italian women in Metropolitan Toronto, for example, often grew vegetable gardens and grapes and put up preserves to cut down on food bills. They took in boarders and minded neighbours' children to add to family incomes.

Women's work was central in establishing a sense of community in small towns or in local neighbourhoods of larger cities. New single-industry towns, such as Kitimat, B.C., and Gagnon, Quebec, were springing up as "suburbs in the wilderness" designed to attract a core group of stable family men as employees. Management believed that such workers would be less prone to mobility and strikes than an earlier generation of single miners. While most of the men worked in the town's main industry, their wives took up the challenge to establish community facilities. A woman who arrived in Flin Flon, Manitoba, in 1926 when the town was still a bush camp, later recalled, "without women this town would be nothing. Women organized the community centre, the schools, the hospital. . . . But most important, women were wives and mothers. They kept the house, raised the children right. . . . Women looked after the home and that's what makes this town great. It's a family town."[16]

From 1920 to 1960, most mothers of young children continued to be engaged in full-time unpaid housework. Older children were expected to help after school. Girls aided their mothers in cooking, cleaning, and washing. They minded younger brothers and sisters while mothers shopped, a daily ritual before modern refrigeration became commonplace in the 1950s. Boys fetched and chopped wood and looked after gardens.

WHAT IS WOMEN'S WORK?

Most women in paid work in the 1950s held poorly paid dead-end jobs. They were tellers but never bank managers, department store salesclerks and cashiers who had no chance of being promoted over their male counterparts. Better-educated women might be teachers or nurses, but few were considered for positions as principals or hospital administrators. The pervasive view that motherhood, not a career, was a woman's destiny helped to block women's advance, but voices demanding equality for women in the labour force were beginning to be heard, particularly from such groups as the Business and Professional Women's Clubs.

In 1944, the clash between feminist and traditionalist views of employment opportunities for women was clear in a disagreement between Laura Hardy, president of the National Council of Women of Canada, and Juvenile Court Judge Helen Gregory MacGill. Hardy sent her executive council members, including MacGill, a list of occupations for which she thought the organization should press governments to establish female training programs. Included were nurses, lab technicians, office assistants for doctors and dentists, household workers, bookkeepers, dressmakers, and switchboard operators. Responded MacGill:

> But these recommendations are for training women to take subordinate positions, yet the men in the Armed Services are offered full professional courses in medicine, law, pharmacy, social service, personnel, engineering, biology, bacteriology, chemistry, etc., graduating not as assistants, but as fully qualified practitioners.
>
> May I beg to remind you that these professions have been opened to women after great struggle and only recently. No opportunity should be lost to give talented women and girls an opportunity to enter any of the professions should they desire.[15]

Hardy ignored MacGill's advice, accepting the mainstream view of "women's work."

Working-class families in many areas tried to reduce spending by raising fowl and sometimes larger animals. In East Vancouver, even in the 1950s, many children fed animals, plucked chickens, and collected eggs. In rural areas, such traditional childhood work was still taken for granted. In town, children scrounged for scrap wood, grass for animal feed, manure for fertilizer, and items—bottles, scrap metal, car batteries—to sell. Some paid work was available to children: girls baby-sat or took sales or clerical work as they got older; boys did odd jobs such as shovelling snow, delivering newspapers, cutting lawns, and painting, later working as packers or delivery boys.

By 1961 it was becoming more common for married women, particularly those with older children or no children at all, to take paid work. In 1941, only 5 percent of married women earned a wage; twenty years later, 25 percent did. Women's paid labour, while still largely confined to low-paying job ghettos in offices and shops, made the difference for many families between just getting by or becoming the owners of houses, cars, televisions, or refrigerators. As children remained in school longer than in earlier generations and enforcement of child labour provisions became stricter, the second incomes of married women filled a gap in the family economy.

• Education

By the 1920s parents who could afford to delay their children's entry into the work force generally encouraged them to complete as many years of secondary schooling as possible. The number of jobs for which high school matriculation was a qualification increased dramatically as employers demanded a literate work force. The national increase in school attendance illustrates the change. In 1921, 27 percent of girls and 22 percent of boys between fifteen and nineteen years old attended school; twenty years later the respective figures were 37 and 35 percent. In Ontario, the secondary school population quadrupled in the 1920s over the previous decade, though the provincial population had grown only 17 percent. By 1959, 47 percent of children of Anglo-Canadian origin in Ontario spent five or more years in post-elementary education. Significantly, only 23 percent of Ontario francophones remained in school that long.

While public schools across the country increasingly emphasized science and mathematics along with literature and grammar in a curriculum that responded to employers' notions of a useful education, Catholic schools in Quebec taught Thomist philosophy, Latin, religion, and humanities. In 1960, there were only 20 seminaries, 60 boys' secondary schools, and 20 girls' schools whose certificates permitted students to enter the Catholic universities. For girls the system taught above all else "preparation for family life, the beauty of the home, its virtues, and its unique position in society."[17] The teachers in Quebec's Catholic schools were less educated than the teachers in the Protestant system. Among the latter, 30 percent had university degrees and 57 percent had more than twelve years of schooling; among the former the figures were 10 percent and 33 percent.

In Quebec, in common with the rest of the country, parents indicated a strong desire to have more money spent on the construction of schools and on the improvement of teaching. An opinion poll conducted for the Social Credit Party in Alberta in 1956 found that the major area in which Albertans wished to see more government action was education. A subsequent provincial royal commission on education reported that schools were plagued by poorly paid and underqualified teachers, crowded classrooms, and a limited curriculum. The commission heard from the Canadian Petroleum Association, manufacturers, and chambers of commerce that there must be "a reduction in pupil–teacher ratios in classrooms, more and better qualified teachers, better materials of instruction, greater efforts to capitalize on the interests of pupils as means of raising the general level of academic attainment, for the purpose of equipping more young people for job efficiency in an age of machines."[18] The appeal of such views caused Alberta's Premier Ernest Manning, then campaigning in the 1959 provincial election, to pledge $350 million in new education spending over five years. Other provinces, while less able than Alberta to spend so generously on education, also substantially increased their education grants to municipalities during the 1950s. Throughout rural areas, the one-room schoolhouses where poorly paid, inadequately trained young women taught eight grades at once gave way to modern, centrally located facilities. For many rural residents, the creation of consolidated school divisions was a mixed blessing because it removed local control over schools and created the need for daily busing of children, sometimes over long distances.

The enthusiasm for more schooling slowly extended to the postsecondary sector but, with university education generally still confined to an elite minority, provincial governments were reluctant to vastly increase spending on universities. University of Toronto students might demonstrate in the late 1930s against spending cuts by Mitchell Hepburn's government, but few ordinary people sympathized with the students' plight. More helpful than governments were private, mainly American, foundations such as Carnegie, Ford, and Rockefeller, which poured money into major universities, as well as funding the Canadian Social Science Research Council, whose grants allowed scholars outside professional facilities to conduct research. Such largesse was generally directed towards anglophone universities in Central Canada to the detriment of universities—both anglophone and francophone—elsewhere. The churches that had founded private universities continued to finance these institutions with little or no state aid before World War II.

Between 1920 and 1940, Canadian university enrolments increased from 23 418 to 37 225. Women's participation jumped from 16 to 24 percent of all enrolments, but their increase was concentrated in areas stereotyped as women's professions: nursing, household science, library science, and physical and occupational therapy. No males were enrolled in any of these areas in the 1940–41 academic year. Men predominated as students in professional areas promising higher salaries and greater independence. In engineering, there were 2851 men enrolled across the country in 1920–21, but only 3 women; twenty years later 4381 men and 13 women were studying in the discipline. Medicine and law were only slightly less solidly male preserves; education and arts were more extensively co-educational.

During the Second World War, the principals of McGill and Queen's were so enthusiastic about the universities' role in producing engineers and scientists for the war effort that they proposed suspending all teaching in commerce, arts, law, and education until the war ended. This did not happen, but it was not the last time that universities would be called upon or would themselves offer to abandon classical notions of scholarly inquiry to become adjuncts of industry and government.

After the war, generous federal grants to veterans wishing to pursue university educations resulted in a doubling of 1944 levels of enrolment by 1947. Federal grants to universities, recommended by the Massey Commission in 1951 and quickly implemented by the federal government, also gave a boost to universities that, despite persistent pressures on the provinces, were receiving only modest funding increases.

In Quebec, the federal grants brewed a storm of protest. Quebec nationalists opposed such grants as interference in provincial affairs. Even federalists such as Pierre Elliott Trudeau, editor of the anti-Duplessis intellectual journal *Cité Libre*, denounced federal intrusion into an area constitutionally reserved for the provinces. Trudeau and other liberals called for Quebec to adequately fund its own universities. Duplessis ignored this demand and accepted federal grants in 1951. Thereafter, however, he yielded to nationalist pressure to reject further federal assistance.

The Catholic Church maintained its hold on Quebec's universities but, especially at Laval, liberal Catholic scholars in the social sciences were much in evidence and influenced an elite-in-training to reject the dogmas of their clerical and political leaders. Protestant-controlled universities in Canada were also less conservative. Brandon College, after being the storm centre of a debate on fundamentalism versus modernism in the 1920s, was abandoned by the Baptist Church for financial reasons in 1938. It survived because of a private endowment and a government grant and eventually became an affiliate of the University of Manitoba. Although its board of governors included many old-line Baptists who had no time for agnostic scholars, Acadia University also became more secular. Its president, Watson Kirkconnell, spearheaded a drive by church-affiliated universities to pry open the Nova Scotia government's coffers.

Technical institutes such as Toronto's Ryerson Institute of Technology, which was established in 1948, were also opened in several provinces as demands for technical rather than academic skills became more important in industry. An obsession with institutional certification made traditional apprenticeship programs an outdated way to pass on skills from one generation to the next. Increasingly, trained teachers and professors were able to create a mystique about their abilities to communicate precise information and to evaluate acquisition of knowledge.

•Culture and Leisure

A better educated public provided an increasing market for Canadian literature. We have seen that mass culture in Canada was dominated by the Americans, whose products and models were also influential in the artistic world. Nonetheless, distinctively Canadian literature and art, admirable in both quality and quantity, continued to be produced.

Both in French and English Canada there was an increased social realism in the literature of the period. While Quebec novels before 1939 maintained the idealization of the land evident in earlier works, there was an increasing recognition by writers like Ringuet (Philippe Panneton) and Claude-Henri Grignon that the traditional Quebec was disappearing and could not be restored. Postwar novelists concentrated on the urban setting within which most Québécois now lived. Gabrielle Roy's *Alexandre Chenevert* (*The Cashier*) (1954), through its portrayal of an unhappy Montreal cashier, depicted the economic and cultural alienation of urban society. Roger Lemelin, creator of *The Plouffe Family* (1948), dealt frankly with issues of social class in several works. Novelists such as Germaine Guèvremont in *Le survenant* (1945) attempted to demystify the rural milieu and demonstrate the ignorant claustrophobia in which many rural dwellers lived. Guèvremont and Roy as well as Yves Thériault were pioneers in including non-francophones in their novels. Roy, who grew up in St Boniface, Manitoba, wrote novels, short stories, and non-fiction articles about her childhood and years as a teacher in the West. Her realistic works are in sharp contrast to *La Belle Bête*, published in 1959 by a young Marie-Claire

Blais. Blais anticipated post-1960 trends in her surreal novel in which both chronology and the boundary between the real and the imagined are deliberately left vague.

In 1948 painter Paul-Émile Borduas published *Refus global*, a rejection of the narrow world of orthodoxy within which artists and writers were expected to work. The manifesto resulted in his exile from Quebec but inspired the Hexagone Group of poets, active from 1953 to 1963, who refused to recognize the traditional boundaries of literary expression.

English-Canadian social realism emerged earlier than its French-Canadian counterpart, and themes such as sexuality, repression of women, and psychological blackmail were present in such classic Prairie novels as Martha Ostenso's *Wild Geese* (1925), Sinclair Ross's *As For Me and My House* (1941), and several works by Frederick Philip Grove. The instinct for survival and resistance during the Depression was celebrated in Irene Baird's *Waste Heritage* (1939) and again in Hugh Garner's *Cabbagetown* (1950). Class strife was the subject of Grove's *The Master of the Mill* (1944).

In the postwar period, a number of Maritime authors, including Thomas Raddall and Ernest Buckler, gained national audiences as did Ontario's Morley Callaghan and Hugh Garner and the West's W.O. Mitchell and Adele Wiseman. Wiseman, although not prolific, created a moving account of the experience of Jewish immigrants to the Prairies in her novel *The Sacrifice* (1956). John Marlyn in *Under the Ribs of Death* (1957) dealt with the experiences of the son of Hungarian immigrants in North End Winnipeg and expressed the confusion of many newcomers as they faced an environment that reviled their native cultures but denied them a firm place within the dominant Anglo-Canadian culture. In her *Confessions of an Emigrant's Daughter* (1939), Laura Salverson gave voice to the troubles of Icelandic settlers in Canada. Hugh MacLennan was one of the most commercially successful and most nationalistic of the modern writers. In *Barometer Rising* (1941), he used the Halifax explosion of 1917 to explore themes related to Canada's colonial past; *Two Solitudes* (1945) focussed on the English–French dualism; and *The Precipice* (1948) examined the impact of American culture on small town values. Despite their didactic tone and Canadian content, the books sold well internationally.

English-Canadian poets before World War II had dabbled in a variety of styles, and many made social criticism central to their work. Dorothy Livesay, F.R. Scott, A.M. Klein, Miriam Waddington, and Louis Dudek were key figures in Montreal-centred social realist poetry. Much of the poetry in the 1950s challenged the materialist values that seemed all-pervasive as Canadians tried to drown memories of depression and war in an orgy of consumerism and status seeking. Some of the leading lights of that decade were Irving Layton, Leonard Cohen, Dorothy Roberts, P.K. Page, and James Reaney.

Canadian painters were also in revolt against conventional subject matter and styles. Emily Carr, who by 1914 had largely given up painting due to lack of both moral and financial support, resurfaced in the late 1920s to become one of Canada's most renowned artists. Abstract and non-objective painting made tentative, if not particularly popular, debuts in Canada prior to the Second World War. Inspired by American and French artists, abstract painters used objects or natural scenes as a base for producing paintings that often bore no direct resemblance to the original object. Non-objective painters began not with objects but with pure imagination to produce their art. In the postwar period, these two movements were embraced by artists in both French and English Canada, although artistic enthusiasm was not reflected in popular success: most Canadians appeared to want a painting to be a simple representation of nature rather than a profound but unfathomable portrait of an artist's soul. For the artists themselves, though only a lucky few made a decent income from their paintings, the new freedom in styles appeared a liberation from the increasingly mechanical character of the larger society of which they were part. Borduas' *Refus global* became the manifesto of the *automatistes* in Quebec who believed that the painter's spirit rather than objects or the imitation of forms should guide the production of art. In English Canada, Harold Town and William Ronald were among noted modern artists. More accessible, at least superficially, was Alex Colville, whose surreal Maritime scenes created a school of magical realism.

In Native communities, artists continued to produce both ceremonial and decorative art and to carry on a modest commerce with collectors who enjoyed their work. In the 1950s, Norval Morrisseau, an Ojibwa from Sand Point Reserve in Ontario, began to do paintings that incorporated the pictography of rock paintings and Ojibwa spiritual themes. This style, labelled Woodland Indian art, would win applause in the white professional art community in the early 1960s and inspire many other Native artists to marry Native and European art forms. Largely due to the promotional energy of Toronto artist James Houston, what is now known as Inuit art was introduced to southern buyers. Beginning in the late 1940s, he encouraged Inuit to produce their ivory and soapstone carvings, and later prints, for market through Inuit co-operatives.

The growing middle class of the postwar period patronized the arts sufficiently to allow many painters, writers, and performers to make a living from their work, though many continued either to live in voluntary poverty or to supplement their meagre incomes from their art with wages from

Emily Carr, 1871–1945, **A Haida Village,** *c. 1929*   (oil on canvas; 82.7 x 60.7 cm; McMichael Canadian Art Collection; Gift of Dr and Mrs Max Stern, Dominion Gallery, Montreal; 1974.18.1)

jobs. Testimony to the expanded importance of the arts in Canadian life was the success of the Stratford Festival and the Banff Centre School of Fine Arts. The town of Stratford, Ontario, demonstrated the potential for theatre in Canada when local business people launched the Stratford Festival in July 1953. Modelling their first theatre in part on Shakespearean designs, the festival's directors provided a blend of Shakespeare and other classics as well as musical concerts aimed at both the Southern Ontario and tourist markets. In Alberta, the Banff Centre School of Fine Arts, begun modestly in 1933 by the University of Alberta Division of Continuing Education, expanded and achieved an international reputation in the postwar period for its programs in drama, music, and art.

Professional theatres opened in most urban centres, generally concentrating, like Stratford, on the classics. Many small-town playhouses closed down, unable to compete with better-financed theatres a short drive away. A few Canadian playwrights, such as Robertson Davies and Gratien Gélinas, had their plays produced on Canadian stages despite the bias of theatre management, and perhaps their audience, for international drama. Radio, mainly the CBC and Radio-Canada, offered others, such as John Coulter and Lister Sinclair, an audience for their work.

Interest in professional sporting events increased among all social classes. Hockey was particularly popular and contests were often emotionally charged, for both players and fans. In March 1955, after the legendary Maurice "Rocket" Richard of the Montreal Canadiens was suspended for the balance of the season as a penalty for brawling, fans at the Forum pelted National Hockey League president Clarence Campbell with food and then took to the streets, breaking windows and looting stores. Not only sports stars but also sports commentators became household names, especially Foster Hewitt, whose play-by-play during radio and television hockey broadcasts, starting in 1931, entertained millions of Canadians as they enjoyed the game in their homes.

Professional sports teams were almost exclusively male, but several female athletes achieved fame in individualized sports. Barbara Ann Scott won the 1948 Olympic figure-skating title and then skated professionally in ice shows. Marilyn Bell was hailed for her swimming achievements beginning in 1954 with her 52-kilometre swim across Lake Ontario when she was only sixteen years old. She later went on to become the youngest swimmer to cross the English Channel and the Strait of Juan de Fuca.

While many Canadians watched the exploits of their sports heroes and heroines only on television, increased prosperity and mobility allowed a greater number of people to pursue sports and recreational activities far from home. Governments opened campgrounds for vacationers and poured more money into museums and art galleries to attract tourists. The convenience of the automobile also made it more attractive for middle- and upper-income urbanites to move away from crowded and noisy inner-city neighbourhoods.

•Suburbanization and Alienation

Suburbs preceded the age of the automobile. Before World War I, developers in Montreal and Toronto were able to make speculative fortunes by acquiring land just outside urban boundaries and convincing—or bribing—city politicians to extend streetcar lines and utilities to these areas. Housing developments were then hurriedly constructed and city dwellers, tired of overcrowded and noisy surroundings, flocked to buy homes in the new areas. The construction of new suburbs ceased in the 1930s when poverty forced families to double and triple up and the formation of new families was delayed by later marriage and fewer children.

Postwar prosperity brought earlier marriages and a baby boom. Demands for more and better housing were common in a generation that had weathered the Great Depression by sharing space and goods. Radio and newspapers, and particularly the advertising they carried, portrayed the suburbs as a world of quiet, privacy, modern appliances, and fine furnishings. It was a world to which many urban residents aspired, and government-guaranteed mortgages, veterans' housing grants, and consumer credit brought it into the purview of a widening group. Little consideration was given to European models of apartment buildings around central shopping and entertainment courts. Canada, after all, was a relatively unpopulated country with enormous territory. The solution favoured by developers, governments, and much of the population was the extension of major urban areas outwards to create suburbs with easy access to the urban centres where jobs awaited.

The new suburbs increased the costs of running the cities. New roads had to be built and maintained for the cars that became indispensable to suburban life. Utility lines and sewers had to be built in the new areas and public transportation provided. More police and firefighters were required, and each new area had to be given its own schools, if pupils were not to be bused to large, centrally located institutions. In the prosperous fifties, the municipalities received some of the funds for such developments from property tax increases and levies on the residents of the new suburbs. They also successfully pressured provincial governments to help by establishing grants to municipalities for construction projects, increasing school grants, and taking over all or most of the costs of looking after indigents.

In most cases, new suburbs initially lacked shopping areas, community centres, theatres, taverns, and other recreational areas. Residents found entertainment in the city centre and friendship via workplace, church, and community organizations that only sometimes were located within their new subdivisions. Many suburbanites and, indeed, increasing numbers of Canadians generally either sought privacy or had it thrust upon them in anonymous settings that brought the term "community" sharply into question. Television replaced community events. Supermarkets, department stores, and malls eventually replaced neighbourhood shops where customers knew each other and the store manager and stopped to talk with one another on streets and in the shops.

It was women who experienced this new privatization most completely and with devastating psychological consequences. Men in paid work often had a sense of camaraderie with fellow workers and certainly had time away from their homes. Many women who worked only in the home lacked any feeling of connectedness with a world beyond their families. For those who were well educated, a sense of uselessness was often most acute. Upper-middle-class housewives were suffering from what Betty Friedan, in her groundbreaking book *The Feminine Mystique* (1963), called "the problem that has no name." Some women, particularly if their children were older or if kin were available to act as child minders, sought refuge in paid work. Others set about in PTAs, YWCAs, and ratepayers' associations to transform the suburban community into something approaching the richness of more established urban locations. Some developed various nervous problems for which a male-dominated medical profession prescribed pills that often created long-term addiction and left the underlying problems unresolved.

Older children too often did poorly in suburban environments where public meeting places were few. A report of the Social Planning Council of Metropolitan Toronto in the 1970s described the dilemma:

> Suburban youth are expected to act as adult consumers. . . . While the market influences youth to consume, it creates an environment which does not enable them to meet some of their basic needs, needs for belonging, needs for expression, needs for social contact. . . . When young people transcend the framework of home and neighbourhood and move out into the larger suburban community they come up against the stark reality that they are almost alone in seeking public forms of community life.[19]

While the idealized images of suburbia were middle class, many new neighbourhoods on the urban fringe were shantytowns. Tarpaper shacks in

Ville Jacques Cartier on Montreal Island, unserviced homes in Bridgeview on the British Columbia lower mainland, and shacks outside St John's without water or sewer facilities, garbage collection, or street lighting demonstrated that many suburbs had greater problems than middle-class angst. Residents of these instant slums were unable to find accommodation in decaying urban cores, where established housing disappeared as office towers and apartments for the middle class encroached upon residential neighbourhoods. The slum dwellers were victims of state housing policies that emphasized aid for middle-class home buyers. As late as 1960, only about 1 percent of housing built in Canada was public housing for families, although a slightly larger percentage consisted of state-subsidized seniors' homes. It was not because public housing was unsuccessful. Toronto's Regent Park, Canada's first large-scale public housing development, was completed in 1947 and, eleven years later, a study suggested that its 1200 families—low-income people whose former neighbourhoods were plagued by crime, alcoholism, poor health, and school absenteeism—had established a relatively peaceful, healthy neighbourhood. While residents complained of a lack of recreational facilites and of the bureaucratic management of the project, their lives had improved as a result of their relocation to roomy rowhouses with excellent sewage and sanitary services.

Opportunities to find decent housing varied particularly dramatically between regions, with Atlantic Canadians, Natives, Northerners, and Gaspésiens, for example, far less likely to live as well as people in Southern Ontario. In Atlantic Canada, there were few suburban developments, and these were generally not prosperous. While less than one in ten new homes built in Ontario during 1960 and early 1961 lacked either a furnace or a flush toilet, over four in ten built in Atlantic Canada during that period lacked one or both of these amenities.

•Reform in the Modern Age

With the loss of a sense of community in many of the new suburbs, people looked elsewhere for ways to participate in a wider community and feel a sense of contributing to general social development. Service clubs, the adult education movement, and political groups attracted individuals who were critical of a life centred on consumerism. The Benevolent and Protective Order of Elks established before World War I and represented throughout the country after 1920, sponsored Boy Scout troops, participated in parades, and raised funds for local facilities such as libraries, swimming pools, community halls, and parks. After World War II, clubs such as the Elks, Kiwanis, and Rotary often received provincial government grants in aid of their community activities.

The Canadian Legion, founded in 1925, attracted war veterans of both sexes and created a sense of community for this large group in its clubhouses across the nation. By 1935 the Legion boasted 160 000 members, including thousands of women in its auxiliaries. The organization became a powerful lobby for veterans' rights, especially in matters relating to education and housing.

Many service clubs were particularly interested in encouraging young people to follow righteous and clearly gendered paths. Boy Scouts, supported by many service groups, promoted traditional notions of masculinity as well as discipline and respect for law. In the 1920s, most Boy Scouts on the Prairies were Protestants of British descent, and attempts to recruit other groups proved largely futile. After World War II, as the link between scouts and the vanishing British Empire became less pronounced, the organization proved a popular training ground in accepted notions of manhood for boys of many backgrounds. Girls, meanwhile, were encouraged before the war to join groups such as Canadian Girl Guides, Canadian Girls in Training, and the Junior Red Cross, all of which trained them to be good mothers, Christians, and British subjects.

While many of the organizations for adult women also assumed limited options for their members, others had broader agendas. The Canadian Federation of Business and Professional Women's Clubs was organized in 1930 to convince the business community's leaders that better training and fairer promotions for women were ultimately in the interest of business. Women's Institutes in British Columbia and the Prairie provinces worked with provincial governments in the 1920s to set up health centres. Black women in Windsor, Ontario, established a club that organized cultural programs, studied black history, and worked for better local race relations. Women also generally led the Canadian Home and School (or Parent–Teacher) Associations that mushroomed from the 1920s onwards and founded the Association of Consumers (after 1962 the Consumers Association of Canada), which grew out of the work of the Wartime Prices and Trade Board to enlist fifty-six women's organizations to monitor prices. After the war, the number of service groups formed by women increased dramatically as women sought to escape the isolation of suburban homes and to improve the quantity and quality of services in their communities.

Women seeking educational challenges as well as career training became an important part of the audience for adult education programs after 1920. Several universities established extension programs aimed first at rural areas and eventually at the non-university population of the cities. E.A. Corbett, who led the University of Alberta's Faculty of Extension in the 1920s and 1930s, felt that his mission was to promote high culture in rural areas. He encouraged local drama productions, and his department lent films, classical music recordings, and books to groups and individuals. Under his leadership, the Faculty of Extension established a radio station to provide educational and cultural programs throughout the province and a summer drama program that later evolved into the Banff School of Fine Arts. McGill and the University of British Columbia established programs along Corbett's model in the 1920s and 1930s. A rather different blend of education and social activism characterized the Extension Department at St Francis Xavier University.

Adult education was not restricted to the universities. Frontier College continued to send university students to camps to provide basic education to workers, particularly immigrants, as it had since Alfred Fitzpatrick, a Nova Scotia-born Presbyterian minister, founded the college early in the century. Trade unions and political parties of the left ran schools for their activists in an attempt to counter the information dispensed by the media, which the left viewed as tools of the capitalist class.

A small but persistent reform element was the pacifist movement. Pacifists shared a repugnance to war as a means of solving national and international conflicts. In the 1930s, many peace activists became convinced that capitalism must be eliminated or reformed if wars were to be prevented. Pacifists became active in socialist and social justice movements, including the CCF, the League for Social Reconstruction, the Fellowship for a Christian Social Order, and the Alberta School of Religion. The rise of fascism and the remilitarization of Germany created a dilemma for many pacifists who valued democracy and equality and did not believe that Hitler could be tamed without recourse to arms. Many joined the Communist-led League Against War and Fascism, formed in 1934. When Spanish fascists under General Francisco Franco began a civil war to unseat the republican government in 1936, long-time pacifist groups formed a Canadian Committee to Aid Spanish Democracy. Among the groups involved were the Student Christian Movement, the YMCA, and the YWCA. The committee sent humanitarian aid to the beleaguered republicans in Spain and gave material and moral support to the 1200 Canadians who risked their lives to save Spanish democracy. One famous participant in the war in Spain was Dr Norman Bethune, who later became a hero of the Chinese revolution in whose cause he died.

Pro-republican activists had feared that a victory for fascism in Spain would flame the ambitions of Hitler and Mussolini and lead to a wider conflagration. They were right. Many prewar pacifists abandoned their former views when the Second World War was declared, but some remained true to their convictions, among them CCF leader J.S. Woodsworth, whose opposition to participation in any war made him part of a tiny minority even in his own party. During the war 12 000 Canadians were classified as conscientious objectors, but 700 of them enlisted either as combatants or non-combatants while most of the rest accepted employment in agriculture or in war-related service jobs.

After the war, more than a decade passed before pacifist voices were clearly heard again. The Canadian Peace Congress was active in calling for nuclear disarmament, but its close affiliation with the Moscow-line Communists made most Canadians in the Cold War era suspicious of its aims. In the late 1950s, a new generation of pacifists, this one leaning more on humanitarian traditions than on the liberal Protestantism of the prewar generation, emerged. They made the dismantlement of nuclear weapons and the establishment of peaceful forums for settling international conflicts their focus. In 1960 the Quakers, a centuries-old pacifist religious sect, established a peace centre on Grindstone Island in Lake Rideau to do research and plan action. That year also witnessed the creation of Voice of Women, a peace and social justice activist group that would endure for many years, conducting highly visible publicity and civil-disobedience campaigns to press its views against war and for a more humane social order.

The foundations of 1960s political activism were thus laid as the decade opened. The new decade could hardly prove a time of less political activism than the 1950s. Political parties enrolled far fewer members than they had in the Depression years, and political life as a form of community involvement was a far less popular choice than participation in service clubs, church organizations, or unions. Prosperity seemed to obviate the need for political action for many Canadians.

• Conclusion:
Towards Consumer Culture

During the Christmas season one Depression year, an Eaton's saleswoman witnessed throngs of little girls admiring Shirley Temple dolls, which were priced at between nine and sixteen dollars, a month's income for a family on welfare.

> Some used to come at opening time and just stand there looking at those pink-cheeked, golden-haired lovely Shirley Temples. Little faces, they needed food. You could see a lot who needed a pint of milk a day a thousand times more than they needed a Shirley doll. They'd stare

for hours. We tried to shush them away, but it didn't do any good. . . . This, mind you, went on day after day, day after day, until some of the [sales] girls thought they would go crazy. One girl had a crying fit over just that, those hundreds of poor kids who would never own a Shirley Temple in a hundred years. They were lucky if they had breakfast that morning, or soup and bread that night.[20]

This moving account of frustrated and clearly gendered juvenile consumerism in the 1930s speaks volumes about how modern media and its creation of dreamy expectations touched most elements of society, including the poor. In the late 1920s, aided by credit purchasing, many ordinary Canadians began to acquire some of the dazzling array of goods that improved technologies made available. When their dreams were dashed by the economic crash, many were angry, but few gave up the hope that prosperity would be restored and a new consumer age would be unveiled. The war required further sacrifices, with rationed goods, but it had virtually eliminated unemployment, and many were earning incomes higher than they could ever have expected. With few goods to buy, they invested their money in Victory Bonds and bank accounts, ready to commence an orgy of spending once peace was declared.

Many of the hapless, ill-fed little girls who could only dream of owning a Shirley Temple doll in the 1930s became mothers of well-fed little girls in the 1950s for whom they could purchase Barbie dolls and an array of other goods. For them, the dream of consumerism was not a fraud, although as "the problem that has no name" invaded their beings, many were puzzled by their apparent unhappiness in a time of prosperity. With one family in four still in poverty, many women were spared such feelings. Some lived in community settings where friendships and activities compensated for poverty; most lived relatively isolated lives, trapped within a consumer culture that promoted a dazzling selection of products, all beyond their reach.

Optimists in 1960 claimed that another generation of economic growth on the scale of 1945–60 would wipe out poverty altogether and usher in an age of abundant leisure for all. But events would soon demonstrate that there were limits to growth. Indeed many of the assumptions of the postwar age of prosperity regarding personal and political morality, the value of consumer culture, and the relative needs of individuals and families for community and privacy would soon be challenged. Canada's blithe imitation of American styles, acceptance of American values and capital investments, unworrying to most in the first period of prosperity, would raise more criticism as a generation that had known neither Depression nor war began to demand centre stage.

• The Commodification
of Culture:
A Historiographical Debate

The transformation of everyday life in the twentieth century has been the subject of studies by scholars in several disciplines. Many questions have been raised: Did increased prosperity bring greater freedom of choice or simply more sophisticated manipulation of average people? Did suburbanization destroy an earlier sense of community or recreate it in a richer environment? Did the triumph of corporate capitalism result in the creation of a value system that encouraged status seeking, or was social and family life insulated from the values that dominated marketplace relations?

These are broad questions that go well beyond the history of a single nation such as Canada. Yet, as historian Paul-André Linteau suggests, in a study of Canadian suburbanization, historians have avoided making broad generalizations, concentrating instead on the "specificity" of individual cases.[21] Suburbanization in Canada, notes Linteau, has not been accompanied by the same degree of destruction of inner-city life as in the United States; nor has racism been as powerful a motive impelling white folk away from the urban core.

Linteau does accept that, on many dimensions, the notion of the "North American city" is applicable to Canada because the patterns of urban and suburban development have been similar in both countries. Political economist Harold Chorney goes further, claiming that in the modern period, there has been a decline in community in cities throughout North America and Europe. Everywhere, lured by a social ethic that emphasizes isolation and privacy in the design of neighbourhoods, transportation systems, and shopping areas, people have become less conscious of belonging to a definable geographical community.[22] Throughout this century, argues Chorney, conservative social planners have emphasized the need to reduce workers' collective solidarity in order to maintain social peace in the interests of the elites.

American historian Stuart Ewen, among others, has traced the growing privatization of life, and the focus on consumer satisfaction, to sophisticated attempts by industry to create markets for a range of products of varying degrees of utility. His history of American advertising demonstrates the extent to which, in an age of mass communication, social values can be shaped by sophisticated manipulators of human emotions.[23]

Feminist historian Dolores Hayden reminds us that alternative visions of community have contended with the developers' creation of the suburb, which generated privacy. In the United States, in particular, "proposals for community kitchens, laundries, dining halls, kitchenless houses and feminist cities"[24] enjoyed considerable support, especially among women, early in the century. For Hayden, the modern suburb as it evolved worked especially against the interests of women, stranding them in their houses as consumers of the goods the media told them they must accumulate in order to be good mothers and the envy of their anonymous neighbours.

The opposing argument to this "community-centred" literature suggests that the new consumer products of this century have lightened women's burden and, with the automobile, given them a mobility that earlier generations of women could never have imagined. The suburban housewife's participation in volunteer activities in a myriad of community groups is used as evidence against the notion that women who lived in the suburbs became atomized and unable to participate in the world beyond the front doors of their homes.[25] Above all, opponents of the pessimistic view of increased commodification of culture have insisted that the alternatives to a capitalism keyed to creating insatiable consumer demands were untenable. The older communities of the inner cities, where the street provided endless human contact and encouraged empathy and co-operation, were also cesspools of overcrowding and disease. The Communist alternative represented by the Soviet Union, in which most citizens lived in apartment buildings and had to share many facilities, was marked by individual powerlessness and minimal satisfaction of consumer demands. But if Chorney, Ewen, and Hayden are correct, there were once other alternatives to all of these models, and their defeat owed as much to the organized opposition of the powers-that-be as to their unpopularity with the masses.

•Notes

[1] National Archives of Canada, Mackenzie King Papers, Vol. 421, June 1947, pp. 382096–99.

[2] Archives of Ontario, George Drew Papers, Vol. 455, File 228-G, 29 July 1946.

[3] Pierre Berton, *The Comfortable Pew: A Critical Look at the Church in the New Age* (Toronto: McClelland and Stewart, 1965), 23.

[4] Quoted in Vera Fast, "The Labor Church in Winnipeg," in *Prairie Spirit: Perspectives on the Heritage of the United Church of Canada in the West*, ed. Dennis L. Butcher et al. (Winnipeg: University of Manitoba Press, 1985), 242.

[5] Harry A. Renfree, *Heritage and Horizon: The Baptist Story in Canada* (Mississauga: Canadian Baptist Federation, 1988), 251.

[6] Herbert Marshall, Frank A. Southard Jr., and Kenneth W. Taylor, *Canadian–American Industry: A Study in International Investment* (New York: Russel and Russel, 1936), 135.

[7] Mary Vipond, *The Mass Media in Canada* (Toronto: Lorimer, 1989), 131.

[8] Michiel Horn, ed., *The Dirty Thirties: Canadians in the Great Depression* (Toronto: Copp Clark Pitman, 1972), 14.

[9] Cited in Dominique Jean, "Family Allowances and Family Autonomy: Quebec Families Encounter the Welfare State, 1945–1955" in *Canadian Family History: Selected Readings*, ed. Bettina Bradbury (Toronto: Copp Clark Pitman, 1992), 429.

[10] Kenneth Coates, *Canada's Colonies: A History of the Yukon and Northwest Territories* (Toronto: Lorimer, 1985), 100.

[11] Gabrielle Roy, *The Tin Flute*, trans. Hannah Josephson (New York: Reynal and Hitchcock, 1947), 74–76.

[12] Health Study Bureau, Toronto, *Review of Canada's Health Needs and Health Insurance Proposals* (May 1946).

[13] Canada, Royal Commission on Medical Services, Brief Presented by Newfoundland Federation of Labour, Oct. 1961.

[14] Joy Parr, *The Gender of Breadwinners: Women, Men, and Change in Two Industrial Towns 1880–1960* (Toronto: University of Toronto Press, 1990), 186.

[15] National Archives of Canada, National Council of Women of Canada Papers, Volume 86, Helen Gregory MacGill, LLD, Vancouver B.C. to Mrs Edgar Hardy, 14 August 1944.

[16] Meg Luxton, *More Than a Labour of Love: Three Generations of Women's Work in the Home* (Toronto: Women's Press, 1980), 29.

[17] Kenneth McRoberts and Dale Posgate, *Quebec: Social Change and Political Crisis*, 2nd ed. (Toronto: McClelland and Stewart, 1980), 53.

[18] Cited in Alvin Finkel, *The Social Credit Phenomenon in Alberta* (Toronto: University of Toronto Press, 1989), 124.

[19] Cited in Harold Chorney, *City of Dreams: Social Theory and the Urban Experience* (Scarborough: Nelson Canada, 1990), 202.

[20] Cited in Veronica Strong-Boag, *The New Day Recalled: Lives of Girls and Women in English Canada, 1919–1939* (Toronto: Copp Clark Pitman, 1988), 13.

[21] Paul-André Linteau, "Canadian Suburbanization in a North American Context— Does the Border Make a Difference?" in *Cities and Urbanization: Canadian Historical Perspectives*, ed. Gilbert Stelter (Toronto: Copp Clark Pitman, 1990), 221. Studies that argue this case further are Michael A. Goldberg and John Mercer, *The Myth of the North American City: Continentalism Challenged* (Vancouver: University of British Columbia Press, 1986); and Caroline Andrew and Beth Moore Milroy, eds., *Life Spaces: Gender, Household, Employment* (Vancouver: University of British Columbia Press, 1988).

[22] Chorney, *City of Dreams*.

[23] Stuart Ewen, *Captains of Consciousness: Advertising and the Social Roots of the Consumer Culture* (New York: McGraw-Hill, 1976).

[24] Dolores Hayden, *The Grand Domestic Revolution: A History of Feminist Designs for American Homes, Neighborhoods, and Cities* (Cambridge, MA: MIT Press, 1981), 302.

[25] A relatively positive assessment of Canadian suburbia is S.D. Clark, *The Suburban Society* (Toronto: University of Toronto Press, 1968). A nuanced attempt to demonstrate contradictory trends within suburbia is Veronica Strong-Boag, "Home Dreams: Women and the Suburban Experiment in Canada, 1945–60," *Canadian Historical Review* 72, 4 (1991).

• Selected Reading

Immigration policies are analysed in Freda Hawkins, *Canada and Immigration: Public Policy and Public Concern* (Toronto: Institute of Public Administration of Canada, 1972). Among excellent works on immigrant experiences are Jean Burnet, ed., *Looking into My Sister's Eyes: An Exploration in Women's History* (Toronto: Multicultural History Society of Ontario, 1986); Helen Potrebenko, *No Streets of Gold: A Social History of Ukrainians in Alberta* (Vancouver: New Star, 1977); and Howard Palmer,

Patterns of Prejudice (Toronto: McClelland and Stewart, 1982). See also Bridglal Pachi, *Beneath the Clouds of the Promised Land: The Survival of Nova Scotia Blacks*, vol. 2, *1800–1989* (Halifax: Black Education Association, 1990). Frank H. Epp, *Mennonites in Canada, 1920–1940: A People's Struggle for Survival* (Toronto: Macmillan, 1982) deals with the history of this ethnic/religious group. Among other useful works on religious topics are G.A. Rawlyk, ed., *Canadian Baptists and Higher Education* (Montreal: McGill-Queen's University Press, 1988); John S. Moir, *Enduring Witness: A History of the Presbyterian Church in Canada* (Toronto: Presbyterian Church of Canada, 1987); N. Keith Clifford, *The Resistance to Church Union in Canada 1904–1939* (Vancouver: University of British Columbia Press, 1985); and W.E. Mann, *Sect, Cult and Church in Alberta*, rev. ed. (Toronto: University of Toronto Press, 1972). James Gray's *Booze: The Impact of Whiskey on the Prairies* (Toronto: New American Library, 1972) and Angus McLaren and Arlene Tigar McLaren, *The Bedroom and the State: The Changing Practices and Politics of Contraception and Abortion in Canada, 1890–1980* (Toronto: McClelland and Stewart, 1986) treat issues that caused endless difficulties for churches. Don Wetherell and Irene Kmet, *Useful Pleasures: The Shaping of Leisure in Alberta 1896–1945* (Regina: Canadian Plains Research Center, 1990) deals with the emergence of various forms of entertainment.

The co-operative movement in the Maritimes and broader struggles against under-development are the subject of Robert J. Brym and R. James Sacouman, *Underdevelopment and Social Movements in Atlantic Canada* (Toronto: New Hogtown, 1979). Acadians' struggles are dealt with in Richard Wilbur, *The Rise of French New Brunswick* (Halifax: Formac, 1989).

Quebec's social evolution is detailed in Paul-André Linteau, René Durocher, and Jean-Claude Robert, *Quebec Since 1930* (Toronto: Lorimer, 1983). On the evolution of Quebec ideologies, see Susan Mann Trofimenkoff, *Action Française: French-Canadian Nationalism in Quebec in the 1920s* (Toronto: University of Toronto Press, 1975) and Michael Behiels, *Prelude to Quebec's Quiet Revolution: Liberalism versus Neo-Nationalism 1945–1960* (Montreal: McGill-Queen's University Press, 1985). The position of French Canadians outside Quebec is described in the *Report of the Royal Commission on Dominion–Provincial Relations*, Books 1 and 2 (Ottawa: Queen's Printer, 1940).

On the media in Canada during this period, see Mary Vipond, *The Mass Media in Canada* (Toronto: Lorimer, 1989), Frank Peers, *The Public Eye: Television and the Politics of Canadian Broadcasting, 1952–1968* (Toronto: University of Toronto Press, 1979), and Paul Rutherford, *When Television Was Young: Primetime Canada 1952–1967* (Toronto: University of Toronto Press, 1990).

The Canadian North is analysed in Kenneth Coates, *Canada's Colonies: A History of the Yukon and Northwest Territories* (Toronto: Lorimer, 1985). Literature on the Native peoples from 1920 to 1960 is summarized in J.R. Miller, *Skyscrapers Hide the*

Heavens: A History of Indian–White Relations in Canada (Toronto: University of Toronto Press, 1989). On the Métis, see Murray Dobbin, *The One-and-a-Half Men: The Story of Jim Brady and Malcolm Norris, Métis Patriots of the Twentieth Century* (Vancouver: New Star, 1981).

The changes in women's lives are outlined by Alison Prentice, Paula Bourne, Gail Cuthbert Brandt, Beth Light, Wendy Mitchinson, and Naomi Black, *Canadian Women: A History* (Toronto: Harcourt Brace Jovanovich, 1988) and the Clio Collective, *Quebec Women: A History*, trans. Roger Gannon and Rosalind Gill (Toronto: Women's Press, 1987). The interwar period for women is studied in detail in Veronica Strong-Boag, *The New Day Recalled: Lives of Girls and Women in English Canada, 1919–1939* (Toronto: Copp Clark Pitman, 1988). Varying experiences of men and women in the work force are discussed in Joy Parr, *The Gender of Breadwinners: Women, Men, and Change in Two Industrial Towns 1880–1950* (Toronto: University of Toronto Press, 1990). See also Diane Dodd, "The Canadian Birth Control Movement on Trial, 1936–1937," *Histoire sociale/Social History* 16, 32 (Nov. 1983): 411–28.

Children's experiences in paid work and housework are described in Neil Sutherland, "'We Always Had Things to Do'": The Paid and Unpaid Work of Anglophone Children Between the 1920s and the 1960s," *Labour/Le Travail* 25 (Spring 1990): 105–41. Paul Axelrod's *Scholars and Dollars: Politics, Economics, and the Universities of Ontario 1945–1980* (Toronto: University of Toronto Press, 1982) describes the climate in which first secondary and then postsecondary education expanded. His *Making a Middle Class: Student Life in English Canada During the Thirties* (Montreal: McGill-Queen's University Press, 1990) examines the content of university education in the 1930s.

Canadian suburbanization is addressed in Paul-André Linteau, "Canadian Suburbanization in a North American Context: Does the Border Make A Difference?" in *Cities and Urbanization: Canadian Historical Perspectives*, ed. Gilbert A. Stelter (Toronto: Copp Clark Pitman, 1990), 208–24; and Veronica Strong-Boag, "Home Dreams: Women and the Suburban Experiment in Canada, 1945–60," *Canadian Historical Review* 72, 4 (Dec. 1991): 471–504.

PART IV

Canada in the Global Village

Time Line

1957–63	– Progressive Conservative government under John Diefenbaker
1958	– European Common Market begins operation
1960	– Contraceptive pill first introduced; Lesage Liberals win Quebec election
1961	– New Democratic Party created
1962	– Canada launches Alouette I; medicare implemented in Saskatchewan; liberalization of Immigration Act
1963	– Major powers sign a nuclear test ban treaty; nuclear warheads for Canada debated in federal election
1963–68	– Lester Pearson leads a Liberal government in Ottawa
1965	– Lester Pearson criticizes American policy in Vietnam; Canada and Quebec Pension plans established; Canada's new flag proclaimed; Auto Pact signed
1966	– Canada Assistance Plan established
1967	– Centennial celebrations; Expo '67 in Montreal; Canada's Immigration Act liberalized
1968	– Parti Québécois formed; formation of National Indian Brotherhood; national medicare implemented
1968–79	– Pierre Elliott Trudeau serves as prime minister
1969	– Official Languages Act; reform of Criminal Code relating to homosexuality, abortion, and birth control; White Paper on Indian policy released
1970	– Report of the Royal Commission on the Status of Women; October crisis; War Measures Act proclaimed
1971	– Canada Development Corporation established
1972	– United Nations Conference on the Human Environment; National Action Committee on the Status of Women created
1973	– OPEC oil embargo sparks an "energy crisis"
1974	– Foreign Investment Review Agency created
1975	– Creation of Petro-Canada; Alberta Heritage Trust Fund created; James Bay Native land settlement signed

1976	–	Parti Québécois forms Quebec government
1977	–	Established Programs Funding replaces block funding for medicare and postsecondary institutions; Berger report on Mackenzie Valley Pipeline released
1979–80	–	Joe Clark heads federal government
1980	–	Announcement of National Energy Program; Quebec referendum rejects sovereignty association
1980–84	–	Pierre Trudeau serves as prime minister
1981–82	–	Major global recession
1982	–	Constitution Act proclaimed
1984	–	John Turner is prime minister from June to September; Brian Mulroney's Conservatives win federal election; Bhopal disaster
1985	–	Alberta Microchip Centre established; Macdonald Commission report
1986	–	Chernobyl disaster
1987	–	Meech Lake accord approved unanimously by premiers; Reform Party created
1988	–	Free trade agreement between Canada and the United States; Conservatives win a parliamentary majority in election on free trade
1989	–	United States–Canada Free Trade Agreement comes into effect; Ottawa establishes Canadian space agency; Audrey McLaughlin becomes first woman to lead federal political party
1990	–	Meech Lake accord dies; Campeau–Belanger commission created in Quebec; federal government sets up Citizens' Forum on Canada; major recession begins in Canada
1992	–	North American Free Trade Agreement signed; Charlottetown Accord defeated in referendum
1993	–	Brian Mulroney resigns as prime minister

THE POSTINDUSTRIAL ECONOMY

At 1:48 Saturday morning, 24 December 1988, the legislation authorizing a comprehensive free trade agreement between Canada and the United States passed in the House of Commons by a vote of 141–111. The debate had begun on 15 December following a bitter November election in which the free trade agreement had been the central issue. Exhausted by the long days of weary debate and the months of wrangling, members of parliament had little energy left to cheer or protest the final result. Even the on-lookers in the gallery were silent. By invoking closure four times during the stormy session, the Mulroney government had ensured that the legislation would pass before the ratification deadline of 1 January 1989. With fewer than half of the 104 senators in the chamber on Friday 30 December, the free trade bill easily passed the Upper House. Governor-General Jeanne Sauvé was in Quebec City, but Supreme Court Justice Antonio Lamer was on hand to give royal assent to the legislation. On 1 January 1989, Canada and the United States became partners in an agreement that would eliminate tariffs on primary and manufactured goods over a ten-year period and ensure free trade in services. Most non-tariff barriers to trade, such as quotas and content regulations, were also slated for elimination.

As we have seen, the pros and cons of free trade with the United States have been debated by Canadians since Confederation, and indeed by British North Americans earlier than 1867. Free trade with the United States dominated the federal election of 1911, but most Canadians rejected the idea at that time and, for most of the twentieth century, had clung to a nationally defined trade policy. What prompted Canada's political leaders to support such a drastic shift in economic policy in 1988?

By the 1980s, the expressions "postmodern," "postindustrial," "global village," and "information society" had become part of the Canadian vocabulary. Such terms reflected the belief that the world had entered a new stage of productivity, interdependence, and social evolution that demanded dramatic new departures. While a host of "futurologists" had spun fantastic visions of how the world would be reshaped, a common focus was the impact that technology, and in particular communications technology, was exerting on human behaviour. Television monitors, satellites, and computers were the harbingers of the Information Age, and one of its most widely quoted philosophers was a Canadian, Marshall McLuhan, founder of the Centre for Culture and Technology at the University of Toronto. It was McLuhan's contention, and that of Harold Innis, upon whose work McLuhan drew heavily, that communications technologies defined the shape and scope of institutions and values, or, in McLuhan's words, that the "medium is the message." For Canadians who experienced the technological revolutions characteristic of the Information Age, the message was abundantly clear: the only certainty was change.

Marshall McLuhan, 1966 (Juster, *Montreal Star*/National Archives of Canada/ PA-133299)

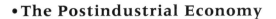

• The Postindustrial Economy

The term *postindustrial* is misleading because Canada remained an industrial nation in the Information Age. In absolute terms, output in primary and secondary industries actually increased in the period between 1960 and 1990. Nevertheless, service industries grew more rapidly. Pundits in the 1960s who trumpeted the arrival of the postindustrial age assumed that the problems of production had been solved and that the only challenge facing industrial nations was to ensure the fairer distribution of wealth while maintaining high levels of economic growth. Such complacency soon disappeared. A new level of economic development characterized by global communications networks, multinational corporations, and international market arrangements resulted in a dramatic restructuring of the industrial order. Ultimately, industrial growth as an end in itself became the source of growing criticism, especially as environmental destruction began to threaten the survival of the planet. By the last decade of the twentieth century, many Canadians had come to accept that there were limits to growth, to the planning capacity of the great multinational corporations that dominated their economy, and to what their governments could do to shelter them from the winds of change sweeping across the economic landscape.

Table 11.1: GDP, REAL GDP, AND REAL GDP PER CAPITA, 1960–90

Year	GDP*	Real GDP*	Real GDP per capita
1960	$ 39 448	$164 126	$ 9 184
1970	89 116	271 372	12 742
1980	309 891	424 537	17 658
1990	667 843	563 060	21 159

*Millions of dollars

Source: Statistics Canada #11-210 (1992).

Table 11.2: SECTORAL DISTRIBUTION OF GDP, 1960–90

Year	Primary	Secondary	Tertiary	Other
1960	12.3	28.7	46.9	12.1
1970	11.1	27.7	50.5	10.7
1980	7.8	26.7	54.7	10.8
1990	7.0	24.4	58.8	9.8

Source: Statistics Canada #11-210 (1992).

Technology and Communications

The Information Age is a child of technological innovation. At no time in human history have people been required to respond to such a barrage of new products and processes. Since 1960, computers, lasers, fibre optics, super-conductivity, genetic engineering, and nuclear science, among other notable developments, have contributed to quantum leaps in productivity and subjected people to revolutionary changes. As new commodities, new production techniques, and new social values burst on the scene, products and approaches considered crucial to the Industrial Age were regularly threatened with obsolescence. Constant adaptation became necessary for economic survival. Since information was the key to diffusing and controlling technological innovation, communications technology—which is itself subject to breathtaking innovation—determined the pace and direction of the postindustrial economy.

Until the end of the nineteenth century, communications were earthbound, requiring copper wire and poles, or underwater cables to transmit signals. Most information was conveyed in print form by stagecoach, train, and steamship. The appearance of the wireless telegraph in 1895, shortwave radio and telephotography (later known as television) in the 1920s, and high-frequency microwave radio in 1946 brought instantaneous global communications closer to reality. With the development of satellite and space communications in the late 1950s and 1960s, signals could be transmitted around the world in a split second. Computers were linked to telecommunications systems in the early 1970s, permitting vast quantities of information to be sent over telecommunication networks. Marshall McLuhan's much talked about "global village" had become a reality, or so it seemed.

Canadians have been closely associated with new developments in communications for at least two reasons. First, because of Canada's tremendous size, improvements in communications have been important in welding the nation together. Governments, recognizing this fact, have usually worked in partnership with private enterprise to develop better communication networks. Second, because of its economic relationship with Britain and the United States, Canada has had easy access to technological innovations that moved the Industrial Revolution forward. Telegraph, telephone, and radio networks appeared in Canada as soon as the inventions on which they were based became practical. It is therefore not surprising that Canadians were among the first people in the world to experiment with the communication technologies that defined the Information Age. In 1958 Canada's television network, stretching from Victoria to Sydney, was the longest in the world. Canada also established cable-television systems more quickly than other nations. When Alouette I was launched on 29 September 1962, Canada became the third nation in space after the Soviet Union and the United States. With its Anik (the Inuit word for "brother") series launched in the 1970s, Canada led the world in the use of satellites for commercial communications. It was also the first nation to establish a digital data network for computer users and pioneered, unsuccessfully as it turned out, in the development of a videotext terminal (TELIDON) designed for computer communications.

At the heart of these revolutionary advances was the computer, essentially a collection of switches that are turned on and off as directed by a program. Originally conceived as an instrument for processing—that is, *computing*—mathematical data, computers soon developed "memories" that enabled them to store information and perform complicated tasks. Virtually every human activity has been altered in some way by computer technology. For this reason, the computer, like the steam engine, electricity, and the internal combustion engine, is considered a *transforming* technology, which cuts a swath across all sectors of the economy leaving massive political and social upheaval in its wake. Computer technology helped to send people to the moon, revolutionized the office, and automated manufacturing processes. By the end of the twentieth century, computers were the centre of an intricate global technology that produced goods and services, influenced the government of nations, and shaped the information people received about the world in which they lived.

The initial research on computers was conducted in Britain and the United States. British scientists sequestered at Bletchley Park used primitive computers to crack German codes during the Second World War. Soon after the war, the Americans began using computers to increase the accuracy of new guns and missiles. Canada's first entry into the computer age was UTEC, developed by scientists at the University of Toronto between 1947 and 1951. A massive structure that filled a whole room, UTEC was powered by electric tubes, quickly over-heated, and experienced more down time than computing time. In 1952, the University of Toronto purchased a British-made computer.

Had innovation stopped with the first generation of computers, the computer revolution would have been stillborn, but the invention of the transistor in 1949 transformed the whole field of electronics. The replacement of vacuum tubes with solid state transistors—ultimately made of chips of silicon sand—allowed computers to become smaller, more reliable, and less expensive to build and operate. Integrated circuitry, developed in 1958, lead to further miniaturization. By 1968 a single silicon chip could hold 256 bits of random access memory (RAM), more than the first generation of computers could cram into a large room. Within another decade, Apple, a microcomputer company based in California, was selling desktop computers to the technology-fixated consumer. By the 1990s, portable computers the size of notebooks enabled people to take the machines with them wherever they went.

Once the commercial potential of the computer was realized, IBM and other big multinational corporations soon dominated the field. A Canadian-based corporation, Northern Electric (later renamed Northern Telecom), eventually carved a niche for itself by producing telephone equipment and switching devices for a global telecommunications market. With a varied production line, sales exceeding $6 billion, and over 46 000 employees in 1986, Northern Telecom had emerged as one of Canada's largest corporations. Other companies produced office automation equipment, digital flight simulators, and the Canadarm, a remote manipulator system used on the American space shuttle. Despite such accomplishments,

Canadarm   (photo courtesy of the National Aeronautics and Space Administration)

the Canadian trade deficit in electronic goods rose from $850 million in 1973 to nearly $6 billion in 1986. Office machines and computers accounted for the bulk of the imports. The vast quantities of capital invested by the United States and Japan in computer technology made it difficult for nations such as Canada to compete successfully in the latest race for economic supremacy.

In the Information Age, even more than in the Industrial Age, technological innovation was the key to economic growth. Recognizing this fact, federal and provincial governments were generous in their assistance to Canadian-based companies attempting to break into the electronics industry or to integrate computer technology into their operations. Support from the federal government was instrumental to most Canadian initiatives in telecommunications. In 1989 Ottawa decided that Canada should have its own space agency and chose Montreal as the site for the venture. The Ontario government established the Ontario Centre for Microelectronics in Ottawa to provide technical assistance and information on computers for industrial uses. Similar government-sponsored centres were located in the Ontario communities of Cambridge and Peterborough to specialize respectively in CAD/CAM (computer-aided design and computer-aided manufacturing) and robotics. In 1983 the Natural Sciences and Engineering Research Council (formerly the National Research Council) initiated a multimillion dollar program to assist universities to explore microchip design and testing. Following a recommendation from the Science Council of Canada, the Alberta Microchip Centre was established in 1985 to give Canada its own microchip manufacturing facility. By the 1990s, Canadians had become accustomed to computerized machines dispensing money from their banks and robots assembling their cars. Who could tell what complicated task the next generation of "smart" computers might perform?

Economic Change in the Global Village

Information Age technology did not develop in a vacuum. It was launched in an economic and political context that shaped the ways innovations were developed and used. By 1960 the Industrial Revolution had triumphed on a global scale. Private capitalism in North America and Western Europe, and state socialism in the Soviet Union and its allied nations, had brought a startling degree of uniformity to the goals and values of the industrialized world. Officially at least, production and consumption of goods and services had become the chief index of human happiness. The planning capacity of large corporations and interventionist governments was a fact of life. Although most consumers rarely bothered to think about it when they bought goods and services, they had become the social creations of the planners. Planners in the recesses of the civil service and corporate sector made most of the decisions about how capital would be spent to satisfy requirements for housing, food, clothing, transportation, education, defence, and leisure. These planners also determined when and how such new products as the transistor radio, the birth control pill, or the computer would be unleashed on the unsuspecting consumer.

While global in its reach, the Industrial Revolution had created a world that was sharply divided on the basis of wealth. In the immediate postwar period, the United States contained only 6 percent of the world's population but consumed over one-third of its goods and services. The economies of Western European nations quickly recovered from wartime devastation and by the 1960s were recording higher rates of growth than Canada and the United States. From their bases in Europe and North America, multinational corporations spread their tentacles around the world buying up cheap resources and selling their products. As "Coca-colonization" became a byword for the economic power wielded by Western corporate capitalism, critics began to ask why orthodox economic theories only seemed to work for industrialized nations. The terms they used embodied a critique of the hierarchy of wealth that characterized the world in the twentieth century. In development studies terminology, the "First World" included capitalist countries of North America and Europe; the "Second World" consisted of the Soviet Union and its European satellites (a universe whose rapid demise from 1989 to 1991 was unforeseeable even a few years before it occurred); while the "Third World" was made up of developing nations in Africa, Asia, and Latin America.

This tri-part economic universe was challenged by the emergence of Japan as an aggressive competitor in the global marketplace. Rising from the ashes of the Second World War, Japan built an extremely efficient industrial sector. The products of Japanese factories were often both cheaper and of better quality than those produced in North America and Europe. Nor did the Japanese remain content with the textiles and small consumer items that they had produced in the immediate postwar period. By the 1970s Japanese radios, televisions, stereo equipment, appliances, computers, and cars were putting North American factories out of business. With huge markets in India, China, and other Asian nations at its doorstep, Japan was poised to become the world's economic leader in the Information Age.

In the wake of the Japanese achievement, Hong Kong, South Korea, Taiwan, and Singapore burst on the scene as industrial nations. Known as the "Four Tigers," these new players in the race for development had risen to prominence, as had Japan, with the help of governments eager to dispense with the image associated with Third World poverty. By the 1980s Japan had surpassed the United States in industrial output, and Japanese banks dominated the world's capital markets. The Four Tigers continued to register impressive rates of economic growth, while Western economies floundered. What at first was whispered only in boardrooms soon rated banner headlines: the focus of the global economy had shifted to the Pacific Rim. Not since the sixteenth century when the economic centre of gravity moved from the Mediterranean to the North Atlantic had such a dramatic geopolitical revolution occurred.

Western nations were astounded by these developments and eager to correct whatever was wrong with their ailing economies. If they could discover the key to Japan's phenomenal success, perhaps they could imitate it to useful effect. A newer industrial base, closer labour–management relations, better planning mechanisms, higher levels of saving, lower military budgets, a smaller public sector, a more competitive educational system— any or all of these factors were put forward to explain Japan's economic edge. Perhaps the Japanese dedication to production was the answer. In North America, corporate managers seemed to be more preoccupied with mergers than with building a better mousetrap. Japanese companies grew to greatness, the argument went, while North American dinosaurs just grew.

The vocabulary of global relations gradually changed to reflect the new economic order. Instead of first, second, and third world, people talked about the disparity between the developed nations, most of them in the northern hemisphere, and the underdeveloped nations of the southern hemisphere. The North–South Institute, a non-profit organization, was established in Ottawa in 1976 to conduct research on Canada's relations with developing countries.

The rise of the Pacific Rim was only one of several shocks experienced by the industrial nations of North America and Europe in the postindustrial age. In 1973, the Oil and Petroleum Exporting Countries (OPEC), dominated by Arab nations angered by Western support of Israel in the Yom Kippur War, declared an embargo on oil exports. The embargo had a devastating impact on industrial nations, which depended upon massive imports of cheap Middle Eastern oil to fuel their economies. Although the embargo was eventually lifted, the price of oil had risen fourfold—from $3 to nearly $12 a barrel—between 1973 and 1975. With both inflation and unemployment rising sharply, "stagflation" became a troublesome new preoccupation of economic planners. How could the unemployment problem be tackled without creating even more inflation and vice versa? When the

Ayatollah Khomeini seized power in Iran in 1979 the price of oil soared again, this time to over $30 a barrel. "Keynesian" economic policies crumbled in the face of such "unplanned" developments.

The Canadian version of Keynes, as shaped by the Bank of Canada and the federal Department of Finance, had focussed narrowly on expanding the money supply and undertaking major public works projects when the economy was in recession. Keynes's belief that such policies would not succeed unless there was significant and permanent government involvement in the economy was ignored by most Canadians, with the exception— for a brief time—of Pierre Trudeau. Having imposed wage and price controls in October 1975, the prime minister suggested that the market economy had to give way to tripartite state–business–labour planning. Business denounced this perspective, and labour accused Trudeau, who had campaigned against controls a year earlier, of ignoring the reality that such policies were mainly effective in limiting wage, not price, increases.

Trudeau's economic policies proved contradictory. Government spending increased dramatically in accordance with Keynesian prescriptions for a stagnating economy but, beginning in 1975, the money supply was severely restricted. Tight money policies were also implemented by the United States and most governments in Europe in an effort to control inflation. The alternative means of reducing inflation was to impose stricter controls over market forces, but ardent free enterprisers, following the lead of British Prime Minister Margaret Thatcher, refused to consider such a possibility. Interest rates climbed and unemployment lines grew longer. By 1981 the global economy was descending into the worst economic slump since the Depression of the 1930s.

The Environmental Challenge

The economic woes of the 1980s were compounded by environmental issues of daunting proportions. Polluted air, undrinkable water, and scorched landscapes had been associated with factory production since the early days of the Industrial Revolution. While inconvenient and even hazardous to those who were forced to live and work in heavily industrialized areas, there had been little concern for the long-term consequences of industrial pollutants. The age of innocence came to an abrupt end in 1962 when American scientist Rachel Carson published *Silent Spring*. In her highly publicized book, Carson provided stunning revelations about the dangers posed by the "tide of chemicals born of the Industrial Age." Rivers and oceans, the air and soil, animal and human species, she argued, were being rapidly destroyed. Lest Canadians should consider their pristine environment immune from such dangers, she singled out the "Rivers of Death" created in New Brunswick and other forested areas of Canada where aerial pesticide spray programs begun in the 1950s were more effective in killing fish than their intended target, the spruce budworm. "We stand now where two roads diverge," Carson concluded. "The road we have long been travelling is deceptively easy, a smooth superhighway on which we progress with great speed, but at its end lies disaster. The other fork of the road offers our last, our only chance to reach a destination that assures the preservation of our earth."[1]

As the environmental movement gained momentum, public and private institutions began to alter their behaviour. The Soviet Union, Britain, and the United States signed an agreement to ban atmospheric testing of

Disposal of toxic waste is a major problem facing the industrialized world.   (© J. Perez, Greenpeace)

nuclear weapons in 1963, and industries built higher smokestacks to diffuse their polluting emissions. Consumers contributed to the environmental cause by avoiding the use of chemical-laden detergents, foods laced with pesticides, and leaded gasoline. Despite such well-meaning efforts, the environmental problem would not go away. Scientists discovered that polychlorinated biphenyls (PCBs), a family of highly toxic chemicals used in electrical equipment, continued to poison the food chain after their use had been discontinued. No one knew how to dispose of the hazardous wastes from nuclear power plants. Even the emissions released into the atmosphere by tall smokestacks came back to earth hundreds of kilometres away as acid rain and snow. In Europe and North America, lakes were literally dying from such long-range transmissions. The oceans too offered evidence of irresponsible use. By the 1990s, North Atlantic cod fish stocks had been exploited to the brink of extinction while people continued to use oceans and lakes as garbage dumps for untreated human and industrial waste.

A United Nations Conference on the Human Environment met in Stockholm in 1972 to discuss the decaying state of the planet. Chaired by a Canadian, Maurice Strong, the conference produced a declaration of environmental rights and established a program to fund and co-ordinate investigations into environmental problems. In the same year, *Limits to Growth*, a study sponsored by the Volkswagen Foundation, and commissioned by the Club of Rome, an independent "think tank" inspired by Italian industrialist Dr Aurelio Peccei, was published. *Limits to Growth* reported the findings of scientists at the Massachusetts Institute of Technology who used sophisticated computer modelling techniques to investigate the "predicament of mankind." They maintained that accelerated industrialization, rapid population growth, increased agricultural consumption, depletion of renewable resources, and environmental deterioration threatened the very future of civilization. If the planet were to continue to support life, the report concluded, a "sustainable state of global equilibrium" must become an urgent priority. A similar message was conveyed by E.F. Schumacher, a German-born economist and progressive thinker, whose book *Small Is Beautiful* (subtitled *The Study of Economics as if People Mattered*) became an instant bestseller when it was published in 1973. Canadian scientist David Suzuki helped to focus public attention on environmental issues through his CBC television series "The Nature of Things."

In the early 1970s, environmental problems still seemed manageable. This illusion was shattered as disasters at Three Mile Island (1979), Bhopal (1984), and Chernobyl (1986) underscored the difficulty of controlling technology. While governments dithered over how best to manage the environment, the list of problems grew alarmingly. The destruction of the ozone layer by chlorofluorocarbons (CFCs), used in aerosols, foam insulation, and super cleaners for electronic equipment, was altering the world's climate and exposing the earth to the unfiltered ultraviolet rays of the sun. The rapid disappearance of tropical rain forests caused further deterioration of the atmosphere. Meanwhile, the superpowers continued to stockpile nuclear weapons, each one capable of wreaking irreparable environmental damage. Seemingly devoid of any sense of social responsibility, France even persisted in testing nuclear weapons in the atmosphere. With both the greenhouse effect and nuclear winter threatening the future of the planet, the limits of technology and of the people who planned it were plain for all to see.

The New Mercantilism

Corporate capitalism in the First World proved remarkably adaptable to the challenges posed in the postindustrial age. In the 1970s, giant corporations, their well-being threatened by the energy crisis and the environmental movement, began moving their production facilities to off-shore locations around the world. Developing countries, desperate for capital investment, offered cheap labour, lower taxes, and fewer corporate and environmental regulations to eat into profits. By transferring assets instantaneously around the world to suit their own purposes, these "transnational" corporations could defy attempts by any one government to control their activities. It was not long before corporate managers could also extract favourable conditions from governments of Western nations anxious to prevent jobs from being exported to other countries.

In the face of these developments, political leaders in the West suddenly seemed incapable of managing their own economies or of maintaining a safe and stable international economic order. One response to this crisis of confidence was the creation of regional trading organizations to secure elusive markets and to balance the growing power of multinational corporations. In 1958, West Germany, Italy, France, Belgium, Luxembourg, and the Netherlands formed the European Economic Community (EEC). Great Britain, Denmark, Ireland, Greece, Spain, and Portugal eventually joined the Common Market too. Canada and the United States signed a Free Trade Agreement in 1989. Three years later, the North American Free Trade Agreement (NAFTA) planned to extend the scope of the North American trading bloc to include Mexico. Both the EEC and individual nations like Japan maintained a variety of tariff and non-tariff barriers designed to protect them from cheap imports. Efforts to eliminate trade restrictions under the General Agreement on Tariffs and Trade (GATT) were hopelessly complicated by these developments. For those who knew their history, the return to closed economic systems seemed like a "new mercantilism," in which economic empires struggled for supremacy. Those who followed the logic of Information Age developments argued that regional alliances were only temporary shelters from the rigorous discipline of the global economy.

By the 1990s, it was becoming increasingly clear that transnational corporations had more power than most nation-states. When the recession descended in 1981, corporations began a massive program of "restructuring" for a leaner and meaner global economy. By automating production processes, reducing the number of workers, and offering a more flexible response to changing market conditions, it was argued, the fittest would survive and triumph. A wave of mergers and takeovers followed, which further concentrated economic power. In Canada, thirty-two wealthy families and nine giant conglomerates controlled over one-third of the country's non-financial assets by 1986. Not only goods-producing industries were involved in merger mania. Global communications companies such as Bertelsmann, Maxwell, News Corp, Time-Warner, and Thomson emerged as giant media conglomerates whose power over the production of ideas was equivalent to the oligarchic control that corporations held in primary and secondary industries. Critics began to wonder about the impact of such concentration in media services. With the world plugged into a global communications network, could a few companies actually control people's minds as well as their material well-being?

In the new climate of corporate concentration and "downsizing," the views of American economist Milton Friedman gained ascendancy among leaders in North America and Europe. According to Friedman and his followers (sometimes called *monetarists* because of their emphasis on monetary policy), government intervention—deficit financing, tax incentives, and the expansion of the money supply—had led to rigidities and inefficiencies in Western economies. The solution was to encourage efficient production, to improve the *supply* of goods and services rather than stimulate *demand* through government spending. If governments simply reduced taxes, controlled inflation, and let the private sector adjust to changing economic conditions, the global economy would right itself soon enough. By the 1980s, Keynesian "demand side" economic theories, eloquently argued by Canadian-born economist John Kenneth Galbraith, were being eclipsed by the tough-minded "supply side" arguments of the Friedman-inspired monetarists.

Supply side economics inspired the policies of Conservative governments in Britain under Margaret Thatcher (1979–90), in the United States under Ronald Reagan (1980–88), and in Canada under Brian Mulroney (1984–93). Although their economies were experiencing the worst dislocation since the 1930s, these leaders attempted to reduce spending on social programs, privatize government activities, cut back the civil service, and exercise tighter control over money supply. In Canada, a Goods and Services Tax was introduced in 1990, continuing the shift in the tax burden to the consumer. Such policies were expected to stimulate the private sector, but they failed to produce the desired results. Instead, the deficit continued to rise ominously, and unemployment levels remained high. Environmental programs were put on the back burner, and the gap between rich and poor yawned ever larger. Meanwhile, austerity programs pursued by industrialized nations and transnational corporations had a negative impact on developing countries whose growing debt load (estimated at $1.3 trillion in 1989) threatened not only to engulf their own economies but to destroy the financial structure of developed nations.

When a new global recession began in mid-1990, it suggested that the politics of austerity was not restoring the mythical market equilibrium promised by the monetarists. Opponents of the "new right" warned that the prescriptions of Friedman and his followers would leave capitalist economies vulnerable to uncontrolled cycles, as they had been before

Cartoonist's view of Brian Mulroney turning his attention from the constitution to the economy   (Gable, *The Globe and Mail*)

TAXATION AND THE DEFICIT

In arguing for cuts to social programs, the federal Conservatives claimed that increased social spending had caused the deficit to spiral out of control under Pierre Trudeau's Liberal government in the mid-1970s. Such arguments were contradicted by Statistics Canada studies. In June 1991, the federal government agency reported that debt payments rose from 10 percent of federal revenues in 1975 to about one-third in 1990. The agency concluded, "It was not the explosive growth in program spending that caused the increase in deficits after 1975, but a drop in federal revenues . . . and rising debt charges. . . . This partly reflects tax reform which shifted the tax burden from corporations to persons, and from income taxes to consumption taxes."[2] An embarrassed federal government forced Statistics Canada to retract its suggestion that federal taxation and interest-rate policies had produced the increased deficit, but the statistical evidence could not be as easily obscured.

1939, and create the potential for another global depression. Unfortunately, the Great Depression was a fading memory, and whatever lessons it taught an earlier generation seemed to have been forgotten.

The capitulation in the early 1990s of the Soviet Union (and its successor states) and Eastern Europe to "free-enterprise" economics was presented as further evidence that there was no alternative to the Thatcher–Reagan model. As they abandoned a corrupt and inefficient system of centralized economic control, these countries appeared unable to conceive of a more democratic model of socialism. In the climate of neo-conservatism, Canada's social welfare system came under increasing attack, and advocates of full employment policies—such as those pursued in Japan, Austria, Sweden, and Norway—were largely ignored.

•Canada's New Age Economy

Canada's small and open economy was subject to all the winds of change in the postindustrial age. At this close vantage point, three trends seem particularly noteworthy. First, like most industrial nations, Canada in the second half of the twentieth century moved increasingly toward a service economy. Second, Canada's economic links with the United States were extended and strengthened, culminating in the free trade agreement. Third, the less privileged more than ever questioned the legitimacy of the uneven distribution of wealth and power in Canada, and tensions related to region, ethnicity, class, and even age heightened.

The Service Economy

In the postindustrial age, seven out of ten Canadians in the labour force were employed in providing services rather than producing goods. The tremendous increase in productivity in primary and secondary industries made such an occupational shift possible. By 1990 twice as many people worked in government as in agriculture, and more people were employed in the food service and accommodation industry than in mining and forestry put together. Because of the expansion of services, economists began to talk about "goods-producing" and "service-producing" sectors of the economy, grouping primary and secondary industries into one category. At the same time, classifications in the service sector—transportation, communications, retail and wholesale trade, finance, real estate, education, health and welfare, recreation, personal services, food, and accommodation—became central to understanding the Canadian economy.

One of the most obvious features of Canada's service economy was the growth of government spending. While the provinces struggled to cope with the demand for more and better schools, hospitals, homes, and highways, Ottawa expanded its involvement in transportation and communications and assumed more responsibility for social security. A Canada–Quebec pension plan and medical care system were added to the roster of welfare programs in the 1960s. The maintenance of a peacetime defence establishment added significantly to federal responsibilities. Finally, governments at all levels expanded their bureaucracies to manage the many services they provided. By the 1980s nearly one in five employed Canadians worked directly for the state or in Crown corporations. Ottawa and the provincial capitals grew in power and population. Although governments produced a wide range of primary and secondary goods, most of their expenditures fuelled the service sector of the Canadian economy.

Government spending had inched slowly upward during the Industrial Age, accounting for 5 percent of the GNP in 1867 and 30 percent in 1960. After 1960, government spending exploded, reaching an astounding 48.2 percent of the GNP by 1985. Nearly half of government expenditure was on goods and services; the rest involved transfer payments, which moved private income from one group of citizens to another (including family allowances, old age pensions, veterans' allowances, medical care, regional development programs, and incentives to business). The balance of government spending also shifted in this period. Between 1960 and

1980, the federal share of GNP rose only slightly—from 14 to 16 percent—while the proportion spent by provincial and municipal governments nearly doubled—from 16 to 30 percent of the GNP—as their responsibilities grew rapidly.

The trend toward urban concentration, typical of the Industrial Age, was consolidated by the service economy. While goods-producing industries were often located near resources, most tertiary industries required a large pool of nearby clients for their services. The West Edmonton Mall, for example, would have had great difficulty generating business in Tuktoyaktuk. Nevertheless, the trend to urbanization began to slow down in the 1970s as people moved away from congested city cores and monotonous suburbs to rural "exurbia." Commuting to work in the cities from exurban homes became a way of life for an increasing number of Canadians. In order to improve their tax bases, many city councils expanded their boundaries into exurbia, becoming vast, sprawling administrative units. Metropolitan growth increased the size and power of Canada's major cities, making Canada little more than a cluster of city states and their economic hinterlands. With the introduction of home computer networks, experts predicted that there would be a wider dispersal of services and population, but in the meantime Canadian cities and their environs continued to be the preferred places to live and work. Three out of four Canadians were classified as urban dwellers in 1971, a figure that remained constant over the ensuing two decades.

While service industries grew in output and employment in the post-industrial age, goods-producing industries remained the backbone of Canada's export economy. Primary resources—crude oil, natural gas, pulpwood, wheat, fish, and other foodstuffs—continued to flow out of the country, mostly to the United States, which absorbed over three-quarters of Canada's exports. Uneasy about their position as "hewers of wood and drawers of water" for their southern neighbours, Canadians in the 1960s began to consider ways of keeping more of the "value added" work in their own country. In 1965, the Liberal government under Lester Pearson signed an agreement with the United States whereby automobiles and automotive parts could cross the border free of tariff duty. Designed as a means of rationalizing the branch-plant operations of the big three North American automotive producers, the Canada–United States Automotive Products Agreement (commonly known as the Auto Pact) provided safeguards for Canadian-based automotive manufacturing. By the 1980s, over one-quarter of the nation's merchandise exports consisted of motor vehicles and parts. Despite this triumph, Canadians continued to import far more manufactured goods than they exported, making manufactured goods the single most important item in Canada's foreign trade deficit.

For most of the period between 1960 and 1990, Canadians ran a surplus on what is called the "merchandise trade account" by exporting sufficient primary products to more than balance the manufactured goods imported. In contrast, Canadians ran a deficit on the "service account." The two most important items on the service account were business services and travel. When branches of such widely patronized multinational corporations as Century 21, McDonald's, and Midas Muffler remitted funds to head office to cover the costs of administration, advertising, product development, and research, they contributed to Canada's service account deficit. The deficit was further increased by travel abroad, Canadians typically spending more money outside the country than foreign visitors spent in Canada. Canada's status as a debtor nation, along with continued high levels of outside ownership, meant that foreigners siphoned off substantial interest and dividend payments. These payments reached a staggering $23.9 billion by 1986, contrasting unfavourably with the $7.1 billion Canadians received from their investments abroad.

The growth of the service sector was one of the major factors contributing to the influx of women into the paid labour force. Prior to the Industrial Revolution, women performed many of the services essential to survival. As services moved from the domestic sphere into the market economy, women moved with them. Domestic work as a paid occupation declined under the impact of household appliances in the twentieth century, but teaching, nursing, secretarial, clerical, and cleaning jobs remained dominated by women. With the expansion of the service economy in the second half of the twentieth century, women's paid employment increased dramatically. Women held 60 percent of the jobs in the service sector by the 1980s and accounted for nearly 40 percent of the labour force. Although women often found jobs more easily than men in the postindustrial economy, they continued to make less money than men and were more likely to be employed in part-time work.

As the forces of postindustrial change worked their way through the Canadian economy, the very concept of *work* came under scrutiny. Increases in productivity in the primary and secondary sectors in the 1960s led to predictions of a four-hour working day. Machines, it was argued, would liberate people to do mainly creative forms of work. Such predictions proved premature. The service economy expanded to absorb the "liberated" labour force, while the rigid prescriptions surrounding hours and conditions of work remained an essential feature of the way most people made a living.

Instead of work and wealth being more widely shared, a new hierarchy of labour emerged. Highly trained, skilled workers in the postindustrial economy held full-time jobs and could supplement their income through contract work. Unskilled service workers, in contrast, survived on a combination of minimum wage work—often defined as part-time work, which carried few benefits—and unemployment insurance. Since much of the work in the service sector turned out to be as monotonous and unchallenging as any assembly line job, the age of creativity failed to materialize for most workers.

Like work, *unemployment* became an elusive concept. The overall workforce "participation rate"—that is, the percentage of people between fifteen and sixty-five who were working or looking for work—rose from 55 to 65 percent between 1946 and 1981, but this was accompanied by a dramatic rise in the unemployment rate. In the 1960s the average unemployment rate was 5.2 percent, in the 1970s 6.7 percent, and in the 1980s 9.9 percent. During the recession of the early 1990s, unemployment rates increased to over 11 percent. The official unemployment rate was considerably augmented by the problem of "structural unemployment," which resulted when workers who lost their jobs proved ill-equipped to take up the jobs that were available. Most unemployed coal miners, for example, lacked the skills to be computer programmers; nor could farmers be readily transferred to jobs in health care industries. Although training programs were implemented to address the problem of structural unemployment, they failed to produce the skilled labour force required in Canada's postindustrial economy. Indeed, many of Canada's most highly trained workers were immigrants. After 1967, Canada's immigration laws substituted educational and occupational biases for ethnic ones, in an effort to attract skilled workers.

The rise of the service economy did little to reduce Canada's vulnerability to the cyclical swings that had plagued its industrial economy. In 1957 lower rates of investment and rising unemployment signalled an economic slump that continued until 1961. From 1962 to 1966 the economy boomed, and all economic indicators—investment, employment, output, standard of living—moved upward. Although unemployment and investment rates were uneven between 1967 and 1973, the economy continued to register impressive rates of growth. Economic indicators began to fluctuate alarmingly in the mid-1970s under the impact of the oil crisis and the rise of the Pacific Rim. With its manufacturing sector under assault and foreign markets rapidly contracting, Canada was particularly hard hit by the recession of 1981–82. The GNP dropped by 7 percent, industrial productivity declined by 18 percent, and unemployment was the fate of 13 percent of the labour force. For young men between the ages of fifteen and twenty-four, the unemployment rate reached a staggering 24 percent. In certain regions of the country, such as industrial Cape Breton, the unemployment rate was even higher. Economic indicators edged slowly upward in the mid-1980s, by which time the larger cycle of development was clear: real economic

---

MASSEY-HARRIS: A CANADIAN SUCCESS STORY?

As we have seen in earlier chapters, the agricultural machinery company founded in 1847 by Daniel Massey went from strength to strength in the late nineteenth and early twentieth centuries. The company moved from Newcastle to Toronto in 1855 and in 1891 merged with its chief competitor to become Massey-Harris, the largest company of its kind in the British Empire. By the first decade of the twentieth century, it had captured a huge share of the rapidly expanding Prairie market for farm machinery and had established branch operations in the United States. When the company ran into difficulties following the Second World War, it was reorganized under the direction of its holding company, Argus Corporation, and continued to prosper. As Massey-Ferguson, it developed a global market and reached annual sales of over $1 billion in the 1960s.

In the difficult economic climate of the late 1970s, Massey's fortunes again began to slip. Conrad Black, the ambitious young head of Argus, became chair of the troubled company in 1978, but the bottom fell out of the farm machinery market in 1980 and Argus wrote off its Massey-Ferguson shares as worthless. In an effort to save the capital and jobs that Massey represented, banks, governments, and shareholders poured $1.2 billion into the failing firm between 1978 and 1984. By 1987, when Massey-Ferguson changed its name to Variety Corp (after the Variety Plough Company, which had been acquired in 1892), it was a third of its former size, but still ranked forty-ninth in Canada with sales and operating revenue of $1.8 billion. Following the signing of the Free Trade Agreement in 1989, it moved its head office to the United States.

---

growth had dropped from an annual average of 5.5 percent in the years between 1956 and 1973 to 2.2 percent from 1973 to 1986. As stock markets slumped, unemployment persisted, and economic growth came to a standstill in the early 1990s, it seemed unlikely that Canadians would ever see another decade like the 1960s.

The Continental Embrace, or Dancing with Wolves

During the Industrial Age, Canadians had become highly dependent upon the United States for the capital, markets, and ideas that fuelled their economy. This reliance became a cause for concern in the Information Age. The debate over Canada's economic destiny was touched off by the Royal Commission on Canada's Economic Prospects, which tabled its report in

1957. Chaired by Walter Gordon, an ardent economic nationalist, the Commission expressed concern over the impact that American branch plants and the high degree of foreign investment were having on the Canadian economy. Branch plants typically hired American managers, devoted little attention to research and development, and remitted a high percentage of their profits to foreign investors. Because they were built to serve only a Canadian market, branch plants often operated inefficiently and were restricted by head office from export opportunities. The high level of foreign investment in Canada contributed to Canada's growing balance of payments problem as capital flowed out of the country in the form of interest and dividends. If Canadians hoped to create a balanced economy and let their manufacturing sector reach maturity, it would be necessary to control the growing American influence.

In the minds of many economic nationalists, free trade was equated with the loss of political sovereignty and the end of a worthy dream to create a more socially responsible nation on the North American continent. This position was passionately argued by Canadian philosopher George Grant in his 1965 classic, *Lament for a Nation*. For others, economic dependency was simply a dangerous posture for a nation as rich as Canada. Excessive dependency, it was argued, made Canada vulnerable to the whims of Washington and the head offices of American-based multinational corporations. Surely this vulnerability could be eliminated if Canadians only had the will to manage their own economy. What other nation with a resource base as rich as Canada's allowed foreigners to have so much control over its economy?

While nationalists supported policies that limited American control of the Canadian economy, classical economists, represented by University of Toronto economist Harry Johnson, argued that economic nationalism was a "narrow and garbage cluttered cul-de-sac." Canada and Canadian workers in particular, he maintained, would benefit by the removal of all restrictions to trade and foreign investment. Only by remaining open to global economic trends could the Canadian economy function at optimal efficiency and therefore provide the best jobs and highest incomes. The free trade option elicited a considerable following among business people and politicians in the early 1960s, but the only tangible result was the Auto Pact. With its quotas for Canadian production, the Auto Pact represented "managed trade" more than unfettered free trade.

Meanwhile, support for a more nationalistic approach to Canadian development was gaining momentum. The majority Diefenbaker administration (1958–62) had talked of restoring the lost British market (though it had no program of action), introduced tax incentives for Canadian-based industries, and incurred the wrath of the United States by trading with communist countries such as Cuba and the Soviet Union. Following the election of 1962, a minority Conservative government felt compelled to implement an unpopular austerity program to deal with a nasty balance of payments crisis. When Diefenbaker refused to co-operate on matters relating to defence policy, the Americans tactlessly intervened in the 1963 election to rid the country of the unco-operative Conservatives. Although leaders in the United States clearly favoured the Liberals under Lester Pearson, they had not bargained for his minister of finance who turned out to be none other than the Prime Minister's long-time friend Walter Gordon.

Gordon's first budget was a highly controversial one. Included among a variety of nationalistic proposals was a 30 percent "take-over tax" on the sale of publicly held Canadian companies to foreigners. Although forced by an angry business community to abandon the tax, Gordon's economic nationalism was gaining widespread public support. A 1964 Gallup poll showed that 46 percent of Canadians felt that Canada had enough capital investment from the United States. In 1964–65, Gordon introduced legislation to protect Canadian banks, insurance companies, and other financial services from foreign control, and steps were taken to reduce American dominance of the Canadian media.

Over the next few years, Canadians became even more nationalistic in their perspective. The growing sense of national achievement coupled with the 1967 centennial celebrations and the coming of age of the postwar baby boomers fostered an unprecedented sense of national pride. At the same time, American involvement in the highly unpopular war in Vietnam (1965–75) helped to consolidate the rising tide of anti-Americanism in Canada. So, too, did American attempts to reverse their own growing trade deficit. On 15 August 1971 President Richard Nixon took American currency off the gold standard and announced a series of measures designed to restore the competitive position of his nation's products. Among these was a 10 percent surcharge on imports to the United States and substantial tax write-offs on the costs of production for export. Although this was not the first time that Americans had pursued a policy of economic nationalism, it was the first time since the Second World War that Canadians were not exempt from such measures.

While Nixon's announcement came as a shock to Canadians, they were psychologically prepared to deal with it. In the buoyant economic climate of the period, Canadians felt confident that they could develop an alternative to the continental embrace that had tightened around them since the Second World War. Canadians also had a leader who was prepared to take a hard look at all aspects of Canadian–American relations.

Shortly after taking office in 1968, Pierre Elliott Trudeau announced in a speech to the National Press Club in Washington that Canada would not project itself as a "mirror image of the United States." His subsequent policy initiatives, including a "planned and phased reduction" in Canada's commitment to NATO and recognition of Communist China, proved that he meant business. Following Nixon's 1971 announcement, Trudeau's Minister of External Affairs Mitchell Sharp issued a statement that committed Canada to what became known as the "Third Option" in Canadian foreign policy. Option one, maintaining Canada's present relationship with the United States, had been tried and found wanting. Option two, closer integration with the Americans, was clearly impossible in the age of Nixon. Option three, reduction of "Canadian vulnerability" to American actions by expanding global political and economic links, seemed the obvious choice.

Three federally sponsored studies conducted between 1968 and 1972 advocated strong measures to combat the adverse effects of American branch plants on the Canadian economy and to control the direction of American investment. Known as the Watkins, Wahn, and Gray reports after the three men who chaired the investigations, they helped to shape federal policy in the 1970s. The Canada Development Corporation (CDC) was created in 1971 to encourage Canadian ownership and management in vital sectors of the economy. In 1974 the Foreign Investment Review Agency (FIRA), under the direction of Herb Gray, was established to screen proposals for foreign takeovers of existing Canadian businesses. When the oil crisis descended, the federal government created Petro-Canada, a Crown corporation with a broad mandate to develop a Canadian presence in the American-dominated petroleum industry. Petro-Canada's role was significantly enhanced by the National Energy Program (1980), which had as one of its main objectives the development of Canadian self-sufficiency in oil. During the first six years of its operation (1975–81), Petro-Canada acquired the assets of four multinationals and emerged as one of Canada's major petroleum corporations.

By the time the National Energy Program was introduced, the tide of economic nationalism had begun to recede. Continuing conflict with the United States over trade, the friction created by FIRA, the shifting global balance of power, and Canada's relatively poor economic performance following the oil crisis, preoccupied Canadian economic planners. The recession of 1981–82 delivered the final blow to the nationalist perspective. With productivity lagging, the deficit rising, and unemployment at levels unknown since the Great Depression, Canadian governments were at a loss as to how to proceed.

In typically Canadian fashion, Trudeau responded by appointing a Royal Commission in 1982 to investigate Canada's "Economic Union and

Development Prospects." Dubbed the "Commission on Canada's Future," most of the commission's thirteen members, including its chair, former Liberal finance minister Donald Macdonald, were acutely aware of the difficulties of generating effective policy responses to the economic and social problems facing the nation. In their three-volume report, released in September 1985, the commissioners argued that Canada had to maintain an adaptive economy, capable of adjusting to global economic change and new technologies. Market mechanisms rather than government intervention, they maintained, provided the best means of ensuring a vibrant Canadian economy. To that end, free trade with the United States offered the only hope for continued economic prosperity, and a guaranteed annual income would replace the hodgepodge of social programs administered by the welfare state. Although the commissioners were not unanimous in support of these recommendations, the majority supported the "second option," underscoring the dramatic shift in economic perspective that had occurred since the early 1970s.

The commission marshalled a broad array of evidence to support free trade. Despite attempts to pursue a "third option" of more diversified trade, especially through an arrangement with the EEC, Canada's dependency on the United States had actually grown in the previous decade. Over three-quarters of Canada's exports were sold to the United States, and half of that trade was between parents and branch plants of multinational corporations (see table 11.3). With over one-third of their GNP derived from foreign trade, Canadians would experience a crisis of

Table 11.3: CANADA–UNITED STATES TRADE, 1980–87

Year	Exports to U.S. % of total Canadian exports	Imports from U.S. % of total Canadian imports	Canadian exports to U.S. as % of Canadian GNP
1980	62.0	66.7	16.3
1981	65.2	65.3	16.5
1982	67.1	67.2	16.3
1983	71.7	68.2	17.1
1984	74.4	68.0	20.1
1985	76.7	68.1	20.4
1986	76.8	66.5	19.4
1987	73.1	67.1	18.5

Source: Jeffrey J. Schott, "The Free Trade Agreement: A U.S. Assessment" in *The Canada–United States Free Trade Agreement: The Global Impact*, eds. Jeffrey J. Schott and Murray G. Smith (Washington: Institute for International Economics, 1988), 10.

unthinkable proportions if the flow of goods across the Canada–United States border was disrupted. The time had come to shake up the industries that remained sheltered behind the old National Policy and to lay the foundations for a new age economy that would serve Canadians well in the twenty-first century.

Leaders of the NDP, labour unions, feminists, church groups, a variety of nationalist organizations, and, eventually, the federal Liberal Party bitterly opposed free trade. They, too, had strong arguments supporting their position. Free trade, they maintained, would allow multinational corporations to consolidate their North American operations in locations with better climates and lower wage levels than those prevailing in Canada. Jobs would be lost in the goods-producing sectors, and the wages of those remaining in the labour force would be substantially reduced. Moreover, Canada's cultural industries would be threatened, and Canadians would be forced to tailor their welfare, environmental, and regional development policies to "harmonize" with the goals of the larger economic partner. Under such pressure, Canada as a nation would surely fall apart. Since American industry was dependent on Canadian resources and markets anyway, economic nationalists argued, there seemed little likelihood of the United States suddenly pulling the plug on trade with Canada. Why use the recession to ram an unpopular and possibly dangerous free trade policy down the throats of the Canadian people?

These arguments tapped deeply rooted national sentiments, and in the 1984 election no party risked advocating a free trade agreement with the Americans. Nevertheless, this option was quickly taken up by the new Conservative administration of Brian Mulroney when it came to office in September 1984. Canada's chief negotiator in the free trade talks was Simon Reisman, a career civil servant who had been instrumental in negotiating the 1965 Auto Pact. With the Canadian business community supporting free trade, the full force of public and private institutions was brought to bear on the issue. The Business Council on National Issues, an organization composed of the chief executive officers of the 150 leading Canadian corporations, most of them multinationals, was fully committed to free trade. The venerable Canadian Manufacturers Association, once the bulwark of the National Policy, came on side. Even the Canadian Federation of Independent Business, which represented the increasingly powerful small business community of Canada, threw its weight behind the scheme.

The details of the free trade treaty were agreed upon in the fall of 1987. Following a year of heated debate, the Mulroney government called an election on 25 November 1988 after the Liberal majority in the Senate made clear their unwillingness to ratify the agreement before the Tories had received an electoral mandate for free trade. While a majority of Canadians opposed the agreement, the Conservatives, who received 43 percent of the votes cast, held the majority of seats in Parliament. In January 1989 representatives of the Canadian and American governments put their signatures on the first comprehensive trade treaty ever signed by the two North American nations. Whatever the Information Age held in store for Canadians, their destiny was now bound more tightly than ever with the United States.

Supporters of the FTA promised Canadians that the agreement would produce new jobs, but they were slow to materialize. Indeed several branch plants, beginning with Gillette, closed their doors in Canada or streamlined their operations. Free trade opponents blamed the agreement, but the firms insisted that their decisions had been made prior to its passage. As another recession descended in 1990, FTA opponents claimed that their dire predictions of job losses were coming to pass. Agreement supporters blamed the federal government's high interest rates and high dollar policies and wondered how the government thought free trade would work in Canada's favour with the high dollar weighing down exports. Cynical opponents of the deal suggested that the high dollar had been part of an informal agreement between the Canadian and American negotiators.

The ink was barely dry on the Canadian–American Free Trade Agreement when the Americans announced that they would be negotiating a similar agreement with Mexico. The Canadian government asked to be included in the talks, which led to a tentative deal in 1992. To the Americans, the North American Free Trade Agreement (NAFTA) was a first step toward free trade with all of Latin America, an opportunity to consolidate their control over the economies of this vast region. The Mexicans hoped that companies from the United States and Canada would relocate in their country to provide badly needed jobs. In Mexico, left-wing forces opposed the deal, arguing that the government hoped to attract new industry to the country by advertising Mexico's cheap wages and minimal environmental and safety standards.

Canadian unions, women's groups, and alliances such as the Council of Canadians and Action Canada Network also opposed NAFTA, arguing that, in the long run, the United States would be the main beneficiary of cheap Mexican labour and vast Canadian raw materials. Some argued that tariffs should only be lowered for countries that implemented social programs, pollution standards, and collective-bargaining legislation similar to that of Canada. The "level playing-field" demanded by free traders ought to be one on which working people and their communities were treated as more than simply "factors of production."

Economic Disparity

"A recession is when your neighbour has to tighten his belt. A depression is when you have to tighten your own belt. And a panic is when you have no belt to tighten and your pants fall down." This remark, attributed to long-time Saskatchewan CCF premier Tommy Douglas, highlights another focus of economic analysis: the distribution of income among individuals and groups within a nation. Canadians in the postindustrial age increasingly called into question the way in which resources and power were distributed under corporate capitalism. Notwithstanding the egalitarian rhetoric underlying the nation's democratic institutions, Canada remained a highly stratified society. The extent of inequality was meticulously chronicled by the science of statistics, which found a powerful new tool in the computer. Economic cycles might come and go, but the structure of inequality remained hauntingly familiar. In the postindustrial, as in the pre-industrial and industrial periods of Canadian history, age, class, ethnicity, gender, and geography remained important factors in determining how one fared in the quest for economic well-being.

The political and social implications of inequality will be discussed in the next two chapters. Here we will look at some of the structural charac-teristics of inequality as a background to these discussions. While it is tempting to see inequality as a natural and inevitable consequence of human interaction, the Canadian experience suggests that purposeful behaviour on the part of people and governments can have a determining effect on how wealth and power are distributed. In one notable case, the standard of living of French-speaking people in Quebec rose dramatically relative to that of anglophones in only two decades. Similarly, postwar baby boomers proved that numbers had a significant impact on public policy. As they progressed through their life cycle, they were sometimes able to pres-sure institutions to bend to their needs, whether it was education, birth control, day care, or old age security.

Despite growth and change in the Canadian economy since the Second World War, the overall distribution of income has remained remarkably static. As table 11.4 indicates, the lowest 20 percent of the pop-ulation has received the same proportion of the national wealth (a little over 6 percent) since 1951. In contrast, the wealthiest 20 percent continued to receive around 40 percent of the national income. Obviously, the welfare state did little to redistribute wealth, although it may have prevented an even greater concentration of wealth in the hands of the rich and powerful. In the Information Age, the old, young adults, and single parents and their children figured prominently in the lowest quintile, highlighting the signif-icance of age and marital status in determining income distribution.

WHO IS POOR?

Social welfare groups often disagree with official government statistics on poverty, claiming that Statistics Canada figures reflect conservative definitions of poverty. In 1987, a relatively prosperous year, Statistics Canada reported that there were 3.5 million Canadians, or 14 percent of the population, living in poverty. Officially, a household was poor if it had to spend at least 62 percent of its income on food and shelter. The remaining money was likely not enough to pay for clothing, transportation, dental care, and presciption drugs or to respond to financial emergencies.

A different definition of poverty was used in a Senate study in the late 1960s: a household was poor if its income was less than one-half the average gross Canadian income for the same type of household. Using this notion of relative deprivation, Senator David Croll, the former chair of the Senate Task Force on Poverty, claimed that there were over five million poor Canadians in 1987, a considerable difference from Statistics Canada estimates for the same year. By any accounting, single women—young and old—were disproportionately likely to be poor. This trend was so marked that analysts began to refer to the "feminization of poverty."

While once there were substantial numbers of elderly people living in poverty, the actual percentage was lower than in earlier periods, owing in part to pension programs. By contrast, the rate of poverty among children was rising, particularly in sole-parent families headed by women. Statistics Canada reported that in 1984, 20 percent of children were living in income-deficient households, up from 15 percent just four years earlier. Although the rate fell to 17 percent in 1987, when the economy was on the upswing, gains were lost in the recession of the early 1990s.

Table 11.4: DISTRIBUTION OF INCOME OF FAMILIES AND UNATTACHED INDIVIDUALS, 1951–86

Quintile	1951	1961	1971	1981	1986
Lowest quintile	6.1%	6.6%	5.6%	6.4%	6.3%
Second quintile	12.9	13.5	12.6	12.9	12.3
Third quintile	17.4	18.3	18.0	18.0	17.9
Fourth quintile	22.4	23.4	23.7	24.1	24.1
Fifth quintile	41.1	38.1	40.0	38.4	39.4

Source: *The Canadian Encyclopedia*, 2nd ed., vol. 2 (Edmonton: Hurtig, 1988), 1051.

The Industrial Revolution and the Information Age had a profound influence on the fundamental demographic structures of Canadian society. Due to lower birth rates and considerably longer life expectancy, the Canadian population was aging. If the present trends continue, fully 20 percent of the Canadian population will be over sixty-five by the year 2031. In the 1980s, nearly half of the single people over sixty-five (the majority of them women) lived below the poverty line.

In the Marxian sense of class, most Canadians in the Information Age belonged to the working class, being forced to sell their labour in order to make a living. About 85 percent of primary income in Canada in the 1980s was derived from wages and salaries; the remainder was made up of interest, dividends, and rents. The number of Canadians who lived off their capital investments or who were self-employed was relatively small. Technically, household production, barter exchange, and underground transactions (such as the drug trade and prostitution) were significant economic activities, but they could not be calculated in statistical analyses. Some economists claimed that this informal economy accounted for over 20 percent of economic activity. No matter how income was measured, it was clear that Canadians differed widely in their share of the nation's wealth. They also derived their income from different sources depending on where they were located on the economic escalator. While over 80 percent of the income of those in the highest quintile came from wages and salaries, those in the bottom quintile increasingly relied on transfer payments for their income and received very little income in the form of interest, profits, and rents.

In 1965, John Porter published *The Vertical Mosaic*, an impressive analysis of stratification in Canadian society. Porter showed that ethnicity and class in Canada were closely interrelated and that an economic elite of less than a thousand men—most of them of British background, Protestant in their religious affiliation, and graduates of certain private schools—dominated the Canadian economy. Even in Quebec, where over three-quarters of the population was French in origin, anglophone elites continued to control the economic structures of the province. Studies conducted for the Royal Commission on Bilingualism and Biculturalism revealed an ethnic hierarchy in Quebec that included francophones among the poorest of Quebeckers. Only Italians and Native peoples had a lower per capita income than French Canadians in 1961. As we shall see in the following chapter, the Quiet Revolution in Quebec did much to improve the status of francophones both in Quebec and elsewhere in the country. In contrast, visible minorities, especially Indians, Inuit, and African Canadians, remained at the bottom of the economic scale.

Women also figured prominently in the ranks of Canada's economically disadvantaged citizens. As one of the last groups to be fully integrated

Native dwellings contrast sharply with houses in Fort George, Quebec.   (John Flanders/
National Archives of Canada/PA-130854)

into the market economy, they were faced with a debilitating double standard in the legal and occupational structures of Canadian society. During
the Industrial Age, women were systematically paid lower wages than men
for doing the same work, and they were barred from professional and management positions. Unless they took great pains to establish themselves as
separate legal persons, they were subject to their husbands in the conduct
of their public lives, and required male approval to borrow money or take
up work outside the home. Women's place, it was argued, was in the home,
rearing and caring for this and the next generation of industrial workers.

The women's movement, which gained momentum in the 1960s,
began the long process of dismantling the barriers to women's equality in
the labour force. In 1970 the Royal Commission on the Status of Women
tabled a report containing no less than 167 recommendations for action.
Equal pay for equal work legislation was passed in federal and provincial
jurisdictions, and quotas on the number of women admitted to graduate
and professional schools were lifted. By the 1980s, Ontario and Manitoba
had introduced legislation to encourage equal pay for work of equal value
as a means of eliminating the low salaries in female job ghettos. Why, for
instance, were female secretaries with years of training and experience paid

While their labour force participation continued to expand, women, such as these typists at the Federal Bureau of Statistics, worked in traditional, poorly paid occupations.
(C. Lund/National Archives of Canada/PA-133212)

less than the men who were hired to sweep the floor in the office? Despite efforts to bring equity to the workplace, women still faced difficulties in their efforts to secure high-paying jobs. "Glass ceilings" seemed to bar their chances for advancement to management positions, and few women were appointed to the boards of major businesses. As table 11.5 indicates, women's full-time salaries as a percentage of men's rose marginally between 1971 and 1982, but the wage gap remained unacceptably wide, even for young women entering the labour force.

Table 11.5: WOMEN'S FULL-TIME EARNINGS AS A PERCENTAGE OF MEN'S, 1971, 1982

Age Group	1971	1982
20–24	74.5	78.2
25–34	65.8	71.3
35–44	57.9	61.6
45–54	55.5	58.7
55–64	64.5	62.2
TOTAL	59.7	64.0

Source: *Women in Canada: A Statistical Report* (Ottawa: Statistics Canada, 1985), 61.

A similar slowness in the direction of change was characteristic of the regional distribution of wealth in Canada. Throughout the second half of the twentieth century, Ontario generally maintained a higher per capita income than other provinces. While the Western provinces fluctuated in their relationship to the average per capita income, the Atlantic provinces remained the poorest region. The persistence of underdevelopment in Atlantic Canada elicited a variety of attempts to "plan" a better economic performance. Generous equalization payments were built into the tax system in 1956, giving all provinces per capita grants based on the average of the two wealthiest provinces, at that time British Columbia and Ontario. The minority Diefenbaker government announced special Atlantic Provinces Adjustment Grants in 1957. During the 1960s "regional development" became part of the larger goal of eliminating pockets of poverty throughout the nation. In the 1970s, Ottawa proclaimed a 200-mile territorial limit at sea and began a massive program to encourage development of the Bank fisheries and off-shore oil. For a few fleeting moments it seemed that the "have-not" status of the Atlantic provinces might soon be over.

The programs to fight regional disparity failed in their stated objective. Like the welfare programs introduced after the Second World War, they served to maintain rather than change the relative distribution of wealth in the country. Critics even suggested that regional programs may have restricted the poorer regions from adjusting to economic realities more efficiently. Most economists and politicians recognized that state-funded regional development legitimized public policies that, of necessity, served the wealthier and more populous regions of the country. Federal planners were loath to pursue monetary and fiscal policy designed to meet the real needs of the poorer regions for fear that Canada's overall economic performance might be jeopardized. How, for instance, could the bank rate be set to meet the needs of the lagging Atlantic region when the Central Canadian economy was facing inflationary pressures? It was easier to make the Atlantic region a dependant of Ottawa—fully half of the region's income was derived from federal transfer payments in the 1980s—than to spend the national resources necessary to make the region more economically viable.

While the Atlantic regional economy lapsed into dependency, the Western provinces experienced a series of booms and busts similar to those that had characterized their economies since the first days of European settlement. The postwar boom in oil and natural gas in Alberta, the discovery of the world's largest deposit of potash in Saskatchewan, the continuing demand for British Columbia's forest products and Prairie grains helped to produce one of the world's richest resource-based economies. With the discovery of oil in the Beaufort Sea in the late 1960s, Westerners revived memories of Yukon gold and dreamed of great wealth from their northern frontier. When the price of oil and other primary products skyrocketed in the 1970s, Westerners were convinced that their time had come. Eastern-based companies established branches in Calgary and Edmonton, workers flocked to take up the jobs that prosperity miraculously spun off, and the balance of power perceptibly shifted westward.

The Western dream faded as quickly as it began. In 1977, the proposed Mackenzie Valley Pipeline was put on hold so that the environmental and social impact of such a project could be properly assessed. Three years later, the Trudeau administration implemented the National Energy Program, designed to transfer some of the profits from the energy producers to consumers and to federal government coffers. The anticipated high price of oil (estimated to rise as high as $95 a barrel by the end of the century) failed to materialize. Instead, the $35 a barrel price began to drop in the 1980s under the impact of OPEC policies, reduced consumption, and the deepening recession. In 1985 two western banks, the Canadian Commercial and the Northland, were forced to close their doors, the first bank failures in Canada since the 1920s. Toward the end of the decade, the centre of gravity had shifted back to Central Canada, where high levels of employment and a rising inflation rate signalled another upsurge in the region's economy.

While the Atlantic and Western provinces were riding to new heights on the resource boom, Ontario and Quebec had laid the foundation of a balanced Information Age economy. The St Lawrence heartland remained the centre of Canada's automobile, aircraft, and steel production and was the favoured location for most of the federally sponsored activity relating to the new communications industries. Together, Ontario and Quebec continued to account for over 80 percent of Canada's manufacturing output. Ontario and Quebec also remained at the heart of Canada's exploding service sector. Although the head offices of many major banks and businesses moved from Montreal to Toronto in the 1970s, Quebec generated its own service sector and exported its financial, engineering, and construction services around the world. Agriculture, forestry, and mining continued to thrive in the two central provinces. Ontario, for instance, led the provinces in the value of its agricultural output, while Quebec's forest industry was second only to that of British Columbia. Even when economic conditions were at their worst, the world continued to consume the minerals of the rich Canadian Shield, and both provinces were exporters of energy. Nothing, it seemed, could long threaten the productivity of Canada's rich St Lawrence heartland.

Then came the recession of 1990–92. Manufacturing jobs disappeared, many because companies went south under the protection of the

THE JAMES BAY PROJECT

The James Bay hydro-electric development was one of Canada's major and most controversial mega-projects to be launched in the second half of the twentieth century. Announced by Quebec premier Robert Bourassa in 1971, the project was designed to produce massive quantities of electricity from the rivers flowing into James Bay. Phase I, completed in 1984, included the world's largest underground powerhouse and a tiered spillway three times the height of Niagara Falls. It flooded a huge area of land, altering the fragile northern ecosystem, and dramatically affecting the lives of many Native people. The second phase was put on hold in 1992, in part because American markets for power had evaporated. Well orchestrated campaigns convinced potential consumers of electrical power from James Bay that the social and environmental costs of the project outweighed its benefits.

Protest against the second phase of the James Bay hydro project   (© Chase Roe)

free trade agreement, and others because companies were "downsizing" their work forces to take better advantage of new technologies. Toronto, where labour shortages had been a problem just a few years earlier, suddenly had double-digit unemployment, and one in five residents of the two biggest cities in the country required unemployment insurance or social assistance at some point in 1991.

At the end of the twentieth century, Canadians could look back on decades of extraordinary economic change. Yet no one doubted that even greater adjustments were necessary. With continental free trade in place and the struggle for global economic supremacy between the United States and Japan a grim reality, the future was anything but secure. A few people even voiced their concern that the twentieth century had indeed been Canada's century as Laurier had predicted. The future, they suggested, was all downhill. Most Canadians refused to accept such a pessimistic outlook and struggled to bring their political and social institutions in line with the Information Age economy. What kind of Canada would emerge from the restructuring process was anybody's guess.

• The Free Trade Agreement:
Who's Right?

It is still too early to offer a historical perspective on the Canada–United States Free Trade Agreement signed on 1 January 1989. At this close vantage point, it is difficult to say whether its supporters or its opponents will be vindicated in the court of history. Nevertheless, it is useful to assess what critics have to say about the impact of the agreement in its first few years of operation.

Opponents of the agreement can be divided into two camps: those who oppose any free trade deal because they feel that it compromises Canada's power to control its economic destiny, and those who support free trade but judge this particular agreement to be fatally flawed. In the former camp can be found people such as Mel Hurtig, a former Edmonton-based publisher and founder in 1985 of the Council of Canadians, an organization dedicated to protecting Canadian sovereignty. Hurtig's book criticizing the Free Trade Agreement is entitled *The Betrayal of Canada*, and he dedicates it to Tommy Douglas, Walter Gordon, George Grant, and Eric Kierans, men whom he feels were instrumental in defining a national agenda for Canada.

In Hurtig's view, "The single most important overall impact of the Free Trade Agreement is already clear—a big decline in the standard of living of Canadians." Hurtig provides wide ranging data, which show that business investment fell in the two years following the agreement and that 264 000 manufacturing jobs were lost as branch plants closed and new operations were located in Mexico and elsewhere. Hurtig predicts that "the future will be much worse . . . the destruction and disappearance of our country."[3] Similar dire warnings were made during the election of 1911, but Canadians, encouraged by business interests, rejected free trade at that time. Although Hurtig assigns some of the blame to big business for supporting the free trade agenda in the 1980s, he places the greatest blame on the Mulroney government for following the dictates of this powerful interest group.

Hurtig's views have been echoed by Maude Barlow, a former Trudeau advisor, who chaired the Council of Canadians in the early 1990s. She and Bruce Campbell argue in their book

Take Back the Nation that under the unequal partnership of the trade agreement, Canadians will be forced to harmonize their labour, social, and environmental policy with the lower standards set in the United States and that Canada's standards will be further eroded with Mexico's inclusion in the agreement. Barlow and Campbell state bluntly that the FTA should be "scrapped":

> *Pragmatically, we have no choice if we want to avoid eventual economic and political absorption into the United States. The costs of getting out—and there will be short-term costs—are far outweighed by the costs of staying in. The longer we're in, the more dependent we become, the higher the costs of getting out, and the more vulnerable we are to U.S. threats to cancel the idea unless we see their way on "unfair" subsidies or other fundamental political choices.*[4]

Other critics of the FTA, including Bill Clinton, elected president of the United States in 1992, profess to support the principle of free trade, but are concerned about specific aspects of the agreement and the problems associated with its extension to Mexico. Although the Liberal Party opposed the FTA during the election of 1988, it was reluctant to support cancellation of the agreement once it was signed. The majority of party members moved to the more comfortable position of support for lowering trade barriers on a global level, and supplementing the economic provisions of the FTA with human and environmental provisions that would raise rather than lower standards throughout North America and elsewhere.

While both radical and moderate opponents of the FTA agreed that it had an unfortunate impact on the Canadian economy and society, supporters of the agreement were less pessimistic. They argued that many of the trends advanced as reasons for cancelling the agreement were not the result of free trade but were caused by larger global forces including a crippling recession, which set in soon after the FTA was signed, and misguided policies on the part of the Bank of Canada. Even without the FTA, supporters maintained, Canadians would have been victims of the restructuring and downsizing policies that were part of global economic strategy. By positioning the nation's producers to gain access to the world's largest market, free trade with the United States and Mexico would ensure the nation's safe transition to the dictates of the global economy.

Free trade advocates such as Thomas d'Aquino, who chairs the Business Council on National Issues, and Peter Cook, who writes for the *Globe and Mail*'s "Report on Business," have their own statistics to throw at the doom sayers. They point to a 16 percent increase in the volume of Canadian exports between 1989 and 1992, the continued success in fighting inflation, and the drop in the value of the Canadian dollar as signs that the Canadian economy is making the necessary adjustments to survive in an increasingly competitive economic environment.[5]

• Notes

[1] Rachel Carson, *Silent Spring* (Boston: Houghton Mifflin, 1962), 244.

[2] *Edmonton Journal*, 20 June 1991.

[3] Mel Hurtig, *The Betrayal of Canada*, rev. ed. (Toronto: Stoddart, 1992), 339.

[4] Maude Barlow and Bruce Campbell, *Take Back the Nation* (Toronto: Key Porter Books, 1991), 168.

[5] Peter Cook, "Free Trade's Turnaround," *Globe and Mail*, 24 Dec. 1992.

• Selected Reading

Robert Bothwell, Ian Drummond, and John English, *Canada Since 1945: Power, Politics and Provincialism* (Toronto: University of Toronto Press, 1981) devote considerable attention to economic matters in their general synthesis, as do Paul-André Linteau, René Durocher, and Jean-Claude Robert, *Quebec Since 1930* (Toronto: Lorimer, 1991) and J.L. Granatstein, *Canada, 1957–1967: The Years of Uncertainty and Innovation* (Toronto: McClelland and Stewart, 1986). See also Kenneth Norrie and Douglas Owram, *A History of the Canadian Economy* (Toronto: Harcourt Brace Jovanovich, 1991); Harold Chorney, *The Deficit and Debt Management: An Alternative to Monetarism* (Ottawa: Canadian Centre for Policy Alternatives, 1989); and Robert M. Campbell, *Grand Illusions: The Politics of the Keynesian Experience in Canada, 1945–1975* (Peterborough, ON: Broadview Press, 1987). A different perspective on this period can be found in Robert Chodos, Rae Murphy, and Eric Hamovitch, *The Unmaking of Canada: The Hidden Theme in Canadian History Since 1945* (Toronto: Lorimer, 1991).

On the welfare state see Keith G. Banting, *The Welfare State and Canadian Federalism*, 2nd ed. (Montreal: McGill-Queen's University Press, 1987); on women's work, see Pat and Hugh Armstrong, *The Double Ghetto: Canadian Women and Their Segregated Work*, rev. ed. (Toronto: McClelland and Stewart, 1984); and Paul Phillips and Erin Phillips, *Women and Work: Inequality in the Labour Market* (Toronto: Lorimer, 1983). Donald Savoie discusses the economic implications of regionalism in *Regional Economic Development: Canada's Search for Solutions* (Toronto: University of Toronto Press, 1986). Thomas Berger's report for the Mackenzie Valley Pipeline Inquiry, *Northern Frontier, Northern Homeland*, rev. ed. (Vancouver: Douglas and McIntyre, 1988) offers a classic statement on the dilemmas for Natives of the development ethic, as do Mel Watkins, ed., *Dene Nation—The Colony Within* (Toronto: University of Toronto Press, 1977) and J.R. Miller, *Skyscrapers Hide the Heavens: A History of Indian–White Relations in Canada*, rev. ed. (Toronto: University of Toronto Press, 1990).

The classic conservative and liberal economic positions which were played out in this period can be found in Milton Friedman, *Capitalism and Freedom*, rev. ed. (Chicago: University of Chicago Press, 1981); John Kenneth Galbraith, *Economics and the Public Purpose* (Scarborough, ON: New American Library, 1975). Several classics in the Canadian free trade debate are still worth consulting, including Kari Levitt, *Silent Surrender: The Multinational Corporation in Canada* (Toronto: Gage, 1971) and George Grant, *Lament for a Nation* (Ottawa: Carleton University Press, 1983). H.G. Johnson, *The Canadian Quandary* (Ottawa: Carleton University Press, 1977) takes an opposing view.

The issue of economic sovereignty was the subject of several publicly-funded commissions including Mel Watkins et al., *Foreign Ownership and the Structure of Canadian Industry*, Report of the Task Force on the Structure of Canadian Industry (Ottawa: Ministry of Supply and Services, 1968); Ian Wahn et al., *Eleventh Report of the Standing Committee on External Affairs and National Defence Respecting Canadian–American Relations* (Ottawa: Ministry of Supply and Services, 1970); Herb Gray et al., *Foreign Direct Investment in Canada* (Ottawa: Ministry of Supply and Services, 1972). This issue is also the subject of Abraham Rotstein and Gary Lax, eds., *Independence: The Canadian Challenge* (Toronto: Committee for an Independent Canada, 1973).

The 1980s is the focus of Stephen Clarkson, *Canada and the Reagan Challenge*, 2nd ed. (Toronto: Lorimer, 1985); G. Bruce Doern and Glen Toner, *The Politics of*

Energy (Toronto: Nelson, 1985); James Laxer, *Leap of Faith: Free Trade and the Future of Canada* (Edmonton: Hurtig, 1986); Diane Cohen and Kristin Shannon, *The Next Canadian Economy* (Montreal: Eden Press, 1984). The pro-free trade perspective of the 1980s is put forward in the three-volume *Report* of the Royal Commission on Economic Union and Development Prospects for Canada. Its seventy-two supporting studies, including Denis Stairs and Gilbert R. Winham, *The Politics of Canada's Economic Relationship with the United States* (Toronto: University of Toronto Press, 1985), are useful for gauging the prevailing economic winds of the decade. Daniel Drache and Duncan Cameron, ed., *The Other Macdonald Report* (Toronto: Lorimer, 1985) offers a dissenting "consensus."

International developments in the environment and economy are assessed by M. Patricia Marchak, in *The Integrated Circus: The New Right and the Restructuring of Global Markets* (Montreal: McGill-Queen's University Press, 1991); Nigel Harris, *The End of the Third World* (London: Penguin, 1986); and Susan George, *A Fate Worse than Debt* (New York: Grove Press, 1988). Growing concern for the environment and uncontrolled technological innovation is discussed in Rachel Carson, *Silent Spring* (Boston: Houghton Mifflin, 1962); *Limits to Growth: A Report for the Club of Rome's Project for the Predicament of Mankind*, 2nd ed. (New York: Universe, 1974); E.F. Schumacher, *Small Is Beautiful: The Study of Economics as if People Mattered* (New York: Harper and Row, 1975); World Commission on Environment and Development, *Our Common Future* (Oxford: Oxford University Press, 1987), otherwise known as the Bruntland Report after the prime minister of Norway who chaired the commission; David Suzuki and Peter Knudtson, *Genethics: The Clash Between the New Genetics and Human Values* (Cambridge, MA: Harvard University Press, 1989).

Biographies of two quite different figures on the post-1960 economic scene are Denis Smith, *Gentle Patriot: A Political Biography of Walter Gordon* (Edmonton: Hurtig, 1973); Peter C. Newman, *The Establishment Man* (Toronto: McClelland and Stewart, 1982).

CANADIAN SOCIETY IN
THE POSTMODERN AGE

In her 1973 autobiography, *Halfbreed*, Maria Campbell describes the dire poverty of her childhood in Northern Saskatchewan. While Métis traditions partly compensated for grim living conditions and racial discrimination, the death of Campbell's mother in 1952 put an end to this source of solace. Only twelve years old at the time, Maria struggled to hold together her family of seven brothers and sisters and her proud but discouraged father. She married at the age of fifteen, but the relationship quickly deteriorated. Campbell drifted across Western Canada, becoming a prostitute and drug addict in Vancouver and later doing low-paid "women's work"— cooking, waitressing, hairstyling. In the late 1960s, she became a militant Native activist in Alberta. Her struggles as a Native person, a woman, and a member of a marginal group even among Native peoples, indicated how much Canada was changing in the period after 1960. While many disadvantaged individuals remained victims of circumstance, the critical spirit of the times caused others to take control of their lives.

People like Maria Campbell derived inspiration not only from their own history but also from the experience of people all over the world who were struggling to improve their circumstances. Although the word *empowerment* became widely used only in the 1980s, it is a useful term to apply to the various anti-colonial struggles and civil rights movements that have swept the globe since 1960. Canadians were in the forefront of many of these movements for change. Taking their cue from the struggle by Algerians to rid themselves of their French imperial masters, some Québécois began to demand independence for Quebec. Students from the baby boom generation followed the example of their counterparts in Europe and the United States in staging protests on a wide range of issues, including unresponsive administrative structures in their schools and universities. Gradually the movement for empowerment touched the lives of most Canadians as women, aboriginal peoples, people of colour, the poor, and even the regions mobilized to claim what they saw as their human rights. This chapter examines the ways in which various groups in Canadian society began to question and attempt to change their status in the postmodern age.

• Cultural Diversity

The Canadian population increased from eighteen million to twenty-seven million between 1961 and 1991, despite the decline of the birth rate below the level of population replacement. The fertility rate hit a postwar peak of 28.3 newborns per 1000 population in 1959 and then declined rapidly to 15.7 in 1976 as more effective contraception became available to Canadian women. That Canada's population continued to grow was due to declining infant mortality, increased life expectancy, and continued immigration.

The dramatic decline in infant deaths since the beginning of the century meant that, in 1990, only 7.9 infants per 1000 failed to reach their first birthday. Life expectancy was seventy-three years for men and eighty years for women; thirty years earlier, the respective figures were sixty-eight and seventy-four. Immigration slowed in the early 1960s, as Canada weathered a recession, and then increased dramatically after 1963 as the economy expanded again. With unemployment rising in the late 1970s, immigration was cut again, although there were significant annual variations. Immigration levels fell below 100 000 per year after the deep recession of 1982, but rose again as the economy rallied. In 1990, despite the onset of a new recession, the government announced that immigration increases to 200 000 per year would be necessary to maintain Canada's population level.

In 1991, no fewer than 16 percent of Canadians had been born abroad. About 94 percent of immigrants lived in the four most populous provinces; Metropolitan Toronto alone accounted for one-third of all immigrants. In both Toronto and Vancouver, 38 percent of residents surveyed in the 1991 census were foreign-born. Their countries of origin were more varied than those of immigrants a generation earlier. While 96 percent of all immigrants to Canada between 1945 and 1960 came from Europe, the United States, and Australasia, by 1985 the percentage of immigrants from these areas had fallen to 70 percent. Eighteen percent of new Canadians were from Asia, 5 percent from the Caribbean, 4 percent

from South and Central America, and 3 percent from Africa, and the per-
centages of Canadians from these regions rose annually.

Revisions of the Immigration Act in 1962 and again in 1967 had
reduced the colour bias that once kept Canada's gates closed to non-
whites. As the economic boom of the 1960s began, it became clear that
Western Europe, back on its feet after postwar rebuilding, would no longer
produce the steady stream of immigrants required to support Canada's
economy. Since the well-educated technical and professional people that
Canada most wanted would not be available in the required numbers,
immigration regulations were changed to open the door to skilled people
from regions other than Europe and the United States. Asians in particular
took advantage of Canada's changing immigration policy. While recent
immigrants, as a group, had once been relatively poor compared to other
Canadians, by 1986 the average immigrant in the labour force earned 9
percent more than Canadian-born workers. This figure masks the poverty
of some immigrant groups, but it demonstrates the extent to which immigrants succeeded in Canada. Among the poorer groups were refugees from
Indochina and Latin America who fled persecution and ethnic discrimination in their war-torn countries.

*Events such as the Chinese Dragon Parade in Vancouver celebrate the cultural diversity
of Canadian society.*   (Vancouver Public Library/79795-A)

Although Canada was changing in the second half of the twentieth century, it remained largely a nation of European origins. In 1985, just under half of Canada's twenty-five million people claimed to be of British or French descent. Almost 20 percent listed a European country other than Britain or France as their nation of ancestry. Only 4 percent claimed Asian, African, or Latin American origins. Just short of seven million Canadians, or 28 percent of the population, reported mixed ethnic origins. While 78 percent of Quebeckers reported French as their ethnic origin and 80 percent of Newfoundlanders claimed only British descent, westerners and Ontarians reported a variety of backgrounds.

In the climate of diversity, groups were more assertive about preserving their cultural heritage. Federal bilingualism and biculturalism programs, which were introduced in 1969, led minority ethnic groups to lobby for federal and provincial grants for what became known as multiculturalism. In 1971, Prime Minister Trudeau appointed a secretary of state for multiculturalism. The federal government and the provinces with the greatest ethnic mix began to fund ethnic organizations and festivals as well as heritage-language instruction in the schools.

Ethnic diversity helped to mute prejudices that were once so prevalent in Canada, and opinion surveys indicated the growth of tolerance among Canadians. Still, discrimination in employment, housing, and other areas continued to face many non-whites, particularly African Canadians and Native peoples. Although human rights legislation in the 1970s ameliorated the situation somewhat, it could not eliminate racism from Canadian society.

Encouraged by the Black Power movement in the United States, African Canadians in the 1960s became more assertive in their struggle against discrimination. A new generation of black leaders, many of them recent immigrants from the West Indies and Africa, refused to accept second-class citizenship. In Nova Scotia, which had over 30 percent of Canada's black population in 1961, blacks faced discrimination in the job market and could expect to live in poorer housing and receive less schooling than whites. Although black organizations, many of them church inspired, had struggled against the most blatant forms of discrimination, including segregation in restaurants and theatres, they were unable to break down the racist attitudes that kept their people in the ranks of the underclass.

The plight of blacks in Nova Scotia received international attention when the City of Halifax decided to demolish Africville. Located on the shores of Bedford Basin, Africville had been home to Halifax's black population since the middle of the nineteenth century. The community had been shamefully neglected by the city authorities, who had provided no water, sewerage facilities, or garbage collection to its homes and had located the municipal dump nearby. In 1961, Halifax City Council decided to remove the 400 citizens of Africville to make way for an industrial development on the site. Residents' protests were ignored; most whites and even a few blacks argued that urban renewal was a necessary prelude to a better future for all Haligonians. Although many residents were compensated for their property and offered alternative housing, they resented not being fully consulted, and they feared the loss of community that would result from the relocation.

In the wake of the demolition of Africville, the Black United Front (BUF) was founded in 1968 to intensify the struggle for change. A visit to Halifax by Stokely Carmichael, a leading African-American militant, served as

Africville in the 1960s   (Bob Brooks, photo; Public Archives of Nova Scotia)

a catalyst for the new organization. In an effort to defuse what appeared to be a growing militancy among blacks in Canada—a student protest against racism at Sir George Williams University (now Concordia) ended in the destruction of the university's computer system in 1969—the federal government offered to fund BUF and other black organizations.

Canadians displayed some complacency on the issue of racism. They were, after all, able to compare their society favourably with that of their southern neighbours, where race relations often boiled over into violence. Such self-satisfaction began to evaporate in the early 1990s. A series of police shootings of unarmed blacks in Montreal and Toronto led to accusations that many police officers were racists who stereotyped all blacks as dangerous criminals. Neo-Nazi skinheads—largely unemployed white male youths—attacked non-whites of Asian and African origin and desecrated Jewish cemeteries. Gays also became targets for violent, even murderous homophobes. Intolerance had its violent side, even in Canada.

For most Canadians, education was perceived as the key to success in the uncertain world that was rapidly unfolding. While groups such as Native and African Canadians continued to lag behind the average, by the 1990s Canadians were far better educated than any previous generation. Over half of Canadians had nine grades or less of schooling in 1951, but only 18 percent had so little formal education in 1986 and, among fifteen to twenty-four year olds, the figure was only 5 percent. There were 1.9 million Canadians with university degrees in 1986 compared to 189 000 in 1951. By the 1980s, about one Canadian adult in ten was a university graduate, and more than one income recipient in three had postsecondary qualifications.

As education levels and income increased, so too did material expectation. Many Canadians were living in consumer heaven, even if it meant lifelong indebtedness. Statistics Canada reported that in 1990, three-quarters of all households had automatic washing machines, clothes dryers, and cable television, and two-thirds had microwave ovens, VCRs, and tape recorders. Sixteen percent had home computers. While fewer homes in poorer regions had all this gadgetry, the spread of high-tech products was on the increase everywhere. Even Quebec, where elites had for so long preached clerical anti-materialism, had become firmly entrenched as a secular, consumerist society.

The nuclear family consisting of a husband, a wife, and several children remained the ideal for most Canadians, but with each census it accounted for a smaller proportion of households. Divorce laws were liberalized in 1969, allowing more unhappy marriages to be dissolved and increasing the number of single-parent households. "The pill," which was widely prescribed in the 1960s, gave women the option of delaying childbirth or indeed of not having children at all. Reflecting somewhat greater tolerance of homosexuality, same-sex couples "came out" in unprecedented numbers. Some employers and provincial governments began to recognize gay and lesbian partners as families for the purposes of benefits and social welfare programs. Common-law marriages, once associated with the poorer classes, became popular across the economic spectrum, particularly among younger adults. Divorce and remarriage substantially increased the number of

GAY LIBERATION

In 1960, the state regarded homosexuality as a crime, the major churches regarded it as a mortal sin, and the medical profession branded it a psychological disorder requiring such treatment as aversion therapy. Gay civil servants, RCMP officers, and members of the armed forces were fired as a matter of policy, and gay men—but not lesbians—were barred from immigration to Canada. Despite such repression, an underground homosexual culture flourished. Lesbians and gay men created social networks that included clubs where they could be themselves without fearing persecution. Gays campaigned to convince politicians, doctors, and church leaders that they were not "deviants" and that sexual preference was a matter of individual conscience. In an atmosphere of growing concern for civil liberties, gays made some progress. In 1969, reforms to the Criminal Code removed some of the legal restrictions against homosexual relations between consenting adults, and sexual preference was removed as a criterion for immigration in 1977. The Parti Québécois added sexual orientation to Quebec's human rights code and, by 1992, Ontario, Manitoba, and the Yukon also prohibited discrimination on the basis of sexual preference. In December 1992, the federal government announced its intention to follow suit for institutions under its jurisdiction.

Right-wing campaigns against homosexuality had their successes as well. Homophobic thugs beat up and sometimes killed gay men. In the 1980s, Toronto's gay newspaper, *The Body Politic*, was slapped with obscenity charges. Police raids on gay bars and bathhouses indicated a continued willingness to harass gays in the name of public morality. The arrest of 300 men in a February 1981 bathhouse raid in Toronto became a focal point for gay organizations demanding legal protection.

The spread of AIDS—Acquired Immune Deficiency Syndrome—which had claimed 3000 lives in Canada by the end of 1991, provided a daunting challenge to the gay community, whose male members initially formed the majority of the victims of the disease. AIDS organizers developed education campaigns to slow the spread of the disease and support systems for persons infected with AIDS. They also pressured governments to fund community groups and medical research to fight AIDS.

Gay activists of the 1990s were often more militant than their counterparts a generation earlier. They won court battles that gave same-sex partners benefits similar to heterosexual spouses. After legal challenges, the Canadian Army agreed in 1992 to end long-standing policies against homosexuals. Gays won the right to be ordained ministers in the United Church. The Roman Catholic Church joined evangelical Protestants in continuing to denounce homosexuality, along with abortion and divorce, as threats to the traditional family.

AIDS Awareness campaign poster   (Canadian AIDS Society)

"blended" families, which might include a couple's biological children as well as each partner's offspring from earlier marriages. Developments in reproductive technology further blurred notions of family. Surrogate mothers, egg donors, sperm donors, and processes like *in vitro* fertilization, sex pre-determination, and embryo screening made reproductive practices increasingly complex and raised fundamental ethical questions about the bounds of medical science.

• Quebec: Modernization and Nationalism

Between 1960 and 1990, Quebec experienced a dramatic transformation. Intellectual ferment in the 1950s was a harbinger of social change, but it took the death of Premier Duplessis in 1959 to remove the bottleneck to political action. In the 1960s, francophones in Quebec began to defy religious injunctions and wrest control of their economy from outside influences. Increasingly, they considered themselves as Québécois rather than Canadians and abandoned their sense of community with French Canadians in the rest of Canada.

If the old Quebec was identified with rural life, spiritual values, and large families, the new Quebec revelled in urbanization, secularism, and small families. By the 1980s, Quebec's birth rate, once the highest in Canada, had fallen to the lowest. Since immigrants in Quebec tended to assimilate to English-language culture, francophones began to fear that they would soon be outnumbered in their own province: large families would no longer offset immigration in determining the demographic balance in the province. Quebeckers also increasingly found little comfort in their Roman Catholic faith. In Montreal, church attendance by Roman Catholics declined from 61.2 percent in 1961 to 30 percent in 1971. Despite reforms designed to appeal to the secular generation, the church had difficulty recruiting enough priests and nuns to minister to their congregations. In 1946 there were 2000 new priests; in 1970 only 100. Sisterhoods, the mainstay of the religious work force, were deserted as jobs opened up for women in the paid labour force and feminist ideology challenged the church's teachings on the role of women.

While leaders in the new secular Quebec embraced modern values relating to church and family, they were less willing to abandon their sense of national mission. They used language to protect their "distinct society" which, ironically, had become more "anglophone" in goals and values. In an effort to forestall the anglicization of Quebec, the provincial government passed strict language laws that, among other things, required non-English-speaking immigrants to educate their children in French-language schools. By producing their own music, art, literature, theatre, and films, francophone Quebeckers developed a separate cultural frame of reference from other North Americans. They thereby ensured that the modernization that outsiders had assumed would submerge national sentiments in the province had the opposite effect.

The state served as midwife to the new secular order. In 1960, the Liberal Party under Jean Lesage won the provincial election and ushered in the "Quiet Revolution." During its six years in office, the Lesage government passed a spate of legislation that fundamentally altered institutional structures in Quebec. The Roman Catholic Church and the anglophone business community bore the brunt of new legislation, which was most impressive in two areas: education and economic development.

Dissatisfaction with the conservative, clerically run educational institutions of Quebec was revealed by the phenomenal success of *Insolences du Frère Untel (Confessions of Brother Anonymous)*, which was published in 1960. Written by Jean-Paul Desbiens, it was a stinging indictment of Quebec education by someone within the ranks of the Roman Catholic Church. The Lesage government appointed a commission to examine the state of Quebec education and make recommendations for improvement. Although the commissioners decided that schools should remain organized along religious lines, they recommended that the state play a larger role in administration and curriculum development.

In 1964, the provincial government established a Ministry of Education, the first since 1875. One of the officials in the new ministry was Desbiens, who had been silenced by his order for his critique of the education system. Under the guiding hand of Education Minister Paul Gérin-Lajoie, new curricula were introduced in Quebec schools, bringing them into line with education systems in the rest of North America. A network of secular junior colleges, or CEGEPs, was created to provide postsecondary vocational and academic training. Between 1960 and 1970, enrolment in Quebec's secondary schools rose 101 percent, college enrolments 82 percent, and university enrolments 169 percent.

The creation of the Centrale de l'Enseignement du Québec, a militant teachers' union, out of the old Catholic teachers' association, demonstrated the continued secularization of education in Quebec. Leaders of the new union issued manifestos inspired more by Marx than by Jesus and easily overwhelmed the rapidly declining numbers of priests and nuns in their ranks who clung to traditional Catholic positions. Conservatives could still mobilize the support needed to win school board elections, for which voter turnout was notoriously low, and they fought off attempts to formally deconfessionalize the school system. In this goal, they had the support of Protestant boards that believed that the dual system defended anglophone rights and the superior schools developed by the wealthier non-Catholic community. Despite its continued existence, few Catholic teachers supported a confessional system, and most taught little differently than teachers in the public schools.

Increased funding for education at all levels was a government strategy to achieve the key goal of the Quiet Revolution: *rattrapage*, or a catching up by Quebec to North American economic standards. As with education, results of purposeful action quickly became apparent. In 1961, there had been a 51 percent gap between the incomes of francophone and anglophone male workers in Montreal. That gap declined to 32 percent by 1970 and 15 percent in 1977.

Although no conscious plan shaped the policies of the Lesage government, the effect of efforts to promote development under francophone control significantly expanded the role of the state. One of the leading exponents of the new *étatisme* in Lesage's cabinet was René Lévesque, formerly a journalist with Radio-Canada. Lévesque waged a successful campaign for the province to nationalize all private hydro companies, making Hydro-Québec a monopoly. With the state in control of the energy sector, strategies that fulfilled nationalist goals of economic development, including the hiring of francophone managers and engineers in massive power projects, could be more easily implemented.

Another major provincial initiative was the establishment of the Quebec Pension Plan in 1965 in response to the creation of the Canada Pension Plan. Lesage argued that a separate provincial plan was needed to provide the government with an investment fund to encourage secondary industries and build the infrastructure required to exploit natural resources. Over time, the fund would be used to give the province minority shares in companies, allowing it to push these companies to invest in Quebec and to increase their francophone representation.

Quebec's desire to run its own social programs soon led to confrontations with Ottawa. In their determination to keep the federal government from using funding arrangements to control areas of provincial responsibility, provincial leaders in Quebec created problems for a reform-minded federal Liberal government under Lester Pearson, which was in office from 1963 to 1968. The solution was to allow Quebec, or any other province for that matter, to opt out of a federal program, retaining its share of funding as long as it established a similar provincial program with the monies. Only

Quebec, in practice, opted out of programs. Pierre Elliott Trudeau, who became prime minister in 1968, rejected the opting-out principle and announced that provinces that pulled out of future federal programs would not be reimbursed.

As the Quiet Revolution worked its way through the fabric of Quebec society, a growing number of Quebeckers became separatists—supporters of a sovereign Quebec nation-state. The major breakthrough for the sovereignty forces came in 1968 when René Lévesque left the Liberals and cobbled together an alliance of nationalist forces to create the *Parti Québécois*. The PQ called for sovereignty association—the creation of a separate Quebec state with the maintenance of close economic links with Canada. Such a state, it was argued, could negotiate with Ottawa *égal à égal*. It was an interesting notion, but its flaw, as both separatists and federalists observed, was that it assumed that the nine remaining provinces and two territories of Canada would be interested in establishing a special economic relationship with a sovereign Quebec and willing to let the federal government represent them in negotiations with Quebec.

The PQ won 24 percent of the vote on a sovereignty-association platform in the provincial election of 1970. In 1973 it increased its popularity to 30 percent and formed the official opposition. Three years later, sensing that the scandal-ridden government of Robert Bourassa was vulnerable, they attempted to broaden their support by promising that a PQ government would only pursue sovereignty association after holding a referendum on the question. In the following election, the PQ won a legislative majority with 42 percent of the vote. The referendum was held in 1980. Quebeckers were asked to give the government a mandate to negotiate sovereignty association with the federal government, but 60 percent voted "*non.*" Despite Lévesque's defeat, the sovereignty issue would not go away. The assertion of Quebec nationalism had dominated the burgeoning music, film, and theatre industries in Quebec throughout the '60s and '70s, and younger francophones felt little emotional attachment to Canada, which increasingly came to mean English Canada. Nonetheless, the emotional letdown after the referendum temporarily knocked the wind out of the separatist sails. Well-educated professionals, particularly in the public service, became cynical about independence, and the PQ government, saddled with debt like most provinces, beat a temporary retreat from the sovereignty option before the 1985 provincial election.

Under their new leader, Pierre-Marc Johnson, who had displaced a dispirited René Lévesque, the PQ proved no match for Robert Bourassa, whose Liberals emerged victorious. Commentators began to claim that young Québécois were less idealistic than the Quiet Revolution generation and that they did not look to the state to secure lucrative careers. With more and more francophones graduating from commerce programs and securing management positions in private companies, the smart view was that capital accumulation, not sovereignty, would preoccupy Québécois. As we will see in the next chapter, events overtook such prognostications.

One of the reasons that the new generation of francophones could pursue their dream in the private sector was the language legislation implemented by the PQ. As embodied in Bill 101, the legislation was designed to ensure the domination of the French language within the borders of Quebec. Many English Canadians, inside and outside Quebec, decried its tough educational provisions that allowed only English speakers born in Quebec to educate their children in English. Allophones—people whose first language was neither English nor French—were required to educate their children in French. Bill 101 also made French the only legal language for signs. For anglophones and allophones this clause symbolized the contempt in which they were held by Quebec nationalists. The efforts of Alliance Quebec, an English-rights organization created in 1982, to stress its acceptance of the primacy of the French language in Quebec, suggested that most anglophones and allophones sought accommodation with francophones, but a history of English-Canadian arrogance often meant that francophones viewed such accommodations as too little too late.

The Federal Government, Quebec, and Francophones

The federal government was not standing idly by as Quebec drifted in spirit outside of the Canadian Confederation. In 1963, the Pearson government established a Royal Commission on Bilingualism and Biculturalism under co-chairs André Laurendeau and Davidson Dunton. The commission confirmed a strong relationship between poverty and French unilingualism in Canada and demonstrated that the rate of assimilation of French Canadians outside Quebec and northern New Brunswick was so alarming as to support Quebec nationalist claims that something had to be done to prevent the disappearance of French culture in North America. Pierre Trudeau, who distrusted Quebec nationalism, or "tribalism" as he called it, was determined to make francophone Quebeckers feel *chez nous* throughout the country.

In 1969, Parliament passed the Official Languages Act, an attempt to put French on an equal footing with English throughout the federal government. The bill created an official languages commissioner responsible for ensuring that federal departments serve the public equally well in both languages. A significant percentage of new civil service hirings required that successful applicants be functionally bilingual, and large numbers of existing unilingual civil servants (usually anglophones) were sent to second-language instruction. By the 1980s, francophone representation in the federal civil service, once quite limited especially at senior levels, corresponded more closely with the percentage of Canadians that had French as their first language.

Through the 1970s, the federal government also tried to expand the use of French across the country by providing funds to support French-language schools, French immersion programs for anglophones, and organizations of francophones outside Quebec. More Canadians than ever before were becoming bilingual, but the success of these programs in strengthening either the French community or national unity was debatable. Francophones outside Quebec complained that economic realities in most of the country still forced them to become proficient in English to escape poverty. Moreover, these communities often lacked francophone cultural facilities and relied instead on English-language institutions. Although Radio-Canada could be accessed on radio and television by most francophones, the centralization of its production in Montreal meant that francophones outside Quebec played little role in shaping its programming. Many of them found the Quebec orientation of its news programs so pronounced that they turned to English-language channels, which had more local content. As for the Official Languages Act, the Fédération des Francophones hors Québec reported pessimistically in 1978 that it had "only slightly, not to say imperceptibly, contributed to the development of Francophone communities outside Quebec."[1]

Francophone organizations outside Quebec opposed separation because of the negative impact it would likely have on their communities, but they generally supported attempts by the Quebec government to limit the use of English in the province, arguing that the strength of *la Francophonie* in Quebec was the linchpin for French-Canadian survival. This led opponents of the extension of French-language rights outside Quebec to argue that French Canadians believed in language rights only when their own rights were at issue.

Encouraged by developments in Quebec, federal support for bilingualism, and the momentum of the times, Acadians in the Atlantic Region experienced their own quiet revolution. The number of Acadians continued to grow in the postwar period, but the rate of assimilation to anglophone culture was high. It soon became clear that, unless Acadians developed institutions and policies to address their needs, they would disappear as a cultural group. As in Quebec, education was identified as a key to maintaining cultural identity. Acadians in the Maritimes pushed for more French-language instruction in their schools and for institutions of higher learning to prepare their children for the new opportunities of the service economy.

In New Brunswick, sheer numbers made the Acadians a force to be reckoned with. Confrontations with Moncton's anglophone mayor, student sit-ins at the Université de Moncton, and a well-attended "Day of Concern" in January 1972 over unemployment brought attention to Acadian demands for programs that would protect their culture and improve their economic condition. In the fall of 1972, New Brunswick Acadians founded the Parti Acadien, whose stated goal by 1978 was to create a separate province of Acadie in the northeastern section of New Brunswick. Although it never won any seats, the Parti Acadien kept politicians on their toes. New Brunswick became Canada's only officially bilingual province, its status declared in 1969 and confirmed in the Constitution of 1982.

An attempt to legislate official bilingualism in 1984 in Manitoba created a backlash so bitter that the NDP government capitulated to tactics by the Conservative opposition to block the legislation. The NDP's bill had represented an agreement with the Société Franco-Manitobaine: the government would provide French-language services to Franco-Manitobans and the Société would abandon its attempt to force the province to retroactively restore services illegally terminated in 1890. The collapse of this agreement put the two parties back in court, which ultimately demanded the expensive translation of all laws passed since 1890.

Opposition to official bilingualism ran deep in English Canada, though polls suggested majority support. While many middle-class families were placing their children in immersion programs, others resented the notion that they had to speak French in order to get certain federal jobs. In popular thinking, particularly in Western Canada, all civil service jobs had become bilingual, the only people wanted for bilingual positions were francophones, and most federal grants were going to Quebec, the spoiled child of Confederation. Sporadic acts of separatist terrorism added to the image of a province where respect for non-francophone Canadians had collapsed.

Resentment against francophone militancy reached new heights during the October Crisis, which erupted in the fall of 1970. On 5 October, James Cross, the British trade commissioner in Montreal, was kidnapped by members of the Front de Libération du Québec (FLQ). Five days later, Pierre Laporte, the Quebec minister of labour and immigration, was abducted by another cell of the FLQ. Although consisting of only a few dozen members, the FLQ had been active since 1963 in pursuing its goals of revolutionary change in Quebec. Associated with over 200 bombings between 1963 and 1970, the FLQ's targets had included such bastions of privilege as McGill University, the home of Montreal mayor Jean Drapeau, and the Montreal Stock Exchange.

The success of the Liberal Party, led by Robert Bourassa, in the provincial election of April 1970 disgusted the FLQ as it did many nationalists in Quebec. From their perspective, Bourassa's victory had been achieved by the anglophone business community and federalists who did everything in

Protest in Ottawa following proclamation of War Measures Act, October 1970 (National Archives of Canada/PA-126347)

their power to steal victory from the PQ. By daring to seize a representative of the British Crown and a Liberal cabinet minister, the FLQ was hitting at the heart of the establishment that they so desperately wanted to topple.

In return for release of the hostages, the kidnappers demanded, among other things, the freeing of FLQ members who were imprisoned or detained and the broadcasting of their manifesto. The manifesto was read on Radio-Canada following the Cross kidnapping, but when the FLQ struck a second time, politicians in Quebec City and Ottawa decided to take strong action. On 16 October, the federal government proclaimed the War Measures Act under which it banned the FLQ, suspended civil rights, and imposed martial law on the nation. This was only the third time in the twentieth century that the War Measures Act had been invoked, and on the two previous occasions Canada had been at war with a foreign country.

The act played little, if any, role in the apprehension of the revolutionaries and the release of the trade commissioner in early December. It may well have precipitated the murder of Laporte, whose body was found in the trunk of an abandoned car on the night of 17 October. Yet most English Canadians and, initially, most francophones accepted claims by Trudeau and Bourassa that the FLQ was planning a full-scale insurrection that had to be nipped in the bud by the imposition of martial law. Ironically, the detention under the War Measures Act of over 450 people, most of whom were never charged with any offence, became another example for Quebec nationalists of the injustice imposed by an English-dominated Parliament. In reality, all francophone members in the House of Commons voted for the War Measures Act, including the Quebec-born prime minister. The sixteen members of parliament who voted against it—fifteen New Democrats and one Conservative—all were anglophones.

Trudeau had less success in attempting to unite Canadians behind his linguistic policies, partly because many people believed the money could be better spent elsewhere, though opponents tended to exaggerate how much the policy cost. Regional grievances were also bound up in the attacks on official bilingualism. Many Westerners and Atlantic Canadians accused Ottawa of being more interested in Quebec's concerns than in issues important to hinterland residents.

•Discontent in the Hinterlands

The discontent that had manifested itself in political movements in the Maritime and Western provinces in the interwar years resurfaced following the Second World War. As in the earlier period, alienation in the hinterlands was fuelled by lower rates of economic development compared to the Central Canadian provinces and by the lack of political power at the federal level to shape national policy. The rapid transformation of primary industries such as farming, fishing, forestry, and mining in the postwar period added considerably to the stress facing these regions. With Ottawa pursuing economic policies geared primarily to the industrial heartland, the outlying regions found it increasingly difficult to manage their vulnerable primary industries. The fact that six of the eight hinterland provinces consistently fell below the national average in investment and income in this period—British Columbia and Alberta were the exceptions—added urgency to the regional cause.

Western Alienation

In many ways, it is misleading to speak of the four provinces west of Ontario as a region. British Columbia has always enjoyed a separate identity from the Prairies and, in the period after World War II, the economies and the political traditions of the three Prairie provinces diverged dramatically. By 1980, Alberta, which had been the least populated of the three provinces before 1939, had a greater population than Manitoba and Saskatchewan combined. Its agricultural sector, while politically important, contributed far less than the energy sector to the provincial economy.

Unlike Alberta, Saskatchewan and Manitoba were have-not provinces, and their relative poverty militated against regional solidarity. During the energy boom from 1973 to 1982, Manitobans were as prone as Central and Atlantic Canadians to see Albertans as "blue-eyed sheiks of the North." Manitoba's economy, while not as vibrant as that of Alberta, was more diversified. Resource production contributed far less to the economy than it did in Saskatchewan or Alberta. Saskatchewan's reliance on agricultural production was vastly more important than in the neighbouring provinces.

Despite these differences, many Prairie residents thought of themselves as "westerners." They felt an allegiance to a region defined by Prairie landscapes and a history of oppression by Central Canada. While a majority of Prairie residents lived either in cosmopolitan cities or their satellites, much in the regional culture suggested a harkening back to rural roots: rodeos, country music, and plays, books, and films with rural themes.

For rural residents, the link with the agricultural past was at once more tangible and more elusive than for their urban counterparts. The number of rural residents was declining precipitously: in Manitoba, what had been a rural majority before the Second World War declined to a minority of 43 percent by 1951; in 1986, less than 28 percent of the population was classified as rural. Only 8 percent of the population farmed, and the number of farms in the province was cut in half from 1941 to 1986. Before 1945, the rural Prairies had been peopled overwhelmingly by small farmers relying on their own efforts and on co-operative marketing and buying to survive. By the 1990s, the average farm was over twice the size of farms in 1945. There was a growing class of farmers whose income and political interest seemed at variance with those of the small farmers, most of whom required off-farm income to survive. The average farm family received federal and provincial subsidies greater than the farmer's net income and many times greater than the payments to a family on welfare.

Farm communities fought hard to preserve schools, hospitals, retirement homes, and other services in the face of declining populations, but small businesses were often forced to close. In bad years, farmers did not buy; in good years, they drove to cities where selection and prices were better. This pattern motivated Eaton's decision in 1976 to close down its huge catalogue-shopping operation in Winnipeg, which for decades had served the whole of the Prairies.

The stresses on farmers and farm communities drove many people to the cities. With uncertain incomes, a high rate of farm accidents, and an increase in diseases resulting from the use of chemicals, many farmers gave up the idea that economic independence was better than wage work. Farm wives, who increasingly worked off the farm as well as on the land and in the household, were often victimized by frustrated farm husbands. Farm women increasingly followed their urban sisters in forming support groups and women's shelters to protect battered wives. They pointed out the particular stresses upon farm women and demanded that governments make day-care and counselling services more readily available in rural areas.

Political battles before World War I had improved the legal position of married farm women. Continuing battles in the 1970s resulted in similar gains for divorced and separated women. The catalyst was the case of Irene Murdoch, a rancher who endured years of physical and mental abuse from her husband while working alongside him on the family ranch. When she left her husband in 1968 after he broke her jaw, her claim to half the ranch was rejected by the courts, which granted her only a paltry maintenance payment. This decision, upheld by the Supreme Court of Canada, elicited much anger, and both farm and city women's groups campaigned for legislation to divide marital assets more equitably.

By the 1980s, some Canadians were beginning to recognize the environmental costs of commercial farming practices. Farmers had been encouraged by tax credits and government experts to ignore crop rotation and nutrient recycling practices in favour of chemicals that intensified production. Many were defensive when critics claimed they were destroying the soil and poisoning or depleting wetlands. Farmers raising livestock found themselves under attack from medical researchers who claimed that Canadians ate an unhealthy amount of red meat and by environmentalists and animal rights activists who charged that livestock farming practices were environmentally unsound and inhumane. Beef farmers fought back with high-profile advertising campaigns. After singer k.d. lang announced in a 1990 commercial that "beef stinks," the farmers of her native Alberta successfully pressured country music stations to boycott her music.

Rural western Canada was no longer completely dominated by farming. Mining, forestry, and even research communities sprouted and flourished as long as the industry that gave them life thrived. Designed to look like a prosperous suburb, Pinawa, Manitoba, was created by the Atomic Energy Commission in 1960 as the home for the mainly professional employees of a nuclear research lab. Somewhat less planned was the expansion of the small Alberta town of Fort McMurray. It began with oil sands development in the early 1960s and continued to spawn new suburbs as skyrocketing petroleum prices briefly created the illusion that oil from the tar sands could be marketed at competitive prices.

Boom towns Lanigan and Colonsay, both in Saskatchewan, were brought into existence by demand for potash. In the early 1990s, with markets sluggish and competition greater, both towns faced an uncertain future. There was no uncertainty for Uranium City, Saskatchewan. Once a community of 3000 residents, it had been abandoned by all but a hundred of its citizens after Eldorado shut down a uranium operation there in 1983. After the late 1980s, uranium companies avoided the creation of permanent communities in mining areas. Fly-in, fly-out commuter camps such as Cuff Lake and Key Lake, Saskatchewan, were seen as the wave of the future for mining "towns."

Resentment against Ottawa ran deep in Western Canada. After 1960, Westerners added bilingualism, the metric system, and resource policy to the roster of grievances that already included freight rates, monetary policy, and federal indifference to the plight of farmers. The oil crisis brought matters to a head. When OPEC began raising oil prices in 1973, the federal government intervened, much to the ire of Alberta and Saskatchewan, both to protect Canadian consumers (especially industrial consumers who were mainly to be found in Central Canada) and to ensure that federal coffers received a portion of the windfall profits of Canadian oil producers. Similar conflicts over gas pricing pitted Ottawa against both Edmonton and Victoria. Alberta's aggressiveness was fuelled by the growth of a provincial bourgeoisie dependent on the energy sector but determined to use the revenues from oil and gas to diversify the Alberta economy and their own personal holdings. The growing provincial bureaucracy sympathized with the views of the new entrepreneurs and expressed in no uncertain terms their frustration with federal arrogance.

The provinces argued that they had the right to control the resources within their borders. They resented the federal government's use of its constitutional control over taxation and interprovincial and international trade to limit provincial control over resources. Although by the late 1970s Alberta had become Canada's wealthiest province, Conservative Premier Peter Lougheed, a former vice-president of the giant Mannix corporation and a representative of the "province-building" bourgeoisie, argued that its prosperity would be short-lived if oil and gas revenues were not used to diversify the economy to prepare for the era when these resources would be depleted. In 1975, his government created the Heritage Trust Fund, into which a portion of oil royalties was committed to provide monies needed to stimulate new economic activity in Alberta. The Fund was not as successful as originally hoped: it invested conservatively and, where it did not, had an uncanny knack of choosing losers.

Saskatchewan had a parallel body set up by an NDP government. Like Quebec's investment fund, it bought shares for the state in private companies in order to encourage economic development within Saskatchewan. It was responsible for establishing a steel-manufacturing firm in Regina, but its limited resources, relative to the Heritage Trust Fund, restricted achievements of this kind.

For both provinces, federal attempts to grab a larger share of resource revenues, so reminiscent of federal land controls before 1930, were unacceptable. Pointing to unresolved regional grievances, both provinces accused the federal government and Central Canadians of exploiting Western Canada and contributing nothing to its development. Humiliated by their experience of having been federal charity cases during the Depression, Prairie residents tended to rally behind their provincial leaders, who promised that economic diversity was achievable if Ottawa would respond to their demands.

The competition for economic development, which seemed to be the primary goal of Western provincial governments of all stripes, allowed corporations to play provinces off one another to provide concessions before deciding where to locate new plants or relocate old ones. Often the desperate desire for economic development led to irresponsible policies. Social Credit, which governed British Columbia from 1952 to 1972 and again from 1975 to 1991, ignored the environmental degradation wrought by resource companies. Preferring short-term prosperity, they followed the lead of their predecessors with lax reforestation policies and indifference to agricultural land lost to industrial development and urban sprawl. As late as the 1980s, only a third of logged land in British Columbia was being reforested. Studies of pulp mills in the province decried a record of poor control over effluents, which seeped into rivers and lakes. Waste coal from strip-mining operations in the East Kootenays fouled the Elk River Valley's creek system, and the stench in cities such as Prince George challenged company claims that they used the best pollution-dissipating equipment. Federal management of the region's fisheries appeared to be no more conscientious. Only when salmon stocks ran dangerously low in the 1980s did the government begin to address the issue of overfishing.

An NDP government in power in British Columbia from 1972 to 1975 made modest attempts to force corporations to control pollution. It also designated agricultural land as resaleable only for agricultural purposes. Although it was environmentally conscious, the NDP depended on support from trade unions such as the International Woodworkers whose boss, Jack Munro, regarded environmentalism as a threat to workers' jobs. By the late 1970s, pressure groups such as Greenpeace, and Native groups angry about resource company encroachments on disputed land, pressured the province to control development. Saving Meares Island, parts of the Stein Valley, and the Queen Charlottes from clear cutting represented only partial success, but the rising consciousness that marked the late 1980s and early 1990s created the possibility that environmental consequences would be taken more seriously when governments assessed economic development. While most environmentalists limited themselves to public education and government lobbying, others resorted to "eco-terrorism." Logging companies claimed that activists spiked trees, endangering the lives of forestry workers. The Squamish Five were sentenced for bombing a B.C. Hydro substation to protest the corporation's irresponsible environmental policies.

In the 1960s, the Conservative government of Duff Roblin in Manitoba had no qualms about mega-projects. Anxious to promote economic development, Roblin and his NDP successor loaned $140 million to a mysterious group of Swiss financiers who agreed to develop a forestry complex in Northern Manitoba. The financiers repaid little of their loans, and the government was forced to take the forestry project under its wing, writing off the loans to bad debts.

The Atlantic Revolution

Atlantic Canada had an even worse record than the Western provinces in managing the development ethic that gripped the world in the second half of the twentieth century. Like Quebeckers, Atlantic Canadians relied heavily on government intervention to stimulate economic development, but they were less successful than Quebeckers in becoming masters in their own house. At the same time, problems facing the region and the programs launched to address them were so wide ranging that they constituted nothing less than an "Atlantic revolution."[2]

The collapse of the region's coal and steel industries and the restructuring of primary industries in the postwar period forced severe adjustments. In the 1950s, the number of workers engaged in the primary and manufacturing sector declined. Unable to find jobs, 82 000 people left the region during the decade. Those who stayed found work in the expanding trade and service sectors. By 1961, direct government employment accounted for over 100 000 jobs in Atlantic Canada, not including the defence activities, which employed as many people as forestry and mining combined. With incomes in the region running from two-thirds to three-quarters of the national average in 1961 and social services severely underfunded, drastic measures were called for.

For a time it seemed as if the region might actually escape the scourge of underdevelopment and dependency. Private enterprise organized the Atlantic Provinces Economic Council (APEC) in 1954 to press for policies that would improve the economic climate in the region. During the Diefenbaker administration in Ottawa, special Atlantic Provinces Adjustment Grants were implemented and an Atlantic Development Board was established to help co-ordinate regional economic planning. Lester Pearson's government was equally committed to regional development. Under Pierre Trudeau, Ottawa decided to extend regional development to other areas of the country, since even the wealthier provinces had underdeveloped regions that needed attention. The Department of Regional Economic Expansion was given a wide mandate to root out pockets of poverty, especially in Quebec, which soon surpassed the Atlantic region in the amount of regional development money it received.

New thinking about the role of the state stimulated ambitious and controversial initiatives in the Atlantic region. In Nova Scotia, the Conservative government led by Robert Stanfield created Industrial Estates Limited to encourage and co-ordinate investment. In the 1960s, New Brunswick's Liberal premier Louis J. Robichaud launched a program designed to raise the living standards in the poorer municipalities of the province, many of them populated by his fellow Acadians. Under the long Liberal tenure of Alexander Campbell, Prince Edward Island was virtually taken over by planners, with the Federal–Provincial Development Plan launched in 1969.

Nowhere was government initiative more visible than in Newfoundland. Having entered Confederation in 1949 with a standard of living even lower than that of the Maritime provinces, Newfoundlanders were determined to catch up to the rest of Canada. Newfoundland's first premier, Joey Smallwood, was an eloquent and energetic champion of economic growth. Assuming the Economic Development portfolio himself, he lobbied any politician or entrepreneur who would listen to invest in his province. He was also prepared to take tough measures with those who resisted the values and institutions of the modern age. Following the advice of the planners, Smallwood's government introduced a program to encourage people to move from their isolated outports to urban centres where they would have better access to services and jobs. What began as a voluntary program in the 1950s became a coercive one in the 1960s. Since jobs were often scarce in the new growth centres, many people felt cheated and demoralized by the bureaucratic processes controlling their lives.

It soon became clear that development in the Atlantic region would not come easily. Although regional incomes remained stable in relationship to the rest of Canada, they failed to catch up, and many of the force-fed industries ended in disaster. In Nova Scotia, millions of dollars were lost in efforts to establish a heavy water plant in Glace Bay and an electronics company in Stellarton. Both communities had been seriously affected by the decline in the coal industry that had previously sustained them, but the new industries failed to take root. Millions of dollars were poured into New Brunswick premier Richard Hatfield's pet project to build a luxury automobile, the Bricklin, but that company too went into receivership. In Newfoundland, Premier Smallwood attracted a variety of entrepreneurs willing to gamble with taxpayers' money, but few of his industrial ventures paid off. An oil refinery at Come-By-Chance, opened with great fanfare in October 1973—the *Queen Elizabeth II* was chartered at a reported fee of $97 000 a day for the occasion—went bankrupt within three years. No one had foreseen the OPEC oil crisis, which would disrupt the best laid plans of Smallwood and his successors.

Atlantic Canada was not alone in the "boondoggle" business, but the bad publicity such investments produced added to an image that the underdeveloped region could ill afford. Negative publicity also dogged successful ventures such as the establishment of three Michelin tire plants in Nova Scotia. By the 1980s, over 5000 people in the province were employed by Michelin, but the price was steep for those who believed in the right of workers to organize to protect their wages and working conditions. In 1979, Nova Scotia's Conservative government led by John Buchanan agreed to pass labour legislation—quickly dubbed the "Michelin bill"—that would make it more difficult for unions to gain a foothold in Nova Scotia's tire industry.

The fisheries and off-shore oil, both declared the salvation of the region in the 1970s, collapsed in the less exuberant 1980s. With most consumer goods and services still produced elsewhere, development money simply flowed out of the region as quickly as it came in. Unemployment rates remained 50 to 100 percent higher in Atlantic Canada than elsewhere in the nation despite continued outmigration and lower labour force participation. Although development programs no doubt helped to keep the region from sinking further behind the rest of the nation and transformed the lives of Atlantic Canadians forever, they failed to solve the problem of regional underdevelopment.

In a region where economic problems remained so persistent, much energy went into maintaining what was achieved rather than fighting for improvements. The citizens of Sydney, with help from Cape Bretoners generally, campaigned tirelessly to prevent their steel mill from closing down in the mid-1960s when it was abandoned by DOSCO. Federal and provincial governments agreed to keep both the steel mill and DOSCO's coal mines at Glace Bay in operation under the auspices of the Cape Breton Development Corporation (DEVCO), which was also charged with seeking ways to diversify Cape Breton's declining industrial economy.

The dramatic rise and fall of the East Coast fisheries perhaps best captures the roller coaster atmosphere of life in Atlantic Canada in the postmodern age. By the 1960s, modern technology made it possible to catch virtually every fish in the sea. Provincial and federal governments poured money into better boats and more fish processing. With the declaration of the 200-mile limit in 1977, the Department of Fisheries and Oceans began to exert tighter control over the fisheries, imposing quotas and licensing limits on most fish stocks. Optimism spurred greater investment in the industry and the continuing exploitation of the resource. By the 1980s, Canadians had become the world's leading fish exporters, but they were running out of fish.

The social impact of the transformation of the fisheries was equally dramatic. As the industry expanded in the 1970s, the more than 1000 coastal communities mostly or wholly dependent on the fisheries received a new lease on life. Wharves, processing plants, and improved social services represented welcome investment in towns and villages that had hitherto been the major sources of the region's migrant labour. As families began to plan around bigger and better incomes, new homes were built and larger vessels purchased.

With growth and optimism prevailing, fisheries workers refused to submit silently to the dictates of corporate organizational structures and government controls. In 1970, fishers in Canso, Milgrave, and Petit-de-Grat launched a fifteen-month strike for the right to unionize under the Nova Scotia trade union act. The Newfoundland Fishermen, Food, and Allied Workers (NFFAW), expelled in the 1950s from the Trades and Labour Congress for its alleged communist leanings, signed up over 28 000 inshore fishers, offshore trawlermen, and plant workers. Under its outspoken president Richard Cashin, it waged a tireless battle for better wages, working conditions, and representation on committees that advised the government on fishing policy.

Even more impressive was the rise of the Maritime Fishermen's Union, which focussed on the plight of the inshore fishers. Originating in the Acadian communities of New Brunswick in the mid-1970s, it soon spread to other Maritime provinces. The MFU forced the New Brunswick government to pass progressive labour legislation and pressured the federal minister of fisheries, Romeo LeBlanc, himself a New Brunswick Acadian, for action favoured by the inshore fishers. Under LeBlanc, who held the fisheries portfolio from 1974 to 1979, the 200-mile limit was proclaimed and programs to promote community stability, provide a fairer share of the quotas for inshore fleets, and improve conservation were implemented.

The fisheries boom quickly turned into a bust. By the early 1980s processing companies were in trouble, and two corporate giants, Fishery Products International and National Sea swallowed up their competitors. With the collapse of the fish stocks in the late 1980s, quotas were cut, fish plants shut down, and many fishing communities faced extinction. People in Canso protested loudly when their fish plant was closed in 1990. Although they won a reprieve, they remained hostages to a corporation whose survival depended on profits not people and whose decisions were determined by forces far removed from the Canso town limits.

In July 1992, the federal government announced that there would be a two-year moratorium on northern cod fishing. This meant unemployment for 19 000 Newfoundland fishers and plant workers. The future of dozens of communities on Newfoundland's east coast became doubtful. Pitiful compensation was offered the workers, and although the levels of compensation were increased after threats by fishers to ignore the moratorium, a bleak future seemed to await families dependent on the fishery.

•Native Peoples Find a Voice

Native people responded to their continued subjugation with increased organization and militancy. Like other groups, they experienced internal divisions, particularly between status Indians, who were beneficiaries of the Indian Act, and Métis and non-status Indians who were not. A catalyst for action by treaty Indians was the unveiling of the Trudeau government's White Paper on Indian policy in June 1969. The government planned to relinquish Native lands while at the same time removing Indians' special status, dismantling the Department of Indian Affairs, and having the provinces assume responsibilities for services to Native people.

The Indian response was overwhelmingly negative. The National Indian Brotherhood (the name was changed to the Assembly of First Nations in 1982), formed in 1968 to speak for treaty Indians, led the attack, claiming that Indians wanted self-government and not the assimilation that becoming ordinary citizens of provinces implied. Native groups argued that, as Canada's first peoples, they had a right to reassert their cultures so long suppressed by government and church policies. The White Paper would be a final nail in the coffin for Native peoples, a policy of cultural genocide. The Trudeau government, surprised at the vehemence of Native reaction, withdrew the White Paper but offered no framework for negotiating Native demands for self-government.

During the 1970s, pressures from the NIB and provincial associations led the government to gradually give Native peoples the responsibility for their own education. The residential system had been phased out in the 1960s and 1970s, though its scars remained. In 1990, the head of the Manitoba Association of Chiefs, Phil Fontaine, made a public issue of claims that had frequently been heard privately: Native children in residential schools had been victims of violence, including sexual abuse, at the hands of members of religious orders as well as lay teachers. In the 1980s, Canadians grew accustomed to revelations about abuse in religious residential schools, orphanages, and reformatories. While not all of the victims were Native children, their plight particularly shocked many Canadians. After 1973, it became increasingly common for Native children to attend local schools controlled by their band councils, particularly in the elementary grades, but many reserves had little success in convincing Ottawa to build high schools close enough so that their children were not forced to either bus several hours a day or live in towns away from the reserve.

Native people who left the reserves for towns and cities rarely were assimilated into the larger society. Undereducated and faced with discrimination, most succumbed to lives in urban ghettos marked by poor housing, poverty, and drunkenness. Indian and Métis Friendship Centres and Native-run addiction programs helped to rescue some Native people from the worst aspects of city life, but, for the most part, aboriginal leaders reckoned that reserves offered their people a better opportunity to live in prosperity and preserve their cultural inheritance.

Unfortunately, reserves often lacked an economic base. This led some aboriginal groups to demand that Native people be trained and hired for work both in the construction and operation of industrial projects near reserves, but companies rarely came through with the jobs, preferring to hire trained personnel from outside. Indians grew angry as they watched industrial developments deplete wildlife and poison waters upon which they depended without offering even employment in return. Increasingly, demands were heard for Native control of industrial developments. Other groups rejected developments that would affect local resources and thereby force Indians to abandon whatever economic self-sufficiency remained to them.

Industrial developments often brought devastation to Native peoples. Northern Ontario pulp mills poisoned the English–Wabigoon River system, which had provided a modest living for Ojibwa fishers and tourist operators. In the 1970s, the prosperous Cree of remote South Indian Lake in Manitoba had their economy destroyed by a hydro development as did several Saskatchewan and Manitoba communities in the 1960s. Even the Inuit and Cree of northern Quebec, who in 1975 received financial compensation from the provincial government in return for a surrender of claims amounting to over one million square kilometres, were living in poverty, according to a federal study in the 1980s.

Native peoples of the Yukon and Northwest Territories were particularly vocal in rejecting the oil and natural gas pipelines proposed in the 1970s to fuel Southern Canada as well as the United States with energy from Alaska and Northern Canada. Neither the Yukon Indians nor the Inuit of either territory had signed treaties with the federal government, and the Mackenzie Valley Indians had treaties but no reserves. While some of the Métis of the Northwest Territories supported a pipeline as a possible source of jobs, in 1975 a large percentage of the Métis joined the Indians of the region to declare the existence of a Dene nation seeking independence within the framework of Canadian Confederation.

The Trudeau government, which supported the proposed pipeline projects, appointed Justice Thomas Berger, a former leader of the New Democrats in British Columbia, to study the impact of a pipeline in the Mackenzie Valley on local residents and the environment. Berger proved sympathetic to the Dene and Inuit who stressed the extent to which they still subsisted on local resources. They made clear their desire to hold off major developments until their land claims had been settled and they were in a position to negotiate with potential investors rather than having the Canadian government impose projects upon them. The government accepted Berger's call for a halt to pipeline developments for a decade, but it was slow in pursuing comprehensive land claims settlements for the North and providing aid to bands seeking to establish local businesses under Native control.

Berger Commission hearings in the Northwest Territories   (Northern News Services Ltd.)

In 1984, the Inuit of the Mackenzie Delta received a land settlement that gave them 242 000 square kilometres, and the Yukon Indians reached agreement with Ottawa in 1988. In November 1992, the Inuit of the eastern Arctic accepted a negotiated deal with Ottawa that provided them 350 000 square kilometres of surface and 36 000 square kilometres of sub-surface mineral rights. At the same time, they voted for partition of the Northwest Territories, with the eastern Arctic to become a separately administered territory called Nunavut (meaning "the people's land" in the Inuktitut language). Within Nunavut's boundaries, 17 500 of the approximate 22 000 residents were Inuit, and many saw Nunavut's creation as a bold experiment in Native self-government.

Outside the territories, the federal government proved even slower to settle land claims made by Indians who lacked treaties or reserves and by treaty Indians who claimed more territory than the government had allotted them. Although there were over 500 claims outstanding in 1990, only three or four per year were being settled. Saskatchewan Indians, for example, claimed that over 400 000 acres of reserve land had been illegally taken from them before World War I. Many Indians became frustrated as their land claims bogged down in bureaucracy and the courts, and militancy became more common. They watched sympathetically as militant

Indians south of the border in the American Indian Movement (AIM) confronted authorities over land claims.

One of the first Canadian confrontations occurred in 1974 when Indians occupied Anicinabe Park in Kenora, claiming that the park, like much of Kenora, belonged to the Native peoples. In the late 1980s, in various parts of British Columbia, Native peoples clashed with loggers whose activities were despoiling traditional aboriginal lands. The province had resisted Native treaties, and the federal government had done little to protect aboriginals when their lands were seized by the province for industrial and urban expansion. In 1985 the Supreme Court awarded the small Musqueam band $10 million in compensation for Indian Affairs' having duped them into granting a golf course a long lease at low rents. Court action might eventually force both Ottawa and Victoria to pay many millions of dollars to compensate the province's Indians for a century of mistreatment. Rather than awaiting monetary compensation once their resources and lifestyle were gone, many Native people in the province preferred to hold off developers who might ruin their lands, even if it meant breaking the law. In 1991, the British Columbia government, responding to growing Native militancy across Canada, agreed to negotiate land issues. If there was any optimism that such negotiations would go smoothly, it dissipated later that year when Judge Allen McEachern issued his decision on the Gitsan–Wet'suwet'en land claim. The judgment reflected long-standing Eurocentric biases and showed the tremendous distance between the two parties.

Pent-up frustrations were evident across the country by 1990. The Lubicon Cree in Northern Alberta, who had been waiting for a reserve for over fifty years, forcibly kept out oil companies wanting to drill on territories claimed by the Lubicon. The Temagami Indians in Ontario, supported by environmentalists, prevented logging on their territories. The Cree of Northern Quebec threatened both court action and possible sabotage if Quebec proceeded with a second James Bay hydro-electric project. Nova Scotia Mi'kmaq pursued their hunting and fishing rights against an unsympathetic provincial government and used an investigation into the wrongful murder conviction of a young Mi'kmaq, Donald Marshall, to expose the racism that they faced on a daily basis. Royal commissions in Manitoba and Alberta concluded, as did the Nova Scotia inquiry, that all components of the legal system, from the police through the judiciary, exhibited prejudice when dealing with Native peoples. The Manitoba Public Inquiry into the Administration of Justice and Aboriginal People had been sparked by two tragic deaths: the murder of Helen Betty Osborne in The Pas in 1971 and the shooting of an unarmed Native leader, John Joseph Harper, in Winnipeg in 1988.

THE MURDER OF HELEN BETTY OSBORNE

On 13 November 1971, the RCMP in The Pas, Manitoba, were alerted to the discovery of the remains of a Native woman in the woods near the town. The body was later identified as Helen Betty Osborne, who was boarding in The Pas while she attended high school. The evening before, Osborne had been kidnapped by four white youths and driven to the woods. She resisted their demands that she have sex with them. They responded by stabbing her more than fifty times.

Although the identity of the murderers quickly spread (one of the youths actually bragged about the incident), none of the town's citizens was willing to give information to the RCMP. It was fourteen years before charges were laid against two of Osborne's four abductors. Of the other two, one was never charged and one was given immunity from prosecution in return for his testimony. In the end, only one man was convicted of any charges.

Roland Penner, the provincial attorney-general at the time of the conviction, claimed that the RCMP would have treated the case with more urgency had the victim been white. The RCMP countered that the real problem was the racist conspiracy of silence within the white community in The Pas.

The most sensational confrontation occurred in the summer of 1990 between the Quebec provincial police and Mohawk Warriors at a reserve near Oka, Quebec. The violent clash left one police officer dead and created a standoff that provoked Canadian military intervention. While the Warriors, who ran gambling casinos and smuggling operations at other reserves, were controversial among the Mohawk, the issue they chose was not: the town of Oka wished to develop a golf course on lands the Mohawk regarded as sacred. The federal government, while denouncing the Warriors as terrorists, was forced to buy the disputed land to make it available to the Indians, but the solution appeared to be a pragmatic reaction to confrontation rather than federal magnanimity toward Native peoples.

Land claims were not the only grievance. Native women who married white men lost their treaty status under a notorious section of the Indian Act that allowed Indian men to marry non-status spouses without loss of status but deprived Indian women of the same right. In the early 1970s, Native women formed two organizations—Indian Rights for Indian Women and the National Native Women's Association—to fight for their rights. Campaigns by Native women were supported by non-Native women's groups.

Together they led the federal government to remove the offending section from the act in 1985. Nonetheless, some Indian leaders blocked the return to reserves by women who had lost their status. The leaders charged that the federal government had done nothing to add to the land base of over-crowded reserves so as to make reintegration of these women and their families possible without creating hardship for existing residents.

On the reserves, women's traditional influence was often eroded. In an atmosphere of hopelessness, Native men struck out at their wives and children. Studies of remote reserves indicated a pattern of physical and sexual abuse in which girls and women were the main victims. On some reserves, almost every woman had been the victim of sexual abuse, usually by a family member, before she reached adulthood. Native women organized support groups and demanded that elected band councils implement programs to counsel men who had abused women and to protect their potential victims. Male band leaders were often resistant to such pressures.

• The Women's Movement

In no area of Canadian life was there more questioning of basic assumptions than in gender roles. Women increasingly challenged sexual stereotypes and demanded that traditional notions of their subordinate place in society be abandoned. Arguing that patriarchal society restricted women, many feminists joined organizations to fight for full equality. Some organizations concentrated on encouraging governments, businesses, and community organizations to involve women equally with men at all levels of decision making. Others claimed that female representation in institutions was not enough; the institutions themselves had to change, as did the behaviour of both men and women.

The feminism of this period is sometimes termed "second-wave" feminism to distinguish it from the "first wave" associated with the struggle for suffrage. Though many first-wave feminists regarded suffrage as only a step along the way toward full equality for women or a feminist restructuring of society, social forces in the 1920s allowed them few victories. Second-wave feminists operated in a more favourable ideological climate, though they too found that the struggle for women's rights was an uphill battle.

The women's movement was preceded by an unparalleled participation of women, including married women, in the paid labour force. Better educated than earlier generations, women had begun to spend a larger part of their lives in paid labour, though in 1960, it was still rare for women to work outside the home while their children were young. By 1981, 49.4 percent of married women whose children were all under the age of six were in paid work; five years later, that rate had risen to 62.1 percent. In 1986, 55.4 percent of all women over the age of fifteen were in the labour force, an increase from 39.9 percent in 1971 and 23.4 percent in 1953.

Although they participated more than ever in paid work, women found that their employment options were limited and that their pay was deflated by notions that women's wages were "pin money," unlike the wages of a male "breadwinner." In reality, financial necessity rather than a desire for pin money motivated most women workers. Liberalization of divorce laws increased the number of self-supporting women. By 1982, one in three marriages ended in divorce; in that year alone 70 000 divorce decrees were issued in Canada. From the 1971 to the 1981 census, the number of single-parent families jumped from 477 525 to 714 005, of which 85 percent were headed by women. In 1979, 40 percent of women workers were separated, divorced, or widowed, and most of those who had children at home were sole providers. With women earning less than two-thirds of men's average income, it is not surprising that the National Council on Welfare reported in both 1975 and 1987 that 59 percent of adults living in poverty were women. It also estimated that the poverty rate for two-spouse families would jump by over 50 percent if all married women left the work force.

While employers and families required women's paid work, social institutions adapted slowly to accommodate the needs of women workers. Despite their new responsibilities, women found that there were virtually no formal arrangements for childcare. Neighbours, relatives, and friends rather than trained childcare workers had to be relied upon to provide a service that society still regarded as a mother's duty. Mothers living in poverty battled with governments to receive day-care subsidies. Single mothers and working wives both returned from work to find the house-work waiting. The "double day" of housework and paid work often left women even less leisure time than their mothers had enjoyed, although their wages sometimes allowed them to purchase labour-saving devices, prepared foods, and off-the-rack clothing. Yet neither at home nor at work did they receive recognition for their contribution. Society did not view housework as "real" work, and those women who worked outside the home were confronted with lack of opportunity for advancement, low wages, paternalism, and outright harassment.

Individual reactions to the obstacles facing women slowly coalesced into political action. In Quebec in 1966, Thérèse Casgrain, a leading figure in the provincial NDP and the peace group Voice of Women, helped to found the Fédération des femmes du Québec, an umbrella group of women's organizations, to fight for women's rights. In English Canada, women's groups, galvanized by leaders such as Laura Sabia, president of the Canadian Federation of University Women, and *Chatelaine* magazine editor Doris Anderson, pressured Ottawa for action. Supported by the Quebec Fédération, English-Canadian women's groups formed the Committee for the Equality of Women whose tactics convinced the Pearson government, spurred by outspoken Cabinet Minister Judy LaMarsh, to create a Royal Commission on the Status of Women. The commission, established in 1967, served as a catalyst to focus complaints from women of every social station in Canada. The National Action Committee on the Status of Women (NAC), an umbrella organization for the many women's groups springing up across the country, was created in 1972. It lobbied governments to ensure that the commission's recommendations—which included

Thérèse Casgrain, 1972 (Archives Nationales du Québec, Direction de Montréal, de Laval, de Lanaudière, des Laurentides, et de la Montérégie)

calls for reforms in education, employment, immigration, criminal and family law, and childcare—would not simply gather dust.

Several of the commission's recommendations centred on birth control. In 1969, Parliament had removed the anachronistic legislative ban on contraceptive devices and information and had liberalized abortion laws. Thereafter, the latter issue proved a particularly hotly contested battleground between those who demanded the complete removal of abortion from the Criminal Code and others who demanded a ban on all abortions, sometimes making exceptions where a pregnancy endangered the woman's life. The former group stressed a woman's right to control her own body while the latter group claimed that a fetus was a living person from the moment of conception and that its right to life outweighed a woman's right to reproductive self-determination. Access to abortion was uneven across the country, leading the Supreme Court to rule in 1988 that the 1969 law, which required abortions to be approved by a three-doctor panel, violated Charter guarantees for equal rights for all Canadians. For a period thereafter, abortions were marginally more freely available, but legislation passed by the House of Commons in 1990 recriminalized abortion, again making physicians responsible for determining whether the procedure was necessary. Anti-choice campaigners threatened to take doctors who performed abortions to court, and many physicians who had offered the procedure announced that they would stop doing so. The Senate rejected the new legislation in early 1991, and Justice Minister Kim Campbell seemed reluctant to reopen what was an increasingly divisive issue. In 1992, a Toronto abortion clinic run by Dr Henry Morgentaler, a tireless crusader for women's right to safe abortion, was destroyed by a bomb blast. While no group claimed responsibility for or was charged with the crime, pro-choice groups pointed to the increasingly desperate methods of anti-choice groups, particularly in the United States, and wondered if such extremism was being exported to Canada.

Women's groups sought to expose the extent of male violence against women and children in Canadian society. Sexual assaults, battering, physical and sexual abuse of children, and sexual harassment in the workplace had generally been regarded as private problems and were often not taken very seriously by the authorities. Indeed, when NDP MP Margaret Mitchell rose in the House of Commons to speak on the issue of wife battering in May 1982, she was greeted with laughter and disparaging remarks from many of her fellow MPs. Such insensitivity shocked many Canadians and helped to bring the issue into focus. Women's groups pressed for battered women's shelters, rape crisis centres, counselling for abusers and their victims, increased court charges, and convictions for rapists and harassers. In

1992, the federal government set up a panel to study violence against women, but the announcement was not greeted with uniform enthusiasm. Some protested that women who were victims of violence did not need another study, they needed specific action. Several feminist groups, including NAC, disturbed by the panel's failure to appoint women of colour and disabled women, withdrew their support from the commission. Issues of inclusion and racism increasingly preoccupied the Canadian women's movement in the 1990s. Women of colour argued that the movement had for too long been a white, middle-class enclave that failed to address— indeed, to listen to—the concerns of those outside this group. Such charges forced white feminists to grapple with the systemic racism that underlies Canadian society.

Many feminist campaigns in the 1970s and 1980s focussed on rectifying women's exclusion from management positions, non-traditional blue-collar

International Women's Day march, 1982   (Canadian Women's Movement Archives/ University of Ottawa Libraries/Nancy Adamson, photographer)

work, and other jobs with high status and good pay. They also continued to pursue both equal pay for equal work and equal pay for work of equal value to increase the pay and prestige of traditional "women's work," which was still the lot of most women. Even within the professions, women tended to enter traditional areas that were less renumerative than those dominated by men. The 1986 census reported that 79 percent of workers in the health professions, sciences, and technologies were women and that, on average, they earned $18 648 per year. By contrast, 94 percent of engineers and applied scientists, a group with an average salary of $38 321, were men.

Changes to education patterns were necessary if women were to pursue non-traditional employment. By the late 1980s, more young women than men were attaining undergraduate degrees, but the majority were still in the arts. Women entering programs such as engineering often had to contend with hostility and puerile sexism passing for humour from other students and even from instructors. "Date rape" became a major problem on college campuses, and feminist attempts to address the issue in "No means no" campaigns were often met with ridicule and threats. On 6 December 1989, an event occurred that forced engineers and male students generally to confront the ugly consequences of sexism on campus. A deranged young man, deluded that feminists had ruined his life, walked into a classroom in the École polytechnique at the Université de Montréal and fatally shot fourteen young women. Public outrage following the Montreal massacre forced many Canadian women and men to re-examine the violent and sexist nature of their society.

•Trade Unions and New Times

"We are not Florence Nightingales," United Nurses of Alberta president Margaret Ethier proclaimed as Alberta's nurses walked the bricks on one of their three illegal strikes between 1979 and 1987. Tired of being exploited by employers—usually the state—women in the "caring" professions began to call into question the stereotype that "women's work" was mainly community service rather than remunerative professional labour. Women in government offices were equally tired of being told that they were servants of the public first and wage earners second. At times consciously feminist, at times not, these women were sufficiently influenced by the ideas of the feminist movement to know that their work was undervalued and that their working conditions required improvement. No longer deterred by arguments that it was unladylike to get involved with unions, women who had the opportunity to do so unionized at a rapid rate.

From 1966 to 1976, four-fifths of Canada's new unionists were women, and in 1978, women accounted for 28.5 percent of organized workers. Although this was a vast improvement from earlier decades, women—who made up 40 percent of all workers—were still underrepresented in union ranks. Joining a union had economic pay-offs: in 1982, it was estimated that the average unionized woman earned 14 percent more than a comparable non-unionized woman worker. It was the public sector that mainly accounted for the growth in women's unionism and, indeed, for the growth in overall unionism in the period after 1960. In 1989, the three biggest unions in Canada were public-service unions: the Canadian Union of Public Employees, National Union of Provincial Government Employees, and Public Service Alliance of Canada represented 825 000 municipal, provincial, and federal workers.

In Quebec, public sector unions in the early 1970s formed a Common Front that used general strikes to improve the position of the lowest-paid workers, most of whom were women. The Bourassa government's attempt to end the 1972 Common Front strike was resisted by the heads of Quebec's three largest union federations, who were all jailed for their efforts. The unions had an easier time dealing with the PQ government during its first term when it was encouraging public workers to vote for sovereignty in the referendum. In its second term, the PQ, gripped by fiscal conservatism, cut public-sector wages and proved as willing as Bourassa to use police and threats to cool the ardour of strikers.

Women faced a struggle within the unions to be heard and to be represented. In PSAC, for example, women accounted for 43 percent of all members but no executive officers in 1983. Even in CUPE—which in the 1970s was headed by the militant and articulate Grace Hartman and included Shirley Carr, the Canadian Labour Congress' first woman president, as one of its members—there were imbalances: while women made up 44 percent of the membership and were well-represented in the executive, only 11 percent of staff representatives in the early '80s were women.

Women in traditional job ghettos outside government remained largely unorganized in 1990. The union movement continued to put few resources into organizing such workers, and their vulnerability during periods of high unemployment made them generally wary of unions. Less than 1 percent of Canada's 145 000 bank employees were organized in 1980 and not many more employees of department stores. The women's movement joined the unions in supporting several strikes by the small numbers of locals in these sectors, including one against Eaton's in the 1980s. Nonetheless, employer determination to break the unions, coupled with weak legislation regarding employers' obligations in first-contract talks, resulted in losses for these militant women. The increased number of women working in small groups in mall chain stores also created problems for union recruiters.

Union growth after 1960 was erratic, despite the increase in unionization of women and public-sector workers. Union membership peaked at 40 percent of the non-agricultural civilian labour force in 1983, but the recession, which ate away many manufacturing and resource sector jobs and even cut into the public-sector work force, caused that percentage to drop beginning in 1984. By 1989, the figure was down to 36.2 percent, which was still an improvement over the 1960 figure of 32.3 percent.

Among the issues that unions faced during the 1970s and 1980s was the traditional conundrum of how to respond to technological change. During the postwar boom, unions largely concurred with management claims that the proliferation of technology created more jobs than it made redundant, but in an environment of economic retrenchment after 1980, such optimism seemed naive. Microprocessors, first introduced in 1971, were displacing blue-collar workers by controlling systems that automatically cut boards, stitched seams, and assembled parts. White-collar jobs, particularly those dominated by women, were even more in jeopardy as file clerks, keypunch operators, and other low-paid workers found their jobs automated and no new positions available. "The chip" devalued the work of many women. "Cashiers are deskilled by the transfer of price information and change calculation into the memory and processing components of the cash register. Like the weaver in the industrial factory, the cashier valued for good price memory and arithmetic efficiency is no longer needed; the cashier becomes a highly replaceable unskilled worker."[3] Unions increasingly called for technological changes to be implemented in ways that would benefit workers rather than employers and the professionals of the computer industries. But they lacked the political clout to force employers to follow policies that protected workers against the effects of technological change.

Unions in the post-1960 period also challenged claims that new machines created a safer environment for those workers who still had jobs. In the mining industry, for example, innovations such as scooptrams meant back injuries and respiratory problems for nickel miners: while the remote-controlled vehicles could have been enclosed to prevent their operators from bouncing about and inhaling diesel fumes, the mining companies resisted the expense that this would entail. The United Steelworkers vividly described the work environment of the mines before an Ontario government commission on the mining industry in 1978. After noting the large number of accidents and deaths in mines, the Steelworkers pointed to such hazards as:

immense pressures from underground rock that is frequently described as "solid" but which in fact is constantly in varying states of flux and change; total absence of natural light; working with heavy equipment which for the most part is designed for maximum efficiency, and not for the protection of the workers using it; the use of high explosives, high noise levels, air concussions, etc. , . . . hygiene, sanitary and health

Workers in fluorspar mine, St Lawrence, Newfoundland   (National Archives of Canada/PA-130784)

dangers arising from dusts, gases, fog, oils, deep holes, falling rock
(loose), runs of muck (broken ores), slippery and unsure footing, and
in some instances (as in Elliot Lake) ionizing radiation.[4]

A tragic reminder of the extreme danger of work in mines where safety regulations were ignored came in May 1992, when a methane gas explosion
killed twenty-six coal miners in the Westray mine in Plymouth, Nova Scotia.

For many industrial workers, the notion of a "postindustrial age"
meant little. For the third of the labour force in blue-collar work, the battles to improve grim working conditions were similar to those fought in
earlier generations. Some gains were made as a result of collective bargaining, but labour also looked to formal politics for legislated changes that
would improve working environments. Since 1961, organized labour had
been formally linked to the NDP, but many members wanted their unions
to do more than back a political party. Unionists also participated in
women's, peace, environmental, and gay rights activities. In Quebec, independence movements created pressures for broader union activism.
Increasingly, conventions were asked to endorse and give funds to campaigns for abortion rights, a boycott of South African goods, or to stop the
testing of American cruise missiles over Canadian territory. Such requests
sometimes provoked dissension. British Columbia's woodworkers were
often at odds with environmentalists inside and outside the union movement; several conservative private-sector unions affiliated with the Quebec
Confédération des syndicats nationaux broke with that federation after it
released a socialist manifesto in 1971 and extolled militant tactics within
the Common Front of public service workers in 1972.

At other times, the trade union movement appeared to be in the vanguard of various progressive groups. In British Columbia, a Solidarity coalition was created in 1983 to fight an ambitious effort by the Social Credit
government to roll back the welfare state and reduce both the staff and
salaries required to deliver government services in all sectors, including
education and social services. Led by unionists, Solidarity quickly became a
rallying force for all those who wanted progressive social change. When the
top union leaders, unhappy with the rank-and-file surge that seemed to
usurp the leaders' authority, came to a settlement with the provincial government without consulting Solidarity, the movement foundered, unable
to find a means of co-ordinating the disparate critics of the government.

The union leaders' dilemma about whether to encourage or discourage militancy, in their own ranks and in society in general, had not been
resolved by the 1990s. While union activists, if not members as a whole,
leaned to the left, the mass character of the movement ensured that it

could not speak with one voice. The election in 1992 of former Canadian Auto Workers' leader Bob White as CLC president encouraged unionists who favoured both on-the-job militancy and social activism.

• Social Movements

Lobby groups were not new in Canadian politics, but pressure groups without strong connections to business, labour, and the churches had had only an embryonic existence before the 1960s. Thereafter, such organizations mushroomed. Although their resources were extremely limited compared to corporate lobbyists, their leaders became skilled in attracting media attention. "Participatory politics" had been a catch-phrase of 1960s student activists, disgusted with the passive roles most Canadians were expected to play in a parliamentary democracy. Anxious for more political involvement, these activists were disillusioned when they found that the political parties offered only minor opportunities for policy discussions. The many organizations that were spawned by the baby boomers reflected a conviction that political parties would require concerted public pressure from outside to ensure effective change.

The women's movement was the largest of the new political pressure groups. It broadened the very notion of politics by asserting that "the personal is political." This meant that personal behaviour, decisions, and relationships reflect the structure of power and subordination in society. The feminist movement combined more informal consciousness-raising groups with formal political lobbying. The National Action Committee on the Status of Women (NAC), the largest feminist pressure group, included over 500 member organizations. Among them were specialized groups such as CARAL, the Canadian Association for the Repeal of Abortion Laws (later the Canadian Abortion Rights Action League) and LEAF, the Women's Legal Education and Action Fund. Groups lobbied for access to abortion services, better provisions for women on welfare, more adequate day-care services and better pay for day-care workers, tougher legislation and stiffer penalties against sexual assault, wife battering, sexual harassment, and pornography, and an end to discrimination based on sexual preference.

Women also figured prominently in voluntary organizations established to protect the environment. The environmental or "green" movement, including such diverse groups as Pollution Probe, Greenpeace, the Canadian Coalition on Acid Rain, the Conservation Council of New Brunswick, and the West Coast Environmental Law Association, performed

a general educative function in addition to its lobbying role with governments. By the end of the 1980s, most Canadians were broadly sympathetic
with the view that clean air, clean water, and healthy workplaces ought to
take precedence over unregulated economic development. Governments
passed legislation that took such sympathies into account, but their overall
practices indicated that corporate, not environmental, concerns were still
paramount. In the late 1980s, the Alberta government, without requiring a
complete environmental assessment, granted licences to several companies
planning major pulp and paper developments in Northern Alberta. Public
pressure forced an environmental assessment in the case of the largest

GREENPEACE

Many voluntary organizations were founded in Canada to respond to the
environmental crisis, but no group has received more attention or caused
more controversy than Greenpeace. In 1970, a small group of American
and Canadian activists in Vancouver created Greenpeace to protest
nuclear testing at Amchitka, in the Aleutian Islands. Although the
Greenpeace vessel, an old halibut boat called the *Phyllis Cormack*, never
reached its destination, the publicity generated by the group prompted the
Americans to abandon their nuclear testing program in the area. Buoyed
by their initial success, Greenpeace conducted similar dramatic non-violent
protests to raise the profile of other environmental issues, among them
French nuclear testing in the South Pacific, the slaughter of whales and
dolphins, the clubbing of baby seals for fur coats, and the dumping of
nuclear and other toxic wastes in lakes and oceans.

By the mid-1970s, branches of Greenpeace had mushroomed throughout the world, and Greenpeace protesters popped up everywhere, precip-
itating incidents for the television cameras. Helium-filled balloons
emblazoned with "End the Arms Race" were released in the Soviet Union;
French movie star Brigitte Bardot was brought to the ice floes of the North
Atlantic to draw attention to the plight of baby seals; Greenpeace crews
intervened between harpoon-throwing Soviet whalers and their intended
catch. In 1985, a Greenpeace member was killed by a bomb planted on
the Greenpeace flagship *Rainbow Warrior* by French agents attempting to
stop a "peace flotilla" protesting nuclear tests on Mururoa Atoll.

While many people were angered by Greenpeace tactics, no one
could deny the organization's effectiveness. The Newfoundland seal hunt
was abandoned, the "Save the Whales" campaign brought reforms to the
whaling industry, and, following the bombing of the *Rainbow Warrior*,

the French minister of defence resigned. By 1985, Greenpeace had more than a million members, and donations had soared to $14 million. Success transformed Greenpeace's organizational structures and prompted a move of its headquarters to Amsterdam. Nevertheless, it retained a strong contingent of Canadian members, many of whom remembered Greenpeace when it operated with one leaking boat on a shoestring budget.

Oil drilling protest in Victoria, staged by Greenpeace (© Heinz Ruckemann, Greenpeace)

development, but the government rejected that study and appointed a pro-development panel to produce a new assessment. The Hibernia oil and gas project in Newfoundland was approved without an intensive environmental impact study, and a controversial dam project in Saskatchewan, the Rafferty-Alameda Dam on the Souris River, was almost complete before the federal government responded to campaigns for a proper environmental assessment of the project.

Opposing the environmental movement were those whose short-term economic interests appeared to be threatened. Big business executives were often able to prevent governments from enforcing their environmental policies. In May 1984, Adam Zimmerman, president of Noranda, effectively circumvented Quebec government demands that the company modernize its copper smelter in Rouyn. He announced that, if forced to comply, he would close the plant, putting 1200 people out of work. Two years later, Kimberley-Clark threatened a shutdown of its Terrace Bay, Ontario, plant if it were held to a pollution-control deadline. The provincial government relented.

Nonetheless, there were victories on the environmental front, such as the fight against acid rain, which was killing many lakes and trees and contributing to respiratory ailments and the erosion of buildings. Since much of the acid rain descending on Canada was caused by emissions from coal-burning factories in the United States, international action was necessary to combat the problem. The Canadian Coalition on Acid Rain played a major role in forcing the Canadian government to pressure the Americans for a formal treaty to reduce emissions. Such an agreement was politically impossible under President Ronald Reagan, whose administration proved generally oblivious to environmental issues. Canada had more luck with his successor, George Bush, who in 1990 signed congressional legislation that was intended to make important cuts in acid rain emissions.

•Cultural Identity

The issues that mobilized many Canadians after 1960 also engaged the nation's artists. Canada's artistic production, particularly in literature, was impressive and included many women and men who received international acclaim, among them Alice Munro, Robertson Davies, Hubert Aquin, Timothy Findlay, Mordecai Richler, and Marie-Claire Blais. Works that gained international popularity often had non-Canadian settings and universal themes. Michael Ondaatje's *The English Patient* (1992), a haunting study of war and its aftermath, won Britain's distinguished Booker Prize. Margaret Atwood's *The Handmaid's Tale* (1985) described a totalitarian state in which absolute patriarchy is realized.

Other writers made broad use of Canadian themes and settings. With the exception of some stories on Africa, the works of Margaret Laurence tended to focus on the fictional town of Manawaka, which was based on Laurence's hometown of Neepawa, Manitoba. Antonine Maillet won France's major literary prize, the Prix Goncourt, for *Pélagie-la-Charette* (1979), a fictional work drawing upon the theme of Acadian explusion. Her earlier work, *La Sagouine,* had gained a wide audience and provided Acadians with a fictional character as enduring as Longfellow's Evangeline. Yves Beauchemin's *Le Matou* (1981), set in working-class Montreal, was a bestseller in Quebec and France and was translated into English as *The Alley Cat.* Joy Kogawa's *Obasan* (1981) recounted the life of a young girl forcibly removed from her coastal home during the evacuation of Japanese Canadians in 1942. It was one of many successful works by visible minority authors, whose numbers included Rohinton Mistry and Bharati Mukherjee. The Mi'kmaq found a voice in the poetry of Rita Joe, while Nova Scotia's black community produced two fine poets in Maxine Tynes and George Elliott Clark.

Works of such variety and quality meant that "CanLit," disdained by Canadian universities before the 1970s, became a mainstay of most English departments by the 1980s. There was also a massive increase in the production of academic works on the history, politics, and sociology of Canada, many of which were assisted by grants from the federally funded Canada Council or Social Sciences and Humanities Research Council.

When universities expanded to accommodate the baby boomers in the 1960s, Canadian nationalists were quick to criticize the hiring of large numbers of foreign, often American, academics who ignored Canadian topics in their teaching and research. In 1972, the Association of Universities and Colleges of Canada established a commission to study and make recommendations on the state of scholarship and teaching relating to Canada in Canadian universities. Chaired by Thomas H.B. Symons, the founding president of Trent University, the commission concluded in its two volume report, entitled *To Know Ourselves,* that students were much more interested in learning about Canada than professors were in teaching about it. Indeed, the commissioners maintained that no country in the world spent so little time studying itself. The Symons Report was hotly debated, and it ultimately helped to convince the federal government to establish programs to encourage Canadian studies in schools and universities and to pass legislation giving preference to qualified Canadians in university hiring.

The government also assisted Canadian recording artists. In 1970, the Canadian Radio-television Commission introduced regulations requiring radio stations to ensure that no fewer than 30 percent of the records they played were of Canadian origin. The regulation helped Canadian artists to establish themselves. In English Canada, some artists, including Joni Mitchell, Neil Young, Bryan Adams, and Anne Murray, crossed over to the American market and produced music that was largely indistinguishable from its American counterparts. Francophone artists were often more original, although the desire to crack the larger market of France, or sometimes North America, could stifle innovation. For all the draw of foreign markets, artists such as Bruce Cockburn, Leonard Cohen, Rita MacNeil, and Gordon Lightfoot remained identifiably Canadian even when their records sold internationally. Felix LeClerc, Gilles Vigneault, Monique Leyrac, and the group Beau Dommage helped to define the contours of the new Quebec nationalism.

In film, it was again francophones who did some of the most impressive work, with Denys Arcand's *Le Déclin de l'Empire Américain* and *Jésus de Montréal* in particular receiving international praise. With some notable exceptions like *Goin' Down the Road*, *The Grey Fox*, and *I've Heard the Mermaids Singing*, English-Canadian films generally imitated American movies and often starred American actors. Few were well received either by critics or at the box office. National Film Board documentaries, by contrast, continued to receive acclaim. A woman's film unit, Studio D, which produced an anti-pornography film, *Not a Love Story*, and an Academy Award winning anti-nuclear documentary, *If You Love This Planet*, were particularly successful. While a few NFB feature films such as Claude Jutra's *Mon Oncle Antoine*, Cynthia Scott's *The Company of Strangers*, and Anne Wheeler's privately produced *Bye Bye Blues* received distribution in theatres, on the whole cinema in Canada continued to be dominated by American products.

Canadian dance companies like Les Grands Ballets Canadiens and the Danny Grossman Dance Company came into their own, and dancers such as Karen Kain and Frank Augustyn of the National Ballet and Evelyn Hart of the Royal Winnipeg Ballet won prestigious international competitions. Canadian playwrights had their works staged at major theatres, which began to intersperse some Canadian fare among the classics and Broadway imports. Moreover, producing new Canadian drama became the raison d'être of many of the alternative theatres, like the Touchstone Theatre in Vancouver, the 25th Street Theatre in Saskatoon, and the Tarragon in Toronto, that opened in the 1960s and 1970s. Playwrights such as Michel Tremblay and Tomson Highway drew heavily on their heritage in their portraits of dysfunctional French-Canadian families and the life and traditions of Native peoples on Northern reserves. Tremblay brought the language of the Quebec streets—*joual*—to the theatre, ending the tradition in which only Parisian French was considered acceptable on stage. The Mummers' troupe and the Mulgrave Road Co-op were the most successful of a number of alternative theatre groups in Atlantic Canada. The Mulgrave troupe, like the Company of Sirens in Ontario, used drama to raise consciousness about child abuse, wife battery, and other little-discussed problems.

In art, as in theatre and literature, regional, ethnic, and gender sensibilities struggled to emerge. On the West Coast, Bill Reid was recognized for his revival of traditional Haida carving. Northwest Coast Native art influenced the work of Jack Shadbolt, a Vancouver surrealist painter, and other non-Native artists. On the Prairies, the major landscape artists were Dorothy Knowles, Wynona Mulcaster, and Ernest Lindner. Esther Warkov of Winnipeg attempted in her paintings to recreate the pre-Holocaust life

Karen Kain and Frank Augustyn in the National Ballet production of "The Sleeping Beauty"   (National Ballet Archives)

of Polish Jews. In a class by himself was William Kurelek, whose lyrical work reflected his attempts to deal with a difficult childhood in rural Alberta and Manitoba.

In Ontario, Joyce Wieland, film maker and artist, produced provocative works that reflected her nationalist and feminist values. Several London artists, among whom Greg Curnoe was best known, created a regional art celebrating local identity and the Canadian struggle to be free of American control. Native artists in Northern Ontario blended traditional Native styles and themes with international influences in a distinctive Woodlands art. The celebrated painter Norval Morrisseau influenced such successful artists as Daphne Odjig of Ontario and Jackson Beardy of Manitoba. Further north, Inuit artists found an ever-growing market for their carvings and prints.

Quebec art reflected a variety of styles and found outlets not only in traditional commercial markets but in such novel sites as the Montreal subway system. Several women including Rita Letendre, Lise Gervais, and Marcelle Ferron painted earthy works that demonstrated the changes that Quebec women had undergone since the Quiet Revolution. A large group of the country's major representational artists lived and worked in the Atlantic provinces. Christopher Pratt, Mary Pratt, and Alex Colville received wide acclaim for their strikingly realistic landscapes.

Canadian and Quebec nationalism and regional identities all helped to recruit audiences for Canada's artistic products. But the cultural importance of both nationalism and regionalism must be seen in perspective. Francophone Québécois, thanks to the language barrier and to growing Quebec nationalism, were far more likely than anglophone Canadians to purchase locally recorded music, watch locally produced television shows, and buy locally written books. Even so, young francophones generally preferred popular American music and dubbed American movies to Quebec-produced or imported French fare.

Heritage conservation became an important means by which national, regional, and ethnic identities could be preserved. Outside of the work of the Historic Sites and Monuments Board founded in 1919, and the National Museum established in 1927, little attention had been paid before 1960 to preserving historic buildings and artifacts. An explosion of conservation and historic reconstruction activities accompanied the Centennial celebrations in 1967 and continued thereafter. Such activities involved all levels of government and were carried out for a variety of reasons. Sometimes the key goal was job creation, as in the federally sponsored reconstruction of Louisbourg as a tourist attraction in Cape Breton in the early 1960s. Provincial projects such as the Acadian Historic Village in

Caraquet, New Brunswick, and the Ukrainian Village outside Edmonton represented a recognition by government of the voting power of ethnic groups. At other times, projects involved attempts to invigorate decaying areas of cities, as in the conversion of dilapidated buildings on the Halifax waterfront and in Winnipeg's warehouse district into fancy shops. In some cases, such as the remains of a Viking settlement at L'Anse aux Meadows and the well preserved buildings in old Quebec City, historical sites received international recognition.

Heritage protection groups achieved many victories. In Saskatchewan, their pressure led the NDP government to proclaim a Heritage Property Act in 1980 that gave both the province and municipalities the right to designate certain sites as historical properties that could neither be torn down nor altered. Within three years, there were over 200 municipal designations, and various old churches, schools, residences, railway stations, and town halls were saved from the wrecker's ball. The government also instituted grants for restoring and maintaining historic properties. Similar programs were soon in place throughout the country. Interest in conservation developed unevenly throughout the country. While Quebec City and Victoria sought to make their core areas historic showcases, Vancouver, Calgary, Edmonton, Winnipeg, and Toronto all proved latecomers to conservation. Their city councils were more concerned with development than preservation, which they often associated with stagnation and fossilization. Even fossils could attract tourists, however, as the citizens of Drumheller learned when Alberta constructed a dinosaur museum in town. Museums, like historical sites, mushroomed after 1960, most focussing on the history of Canada or its regions.

Canadian interest in sports—as both participants and spectators—continued to thrive. As in other nations, sports in Canada became increasingly identified with the "national interest." In 1961, the Fitness and Amateur Sports Act was passed, which made federal funds available for sports activity. Amateur sports became more bureaucratized, presided over by paid administrators rather than enthusiastic volunteers.

While studies bemoaned the lack of fitness of the population as a whole, Canada produced an impressive range of athletes. Canadian figure skaters built on the tradition of Barbara Ann Scott and produced a long list of world champions and Olympic medallists including Donald Jackson, Barbara Wagner and Robert Paul, Karen Magnussen, Toller Cranston, Barbara Underhill and Paul Martini, Elizabeth Manley, Brian Orser, and Kurt Browning. Speed skater Gaeten Boucher captured three medals at the 1984 Olympics. Swimmers Elaine Tanner, Victor Davis, and Alex Baumann brought Commonwealth, Pan-American, world, and Olympic medals to

Canada as did Carolyn Waldo and Sylvie Frechette in synchronized swimming. Skiers Anne Heggtveit, Nancy Greene, Ken Read, and Steve Podborski turned in winning runs on the slopes while sprinter Harry Jerome, rower Silken Laumann, and gymnast Curtis Hibbert dazzled spectators at international competitions.

While many young Canadians dreamed of becoming sports celebrities, studies suggested their chances were best if they were Anglo-Canadian males with professional or white-collar parents. The costs involved in training athletes who could compete in national and international events excluded most working-class children. Girls faced particular challenges as sexual segregation continued to make sports a largely male preserve. Attempts by girls and women to share the same opportunities as boys were mightily resisted. In 1985, the Ontario Hockey Association barred thirteen-year-old Justine Blainey from participating on a leading boys' hockey team. Several courtrooms and thousands of dollars later, Justine got her wish in 1987. But the OHA continued to grumble that the bodychecking and slapshots of the boys' league made the inclusion of girls inappropriate. Such stereotypes prevented most girls with athletic talent from following Justine Blainey's example.

For many, civic identity was bound up with local sports teams. In big cities, the presence of a major league franchise was a source of pride, even if no one on the hockey, football, or baseball team was a resident of the city. In smaller towns, where sports teams were composed of local people who played in amateur leagues, sport meant more than vicarious satisfaction from the performances of highly paid professionals. The death of four young members of the Swift Current Broncos in a bus crash in 1986 was a cause for mourning in the whole community, and the team's win of the junior hockey Memorial Cup a few years later was seen as a fitting tribute to the dead boys' memory.

Two radically different events can be seen as symbols of Canadian participation in sports in this period. The first was the dramatic ending to the first Soviet–Canada hockey series in 1972. Canadian coaches, players, promoters, and fans had long insisted that Canadians were the best hockey players in the world and that their unimpressive showings at the Olympics and other international amateur competitions were due to strict definitions of amateurism that excluded players in the National Hockey League. National pride was on the line when a series was arranged between the Soviets and the best Canadian players in the NHL. Paul Henderson's famous series-ending goal has come to be seen as one of the classic moments in Canadian sports history.

National pride turned to shock in the steroid scandal that followed sprinter Ben Johnson's initial victory at the Seoul Olympics in 1988. In the media circus and official enquiry that followed, Canadians learned that many athletes used performance-enhancing steroids, ignoring ethical issues and endangering their personal health in order to win. Questions of amateurism that had plagued earlier international competition seemed rather quaint as sports took on a big-business atmosphere where millions of dollars in endorsements could await Olympic gold medallists.

Big-business baseball also came to Canada as first Montreal and then Toronto sponsored major league teams. In 1992, the Toronto Blue Jays spent almost $50 million on player salaries in their successful quest for Canada's first World Series. There is much that could be said about Canadian sports fans rallying around an "American League" team that had not a single Canadian player on it. Was it yet more evidence that Canada was slowly being annexed economically and culturally into the United States? Or did support for the Toronto team reflect a healthy anti-Americanism and nationalistic glee at having beaten the Americans quite literally at their own game?

Two stories vied for Canadian headlines in mid-October 1992. The first was baseball. The second was the upcoming referendum on the Charlottetown Accord. Special interest groups of every description campaigned with equal fervour both for and against the accord. They represented a cross-section of the regional, ethnic, political, class, and gender divisions that we have described in this chapter. The final chapter further analyses the forces that have contributed to a national purpose in the period since 1960 and the opposing forces that have led to our present national malaise.

• Contemporary Regionalism:
A Scholarly Debate

Regional antagonism has been particularly sharp in Canada since the 1970s. Westerners and Atlantic Canadians blamed many of their problems on Central Canadian control over the federal government. Within Central Canada, Quebec and Ontario accused one another of reaping all the benefits of Confederation. Clearly, not everyone could be right.

There is ongoing debate among scholars about what defines the identity of Canada's geographical regions, the degree to which residents of the regions think of themselves in regional rather than provincial or national terms, and the extent to which calls for more power for the regions reflect progressive or reactionary political tendencies within Canada. There is often dispute about the extent to which regions are unique or are variants on common Canadian themes.

The claim that Quebec is a distinct society is well known, but strong cases for uniqueness can also be made for other regions. Historian Douglas Cole, commenting on the exclusion of British Columbia from many discussions of national character, offers a provocative analysis of that province:

> *Nature is different, heritage is different, character is different. Perhaps then the mind is also different. . . . What [British Columbia] shares with English Central Canada it probably shares almost equally with other English-speaking countries, more especially with settlement colonies. In this sense, Tasmania may be as comparable to British Columbia as Ontario.*[5]

Scholars have debated the role that the creation of myths plays in defining regions. For some, myths are a positive element, enabling people to comprehend their region's history and collectively determine its future. Historian Douglas Francis recognizes the role that scholars play in shaping such myths, and he applauds recent intellectual and cultural histories of the Prairies for their "ongoing search for a prairie myth, some *Weltenschaung* which can be said to be uniquely Western Canadian."[6]

Other scholars argue that mythologies are simply smoke-screens concocted by regional elites to enlist popular support for struggles against other regional elites. Sociologist John Conway criticizes the myth-makers whom he accuses of creating a "blind regionalism." In Alberta, for example, Premier Lougheed "bashe[d] the 'feds' and [won] overwhelming mandates while ignoring the fact that his provincial economy is the near-private preserve of the multinational oil companies."[7] For Conway, a regional politics that mobilizes people from various social strata behind the regional elites is bankrupt: it obscures the oppression of workers and farmers by these elites and precludes subordinate groups in one region from making common cause with their counterparts elsewhere. While Francis suggests that cultural images shape Western regionalism, Conway argues that economic considerations are more important. Western regional solidarity, he argues, is based on "the inevitable insecurity that haunts resource-based economies."[8]

Economist Paul Phillips counters that, in the period since the Second World War, the economies of the three Prairie provinces have diverged, and it is therefore misleading to speak of a Prairie region with common interests and a common vision.[9] Phillips' observations may help to explain why voting patterns in the three provinces have differed and why there was no unity among the three provinces on such issues as the National Energy Program and free trade with the Americans.

Similar debates have marked scholarship on the Atlantic provinces. Much recent scholarship claims that local elites in the region emphasize cultural uniqueness as a means of avoiding issues of poverty and stagnation. Sociologist James Overton, analysing the underlying ideology found in the report of the Newfoundland Royal Commission on Employment and Unemployment in the 1980s, notes that "at a time when the state is retreating from responsibility for both employment creation and support of the unemployed, the virtues of outport culture have been rediscovered and presented as essential to the construction of a 'post-industrial society.'"[10]

Overton and many other scholars of the Atlantic region defend national programs that redistribute income toward poorer areas such as Atlantic Canada, although most decry Ottawa's bureaucratic impulses that frequently limit local participation in the determination of provincial economic programs.[11] In contrast, neo-conservative scholars believe that redistributive programs simply create dependency and prevent Atlantic Canadians from taking their destiny into their own hands. Even if that destiny for many is migration from the region, there would be fewer but better Atlantic Canadians.[12]

Debates about the national question in Quebec have similarities to the debates about regionalism elsewhere. Social work professor Eric Shragge suggests that provincial elites were shaping the contours of Quebec's nationalist movement much as regional elites were shaping regional perspectives elsewhere in the country. Argues Shragge:

The identification of the nationalist movement with the state creates a vested interest of those who hold a stake in expanding the power of the Quebec state. Given the acceptance of a neo-conservative ideology by those who have held state power in Quebec for the last ten years, and the lack of a dissenting voice from within the state apparatus, the nationalist movement has become too close to the Quebec state to have the possibility of promoting an agenda for social change.[13]

Most Quebec francophone intellectuals reject this position, noting that debate within nationalist circles about the direction of a sovereign Quebec is robust.

•Notes

[1] La Fédération des Francophones hors Québec, *The Heirs of Lord Durham: Manifesto of a Vanishing People* (Toronto: Burns and MacEachern, 1978), 70.

[2] Margaret Conrad, "The Atlantic Revolution of the 1950s" in *Beyond Anger and Longing: Community and Development in Atlantic Canada*, ed. Berkeley Fleming (Sackville and Fredericton: Centre for Canadian Studies and Acadiensis Press, 1988), 55–96.

[3] Heather Menzies, *Computers on the Job: Surviving Canada's Microcomputer Revolution* (Toronto: Lorimer, 1982), 56.

[4] Quoted in Wallace Clement, *Hardrock Mining: Industrial Relations and Technological Changes at INCO* (Toronto: McClelland and Stewart, 1981), 227–28.

[5] Douglas Cole, "The Intellectual and Imaginative Development of British Columbia," *Journal of Canadian Studies* 24, 3 (Fall 1989): 74–75.

[6] R. Douglas Francis, "The Search for a Prairie Myth: A Survey of the Intellectual and Cultural Historiography of Prairie Canada," *Journal of Canadian Studies* 24, 3 (Fall 1989): 60.

[7] J.F. Conway, *The West: The History of a Region in Confederation* (Toronto: Lorimer, 1983), 228.

[8] Ibid., 233.

[9] Paul Phillips, "The Canadian Prairies—One Economic Region or Two?": Implications for Constitutional Change with Particular Reference to Manitoba" in *The Constitutional Future of the Prairie and Atlantic Regions of Canada*, ed. James N. McCrorie and Martha L. MacDonald (Regina: Canadian Plains Research Center, 1992), 37–49.

[10] James Overton, "A Newfoundland Culture?" *Journal of Canadian Studies* 23, 1 and 2 (Spring/Summer 1988): 19. An excellent article in the same vein as the Overton piece in the same issue is Ian McKay, "Among the Fisherfolk: J.F.F.B. Livesay and the Invention of Peggy's Cove," 23–45.

[11] The view that Ottawa has been overbearing in its dealings with the provinces, particularly the Atlantic region, is outlined in David Milne, *Tug of War: Ottawa and the Provinces Under Trudeau and Mulroney* (Toronto: Lorimer, 1986).

[12] See, for example, Thomas J. Courchene, *Equalization Payments: Past, Present and Future* (Toronto: Ontario Economic Council, 1984). A left-wing critique of both existing regional development programs and the neo-conservative solution is found in Ralph Matthews, *The Creation of Regional Dependency* (Toronto: University of Toronto Press, 1983).

[13] Eric Shragge, "Avoiding the Social Question in Quebec," *Canadian Dimension* (Jan. 1992): 19.

• Suggested Reading

On post-1960 immigration, see Freda Hawkins, *Canada and Immigration: Public Policy and Public Concern*, rev. ed. (Toronto: The Institute for Public Administration of Canada, 1987); Alan G. Green, *Immigration and the Postwar Canadian Economy* (Toronto: Macmillan, 1976); and Gerald E. Dirks, *Canada's Refugee Policy: Indifference or Opportunism?* (Montreal: McGill-Queen's University Press, 1978). On the reception immigrants received see Jean Burnet with Howard Palmer, *Coming Canadians: An Introduction to a History of Canada's Peoples* (Toronto: McClelland and Stewart, 1988). See also Bridglal Pachai, *Beneath the Clouds of the Promised Land: The Survival of Nova Scotia's Blacks*, 2 vols. (Halifax: The Black Educators Association, 1987/90).

On the universities of the period, see Paul Axelrod, *Scholars and Dollars: Politics, Economics, and Universities of Ontario 1945–1980* (Toronto: University of Toronto Press, 1982) and Thomas N.B. Symons et al., *To Know Ourselves: Report of the*

Commission on Canadian Studies (Ottawa: Association of Universities and Colleges of Canada, 1976).

Developments in Quebec from the Quiet Revolution through the René Lévesque premiership include Paul-Andre Linteau et al., *Quebec Since 1930: A History* (Toronto: Lorimer, 1991); Kenneth McRoberts, *Quebec: Social Change and Political Crisis*, 3rd ed. (Toronto: McClelland and Stewart, 1988); Graham Fraser, *PQ: René Lévesque and the Parti Québécois in Power* (Toronto: Macmillan, 1984); René Lévesque, *Memoirs* (Toronto: McClelland and Stewart, 1986); Ronald Rudin, *The Forgotten Quebecers: A History of English-Speaking Quebec, 1759–1980* (Quebec City: Institut québécois de recherche sur la culture, 1985); Henry Milner, *The Long Road to Reform: Restructuring Public Education in Quebec* (Montreal: McGill-Queen's University Press, 1986); and William Coleman, *The Independence Movement in Quebec, 1945–1980* (Toronto: University of Toronto Press, 1984).

On the views of Quebec's most noted federalist, see Pierre Trudeau, *Federalism and the French Canadians* (Toronto: Macmillan, 1977). Among useful works on francophones outside Quebec are Richard Wilbur, *The Rise of French New Brunswick* (Halifax: Formac, 1989); la Fédération des francophones hors Québec, *The Heirs of Lord Durham: A Manifesto of a Vanishing People* (Toronto: Gage, 1978); Sally Ross and Alphonse Deveau, *The Acadians of Nova Scotia: Past and Present* (Halifax: Nimbus, 1992); and Georges Arsenault, *The Island Acadians, 1720–1980* (Charlottetown: Ragweed Press, 1989).

Atlantic struggles are discussed in Gary Burrill and Ian McKay, eds., *People, Resources and Power in Atlantic Canada: Critical Perspectives on Underdevelopment and Primary Industries in the Atlantic Region* (Fredericton: Acadiensis, 1987); David A. Macdonald, *'Power Begins at the Cod End': The Newfoundland Trawlerman's Strike, 1974–1975* (St John's: Institute of Social and Economic Research, Memorial University of Newfoundland, 1980); and Wallace Clement, *The Struggle to Organize: Resistance in Canada's Fisheries* (Toronto: McClelland and Stewart, 1986). Financial boondoggles are outlined in Phillip Mathias, *Forced Growth: Five Studies of Government Involvement in the Development of Canada* (Toronto: Lorimer, 1971).

The post-1960 Prairies are analyzed in Gerald Friesen, *The Canadian Prairies: A History* (Toronto: University of Toronto Press, 1984); John Richards and Larry Pratt, *Prairie Capitalism* (Toronto: McClelland and Stewart, 1979); and Larry Pratt and Garth Stevenson, eds., *Western Separatism: The Myths, Realities, and Dangers* (Edmonton: Hurtig, 1981). On British Columbia see Jean Barman, *The West Beyond the West: A History of British Columbia* (Toronto: University of Toronto Press, 1991); Rennie Warburton and Donald Coburn, eds., *Workers, Capital and the State of British Columbia: Selected Papers* (Vancouver: University of British Columbia Press, 1987); and Patricia Marchak, *Green Gold: The Forest Industry in British Columbia* (Vancouver:

University of British Columbia Press, 1983). On the Reform Party see Murray Dobbin, *Preston Manning and the Reform Party* (Toronto: Lorimer, 1991).

The lives of Canada's Native peoples are explored in J.R. Miller, *Skyscrapers Hide the Heavens: A History of Indian–White Relations in Canada*, rev. ed. (Toronto: University of Toronto Press, 1991); Kenneth Coates, *Canada's Colonies: A History of the Yukon and Northwest Territories* (Toronto: Lorimer, 1985); Boyce Richardson, *Strangers Devour the Land*, 2nd ed. (Vancouver: Douglas and McIntyre, 1991); Sally Weaver, *Making Canadian Indian Policy: The Hidden Agenda 1968–1970* (Toronto: University of Toronto Press, 1980); and Celia Haig-Brown, *Resistance and Renewal: Surviving the Indian Residential School* (Vancouver: Arsenal Pulp Press, 1988).

The comprehensive women's histories of Canada and Quebec, by respectively Alison Prentice et al. and the Clio Collective, provide coverage of the post-1960 period. Among specialized works, see Jeri Dawn Wine and Janice L. Ristock, eds., *Women and Social Change: Feminist Activism in Canada* (Toronto: Lorimer, 1991); Naomi Herson and Dorothy E. Smith, eds., *Women and the Canadian Labour Force* (Ottawa: Social Sciences and Humanities Research Council, 1982); Rosalie Abella, *Equality in Employment* (Ottawa: Minister of Supply and Services, 1984); Paul Phillips and Erin Phillips, *Women and Work: Inequality in the Labour Market* (Toronto: Lorimer, 1983); Heather Menzies, *Computers on the Job: Surviving Canada's Microcomputer Revolution* (Toronto: Lorimer, 1982); Pat Armstrong and Hugh Armstrong, *The Double Ghetto: Canadian Women and Their Segregated Work*, rev. ed. (Toronto: McClelland and Stewart, 1986); and Angus McLaren and Arlene Tigar McLaren, *The Bedroom and the State: The Changing Practices and Politics of Contraception and Abortion in Canada* (Toronto: McClelland and Stewart, 1986).

On the male labour force, see Wallace Clement, *Hardrock Mining: Technological Changes and Industrial Relations at Inco Ltd.* (Toronto: McClelland and Stewart, 1981) and his *The Struggle to Organize: Resistance in Canada's Fisheries* (Toronto: McClelland and Stewart, 1987); Bill Freeman, *1005: Political Life in a Union Local* (Toronto: Lorimer, 1982); Sue Calhoun, *A Word to Say: The Story of the Maritime Fisherman's Union* (Halifax: Nimbus, 1992); and Silver Donald Cameron, *The Education of Everette Richardson: The Nova Scotia Fisherman's Strike, 1970–71* (Toronto: McClelland and Stewart, 1977).

On gay liberation and AIDS organizing see Gary Kinsman, *The Regulation of Desire: Sexuality in Canada* (Montreal: Black Rose, 1987) and David M. Rayside and Evert A. Lindquist, "AIDS Activism and the State in Canada," *Studies in Political Economy* 39 (Autumn 1992): 37–76.

FORGING A NEW CONSENSUS

13

On 25 October 1992, one day before a national referendum on the Charlottetown Accord, a young Native woman, a single mother from Edmonton, called an open-line show to express her confusion about the constitutional debate. Like at least 1.5 million other Canadians, she was unemployed. If she found work, it would likely be at the minimum wage, and day-care expenses, though subsidized in Alberta, would ensure that she remained poor. Was there anything in the constitution, she asked, that would guarantee jobs or a decent income for Canadians? If not, why not?

The simple wording on the referendum ballot—"Do you agree that the Constitution of Canada should be renewed on the basis of the agreement reached on 28 August 1992?"—belied the complexity of the deal worked out by the prime minister, the ten premiers, the territorial leaders, and heads of several Native organizations. Throughout September and October, Canadians were bombarded by contradictory claims from groups that supported or opposed the accord. It either enhanced Native rights to self-determination, or it jeopardized existing rights and threatened the position of Native women. It committed governments to protection of social programs, or it cleared the way for the elimination of such programs. It weakened federal authority, giving more powers to the provinces, or it largely maintained the status quo in the federal–provincial division of power. It made important concessions to Quebec, recognizing its uniqueness within the Canadian family, or it made only symbolic gestures toward the province. It weakened gains made by women under the Canadian Charter of Rights and Freedoms, or it left them untouched. Who were voters to believe? In the end, most Canadians, often for opposite reasons, decided that the compromise did not reflect the principles that they wished to see enshrined in the Constitution.

Many regarded the constitutional process that had led to the referendum as an anti-democratic exercise in elite accommodation. Some defenders of the process suggested that divisions among politicians reflected even deeper divisions among the Canadian people. A more truly democratic procedure, they suggested, would have produced chaos rather than consensus.

The 1992 referendum gave few clues as to what—if any—constitutional arrangement might be accepted in a country with profound regional, class, ethnic, and gender divisions, but it was clear that brokered deals among elites had lost much of their legitimacy. The issues discussed in the referendum debate, and Canadians' willingness to reject a pact endorsed by leading politicians, demonstrated the change in Canadian politics since 1960. At that time, neither Native concerns nor women's issues received much attention. The welfare state was still in its infancy. Formal politics was the preserve of upper-class male Anglo- and French-Canadian elites. In the consensus atmosphere of the 1950s, citizens appeared to accept that the marking of a ballot every four years was the extent of their participation in public policy making. Beginning in the rebellious 1960s, the growth of social protest movements and the demystification of elites changed not only the issues under discussion but the way people viewed politics and politicians.

Despite the political questioning of the era, the two traditional parties—the Liberals and Progressive Conservatives—continued to dominate federal politics. In 1961, the New Democratic Party was born of a union between the old CCF, the Canadian Labour Congress, and New Party clubs. A democratic socialist party designed to appeal to labour and urban voters, the NDP abandoned some of the radical rhetoric of the CCF's Regina Manifesto and entered the new political age under its leader Tommy Douglas, the former CCF premier of Saskatchewan. While the NDP belonged to the Socialist International and continued to press for a more equitable society based on social democratic principles, it pruned itself of its more radical elements—the Waffle—in the early 1970s. Always the third party at the federal level, the NDP had more success at the provincial level, governing, at one time or another, British Columbia, Saskatchewan, Manitoba, Ontario, and the Yukon.

Other alternative parties were created during this period, including the Western Canada Concept, the Reform Party, the Green Party, even the Rhinoceros Party. The Feminist Party of Canada was founded in 1979, though it attracted only a few members and never fielded candidates in an election. Women seemed to prefer working within the established parties rather than pursuing a separatist strategy. There were many notable achievements for women in politics. Several women—Alexa McDonough, Sharon Carstairs, Rita Johnson, Lyn McLeod, and Catherine Callbeck—

were elected to lead their respective provincial parties. With her brief administration in British Columbia, Johnson became the first woman premier in Canada. In 1989, Audrey McLaughlin won the leadership of the federal New Democrats.

Atlantic Canadians remained unwilling to turn to third parties, whether of the left or the right. This was not because they were happy with the two major parties. While a large proportion of Atlantic Canadians turned out on election day, polls showed that they were the most cynical of Canadian voters. They neither expected their politicians to represent them effectively, nor did they believe in their own ability to effect change through the political process. In the face of such cynicism, Atlantic Canadians were less likely to throw their energies into political reform. As a result, their political culture retained aspects of personal patronage that had given way in other regions of the country to a more corporate, though not necessarily less corrupt, approach to the political process.

• Defending the Welfare State

From their inception, social welfare programs in Canada had been generally accepted as a means of offsetting socio-economic inequities and of securing mass acceptance of capitalism. In formulating social programs, the federal government attempted to deflect both the demands of social democrats for policies that would truly redistribute wealth, and the criticism of the right wing, which claimed that public programs robbed people of initiative, cost too much money, and led to too much government involvement in people's lives. In the early 1980s, with economic growth slowing and neo-conservative politicians such as British Prime Minister Margaret Thatcher and American President Ronald Reagan promising to "downsize" government, Canadian conservatives argued that Canada's global competitiveness depended upon following suit. They had a particularly sympathetic audience in the Progressive Conservative government of Brian Mulroney, elected in 1984.

Critics of big government pointed to the rapid increase in Canadian social expenditures, which rose from 12.1 to 21.7 percent of gross domestic product from 1960 to 1981, according to the Organization for Economic Co-operation and Development. Less publicized was the modest extent of government spending on social programs relative to other OECD countries, including some of the world's most competitive trading nations. West Germany had had the OECD's largest per capita social expenditures in

1960, and yet it continued to post the greatest productivity gains of any OECD country. Sweden, Italy, Austria, and the Netherlands, all successful nations in global trade, also out-distanced Canada in growth and volume of social expenditures (see table 13.1).

Table 13.1: SOCIAL EXPENDITURES BY COUNTRY (Percentage of Gross Domestic Product)

Country	1960	1981
Belgium	17.0	38.0
Netherlands	16.3	36.1
Sweden	14.5	33.5
Germany	20.5	31.5
Italy	16.5	29.1
Denmark	10.2	29.0
Austria	17.9	27.9
Ireland	11.7	27.1
Norway	11.7	27.1
United Kingdom	13.9	24.9
France	13.4	23.8
Canada	12.1	21.7
United States	10.9	21.0
New Zealand	13.0	19.6
Australia	10.2	18.6
Japan	8.0	17.5

Source: OECD Bulletin, No. 146 (Jan. 1984), reprinted in Andrew Armitage, *Social Welfare in Canada: Ideas, Realities and Future Paths*, 2nd ed. (Toronto: McClelland and Stewart, 1988), 22.

Pensions are a case in point. By 1981, Canada devoted less of its gross domestic product to public pensions than any other OECD country. The Canada Pension Plan (CPP) was introduced by the Pearson government in 1965, but its rates were kept low to appease private insurance companies. Even with the Guaranteed Income Supplement, introduced in 1966 as an add-on for needy pensioners, the elderly could not maintain a decent standard of living without other income. Private pensions failed to make up the difference: among western democracies, only the United States had less private pension protection than Canada. In 1980, 44 percent of paid workers in Canada had private pension plan coverage. By contrast, 90 percent of Swedish workers, 80 percent of French workers, 60 percent of West German workers, and 50 percent of British workers enjoyed such coverage. The lowest-paid workers were most likely to have no pension coverage at all. While only 9.4 percent of Canadians earning under $7500 in 1979 had pension plans, 76.4 percent of those earning over $30 000 had coverage. Lack of portability of most plans meant that many workers nominally covered by pension plans would never collect from them.

In the early 1980s, the federal government was confronted by a variety of lobby groups favouring increased pensions. Women's groups called for homemakers to be allowed to contribute to CPP and for old-age pensions to be set above the poverty line. Since women lived longer, they considerably outnumbered men among the elderly. In 1980, Statistics Canada reported that 27 percent of seniors lived on "limited incomes" (the euphemism for poverty), and the percentage of elderly women in poverty was even higher. Labour, pensioners' associations, and welfare organizations joined the chorus pressuring the government to increase pension payments. In response, the Trudeau government increased the Guaranteed Income Supplement, and by 1985, the rate of poverty among the elderly had dropped to 19 percent. At that point, Prime Minister Mulroney, testing the waters for his neo-conservative agenda, announced that pension payments would no longer be fully indexed to inflation. Vocal protest forced Mulroney to retreat, but it was clear that his government would do little to bring payments to the elderly up to OECD rates.

Seniors protesting the Conservative government's proposal to deindex old-age pensions (Ron Poling/Canapress)

Canada could be prouder of its national health program than its record on pensions. "Medicare" was pioneered in Saskatchewan, which was also the first province to introduce hospital insurance. Bitterly opposed by that province's doctors, who went on strike in an attempt to kill the plan, Saskatchewan's NDP government introduced medicare in 1962. While physicians argued that doctor-controlled and voluntary private insurance schemes were preferable to a state program forcing all doctors and patients to enrol, national public opinion had long been against them. In 1944 and again in 1949, 80 percent of Canadians indicated their approval of a federal health plan that covered complete medical and hospital care for a monthly flat rate.

John Diefenbaker established a Royal Commission on Health Services in 1961. Its report, submitted to the Pearson government in 1964, called for a universal medicare scheme, strengthening the hand of reformist Liberals like Walter Gordon and Judy LaMarsh. The Liberals made medicare an issue in the 1965 election and, on their return to office, proceeded to announce a national shared-cost health insurance program that adhered to four principles: universality of coverage; coverage of most medical treatment; portability of benefits; and provincial administration. Only Saskatchewan and British Columbia offered no criticism of the medicare plan. Nonetheless, by 1970 all provinces had established programs embodying the four federal principles.

Attempts by some provinces to allow doctors to "balance bill" when they felt that the payment for a medical treatment was too low met a stiff federal response in the early 1980s. Health and Welfare Minister Monique Bégin successfully stared down the premiers of Ontario, British Columbia, and Alberta after penalizing their provinces financially for allowing extra billing. The original principles of medicare enjoyed too much national support for any premier to win much favour—outside the physicians' lobby—for a defence of extra billing in the name of provincial rights.

Income security programs, other than old-age pensions, enjoyed less support from the population. The Canada Assistance Plan (CAP) of 1966 built upon an earlier federal–provincial agreement to establish national guidelines regarding rights of citizens to provincial welfare programs that were partly funded by the federal government. There is no doubt that CAP produced improvements in the lives of poor Canadians. Marion Dewar, executive director of the Canadian Council on Children and Youth and former mayor of Ottawa, recalled in 1990:

> When I was nursing with the Victorian Order of Nurses in the early
> 1960s, it was a very different society from the one we live in today. We
> gave bed baths to elderly people living in cold rooms, or living with

relatives who refused to feed them. I particularly recall one woman who had suffered a stroke. She had lost her ability to speak. I went in once a week to see her at first. Each visit she clutched my uniform and pointed to her mouth. I realized she was hungry. I started going in two or three times a week. I would bring her soup and feed her. When government assistance became available, she went to live in a nursing home.

It was during this period that a three-month-old baby living in downtown Ottawa had its face chewed by a rat.

In those days welfare was granted to those persons whom local politicians decided to give it to. If you were a young person out of work, very often having run away from an abusive home, you could be refused welfare. If you were a juvenile, you could be sent to one of the "reform schools," in some of which, we are hearing today, the young people were abused.[1]

The Canada Assistance Plan helped to systematize welfare, but it had only a minimal impact on poverty. The persistence of poverty led some social welfare activists to campaign for a guaranteed annual income (GAI) for Canadians. Arguing that most poor people chose neither to be unemployed nor to receive low wages, advocates of GAI claimed that a minimum, decent standard of living ought to be a right of citizenry. In the late 1980s, some conservative business organizations also picked up the GAI theme, after it was outlined by the Macdonald Commission. The Business Council on National Issues argued that the GAI could replace unemployment insurance, CAP, the Guaranteed Income Supplement, and other such programs to streamline administration of the Canadian welfare state. It also contended that the GAI rate should be set considerably lower than the minimum wage. This reflected the growing concern that poverty was the result of shiftlessness and that there was a large class of undeserving "welfare bums" who preferred government handouts to hard work. Such views overlooked the fact that individuals, much less families, could barely support themselves on minimum wages, which rose less quickly than inflation. Indeed, increasing numbers of social welfare recipients were part-time and even full-time minimum-wage workers.

The inadequacy of minimum wages and the Canada Assistance Plan meant that many families ran out of money before their next welfare payment or pay cheque was due. Children whose parents were unable to afford even basic groceries regularly went hungry the last week of the month before the welfare cheque arrived. Such families were forced to rely on private initiatives such as food banks to survive. Food banks started modestly in the early 1980s in some urban centres. By 1992, 150 000 people were served each month by the Daily Bread Food Bank in Toronto alone, and an estimated two million Canadians relied on food banks at some point that year. While the churches and volunteer groups that ran food banks regarded their continuous expansion as an indictment of society, some conservative politicians did not agree. Alberta premier Don Getty cheerily suggested that food banks were a positive force allowing people to factor free food into their budget planning. Many Canadians were also apparently factoring in the savings that resulted from living in church basements, charitable hostels, and even on the streets.

Increasingly, by the late 1980s, organizations supporting expanded social welfare programs were on the defensive. The Conservative government, obsessed with the national debt and unwilling to tax the corporate sector more heavily, looked to cut costs rather than institute new programs.

THE DAY-CARE CRISIS

By the early 1990s, a majority of mothers with children under twelve worked outside the home, but good affordable day care was available only to a minority. Not only was day care expensive, but the hours when it was available often failed to match the needs of parents who were forced to work evenings or weekends.

Horror stories of unlicensed babysitters sexually assaulting or beating children in their care were common. Even more frequent were reports of private day-care facilities that were unclean, overcrowded, understaffed, and poorly equipped. In North York, Ontario, in 1977, a couple was fined $1000 for operating an unlicensed day home in which thirty-nine children spent their days on mattresses in the home's three bedrooms. One of the children had been placed on a wet mattress in a closed cupboard. The police reported that the home was filthy and depressing and had no toys, books, or equipment for the children. Parents, desperate for affordable day care, had taken what was available.

The 1970 report of the Royal Commission on the Status of Women had set guidelines for a national day-care program. The report made clear that equality for women was impossible without a recognition that the care of children was the joint responsibility of fathers, mothers, and society. "Parents require supplementary help, and society may legitimately be called upon to contribute to community service for its younger generation. The equality of women means little without such a program."[2] More than twenty years later, affordable, accessible, quality day care remained elusive for most Canadian families, and the day-care lobby was dealt a serious blow when the Mulroney government reneged on its campaign promise for a national day-care program after it was re-elected in 1988.

Federal transfer payments to the provinces were a major target for those wishing to cut the costs of social welfare programs. Attempts by the federal government to limit growth in grants to the provinces had begun in 1977 when block funding replaced equal federal–provincial sharing of medicare and postsecondary education costs. The Trudeau Liberals called the new arrangement "established programs financing" and gave the provinces a percentage of federal income and corporate taxes plus a cash grant to replace the old formula. While cash grants initially were increased by the annual rate of inflation, the Trudeau government set limits to increases in federal spending on postsecondary education for 1982 and 1983.

In 1986, the Mulroney administration announced that federal cash grants for medicare and postsecondary education would be reduced by 2 percent annually. Though Mulroney had claimed in the 1984 election that Canada's universal social welfare programs were a "sacred trust," his government continued a process of cutbacks that the provinces claimed cost them $11 billion in medical financing from 1982 to the end of 1988. Concerns were voiced that Canada's medical system was deteriorating: line-ups for surgery grew and provinces increasingly complained that they were unable to hire medical specialists, purchase new medical equipment, or add hospital beds. Conservatives claimed that the elimination of deterrent fees meant that too many people were taking advantage of the system; progressives claimed that physicians were overpaid. There was a growing belief that the existing health-service model gave too much power to physicians and relied too heavily on costly laboratory tests, large hospitals, and expensive drugs. Some reformers called for more holistic approaches to medicine, which not only treated physical ailments but addressed those aspects of life—poverty, pollution, stress, and poor nutrition—that contributed to disease.

In the 1988–89 fiscal year, federal transfers of all kinds totalled over $32 billion. This included more than $17 billion for established programs financing, $1.3 billion for extended health care services, and just under $5 billion for expenditures under the Canada Assistance Plan. In 1990, the Conservatives, at the behest of big business organizations, introduced a bill that would speed up federal withdrawal from established programs financing. The cash transfer of $9 billion in the 1989–90 fiscal year would be reduced progressively to zero in the year 2004. The federal government seemed less concerned with reducing the deficit than transferring it to the provinces.

Sacred trust or no, other federal programs were also in jeopardy in the late 1980s. Child benefits were partially de-indexed from inflation, federal supplements for hiring and training workers were cut, and a program to help municipalities maintain low-cost rental units was eliminated. The principle of universality was removed from family allowance and old age security payments; a cap was placed on increases in Canada Assistance Plan funding; and unemployment insurance benefits were cut and requirements stiffened so that many people who quit their jobs were no longer eligible for benefits.

These policies met strong resistance from organizations as varied as the social planning councils of major cities, the Salvation Army, the National Action Committee on the Status of Women, the National Anti-Poverty Organization, labour federations, and the National Pensioners and Senior Citizens Federation. By 1990, these organizations were campaigning together to defend and extend Canada's social programs. The Canadian Conference of Catholic Bishops demanded that an ethic of sharing and a determination to end poverty take precedence over profit making and individualist consumption, but this message carried less weight with the federal government than did the big business agenda. The social welfare lobbies had varying degrees of success with provincial governments. The election of the New Democrats in Ontario in 1990, and British Columbia and Saskatchewan in 1991, created huge expectations among social welfare advocates, but it was clear that, with a recession plaguing the country, governments of all political stripes would be reluctant to create new programs or increase expenditures on old ones. Even the New Democrats were influenced by the neo-conservative ideology that rejected Keynesian notions of allowing deficits to rise during recessions.

•Co-operative Federalism?

As we saw in earlier chapters, federal social programs were often sore points in federal–provincial relations. There were many reasons for the conflicts, though they usually boiled down to power and money. Under the constitution, social programs were an area of provincial responsibility, and several provinces, notably Ontario and Quebec, were reluctant to hand their prerogatives over to the federal government. Cost-sharing arrangements could lead to fiscal problems for the provinces, not the least of which was federal inconstancy in financing. Moreover, as federal expenditures grew, Ottawa attempted to increase its share of revenues from provincially controlled resources. Finally, as in the case of medicare, provinces simply objected either to the principle or the details of proposed programs.

From the federal point of view, particularly during the Trudeau years, Ottawa was only trying to establish a balance between federal and provincial powers. Federal expenditures had grown far more slowly than provincial spending in the post-war era. Increases in Ottawa's expenditures were necessary if the federal government was to continue to play a meaningful role in the lives of citizens. Once the federal government began spending money on programs administered by provincial governments, it had a duty to ensure that national norms were observed. This made sense to Canadian nationalists, and many accused the provincial governments of trying to create ten autonomous states. Supporters of greater provincial autonomy denied that Trudeau had merely restored balance in the relative powers of the provinces and the central government. Regional economic development policies in Prince Edward Island meant that the federal government had a virtual veto over most areas of policy previously under provincial jurisdiction.

In the late 1970s the large Hibernia oil field was discovered off Newfoundland. Brian Peckford, Newfoundland's Conservative premier, insisted that the province have equal control with Ottawa over offshore developments. He argued that the province was more sensitive than Ottawa to the need to balance oil developments with protection of the fishery and to use the new economic activity to foster spinoffs throughout the provincial economy. Trudeau resisted these demands and was supported by the Supreme Court, which ruled in 1984 that the federal government need not share control over oil development with St John's. That same year, the Mulroney Conservatives were elected, campaigning on a promise to restore "co-operative federalism" after years of confrontation between Trudeau and the provincial premiers. Mulroney agreed to Newfoundland's claims for co-management of offshore oil developments. Peckford's successful use of the provincial rights issue in several elections demonstrated that citizens were more likely to accept such arguments in the area of economic development than in social programs.

This was also true of the National Energy Program. Announced by the Trudeau government in 1980, it brought forth a particularly belligerent response from Alberta's Peter Lougheed. Sputtering angry anti-Ottawa rhetoric, the provincial government cut its oil production to force negotiations. Within a year, a deal had been struck that preserved essential features of the NEP—a "made in Canada" price for oil, larger federal revenue from energy production, and greater Canadian ownership of the energy industry—but increased energy prices and jettisoned a natural gas export tax.

Trudeau claimed that the NEP was an instrument of nationalism but, if so, it was more Central-Canadian than pan-Canadian nationalism. Its goal to provide cheap energy meant that energy-producing provinces, along with the multinationals that dominated the sector, had to sacrifice revenue to fuel the industries of Central Canada. There was nothing in the policy that would aid Western provinces anxious to use energy revenues to foster secondary industry. Ultimately the policy was a costly one for all Canadians: the grants and tax incentives offered to Canadianize the industry proved expensive for the public purse, particularly at a time when deficits were beginning to soar.

Politically, too, the NEP had its costs. Angry small business people, who depended on the success of the major oil companies, began to reject not only the Trudeau government but Canadian Confederation. A right-wing separatist party, the Western Canada Concept, held huge rallies in Calgary and Edmonton and elected an MLA in a provincial by-election in 1982. Although personality conflicts quickly tore it apart, the WCC struck a responsive chord among rural Albertans and some urban small business people with its repudiation of the welfare state, bilingualism, and alleged federal attempts to appease Quebec at the expense of Western Canada.

Only a small minority of the Westerners who were alienated by Trudeau rejected Canada altogether. Others wished to reshape the country to reflect an imagined golden age during which white Christian men had carved a living out of the wilderness, untrammelled by big business, big government, and big labour. Such sentiments helped to produce the Reform Party in 1987. Led by Preston Manning, son of Alberta's long-time Social Credit premier Ernest Manning, the Reformers declared that the West did not want out of Confederation: rather it wanted in, and it wished to reconstruct that Confederation to better reflect the regions. While they were anti-separatist, Reformers shared the WCC's right-wing agenda. They wanted the federal deficit slashed even if it meant sacrificing subsidy pro-grams to farmers and abandoning universality in social programs, and they wanted Canadian immigration policy to favour Europeans as it had before 1962. Manning's increasingly centralized control of the party and his attempt to woo Ontario support partially tarnished Reform's image in the West, but it was a force for both the Alberta and federal Conservatives to reckon with.

When Mulroney abandoned the NEP, he undoubtedly was influenced by political protest in the West, and he used the rhetoric of provincial rights to justify his actions. But, to a large extent, he was capitulating to the interests of American energy companies who had chafed at a policy that encouraged Canadianization of their assets within Canada, kept Canadian prices for oil below world levels, and increased federal taxation of the energy industry.

Battles over energy development, regional development grants, and shared-cost programs during the Trudeau period suggested that Canadian federalism was more competitive than co-operative. Federal relations were particularly poor with Quebec after the election of the Parti Québécois in

1976. Ottawa announced several major regional development programs without the approval of the Quebec government and, in general, appeared to be trying to appeal to the province's population over the heads of its provincial administration. Partisan considerations also soured federal–provincial relations with other provinces, few of which had Liberal administrations during Trudeau's years in office. It was unsurprising, then, that the provinces proved hostile to Trudeau's plans to patriate the Canadian constitution with a Charter of Rights and Freedoms and an amending process that could be construed as threatening to provincial rights.

•Patriating the Constitution

During the 1960s and 1970s, several attempts were made to "patriate" the British North America Act—that is, to make the constitution a Canadian document and remove the last vestige of British control over Canada. The housing of the constitution in Britain had become purely symbolic once the Canadian Supreme Court replaced the Judicial Committee of the Privy Council as the high court of the nation in 1949. Nonetheless, the fact that the Canadian constitution was simply an act of the British Parliament bothered some federal politicians. Moreover, the constitution contained no amending formula. Amendments to allow federal unemployment insurance and old-age pensions had been passed with the support of all provinces and the federal government. Federal politicians, supported by social welfare proponents, believed that an amending formula requiring unanimity would prove an obstacle to further expansion of federal powers.

In the early 1960s and again in 1971, the federal and provincial governments almost agreed on patriation of the constitution, with an amending formula added. The holdout on both occasions was Quebec, where a consensus was building in favour of greater constitutional powers for that province. In the 1966 provincial election the provincial Liberals and the Union Nationale appeared to rival separatists in their calls for special status for Quebec.

The Lesage Liberals, who lost the election, sought provincial control over family allowances, Canada Manpower, and the new Guaranteed Income Supplement for pensioners. They also wanted the federal government to rebate to Quebec monies that would have been spent in the province on shared-cost programs from which Quebec opted out. The Union Nationale, under Daniel Johnson, called for a new Canadian constitution with special status for Quebec. In the new Canada, the federal government would collect no income, corporate, or death taxes in Quebec and would yield to that province total control over all social programs. As premier, Johnson sent "national" delegations to international conferences, causing rows with Ottawa, toyed with the idea of establishing a separate Quebec currency, and made clear that Quebec reserved the right to separate if Canada did not accede to its demands for special status.

A number of members of both the federal Conservative and New Democratic parties in the late 1960s appeared to believe that accommodation of Quebec's demands was necessary to keep the country from falling apart. The election of Pierre Trudeau in 1968, with a tough federalist line, caused all three national parties to reject notions of radical constitutional change. Trudeau's popularity in Quebec suggested an ambivalence on the part of a population whose leading provincial politicians were all Quebec nationalists but who had sent Trudeau and other prominent federalists to

Quebec Liberal leader Claude Ryan and Parti Québécois leader René Lévesque (*Montreal Gazette*/National Archives of Canada/PA-117480)

Ottawa. Trudeau's promotion of French Canadians within the civil service and his spending of considerable federal monies in Quebec caused many to vote for "French power" in Ottawa, but many of the same people had little difficulty supporting provincial politicians who wished to erode or even end Ottawa's power within Quebec.

In Quebec provincial politics, both federalists and supporters of sovereignty association sought to drastically limit the powers of the federal government. The Quebec Liberal Party, leading the "*non*" campaign in the 1980 referendum on sovereignty association called by the Parti Québécois, advocated a renewed federalism that would give Quebec control over social programs and most economic policies, leaving the federal government in charge of foreign affairs, defence, and monetary policy. This was a far cry from Trudeau's advocacy of federal control in any area involving the national interest.

A 1979 federal task force on national unity, chaired by former Trudeau Cabinet minister Jean-Luc Pépin and former Ontario premier John Robarts, had also advocated a "soft" federalism that would give more powers to all provinces, not just to Quebec. Trudeau rejected such a decentralized vision of Confederation. From his point of view, Ottawa already housed a weak central government, and the provincial politicians who played on alienation from Ottawa were demagogues after more personal power.

Once the referendum was over, Trudeau announced that the federal government was tired of endless constitutional consultations with the provinces and of Quebec's inevitable vetoes of attempts to patriate the constitution. With or without provincial approval, Ottawa planned to ask the British government to place the constitution in Canadian hands. The patriated constitution would include a Charter of Rights and Freedoms and a new amending formula. If the government of either Ontario or Quebec or a majority of Western and Atlantic provinces objected to an amendment, Ottawa could call a referendum where voters could effectively veto their provincial government. Undoubtedly, Trudeau's emphasis on civil liberties and participatory democracy in the constitutional package was an attempt to improve the image of the federal government.

Most provinces resisted Trudeau's initiative, seeing it as a bid to weaken provincial rights. Only Ontario and New Brunswick, which had few grievances with Ottawa at the time, supported the plan. Quebec Premier René Lévesque had the support of seven other premiers in opposing Trudeau. The eight provinces agreed to stand together in challenging the procedure in the courts.

The Supreme Court ruled in September 1981 that "substantial consent," but not unanimity, of the provinces was needed for patriation. With

Prime Minister Margaret Thatcher unwavering in her declarations that Britain would accept a request by the Canadian government for patriation, the premiers began to fear that patriation would be achieved without the provinces winning any concessions. On 5 November 1981, nine premiers came to terms with Trudeau, leaving René Lévesque to claim betrayal. The premiers of the three westernmost provinces and Newfoundland had been won over by Trudeau's agreement to strengthen provincial control over resources, while Manitoba Premier Sterling Lyon, in the middle of a hard-fought election campaign, recognized that his longstanding opposition to the Charter of Rights and Freedoms was a political liability.

That deal created the Constitution Act, which consisted of the renamed British North America Act, an amending formula, and the Charter of Rights and Freedoms. The amending formula allowed the federal government to change the Constitution if it had the approval of the federal Parliament plus two-thirds of the provinces representing a combined population of at least 50 percent of all Canadians. Unanimous consent of all provinces as well as both houses of Parliament would continue to be required for amendments affecting representation in the House of Commons, Senate, and Supreme Court and for changes affecting the use of the French and English languages. Furthermore, a province that believed that its legislative or proprietary rights were attacked by an amendment could declare the amendment null and void within its boundaries. A province would also have the right to opt out with full financial compensation from a program established by amendment that affected educational or cultural matters. As a concession to Atlantic Canada, section 36 of the constitution committed Canadian governments to the principle of equalization to "ensure that provincial governments have sufficient revenue to provide reasonably comparable levels of public services at reasonably comparable levels of taxation."

The Charter guaranteed Canadians freedom of speech, association, conscience, and religion and prohibited discrimination on the basis of colour, sex, or creed. Enshrined were voting rights, rights to legal counsel, and protection against arbitrary arrest. While the courts could be used to protect various rights that governments had at times infringed in the past, there were several restrictions on Canadians' constitutional freedoms. Legislatures could place "reasonable limits" on citizens' enjoyment of rights. Provinces could also override constitutional rights by passing a law that specifically indicated that it applied notwithstanding a Charter provision. Indeed, Quebec quickly acted to exempt all of its legislation from the Charter, claiming that its own human rights code protected citizens better than the federal version. The Charter guaranteed Canadians the freedom to live and work anywhere in Canada, although provinces with high unemployment rates retained the right to give existing residents preferential treatment.

Section 28 declared that Charter rights "are guaranteed equally to male and female persons." This section owed its existence to concerted pressure from women's goups, as the proposed Charter had originally said nothing about gender equality. Effective feminist lobbying also succeeded in exempting section 28 from the override provisions of the Charter. Women's struggle for Charter rights was a difficult one given lack of government support and the partisan disagreements among feminists. Many Liberal women were torn between support for the government and the desire for constitutional change. It is not surprising, then, that Charter equality provisions fell short of the demands of women's groups: a preamble to the Charter in which equal rights for women and men were delineated in a statement of purpose; the addition of marital status, sexual orientation, and political beliefs to religion, race, age, and sex as illegitimate grounds for discrimination; equal representation for women in the Supreme Court; and the explicit right to reproductive freedom.

Native lobbies were likewise only partially successful in pressuring for changes to the constitution. Their attempts to win the right of self-determination failed, but the Charter did acknowledge aboriginal concerns by guaranteeing that nothing in the document would affect existing treaty rights or prejudice later land settlements. A constitutional conference on Native rights was to be called within one year of the proclamation of the constitution.

Though much of the Charter focussed on individual rights, the section on Native peoples recognized collective rights as well. So did a subsection of the non-discrimination clause that recognized the validity of affirmative action programs on behalf of women and minorities. Language rights also received some recognition. English and French were inscribed as the official languages of Canada and New Brunswick, while Quebec and Manitoba's existing constitutional obligations in the area of language were left intact. The right of English and French minorities to education in their own language, where numbers warranted, was enshrined.

Quebec denounced a clause that undid the provision in Bill 101 limiting instruction in the English language to children of anglophones born in the province. The right to be educated in English was extended to the children of anglophones born elsewhere in Canada: immigrants were subject to provincial rules regarding language of instruction.

Arguably, the new constitution did not otherwise limit Quebec's existing powers or its ability to protect the French character of the province. Even so, the francophone community was generally disappointed with the results of the constitutional negotiations. *Indépendantiste* political scientist Daniel Latouche summed up provincial reaction:

> For the sovereignty group, the *Constitution Act, 1982* spelled failure for the very concept of sovereignty association, not so much by the act's substance as by the process and play of forces that had produced it. How could there be association if English Canada refused even to acknowledge the existence of a distinct political collectivity?
>
> The disappointment was no less keen for the proponents of renewed federalism, who could have had serious hopes of seeing their ideas used as a basis for future constitutional discussion. After its referendum victory, the federal government hurried to pass the *Constitution Act, 1982* without really asking their opinion or, worse still, waiting for them to get back into office. This could only mean a fixed resolve in the rest of Canada to reject any notion of different, particular or national status for Quebec.[3]

For women and Native peoples too, the new constitution would prove a disappointment, at least during its early years. Charter equality and non-discrimination rights only came into force in 1985. Early constitutional

Pierre Trudeau and Queen Elizabeth II completing the patriation of Canada's constitution (Robert Cooper/National Archives of Canada/PA-141503)

decisions regarding gender rights suggested that the courts, dominated by men, were blind to the differences in social power between the sexes. In 1989, a study prepared for the Canadian Advisory Council on the Status of Women reported that "women are initiating few cases, and men are using the Charter to strike back at women's hard-won protections and benefits."[4] While feminist lawyers, notably in LEAF (the Women's Legal Education and Action Fund), were working to change this situation, it was clear that women would have to lobby for legislative changes rather than rely on the courts to gain equality.

Native people were no more successful. Three first ministers' conferences yielded nothing on Native attempts to win an amendment guaranteeing self-government. Seven provinces, including either Ontario or Quebec, had to be on side, and Quebec refused to consider constitutional amendments on the grounds that it had not signed the new constitution and therefore did not recognize its legitimacy. At the third conference in 1987, British Columbia, Alberta, and Saskatchewan, all with Conservative or Social Credit governments, claimed that Natives' demands for entrenchment of aboriginal rights in the constitution were imprecise. They feared that their provinces' rights to control resources would be inhibited by such an amendment. In all four holdout provinces, the record indicated that developers' rights had been generally favoured over aboriginal rights. By 1992, the strength of the Native lobby, led by the Assembly of First Nations, forced a reconsideration of the notion of inherent rights for Native peoples.

If the Constitution Act was meant to bind Canadians more closely together, it has demonstrated little success. Three issues, free trade, the Meech Lake Accord, and the referendum on the Charlottetown Accord, revealed the depth of disagreement among Canadians regarding the role of the federal government in Canadian Confederation.

• Free Trade Debate

Brian Mulroney's Conservatives came to power in 1984 in a climate of increasing concern about the security of Canada's export trade. Mulroney had promised "jobs, jobs, jobs" to a nation that had suffered high unemployment for a decade. Unemployment had skyrocketed during the 1982 recession, and when Mulroney took office, 1.4 million Canadians were officially unemployed. Many others had given up looking for work or had settled for part-time jobs. When the statistics were all boiled down, about one Canadian in five was either underemployed or not employed at all.

Mulroney promised that jobs would be created if the Liberal fetters on the marketplace were removed and investor confidence restored. Significantly, he did not mention free trade in the 1984 election and, indeed, had flatly rejected the idea when he was elected Conservative leader a year earlier. It was inevitable that he should change his position when faced with growing corporate support for free trade. Mulroney was a former president of Iron Ore Company of Canada, an American subsidiary, and was rarely at odds with big business interests or, for that matter, with the wishes of American President Ronald Reagan, who first proposed free trade in 1980.

Formal negotiations for a free trade pact began in 1986. As the talks progressed, it became clear that the Americans were interested in breaking down barriers to American investment in Canada, assuring availability of Canadian energy and water supplies and other resources, and guaranteeing access for American service industries. Because of GATT agreements, tariffs affected only about 20 percent of trade between the two nations and the Americans were happy enough to remove those that remained. They were less keen to dispense with the countervailing duties (the penalties that they imposed on imports to compensate for alleged unfair advantages over American products) that obsessed Canadian negotiators.

In the final agreement, each party had the right to impose countervailing duties. A disputes mechanism was put in place to resolve claims of unfair subsidies and other problems that might arise, but the commission that would rule on complaints could not bind governments to follow its rulings.

The two sides failed to agree on the definition of "unfair subsidies." American negotiators regarded Canadian regional development grants, lower timber stumpage fees, and even medicare as subsidies (the latter because American firms often agreed to pay their employees' private medical insurance fees). Meanwhile, the Americans pointedly exempted military expenditures from the agreement. This meant that they could continue to aid the country's underdeveloped regions through military expenditures while at the same time decrying Canadian regional development policies that relied far less on military expenditures. They also excluded discussion of subsidies to grain farmers, arguing that similar European subsidies had to be addressed first.

In pursuing the FTA, corporate Canada had two related goals: greater access to the American market and greater tools with which to resist pressures for a strongly interventionist state. "The alternative to free trade is a controlled economy," claimed supporters of the deal.[5] At the same time, they denied charges that the nation's ability to choose its own economic destiny had been traded away. They rejected claims that

Canada's social programs were in jeopardy, that its state-protected cultural industries were made vulnerable, and that regional development programs had been sacrificed.

If staunch free-enterprisers formed the core of the agreement's supporters, opponents were united by a belief that Canada's separate existence justified a state presence in the economy. The major industrialists who supported this view were few, but they were often quite vocal. Frank Stronach, founder of Magna International, and Harrison McCain, head of the multinational food giant, McCain's, spoke against the agreement; Stronach even ran unsuccessfully for the Liberals in the 1988 election. Canadian Steamships chair Paul Martin Jr was a successful Liberal candidate, though a more lukewarm opponent of the agreement. Most of the industrialists who opposed the agreement advocated freer trade but claimed that the Mulroney–Reagan agreement gave away too much sovereignty in return for too few concessions.

Dominating the anti-free-trade coalition were groups that favoured an expanded Canadian welfare state and questioned the ability of uncontrolled markets to ensure social justice. These included organized labour, women's groups, and social justice groups within the churches. Members of Canada's cultural industries were also largely against the agreement, with celebrities such as Margaret Atwood, Pierre Berton, and David Suzuki particularly vocal opponents. The agreement's vague exemption of cultural industries from its provisions provoked cries of a cultural sell-out.

Labour and women's groups claimed that women workers, many of whom were employed in service industries, would be particularly vulnerable if the agreement passed. The agreement would allow Americans to further penetrate Canadian banking, accounting, transportation, marketing, advertising, health, and day-care industries. Indeed, the final agreement gave service firms the right to establish themselves in both countries and to import "temporary" staff for as long as required. Political economist Marjorie Griffin Cohen predicted in 1987:

> free trade in services will adversely affect women. One result will be increased job losses, as imported services replace domestic ones. But another significant problem, which will result from the demand for the right of establishment and national treatment, will be the amount of control Canada will be able to maintain over the direction of social, economic and political development. This, in turn, will have an effect on both the conditions of work, and the nature of the provision of certain types of services.[6]

Although only a quarter of the manufacturing labour force, women were concentrated in textiles, clothing, footwear, and food industries, all of which enjoyed tariff protection. The labour movement, a vigorous opponent of the deal, claimed that the removal of tariffs would cause many American branch plants in Canada to close. There were also fears that Canadian investors, taking into account the lower rates of pay in many American states, would either flee the country or cut the pay of their Canadian workers. Ultimately, Canadian workers would be forced to accept a lower standard of living and fewer benefits so that Canadian companies could compete with American firms. The country's social legislation, minimum wage provisions, and relatively strong unions could thus all be jettisoned in a free trade environment.

Opponents of the agreement differed regarding economic strategies for putting Canadians back to work, the ostensible aim of the free trade supporters. The federal Liberals at times called for a re-negotiation of the agreement and at others for a return to sectoral bargaining. On the whole, the Liberals appeared to lack an industrial strategy and were criticized by the Conservatives as offering only the status quo as an alternative to free trade. The New Democrats had, over the years, proposed greater government intervention in the economy, but in the election they chose to concentrate on their social and environmental programs and their popular leader, Ed Broadbent. Such questionable strategy meant that John Turner's Liberals easily upstaged the party on the main issue of the election. Perhaps the most memorable moment in the election campaign belonged to Turner who, in a heated exchange with Brian Mulroney during the televised leaders' debate, accused the prime minister of selling out the country. Since the Liberals and NDP apparently failed even to consider working together to elect an anti-free-trade majority, the odds were in the government's favour.

In the end, voters in only two provinces embraced free trade. Alberta's endorsement was overwhelming. Anxious for markets for their oil and gas, and resentful that their economy remained sluggish while Central Canada was experiencing a boom, Albertans responded positively to the expensive campaign their provincial government sponsored in favour of the agreement. Quebec's once protectionist business community also endorsed free trade. Companies such as Bombardier and Power Corporation, which had international investments and markets, did not share the views of manufacturers in long-established sectors who worried mainly about the home market. The opportunity to invest and sell in the United States on the same basis as American firms appealed to the large Quebec corporations, many of which had prospered because of generous provincial grants and loans. Quebec's two main provincial parties both campaigned for the agreement. For the Parti Québécois, support for free trade was as much a strategy in their battle for sovereignty as a judgment on the wisdom of open markets.

This party, whose first term in office had been marked by economic interventionism, now proclaimed from the opposition benches that free trade would end the threat of Canadian economic blackmail against an independent Quebec. Provincial premiers had informed Quebec during the 1980 referendum that their markets would not be freely open to protected Quebec manufactures such as footwear, clothing, and textiles if the province left Confederation. With protection gone, argued *indépendantistes*, Canada would be unable to scare Quebec into remaining in Confederation by threatening the economic consequences of a rupture.

Outside Quebec, each region showed a degree of division over free trade. Ontario gave slightly less than half its seats to the Conservatives. In the West, while Alberta heavily supported free trade, a majority of the electorate in Saskatchewan, British Columbia, and Manitoba voted against the agreement. In Atlantic Canada, three provinces rejected the agreement, angry that it appeared to threaten regional development grants and offered no new protection for their fisheries. Only in New Brunswick, where Liberal Premier Frank McKenna gave the agreement a lukewarm endorsement, did the seats split evenly between supporters and opponents of the FTA.

Foreign economic control, of course, was not the only issue in the 1988 election. Constitutional matters continued to haunt the political scene and influence political choices.

• Meech Lake and Its Aftermath

Quebec never signed the 1982 Constitution. Although its approval was unnecessary to give the legislation effect, Brian Mulroney was determined to bring Quebec into the constitutional fold. Robert Bourassa, the Quebec premier, presented five demands that had to be fulfilled before Quebec would sign the constitution. The first was a clause recognizing Quebec as a distinct society. The second was a Quebec veto for constitutional amendments. The remaining three would give all provinces a greater role in immigration, would allow them to remain outside any new cost-sharing programs without financial penalty, and would have the federal government choose Supreme Court judges from lists provided by the premiers. A first ministers' conference held at Meech Lake, near Ottawa, in April 1987 tentatively approved a package that met Quebec's demands and incorporated concerns expressed by other provinces. The final agreement, worked out in an all-night session in Ottawa on 3 June 1987, embodied a vision of Canada strongly at odds with that of postwar Liberal federalism.

Demands for Senate reform, particularly from Alberta, were dealt with by giving the provinces the right to present Ottawa with a list of names from which senators would be drawn. Annual first ministers' meetings to discuss constitutional change were entrenched in the Accord. To win support from premiers who balked at the idea of Quebec having a veto over constitutional change, Mulroney granted all provinces a veto. The Meech Lake Accord would be the first test of whether an amendment could muster the consent of the federal Parliament and all provincial legislatures.

Despite the unanimity of the first ministers and support for the accord from the three national party leaders, Meech Lake had its opponents. Many groups attacked the lack of involvement of ordinary Canadians in the constitution-making process, particularly after Mulroney announced in late June that no amendments to Meech Lake would be considered: it had to be ratified within three years by Parliament and by all ten provincial legislatures without a word changed.

Quebec *indépendantistes* denounced the agreement, ridiculing the distinct society clause and claiming that Quebec was a nation that ought to have sovereignty. PQ leader Pierre-Marc Johnson and his successor, Jacques Parizeau, asked, as did many English-speaking Canadians, what the nebulous words "distinct society" meant in legal terms.

Former prime minister Pierre Trudeau, a lonely federalist voice in francophone Quebec, denounced the accord as a sell-out of federal powers to power-hungry premiers. Mulroney tried to calm federalists by claiming that the distinct society clause was largely symbolic. Trudeau noted that if this were the case, it would disappoint Quebec nationalists who would continue making constitutional demands for more provincial powers. If, on the other hand, court decisions allowed Quebec to legislate in areas reserved for the federal government in order to preserve a distinct society, Mulroney's assurances were worthless. How the courts would interpret the distinct society clause was hypothetical, but Meech opponents, both federalist and separatist, rejected a clause that appeared to abandon such an important question to the courts.

Apart from the distinct society clause, the two aspects of the accord that drew the most fire were cost-sharing provisions and the unanimity requirement for constitutional amendments. The latter was criticized on a number of fronts. Canadians were becoming sceptical of constitutional processes by which eleven white men meeting behind closed doors could decide the future of the nation. A wide range of individuals and special interest groups were beginning to demand that their voices be heard. Supporters of particular amendments believed that the unanimity clause would permanently dash hopes of reform. For the aboriginal peoples, who had been one province short of a crucial amendment just months before

Meech Lake was announced, the unanimity clause was a particularly bitter pill. Aboriginal self-government appeared to have been sacrificed on the altar of provincial rights. Senate reformers in Western and Atlantic Canada also believed that the accord doomed their hopes, though even the 1982 constitution had required unanimity for changes to the Senate.

Supporters of the welfare state were not pleased with the provision that allowed provinces to exempt themselves from new federal cost-shared programs, provided they set up a similar program. The language of the accord made no reference to national standards in such cases. Indeed, groups working for new national policies, particularly in the child-care area, suspected that provincial opposition would block the establishment of new shared-cost programs. After all, medicare had been imposed with popular support, but with limited enthusiasm from provincial governments. Similar opposition to a national child-care program would result in federal abandonment of the notion or a hodge-podge of "opt-out" programs with federal money but no national standards.

National women's groups objected to the weakening of federal powers and demanded that women be included in a clause that exempted aboriginal people and multicultural groups from the application of the clause recognizing both linguistic duality across Canada and a distinct society in Quebec. Quebec women's groups were divided on the issue. Many feminist nationalists decried the suggestion that a Quebec government might use the distinct society clause to limit women's abortion rights or to bar women from certain occupations. They claimed that anglophone women who feared that Quebec might revert to Catholic conservatism and roll back women's victories were out of touch with modern Quebec, which had the most progressive women's legislation in Canada.

Much of the Meech Lake debate might have become academic had three elections between 1987 and 1989 not changed the provincial arithmetic. First came the election of Liberal Frank McKenna in New Brunswick. McKenna was a Meech Lake opponent and, with his party in control of every seat in the provincial legislature, he was in a position to prevent passage of the accord.

In 1988, Manitoba's NDP administration was succeeded by a Conservative minority government led by Gary Filmon. The Liberals under Sharon Carstairs, a passionate opponent of Meech, had over one-third of the seats in the legislature and threatened to topple Filmon over the issue. NDP leader Gary Doer eventually joined Carstairs in opposing the accord, arguing that the combination of the Free Trade Agreement and the Meech Lake Accord would leave the federal government an empty shell. Such an argument was common, although, in fact, many opponents of free trade, including John Turner, Ed Broadbent, and Ontario Premier David Peterson, supported Meech Lake.

Filmon added his party, which was divided on the accord, to the column of those demanding amendments after Quebec used the notwithstanding clause to nullify a Supreme Court decision regarding the language on signs. The Court had ruled that a request by some merchants to include English on a store sign was reasonable, particularly since the French words would dominate. Premier Bourassa, faced with nationalist demands to uphold the integrity of Bill 101, invoked the notwithstanding clause and ruled that languages other than English could be used on signs only inside shops. Filmon appeared to take up the cause of the anglophone minority, but Quebec politicians pointed out that he had been part of the Conservative caucus that had opposed linguistic equality for Manitoba francophones.

The election of a scrappy opponent of Meech Lake in Newfoundland in 1989 marked a further milestone in Meech's progress. Clyde Wells wanted a strong federal state and opposed special powers for any one

Clyde Wells and Brian Mulroney, 1992   (Ron Poling, Canapress)

province, but he wavered between outright opposition to special status for Quebec and a willingness to accept the distinct society clause if the first ministers agreed to an elected Senate with equal representation from all provinces. When Mulroney appeared intransigent, the Newfoundland legislature rescinded its ratification of Meech Lake that had been secured under Brian Peckford.

Although Northerners had no direct voice in the constitutional amendment process, most were relieved at the growing provincial opposition to the accord. Residents of the Yukon and the Northwest Territories could hardly support an accord that would virtually preclude them from becoming provinces. Without provincehood, they would have no right to nominate senators or Supreme Court judges and they would have no say at constitutional conferences or regarding constitutional amendments.

By early 1990, polls indicated that a majority of Canadians opposed the Meech Lake Accord, despite the fact that over 70 percent admitted they knew little or nothing about its provisions. Interestingly, while even fewer Quebeckers claimed to be familiar with the accord's contents, an overwhelming majority believed that it ought to be passed. More ominously, growing numbers of Québécois—a majority by spring 1990—thought the province should embrace sovereignty, or at least sovereignty association, if the accord was not ratified by the 30 June 1990 deadline.

Aware of the strength of this opinion in Quebec, some Canadians believed that the accord, flawed or not, should be passed to keep Quebec within Confederation. Others opposed the accord specifically because they thought it gave too much power to Quebec. Many Canadians joined Pierre Trudeau in defending the federal state from its presumed attackers, but they did not always agree on what elements of Meech eroded federal power. Some Canadian nationalists were prepared to accept special status for Quebec but could not accept increased provincial powers and an inflexible amending formula.

The Mulroney government stuck to its hard line that not a word of the accord could be changed. Frank McKenna emerged as a possible conciliator, proposing a "parallel accord" that would deal with Meech opponents' concerns regarding women, aboriginal peoples, Northerners, and the distinct society clause. Just weeks before the ratification deadline, Mulroney reassembled the premiers and used the threat of Quebec separatism to try to force the dissenters to accept the accord with an accompanying statement that granted a degree of Senate reform and acknowledged the views of several constitutional lawyers regarding the scope of the distinct society clause. It almost worked. McKenna, who had come to believe that ordinary Quebeckers would misunderstand Meech's rejection, asked his legislature to ratify the accord with its accompanying statement.

The three Manitoba party leaders, who had worked together to produce a set of changes to the accord that would preserve a strong federal government and protect the rights of women, aboriginals, and Northerners, accepted the agreement under pressure. This was particularly galling for Sharon Carstairs, since she had opposed the accord from the beginning and could not pretend that the first ministers' meetings had changed the intent of the document. Still, neither she nor the "two Garys"—Filmon and Doer—wanted to be responsible for the collapse of Confederation.

Clyde Wells was displeased with Mulroney's tactics and Bourassa's unwillingness to budge. He wanted Newfoundlanders to decide in a referendum whether the legislature should ratify the accord. When Quebec refused to extend the deadline, Wells resolved instead to have a free vote on the revised accord in the Newfoundland legislature.

Meanwhile, Elijah Harper, the lone Native member in the Manitoba legislature and a former NDP cabinet minister, used procedural methods to prevent the accord's passage in Manitoba before 30 June. The party leaders could have changed the procedures to force a vote on time, as Ottawa pressured them to do, but they decided to let the agreement lapse. Manitobans had generally disapproved of the province's capitulation at the constitutional conference, and Harper's last stand for Native peoples seemed a fitting way to let the accord die. When it became clear that Manitoba could not pass the accord in time, Clyde Wells called off the

Sharon Carstairs and Elijah Harper (Office of the Leader of the Manitoba Liberal Party;
Office of Elijah Harper)

Newfoundland vote. Meech Lake was dead, killed by the misgivings of several have-not provinces and aboriginal peoples.

Bourassa was furious, arguing that the idea of the accord had been to meet Quebec's demands and not to address the discontent of all the other provinces. He felt that Quebec had been humiliated, and he assured Quebeckers that the province would never again attend a constitutional conference with other premiers. Rather, it would seek new provincial powers through direct Ottawa–Quebec City negotiations. Support for independence for Quebec had never been stronger than it was in the wake of the Meech defeat. In the fall of 1990, Bourassa established a commission on the future of Quebec. Headed by businessmen Michel Bélanger and Jean Campeau, it filed a majority report in 1991 that favoured Quebec remaining in Confederation only if Ottawa recognized its sovereignty in most jurisdictions. Some nationalist MPs from Quebec formed the Bloc Québécois, a federal party supporting an independent Quebec and attempting to defend Quebec rights in Ottawa until such time as independence was achieved. The party was headed by Lucien Bouchard, a renegade Conservative Cabinet minister.

Although Bourassa continued to support federalism, his party adopted a tough constitutional policy demanding that Quebec have absolute jurisdiction in many areas of economic and social policy where the federal government had total or shared power. To appease separatists and put pressure on the rest of the country, the National Assembly passed legislation calling for a referendum either on sovereignty or an offer of constitutional renewal from the rest of Canada.

Outside Quebec, Canadians appeared to have little to say on constitutional issues in the early post-Meech period. Mulroney established a national citizens' forum on Canada's future, headed by CRTC chair Keith Spicer, to determine what Canadians wanted in their constitution. Given the political climate, many Canadians greeted the creation of the commission and its 1991 report with a great deal of cynicism.

The Referendum

As the clock ticked toward Bourassa's referendum deadline, he decided to return to the bargaining table. A marathon session attended by the premiers and some Native leaders produced the Charlottetown Accord of 28 August 1992. The accord was a complex document that included concessions to each of the players in the room. Quebec was to receive much of what it had been promised during the Meech Lake discussions, but it did not gain important new powers. The federal government agreed to turn over certain areas, such as housing and forestry, to the provinces, but this fell far short of Quebec demands.

To achieve agreement on special status for Quebec, Bourassa had to make a concession that was galling to most Quebec nationalists: equal provincial representation in the Senate. In the 1980s, the government of Alberta had begun to demand a "triple-E"—equal, elected, effective— Senate with powers equal to those of the Commons, but in which representation would be by province rather than by population. The Senate could then become the means by which the peripheral regions could force Central Canada, which dominated the House of Commons, to be more sensitive to their needs. The smaller provinces embraced such Senate reform, but Quebec rejected its underlying assumption of a nation of ten equal provinces rather than two founding peoples. Bourassa finally agreed to the triple-E Senate after its powers were whittled down. The other provinces agreed to guarantee Quebec that its representation in the House of Commons would not fall below 25 percent, its approximate percentage of the population of the country in 1992.

The premiers recognized Native rights to self-government, but the perimeters were to be determined in subsequent political negotiations. A social charter, the brainchild of Ontario's NDP government, was included in the accord, committing governments to maintain existing social programs. Since conservative administrations in Ottawa and some provinces were more in favour of cutting social spending, these commitments were "non-justiciable": no one could take a government to court for failing to live up to the social commitments in the constitution.

When the Charlottetown agreement was first announced, polls suggested that a majority of Canadians in every province supported it. Several provinces, including Quebec, had agreed to test support for any constitutional agreement in binding referenda. The Mulroney government had previously opposed popular consultation on constitutional changes but, faced with the prospect of a variety of provincial tests, it decided to hold a national referendum. The federal Liberal and New Democratic leaders joined Mulroney in supporting the accord, and its smooth passage by a constitution-weary electorate seemed assured.

Soon, however, various provisions in the accord began to draw fire, and the public's growing distrust of politicians—particularly Mulroney— put the "Yes" forces on the defensive. Mulroney opened the referendum campaign in Quebec with a speech in which he ripped up a copy of the accord and threatened that its rejection would be the beginning of the end of Canada. Such scaremongering backfired: the "Yes" forces were widely seen as trying to blackmail Canadians into supporting the accord.

The "No" forces—made up of the right-wing Reform Party, centrists represented by Pierre Trudeau, and progressive organizations such as the National Action Committee on the Status of Women—opposed the accord, but for different reasons. Reform Party leader Preston Manning argued that the agreement went too far in conceding group, as opposed to individual, rights. NAC countered that the accord did not go far enough, that it ignored the rights of women generally and aboriginal women in particular. Manning claimed that the constitutional proposal would discourage governments from cutting social spending. NAC argued that the accord should have protected social programs, but that the watered-down social charter failed to do so. Some opponents insisted that the agreement gave too much to Quebec; others that it gave too little. Quebec nationalists were well represented in the latter camp. While separatists dominated the "No" coalition in Quebec, an important group of Liberals led by MLA Jean Allaire, who had drafted the constitutional position of his party, also opposed the accord.

The "Yes" side was no less disparate. The language of the accord was ambiguous enough to attract support from such ideologically opposed organizations as the Canadian Labour Congress and the Canadian Chamber of Commerce. What generally united supporters was the belief that the accord

Editorial cartoon the day following the referendum on the Charlottetown Accord (Gable, *The Globe and Mail*)

NATIVE PEOPLES AND THE CHARLOTTETOWN ACCORD

Four of the seventeen people who signed the Charlottetown Accord were Native leaders, representing status Indians, non-status Indians, Inuit, and Métis. The latter three groups generally supported the agreement, but only a minority of status Indians voted in favour of the accord. The Native Women's Association of Canada, claiming it had been wrongfully excluded from the negotiations, went to court in an unsuccessful bid to prevent the referendum from taking place. What in the accord provoked such disparate reactions among aboriginal peoples?

The accord called for "the recognition of the inherent right of self-government" for all Native peoples. "Aboriginal governments" were to form an undefined third order of government in Canada to preserve Native "languages, cultures, economies, identities, institutions, and traditions." Their powers were to be negotiated with the federal and provincial governments. Failing agreement, Native peoples could, after five years, resort to the courts to assert their right of self-government. The accord confirmed existing treaty rights and stated that section 35(4) of the Constitution Act, which guaranteed these rights equally to both sexes, should be retained. The Métis, whose aboriginal rights had never been guaranteed under the constitution, were to negotiate with the federal government and the five most westerly provinces on self-government, land and resources, cost sharing, and transfer of some aboriginal programs and services to the Métis.

Politicians hostile to Native rights began to make outlandish claims about the accord. Despite a clause that limited land claims, Preston Manning and Parti Québécois leader Jacques Parizeau both suggested that aboriginal peoples might end up controlling most of the land in the country. By contrast, many Natives opposed the accord precisely because it did nothing to speed up land claim negotiations. Some status Indians maintained that Natives were sovereign peoples who should govern themselves as they saw fit. They rejected the notion that they should have to negotiate a political accord with the federal and provincial governments. Métis and non-status Indians, lacking the secure land base of many treaty Indians, generally rejected this perspective. While the gender rights clause appeared to protect aboriginal women, the Native Women's Association of Canada charged that the accord gave self-government precedence over gender and other rights. Accord supporters argued that opponents distorted the agreement, producing improbable worst-case scenarios, but status Indian distrust of white governments and Native women's distrust of male aboriginal leaders was the product of bitter experience.

represented the best possible compromise in a country of endless divisions. They argued that the constitutional obsession had to end so that the government could concentrate on the country's economic problems.

Ultimately, the "Yes" forces could not withstand the many-pronged "No" campaign. Many Canadians felt left out of the constitutional process. Many more did not like certain features of the accord and resented being told that they had to accept the deal as a package. Weary of continued constitutional impasse, disillusioned by political dishonesty, incompetence, and scandal, and uneasy because of the long recession that showed no sign of lifting, many Canadians simply wanted to send their politicians a message. Three have-not provinces—Newfoundland, Prince Edward Island, and New Brunswick—supported the accord in the hope that constitutional bickering could be put to an end, but Ontario voters were split virtually down the middle. In the remaining six provinces, the accord suffered a clear defeat.

Popular disillusionment with the constitutional process and politics in general was directed particularly at the prime minister. Through 1991 and 1992, polls indicated that fewer than 20 percent of Canadians were prepared to re-elect a government led by Brian Mulroney. His resignation as prime minister, announced early in 1993, was applauded by many Canadians. Popular or not, in 1991 Mulroney committed Canadians to active participation in a war in the Middle East. For many it seemed that such a position was in line with one of growing Canadian subordination to American foreign policy.

•Foreign and Defence Policy

In the early 1960s there were indications that Canada might chart an independent course on defence rather than continue to offer unquestioning support to the Americans. Prime Minister Diefenbaker appointed Howard Green, well known for his support of disarmament, to the position of secretary of state for external affairs in 1959. Both Green and Diefenbaker grew increasingly impatient with the strong-arm tactics of American politicians and diplomats, as well as their own Canadian defence experts, who argued that Canadians had to adopt nuclear weapons as part of their commitment to NATO and NORAD defence strategies.

The issue of nuclear weapons divided Canadians and caused dissension in the ranks of both the Liberal and Conservative parties. Under Lester Pearson, the Liberals had declared against nuclear weapons, but some members of the party were uncomfortable with this position. Diefenbaker's cabinet was divided on the issue: External Affairs Minister Green was firm in his conviction that Canada should not join the nuclear club, while Defence Minister Douglas Harkness was equally convinced that Canada should adopt the most up-to-date military equipment. As long as the question remained academic, Diefenbaker could stall in the hope that events would make such a difficult decision unnecessary. The Cuban missile crisis forced his hand.

In 1959, troops led by Fidel Castro toppled a corrupt military regime in Cuba and ushered in a socialist revolution. The Kennedy administration in the United States supported a military expedition to undermine Castro in 1961, but it was decisively repulsed at the Bay of Pigs. In the aftermath of the attempted invasion, Soviet missiles were sent to Cuba. Still rankling from the defeat at the Bay of Pigs and determined to keep the western

John F. Kennedy, Governor-General Georges Vanier, John Diefenbaker, Jacqueline Kennedy, and Olive Diefenbaker in Ottawa, 1961   (National Archives of Canada/ PA-154665)

hemisphere free from communism, Kennedy demanded, in October 1962, that the Soviet Union remove its missiles from Cuba. He also called upon his Canadian allies to put their NORAD forces on alert in the event that the Soviets refused to back down.

On the evening of 22 October, Lester Pearson rose in the House of Commons to demand a statement from the prime minister concerning President Kennedy's television broadcast announcing the missile buildup in Cuba. Pearson was not the only one wondering about Canada's official role in the dramatic developments that threatened to precipitate a third world war. Concerned that Kennedy was being too belligerent with the Soviets, Diefenbaker waited three days before announcing that Canadian forces were on alert. No one had any way of knowing that the defence minister had secretly placed Canada's forces on alert immediately after Kennedy's request. As events unfolded, Canada's half-hearted public response was of little immediate consequence: the Soviet Union agreed to withdraw the offending missiles. However, Diefenbaker's truculence annoyed the Americans who were now determined to topple a Canadian prime minister who refused to do their bidding.

In the months preceding the 1963 federal election, statements from the American State Department and from a retired American NATO leader attempted to discredit Diefenbaker's admittedly inconsistent foreign policy. Diefenbaker decried American interference in a Canadian election and finally made a commitment to reject nuclear weapons for Canada, but his unpopular government went down to defeat by Lester Pearson's Liberals, who had abruptly changed their position on the nuclear question following the missile crisis. Once in office, the Liberals followed through on their commitment to the controversial nuclear warheads. Pearson's secretary of state for external affairs, Paul Martin, had made it clear that Canada's acceptance of nuclear weapons for its NATO and NORAD forces helped the country obtain special consideration from the Americans on economic issues, noting that "One of the functions of Canadian diplomacy has been to ensure that the United States will always harbour a special regard for Canada."[7]

During the Pearson years, the only episode that jeopardized Canada's status in Washington was a speech made by the prime minister in 1965 at Temple University in Philadelphia. Pearson advocated that the Americans temporarily cease bombing North Vietnam in an effort to seek diplomatic solutions in Indochina. President Lyndon Johnson, meeting Pearson afterwards, grabbed him by the shirt collar and shouted, "You pissed on my rug." It was a rough reception for a prime minister whose country had compromised its role in the International Control Commission to defend

America's view of the Vietnamese conflict and to spy on North Vietnam for the Americans. A report in 1962 prepared by Canada and co-signed by India, desperate for American goodwill because of border wars with China, was regularly produced by American officials wishing to demonstrate North Vietnamese atrocities, of which there were no doubt many. That the report ignored the equal or greater human rights abuses in South Vietnam appeared to be of as little interest to official Canada as it was to the United States.

When Pierre Trudeau came to power, there was talk of a reassessment of Canada's NATO and NORAD commitments. In the end, Canada's NATO troops in Europe were cut in half while its NORAD commitment remained unchanged. In addition, the obsolescence of the nuclear warheads used by Canadian forces allowed Trudeau to return to Canada's earlier status as a nation without nuclear weapons. While Trudeau campaigned to slow down the arms race, he continued to support the concept of nuclear deterrence. His agreement to allow cruise missile tests over Canadian territory appalled the growing peace movement and suggested that the desire to appease the Americans remained strong in Ottawa. Nevertheless, there were disagreements between Ottawa and Washington. Trudeau denounced the American invasion of Grenada in 1983 and called for international efforts to improve the imbalance in wealth between the North and South. The Americans responded cooly to such efforts.

Overshadowed by the dominance of the superpowers, Canada's involvement in international affairs was modest. Canadians took considerable pride in the fact that Nobel Prize winner Lester Pearson set Canada on a course of peacekeeping activities in hot spots around the world but, in reality, the Canadian peacekeeping role was a modest one too. In the 1960s, Canadian peacekeeping forces were committed to the Congo, Yemen, and Cyprus, but they were expelled from Egypt by President Nasser in 1967 and had little success when they attempted to keep the peace between warring factions in Eastern Europe following the collapse of the Soviet Union. The numbers involved in peacekeeping forces were never very large, certainly not compared to the numbers committed to NATO and NORAD duties. Historian J.L. Granatstein concluded that Canadian peacekeeping was "only a minor role performed by the military forces of a minor power."[8]

Canada's role as a champion of foreign aid and international human rights also does not bear close scrutiny. Since 1960, Canada's foreign aid commitments never reached the goals set by the United Nations, and the assistance that was granted usually had strings attached and went to countries with politically acceptable regimes. Similarly, Ottawa had a tendency to denounce human rights violations that occurred in nations unfriendly to the West and ignore them in the sometimes brutal regimes that supported Canadian—or American—interests. These tendencies in foreign policy were not unique to Canada, but they undermine any claims that Canadians were somehow more high-minded than people of other nations in the way that they conducted themselves abroad.

In the Mulroney years, Canada and the United States moved even closer on foreign policy issues. As the Cold War thawed in the late 1980s, neither country seemed to have a clear vision of what diplomatic issues were likely to preoccupy the "new world order." Iraq's invasion of Kuwait, an American ally, in August 1990 marked the first major post-Cold War incident. Canada supported a tough United Nations embargo against Iraq and appeared ready to endorse American plans for an invasion of Iraq should it refuse to withdraw from Kuwait. Iraq proved intransigent, and the United States led massive strikes against the country. The Gulf War was enormously popular in the United States, but less so in Canada. Nonetheless, Mulroney lent his full support to President George Bush, extending him a hero's welcome when he visited Ottawa after the war. Mulroney had also refused to criticize the United States for its invasion of Panama in 1989 and seemed incapable of viewing American foreign policy, however belli-cose, with anything but uncritical approval.

The morality of Canadian external policies appeared particularly sus-pect in the area of arms sales, including sales to both Iraq and Iran as the two countries waged a territorial war in the 1980s. Canada sold $1.9 billion in military commodities in 1985, a substantial increase from the $336.2 mil-lion sold in 1970. Almost 90 percent of these arms were sold to the Americans, with whom the Defence Production Sharing Agreement contin-ued to provide a stable market. Particularly in the Vietnam era, critics of Canadian foreign policy accused the government of blindly following American defence policies because they produced benefits for Canadian armaments manufacturers. The federal government continued to subsidize defence industries, even though studies suggested that the expenditures would create more jobs in other areas of the economy.

Apart from selling arms to willing buyers, Canada, a signatory in the 1960s of a nuclear non-proliferation treaty, peddled nuclear reactors pro-duced by Atomic Energy of Canada Limited, a Crown corporation. Such sales were ostensibly meant to encourage only peaceful uses of the atom, but when India, a client for AECL's Candu reactors, detonated a nuclear device in May 1974, the questionable effectiveness of Canadian safeguards on its nuclear sales was demonstrated. It took Canada another two years to sever its nuclear relations with India. In the meantime it attempted to stiffen safeguards, only to be defeated in 1977 after European Economic Community complaints.

All of this discouraged the Canadian peace movement, which included church, union, student, and professional groups as well as broad-based coalitions. While activists breathed a sigh of relief as the Cold War ended, in some respects the resolution of such a long, broad conflict complicated the pursuit of global peace. The peace movement was ill prepared to deal with the variety of regional conflicts in the Persian Gulf, the Middle East, Somalia, and the former Yugoslav republics. For many peace activists, the most important goal was removing the economic inequalities and ideological hatred that caused people to resort to violence.

• Whither Canada?

Canada in the early 1990s appears to be in danger of falling apart. Its squabbling provinces continue to reopen historic wounds and are little disposed to celebrate collective achievements. Although Canadian prosperity is envied by much of the world, within Canada, the unequal distribution of wealth inevitably has created contention. Immigrants and refugees apply in droves for the chance to come to Canada, and those lucky enough to be chosen sometimes puzzle at the bitterness that appears to be tearing the nation asunder. Whether Canada can be reconstituted as a viable nation and, if so, what balance of federal and provincial powers will create relative harmony, remains an unknown. As the federal government, which promoted free trade and greater provincial powers cheerfully abandoned rail lines, air links, and CBC outlets that united distant parts of this far-flung country, some questioned whether Canada was too expensive an undertaking to sustain. Was it worthwhile ignoring marketplace principles to provide the funds that allowed Prince Edward Island to have a university, northern Manitoba to have hospital services, and Alberta to have a French-language CBC? Only the collective wisdom of the Canadian people would decide. The struggles of ordinary people, as we have seen, as well as the activities of elites had shaped the character of Canada and would continue to do so.

• If Quebec Leaves:
The Academic Debate

Increasingly, social scientists—if not governments—have been prepared to speculate on the political and economic impact of Quebec sovereignty on both Quebec and the remaining Canadian provinces. Historian David J. Bercuson and political scientist Barry Cooper have marshalled arguments as to why the rest of Canada would be better off without Quebec. They argue that Quebec nationalism is incompatible with the liberal-democratic values that they believe are central to English-Canadian politics. Quebec nationalists, they maintain, place the rights of French Canadians above both majority and individual rights. Bercuson and Cooper suggest that majority rule ought to be—and, without Quebec, would be—the essential principle of governance in Canada.[9]

Some authors point to liberal democracies that accommodate minority communities without losing their liberal character. Political scientist Alain Gagnon cites the examples of Switzerland and Belgium, where regional governments "have the right and the obligation to protect and promote their respective linguistic community against any infringements." Gagnon labels this "a charter of rights and freedoms whose application varies according to specific regions."[10]

Bercuson and Cooper reject such regionalism, and they suggest that a Quebec-free Canada could avoid decentralization by giving each province equal representation in the Senate. Other scholars are sceptical that such a proposal would be acceptable to Ontario. They predict that, if Quebec left Confederation, Canada would begin to fall apart. Economist Tim O'Neill observes that Ontario's dominance in population and economic activity could lead other provinces to "forge separate regional and interregional alliances with other provinces and possibly with contiguous areas of the United States."[11]

Federal bilingual policy is a sore point for many scholars. Bercuson and Cooper scoff at those who claim that "what makes us great is official bilingualism and French on our cereal boxes."[12] While few other anglophone scholars share this rejection of legislated bilingualism, many Quebec nationalists do.

They argue that Quebec's government should operate only in French while governments outside Quebec should offer services in French only in heavily francophone areas. Sociologist Hubert Guindon, a nationalist who supports a popular campaign for unilingualism in Quebec, argues that "the official bilingualism adopted by the Canadian state was politically irrelevant."[13]

Bercuson and Cooper argue that a Canada without Quebec would be more prosperous than today's Canada. Adopting the neo-conservative view that the federal government's spending has been out of control for several decades, they suggest that Quebec pressures have played a key role in preventing the government from trimming its programs. Although they provide no figures to corroborate this view, they conclude: "By ending the wasteful transaction costs of official bilingualism and especially the ongoing transfer of wealth from Canada to Quebec, the citizens of Canada would undoubtedly be more wealthy, not less."[14]

Quebec economists of a nationalist bent have rejected the view that Quebec is a net gainer from tax transfers in Canada. Georges Mathews has produced a "balance sheet of federalism for Quebec," which claims that Quebec had a marginally favourable balance from 1973 to 1986 but afterwards was a net loser.[15] Pierre Fortin also argues that Confederation continues to have a negative economic impact on Quebec. He claims that the federal debt, failed federal development policies, and monetary instability as well as duplication in powers between the federal and provincial governments have hurt Quebec's economy.[16] Indeed, such wrong-headed policies hurt every province's economy, and Fortin suggests that radical decentralization might be of benefit to the whole country. If emotional attachments to Canada make residents of other provinces reluctant to support decentralization, then Quebec must either receive special status or become sovereign.

Scholars in have-not provinces, especially Atlantic Canada, have been less sanguine about the economic prospects of their provinces should Quebec leave. Tim O'Neill notes that "neither extensive decentralization nor separation will have a positive impact on Atlantic Canada" because the region now depends more on federal transfers than other areas.[17] O'Neill also observes that notions that either Quebec or the rest of Canada will benefit economically from a break-up take as a given that the break-up will be amicable and cause little short-term economic disruption. There has already been an indication that the two sides would have difficulty determining how to divide up the national debt.

Political scientist Peter Russell suggests that the aftermath of Quebec sovereignty might well depend on how it is achieved. If it comes through a unilateral declaration of independence rather than through a long process of negotiation, "the climate of uncertainty and tension generated by such a move will reduce international confidence and put severe strain on the Canadian economy."[18] Opponents of independence, particularly anglophones and aboriginals, "might insist on federal protection of their rights against a Quebec government operating outside Canadian law. Civil disobedience and violence cannot be ruled out." While such views strike many as alarmist, some Quebec nationalist intellectuals readily concede that the sovereignty-association formula is probably impossible. There is no guarantee that the rest of Canada would negotiate a common market with a seceding province. Hubert Guindon, reflecting on the debate in the 1980 Quebec referendum, observes: "The common myth shared by both those opposed to sovereignty association and those in favour was that should the 'oui' forces have won decisively, it would have led automatically to the creation of a sovereign state with association with Canada. . . . Such naivety, in a sense, honours us. But it augurs poorly for the kind of sophistication that will be required to inch our way towards sovereignty."[19]

The accuracy of these analyses will only become apparent if Quebec does in fact leave Canada. While the "constitution industry" and most Canadians, including most Quebeckers, still hope that accommodation is possible, Quebec's leaving is no longer unthinkable. It is therefore only natural that scholars continue to paint scenarios of Canada without Quebec and Quebec without Canada.

•Notes

1 Quoted in Canadian Council on Social Development, "Canada's Social Programs Are in Trouble" (Ottawa: CCSD, 1990), 5.

2 *Report of the Royal Commission on the Status of Women in Canada* (Ottawa: Information Canada, 1970), 261.

3 Daniel Latouche, *Canada and Quebec, Past and Future: An Essay* (Toronto: University of Toronto Press, 1986), 57.

4 Gwen Brodsky and Shelagh Day, *Canadian Charter Equality Rights for Women: One Step Forward or Two Steps Back?* (Ottawa: Canadian Advisory Council on the Status of Women, 1989), 3.

5 Earle Gray, ed., *Free Trade, Free Canada: How Free Trade Will Make Canada Stronger* (Woodville, ON: Canadian Speeches, 1988).

6 Marjorie Griffin Cohen, *Free Trade and the Future of Women's Work: Manufacturing and Service Industries* (Toronto: Garamond Press, 1987), 51.

7 Paul Martin, *A Very Public Life*, Volume 2, *So Many Worlds* (Toronto: Deneau, 1985), 389.

8 J.L. Granatstein, "Canada and Peacekeeping: Image and Reality" in *Canadian Foreign Policy: Historical Readings*, rev. ed. (Toronto: Copp Clark Pitman, 1993), 281.

9 David J. Bercuson and Barry Cooper, *Deconfederation: Canada Without Quebec* (Toronto: Key Porter Books, 1991), 15–16.

10 Alain Gagnon, "Other Federal and Nonfederal Countries: Lessons for Canada" in *Options for a New Canada*, ed. Ronald L. Watts and Douglas M. Brown (Toronto: University of Toronto Press, 1991), 232.

11 Tim O'Neill, "Restructured Federalism and Its Impacts on Atlantic Canada" in *The Constitutional Future of the Prairie and Atlantic Regions of Canada*, ed. James N. McCrorie and Martha L. MacDonald (Regina: Canadian Plains Research Centre, 1992), 63.

12 Bercuson and Cooper, *Deconfederation*, 134–35.

13 Hubert Guindon, *Quebec Society: Tradition, Modernity, and Nationhood* (Toronto: University of Toronto Press, 1988), 143.

14 Bercuson and Cooper, *Deconfederation*, 140–41.

15 Georges Mathews, *Quiet Resolution: Quebec's Challenges to Canada* (Toronto: Summerhill Press, 1990), 139–40.

[16] Pierre Fortin, "How Economics Is Shaping the Constitutional Debate in Quebec" in *Confederation in Crisis*, ed. Robert Young (Toronto: Lorimer, 1991), 35–44.

[17] Tim O'Neill, "Restructured Federalism," 63.

[18] Peter H. Russell, "Towards a New Constitutional Process" in *Options for a New Canada*, 148.

[19] Hubert Guindon, *Quebec Society*, 166–67.

•Selected Reading

There is a large literature on the post-1960 welfare state. Among useful works are Dennis Guest, *The Emergence of Social Security in Canada*, rev. ed. (Vancouver: University of British Columbia Press, 1985); Shankar Yelaja, ed., *Canadian Social Policy*, rev. ed. (Waterloo, ON: Wilfrid Laurier University Press, 1987); Andrew Armitage, *Social Welfare in Canada*, 2nd ed. (Toronto: McClelland and Stewart, 1988); Allan Moscovitch and Jim Albert, eds., *The Benevolent State: The Growth of Welfare in Canada* (Toronto: Garamond Press, 1987); Keith Banting, *The Welfare State and Canadian Federalism*, rev. ed. (Montreal: McGill-Queen's University Press, 1987); Malcolm G. Taylor, *Health Insurance and Canadian Public Policy*, rev. ed. (Montreal: McGill-Queen's University Press, 1987); and Jacqueline S. Ismael, ed., *Canadian Social Welfare Policy* (Montreal: McGill-Queen's University Press, 1985).

On federal–provincial relations, good works include David Milne, *Tug of War: Ottawa and the Provinces Under Trudeau and Mulroney* (Toronto: Lorimer, 1986); Garth Stevenson, *Unfulfilled Union: Canadian Federalism and National Unity*, 3rd ed. (Toronto: Gage, 1988); G. Bruce Doern and Glen Toner, *The Politics of Energy: The Development and Implementation of the NEP* (Scarborough: Nelson, 1985); and J.O. House, *The Challenge of Oil: Newfoundland's Quest for Controlled Development* (St John's: Institute of Social and Economic Research, 1985).

The evolution of the Constitution Act, 1982, is assessed in David Milne, *The New Canadian Constitution* (Toronto: Lorimer, 1982); Edward McWhinney, *Canada and the Constitution* (Toronto: University of Toronto Press, 1982); Roy Romanow, John Whyte, and Howard Leeson, *Canada Notwithstanding: The Making of the Constitution, 1976–1982* (Toronto: Carswell/Methuen, 1984); and Keith Banting and Richard Simeon, eds., *And No One Cheered: Federalism, Democracy and the Constitution Act* (Scarborough: Nelson, 1983). The flavour of the Meech Lake Debate is sampled in Michael D. Behiels, ed., *The Meech Lake Primer: Conflicting Views of the 1987 Constitutional Accord* (Ottawa: University of Ottawa Press, 1989). Andrew Cohen, *A*

Deal Undone: The Making and Breaking of the Meech Lake Accord (Vancouver: Douglas and McIntyre, 1990), provides a journalistic account of the accord's demise.

On Native issues, see *Nation to Nation: Aboriginal Sovereignty and the Future of Canada,* ed. Diane Engelstad and John Bird (Toronto: Anansi, 1992). On the 1992 constitutional debate, see Pierre Trudeau, *A Mess That Deserves a Big No* (Toronto: Robert Davies Publishing, 1992); Laurier La Pierre, *Canada, My Canada: What Happened?* (Toronto: McClelland and Stewart, 1992); and George Fallis, *The Costs of Constitutional Change: A Citizens' Guide to the Issues* (Toronto: Lorimer, 1992).

On the great free trade debate, see Duncan Cameron, ed., *The Free Trade Papers* (Toronto: Lorimer, 1986) for opinions of opponents and Earle Gray, *Free Trade, Free Canada: How Free Trade Will Make Canada Stronger* (Woodville, ON: Canadian Speeches, 1988) for the views of supporters. Women's concerns regarding the agreement are presented in Marjorie Griffin Cohen, *Free Trade and the Future of Women's Work: Manufacturing and Service Industries* (Toronto: Garamond Press, 1987).

Among useful works on Canadian foreign policy after 1960 are Ernie Regehr and Simon Rosenblum, eds., *Canada and the Nuclear Arms Race* (Toronto: Lorimer, 1983); Victor Levant, *Quiet Complicity: Canada and Vietnam* (Toronto: Between the Lines, 1986); Douglas A. Ross, *In the Interests of Peace: Canada and Vietnam 1954–1973* (Toronto: University of Toronto Press, 1984); J.L. Granatstein, ed., *Canadian Foreign Policy* (Toronto: Copp Clark Pitman, 1986); and George Ignatieff, *The Making of a Peacemonger* (Toronto: Penguin, 1987).

I N D E X

Printed in Canada